# Sikunder Burnes

# There Was Something about Alexander Burnes

'The most unaffected, gentlemanlike, pleasant and amusing man that I have had the good fortune to meet.' Field Marshal Sir Neville Chamberlain

'He is one of the most agreeable persons I ever met with; and the banks of the river, dull at all times, are doubly so now that he has left us.' General Sir Henry Fane

'The winning smile, and frank and courteous manner appeared to have gained for him a degree of consideration which no other European could boast of.' Lieutenant William Taylor

'Of the great minds which I have been allowed to study, the distinguishing characteristic was their simplicity and naked truth; and in this essentiality of greatness Sir Alexander is most especially modelled.' Surgeon General Dr Richard Kennedy

'I confess I shall be confident of any plan he undertakes in this quarter of India.' General Sir John Malcolm

'From long personal acquaintance and experience of his habits, there is no officer of whatever standing or rank in the Bombay Army who is so peculiarly qualified.' Colonel Sir Henry Pottinger

'In all his changes of fortune, he was never known to overlook a kindness, or forget his early friendships.' Major T. B. Jervis

'Really Sir, you are a wonderful man.' King William IV

*To Martin,*
*with Best Wishes*

# SIKUNDER BURNES
## MASTER OF THE GREAT GAME

CRAIG MURRAY

First published in Great Britain 2016 by
Birlinn Ltd

West Newington House
10 Newington Road
Edinburgh
EH9 1QS

www.birlinn.co.uk

ISBN: 978 1 78027 317 4

Copyright © Craig Murray 2016

The right of Craig Murray to be identified as the author of this work has been asserted by him in accordance with the Copyright, Designs and Patents Act, 1988

All rights reserved. No part of this publication may be reproduced, stored, or transmitted in any form, or by any means, electronic, mechanical or photocopying, recording or otherwise, without the express written permission of the publisher.

*British Library Cataloguing-in-Publication Data*
*A catalogue record for this book is available on request from the British Library*

Typeset in Adobe Arno by
Koinonia, Manchester
Printed in Malta by
Gutenberg Press Ltd

# Contents

*Preface: Historian, Interrupted*     vii
*Acknowledgements*     x

| | | |
|---|---|---|
| 1 | Montrose | 1 |
| 2 | A Rape in Herat | 8 |
| 3 | Scottish Patronage, Indian Career | 10 |
| 4 | A Griffin in India | 18 |
| 5 | Dawn of the North-West Frontier | 31 |
| 6 | The Indus Scheme | 50 |
| 7 | The Shipwreck of Young Hopes | 58 |
| 8 | The Dray Horse Mission | 69 |
| 9 | The Dazzling Sikhs | 75 |
| 10 | Rupar, The Field of the Cloth of Cashmere | 89 |
| 11 | Journey through Afghanistan | 97 |
| 12 | To Bokhara and Back | 113 |
| 13 | The Object of Adulation | 123 |
| 14 | Castles – and Knights Templar – in the Air | 136 |
| 15 | To Meet upon the Level | 146 |
| 16 | Imperial Rivalry in Asia | 149 |
| 17 | While Alex was Away | 154 |
| 18 | Return to the Indus | 161 |
| 19 | The Gathering Storm | 172 |
| 20 | Peshawar Perverted | 186 |
| 21 | The Kabul Negotiations | 194 |
| 22 | Stand-off | 208 |
| 23 | 'Izzat wa Ikram' | 221 |
| 24 | Regime Change | 228 |
| 25 | Securing Sind | 254 |

| | | |
|---|---|---|
| 26 | The Dodgy Dossier | 270 |
| 27 | Kelat | 275 |
| 28 | A King in Kandahar | 287 |
| 29 | Death in St Petersburg | 292 |
| 30 | Ghazni | 295 |
| 31 | Mission Accomplished | 304 |
| 32 | Kabul in Winter | 312 |
| 33 | Dost Mohammed | 328 |
| 34 | Discontent | 339 |
| 35 | Dissent and Dysfunction | 355 |
| 36 | Death in Kabul | 363 |
| 37 | Aftermath | 374 |

*Notes* 383
*Bibliography* 412
*Index* 422

# Preface: Historian, Interrupted

To anticipate the critics, this is history written by a bureaucrat. The story is told not just of Burnes' adventures, but of the accounts and reports he had to file. The Byzantine jealousies and turf battles of British officials are uncovered. For this was the very stuff of Burnes' life in India, what pre-occupied him day to day, and what is missing from romantic accounts of the Great Game. Equally I have tried to give full weight to two major aspects of the lives of British rulers in India – sex and freemasonry – to which most histories turn a blind eye.

It is thirty years since I graduated from the University of Dundee with a First in Modern History. I had a place for a PhD. Then, to my intense surprise, I won a position in the Diplomatic Service. Being about to get married, I needed the money. Whether history suffered any loss you can judge from this book.

I had already encountered Alexander Burnes as the star among the real life characters of George MacDonald Fraser's *Flashman*. Burnes ranked with Burton and Livingstone in his fame as a nineteenth-century explorer. His books were best-sellers. He was received by kings. He won the gold medal of the Royal Geographical Society and its continental counterparts. He was knighted for his services and made a Companion of the Bath and Fellow of the Royal Society. He was a colourful and controversial character, a major figure in the First Afghan War, whose opinions could still cause a full parliamentary debate twenty years after his death. And he was the great-nephew of Robert Burns.

Yet there is no recent biography of Burnes. In 1969 Philip Lunt produced the slim *Bokhara Burnes*, mostly a précis of Burnes' travel writing. There has never been a study of Burnes' origins and motivations. Crucial questions, such as why he changed his views to support the disastrous invasion of Afghanistan, have been given only cursory consideration. Burnes' sex life is widely cited as a contributing factor in sparking the 1841 Kabul uprising against the British, but this claim has never been properly examined.

Burnes has been treated more kindly by fiction than biography. *Flashman* brought him to a wide audience. He is compellingly imagined as the hero of Philip Hensher's *The Mulberry Empire*, while in John C Griffiths' *The Queen of Spades*, a direct descendant named Alexander Burnes fights off the 1980s Russian occupation of Afghanistan. Burnes was the major influence for Kipling's *The Man Who Would Be King*, not least in its Masonic themes. At least four other novels feature Alexander Burnes.

Burnes naturally is very prominent in accounts of the Great Game, but these rehearse the same limited sources. Burnes is a major figure in William Dalrymple's beautifully written history of the First Afghan War, *Return of a King*.

I became conscious during months of transcribing manuscripts, particularly in India, that nobody had looked at them for decades, sometimes over a century. One vital folder of Burnes' letters in the National Archive of India had crumbled beyond reading. This influenced a decision to include much direct quotation.

I admit I identify with Burnes to a considerable degree. We were both East Coast Scots, from similar social backgrounds, who sought a living abroad primarily for economic reasons. When offered the Ambassadorship in Tashkent, following in the footsteps of Burnes was directly on my mind.

Both Burnes and I met career disaster when policy changed radically between our being appointed as Envoy and taking up our posts. Burnes was sent to Kabul to increase British influence with his friend, the Emir Dost Mohammed, as a buffer against Russian encroachment. After Burnes' mission was under way, the Governor General had undergone a complete change of mind, and had decided Dost Mohammed needed to be replaced, not allied. Burnes' mission was thus doomed to failure.

In summer 2001 I was appointed British Ambassador to Tashkent, based on my work in promoting human rights and democracy in Africa. Uzbekistan was seen as a tyranny in need of being shoved towards reform. But in the year between my appointment and my arrival in Tashkent in August 2002 came the 9/11 attack and our most recent invasion of Afghanistan. President Karimov of Uzbekistan went, in the official view, from being a tyrant to being our indispensable ally in the 'War on Terror'. My job changed from pushing for human rights to facilitating Karimov's clampdown on opposition. Like Burnes, I was completely unsuited by belief and temperament to the new policy.

Burnes has been much criticised by historians for backing down and switching to support the invasion. I know the pressures on you to conform, particularly in time of war, and do the 'patriotic' thing. Burnes and I made opposite decisions in the same dilemma. Burnes is criticised for not sticking to his principles against his government; I am criticised for deserting my government for my principles. You can't win.

There are continuities in British social attitudes and institutional practices. Future historians will find the survival of British class and social attitudes more remarkable than their mutation, and I worked as a fairly direct institutional descendant of Burnes. The Diplomatic Service of my time retained some of the feel and style of the India Office from which it in part descended; several of the despatches and arguments of Burnes and his colleagues could have been written in my period, right down to the phraseology. I especially recognise the intra-institutional relationships and turf battles.

If it were a novel this story would be in danger of being deemed too fanciful. It is the tale of a hero rising from obscurity to fame via fabulous adventures involving shipwreck, a thousand-mile river journey through India on a spying mission improbably disguised as the transport of English carthorses, secret agents and exploration through the oriental extravagances of Central Asia, the seduction of numerous women, and finally overreach, hubris, a terrible death and the annihilation of an entire British army. Burnes is an extraordinarily gifted hero of this tale.

There are of course striking parallels between the disastrous British invasion of Afghanistan in 1839, and the latest occupation of that country. In 1840 we sought to prop up a puppet Pashtun ruler, from the Popalzai khail of the Dourani tribe, promoting pro-western policies inimical to most Afghans. This led to revolt by major elements of the Pashtun tribal structures and Sunni religious leaderships, as opposed to indifference or support for the invaders from parts of the Tajik and Hazara minorities. That precisely described the situation in 1840 or 2010. Will we never learn?

Craig Murray<br>
*Edinburgh*

# Acknowledgements

Grateful thanks are due to the staff of the Montrose Museum, Montrose Library and the *Montrose Review* archive in Forfar, and the archives and pictures staff of Angus Council, for their enthusiastic and unstinting support.

In India the National Archives staff in Delhi and the Maharastra State Archive were unfailingly attentive and helpful. The curators of the Rao's Palace Museum in Bhuj were a mine of information joyously shared. In Mumbai, the officers and staff of the Mumbai Asiatic Society show great dedication to an astonishing institution. At Freemason's Hall, Mumbai, the access and unlimited tea given to a non-Mason was most kind.

The National Library of Scotland was a joy to work in. The National Archive of Scotland gets the prize for fast production of manuscripts. Bob Cooper of the Grand Lodge in Edinburgh was enthusiastic, and thanks to Louise Yeoman for information and advice. Bruce Gorie of the Lyon Office was courteous and efficient.

Worcester College Library, Oxford, was very welcoming and showed a genuine interest. The British Library building at St Pancras is a marvel.

Many thanks to the toilers in the same vineyard who advised and swapped transcriptions, particularly William Dalrymple, Farrukh Hussain, Alexander Morrison and the late Christopher Bayly.

Researching this book has been a labour of love which has taken half my working time for six years, unfunded, and cost a lot of money in travel and accommodation. There has been a huge impact on the finances of my family. So I owe them much more than just the run-of-the-mill thanks for their support and understanding.

CHAPTER ONE

## Montrose

Alexander Burnes has no grave and no memorial. When hacked to death in the Residence garden in Kabul, the bodies of Alexander and his younger brother Charles disappeared. Unlike other victims of the uprising, no severed body parts were hung in the bazaar by triumphant Afghans or paraded on spears to taunt British prisoners. Burnes' boss, William Macnaghten, was to be displayed in parts through the city, but somehow, a year of vicious war later, enough bits of him were reassembled by the British for a burial ceremony. There is no definite evidence of what happened to the remains of Alex and Charlie, and nobody in the British army tried to collect them.

Nor did their family put a plaque in the local kirk of Montrose. This is something of a mystery. The churches of the United Kingdom are replete with memorial tablets to those who fell in the Empire's wars, many very much less distinguished than Lieutenant Colonel Sir Alexander Burnes KCB, FRS, FRGS, Légion d'Honneur, Knight Commander of the Royal Dourani Empire. Not to mention, a greater honour than all that in Alex's own estimation, great-nephew of Robert Burns.

Montrose is a bustling and handsome market town on the East Coast of Scotland, with the county of Angus as its hinterland. Services to the North Sea oil industry have attracted corporate outposts and a technical training industry and given new life to its port. It is neither sleepy nor backward looking, and retains virtually no memory of Alexander Burnes.

This is a shame because Burnes never forgot Montrose, and he had the *Montrose Review* sent out to him in Bombay, Bhuj and Kabul. He was Montrose through and through. His father, brother and grandfather were all Provost and his mother's cousin was the minister.

The Burnes family had lived in north-eastern Scotland for at least 200 years. We know rather a lot about Alexander Burnes' ancestors because, being also Robert Burns' ancestors, they are the second most studied family in Scottish history. Alexander's brother James was to become an obsessive genealogist, for the most curious of reasons.

At the beginning of the eighteenth century the Burnes family had been tenant farmers on the fertile coastal lands of Earl Marischal Keith; sufficiently well-to-do to intermarry with junior brides of the Keith family.[1] Unfortunately, as the hereditary leader of the King's military forces in Scotland, the Keith raised the standard of Jacobite rebellion in 1715, when Westminster proclaimed the German and unpleasant but Protestant George I as the replacement for the last Stuart monarch, Anne. The Burnes family followed the Stuarts loyally in both 1715 and 1745, and suffered despoilation and deprivation as a result. As Robert Burns put it:

> What they could, they did, and what they had, they lost: with unshaken firmness and unconcealed Political Attachments, they shook hands with Ruin for what they esteemed the cause of their King and their Country.

Robert Burns' view of family history tallies exactly with the later manuscript researches of James Burnes, who specifically mentions Robert Burnes of Clochnahill as fighting at Sheriffmuir and Fetteroso.[2] Some writers on Robert Burns have dismissed his Jacobite ancestry as romantic speculation. But it is now plainly understood that the majority of Jacobite volunteers were in fact from north-east Scotland rather than the Highlands proper, and were not Roman Catholic.[3] Their motivation was primarily nationalist.[4] If the Burnes family were not out, who would be? Besides, as chief tenants of Earl Keith, they would have been expected to follow him into the field.

The diagram shows Alexander Burnes' relationship to Robert Burns.[5]

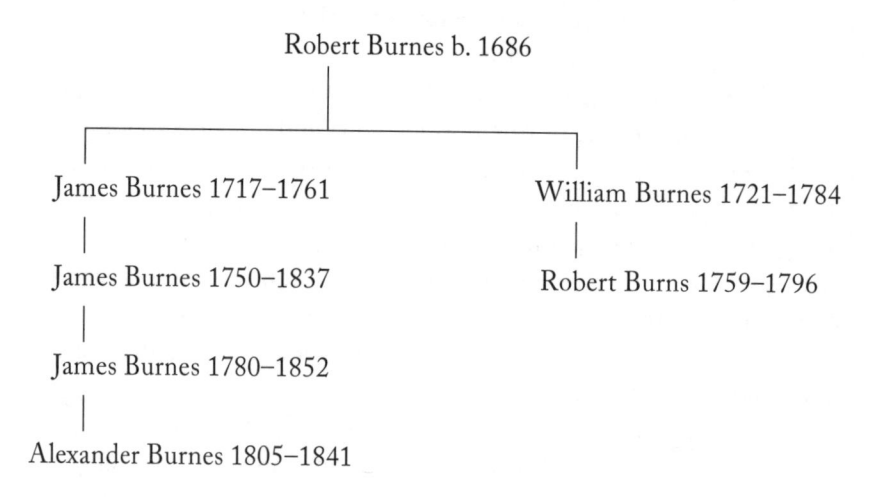

```
                    Robert Burnes b. 1686
                           |
         ┌─────────────────┴─────────────────┐
  James Burnes 1717–1761            William Burnes 1721–1784
         |                                   |
  James Burnes 1750–1837            Robert Burns 1759–1796
         |
  James Burnes 1780–1852
         |
  Alexander Burnes 1805–1841
```

Alexander's eldest brother was also a James Burnes (b. 1801). Historians have previously made the relationship between Alexander and Robert closer, claiming Alexander Burnes' grandfather and Robert Burns' father as brothers. This seems to have been done by collapsing James Burnes 1750–1837 and James Burnes 1780–1852. This mistake is easily made as father and son worked for thirty years in the family law firm, both were on Montrose town council, and one married a Miss Greig and the other a Miss Gleig.[6]

The poet was the first in the family to drop the 'e'. His father William moved to Ayrshire where the surname was usually spelt 'Burns', and that is probably why Robert changed. William had left Angus when his father's farm at Clochnahill failed and, via Edinburgh, moved to Ayr and life as a landscape gardener and farm improver. Robert Burnes – as his baptism record spells it – the future poet, was born in Alloway on 25 January 1759.[7]

On leaving Clochnahill, William's brother James moved to Montrose, where he worked as a builder and achieved respectability as a member of the town council. His son, also James, studied law in Edinburgh[8] and eventually established his own law firm in Montrose, and set his son James on the same path. This James, b. 1780, was a contemporary at Montrose Academy of Joseph Hume and James Mill; after studying law at Edinburgh he became apprenticed to his father and entered the family law firm.

In 1793 James Burnes (b. 1750), Writer to the Signet, built a house at Bow Butts, a name denoting the archery range. The Burnes house today stands neglected and on the buildings at risk register.[9] It is a solid home in a vernacular take on classical architecture. The ceilings are low and the building a little squat, hunkered down against the icy winter blasts on this north-eastern coast. Extended later, in Alexander's boyhood it had four bedrooms, three reception rooms and a kitchen. In its day, Bow Butts would have been one of the major houses of Montrose.

I commissioned an architect's report in 2008 which commences: 'The house is in a fairly dilapidated state with many areas of water penetration and broken and built-up windows. There is quite a bit of internal damage and mild vandalism and there are many dead pigeons [. . .]'[10] Most of the architectural features have been robbed out. All the land with the house was sold, and later buildings have been constructed right up against it. The Provost lamp[11] which is recorded as being above the front gate has been removed. The house is not listed for protection.

James (b. 1750)'s wife, Anne Greig, died in 1796. In 1800 his nineteen-year-old son brought home a seventeen-year-old bride, Elizabeth Gleig, daughter of the Provost of Montrose, to his widowed father's home, shared also with the groom's three sisters and brother. None of these married or lived past thirty. They remained in the home, which James and Elizabeth started to crowd further with many children. Alex was to reminisce that his bedroom was the cupboard under the stairs.[12]

On 12 February 1801, seven months after her marriage, Elizabeth Gleig gave birth to non-identical twins. They were baptised James and Anne. Anne survived baptism only a few days. James grew up to become a doctor.

In February 1802 Elizabeth gave birth to another healthy son, named Adam, who was to become the third generation in the family law business. In 1803 Robert arrived; he died aged twenty-two. No children were born to Elizabeth in 1804, but on 16 May 1805 Alexander, our hero, came into the world.

He was premature and baptised quickly in case he did not survive, but grew into a robust child. He was to have plenty of company; the fifth surviving sibling, David, was just a year younger and their first surviving sister, Anne, brought what must have been a welcome feminine touch to the brood. One year later she had a sister, Elizabeth, to keep her company. The next year, 1810, they were joined by Jane. In 1812 another boy came along, Charles, of whom Alex, seven years older, was extremely fond. It was 1815 before Cecilia joined the family. William was born in 1818, and Edward in 1819.

So when Alexander left home in 1821 he had eleven living siblings, while his grandfather also lived at home with with his mother and father. His three unmarried aunts, who had lived with them, had all died in their twenties, which gave Alexander early acquaintance with death. Yet another brother, George was born in 1822, though, with the two toddlers, William and Edward, he died the same winter. A final sister, Margaret, born 1824, also only lived a few weeks.

As Alexander grew up, his father was at the centre of the social life of Montrose. He had married the daughter of the Provost. He joined Montrose burgh council on 11 December 1817, became Chief Magistrate on 23 September 1818 and was himself elected Provost in 1820 and re-elected in 1824.[13] Scottish burghs were extremely corrupt and literally self-perpetuating, the only voters for a new council being the councillors. But the Montrose election was the only exception in Scotland for fifty years, the burgh having obtained a royal warrant for election by all burgesses – a much wider but still limited franchise. James Burnes eventually became Justice of the Peace for Forfarshire, and 'took a leading part in all the agricultural and municipal improvements which were effected in the eastern district of his native county'.[14]

Here he is Secretary of the Central Turnpike Trust, meticulously keeping the board minutes and accounts of the project to build a new high road through Angus to Dundee. Here he is Secretary of Montrose Circulating Library, persuading the publisher Constable to provide books at trade prices.[15] On 1 February 1799, when the Montrose Loyal Volunteers are raised to fight against any Napoleonic invasion, the General Order commanding their establishment is recorded in the meticulous hand of James Burnes, their newly commissioned adjutant.[16] He was Master of St Peter's Lodge of Freemasons, as had been his father before him.[17] Alex Burnes' family were local movers and shakers.

James also played a wider political role in electing the town's Member of Parliament. A single member represented the burghs of Montrose, Arbroath, Forfar and Brechin, and again the only electors were the councillors of each burgh. There was therefore much political negotiation, fixing and corruption. The town's democratic sympathies were generally radical, and fifteen-year-old Alexander enthusiastically recorded in his diary the jubilation at the acquittal in 1820 on adultery charges of Queen Caroline: 'A most brilliant illumination [...] on the ground of the glorious triumph the Queen had obtained over her base and abominable accusers.' Support for the Queen against the King had become a symbol of radical and anti-monarchical feeling.

The agricultural improvements in which Provost Burnes was involved increased productivity but had profound social effect. In Forfarshire adoption of turnips and clover as rotation crops led to an increase in cattle on previously arable land, raised in the hills to the west then fattened in the lowlands. This led to better manured and more intensively farmed soil and increased grain production. It also meant the end of the run-rig system and the removal of cottars, who lost their smallholdings amidst the inclosure of commonalities. In 1815, fully two-thirds of Scotland was common land, but it was to be grabbed quickly[18] by the aristocracy. Lawyers like James Burnes were central to agricultural 'improvement', because their role was to dispossess cottars and traditional tenant farmers – who had very little protection under Scots law – and to execute inclosure. The Ramsay family's Panmure and Dalhousie estates were leading examples of agricultural improvement, and it was chiefly for the Ramsays that James Burnes undertook this work. The Burnes/Ramsay relationship was to extend to India and to Freemasonry and forms a major subject of this book.

The most important buildings in the Montrose lives of the Burnes family are still there, and it is instructive to walk around them. In one sense their world was highly circumscribed. Provost Burnes could walk past his home, his legal office, his kirk, his town hall, his Masonic Lodge in under three minutes. At the bottom of the Burnes' large walled garden was Montrose Academy, where the children went to school, and next to it the links where they used to play.

Yet in another sense this little world of Montrose was extraordinarily wide. In that three-minute walk, Provost Burnes would pass the homes of the Ouchterlonies, the Craigies, the Ramsays, the Leightons and the Humes. Every one of these families had sons serving as military officers in India. Their residences, behind severe stone exteriors, were ornamented with oriental hardwoods, high ceilings, fancy plaster-work and marble. Their contents were bought with remittances from India and profits from Arctic whalers and Baltic timber, jute and tobacco vessels that lined Montrose's wharves. In the year of Alex's birth 142 vessels were registered to Montrose, totalling over 10,000 tons. The town had five shipyards. Young Alex would have run down to see the huge whalers coming in, and joined the crowds that waved out the Baltic brigs which set off as an annual fleet when news arrived that the ice had broken at Riga. Montrose exported the grain and cattle of Angus to Europe and was a centre of Scotland's booming linen industry. By 1815 Montrose had two steam-powered mills weaving linen from imported flax, as well as a continuing industry in homes and small workshops throughout the town and surrounding countryside. In the period 1818–22 Scotland produced on average over 30 million yards a year of linen cloth. The linen mills of Montrose were some of Scotland's very first factories.[19]

But there was insecurity in the Burnes' world as well. Montrose had suffered during the Napoleonic period, with the continental system of economic blockade hitting the crucial Baltic trade. Throughout Alex's childhood, Montrose was the scene of repeated rioting as the hungry poor attempted to stop the loading of grain onto ships for export. In fact the town had a remarkable hundred-year tradition of mobs sacking the excise warehouses.[20] In 1813, 200 troops were sent to put down such revolt, and fifty special constables sworn in; finally a full regiment was offered from Stirling.[21] Then the great post-war recession after 1815 hit Montrose hard. The years 1817–20 saw a slump in both manufacturing production and commerce. We see some of the effect in surviving correspondence of James Burnes senior – as a lawyer he was involved in action against James Watt,[22] bookseller, and James Deuchars, cabinetmaker, both of Montrose and bankrupted in 1817 and 1818 respectively. In depressed times for the entire country, the Burnes family had a large number of mouths to feed.

In 1825 James Burnes resigned as (honorary) Provost to be appointed Town Clerk. This was a drop in social prestige, but brought a regular salary and we may surmise that the decision is indicative of some financial strain. The year 1825 was one of economic collapse in Scotland, which resulted in the bankruptcy of many professional men, including Sir Walter Scott.

Montrose may have been small, but at a time when Scotland's schools were among the best in the world, Montrose Academy had a national reputation.[23] When Alex was ten it moved to splendid new neo-classical premises.

The town council had voted a very substantial £1,000 to its foundation, and construction had naturally been started with a full Masonic ceremony.[24] Alexander was to become one of four Fellows of the Royal Society produced within a generation. But the masters could be sadistic, as one of Alex's classmates recounted:

> Mr Calvert was the one that we stood most in awe of, for he was a powerful man, and it was no joke to occasion his displeasure [. . .] it was in fact sometimes a reign of terror [. . .] his fun was sometimes worse than his earnest, for he [. . .] thrashed us, at first in a playful mood; but if any had winced under the lash, or lifted up his trousers to save his skin, he would have laid on harder, and sometimes got angry.
>
> We were always glad of a visit from Provost Burnes, for when he looked in it was always with a smiling face [. . .] if we had any fear, it always left us when the Provost made his appearance, and we felt happy[25]

To a modern eye, there is a psycho-sexual motive here, particularly in the 'playful' beatings. Another teacher, Rintoul, was so feared that the boys held a bonfire to celebrate his death.

Burnes was a bright but not a brilliant child. He read widely and participated enthusiastically in the school debating society. He lived a healthy, outdoor life and did not hang back from rough and tumble games with his friends. He recalled to his old friend David Mitchell: '[w]e went to the North Water [. . .] to catch podlies [coalfish] at the pier or use our skatchets [ice skates] at the Cruizers.' Mitchell remembered a rumbustious playmate: 'He was a rough boy at school, often running with his bootlaces untied, and falling over in the chase, as well as the foremost in bold adventures.' Burnes was more prominent at play than in class: 'I never got a prize in my life' he reminded Mitchell, who remarked, 'Having known him so well as a school companion and playmate, his brilliant career in India struck me with surprise.'[26]

CHAPTER TWO

## A Rape in Herat

In 1818, while Alexander ran and played on the links of Montrose, a young princess was raped 4,500 miles away in Herat, Afghanistan. That rape reignited a blood feud between Afghanistan's two most important families, and was to have a profound effect on the destiny of young Alexander.

Shah Mahmoud of Afghanistan was angered by his half-brother Prince Firozuddin, the Governor of Herat, a beautiful city in a rich and fertile province and the subject of a dispute between the Persian and Afghan monarchies, united for almost two centuries, but no more. Firozuddin had agreed to resume Herat's lapsed tribute payment to the Shah of Persia. Mahmoud, who had gained, lost and regained his throne by war, each time deposing a half brother, feared Firozuddin's alliance with Persia may be a preparation for an attempt on his throne of Kabul.

Mahmoud, of the Dourani royal family, the Saduzais, owed his throne to the support of Afghanistan's militarily strongest family, the Barakzais. Their leader, Futth Khan, was his Wazir (Prime Minister), and Supreme Commander of the royal armies.[1] Futth Khan, with his younger brother Sirdar Dost Mohammed Khan was despatched with an army ostensibly to support Prince Firozuddin, with whom the breach was not open, by dispersing Persian forces around Herat.

Futth and Dost Mohammed defeated the Persian forces in a hard-fought battle, in which Futth was injured, and Mohammed distinguished himself. Mohammed then entered Herat with his Kohistani forces, largely ethnically Tajik. These were billeted on the nobility, and at dawn seized their hosts, while Mohammed captured Firozuddin and massacred the palace guard before his eyes. The city was then given up to wholesale rape and pillage.

Dost Mohammed took the royal valuables as his share. He stormed into the zenana (royal harem) to loot the jewels. And then he went too far – he raped a royal princess, one thing the senior aristocracy of Afghanistan did not do.

This was not anything to do with respect for non-combatants. When Mahmoud's immediate predecessor, Shah Shuja came to power, he took revenge on Mullah Aushik, a powerful Shinwari chieftain who had on behalf of Mahmoud captured and blinded Shuja's elder and only full brother, Shah Zeman. This included strapping all Aushik's wives and children across cannon mouths and blowing them into pieces.[2] Aushik himself was strapped to a chair and had gunpowder poured down a tube into his stomach until it overflowed from his mouth, which was then ignited by firing burning cotton wads at him from a pistol. The great Koh-i-Noor diamond, now the glory of the British crown, was recovered from a crack in Aushik's dungeon, where Zeman had hidden it just before his blinding.[3]

The rape of a royal woman was different. It broke the Pushtun-wali – the Pathan code of conduct – in a way that startled Dost Mohammed's peers.

Mohammed may have been carried away by lust after his wrenching off her jewels left the young Princess naked:

> He commenced to plunder and to gain possession of all the jewels, gold, and treasure [. . .] and committed an unparalleled deed by taking off the jewelled band which fastened the trowsers of the wife of Prince Malik Qasim [. . .] and treated her rudely in other ways. The pillaged lady was the sister of Kam Ran, to whom she sent her profaned robe.[4]

Mohan Lal was writing for a Victorian British audience, but it seems pretty clear that 'treated her rudely in other ways', means at least sexual molestation, particularly combined with 'profaned robe'. A contemporary British historian said she was 'dishonoured'.[5]

The princess – nobody recorded her name – was the King's daughter, the full sister of Crown Prince Kamran and, in the world of Royal Dourani inter-marriage, first wife to the King's nephew. Mohammed Khan Barakzai had insulted the entire khail of the Saduzais' in the most profound way possible. The consequences were immense.

Futth Khan was to be first blinded then tortured to death by a vengeful Shah Mahmoud and his son Kamran. It gives some idea of the enormous complexity of the Afghan civil wars that Futth Khan had previously blinded Mahmoud's brother Zeman to set Mahmoud on the throne, while Zeman had himself earlier blinded and murdered Futth Khan's father Sirafrauz Khan.[6] Into this vicious feuding in distant Afghanistan was the young Alexander destined to be thrust.

CHAPTER THREE

## Scottish Patronage, Indian Career

James Burnes turned to his childhood friend Joseph Hume for patronage for his sons. Hume had returned from a career in the East India Company with the fortune that had enabled him to become an influential figure in politics. He had clout with the EIC, where the directors were permitted to nominate young men to cadetships. Now MP for Aberdeen, and later with James' help MP for Montrose, Hume was able to help two of James' sons. This was a well-trodden career path. As Sir Walter Scott put it, the EIC was 'the Corn Chest for Scotland where we poor gentry must send our youngest sons'.[1]

The post of civilian writer was the most coveted starting position available. These positions carried high salaries and offered extraordinary opportunities for corruption. An inquiry at the time of the renewal of the EIC's charter in 1813 had found that appointments to a writership were being sold on for around £3,500, a very large sum.[2]

An appointment as a cadet to the army of the East India Company was less attractive though still valuable. Salaries were lower and there was less chance to supplement your income through corruption. Promotion could be very slow. But there were opportunities for those with skill and industry, and always the prospect of prize money from the loot of some Indian town. It was an opportunity to become an army officer without purchasing your commission, still required in the regular army. So the family seized on Joseph Hume's offer to find a cadetship for fifteen-year-old Alexander, and he was sent to London to prepare. At least he would be joining James, a graduate of the University of Edinburgh, then the world's most advanced medical school, who was in his second year of specialist Indian medical study at Guy's and St Thomas in London, preparatory to joining the Company's surgeon corps.

The opportunity came suddenly. On 6 March 1821 the boy was put on a Dundee smack, the fastest passenger transport between north-east Scotland and London. There were several competing companies, at least two of which had several sailings a week from Dundee. Fares ranged from £2 12s 6d cabin class to £1 1s deck class.³ Nine days later Alex was met at Hoare's Wharf by Joseph Hume and taken to his home. The next day, Joseph took him to meet Stanley Clarke, a director of the EIC, who was willing to nominate him for the Company's Bombay army.

Alexander wrote two remarkable letters home, which tell us a great deal about his preparations for India.

Mrs Burnes
James Burnes Esq
Writer⁴
Montrose

London March 1821

My Dear Mother,
[...] I have spent a week in Chingford; instead of being only ten miles from London you would rather suppose a hundred, for we did not meet a human soul until we arrived at Uncle David's house, there is neither schoolmaster, doctor, lawyer, banker, taylor or any other business except farmers and vintners – uncle David performs the office of Mr Rintoul, and Aunt Glegg that of Mr Beattie⁵

[...] My nature would not allow me to stop in the house, for I explored all the surrounding neighbourhood in which I found a hunting seat of Queen Elizabeth's near Epping Forest, now inhabited by the forester

[...] My detention and that of James for two months would perhaps astonish you, and more so on account of my sudden departure, but [...] the advantages which will accrue from my attending Dr Gilchrist, I have no doubt will satisfy you.

James introduced me to Dr Gilchrist [...] I am to commence attending his classes on Tuesday first [...] by so doing, in this country I may acquire the principles of the language and in India how to speak it.

James and I dined at Mr Hume's on Sunday last. What had induced you all to think I had a rough passage up I know not, for there was never a more pleasant passage performed and I would be perfectly satisfied with such weather in our passages out, but that cannot be expected because the fate of poor Paterson's vessel off the Cape shews what weather we have to expect [...]

There is one fortunate thing [...] a vessel is set to sail for Bombay about the middle of May, commanded as Dr Gilchrist told us by a friend of his – and Mr and Mrs Gilchrist will be able to get James appointed surgeon, and as the passage money is moderate, we should perhaps be able to save all now living in London.

On Saturday we received through Mr Hume a letter from Lord Gillies, enclosing one to Governor Elphinstone I here send you a copy of his Lordship's letter

*Edin Mar 21 1821*

My Dear Sir,

I have the pleasure of sending you enclosed a letter of introduction in favour of you and your brother from Admiral Fleming to his brother Mr Elphinstone, the Governor of Bombay [...]

I applied to Admiral Fleming in consequence of a letter from your father, asking me whether I had any friends at Bombay to recommend you to them. I have no friends there and have not the honour of knowing Gov. Elphinstone but his brother the Admiral is a friend of mine. This letter I trust will be useful.

Believe me yours very truly,

Ld. Gillies
To James Burnes
Assistant Surgeon in the service of the East India Company

So if we do not get forward it will not be for want of recommendatory letters [...]

Believe me
Your Truly Affectionate Son
Alex Burnes

PS I hope you make them feed the hawk and crow and also take care of the tulips and other flowers I had.
NB William Ross has my Greek dictionary which you can get from him when he's done with it but not till then for you know well the circumstances of his father.[6]

James Burnes Esq
Writer Montrose
London April 1st 1821

My Dear Father,

This being your birthday I take up my pen to express James's wishes and mine for your health and happiness – and as the four of your sons are now separated from you, your health was not here and I suppose not at home omitted – would that my birthday had come for from that day I hope never to be a burden to anyone.

Fortunately my birthday happens on Wednesday which is account day so I will be entitled to pay the very day I am sixteen. Remember Burns when my birthday comes

> 'That request permit me here
> When yearly ye assemble
> One round I ask it with a tear
> To him the son that's favoured'

I am astonished by your silence for except a few lines from [Shannon?] and a letter from you returning the certificates, I have not received a scrap from father, mother or brother.

Mr Hume has given me a state of James' expenditure in London which I now transmit you [. . .]

James amounts to £84 and mine to £101 odd, but the reason for the disparity is my getting all my accoutrements such as sword, cap and so in London, which James had not. This is really a great sum, but the amount which you intended to send up for James alone makes me suppose you will think this moderate. I cannot yet tell you exactly how much it will cost to land us in India as there may yet be some things required here, but by the statement you sent there appear to be in the hands of Mr Hume about £145 so our equipment will amount to £40 more. £200 will equip us both, after which the expense of our living in London since I arrived (for James paid Mr Scroggie about a week ago all demands) and the passage money (which we do not yet know but will be informed of it as soon as James sees the captain of the Sarah) must be paid – these demands (altho' comparatively speaking moderate) will perhaps startle you. Should ever the fickle goddess Fortune shine upon me it will also afford me much pleasure to repay you all my expenses.

From a book, called *The Cadet's Guide to India* [. . .] it appears that a cadet (which I do not hope to be for long) can live comfortably and yet save £120 per annum, but my desire in going to India never was a lust after money, but to lead a comfortable [. . .] life in a delightful country from which I hope to return after some years with a competency.

It would give me very much pleasure if it were in your power to assist Mr Christian in getting a situation of the same kind he is now trying for [. . .] for he is a very clever, deserving young man, and I am sure will give satisfaction to whatever situation he is appointed.

[. . .] I went for the first time to Dr Gilchrist, and [. . .] the language [. . .] doesn't appear so difficult as I was at first led to imagine [. . .]

On account of the great distance Mr Scroggie's is from Dr Gilchrist's classroom, Dr Gilchrist and Mr Hume have both recommended me to remove to No. 8 Buckingham St, Strand, where Dr Gilchrist's pupils meet daily and where I am boarded for 25s per week so that all letters you send me thro' Mr Hume can be directed as above. Are you to send the Montrose newspaper while I am in London or only when I go to India? I should like it in both places. Mr Hume says when you send them to India they should go in parcels.

Expecting soon to hear from you,
Believe me,

Your Truly Affectionate Son,
Alex Burnes[7]

Joseph Hume was acting like family, looking after the brothers, receiving their mail, inviting them to dinner, handling their accounts, advancing money where required and effecting useful introductions. Dr Gilchrist was the foremost British Hindu scholar of his day, and had invented the then most widely followed transcription of Hindi sounds into English letters. It was not compulsory for new cadets to take private lessons in Hindi before travel to India, but most did as command of languages was a recognised path to professional advancement.

*The Cadet's Guide to India*'s opening sentence reads: 'Before entering into details, let me caution parents or guardians against sending young men to India without letters of introduction [...]' It was, in polite society, an impropriety to speak to someone to whom you had not been formally introduced. With an introduction to the Governor or Commander-in-Chief from somebody on an equivalent social level, a cadet could be confident of receiving at least one invitation to a social function, which is why such letters were known in Company slang as 'soup tickets'.[8] From there a wider circle of senior people might take an interest in a cadet's career. Without such connections a cadet might languish in his quarters.

Alex had such letters from Joseph Hume himself. There was a striking willingness among Scots to give a hand up to fellow Scots. It was good of Admiral Fleming (he had changed his surname to inherit an estate)[9] to provide the Burnes brothers with a letter of introduction to his brother Mountstuart Elphinstone, at the request of his friend Lord Gillies. Adam Gillies of Brechin was a senior Scottish judge, whom James knew in that capacity and as a part of the Radical interest in Forfarshire. This was how the Scots network functioned. The key boost to Alexander's career was to be given by Sir John Malcolm, of whom it had been complained: 'Malcolm like a true good Scotchman, has a happy knack at discerning the special merits of those born north of the Tweed.'[10]

The cost of equipping his sons was a substantial burden for James senior - £200 would have been half a year's income for most Scottish country lawyers in 1821. *The Cadet's Guide* gives a very long minimum outfitting list:

4 dozen frilled calico shirts
1½ ditto Night-shirts
4 pair white cotton half-hose
8 pair Web Pantaloon Drawers
2½ dozen Towels
2 pair Flannel Drawers
1 Flannel Dressing-gown
1½ dozen single Night-caps

4 Black Silk Neck-handkerchiefs
3 pair strong stout Gloves
Foraging Cap to wear on board ship
A round Hat to land in on arrival
Sea Cot with two Cot Screws
Hair Mattress
2 Feather Pillows
8 Pillow-cases
4 pair full-sized sheets
1 pair Blankets[11]

The list goes on a lot further.

We can trace from these letters three qualities which were to be the mark of the young Alex. Firstly, 'My nature would not allow me to stop in the house, for I explored all the surrounding neighbourhood.' Secondly, on first encountering Urdu or Persian he says 'it doesn't appear so difficult'!

The third is kindness. For a fifteen-year-old he spends a lot of time thinking about others. Alex is concerned for the impecunious Willie Ross, for 'poor Paterson', whose family is always close to distress and for Mr Christian who needs a position as a schoolteacher. And Alex is very concerned about the financial costs that James and he are causing. He is glad he will no longer be a financial burden on the family. In fact, money worries run here as a theme, affecting all the named families, portraying Montrose as a community under stress.

Alex was homesick and upset he had not been receiving letters from his family. All his references to home reflect nothing but fondness: he is worried about his plants and pets, concerned about schoolfriends. He wanted the *Montrose Review*. While the Alexander Burnes who left for India was remarkably self-possessed, he was also just a homesick fifteen-year-old boy.

The five-month voyage out to India, around the Cape of Good Hope, could be hazardous. The *Emma*, on which Paterson had sailed, was a privately-owned India packet of 467 tons. It had gone down in Table Bay in a hurricane, on 4 January 1821, along with the *Dorah* of Calcutta. Fortunately there were no casualties, the ships having been abandoned.[12] A future colleague of Burnes, Henry Durand, lost all his possessions on his passage in 1828 when the *Lady Holland* struck Dassan island.[13]

Alex had to pass an examination to be admitted as a cadet and sat it, as was usual, on his sixteenth birthday, 16 May 1821. There were also a number of declarations required as part of Pitt's reforms aimed at reducing corruption in the Company. The docket survives in the East India Company's military records.[14]

To the Honourable Court of Directors of the United East India Company

The humble petition of Alexander Burnes

Sheweth, that your petitioner is desirous of entering the Military Service of the Company, as a Cadet for the Bombay Establishment to which he has been nominated by William Clarke Esq, at the recommendation of Joseph Hume Esq, and should he be so fortunate as to appear to your Honours eligible for that station, promises to conduct himself with fidelity and honour.

That your Petitioner has been furnished with the Articles of War, has read the Terms, and also the Resolution of the Court of the 9th August 1809, to which he promises to conform; as also to all the Rules[. . .] which have been [. . .] established by the Honourable Court [. . .]

And your Petitioner, as in duty bound, will ever pray.

Alexr. Burnes

**Director's Nomination**
I William Stanley Clarke Esq., being one of the Directors of the East India Company [. . .] do declare, that I have inquired into the character, connexions and qualifications of Mr Alexander Burnes and that in my opinion he is a fit person to petition the East-India Company for the appointment he now herein solicits.
Recommended to me by Joseph Hume Esq.

Wm Stanley Clarke East India House

Examined and Passed the 16th May 1821 by John Morris

Examination
[. . .]
7. Do you believe that any person has received, or is to receive, any pecuniary consideration, or anything convertible, in any mode, into a pecuniary benefit, on account of your nomination?
No – Certainly Not
8. Are you aware, that if it should be hereafter discovered, that your appointment has been obtained by improper means, you will be dismissed, and rendered ineligible to hold any situation in the Company's service again?
Yes.

Alexander Burnes

There is also a copy of Alexander's baptism record and a sworn statement from both his father and from Joseph Hume that no money had changed hands.

The twenty-year-old James was entering as an assistant surgeon, so went through a different process. In December 1820 the distinguished Scottish surgeon W J Chambers gave James a certificate from Guy's Hospital that he was 'qualified in physic to serve as an Assistant Surgeon at any of the Company's presidencies in the East Indies'. James then had to make his declarations before the Lord Mayor of London, which he did on 7 March 1821. James' nomination was from Robert Hempsall, another director.[15] Hume had been calling in favours.

It is worth noting one other cadet who joined that year. Nine days after Alexander, George LeGrand Jacob arrived at Leadenhall, the day after his sixteenth birthday which had fallen on a Sunday. He was nominated by the Scots director James Pattison, and his father was noted as 'a gentleman residing on his estate at Guernsey'. Jacob was to travel out with the Burnes brothers, and become Alexander's closest friend.

We have no record of Alexander and James' voyage, but many others recorded their impressions. Sleeping quarters for a cadet were typically little more than a plank about fourteen inches wide, in a tiny room with five others. An industrious cadet had five months to study his Indian languages and to ask questions of the old hands. Sir John Malcolm, returning to India as Governor of Bombay, entranced the young cadet Henry Rawlinson with endless anecdotes. Fellow cadets had an intense bonding experience at sea, as Alexander with George Jacob.

James' application docket includes a copy of the Company's passage regulations. The cadets had an important choice – a Captain's Table passage at £110 or a Third Mate's Mess passage at £70. This would make a large difference to status on ship, and on arrival. Probably the Burnes had to go for the cheaper option. The regulations stress that it was forbidden for cadets to purchase any further privileges from the Captain. Baggage allowances were the same for all and strictly enforced. These were tight considering cadets were starting a completely new life: one chest, of which the maximum depth and width was twenty inches, two smaller trunks, a box of books and a hat-box.

The start of the voyage was rendered unpleasant by sea-sickness among the passengers, horrid in cramped conditions, and hangovers among the sailors, inebriated on departure, an accepted feature of seafaring life. Thereafter there was reading, chess and amateur theatricals, but also boisterous deck games, plus fishing, and harpooning sharks. Albatrosses were caught with baited lines, and happily eaten, contrary to myth. Cadets were entertained by the sailors with stories of sightings of the Flying Dutchman and other yarns. The antics of the cadets would wear on the nerves of older passengers. The ship's master included bed and board in what he charged; generally the food was very bad and the wine execrable.

CHAPTER FOUR

## A Griffin in India

The *Sarah* reached Bombay on 31 October 1821.[1] After the stultifying ship, the crowds, bustle, sights and smells of Bombay crammed in upon them. Alexander felt a moment of comfort as the *Sarah* eased through the apparent chaos of masts to its berth; they passed a vessel from Montrose's neighbouring port of Arbroath. Suddenly, home did not seem quite so far away.[2]

Sporting the 'round hat to land in on arrival' specified, cadets were amazed by the jostling crowds of people trying to sell, or to be taken on as servants; and by the filth, the flies and the heat.

On 9 November Alex was posted to the 1st Battalion of the 3rd regiment of Native Infantry (NI). Four days later James was posted to the artillery at Malunga as assistant surgeon. On 18 November Ensign Alexander Burnes appeared on parade for the first time.

That careful letter of introduction from Admiral Fleming to his brother Mountstuart Elphinstone, now Governor of Bombay, paid dividends:

> The Governor [...] invited us to the most splendid fête I have ever beheld [...] and was extremely affable and polite, which, among a party of a hundred, and the most part general and great men, was a great deal [...] [a] grand public ball was given to Sir John Malcolm, on his leaving India [...] I had the honour of receiving an invitation; but where it came from I know not. It was, if anything, grander than Mr Elphinstone's, and held in a house [...] about the size of the old Council House at Montrose, illuminated with lamps from top to bottom.[3]

Alex wrote home that he found his fellow officers pleasant and gentlemanly. But, 'How dearly should I like to see little Cecelia or Charley trudging in to my canvas abode. But ah! That is far beyond probability. However, I may yet see Charley in India, for he seems a boy made for it.'[4]

On 30 April 1822 Alex wrote home again, expressing his hope that his regiment would go to China to take part in a war that appeared imminent. Otherwise he would volunteer to go on attachment, 'for if a man does not push on he will never see service, and, of course, will never be an officer worth anything. And what will the old maids of Montrose do for want of tea?' War was delayed, but it shows Alex was both active and ambitious.

Local languages were a key requirement for employment outside a garrison camp. Alexander studied assiduously, and instructed his servants not to speak English with him. In May 1822 he passed his interpreter's examination in Hindustani. He had taken on the added burden of learning Persian, which he found 'one of the most delightful languages that can be conceived'. By September he was enthusing over his love for Persian poetry.

That same month, Alex was posted to the 2nd Battalion, 11th NI, which was immediately ordered to Pune. There he greatly enjoyed the mountain scenery and the leisure pursuits of garrison life – he reported excitedly that he had an excellent horse and had killed his first hog with a spear during a three-day hunt. But he also commented on another aspect of local British society, 'which is very pleasant for India there being no less than 17 ladies in the cantonments almost all of which I have visited you may be astonished but I am turning a gay character.'[5]

The wife of his CO, Major Brooks, attracted officers like bees round the honeypot: 'Mrs Brooks is a great rider on horseback and [...] is a beautiful woman. She is rather young being only 27 and never goes out in the evening but she is attended by some of us, I have seen a troop of 12 Officers with her [...]' There is a hint of something racy about Alex's calls on the British wives of Pune. Sexual morality in the early 1820s was loose throughout all classes, and certainly in British India.

The tone at Pune had been set by the Resident and Commissioner Mountstuart Elphinstone, before he left in 1820 to become Governor of Bombay. He was the fourth son of Lord Elphinstone, an ancient Scottish title. His uncle had been a director of the EIC, and another uncle Admiral of the Company's navy. He never married, and carried on sexual liaisons with British and Indian women with the relish of a true Georgian, ranging from prostitutes to well-born ladies. Unsurprisingly, he occasionally contracted venereal diseases, which he treated with ointments of sulphur and mercury.[6]

One of Elphinstone's late Victorian biographers uses the lightest of disguise on his adventures in Pune:

> Bombay was near enough to bring a constant succession of visitors, among whom we hear of several ladies [...] He delighted in taking them on little tours through the Deccan, to visit old ruins or romantic scenery.[7]

Chief among these ruins were the nearby Ellora caves, with their sexually explicit sculptures. While British girls were supposed to be virgins on marriage, a great many were not. After marriage, fidelity in married women, particularly after they had produced the first male child,[8] was considered less important than it was to become. There was also little distinction in behaviour in the 1820s between the middle class and the aristocracy. Middle-class morality was not yet a dominant concept.

Emily Eden writes of the visit of the Governor-General's camp to Kurnaul, where she explains there were a great many 'single' British women whose husbands were away with the army:

> I never saw anything so happy as the aides de camp were at Kurnaul; flirting with at least six young ladies at once [. . .] there were dinners, balls, plays etc., and they always contrived to get a late supper somewhere, so as to keep it up till four in the morning. I dare say after four months of marching, during which time they have scarcely seen a lady, that it must be great fun to come back to the dancing and flirtation [. . .][9]

This open flirtation with married women is retailed as healthy fun by Emily Eden, who well knew that these supper assignations lasting until 4am were not all innocent. It was often hinted that officers' wives in India were not all they should be:

> The military ladies [. . .] are almost always quite young [. . .] showily dressed, with a great many ornaments, and chatter incessantly [. . .] While they are alone with me after dinner, they talk about [. . .] the disadvantages of scandal, 'the Officers' and 'the Regiment', and when the gentlemen come into the drawing-room, they inevitably flirt with them most furiously.[10]

The majority of British sexual relationships in India were between British men and Indian women. William Dalrymple states 'up to the nineteenth century, but perhaps especially during the period 1770 to 1830, there was wholesale interracial sexual exploration'.[11] As Lord Wellesley, a Governor-General who kept a number of Indian concubines and enjoyed sex with British community wives wrote: 'I assure you that this climate excites one sexually most terribly.'

Even as late as 1838 local mistresses could still be invited to a formal ball in Delhi in the presence of the Governor-General and his sisters: 'Englishwomen did not look pretty at the ball [. . .] and it did not tell well for the beauty of Delhi that the painted ladies of one regiment [. . .] were much the prettiest people there, and were besieged with partners.'[12] In 1810, writing the *East India Vade Mecum*, the standard background reading published by the East India Company for cadets, Captain Thomas Williamson took it for granted that officers would have local sexual companions. The main question was how many:

> When more than two ladies are retained by the same gentleman, the whole generally become perfectly passive, [...] appearing to associate with tolerable cordiality ... I have known various instances of two ladies being conjointly domesticated; and one, of an elderly military character, who solaced himself with not less than SIXTEEN, of all sorts and sizes.[13]

We learn from Williamson that local concubines of British officers expected two or three female attendants, perfume and jewellery. Ninety per cent were Muslim, they were good housekeepers, prone to jealousy, useful walking dictionaries, and total costs were about Rs40 per month. This was a small fraction of the cost of keeping a European wife. We do not know if Burnes kept a local partner, but he probably did.

Pune had been the capital of the Mahratta Confederacy which dominated much of India in the late eighteenth century and effectively ended the reign of the Mughal Emperors.[14] The Mahrattas had been the fiercest military opponents of British expansion in India, subdued only five years previously after forty years of bloody resistance. Indeed on 5 November 1817 Baji Rao, the Peshwa of Pune, an unwilling British puppet, made a last bid for independence, attacking the Residency with an army of 18,000 Mahratta horse and 8,000 infantry, mostly officered by European mercenaries.

At the battle of Kirki, four miles from Pune, Mountstuart Elphinstone had taken effective military control (he had been military secretary to Arthur Wellesley, later Duke of Wellington). General Sir John Malcolm with a strong force then tracked down the Peshwa, who was packed off to Kanpur on an annual pension of Rs8 lakhs. Pune was formally annexed in 1818 and was now British territory. These events were still fresh as young Alexander Burnes arrived. Alex himself used to ride the battlefield of Kirki and imagine the cavalry charges.[15]

Mountstuart Elphinstone described in 1819 the widespread hatred the British usually preferred to under-report:

> The desmukhs and other zamindars, the patels and other village authorities, who lose power by our care to prevent exactions ... The whole of the soldiery and all connected with them – all who lived entirely by service, all who joined service and cultivation, all who had a brother in employment who is now thrown back on the family, and all who had horses and were otherwise maintained by the existence of an army – detest us and our regular battalions, and are joined by their neighbours from sympathy and national feeling.[16]

Elphinstone's spies uncovered a plot headed by the priestly caste of Pune to massacre the British residents and seize the forts. He had all alleged plotters blown from guns without process. This increased the 'national feeling'.

On Christmas Day 1822 Alex was appointed as interpreter to the First Extra Battalion at Surat. This was his third regiment in an army career of just two years. But within a further year there was a fourth; at both Pune and Surat he had been on good terms with a Colonel Campbell, who offered him the position of Adjutant of the 21st Bombay NI. This was a promotion with an allowance of Rs600 a month. Campbell had been diffident in offering as he thought Alexander was looking for political rather than regimental duties, but Burnes declared: 'No man in his sound senses would refuse a situation of fifty or sixty guineas a month.' He was banking monthly savings of Rs53. At Surat he took on a servant, Ghulam Ali, who proved exceedingly loyal. Alex now wrote to his father urging him to send his brother Charlie out to a cadetship, as he could pay all expenses. But the family were unable to obtain a nomination. On 16 October 1823 Burnes was proud to remit £50 to his father in Scotland.

Four days later, gambling at cards, Burnes was horrified to find himself down six months' salary. Gambling debt was a routine scrape into which most cadets fell through boredom. Lord Valentia warned, 'There are a few steady and practised gamblers, who encourage every species of play among the young servants of the Company, and make a considerable profit by their imprudence [...]'[17]

Burnes was able to recover the money by the end of the evening, but he was shaken and does not appear to have had further gambling habits. Alex genuinely enjoyed the companionship of the mess. But he realised he was not entirely suited to regimental life. He confided to his diary:

> I am different from all around me. I dislike all gymnastic and athletic exercises. I like argument much – a jolly party only now and then; much study, and very partial to history, but dislike novels extremely, even Scott [...] I ought not to have been a soldier, though I glory in the profession, for I am too fond of pen and ink.

All his reading and thinking, particularly on scientific topics, combined with exposure to Islamic thought and culture, led Alexander to reject the narrow form of Christianity in which he had been brought up. He recorded:

> I have of late been deeply pondering in my own mind the strange opinions I begin to imbibe about religion [...] Would to God my mind were truly settled on this important subject! Could I be convinced fully of it, I would not believe in a future state: but it is an improbable thing to believe God has made man gifted with his own reason, after his own image, and yet to perish ... I lead a happy life [...] but I entertain different ideas of religion, and am afraid they will end in my having no religion at all.[18]

Like many in British India, Burnes was to attempt to reconcile his spiritual sense with rationalism and the claims of comparative religion through Freemasonry.

Alexander was next appointed interpreter to the Sudder Adawlut, or Civil Court of Appeal, in Bombay, where he assisted the British judges in determining disputes in accordance with local legal practice, and could enjoy the much wider society of Bombay, where James was now posted. James was elected a member of the Bombay Literary Society on 26 June 1823.[19]

\* \* \*

In Vilnius, Jan Prosper Witkiewicz had led a rather more privileged life than Alexander Burnes. He was a member of the old aristocracy, whose ancestors had ridden with Jan Sobieski and stemmed the tide of Muslim conquest before the gates of Vienna. He was just one year younger than Burnes, but after Alex had already been in India for three years was still in school in Krozach.

The Polish/Lithuanian state had been one of the great powers of Europe, but the political dysfunction of its institutions had led to it being devoured by neighbouring states. Napoleon had given a boost to Polish nationalism by reuniting the Grand Duchy of Warsaw and benefiting from its military potential. But Poland had died with his empire, and again been partitioned, the Russians claiming the greatest share. Polish nationalism survived; its growth coincided with the Romantic movement and struggle for re-emergence of political liberalism, which were to impart to Polish nationalism its distinctive character.

Six young noblemen of Witkiewicz's school formed a secret society to promote independence, the 'Black Brothers'. Being sixteen- and seventeen-year-olds, the figures of authority they knew were their schoolteachers, so they sent them anonymous letters supporting independence. They wrote anti-Russian graffiti on the walls. In November 1823 the boys were arrested and interrogated, roughly. They were tried by the Russian authorities in Vilnius as revolutionaries. On 6 February 1824 three were sentenced to death and three were sentenced to be knouted – often fatal.

The Russian Viceroy in Poland, Grand Duke Pavlovich, commuted their sentences to transportation. All were stripped of nobility and treated as peasants. Four, including Witkiewicz, were sent straight to Orenburg, the most remote Russian outpost, and there enlisted as common soldiers. The two oldest were to complete ten years of hard labour in Siberia before suffering the same fate.[20]

\* \* \*

Britain was again extending its borders in India. Unrest in Cutch, the maritime state on its north-west frontier, led to Company invasion. The 21st Bombay NI was among the first British forces ordered in, and Burnes went along as interpreter. In April 1825 the 21st were involved in fighting and Burnes found himself working closely with the British Resident, Captain Walter. He was regarded as having distinguished himself.[21]

The Cutch field force reunited James and Alexander. James had been at the convalescent hospital in the hills of Severndrug, then Malligaum and the 5th Madras NI – where his three predecessors had died of cholera. Having stemmed the epidemic through sanitation, he was viewed as having expertise in cholera, and appointed to Bombay to try to check its ravages amongst the 18th Bombay NI. He was then made Superintendent of a new Bombay Cholera Institute, and then appointed Surgeon to the British Residence in Bhuj, Cutch. This was a promotion and a key frontier post. James obtained this promotion through a competitive examination in local languages.

In April 1825 the Assistant to the Resident in Bhuj wrote to the government of Bombay that an army of 6,000 had gathered in Sind ready to sweep down on the small British garrison. He also believed that fifty assassins had been despatched to Bhuj in various disguises, while another army was preparing to fall on Luckput, and Ali Murad Talpur of Sind was urging his fellow Amirs that the time was right to raise their vast army and annex Cutch.

The letter also gives harrowing detail of the effects of the wars on the local population:

> the ryots have been deprived of the scanty pittance which remained to them after two years of famine – Not content with carrying off their grain and cattle, their houses and implements of husbandry were burnt to the Ground [. . .] I am afraid a final emigration will ensue [. . .] All trade has been suspended, the merchants have only been restrained from leaving the town in a body – by a promise which I have made to visit them [. . .][22]

The officer asks for permission to spend official money for relief – but concludes that Cutch's only hope was to be 'taken under the protection of the Honorable Company'. Britain's next annexation was in train.

Britain's move to take Cutch caused consternation to the Amirs of neighbouring Sind. They had ambitions of suzerainty over Cutch themselves, and were not prepared to allow local civil wars to pass without an attempt to impose their own interests. Sindian irregulars started to pour through the Thar desert into Cutch via the Nagar Parkar oasis, and there was suspicion that these were stiffened by Sindian royal levies. It seemed that a British territorial advance was likely to lead into a further advance into the neighbouring state, for the sake of 'stability' in their newly conquered territory, and in 1825 a field force of 8,000 was gathered for the invasion of Sind. Both Burnes brothers immediately volunteered. James was appointed assistant surgeon – his superior, five years older, was Dr John McNeill of Argyll. Alexander obtained the coveted position of Persian interpreter. It would put him right next to the commander.

Still anxious to assist the Burnes brothers, in January 1825 Joseph Hume had sent them letters of introduction to General David Ochterlony, also of Montrose parentage. Unfortunately Ochterlony, despite a highly distinguished history, had been relieved of command following disagreements with Calcutta. But Alexander replied to Hume, informing him that war with Sind appeared inevitable, and that:

> I am proud to say that the same good fortune which I had at the commencement of my career seems still to attend me, and that the late disturbances have elevated me from the regimental to the general Staff, having been appointed Quartermaster of Brigade to the Cutch Field Force [. . .] which makes my pay and allowances 400 Rupees a month.

Alexander now compiled a statistical paper on the district of Wagur. Statistics were the engine of British India, enabling revenues to be assessed and collected, troops to be raised, moved and supported, and economic development to be planned. Alexander's work was viewed as a model and submitted up the military hierarchy, eventually bringing Alexander to the attention of the newly arrived Governor, Sir John Malcolm, who approved a welcome financial bonus.

We have already bumped into John Malcolm several times; as Henry Rawlinson's companion on the passage out to India, as Ambassador to Persia in 1809, and as the Brigadier General who accepted the surrender of the Peshwa. At the fierce battle of Mahidpur on 21 December 1817, Brigadier Malcolm had with great personal courage led a frontal attack on the massed Mahratta cavalry.[23] Alex in his first Indian weeks had attended a Bombay farewell party for Malcolm, who was now back. Malcolm noticed Alex's work favourably. As did the Commander in Chief of the Bombay Army, General Sir Thomas Bradford, who instructed that Burnes attend Major T B Jervis to be taught surveying and mapping techniques to equip him for more political and intelligence work.[24]

In collecting detailed statistics for a survey of Cutch and Kattiawar, one fact leapt out at Burnes. In 112 towns and villages inhabited by Rajput tribes, there were nearly six male children for every female; not a single village had more girls than boys. Saira in the district of Dang had twenty boys and no girls, while Bibar in the district of Pawar had forty boys and five girls. Burnes was shocked by the prevalence of female infanticide, and produced a paper which baldly stated that British claims to have reduced the practice were unfounded.

This paper gives a vital insight into the mind of the twenty-one-year-old Burnes. He does not, as his contemporaries were increasingly inclined to do, write a homily about spreading Christianity among the heathen. His approach is humanistic. He explains the social causes of female infanticide: the Rajputs were an elite social group of landholders, with a non-Rajput peasantry beneath them. Their landholdings were by law divided equally among sons. To maintain their economic position, they wished to limit subdivision by preventing marriage. They had strict rules of caste which prevented females from marrying outside a very narrow group, in addition to which their rules on incest were extensive; potential husbands were therefore scarce. Unmarried women normally became to European eyes, prostitutes entailing a degree of disgrace. Burnes' perception was not one of orientalist misconstruction – even senior female members of the Bhuj royal family were sometimes compelled into prostitute status. All of these factors combined to result in 80 per cent of Rajput girls being killed at birth.

Most males therefore remained unmarried, or with lower-caste partners whose children could not inherit land, which was the social purpose of the abhorrent system – to keep landholdings together. Burnes argued that to tackle the practice of female infanticide, preaching or exhortation were insufficient and police action impractical, and what was needed was economic reform to address the fear in Rajput society of loss of status

This scientifically-based approach seems startlingly modern. There is nothing in Burnes' paper which could not have been written by a modern development agency. He was acutely aware that those who try to analyse and explain, rather than simply condemn, are often called apologists: 'By these remarks I am very far from advocating the barbarous custom of female infanticide. I wish merely to give an outline of the changes which our measures may, and will, produce.' His paper was submitted to the Governor, who ordered it read at the Bombay Asiatic Society. That Society forwarded it with a commendation to the Royal Asiatic Society in London, who published it.[25] Young Burnes was building an intellectual reputation.

He was also burgeoning socially. The Asiatic Society was the social hub of Bombay. The Literary Society, Geological Society and Geographical Society shared the same premises, which are still a joy to visit. The Asiatic Society had been founded by the Scottish lawyer and philosopher Sir James Mackintosh, with the aim of making the oriental knowledge of Company servants available to a wide European audience. John Malcolm was not just patron, but a prolific contributor.[26] On 27 June 1827 Alexander Burnes was elected to membership of the Bombay Literary Society, proposed by his brother James and seconded by Major Henry Pottinger.[27]

Burnes was entering public life in the tradition of a specifically Scottish school of imperialist and orientalist thought led by Malcolm, Elphinstone and Munro. This rejected Christian conversion and European institutions, and had an innate respect for Indian culture.[28] It was under strong challenge, not so much intellectual as emotional, from the Britnat evangelising ideology which was to replace it.

Another central social institution for the British of Bombay was the Masonic Lodge. Sir John Malcolm became a member of the Benevolent Lodge in Bombay on his arrival as Governor in November 1827, and Alexander Burnes, firmly in the family tradition, the following year.

The Benevolent Lodge was regarded as 'aristocratic'. Thirteen freemason NCOs of the Bombay Horse Artillery were posted to Bombay from Pune, where the Lodge was more democratic. They started holding meetings in the Apollo Gate of Bombay Fort. The Benevolent Lodge learnt of this, and invited them to join as honorary members. At their first meeting, the NCOs were told there were refreshments for them downstairs, while the officers were to dine upstairs. The men walked out.[29]

The next day the 'ringleader', Sergeant Willis, was summoned by the Colonel of the Horse Artillery. Willis stood his ground: the first law of freemasonry was that Masons 'meet upon the level'. Against much officer opinion, Malcolm insisted the men should join as equals. A decade later the Lodge split over the admission of Indians, which Burnes actively supported. It is reasonable to presume he was on Malcolm's side over the admission of non-officers.

In late 1827, Burnes' training in surveying techniques completed, he undertook a geological survey of Cutch, with particular attention to changes caused by the great earthquake of 1819. This had reshaped the Indus delta, and the Runn of Cutch, a great salt desert, was now under sea-water for much of the year. It allowed Burnes to apply his formidable scientific mind, and his talents as a draughtsman. It also was an adventure for a twenty-two-year-old, involving riding alone through new British territories still potentially hostile.

At the submerged town of Sindri, Burnes journeyed by boat for thirty miles along a salt lake that had recently been arable land. At the submerged fort, he stood on the top of battlements which rose to only two inches below the surface, and drank in the 'novel sensation'; no land was visible to the horizon, around all 360 degrees. He found that 2,000 square miles had been inundated, while westward a mound fifty miles long and up to sixteen miles wide had been raised. Burnes also noted the new channels the Indus had cut to the sea since 1819, scouring through the newly raised land formations. He carefully drew the new geological sections.

Burnes returned in 1828 to complete this survey. His work was so good it was used as the base for UN scientific studies of the next great Cutch earthquake in 2002. Published at Malcolm's request by the Bombay Asiatic Society, it caught the attention of the great geologist Sir Charles Lyell, one of the founders of the modern science. In his *Principles of Geology* he quotes from Burnes' study, and uses his maps and illustrations.[30]

Lyell's popular work did much to foster a fashion for geology, but also did a great deal to advance rationalism and undermine improbable religious beliefs. Lyell had the most direct influence on Darwin – he was his tutor at Cambridge. An understanding of the processes of geological change was incompatible with the belief that the earth was but a few thousand years old. Burnes had a great interest in geology and palaeontology, and a modern outlook. This may have related to his religious scepticism.

Burnes continued to pay close attention to geology, beyond his obligation to report to the Company on exploitable minerals. Charles Lyell was to be a signatory of Burnes' nomination to a Fellowship of the Royal Society, along with John Franklin.[31] Burnes and Lyell met a number of times in London including at the Geological Society in February 1835.[32] They became regular correspondents and Burnes sent back interesting discoveries, particularly fossils. In the New York edition of the *Principles of Geology* of 1868, Lyell acknowledged 'my friend the late Sir Alexander Burnes'.

Alexander also became a friend and collaborator of the great palaeontologist Hugh Falconer and his associate Proby Cautley as they went about classifying 80 per cent of then known species of dinosaur.[33] Falconer originated the evolutionary theory of punctuated equilibrium, now scientific orthodoxy. Burnes was able to discuss palaeontology with them and continually sent samples.[34] Lyell and Falconer were, like Burnes, from north-east Scotland, Lyell from Kirriemuir and Falconer from Forres.

In his wide-ranging intellectual interest and cool rationalism, Burnes was very much a product of the Scottish Enlightenment. This attitude combined with his unabashed joie de vivre mark him out as the pre-Victorian he was. Had he lived longer, perhaps like his acquaintance Charles Trevelyan, Burnes would have learned to cloak his past in Victorian hypocrisy. Burnes wrote to Charles Masson that in 1837 Trevelyan was travelling in India with four wives.[35] Burnes' early death exposed him to the full wrath of censorious Victorian historians in the immediately succeeding generation.

In his paper on the Cutch earthquake, Lieutenant Burnes did not forget he was surveying for military intelligence:

In a military point of view I do not think we have benefited from the alterations in the river [...] it is ill adapted for military operations [...] the approach to the country of the Ameers [is] more difficult to a regular army than ever [...] in invading Sinde it would always be advisable to reach the Indus as high up at its delta as possible as rivers will be less frequent in the march of an army [...][36]

The Bombay Asiatic Society forwarded this paper to the Royal Asiatic Society in London, where on 5 February 1831 it was read to a meeting by Alex's proud sponsor, Joseph Hume.

The Amirs of Sind were determined to keep the British as distant as possible; it was obvious that they were next in line for annexation. It was therefore a surprise and an intelligence-gathering opportunity when on 23 October 1828 Henry Pottinger received a letter from Murad Ali Khan, the principal Amir, requesting the help of a British doctor. Forty-eight hours later James Burnes was on his way, with a substantial escort.

James won the goodwill of the Amirs of Sind and put their relationship with the British on a friendlier footing than it had been for decades. However his report was scant of information on military resources, fortifications, revenues, trade and navigation, which the British government required. Pottinger described it to Malcolm as 'most unsatisfactory and meagre.'[37] Malcolm thought it of sufficient interest to order it published by the Bombay Asiatic Society, but agreed regarding its political and military content. In this period a number of Company surgeons were being transferred into the much sought-after Political Department after producing useful work, but James was not offered the chance. He was exceptional as a medical man; the Government of Cutch observed that 'there was no one of any class or rank who would not, if sick, reckon upon his services at midnight.'[38]

Alexander's work was attracting glowing opinions. In December 1827 General Bradford forwarded more results of his surveying to Malcolm with a striking commendation:

> In handing up for the information of [...] the Governor [...] the accompanying Supplementary Memoir to the Map of the Eastern branch of the River Indus by Lieut Burnes [...] I have again the gratifying task of recording His Excellency the Commander in Chief's unqualified approbation of the indefatigable zeal, talent and perseverance of that officer, whose labours have already on several occasions received [...] the favorable notice of Government[39]

Again Malcolm forwarded the work to the Bombay Geographical Society for publication[40] with his public comment that it 'affords a very creditable proof of Lieutenant Burnes's disposition to combine the advancement of general knowledge with a satisfactory performance of his public duties'.[41] Malcolm was an ardent fan of Robert Burns, and always travelled with a book of his poetry. This helped his increasingly warm relationship with the poet's young relative. Alexander's prodigious output continued. In August 1828 the Society received his paper on the alum mines of Mahore, together with geological notes of various strata revealed by the mining operations.[42] Promoted now to Assistant Quartermaster-General, his monthly salary had reached Rs800, approximately £1,000 per year, which made him one of Montrose's wealthiest citizens. On 25 February 1829 Alexander was elected to the Committee of the Literary Society; at the same meeting young Lieutenant Henry Rawlinson became a member.[43]

CHAPTER FIVE

## Dawn of the North-West Frontier

British India had benefited from a decade of comparative peace and consolidation after the great period of expansion culminating in the conquests of Wellesley in the Mahratta wars. The Governor-General, Lord Bentinck, was interested in internal reform and ideologically opposed to aggressive war. Second son of the Duke of Portland, the family were so wealthy that his career had been unimpeded by two major crashes.

In 1807 he had been dismissed as Governor of Madras after being blamed for the Vellore mutiny. Then, appointed Captain-General of Sicily (1812–15), he had ignored urgent orders to support Wellington in Spain, and instead pursued Quixotic schemes with Louis-Philippe d'Orleans for the unification of Italy. Returning to Sicily in 1815 after campaigning in Tuscany, he was forcibly prevented from landing on the orders of British Foreign Secretary Lord Castlereagh.

On appointment as Governor-General of India in 1827, he told the Montrose utilitarian James Mill, Secretary of the Board of Control, 'I am going to India, but I shall not be Governor-General, you will.' Less quoted is Mill's view of Bentinck: 'a well-intentioned but not a very well-instructed man'.[1]

During Bentinck's pacific rule, the eyes of the leaders of British India turned to far horizons, where they dimly perceived a new threat. Despite decades of Russian encroachment, in 1820 Persia still ruled a territory much larger than present Iran, extending into Muslim territories in the Caucasus. The Russian Empire was in successive wars capturing more of this territory. By the Treaty of Turkmenchai of 1828, Russia consolidated advances including the strategic fortresses of Yerevan and Nakhchivan. Russia now had full control of the Caspian. The articles of the treaty on stationing Russian Consuls throughout Persia, and Russian training of the Persian military, reminded British officials of the terms they themselves imposed on Indian states they were preparing to subsume. In addition Russian expansion was to be subsidised by Persia with

£4m, precisely the device the British used against indigenous states.[2]

In September 1828 Bentinck wrote to Malcolm:

> The fact is, that Persia is now little better than [...] a Maratha power [...] she is completely at the mercy of Russia; and if Russia should take it into her head to invade India, she will begin, not by the invasion of Persia, but [...] by a close alliance.[3]

Britain was bound by the treaties of 1809 and 1814 to assist Persia if attacked by a European power and had failed in this.[4] Persia concluded Russia was a better bet.

Not by coincidence, Alexander Burnes was now given his chance to explore the new boundaries of British India, towards Persia. As an officer of the Quartermaster-General's Department it was his duty to know the supply of provisions and facilities for quartering British troops, and he was ordered to journey to the mountain of Abu – which Burnes called 'the opportunity of exploring the whole North Western Frontier of the Bombay Presidency'. The twenty-three-year-old's report recommended further work as 'it was considered as the most probable line of route by which our Eastern possessions might be invaded by a European power'.[5]

Alex therefore made to General Bradford an audacious proposal, to move from surveying the Company's new territories to exploration beyond the frontier:

> Camp Bhooj 14 July 1828
>
> Sir,
> I herewith do myself the honor to transmit a Military Memoir [...]
>
> 1. [...] I have been forcibly struck at the meagre and uncertain knowledge we possess of the large tract of country to the Northward of that which I have traversed and [...] I am most anxious to explore at the opening of the ensuing season the unknown regions –
> 2. [...] the banks of the Loonee River [...] and [...] Jissulmere which has never yet [...] been visited by a European, tho' it must be an object of some interest [...] as being one of the points thro' which the French contemplated the invasion of our possessions during the late war.
> 3. A reference to the Map will show the vicinity of Jissulmere to the Indus [...] and did it appear [...] that it was possible to extend my journey to that point I should also feel most thankful for permission [...]
> 4. I [...] further [confess] a most ardent desire to descend the Indus from the point last mentioned to the Sea [...] My brother's late visit to their Capital has shown these rulers in so different a light [...] that I humbly believe there must be some chance of success.
> [...]

6. The opportunities which I have already enjoyed of gaining a knowledge of the character of the Natives [...] and the total absence of any complaints against either my servants or myself during that period will I trust be a sufficient safeguard to Government that I will not interfere with the prejudices of the people [...]

I have the honor to be
Sir
Your most Obdt Servant
Alex Burnes
D A Qmr Genl in Cutch[6]

Burnes was positively initiating exploration beyond the frontiers. Bradford strongly approved, writing to Malcolm with a further unequivocal commendation:

> The application contained in that officer's letter [...] His Excellency conceives (undertaken by this intelligent young officer) would prove productive of great and important benefit to the Public Service
> [...]
> The zeal, talent and indefatigable industry of Lieutenant Burnes, His Excellency has already on several occasions much pleasure in bringing to the Knowledge of Government.[7]

Unfortunately, establishment of garrisons of the Bombay Army in Cutch required a great deal of work and several officers senior to Burnes in the Quartermaster-General's Department were off sick. Burnes could not be spared. Believing this would end his cherished project for exploration, he conscientiously set out hand-over notes for somebody else:

Bombay 7th November 1828

Sir,
[...]
2. From Bhooj I proposed crossing the Runn to the outpost of the Deera Brigade [...] and there instituting inquiries into the state of Parkur which, from its constant cabals, I would not assuredly have visited without previously ascertaining [...] it is of some importance as being one of the few cultivated places in the desert and the resort of the disaffected from the surrounding countries [...]
3. From Parkur I should have proceeded round the head of the Runn north easterly [...] the Runn would have been an object of most minute inquiry – It has been represented on all our maps as 'never passable' but the information I received when in that neighbourhood in March last induced me to alter 'never' to 'seldom' [...] cattle are abundant about the Loonee and their utility in a military point of view I had hoped to determine
[...]

8. On reaching Jesselmere I would have waited on the Rajah who is one of the five Rajpoot chiefs [...] Jessulmere is said to be built as a hill fort, a plan of which would be desirable. It is also on the high road from Ajmere and indeed Hindoostan to Sind and through this channel much opium and goods are transported. Enquiries into the commerce would have occupied my minute attention [...]

I have the honour etc.
Alex Burnes
D A Q M General[8]

Having received these notes from Burnes, Bradford wrote to Malcolm suggesting that Lieutenant James Holland, Persian interpreter on his staff, conduct the exploration.[9]

Burnes had been working closely with the new Resident, Pottinger, who had the direction of British policy in Cutch. Pottinger now came to young Burnes' rescue, arguing to Malcolm that Burnes should go instead, with an analysis of Burnes' methods as an intelligence officer which is crucial to the understanding of this biography:

there is no officer [...] who is so peculiarly qualified [...] to give full effect to the plan he has himself suggested. The manner in which he has on all occasions conducted his statistical investigations [...] amongst various tribes of people naturally suspicious, deserves to be noted, and the happy tact that he possesses of conciliating and gratifying the natives by the kind and friendly tone of his intercourse with them at the very time he is acquiring by that intercourse, information from them [...] strikes me to be peculiarly worthy of [...] commendation.[10]

Malcolm agreed, adding that he would prefer delay to the journey being deputed to somebody other than Burnes. Bradford suggested that James Holland might then assist Burnes, and Holland's letter makes plain that Burnes was regarded as a star: 'I have not the presumption to suppose my exertions can ever be of the same service to Government as those of that talented officer, but I cannot refrain from expressing a belief that the exertions of two young officers [...] would be of greater avail, than those of one unaided.'[11]

Malcolm was so impressed that he decided to transfer Burnes into the elite Political Branch, initially on an acting basis, as assistant to Pottinger. As Cutch was so recently under British control, this was a good appointment. Burnes' elation was tempered by the financial stipulations. He was to be Assistant Resident at Bhuj and continue as Deputy Assistant Quartermaster-General of the Army, but draw only one salary. He was not to be eligible for the normal substitution pay when Pottinger was absent – which Malcolm noted was 'almost always'.

Malcolm stated these conditions would annually save the Company – and cost Burnes – over RS6,000, about £600. Burnes' sole additional remuneration was to be RS300 per year over his army salary. Malcolm made plain that exploration beyond the frontier was the priority, and instructed Pottinger that it must 'appear that the survey is of a secondary object [. . .] [which] will tend greatly to allay that jealousy and alarm which might impede [. . .] the progress of his topographical inquiries[. . .]'[12] Indian princes were well aware that the purpose of such surveys was to prepare for the movement and operation of British armies.

Holland was already living at Bhuj with James and Alexander. The Company army had taken over the massive hill fort. The surrounding walls and towers still stand, connecting the peaks of a cluster of hills above the separately walled city. The British army encamped inside the fort, and stayed a long time – the few surviving internal buildings are barracks from the early twentieth century. The Resident lived just beneath the fort. Pottinger's Residence stood until the earthquake of 2002; it was from 1946 in use as the Indian Army Officers' Mess.

The armies of the Company moved their major north-west frontier post forward as British India steadily expanded. First Surat, then Kheda (Kira to the British) and then Bhuj was the military headquarters, reaching Karachi in 1839. Alexander was intimately concerned in each of these movements. He was posted in Surat from 1823 to 1824. The Cutch expeditionary force with which Alexander and James served was based in Kheda. It was there in 1828 that Alexander was initiated as a Freemason, in Benevolent Lodge No. 480, Kira.[13]

Today there is no memory in the town of Bhuj of a large British garrison. At the Old Palace museum, I told the curator I was researching Burnes. 'Alexander or James?', he immediately replied. But even he did not realise how large the British presence had been, and I am not sure he quite believed me.

The British garrison in Bhuj peaked in 1826 while war with Sind threatened. The Distribution Return of the Bombay Army gives the figures shown for Bhuj:[14]

| Date | Europeans | Natives |
| --- | --- | --- |
| 1 January 1823 | Foot Artillery 38 | Gun Lascars 33 |
| | Infantry 3 | Infantry 1719 |
| | | Pioneers 13 |
| 1 January 1826 | Dragoons 543 | Gun Lascars 114 |
| | Horse Artillery 74 | Infantry 4990 |
| | Foot Artillery 90 | Pioneers 11 |
| | Infantry 685 | |
| 1 January 1828 | Infantry 35 | Gun Lascars 69 |
| | | Infantry 3147 |
| | | Pioneers 13 |
| 1 January 1830 | Infantry 107 | Gun Lascars 89 |
| | | Infantry 1866 |
| | | Pioneers 26 |

While Bhuj was a remote and dusty outpost, it was nonetheless a bustling one. There would have been quite a social life among the officers of the garrison, who would change as regiments were rotated. Malaria was endemic and a visit to the British cemetery is sobering. But it also reveals that not only officers but other ranks sometimes had wives at the station, and there were British children too. The cemetery is locked and difficult to access, and inhabited by a pack of wild dogs. I was not able to stay long, but enough to get a sense of the community in which the Burnes brothers lived.

The youth of those buried is shocking, most in their early twenties. James must have been fraught as the community doctor. Emily Eden notes: 'It is melancholy to think how almost all the people we have known at all intimately have in two years died out [. . .] None of them turned fifty; indeed all but Mr S between thirty and forty.'[15] She added that John Colvin was posted to Delhi in 1826 as one of 'a very large party of young men'. Age thirty-six, he was the sole survivor.

We can imagine Bhuj society as typical of other British stations. Any military and political work would largely be conducted in the fresh hours after dawn. The afternoon was often devoted to sports or social calls.

We know that the Burnes group gathered for regular dinners, including some modelled on the revelrous *Noctes Ambrosianae* portrayed in *Blackwood's Magazine*. Burnes got these up with the help of the chaplain James Gray, who had participated in the original Edinburgh *Noctes*. Gray had been a figure on the Edinburgh literary scene; the brother-in-law of James Hogg, he was

Robert Fergusson's editor and one of Robert Burns' friends in Dumfries, and had taught Burns' children.[16] The Burnes brothers could not have hoped to find such congenial company in Bhuj. Alex played the role of chairman in the literary debates and repartee.[17] James and Alexander would be joined by Gray, Holland and other officers, with the Burnes sisters and any other available ladies. Anglo-Indian dinners were big formal affairs with huge quantities of meats, curries, wines and spirits being consumed. Each guest brought their own khitmutgar to serve them.[18] It was common for a European household to have two dozen servants.

In Bombay on 28 March 1829 James Burnes made a good marriage to Sophia, daughter of Major-General Sir John Holmes. The happy couple settled down in Bhuj in a bungalow in the British lines, and there were born George (1829), Fitzjames (1830), Sophia (1832) and Holland (1833); little Sophia died just after her first birthday.[19] I took flowers, but could not find her grave.

Alexander and James paid for each of their sisters, Anne, Elizabeth, Jane and Cecilia, to come out in turn to India. This was a fairly certain way for them to find husbands. They stayed with James and Sophia in Bhuj, and all caught and married their army officer. On 3 March 1831 Elizabeth married Major Richard Whish in Bombay. Ann married Captain William Ward at Bhuj on 6 April 1833, a relief after three years. On 11 July 1833 Jane married James Holland in Ahmedabad. Finally Cecilia, ten years younger than Alex, married Captain John Major at Bhuj on 12 November 1839. Thus the Burnes family was based in Bhuj for at least thirteen years.

Pottinger had made his name in 1809 as a young Lieutenant with a very daring exploration through Cutch, Sind and Kelat into Persia, then as Envoy to Persia. The journeys of Pottinger and his companion Captain Christie were the prototype of the Great Game. They travelled as Tartar Muslims, disguised as horse dealer or pilgrim. At Kelat they split and made rendezvous in Isfahan, over three months of dangerous travel later. Pottinger secretly mapped 2,412 miles, mostly never travelled by the British before.[20] Christie took a more northerly route through Herat, and the conclusion they brought back to Malcolm was that a European invasion of British India through Herat was possible, through Kerman and Kelat not. Pottinger was only twenty and became Malcolm's most trusted officer. His twenty-three-year-old companion, Captain Christie, two years later became one of the first casualties of the Great Game, dying at the head of a battalion of Persian infantry, trying to halt the advance of Russian forces. Russia had been given a formal assurance British 'advisers' would not fight them. In consequence, when Christie was found wounded on the field, they sabred him.

It is difficult to know what restraint the presence of his sisters and James' wife placed on Alex's sex life. There is no indication of a permanent local companion for Alex in his bungalow. This does not exclude there having been one. Charles Metcalfe, an Acting Governor-General, had a Sikh wife and three acknowledged Eurasian children. The doyen of Victorian Indian historians, Sir John Kaye, in 1854 wrote a two-volume biography of Metcalfe which completely omitted his racially unacceptable family. For Alex to inhabit a Scottish family circle in Bhuj was not incompatible with an unmentioned local sexual companion. As Durba Ghosh puts it, 'For many men in colonial settlements, sexual relationships with native women were a type of public secret [...] but native companions and their children were rarely seen, acknowledged or entertained at public events.'[21]

Pottinger was active sexually throughout his colonial career. We have no details for Bhuj, but in 1843 as Governor of Hong Kong he conducted an open affair with 'Pretty Mrs Morgan, fair, fat and forty' which contributed to the arguments with British merchants that led to his resignation.[22] In 1847 he was quickly removed as Governor of Cape Colony because British Indian sexual behaviour was not acceptable in South Africa.[23] The Cape Coast archivist recorded, 'No other Governor of this colony ever lived in such open licentiousness as he. His amours would have been scandalous in a young man, in one approaching his sixtieth year they were inexcusable [...] a cold, calculating, sneering, unsympathetic demeanour prevented men of virtue being attracted to him.'[24]

Malcolm and Pottinger agreed that British India needed to expand to the north-west to reach secure borders. They now sent Alexander and James Holland to explore beyond the frontiers, on the pretext of persuading the Soda tribes to stop harbouring marauders who launched regular raids into Cutch. They were to survey routes for future British army movements and positions for the defence of the frontier, and assess the political and commercial structures of neighbouring states.

On 29 September 1829 Burnes received his orders to start.[25] He had been appointed Acting Assistant Quartermaster-General, a brevet Captain. Official correspondence to Burnes varies spasmodically between 'Captain' and 'Lieutenant' from 1828 to 1831.

This mission was Burnes' first diplomatic assignment. His instructions were loose, encouraging him to survey routes over the Runn of Cutch to the Indus, to survey as much of that river as he could, and if possible press on into Sind itself. Parkar was strategically important as its oasis defined the only military route through the vast and desolate sands of the Thar desert.

Pottinger provided guidance notes. The Parkar chiefs were to understand that now the British controlled Cutch, the world had changed. On the other hand, Burnes must avoid 'angry remonstrance' as the chiefs were dangerous murderers. They should not stay in Parkar long, so as not to give time to the Amirs of Sind to react. They should then explore the Luni river up to Pali, on the pretext of investigating trading opportunities in opium. Pottinger would send a qasid (messenger) to meet them at Parkar with harmless instructions which they might show if challenged. Surveying must be done in secret.

> you are to remember that [. . .] your [. . .] safety is a consideration paramount to everything else [. . .] [you] [. . .] should [not] go furnished with any scientific apparatus, or instruments, beyond compasses and small pocket sextants to take altitudes etc. It would no doubt be very desirable to have perambulators and theodolites, but I look on it that they would excite so much suspicion and surprise, as would counteract all other precautions.[26]

The opium trade figures prominently in all of Burnes' explorations. In 1828, the monopoly on sales of opium from British India accounted for 16 per cent of the EIC's revenue. Opium sales to China through agents (it was against Chinese law) paid for the vast amounts of tea the Company exported from China to the UK. Duty on this tea accounted for an astonishing 10 per cent of government revenue in London. Opium trade routes were therefore commercial information of national importance.[27] The trade was so valuable the Company gave its opium agents the colossal pay of £7,500 p.a. – more than the Chancellor of the Exchequer, the highest British government salary. Shipping of opium in Portuguese vessels from Karachi was a major breach in the Company's monopoly, and a major driver behind interest in Burnes' explorations.

The raids of Khosa tribesmen on British trade had been an irritant to Bombay and Calcutta since at least 1814, when Captain Holmes had been sent to attack Khosa raiders. These raiders were part of the excuse for British treaties in 1814 and 1819 which made Cutch a British protectorate. The British had always believed the Khosa were instigated by their nominal sovereigns the Amirs of Sind, and in 1820 a British force had marched on Parkar and attacked both the Khosas and forces of the Amirs. The Governor-General had intervened to prevent Mountstuart Elphinstone, then Governor of Bombay, from launching a full invasion of Sind.[28] Alex and James Burnes had operated against the Khosas with the Cutch field force.

Burnes and Holland finally left Bhuj on 1 December 1829. At twenty-four, Burnes was the elder by two years. As they rode out into the vast, scorching, wind-blown dunes of the great desert, they were thrilled at this opportunity. They became lifelong friends; three years later Holland married Jane Burnes.

If Burnes performed well it might open up permanent appointment to the Political Branch. The reports he submitted are therefore painstaking. In the first, marked 'Camp at Keerawow, 14th December 1829',[29] he apologised for reporting in such detail. He noted he was the first European ever to visit other than on a punitive raid, and added he was motivated by a 'great anxiety to shew myself worthy of the honour and trust which the Government have conferred upon me'.

He lived a great deal of his life in tents, and it is important to form a picture of these camps. British officers had large, individual tents. These would be taken ahead by bearers and pitched, ready for the officers' arrival in the evening. Their escort and servants would inhabit numerous tents around them. The camp would be very diffuse, as men of differing castes could not share a tent or cook their food together. Camp-fires were therefore numerous and small. Horses and baggage animals would be pegged or corralled on the margin of the camp.

The kind of tent in which Burnes slept would have had both an inner and an outer; valets and bodyguards were sometimes allowed to sleep in the space between. At the entrance and ventilation points would be hung additional screens called tatties, kept soaked to provide cooling through evaporation. In very hot weather the British sank a pit under the tent. The floor was covered with rich carpet. The official issue tent for a subaltern, the most junior officer, was a substantial twelve feet square, but many officers used larger, private tents.[30]

A contemporary traveller in India, Charles Hugel, had a tent with poles twenty-five feet high – like a modern British telegraph pole. The outer roof alone of Hugel's tent weighed 600lb, and the fabric needed six horses to carry it. William Hough wrote that when a regiment's tents were brought down by a storm, sleeping officers were in danger of being killed by falling tent poles. There are numerous references to marches delayed by heavy rain, because the wet tents were too heavy to be lifted.

Burnes arrived at Nagar, capital of Parkar, on 10 December 1829, and the Rana of Nagar, Jugaji, came to meet him: 'He brought along with him most of the inhabitants of Nuggur', an indication of how unusual was a visit from a British officer. Jugaji believed that Burnes had come to arrest him for the murder of his predecessor. In his report, Burnes makes light of any danger, but plainly the situation must have been tense. Burnes' instructions were to force Jugaji to stop giving shelter to bandits with whom he was closely linked. It was a difficult position.

Burnes was a model of tact, combining reassurance with threat:

> I told him, that I was not sent to interfere with the politics of the state and that I was happy to hear he had been confirmed in the title of Parkur by the Ameers of Scinde [...] but I evaded all allusion to the foul murder which he had committed [...] to achieve it. I said, that tho' Parkur was no longer the den of thieves which it had been [...] yet it was still a cause of much dread to the neighbouring countries [...] generally to impress upon his mind, that a continuance of such practices must one day bring ruin upon him.[31]

The Rana offered to hand over to the authorities in Cutch any named fugitives, and to take stringent measures on his frontiers to prevent the further passage of plunderers. He represented a number of dissident groups who had fled from political persecution in Cutch or Sind, and said that he had given them land to farm. Burnes replied that he 'was not instructed to prevent his shewing acts of civility and hospitality to men in distress', but that he should beware the danger of sheltering the wrong people. He promised that good actions would be rewarded, and presented a pair of fine pistols.

Burnes then moved on to Virawow, where he met the chief of the Soda tribe, Punjaji. Here Burnes made an explicit promise of cash reward in return for the suppression of banditry. Punjaji had a considerable revenue from the possession of the God, Gricha, to whom pilgrims came from a wide area. Punjaji's father had killed a neighbouring Soda ruler, Thakur of Pitapur, forty years previously to seize the idol, and a deadly feud had continued ever since.

The Amirs of Sind claimed suzerainty over the Sodas, and enforced a tribute on the resentful Punjaji through annual visits – the *thanna* – by a troop of Baluchi warriors. Burnes was able to witness one:

> A thanna of sixty Beloochees has been at Veerawow for the last week to demand the annual tribute [...] Last year the tribute paid amounted to eighty 'rulsees' of grain, which is always sold in the country and may yield the paltry sum of a thousand rupees to the Chief Ameer of Scinde [...] some one of the Sirdars of the court of Hyderabad receiving an order to proceed to Parkur and collect as much money as possible, and if their demands be not complied with, they always help themselves to a portion of cattle.[32]

Burnes was able to show goodwill by assisting the Sindian party with medicine. His political report on Parkar was followed by thirty close-written pages on geography, topography – with a particular eye to facilities for a passing army – geology, commerce and anthropology. The whole is an impressively clear piece of work. Pottinger was pleased and passed it on to Malcolm. The reply of 12 January 1830 is entirely approving:

> you will be pleased to convey to that officer the satisfaction of Government with his interesting and useful account of Parkur as well as for his discreet and conciliating attitude towards the chiefs of that district. Nothing can more fully

evince the expediency of combining political duties with those of geographical research [...] and if [...] the incursions of plunderers cannot be prevented, we shall at least become possessed of information that will enable us to defeat them.[33]

More importantly for Burnes, Malcolm was so impressed that he forwarded the report on for the attention of the Governor-General in Calcutta.[34] Alexander Burnes was being noticed in high places.

On 24 December Burnes was able to report that they had now crossed the Thar desert and followed the Luni river up to Chitalwana. They intended to make a further loop through the desert to explore the oases before continuing to Pali.[35] Alexander recorded in his official journal a fascinating account of how he carried out his survey, and especially his technique of pumping people for information:

> I march exactly at daylight and survey till about 10 o'clock which, in the mildness of the cold season, can be borne without inconvenience. On the road I always enter into conversation with the village guides whose extreme simplicity fits them well to convey information about themselves, their country and their customs.
>
> By 2pm the survey of the morning figures on the map and the latitude is determined to correct it, when [...] two or three [...] villagers are invited into my tent to talk with me till within half an hour of sunset. I ask the distances of all the villages around within ten miles the road to each and the cross distance of one to another which I sketch roughly on paper [...]
>
> The information on these points is acquired slowly in the intermediate spaces between conversation with the villagers who are generally so delighted to have a hearing granted them to all they have to say, that all suspicion is banished [...] I have heard, I believe, in almost every village, the private history of its owner, the legends of its gods, the notions of the people and their minute customs and prejudices and with due heed to such matters one will readily find that the number of cosses[36] and the number of houses of each village will soon follow [...]
>
> In the evening I take the angles to all hills and towns in sight of my encampment and also a series of bearings to such as are beyond view by a guess on the direction being pointed out by a villager [...]
>
> On the march I take three or four series of similar angles [...] and, with the assistance of the native information [...] can easily construct the map.[37]

When he submitted the map to government, he added:

The latitudes throughout have been determined by the sextant with the false horizon. Observations were taken daily by two different sextants and, in most instances, the mean of the two laid down as the correct parallel after the necessary corrections for refraction parallax etc. etc. had been made.

> The parallels of latitude have been laid off on the scale of [damaged] statute miles to a degree; the meridians of longitude on the other hand are given according to their value calculated by their distance from the equator [...]
>
> It was indeed prudent to avoid [...] carrying any instruments or apparatus which might excite the suspicions of the people, perambulators and theodolites were therefore dispensed with and the valuable compass by Smalehalder substituted [...]
>
> The rate of march was previously determined by perambulator [...] to be a few yards less than four miles an hour [...] There were many opportunities occurred by cross-bearings from other hills at a considerable distance to judge of the justice of this calculation and it has been verified both by them and by latitude.
>
> The survey [...] laid down in this map was much facilitated by the hills with which they are studded, Some of them were visible from a distance of forty-five miles and became thus, as so many points to check the different portions of the survey, and which have rendered the map trigonometrical.

Behind the published accounts of all of Burnes' travels lay this continual, intensive survey work, in addition to all the commercial, political, historical, cultural, ethnographical, geological and archaeological information collected. It is not an accident of nomenclature that while most of the correspondence on Burnes' travels and negotiations was addressed to the Political Committees of the EIC in Bombay, Calcutta and London, the surveys are always addressed to the Secret Committees. This is the kind of information which accompanied the maps:

> Parkur is open to attack from all sides and could be approached by an army with heavy guns from the South East by 'Nurrabate' but any advance made into the country with ultimate intentions on Sinde would be inadvisable as the road is not passable beyond Parkur. Guns might be dragged along the Runn banks but the desert would be rendered impregnable in a day by filling up or concealing the wells [...] The roads before Parkur are passable for carts but beyond none but beasts of burden travel. Water is abundant in the district and might be found about ten feet beneath the surface.[38]

Unfortunately, while the quality of Burnes' work in Parkar was undoubted, the expedition was not welcome in the Governor-General's offices. Calcutta did not share Pottinger's view that a detailed knowledge of what lay beyond its north-west frontier was essential to the security of British India. They were primarily concerned with reducing expenditure and making the Company profitable. Sending two young officers exploring, who might get themselves killed and cause problems, was not on the agenda.

There was also a turf battle here. Relations with foreign states were strictly the preserve of the Governor-General and the Supreme Government in the

Bengal Presidency. The Governors of the Bombay and Madras Presidencies were not permitted to run their own foreign policies, and Bombay officers like Burnes and Holland were not allowed on missions in foreign states without the express permission of the Governor-General. This had not been sought. This, and the ramifications of being 'only' a Bombay officer, affected Burnes' career.

Even before Burnes had reached Parkar, a letter had been sent from Calcutta to Bombay curtly ordering the end of the mission. On 26 January 1830, having just received that instruction, Charles Norris, the Chief Secretary in Bombay, wrote to Pottinger and Burnes ordering a stop.[39] But Burnes was 700 miles away before the order reached Bhuj.

Pottinger by then had written to the British political agents – officers detached to foreign capitals – in Jaipur, Ajmir and Udaipur, asking them to assist Burnes.[40] This compounded the problem. While there was a tacit acceptance in Calcutta of Pottinger's intelligence gathering in Sind and Kelat, the Rajput states were very different. These political agents were Bengal officers.

On 4 January 1830 Pottinger had sent further instructions to Burnes and Holland to push on:

> I have now to request, that you will continue your survey and inquiries in the direction of Jessulmere and Ooch.
> It is [. . .] impossible that at this distance I can even form a conjecture of the serious obstacles that may oppose your advance [. . .] I must therefore [. . .] leave everything to your sound discretion and judgement, and only
> [. . .] remind you, that you are neither to run into difficulties, nor to endanger your lives [. . .]
> The project of your descending the Indus [. . .] into Scinde I consider to be almost hopeless, for I feel certain, from the interest your visit to Parkheer has already attracted, that the Ameers would never consent to your entering their dominions [. . .] I cannot disguise from myself that means might be taken by them to make away with you in such a manner as to render it impossible to prove that you had not been waylaid and murdered by robbers.
> You had better continue to despatch [. . .] sketches of your routes and notes on the tracks through which you pass, for the purpose of being deposited at this place till your return.[41]

This letter reveals how dangerous the experienced Pottinger considered this expedition to be. A copy to Malcolm drew an instant reply stating that in view of the dangers, Burnes and Holland must immediately be ordered not to cross the Indus.[42]

On 8 January 1830 at 5pm, Burnes and Holland rode up to the gates of Jaysulmir with their small escort of local horsemen. Burnes described the fortress as 'commanding and magnificent', crowning a rocky hill, triangular in shape with sides three hundred yards long, and having three or in places four concentric walls and 175 towers and bastions.

At the gate of the castle, Burnes' party were detained and only Burnes and Holland allowed to enter. It must have been an intimidating experience:

> We continued to advance on horseback and passed through four strong gates till we alighted [...] and were conducted [...] through five or six courts and as many more now very dark staircases [...] Every place [...] was lined with the guards of the Prince [...] the Seiks, I noticed, were nearest the person of the Prince. Two flights of steps from the summit we were met by the Prime Minister of the Rawul, a Brahmin, and introduced by him to the durbar. On entering, Guy Sing rose from his throne [...] and advancing a few steps on a cushion stretched out his open hand (which is simply touched by the person) and then desired us to be seated on a cushion spread out in front of his jaddee and nearly on a level with it. On both sides sat his chiefs and men of weight in the community arranged in regular order, behind him were his relations and domestics and on his right hand stood his minister [...] strict silence was preserved and this, with the cleanly whiteness of their garments, gave a considerable solemnity to the scene. The appearance of the Rawul himself was most dignified, he is rather stout, but has both an intelligent and pleasing complexion. He was plainly dressed, without any other ornament than a pair of elegant gold bracelets and a 'sirpeesh' of rubies and diamonds on his turban [...][43]

They found the Rawul affable and full of questions about British customs and technology, but without pausing in his flow for an answer. The meeting concluded with expressions of his desire for friendship and co-operation.

Pottinger was now fighting Bentinck's instruction to terminate the mission. In sending Malcolm the Jaysulmir reports, Pottinger suggested 'these documents might be sent [...] in order that His Lordship the Governor-General-in-Council may see how well Lieutenant Burnes and Holland have already acquitted themselves [...] and perhaps, in consequence, be induced to modify the intimation contained with Chief Secretary Swinton's letter of the 4th December 1829.'[44]

By 9 February Burnes and Holland had reached 'Gajussoor 14 miles beyond Pallee'. They were in the territory of the Raja of Jodhpur, who had sent them an escort, and wished them to visit Jodhpur itself. But as Jodhpur was east and their goal was north-west, they politely declined. They now sent back to Pottinger very extensive notes, journals and maps, and Burnes set out their future route to Uch, from where they intended to descend the Indus by boat.[45] Pottinger meanwhile was at pains to state to Malcolm that Bentinck's instruction to terminate 'Was dispatched from the residency to Lieut Burnes on the 21st [...] but owing, I presume, to the rapid manner which that officer has moved from one part of the country to another, it had not reached him'.

The young men arrived in Pali on 1 February, where they wrote reports on the opium trade. They reached Gagara on 7 February and Ajmir on 17 February. They stayed there three days, preparing to strike out across the desert to the Indus. Finally, on the very eve of departure, the instruction from Bentinck caught up with them and they had to turn for home.[46] They returned through Bimalia to Bhuj. On 19 March Alexander wrote to his sister Anne in Montrose a breathless account of his adventures.[47]

The formal reports they prepared – all 199 crammed pages of them – appear entirely to be in Burnes' hand. They include records of temperatures taken at 6am, 10am and 2pm daily in ninety-seven different locations, the analysis of 216 geological samples, reports on commerce and trading routes, navigability of the Luni, practicality of roads for artillery, fortifications, revenue and availability of forage and the height of hills. His map was accompanied by a (mostly) alphabetical gazetteer giving information on 253 villages. Here is an extract:

> **Siew**  A village of 100 houses belonging to a Bhattu chieftain 50 miles E.N.E. of Jaysulmere, and noted for harbouring a set of thieves [. . .] The Daoodpootras lately revenged themselves on the place by filling up the wells and throwing down its gurry.
> **Sutteesa**  A village of 60 houses, 40 miles E.N.E. of Jaysulmere, similarly situated to the village of Siew above described. The chief of it is a relative of him of Siew.
> **Syad**  A village of 25 houses, 9 miles E of Jaysulmere, belonging to Jessore Rajpoot. It is built on the brow of a Rocky Hill, and as the houses are terrace roofed, it has at a distance the appearance of a fort. Water is to be had from pits dug in the bed of a tank.
> **Taitra**  A village of 100 houses now nearly deserted, the residence of a Bhattee chief 70 miles N.E. from Jaysulmere. Its chief like him of the neighbouring place of Barras. Indeed all the Bhattees are plundering characters. Taitra is about 12 miles S. of Pohura.
> **Tunmote**  A frontier and small strong fort about 100 miles N.W. of Jaysulmere. It is a subject of dispute between the Daoodpootras and the Rawul of Jaysulmere.[48]

The disappointment which Burnes and Holland felt at having to terminate their mission had to be subsumed in the major task of writing up the reports and preparing their maps. These were submitted to Malcolm under a secret dispatch of 6 July 1830[49] forwarded on by him to the Governor-General under a minute of 9 August,[50] drafted by Burnes, who had joined Malcolm in Dupuri.

For letters to be exchanged with London at this time took a year. Burnes did not know it yet, but for the first time he was being noticed with approval at the EIC headquarters in Leadenhall Street, not for this mission, but for the map and memorandum of the Mouth of the Indus completed a year previously. On 10 March 1830 the Military Committee of the Court of Directors wrote to the Governor-General commending 'the zeal and talents of Lieut. Burnes'.[51]

James and Alexander had meantime been in correspondence with their father on bringing out their two sisters, twenty-one-year-old Elizabeth and twenty-year-old Jane. Their eldest sister Anne remained in Montrose another year, to help her mother with the younger children.

James Burnes senior became worried as to whether the girls had made the passage safely. The *Fortune* had left the Clyde on 12 April 1830[52] for Bombay and on 25 April Jane had sent back a letter from the Scilly Isles, but no other letters had reached home from Mauritius, St Helena or the Cape. Perhaps the girls, having escaped that cramped Montrose home, were having too much fun to write. But their parents were distraught. Death from disease or shipwreck was a serious risk. James senior wrote:

> all our feelings are absorbed in the overwhelming anxiety to hear of the safe arrival of our dear Elizabeth and Jane. We hoped that they would reach Bombay about the beginning or middle of August and as Alexander would be there [...] we were hopeful that they would at once receive the countenance and protection of a brother [...] Not a paper has once mentioned the *Fortune* [and] the suspense has become absolutely harassing – God send that in a few weeks we may know that they are both well and with you, and that Mrs B and you are both pleased with them.[53]

In fact by the time he wrote the girls had been for two months the toast of the Bhuj garrison, the *Fortune* having arrived in Bombay on 21 August after an uneventful passage. Elizabeth was married at Bombay Cathedral to Captain Richard Whish within six months of stepping on the dock.

In Montrose, the account of James' mission to Haidarabad was being prepared for publication by his father, who had engaged Dr Browne, former editor of the *Caledonian Mercury*, to see it through the press. James was self-publishing and 500 copies would cost 'considerably more than 120 pounds', a substantial sum. Two hundred copies were to go to James in India, and the rest they would try to sell in the UK as 'I hope to establish your reputation as a literary man'.[54]

The small-town squabbles of Montrose must have seemed a world away to James junior as he read his father's letter in the heat and dust of Bhuj:

> Cap. Leighton arrived here a few days after your packet and sent down his [visiting card] on the 18th. He called on the 19th [...] Mrs Leighton tho' here

did not call. She did not call at all the last time she was here, tho' your mother and sister called on her. This is very vexing to us, but we cannot counteract that low and desperate jealousy on the part of the Leightons here [...]

The other news was that their brother David, having qualified in medicine, had on 2 November 1831 been appointed a ship's surgeon on the frigate HMS *Undaunted*, while Adam was joining the family law firm. James senior's long letter was posted at Montrose on 18 November 1830 addressed to 'Dr James Burnes, the Residence, Bhooj, Cutch via Forbes and Company, Bombay'. It was stamped in London on 1 December 1830 and is marked as received at Bhuj 24 June 1831.

Forbes and Co. were the Burnes' agents in Bombay. They acted as bankers; receiving and holding salaries and honouring bills. They were also postal and shipping agents and suppliers, bringing in foods, wines and other goods against specific orders from a catalogue. Remarkably the company still exists in Mumbai. I called on them, but they denied any knowledge of company archives.

James senior's letter was posted as a single sheet – that is to say one piece of paper, folded and sealed with wax, with no envelope. This was the cheapest way to send. As there was a great deal to say, not only was every margin written over, but after a side was completed, it was turned ninety degrees and then completely overwritten. You must read it first from one angle then the other, but the tangle of crossed handwriting is difficult to decipher. Perhaps money was still tight in Montrose.

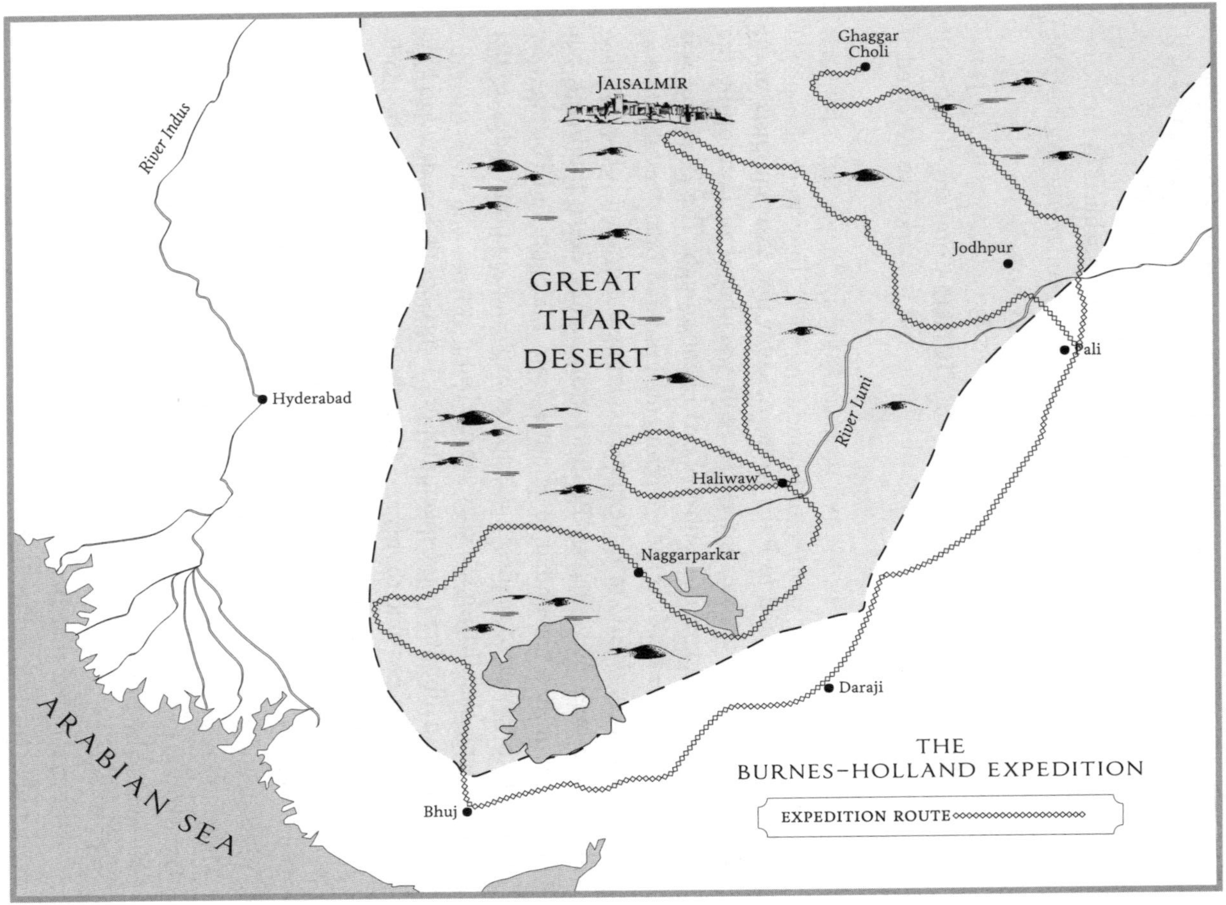

THE
BURNES–HOLLAND EXPEDITION
EXPEDITION ROUTE
Ghaggar Choli
JAISALMIR
River Indus
GREAT THAR DESERT
Jodhpur
Pali
Hyderabad
River Luni
Haliwaw
Naggarparkar
Daraji
Bhuj
ARABIAN SEA

CHAPTER SIX

## The Indus Scheme

Burnes was delighted to learn from Malcolm that their enthusiasm for exploration of the north-west frontier was shared in London by the President of the Board of Control, Lord Ellenborough. The President was a cabinet minister heading the government appointed Board, established in 1784 to control the EIC in its territorial administration and foreign policy. Burnes had been prevented by Bentinck from sailing down the Indus, but Ellenborough had responded to minutes from Malcolm and Pottinger by writing to Bentinck to request a mission of exploration up the Indus, to the banks of which no British territory yet reached.

Burnes had submitted a prospectus for precisely this mission, dated 30 June 1830, setting out possible routes and the political arrangements to be made with rulers.[1] He suggested that the suppression of cross-frontier brigandage should again be the cover story, plus concern at recent Sikh incursions to the South. Burnes suggested that the Amirs of Sind should be informed of this mission late, making interception difficult. Pottinger forwarded this plan to Malcolm on 30 July 1830. Malcolm suggested that it would be best to avoid Umarkot, as just too dangerous, while 'I do not find myself quite as sanguine as Lieutenant Burnes appears to be [. . .] but there is nothing glaringly impossible'.

Pottinger noted that Burnes' mission to Parkar had actually succeeded in stopping the brigandage there, and believed that could be the excuse for sending him further afield. Pottinger thought the most important part of the Indus survey was from Uch to Haidarabad and that Burnes was likely to be prevented from proceeding down river from Haidarabad. His alternative:

> dispatching some very bulky Present (a Carriage for instance) which could not be transported on Camels, to the Ameers, or requesting their Highnesses sanction to forwarding through their country a similar token of friendship to Runjeet Sing and stating why it must be transmitted by Boat. One or two

officers qualified for collecting the desired information would in either case naturally proceed in Charge of the Present [...]²

This was the origin of perhaps the most famous of all spying ruses.

Malcolm needed to get the plan past the very significant obstacle of Lord Bentinck. In his minute of 9 August Malcolm queried the cancellation of Burnes' recent expedition:

> no bad impressions were made or jealousy excited, and from the information given me by Lieut. Burnes [...] he would have come down the Indus and ascertained all the objects we are so desirous to know with little or no trouble [...]

He then addressed head on the turf war with Bengal:

> The qualifications of Lieut Burnes [...] may be equalled or perhaps surpassed by many officers of the Quarter Master General's Department in Bengal, who would, no doubt, be forward to explore provinces where Lieut Burnes went [...] from these provinces being subject to the Bengal Presidency [...] but [Burnes] had been appointed and done duty as an assistant in the Political department in Cutch. This gave him an introduction and influence in the countries he traversed [...] which, added to his former acquaintance with many of the inhabitants and his temper and habits and unimpaired health, enabled him to make a progress which would have been difficult for an individual without similar advantages [...]
>
> Lieut Burnes passing through part of the territories of Joodpoor and Jaysulmere was necessary for the completion of other more important parts of his survey. He was authorised to proceed as he did by me without the most distant idea on my part of any usurpation of authority.³

This turf battle was a major obstacle to getting Bentinck to agree that Alexander should lead the exploration of the Indus ordered by Ellenborough.

I know from professional experience that carving out and defending their personal area of influence is a chief motivator of ambitious civil servants. This is a central point – M E Yapp argues that the pushing of projects of border expansion by officers who gained personal career advancement was the prime driver of the Great Game. Yapp describes Malcolm as 'a skilful and merciless intriguer, ready to grasp at any prospect of advance'.⁴ On Yapp's reading, Malcolm sending Burnes into Bengal's sphere of influence was an internal British power play that led on to major territorial acquisitions.

Malcolm justified his choice: 'Having had my attention much directed [...] during these thirty years to the exploring and surveying of countries in Asia [...] I have gained some experience in the qualities and habits of the individuals by whom such enterprises can be undertaken and of the pretexts and appearances necessary to give them success'[5] and noted that in 1828 and 1829 he had delayed the exploration until Burnes became available.

London was enthusiastic. This mood had been bolstered from an unlikely direction. The fiery Irishman Colonel George de Lacey Evans was a real fighting soldier and had been at Waterloo. He had entered Parliament and become known as an advanced radical, advocating universal suffrage and the right of workers to combine. He was even heard to wonder why women might not vote, which led Palmerston to conclude he was mad.

Evans drew popular attention to the rapid expansion of the Russian Empire, and argued that it posed a threat to British India. In his books *On the Designs of Russia* (1828) and *On the Practicability of the Russian Invasion of India* (1829) he argued that Russian armies could advance to India in just two years. He projected Russia's principal line of advance as from the Caspian to Khiva and then by the Oxus to Balkh and across the Hindu Kush to Kabul, thence through the Khyber pass to Peshawar.

Events seemed to bear Evans out. The Treaty of Turkmenchai in 1828 had consolidated Russia's position across the Caucasus, making deep inroads into Persia's Caspian territories and seizing important military positions. Then, in the year between Evans' two books, Russia had taken the key fortresses of Varna, Kars and Erzurum and the city of Adrianople from the Turks.[6] In the period 1828–30 Russian territorial gains throughout Eurasia were larger than France and England combined.

Evans made the crucial point that a Russian threat to India was potent, not because of the strength of the Russian army, but because of the disaffection of the Indian people themselves with British rule. He argued that it was therefore essential that no potential threat was allowed near India as 'the defence of dependencies held by the sword rather than the affection of its inhabitants, can only be advantageously made in advance of their frontiers.'[7]

He called for the establishment of a British Agent at Kabul, which state could be a buffer against Russia; he also advocated a commercial consulate at Bokhara, and a thorough survey of the routes from Peshawar to Khiva.[8] In short, Evans plots out Alexander's future career. His books crystallised the thinking of the ruling establishment on the strategic defence of British India, and Burnes was to be a key player in advancing their aims.

Evans was read by everyone who mattered. The Duke of Wellington was Prime Minister. Evans, despite his radical politics, was one of the few politicians the Iron Duke did not actively despise. Wellington viewed the advance of Russian armies on India as impracticable, but was alive to the dangers of Russian advances stirring up latent disaffection there. Wellington was a friend of Malcolm, who had served alongside him in the Mahratta Wars and resided with him in Paris after Waterloo. From Persia, the British Ambassador MacDonald reported with alarm proposals for a joint expedition with 20,000 Russian 'auxiliaries' to invade the Turkmen lands and Khiva to counteract slave raids.[9]

Lord Ellenborough shared Evans' views. Ellenborough was a strange character, whose personal identification with the anti-Russian cause was not quite healthy. When Russia took the Turkish fortress of Erzurum, he wrote: 'Every success of theirs in that quarter makes my heart bleed. I consider it a victory over me, as Asia is *mine*.'[10] He recorded his dream of commanding a British army in battle against the Russians on the banks of the Indus. He had been inspired by James Burnes' book on Sind, and written of it 'no British flag has ever floated upon the waters of this river! Please God it shall, and in triumph, to the source of all its tributary streams'.[11]

In fact, there had once been significant British connection with the Indus. Bornford and Wilde had sailed down from Lahore to the sea in 1638.[12] Company factories had been established on the Indus from 1639 to 1662, and local commodities proved profitable exports. In 1727 Capt. Alexander Hamilton described the Indus as 'navigable as far as Kashmir'. The British tried again with a factory at Thatta in 1758–75 but had been expelled by the rulers of Sind.[13]

Wellington himself now authorised the British push to explore Central Asia. Ellenborough recorded:

> The Duke then said we must look not to India only, but to all Asia, and asked me if I had read Evans' book. I told him I had; that forty-eight hours after I had read it I sent a copy to Malcolm and to Macdonald. I told him all the views I had with regard to the navigation of the Indus and the opening of a trade with Cabul and Bokhara. He said our minds appeared to have been travelling the same way.[14]

The Secret Committee of the EIC obliged. Britain could oust Russian influence from Central Asia through trade domination. On 12 January 1830 the Secretary of the Secret Committee drafted clear guidance for the Governor-General:

> if the produce of England and of India could be sent at once up the Indus to such points as might be convenient for their transport to Cabul [. . .] we might succeed in underselling the Russians and in obtaining for ourselves a large portion at least of the internal trade of Central Asia [. . .] direct your attention with a view to the Political effects [. . .][15]

The Board of Control also set out for Bentinck six subjects about which it wanted information.

The tonnage of vessels in the ports on the Caspian, the size of the Russian navy there and the volume of Caspian trade with Russia

The route and time taken by caravans from Orenburg to Bokhara, the size of caravans and the number each year, the terrain covered

Details of Russian settlements on the East Coast of the Caspian

Details of Russian Moves towards the Aral Sea

The military and political state of Khiva, Bokhara and Kokand

Annual returns of the trade of Central Asia[16]

This letter was sent to Bentinck and Malcolm. This request is essential background to Burnes' journey up the Indus. Even before Burnes left Bhuj, the requirement was always there to survey to Kabul, Bokhara and the Caspian. And his route after Bokhara was key: through Khivan territory and disputed Khorasan and right on to the eastern shore of the Caspian and the Russian sphere; then return to India via Tehran. It is plain that Burnes was systematically meeting the precise requirements of the Board of Control.

Forced by Wellington to this policy, Bentinck now abdicated responsibility and passed the buck to Malcolm. There was already bad blood between Bentinck and Malcolm, who had accepted the post of Governor of Bombay on an understanding that his area of control would be extended over Central India; he was furious with Bentinck for blocking this. The Governor-General now preferred to avoid tempering Malcolm's ambition on the north-west frontier.

Another Company civil servant, Edward Stirling, had just become one of the first Europeans since Alexander to cross over the high passes through the Hindu Kush. Stirling fell victim in Calcutta to the disapproval of such adventures by Bentinck. He was however sent from London a list of questions about his journey, most of which are precisely the same as those given Burnes.[17] There was therefore a systematic basis to these inquiries.

Ellenborough suggested, at the instigation of Henry Ellis, Chairman of the Court of Directors, that a pretext for the mission might be to send two English dray horses to Ranjit Singh, who was inordinately fond of collecting bloodstock. Malcolm varied this improbable cover story for a spying mission:

> it would perhaps be still better to send [. . .] a large carriage which, from the size of the package, could obviously not be conveyed by land. This might be shipped with a letter to the Ameers of Sinde, requesting they would assist in forwarding the present which the English government had sent to Runjeet Singh, and the dray horses, if they came in time, might accompany it.
>
> I should desire, if this is approved, to send Lieut. Burnes in charge, writing to the Ameers that he had been selected [. . .] to concert measures against any future excesses of the Khosas and to find out any bands in the Tharr.

## The Indus Scheme

> It would be advisable, if this plan is adopted, that it be kept perfectly secret [...]

Malcolm argued, 'I confess I shall be confident of any plan he undertakes [...] and provided a latitude is given to him to act as circumstances may dictate, I dare pledge myself that the public interest is promoted.' Burnes justified and needed a free rein. But Malcolm had another reason for selecting Burnes – he was cheap!

> The employment of Lieut. Burnes has another recommendation – it will be attended by little expense. He may perhaps have an officer with him and two or three servants but his guard will be people of the country he visits and is familiar with. He presses such on the justest grounds [...] they disarm that jealousy which the appearance of our troops excites. They form also a means of contacts with the natives of the districts through which he has to pass. With respect to any personal allowance Lieut Burnes is satisfied with what he has and never has [...] raised a question upon that subject, being much more anxious to obtain reputation than money.

Malcolm continues:

> Should serious setbacks oppose the progress of Lieut Burnes beyond Hyderabad and yet the Ameers be willing to allow the presents to go on I should take care that he is accompanied by native surveyors, in the character of servants, whose fidelity could be relied upon and who were quite equal to make a good report of the river and the countries they passed.

Malcolm and Pottinger had since 1828 been involved in training a group of Indians in secret surveying and conveying of messages and maps. Burnes would be accompanied on all his successive travels by such Indian surveyors, usually disguised as domestic servants or fellow travellers. They would branch off to survey neighbouring districts or topographical features, and this accounts for the great volume of ground covered by Burnes. This type of secret surveying was being undertaken some thirty years before the date generally noted as the establishment of the corps of pundits.[18]

One of the native surveyors selected to accompany Burnes was Mohammed Ali, appointed sub-assistant surveyor. He was paid a monthly salary of Rs45 and field allowance of Rs85 while on mission.[19] That was higher than the most senior Company native NCOs and reflects the danger of the job and the skill and status of the corps of local surveyors.

While Alexander was selected in India to be the agent who kicked off the Great Game, Ellenborough had chosen a young cavalry officer to tackle the same task from the other end. Arthur Conolly had been in England on leave, and was now asked to return overland, from St Petersburg to Calcutta via

Persia, to check out the Russian advance dispositions. The careers of Conolly and Burnes were to run parallel for the next decade, and take on an oppositional aspect.

In Calcutta, Bentinck's most senior adviser, Sir Charles Metcalfe, was out of sympathy with all this spying. On 25 October 1830 he wrote a minute attacking the entire plan, arguing that 'we ought not wantonly to offend intermediate states, by acts calculated to rouse hostile feelings against us, but rather to cultivate friendly dispositions [. . .]'[20] The scheme for sending the horses up the Indus was a dangerous ruse which could provoke a war, 'It is a trick in my opinion unworthy of our government, which cannot fail when detected, as most probably it will be, to excite the jealousy and indignation of the powers on whom we play it.' Metcalfe added that twenty years earlier, fear of a French invasion had been the great 'bugbear' and the Russian scare was no more realistic.

However, Ellenborough and Malcolm had the bit between their teeth as surely as dray horses. On 30 November 1830, Burnes received his marching orders from Malcolm:

> The Honorable the Governor-in-Council, being desirous of obtaining full and correct information regarding the navigation of the River Indus and the chiefs and tribes possessing the territories on its banks, has resolved to employ you on the prosecution of that design [. . .]
>
> The plan adopted will be to dispatch from hence [. . .] a large carriage which is intended as a present to Runjeet Singh and in charge of which you will proceed up the river Indus. The ultimate destination of the package to be kept secret, until the boats which may be required shall have sailed from Mandavee when letters to the Ameers of Scinde will be despatched, but so as to arrive too late to prevent the receipt of any answer having for its object the prevention of the mission [. . .]
>
> The depth of water in the Indus, the direction and breadth of the stream – its facilities for steam navigation, the supply of fuel on its banks, and the condition of the princes and people who possess the country bordering on it, are all points of the highest interest to the Governor in Council [. . .] [your] slow progress [. . .] will [. . .] give you every opportunity to pursue your researches.
>
> The Governor General is now in the Upper Provinces of Bengal: you will therefore on proceeding beyond Hyderabad open a communication with the Secretary with his Lordship, and act according to such instructions as you may receive from him [. . .]
>
> A dray horse and four dray mares have arrived from England as presents from the Honorable the Court of Directors to Runjeet Singh; those shall be forwarded as soon as they shall have had sufficient rest after their voyage [. . .] it will not however be necessary for you to delay your departure from Kutch on that account.[21]

So the carriage was viewed as the gift, and Ellenborough's carthorses an optional extra. The present of a carriage was commonplace – Mountstuart Elphinstone had given Ranjit Singh one in 1809.[22] Malcolm stipulated to Pottinger that while suppression of the Thar and Parkar bandits was the diplomatic pretext for calling in at Haidarabad, discussions on this point must not be allowed to delay the survey.[23] Burnes took meticulous note of all this instruction. But his overwhelming feeling was of delight; his cherished proposals for the exploration of the north-west frontier were coming true, and he was off on the journey – and career opportunity – of a lifetime.

CHAPTER SEVEN

## The Shipwreck of Young Hopes

Burnes was selected for the Indus mission because he had over six years impressed his superiors. He had done so on active service with the Cutch Field Force and then in undertaking the provisioning and carriage of the 8,000 strong Sinde Field Force. He had carried out a series of geographical, geological and surveying operations, and produced maps which greatly increased the knowledge of important lands immediately on the Empire's frontier. Finally he had accomplished, with Holland, the sensitive exploration of the land and resources of important Indus territories. He had been aided in all this by his achievement of proficiency in the Hindustani and Persian languages.

He had shown initiative in getting permission for these activities, and then bureaucratic assiduity in producing reports, statistics and beautifully drawn maps to make these labours useful to government. Alexander Burnes was, with good reason, the rising star of the Bombay Presidency.

Bentinck agreed with Malcolm's proposed arrangements for the dray horse mission, although with what reservations is unknown as Malcolm told his Secret Committee he had mislaid Bentinck's letter. Bentinck was replying to Malcolm's self-exculpation for having sent Burnes trespassing all over Bengal territory, perhaps in terms Malcolm did not want broadcast.

Malcolm told the committee:

> I had several communications with Lieut Burnes as to the aid he might require. He had no wish but that a young officer might accompany him who might he thought be in many cases useful [. . .] He concurred with me that Ensign Leckie of the 22nd was from youth, good constitution and temper quite suited for this service.[1]

Malcolm had hit upon another deserving young Scotsman. Launching the mission was the last significant act of Malcolm's Indian career, as he left Bombay for good on 5 December 1830, to be replaced by John Fitzgibbon, the Earl of Clare, who took over on 21 March 1831. Clare notoriously had shared an intense schoolboy passion with Byron. Remarkably Clare was to accuse Malcolm of deliberately impeding his arrival.[2] Burnes lost an important sponsor at a crucial moment. In the interim General Beckwith was Acting Governor General for a fortnight before dying of fever. John Romer then took over temporarily. So Burnes was without consistent support from Bombay.

The dray horses, now in Bombay, were grazing for a month under Leckie's supervision, recovering from their long sea voyage. Burnes was at Mandvi, the port of Cutch, arranging shipping.

Pottinger believed 'The construction of the boats in question is particularly favorable for the transportation of the horses, and they can either be covered in; or left open above as the temperature and climate may render desirable [. . .]'[3] Regrettably this is the only surviving snippet on the management of the horses. They were certainly resilient, but we know nothing of their routine of food, grooming, mucking out or exercise, or if Burnes visited or talked to them.

Typically, in the midst of these preparations Burnes managed to conclude a report for the Bombay Asiatic Society of an archaeological survey he had conducted of the great Temple of Somnath.[4] On 30 December Leckie was ordered to sail to Mandvi from Bombay with the horses, and given an allowance of Rs800 for immediate personal expenses.[5]

The Amirs of Sind had seen the frontiers of British rule move steadily towards them. In 1808 Captain David Seton, British Resident at Muscat, had concluded a treaty of trade and mutual defence with the Amirs, only for it to be repudiated by the Governor-General Lord Minto. The following year, one of Napoleon's generals, Gardane, was in Tehran promoting a joint Franco-Persian attack on India through Herat. Minto sent embassies to Persia, Afghanistan, Sind and Lahore to shore up diplomatically British India's north-west frontiers. Mountstuart Elphinstone, Envoy to Shah Shuja of Afghanistan, had floated the idea that Britain purchase for £200,000 the sovereignty of Sind, arguing that, unlike Shuja, Britain had the military muscle to subjugate the Amirs and would thus secure a firm border on the Indus. The Amirs learnt of this and saw the British were insincere.

On 28 January 1831 Burnes and Leckie set sail from Mandvi with a small fleet of native boats plus a British cutter.[6] I visited Mandvi port and went around the local shipyards, where large wooden boats are still constructed, though now fitted with an engine. They are substantial vessels, constructed around a framework of enormous hewn beams. As in Burnes' day, they conduct coastal trade in the Persian Gulf, Red Sea and East Africa. Many of the builders I met knew of Alexander Burnes, and all claimed their families had sailed with him.[7] Alice Albinia had a similar experience on the Indus, where she found detailed knowledge of Burnes' visits among local boatmen.[8] Burnes left a positive impression. In 1858 George Jacob, as a General, was to visit Mandvi where: 'The Lukput came out to meet me [. . .] an intelligent man, of pleasing manners: he had accompanied Burnes to Sind: repeated several of his sayings, and spoke highly of him.'[9]

Pottinger wrote to Romer to inform him that Burnes had started. He pointed out that at this time of year the journey up the Indus would be particularly slow, as the river was low, and the wind contrary. He had provided the expedition with a small 'bunder [harbour] boat', carrying twenty-four oars. It 'will always put it in Mr Burnes' power to sound or even measure the river on various pretences, such as going out in her to fish or shoot or look for a better channel for his fleet'.[10]

Burnes had decided on no escort. He viewed the venture as hazardous, but argued that 'no escort of any moderate detail could provide the necessary protection, and at my urgent request, I entered upon it [. . .] believing that we could trust to the natives of the country and form [. . .] a link of communication with the country that could allay suspicion'.[11] This was brave, and unusual – both Malcolm and Elphinstone had gone on their 1809 missions with escorts of 400 Company troops. Burnes was right that an escort puts a distance between you and the communities you encounter, and reduces your information gathering potential. Burnes' non-threatening demeanour was essential to his success.

He had also decided to travel with very little money, but rather carried hundis, or bills of exchange, to be drawn on local merchants who operated as informal bankers.[12] It displays the sophistication of the indigenous commercial system that Burnes could set off beyond British India carrying little cash. Burnes' hundis were to be drawn in:

Tatta Rs1,500
Hyderabad Rs2,000
Shikarpur Rs1,500
Bhawalpur Rs1,500
Multan Rs2,000

This would involve a number of different currencies,[13] again evidence of the sophistication of the system. Pottinger wrote to Romer apologising for the loss to the Company from the exchange transactions.[14]

In addition to the carriage and carthorses the party also carried presents for rulers to be met on the route. In Montrose Museum survives the packing list of the presents for the Amirs of Sind:

List of Packages
No. 1
2 Maps of the Globe in Persian
2 Ditto of Hindoostan in Persian
2 Books of Umvari Sohilee in Persian

No. 2
1 Table Clock

No. 3
2 Pairs English Shawls (yellow and white)
1 Gold Hunting Watch with Chain, 2 seals and 2 keys
2 Telescopes
14 Scissors
4 Razors
4 Penknives

No. 4
1 Double Barrelled Gun in Case

No 5
1 Pair Single ditto Pistols ditto

No 6
1 Piece of Superfine Thick Scarlet Cloth being 20½ yards
1 Ditto Ditto Black 18¼ yards

No 7
2 Pairs cut Glass candle sticks with drops

No 8
4 Coloured Table Shades for Ditto

(Signed) R Money
Actg Pr Secy to Govt.[15]

Pottinger warned Burnes to be cautious:

> I cannot allow myself to suppose [. . .] that the Ameers of Sinde will refuse to allow you a passage [. . .] but [. . .] you are fully apprized of the necessity for being most careful that no act of yours, such as frequently and <u>openly</u> sounding and measuring the river, surveying the banks as you pass, or even writing too much in public, should excite their suspicions.[16]

Pottinger had arranged for Pitumba Thakuri, the British Agent in Mandvi, to accompany Burnes. Thakuri had been Pottinger's companion in his youthful exploration to Sind and Kelat. Pottinger's final injunction to Burnes was typically British: to be sure to send back receipts for expenditure in duplicate.

Pottinger then wrote on 18 February 1831 to Murad Ali Khan, principal Amir, informing him that Burnes was coming with presents for Ranjit Singh by river as 'it would be utterly impossible to transport them by land'. Pottinger requested that the Amir provide suitable river vessels and a local guard of up to twenty good men, whose wages Burnes would pay. Pottinger informed Ali Khan that Burnes had instructions to discuss joint measures for the repression of Khosa banditry.

Bentinck now wrote to Ranjit Singh to tell him the gift was coming.[17] His letter was sent to Ludhiana, where the Resident, Captain Claude Wade, was the accredited Representative to Ranjit Singh's court of Lahore. Wade set off for Lahore on 15 July, accompanied by a strong cavalry escort.[18] The Governor-General told the Maharaja that, by the time the letter reached him, Burnes should be approaching. That proved highly optimistic.

While Burnes was still at sea, Jetta Ahmed, British Native Agent at Haidarabad, had delivered Pottinger's letter announcing Burnes' coming to the Amir. The answer was instant and unequivocal:

> The Ameer observed that no English gentleman had ever come to Scinde in this manner nor had it ever been permitted that they should land at any of the sea ports of the country [...] Captain Burnes would not [...] be allowed to disembark, and that [...] the Scinde government would be instructed to send him back. That he might then proceed by land, or any other way he liked, but that he never would be allowed a passage through the Scinde territories.[19]

The Amir added that the treaty of 1809 stipulated that none of the Amirs' families were allowed to go to Bombay, and no British were allowed to go to Sind. Jetta Ahmed suggested that Burnes was only passing through as a traveller, but this cut no ice. Ali Khan added that boats never had been successfully dragged against the stream to Lahore.

Jetta reported that the Amirs suspected that Burnes was really coming to map the roads and sound the river, to prepare the way for an army. The following day Ali Khan summoned Jetta again to repeat his negative 'with great warmth of expression'. Pottinger sent this report immediately to Romer, with a thunderous proposal that in response to the Amirs' 'threatening and insulting' behaviour 'we may by blockading their harbours for a short time [...] and forbidding all vessels from Scinde from entering any of the ports in the Company's territory, reduce these ignorant and semi-barbaric rulers to [...] making whatever apology or reparations we choose'.[20]

The Amirs were castigated by British officials for being 'suspicious', 'jealous' and 'insulting'. There seems an absence of self-awareness in the British. Amongst themselves they quite openly avowed that Burnes was on a spying mission, and yet they were indignant that any 'Native' would accuse them of it.

Murad Ali Khan changed tack and wrote to Pottinger alluding regretfully to the physical impossibility of going up the Indus. It was too shallow, too fierce, the winds contrary, it had never been done before. He suggested Burnes go by land through Jaysulmir, there was grazing all the way [. . .][21] Pottinger wrote to Romer that the Indus being unpassable was a lie; but to Murad Ali Khan he wrote diplomatically suggesting that even small boats could take a single horse, and that these horses were not fit for crossing deserts, while the carriage was so heavy an elephant could not take it.[22] Romer wrote to Haidarabad in similar vein.[23]

Ignorant of these problems, the Burnes flotilla sailed north, noting eleven mouths of the Indus delta, and conducting a brief survey of the largest eastern mouth. Eventually they reached the western mouth, and anchored in the river known here as the Pitti, with the white fort of Karachi visible and the Hala mountains beyond, which Burnes identified with the Mount Irus of Alexander's admiral Nearchus.[24]

On 29 January 1831, they sailed sixteen miles up the Pitti and anchored in fresh water. Burnes received a message from the local authorities asking him to halt pending orders from Haidarabad. The following morning a group of officials arrived from the Nawab of Karachi. Burnes allowed them to search the boats and found them 'very civil'. On 1 February Burnes sent men ashore to obtain provisions; they came running back in panic. They had been manhandled; a rumour was widespread that the flotilla was hiding an army and being followed by a warship of 300 guns.

Armed parties began to arrive, totalling fifty men. With Burnes' permission the customs authorities from Daraji boarded the boats, and searched all goods and stores, listing everything. They suspected the huge wooden crate of the carriage contained artillery, and smaller crates held explosive devices.[25] They opened everything, but were again civil. They instructed Burnes to drop back a few miles into salt water, and promised him supplies, while they sent the list of cargo to Haidarabad and awaited orders. Burnes complied.

The following day, three boatloads of armed men arrived from Karachi and insisted that Burnes return to sea. They refused water or provisions, or to allow anyone onshore. Burnes' party was now being treated 'grossly and contemptuously' and 'with all manner of insult'.[26]

Pitumba, Pottinger's old travel companion, discovered that HMS *Challenger* had indeed just appeared off Karachi; an unfortunate coincidence, but it reinforced Sindian fears concerning Burnes' appearance. While Burnes was in tense discussion with the armed Karachi men, the customs boat from Daraji returned. The officer in charge showed Burnes orders confirming that the command to turn them back came directly from Amir Murad Ali Khan.

Burnes replied that it was international custom that an Envoy could not be dismissed without a personally addressed instruction from the ruler. The angry retort was that in Sind, customs were different. Tempers flared on the sweltering boat. Matchlocks were fingered, and some of the Karachi men started yelling 'Hunkar! Hunkar!' which Burnes translates politely as 'Move off instantly.' Burnes offered to be taken hostage, until orders came from Haidarabad. But the Jemadar in charge replied: 'I have orders to turn you out and all Feringees and you may consider yourself fortunate in being so well treated.'

Burnes had no alternative but to turn back. His requests for water, food, fuel and forage were denied.[27] He weighed anchor and dropped another mile downriver, then attempted to stop and gather firewood. The following Karachi dinghies opened fire, causing Burnes to move on: 'It is evident we must either stand our ground by force or move on in peace.'

Burnes sailed back to Cotasir in British-controlled Cutch, to reprovision. On the way the carthorses had to be fed on the men's rice, and the oars of the bunder boat cut up for firewood. Pottinger was furious not just with the Amirs, but with Burnes. He wrote to Romer that Burnes 'from an over-anxiety to avoid anything like a quarrel, was induced to come back'.[28]

The mission was going horribly wrong. All the correspondence was copied to Bentinck. His Private Secretary wrote to Clare on 11 March that 'His Lordship awaits with anxiety the receipt of further intelligence.'[29] Bentinck had never been keen on this mission, and it now threatened conflict with Sind. Pottinger wrote to the Amirs with the scarcely veiled threat that he hoped 'they will guard against any of their officers [. . .] committing any act towards the Mission which might compromise the longstanding friendship between the two governments.'[30]

On 10 February Burnes received from Pottinger a copy of Murad Ali's letter, in which the Amir did not forbid sailing up the Indus, merely cautioned it was physically impossible. Burnes took this as permission to try, and set out again to sea.

For days the flotilla made little progress in a calm. Then a tempest struck at 2 am on 14 February. Even from the dry account of Burnes' official journal, it was terrifying as the boats were 'taken aback'. A sudden fierce wind from the opposite direction exerted force on the sails the reverse way to which the mast stays and tackle were braced. One boat had its mast ripped out. Burnes' own boat was knocked on its side, the mast dragging in the water. As men, clinging desperately to the vertical deck, sought to cut away the mast, the rowed bunder boat appeared. A line was got across and the bunder boat, assisted by the small rowing boat from Burnes' own vessel, hauled Burnes' boat upright, an astonishing operation in 'mountainous' seas, and testament to the skills of the Mandvi sailors.[31]

The full force of the storm lasted thirty-six hours. Burnes' boat had sprung leaks and was being furiously pumped; its smaller sail was split. But although the winds continued fierce, at noon on the 15th Burnes was able to get a sextant reading through breaks in the cloud, and set a course for Daraji. On the 16th they anchored there, and Burnes sent Pitumba and Mohammed Ali ashore to speak to the authorities. They returned with dispiriting news: the Kinchi of Daraji had replied that he had orders from Murad Ali's own hand, that he must never allow Burnes an inch up the river. Burnes sent a note to Jetta Ahmed to intercede with the Amir.

Three of Burnes' boats were storm-scattered. Two returned to Mandvi, with the stallion and two mares. Pottinger sent these back to rejoin Burnes under command of a 'steady old officer', Lieutenant Morris of the 24th NI, who returned to Cutch immediately he had delivered the horses.[32] On 18 February Burnes was happy to see the missing boat limping towards them. It had cut away its mast and been driven past Karachi, but had survived.

After ten days at sea, they were almost out of fresh water. Burnes noted defensively in his official journal that padlocks had been placed on the water tanks from day one; the men were reduced to a daily 'pittance'. Burnes could not have expected to be kept at sea so long. But they had encountered serious problems from the Sind authorities over water the first time, and it is difficult to understand why Burnes had not taken more vigorous measures to ensure greater stores when replenishing in Cotasir.[33]

Burnes sent off the bunder boat, into what was still a storm, with two tanks to get water, noting 'I expect nothing less than a point blank refusal from the villagers.' This they got, and it was midnight before the exhausted rowing crew could get back again. Burnes tried giving money to a passing boat, asking them to return from Cutch with water. He never saw it again.

On 21 February the Reis of Daraji, the most senior official yet, summoned Burnes to a meeting on the beach. He stated unequivocally that Burnes was not permitted to enter Sind. The Amir had no confidence in the mission due to the appearance of HMS *Challenger*. Burnes explained that the party were now in distress for lack of water, but the Reis said his orders were to refuse supplies. Burnes refused to leave, but this was bluff. He wrote: 'We must sail [...] not having a sufficiency of water for one whole day [...] much less for a voyage to Mandavie [...].'[34]

Burnes was now in a quandary. They had no water, but a storm force wind still blew in the wrong direction for sailing out over the sandbar at the mouth of the river. The terrifying experience is written up in his journal:

we weighed anchor at daylight and in half an hour both the vessels were given up as lost and we despaired of our lives. The current cast us on the breakers, the sea rolled over us with terrific force sweeping us out of our cabin and inundating the stranded vessel. The tide and waves swept us along rubbing the ground and when the sails had been cast aside as useless and we thought only of saving our lives we were unexpectedly driven beyond the bank and by 7 am were in safe anchorage. The sailors behaved nobly and every hope of escape, had we continued in our situation, was gone for our bunder boat was likewise on shore [...][35]

Another boat containing two dray horses was firmly stranded on a sandbank. Burnes left Mohammed Ali and the bunder boat crew, with a substantial sum of money, hoping fervently they would not be maltreated. The dray horses were got out to graze by the shore. Burnes then sailed, without water, for Mandvi and by great good luck had perfect conditions, making a five-day journey in thirty-three hours.

It was a bitter blow to Burnes to return to Mandvi after the failure of this second attempt. He reported back to Pottinger, 'It is with much concern that I proceed to make you acquainted with our return to Cutch.'[36] The great career opportunity was receding. Alex wrote anxiously 'I trust, most respectfully, that the line of procedure which I adopted will be judged fitting and correct [..,] I had to encounter obstacles that never entered my contemplation [...]' On 27 February 1831 Pottinger wrote defending Burnes to Clare, stating that 'no argument or exertion has been left untried to secure the success of the mission.'[37]

There could now be no doubt that the mission had been blocked by Murad Ali Khan in person. Pottinger suggested withdrawing Jetta Ahmed and again a naval blockade.[38] He also recommended that Ranjit Singh be informed of the delay to his presents; this was to prove the most practical step. Pottinger still resented his personal experience of being detained by the Sind authorities on the Indus in 1808. He now wrote in fury to one of the Amirs, Ishmael Shah:

I am perfectly acquainted with the state of the roads and rivers of Sindi [...] the Ameers have needlessly [...] laid the foundations of falsity and unfriendliness equally with the British Government and that of Maharaja Runjeet Sing [...] the fact of twice turning back a vakeel charged with Royal presents is [...] an act of barbarous incivility [...][39]

An enclosed memorandum, addressed to Murad Ali, was incandescent:

Captain Burnes was absolutely refused fresh water and food for himself and his people, and was forced to come away the second time from the want of the necessaries of life [...] Is it the way to receive a vakeel from a friendly state by keeping him on board a boat in the open seas amidst storms and quicksand for days, to refuse to supply his urgent wants for water and food and finally to drive him out?[40]

Pottinger told Clare that, in view of the brazen behaviour of the Amirs, 'I considered it unnecessary to disguise my sentiments' in drafting this memorandum which he characterised as not 'strictly official'. He justified not consulting Clare as trying to solve the matter 'in a manner that should neither compromise the dignity, nor yet call for the interference, of my superiors'.[41] Clare ignored Pottinger's suggestions about naval blockades, and firmly rejected the idea of withdrawing Jetta Ahmed.[42]

Ranjit Singh was impatient to see his horses. He had moved troops from Derajat to threaten Shikarpur, the commercial centre of Sind. This town, reputedly harbouring enormous treasure, was a major goal for Ranjit. His troop movement was unrelated to the passage of his presents, but it certainly reminded the Amirs that it was unwise to provoke the Sikh ruler. Ranjit summoned the Sindian ambassador and urged him to explain to his masters the 'necessity' of assisting Burnes.[43] He sent an accredited Sikh envoy into Shikarpur to make pointed enquiries about Burnes' progress and express the Maharaja's 'disappointment and surprise'.[44]

While Burnes had been stuck off Pitti, Jetta Ahmed had been trying to argue the British case with the Amirs. Ahmed was a prosperous Hindu merchant. He took on the role of British Agent for the prestige and access it gave him, more than for the honorarium. Now he was the focus in Haidarabad of intense suspicion that threatened to ruin his business and endanger his safety. Murad Ali was ominously referring to him as a 'Hindu intriguer'. In the circumstances, Jetta's loyalty and the coolness of his reports are commendable. So was his persistence. For a week he tried every day and every route to get to the Amir, constantly being rebuffed with excuses that the Amir was getting his hair dyed or fingernails painted. Finally Jetta managed to see him, and he reported that Murad was in a dilemma:

> the Ameer of Sindh avoids giving any reply lest he should be involved in perplexity; he has stopped his ears with the cotton of absurdity, and taken some silly notions into his head that if Captain Burnes should now come he will see thousands of boats on the River Indus and [. . .] will conclude that it is the custom of the Ameers of Scinde to deceive [. . .][45]

Having said passage was physically impossible, how could Murad now say yes? Pottinger thought this vacillation sufficient to try again, and wrote a further letter on 1 March. That crossed with another from Jetta dated 22 February 1831, recording that the Daraji authorities had reported that they had turned Burnes away, but received orders by return that they should let him come upriver to Lucput. Furthermore Murad Ali's cousin, Amir Rustam Khan of Khairpur, had written to Murad to say it was wrong to block an ambassador.[46]

At last, the wind seemed to be changing in Burnes' favour. A letter from the Governor's office, stating that Clare approved of the 'judgement and temper he displayed in the difficult situation in which he was placed in negotiating with the Scind authorities'[47] must have eased his career worries.

CHAPTER EIGHT

## The Dray Horse Mission

In Orenburg, across the Hindu Kush, Jan Prosper Witkiewicz had survived six years in the frontier garrison as a soldier of the Russian Imperial Army. Like Burnes, he had devoted himself to the study of native languages. He could speak Kazakh and Kirghiz fluently, and had a good grasp of Persian. He had also gained a thorough understanding of local customs, living in nomadic encampments. How he had managed to accomplish all this as a common soldier in penal service, is not entirely clear.

An important Russian colonist, Count Khotkiewicz, had secured the services of Witkiewicz on his huge estate, and knew his background. Khotkiewicz used him to negotiate with Kazakh and Kirghiz nomads whom he wished to exclude from his land, and appreciated Witkiewicz' skill. He recommended him to the Governor-General, Count Pavel Sukhtelen, and Witkiewicz was attached to the Governor's office and the Frontiers Commission. In 1829 the natural philosopher Alexander von Humboldt visited Orenburg and was impressed by the young soldier's talents, which he pointed out to Sukhtelen.[1] In October 1830 Witkiewicz was made a Warrant Officer, and in 1831 commanded a small force which routed a tribe of 2,000 Kazakhs.

Sukhtelen recommended Witkiewicz for promotion to full officer – but included the caveat that Witkiewicz was sometimes very secretive.[2] In 1830 the Polish rose against Russian rule. There were many Poles in Orenburg, including a substantial number like Witkiewicz condemned as nationalist sympathisers. Rather than promoted, Witkiewicz was imprisoned as one of the suspected ringleaders of a proposed local Polish insurrection. But there was no hard evidence against Witkiewicz and he was cleared in November 1833. Whether he had been in close confinement for these two years is uncertain; it seems unlikely as he was immediately deployed on missions of great trust.

\* \* \*

On 29 March 1831 Burnes decided he must leave the boats and travel overland to Haidarabad in order to negotiate with the Amirs. He set out with only Pitumba. Arriving at the city of Tatta, he was met by an Envoy from the Amirs who told him that permission had been obtained for the entire party to come to Haidarabad and proceed overland through Sind to Lahore. Burnes declared this unacceptable, and remained at Tatta a week in negotiation.[3] On 8 April Burnes reported to Pottinger triumphantly that the Amir had agreed to the mission travelling up the river right to Lahore.[4] To the Amir he wrote with great tact, thanking him for playing the part of a true friend in pointing out the dangers of the river, but then assisting him to overcome them.[5]

Burnes rejoined his boats on 10 April. They now transferred from the Mandvi sea-going vessels into six dundis, large flat-bottomed sailing barges used widely on the Indus, 'not unlike Chinese junks – very capacious, but most unwieldy'.[6]

On April 18 at 10am, Burnes' flotilla finally anchored at Haidarabad. They were immediately greeted by representatives of the Amirs, and that evening Burnes and Leckie were lodged next to the house of the absent Nawab, Mohammed Khan Logari, whose son Ahmed acted as host. Frequent messages of goodwill poured in from the Amirs. Burnes was surprised by one from Murad Ali Khan, asking him to bring all the presents straightaway, and not tell any of the other Amirs about them.[7]

The next morning there was a diplomatic misunderstanding. Ahmed Khan arrived at daybreak to conduct Burnes to a durbar with Murad Ali, but Burnes explained the appointment had been fixed for after lunch. Burnes chose to regard the dawn summons as an insult, while Ahmed explained that it was an honour that Murad was anxious to see him. Other Ambassadors waited days for an audience. Burnes refused to go; Murad Ali sent apologies for the misunderstanding along with fruits and sweetmeats.

Murad behaved the more gracefully, but Burnes felt he had made a point:

> There is nothing more necessary, I observe, in dealing with the authorities of this country, than to meet insolence and pride with their own weapons. It is certainly disagreeable but I find that civility certainly follows. The Khan was in pretty good humour before he left, but I learned afterwards that he declared his astonishment at being so sharply answered, as he said, by a 'koodak' (youth).[8]

Burnes had been embittered by his experience on the boats. But a combination of his youthful charm, and the genuine gratitude Murad felt for James' medical services, helped overcome the frost, and next day discussions were rattling along.

At the durbar Murad Ali was with his nephews Sobdar Khan and Mohammed Khan. Murad called Alexander forward to sit on his cushion, and much admired Burnes' dress uniform, particularly his cocked hat.[9] He then apologised for all the difficulties Burnes had encountered, referring to himself as a 'simple soldier' who had to react to the fact that Burnes' coming up the river – and Murad made plain that he realised Burnes was surveying – was a breach of treaty obligations. However, now there would be friendship between them. Murad would provide his own state barge for Burnes to travel through Sind. Boats, camels, palanquins and elephants would be at the party's disposal. Britain would understand that the Amir of Sind was a firm friend. On the ostensible reason for negotiation, he readily agreed to station forces for the suppression of banditry from Thar and Parkar.

Burnes tactfully replied that 'I forgot in the agreeable interview which was now passing the difficulties which I had encountered, that it was not in the hand of man to avert calamities by sea [. . .]' and reported to Calcutta that he viewed the Amir's position as satisfactory, whether the motive was amity or fear. The Amirs were preoccupied by Britain's friendship with Ranjit Singh; as they viewed both Britain and the Sikh empire as a major threat, their alliance caused great concern.

Murad told him that the gifts were most welcome, but the clock and table shades were no use and perhaps he could have more pistols instead. Burnes' indignant refusal was not understood, and a messenger sent the next morning with the identical request.[10] I have felt precisely the same when Central Asians have spurned gifts; we view it as rude; they view it as practical.

Certainly Burnes received gifts much more valuable than he had given, including a beautiful gold and jewel-encrusted Damascus sword, and 1,500 gold Rupees. He divided 200 of these between his own servants and those of the Amir. The gifts had to be surrendered to the Company treasury; the Company might allow the recipient to keep them, but this was increasingly rare. James had been allowed to keep his gifts from Sind.

On 21 April the flotilla left Haidarabad with Burnes and Leech comfortably ensconced in the silk-lined pavilions of the Royal jumli, a vessel with sails and twenty oarsmen, which Burnes noted was just the kind of boat which the Amir had assured them it was impossible to sail up the Indus.[11]

Murad Ali Khan wrote to Lord Clare detailing the arrangements he was making and that 'If the wind is fair in 6 or 8 days he will be beyond my borders, and my attendants receiving from him a letter acknowledging their services shall then return. Captain Burnes will have written to tell you all that I have done in friendship.'[12] Clare forwarded this and copies of Burnes' official journal to Bentinck in Simla.

Alexander got no praise for his diplomatic success at Haidarabad. The response handed down from the mountain was distinctly chilly: 'the above dispatches do not at present call for any particular order or remark from His Lordship.'[13]

As the party sailed on through Sind, they attracted large crowds. Burnes had a policy of openness: 'We saw much of the Sindians on our way up the river and did everything to encourage their approach by granting free admission on board [. . .] and it was attended with the happiest results and facilitated our intercourse with the natives.'[14] He had a great many conversations with senior visitors, gently probing them for information and found almost universal scepticism that he needed to sail up the river to bring the presents; everybody realised this was a ruse to survey the river.[15] The party sailed out of the territories of Murad Ali Khan and into those of another of the Amirs of Sind, Rustam Khan, whose feudal seat was at Khairpur. They received a less alloyed welcome than in Haidarabad. Rustam, a burly bearded man, received them formally in durbar and invited them to return later in the day. He surprised Alex with his knowledge of woad:

> In the evening we [. . .] found him seated on a terrace spread with Persian Carpets surrounded as before by his numerous relatives – he made a long address to me regarding his respect for the British Government [. . .] The Ameer asked numerous questions about England and its power, recalling that he had heard that we were not formerly a military power, and that a few hundred years ago we went naked and painted our bodies. I told him that what he said was true and that we had risen by means of commerce to riches and military renown. On religion he was very inquisitive, and when I said I had read the Koran, he made me repeat the 'Kulma' in Persian and Arabic to his inexpressible delight [. . .] He examined my sword, a small cavalry sabre, and commented that it would not do much harm; but I rejoined that the age of fighting with this weapon had passed, which drew a shout and a sigh from many present [. . .] There was such mildness in all that the Ameer said, that I could not believe we were in a Belooch court.[16]

Repeating the Kalima is the formal act of declaration you are a Muslim. That is why Rustam was delighted, and there is no doubt Burnes knew this. Burnes most certainly had great respect for Islam, but his precise religious views remain uncertain in the absence of his private diaries.

The Baluch tribes still fought with the sword, which was fundamental to their culture:

> The Beloochees are a particularly savage race of people, but they are brave barbarians. From childhood they are brought up in arms and I have seen some of the sons of chiefs who had not attained the age of four to five years, strutting about with a shield and a sword of a small size [. . .][17]

The Baluch sword's redundancy was something the British were to prove.

Ten sheep a day were provided for Burnes' party, while nightly meals of seventy-two different dishes were provided for Burnes and Leckie. They left Khairpur with regret.

> Before starting the Ameer and his family sent me two beautiful swords, with belts ornamented by large masses of gold [...] To these were added many cloths and native silks – also a purse of a thousand rupees which I did not accept, excusing myself by the remark that I required nothing to make me remember the kindness of Meer Roostum Khan.[18]

Burnes was perturbed, however, by the gulf between the lifestyle of the Amirs and the abject poverty of their population: 'They wallow in wealth amidst one of the most miserable bodies of subjects in any land.'

The Indus was a mighty river, in places two miles across. Burnes was impressed when they arrived at Rori, where it narrowed to a historically important ferry crossing, though the current was fierce. In the middle of the river stood the rock outcrop of Sukkur, with its fortress of Baikhar commanding the crossing. Burnes realised that, if the Indus were to become Britain's western frontier, this was a key defensive position.

Rustam Khan's vizier had accompanied Burnes, and that evening they sat on the riverbank, looking at the fortress island by moonlight. The vizier chose this moment for a 'curious interview'. He said that Rustam Khan wished to have a formal treaty with the British, independent of his cousins at Haidarabad. Neighbouring states such as Daudputra, Jaysulmir and Bikaner had treaty relationships with Britain, and Khairpur felt disadvantaged. Looking at the stars, he said that Rustam had been told by his astrologers that one day the British would possess all India. The British might then ask why Khairpur had not offered allegiance, so they wished to do that now. Burnes replied that the British had no intention of ruling all India, and he had no powers to discuss treaties, but the British authorities would be grateful for this proof of friendship.[19] On departing Burnes wrote directly to Bentinck commending 'Meer Roostum Khan of Khyrpor who had never before seen an European, but evinced by his acts towards us most cordial attachment to the British government.'[20]

On reaching the frontier of Sind, Burnes bade farewell to his escort, and removed the horses, carriage and parcels from Rustam Khan's state barges. Waiting for them was the Nawab of Dera Ghazi Khan with a fleet of fifteen boats – the fifth set of boats they had used. They had been awaiting Burnes for three months, and immediately summoned their ruler, Bhawal Khan of Bhawalpur, chief of the Daudputras, who hastened in one day forty miles to join them from his capital of Uch.

Burnes declined with difficulty Rs2,000 from Bhawal, but the Khan insisted on providing Rs100 a day plus all their food and drink, and servants even for Burnes' boatmen. The royal party rode along the shore as the flotilla proceeded upriver to Uch, where there was the customary exchange of gifts, and an eighty-gun salute from the fortress. On 6 June 1831 Burnes wrote to Pottinger:

> I presented him with a gun, a watch, a brace of pistols, with several other articles of European manufacture, but he gave me presents of fourfold value, which I could in no way refuse; he sent two horses with rich silver and enamel trappings, his own matchlock, ornamented with gold, and one of his hawks with several Cashmere shawls [. . .]
>
> His liberality amounts to munificence, and his hospitality exceeds all bounds, nor was it coupled with a single request on his part [. . .] The British, he said, were his friends.[21]

The Khan had reason to be friends with the British; he was under intense pressure from Ranjit Singh. Burnes noted, however, the Daudputras had traditionally been friendly and Bhawal Khan's grandfather had assisted Mountstuart Elphinstone on his mission in 1809. As with Rustam, Burnes forged a genuine friendship with Bhawal.

Burnes copied his report to both Clare and Bentinck, and suggested that the Governor-General might send some presents to make up for the disparity in gifts. This expense was declined in Simla, and instead a letter of thanks was sent from Bentinck's Deputy Secretary.[22] The letter made plain that Bhawal should communicate only with the Bengal Presidency, through the Resident in Delhi, and not with Alexander Burnes and Bombay.[23] Bentinck remained indifferent to Burnes' mission, verging on hostile.

In Uch, Burnes had a life-changing encounter, when he met traders and financiers, a mixture of Muslim, Hindu and Jew:

> we were visited by some of the principal Merchants of Bhawulpoor [. . .] I was much struck with the intelligence of these people, and the wideness and extent of their travels. Most of them had traversed the Kingdom of Cabool, and visited Balkh and Bhochara, some had been as far as Astracan, and they used the names of these towns with familiarity as if they had been Indian. They had met Russian merchants at Bhochara [. . .] The intervening countries they represented as perfectly safe; and bestowed the highest commendations on Dost Mohammed of Cabool, and the Uzbecs, who encouraged commercial communication.[24]

Suddenly the fabled lands of Central Asia appeared tantalisingly close.

CHAPTER NINE

## The Dazzling Sikhs

The next frontier handover was much more difficult. The Sikhs had recently attacked Bhawal Khan and annexed territory. His vizier was loath to allow the boats to meet the Sikhs, for fear of looting. But Burnes eventually prevailed, and the tense transfer went without trouble.

The Sikh nobles who awaited Burnes gave him a copy of the parwana they had received from Maharaja Ranjit Singh. It demonstrates the importance Ranjit placed on the mission:

> When Mr Burnes approaches, you are immediately to dispatch an elephant with a silver houda, in charge of the Diwan, who is to state that the animal has been sent for his own express use [. . .] then shall the sirdar Lann Sing, and Sarwar Mull, seated on other elephants, approach and have an interview with that Englishman, paying him every manner of respect [. . .] and Congratulating him in an hundred ways on his safe arrival [. . .] distributing at the same time 225 rupees to the poor. You are then to present a handsome bow, and each of you 11 gold Venetians, and conduct him to the halting place, and there set before him one thousand one hundred rupees and fifty pots of sweetmeats. You are then to supply the following articles – grass, grain, bran, milk, eggs, fowl, sheep (doombas), curds, vegetables, fruit, roses, spices, water vessels, beds and every other thing that might be necessary, in quantities without bound [. . .] When you visit, you are to parade the two companies, and the horse, and place guards according to Mr Burnes' pleasure.
>
> When you reach Shoojuabad you are to fire a salute of 11 guns, and furnish everything as before directed, and present one thousand one hundred rupees, with sweetmeats and fruits [. . .] If Mr Burnes desires to look at the fort of Shoojuabad, you are to [. . .] shew it [. . .]
>
> On reaching Mooltan, you are to conduct Mr Burnes with great respect and pitch his camp in whatever garden he should select [. . .] You are then to present him with a purse of 2,500 rupees, and an hundred pots of sweetmeats, and fire a salute of 11 guns from the ramparts of the Fortress [. . .]

> In quitting Mooltan, you are to load one hundred camels with provisions for the supply of Mr Burnes to Lahore, and Soobudar Sarwan Mull is to attend him in person for the first stage [. . .][1]

The document does not reveal that Lehna Singh had been chosen by Ranjit Singh to greet Burnes because of his strong scientific knowledge, to learn as much as he could about Burnes' survey of the Indus.[2]

At Sikh request, Burnes had the drays landed for inspection. The Sikhs were amazed to see such 'little elephants'. The horses were a dappled gray, considered highly desirable. There was, however, a lack of understanding of the function of a carthorse 'and for the first time a dray horse was expected to gallop and canter and perform all the movements of the most agile animal'. The shoes were found to weigh four times as much as ordinary horseshoes, and a courier was immediately sent galloping off with one for the Maharaja.[3]

Leaving the Indus on 12 June, they continued along the Ravi, which meandered through a broad valley. The party were now in twelve boats the Sikhs had provided. These were small and uncomfortable, simply ferries for river crossings, as the Sikhs did not use the river for transport. After a tedious five-week passage, including a lot of stranding, finally on 17 July the tall minarets of the King's mosque at Lahore came shimmering into view. Burnes was entranced. 'As the sun set I descried for the first time the lofty mountains which encircle Cashmere, clothed in a mantle of white snow. I felt a nervous sensation of joy as I gazed at the Himilaya, and was about to forget the duties which I owed to the Sirdar, in contemplating the mighty works of nature.'[4]

They camped outside while a ceremonial entry was prepared.[5] This was worth the wait. Ranjit Singh's chief minister, Aziz al Din, and most powerful noble, Raja Ghulab Singh, arrived accompanied by uniformed cavalry in plumes and cuirasses, and a smart regiment of European style infantry. With them came Claude Wade, British Resident at Ludhiana, accompanied by Dr Murray.

Wade had a strong motive to be there, and assiduously attended all Burnes' formal meetings with Ranjit Singh, although he was absent from some of the ensuing drinking bouts. The short, pugnacious Wade had just won the right to report directly to the Governor-General, rather than through the Resident in Delhi, a major boost to his deep-seated ambition to control British frontier policy. Wade dispensed money to Sikh informers at Lahore with such abandon the Sikhs called him 'Baksheesh Sahib'.[6] To have young Alexander Burnes [. . .] steal his thunder was intensely galling. As Malcolm Yapp put it: 'In the context of this struggle for the control of British north-west frontier policy [. . .] the choice of Alexander Burnes, the assistant at Bhuj, to conduct a mission to Lahore in 1831, posed a significant threat to Wade's authority.'[7]

Wade had therefore come armed with a letter from Bentinck stipulating that he was to be present at Burnes' interview with Ranjit Singh. The shrewd Maharaja's diplomatic reply was that 'Your Lordship's permission to Captain Wade to be present at the reception by me of Lieutt Burnes and Mr John Leckie has been the source of much pleasure and satisfaction.'[8] Wade had also suggested that he, not Burnes, should present Ellenborough's letter to Ranjit Singh, but been overruled by Bentinck.[9]

Bentinck was becoming more positive about the notion of a forward policy towards Central Asia. This was from the influence of young Charles Trevelyan, who with Arthur Conolly had written a series of papers on the prospects of expanding British influence by Indus-borne trade. They proposed a strong Afghanistan as the key buffer state between Britain and Russia. Bentinck was also influenced by fellow Whig, Charles Grant, who had replaced Ellenborough as President of the Board of Control in a new government. Grant, a key member of the evangelical 'Clapham sect', favoured spread of British influence in Central Asia on grounds of the march of 'civilisation'. This encouraged Bentinck away from Metcalfe's isolationism. Bentinck noted that Ranjit was the strongest power on the Indus. Therefore a commercial treaty with Ranjit should be the lynchpin of his new policy.[10]

While the British had a treaty relationship with Ranjit Singh, it was uneasy. Metcalfe's mission to Lahore in 1809 had been an exercise in brinkmanship that came close to war before the Sutlej boundary was agreed. Moorcroft's diplomacy in 1821 had heightened Ranjit's distrust. In 1830 Jacquemont had written delightedly that the 'English are nothing' at Lahore, while Ranjit had a deliberate policy of employing French and other nationals precisely because he viewed them as 'inimical to the English'.[11] The British had allowed the open collection of money, arms and recruits from their territories for the anti-Sikh jihad of the Wahabi Syed Ahmed, who had just been defeated in May 1831. More positively, a Sikh delegation led by Ranjit's minister Aziz al Din and General Hari Singh had been warmly received by Bentinck in Simla in April 1831, and Bentinck had conceived the idea of meeting directly with Ranjit Singh, and instructed Wade to arrange this.

Burnes, Leckie, Wade and the party now moved on towards Lahore until they came to the residence of Chevalier Allard, since 1822 Commander of Ranjit Singh's regular cavalry and one of a number of former Napoleonic veterans whom the Maharaja employed to train his army. Allard had risen from the ranks to become Sergeant Major of Joseph Bonaparte's bodyguard, and by Waterloo a Captain of Curaissiers. Burnes found Allard 'engaging and gentlemanlike'. Ranjit Singh employed over 100 Europeans, of at least eighteen different nationalities, to officer his army. Most were in the artillery and the largest group were British deserters, while the most senior were Napoleonic French or Italian. Their contracts insisted that they commit to the country by taking a local wife (almost all took several) and allowing their beards to grow.[12]

Allard lived in great style on an annual salary of Rs60,000, over £6,000, although salaries were greatly in arrears. He had a single, beautiful Kashmiri wife, to whom he was devoted – however, she gave birth to their first child at twelve years old.[13] In an upper room of which walls and ceiling were covered entirely in mirrored mosaic, Burnes and Allard ate a buffet breakfast of finest French cuisine, washed down with champagne. The trumpeters of Allard's Sikh cavalry played; probably not the ideal accompaniment to breakfast.[14]

On 20 July, Burnes and Leckie were taken to see Ranjit Singh, with a massive escort of Sikh regiments, augmented by Wade's own escort of Bengal sepoys, although Wade himself had gone ahead to take his place in Ranjit Singh's durbar:

> The Coach headed the procession and in the rear of the dray horses we ourselves followed on elephants with the officers of the Maharaja [. . .] The streets were lined with cavalry, infantry and artillery, all of which saluted as we passed; the concourse of people was immense [. . .] On entering the first court of the palace we were received by the Raja Dihan Sing, a fine soldier-looking person draped in armour
> [. . .] At the very threshold I found myself in the [. . .] embrace of a diminutive old looking man, the great Maharaja Runjeet Sing – he was accompanied by two of his sons who likewise embraced me, when the Maharaja conducted me by the hand to the interior of his court [. . .] We found Captain Wade and Dr Murray in the durbar and all of us were seated on chairs in front of his highness.[15]

Ranjit Singh's hall of audience was built entirely of fine white marble. A huge silken canopy, studded with glittering jewels, covered most of the hall. Ranjit himself wore a necklace, armlets and bracelets of myriad emeralds, some of which were very long, and his gold sword hilt and scabbard were encrusted with diamonds and rubies. Many of the nobles wore almost equally stunning jewels, and all were dressed in fine silk of a bright yellow, the favoured colour of the Court. Burnes found the overall effect gaudy but magnificent.[16]

Burnes now handed over Lord Ellenborough's letter, which as an extravagant cover for spying must be one of the most peculiar ever issued by a British cabinet minister:

> His Majesty Maharajah Runjeet Singh
> Chief of the Sikh Nation and
> Lord of Cashmere

The King my most Gracious Master, has Commanded me to express to your Highness, His Majesty's acknowledgement of Your Highness's attention in transmitting to His Majesty [. . .] the splendid Manufactures of your Highness's subjects of Cashmere.

The King, knowing that your Highness is in possession of the most beautiful horses of the most celebrated breeds of Asia, has thought that it might be agreeable to your Highness to possess some Horses of the most remarkable breed of Europe, and [. . .] has commanded me to select for your Highness, some horses of the gigantic breed, which is peculiar to England. These horses, selected with care, requiring much time, I now send to your Highness, and as their great weight makes it inexpedient that they should undergo the fatigue of a long march in a hot climate, I have decided that they should be conveyed to Your Highness by the Indus and such River of the Punjab, as may be most easy of navigation [. . .]

Ellenborough
June 21st 1830[17]

Ranjit Singh had the letter read out to the durbar. Ambassadors from neighbouring states had been summoned, to witness how close was Ranjit's alliance with the British. Ranjit gave theatrical expressions of delight, and reinforced this by an enormous artillery discharge of sixty guns, each firing twenty-one times.[18]

Ranjit Singh's reply is equally remarkable:

From Maha Rajah Runjeet Singh Bahadoor
to The Minister of His Majesty the King of England for the Affairs of India

At a happy moment when the balmy zephyrs of spring were blowing from the Garden of Friendship and wafting to my senses the grateful perfume of its flowers; Your Excellency's Epistle, every letter of which is a new blown rose on the branch of regard, and every word a blooming fruit on the tree of esteem, was delivered to me by Lieutenant Burnes and Mr John Leckie, who were appointed to convey to me some horses of superior quality, of singular beauty, of Alpine form and elephantine stature [. . .] which had been sent as a present to me by His Majesty the King of Great Britain, together with a large and elegant carriage – these presents [. . .] have arrived by way of the River Sindh in perfect safety, and have been delivered to me [. . .] by that nightingale of the garden of eloquence, Lieutenant Burnes – and the receipt of them has caused a thousand emotions of pleasure and delight to arise in my breast [. . .] these animals in beauty, stature and disposition surpass the horses of every city and every country in the world. On beholding their shoes the new moon turned pale with envy and nearly disappeared from the sky – such horses the eye of the sun has never before beheld in his course through the universe. Unable to bestow upon them in writing the praises which they merit, I am compelled to throw the reins on the neck of the steed of description [. . .][19]

In the durbar, Ranjit declared delight at their size and colour, insisting his nobles took turns to sing their praises. He then displayed horses from his famous stud, but Burnes was surprised that these did not seem to him very good, though caparisoned in fabulous jewels and from bloodlines which Ranjit Singh could recite.

Ranjit became fond of his drays, and had them trained to be ridden. According to Ranjit's physician John Martin Honigberger, who was in charge of their veterinary care 'Alex Burnes had brought them up the Indus, and they were much admired for their size and uncommon height. One of them became the famous riding horse of the Maharajah, who being of very low stature, appeared when on the back of the animal [...] on an elephant.'[20]

Charles Hugel saw them in 1836, and wrote, 'The equipage is by no means splendid [...] an old coach, lined inside with blue velvet, and coarsely painted without [...] to send four brewers' horses and a monstrous dray horse to a prince who has a peculiar fancy for the most elegant saddle horses, is something like giving a man who loves rare flowers a cart-load of potatoes.'

Hugel was scathing of the idea that local rulers were taken in by Burnes' mission. 'The Amirs of Sindh were as little to be deceived by the pretext as Ranjit Singh himself; and it certainly did evince great ignorance of the circumstances and affairs of India [...]'[21] Hugel was right; nobody was fooled by the subterfuge. But nevertheless, the pretext worked. Nobody cared absolutely to call the British bluff, and so the survey was made.

During the hour and a half of the presentation ceremony, Ranjit asked penetrating questions of Burnes. He was particularly interested in the navigation of the Indus and the depth of its water, making crystal clear he knew Burnes was surveying. He also asked about the rulers and the political, economic and military strength of their states, and discussed 'the riches of Sinde which seemed to excite his utmost cupidity'. Ranjit asked Burnes straight out what the British attitude would be to his annexation of Shikarpur. Burnes replied that it was 'too grand a subject for me to answer'.[22] It was scarcely a secret that Ranjit coveted lands for his still expanding empire. Claude Wade had just reported that Ranjit had received a proposal from Mehrab Khan, ruler of Kelat, that they should join forces and take both Haidarabad and Kandahar.[23]

The Maharaja was in poor physical health and Burnes gave a perceptive little pen portrait of this remarkable man:

> The exertions which H. H. underwent appeared to exhaust him [...] Nature has indeed been sparing in her gifts to this personage and there must indeed be a mighty contrast between his mind and body. He has lost an eye, and is pitted by the small pox, and his stature does not certainly exceed 5 feet 3 inches. He

is entirely free from pomp and show, yet the studied respect of this Court is remarkable, not an individual spoke without a sign [. . .][24]

Ranjit Singh invited his British guests to a military review the next day. Before going to bed, Burnes wrote to Bentinck, copied to Clare, informing them of the successful completion of his river journey and his warm reception. He must have been delighted when he received the reply from Bentinck's Secretary, H T Prinsep, which began 'I am instructed [. . .] to convey to you the Governor-General's congratulations on the successful issue of the enterprise [. . .] his conviction that the government is greatly indebted to your skill and prudence for this important result.'[25] The hostility was over.

The following morning they met Ranjit in front of five regiments of infantry, drawn up on the parade ground outside the city walls. They were dressed in European-style uniforms, white with black cross belts, and bore muskets, which Ranjit explained were manufactured locally at a cost of Rs17 each. Burnes accepted an offer to review the troops, after which they went through a series of manoeuvres under a Sikh general, all the commands being given in French. Burnes was highly impressed, considering them the equal of Company troops.

Ranjit Singh now spoke of his newly conquered territory of Kashmir, taken from Kabul. He had received Rs36 lakhs of revenue this year. He complained, 'All the people I send to Cashmere turn out rascals (haramzada).'[26] They became corrupted by the pleasures of that country. He would either have to govern in person, or send one of his sons. Ranjit Singh's difficulties in governing Kashmir and Peshawar became the hinge on which Burnes' career turned.

In Lahore, Burnes and Leckie lived in the absent Ventura's house, an elaborate building supposedly in the style of an English cottage, with a beautiful garden containing ninety fountains. Ventura, from Modena, had been a Colonel of infantry at Waterloo, having survived the march to Moscow and back with Eugene de Beauharnais' Italian army. He kept many concubines, who lived behind the house in the marble tomb of Anarkali, the assassinated wife of Akbar the Great, while his stunning half French, half Armenian first wife lived in the main home with their children. She left him at around the period of Burnes' visit, to live as one of the peculiar collection of British government pensioners at Ludhiana.

Burnes spent much time with another of the Maharaja's Frenchmen, M. Court. Another Napoleonic veteran but also a distinguished scholar and graduate of the Ecole Militaire, Court had served the King of Persia before travelling in disguise through Central Asia to join the Sikhs. His principal work for Ranjit Singh was in the ordnance department, designing and producing cannon and shells for the formidable Sikh artillery.

Burnes and Court discussed at length the plan Burnes was forming of a journey to the forbidden city of Bokhara. Court showed Burnes his own extensive maps which much surpassed anything available to the British government. They talked of Russian influence in Persia and the possibility of a Russian invasion. They discussed passes, forage and baggage trains, and routes for heavy guns. Court freely gave advice, furnishing Burnes with specially written notes for his projected journey. At Burnes' suggestion, the Company purchased Court's papers for the considerable sum of Rs5,000.

Much of the entertainment Burnes received was plainly of a sexual nature. Nautch girls sang and danced, but were essentially prostitutes, albeit originally in the service of temples. George Hadley recorded what common sense tells us must be true: 'When a gentleman gives an entertainment, he often gives a dance "nautch" [...] The entertainer generally compliments his guests with the liberty of chusing their partners for the night.'[27]

Ranjit paraded a 'regiment' of women in uniform, which was overtly sexual, as was a fight between girls he staged for Burnes. There are many accounts that Ranjit liked to watch the performance of sexual acts. As a young man he would have sex in front of his court if the fancy took him.[28] The public display of potency may have been a considered act. One young wife, Rani Chunda, had many lovers, some of whom were encouraged by Ranjit: 'To give a detail of these affairs and of scenes acted in the presence of the old Chief himself and at his instigation, would be an outrage on common decency.'[29]

While we may doubt whether Burnes participated in open orgies, it is most probable that he accepted women. In 1809 an earlier British Envoy, the principled Charles Metcalfe, had been provided by Ranjit with an Indian mistress, who became his wife. Captain William Osborne recorded this conversation with Ranjit Singh:

> 'Did you see my Cachmerian girls?' 'How did you like them?' 'Are they handsomer than the women of Hindostan?' 'Are they as handsome as English women?' 'Which of them did you admire most?' I replied that I admired them all very much, and named the two I thought handsomest. He said 'Yes, they are pretty; but I have got some more that are handsomer, and I will send them this evening, and you had better keep the ones you like best.' I expressed my gratitude for such unbounded liberality; his answer was: 'I have plenty more.' He then led the conversation to the subject of horses.

Osborne recounts the story of a beautiful dancing girl nicknamed 'The Lotus', with whom Ranjit fancied himself in love. General Ventura was much taken with her. The Maharaja bet Ventura a substantial sum that he could not seduce her. Two days later Ventura was collecting on the wager. The girl was then enrolled as an officer in Ranjit's female 'regiment'. William Osborne was fascinated by her, and in 1838 gave her a pearl brooch presented to him by Ranjit, drawing a reprimand from Macnaghten, Political Secretary to the Governor-General at Simla, as gifts to officers were the property of the Company. The Lotus was to be burnt alive on Ranjit's funeral pyre.

Ranjit rather liked his guests enjoying sex with his women.[30] This is not a diplomatic practice that has died out. I was offered girls on a number of occasions in my diplomatic career, routinely though not only in Central Asia and the Middle East. The young lady and I would normally agree to pretend we had sex, in order not to cause her any trouble with my host. Burnes was in Lahore when George IV, formerly Prince Regent, was on the throne and British sexual morals were extremely loose; even more so for the British in India. We can be confident he accepted sexual entertainment in Lahore.

It was not just the Maharaja himself who was thoroughly debauched, it was his entire court. This was openly bisexual, which exceeded British tolerance:

> Suchet Singh was, from his early youth, remarkable for his debaucheries. Like his brother, Dehan, he had risen to favour and station in the court of Runjeet by the most infamous of means. They both attracted the eye of the old monarch by the beauty of their person, and secured his patronage by the most criminal compliance with his desires.

Victor Jacquemont, a French visitor this same year, noted that Ranjit had 'le bon esprit d'être amoureux de moi (en tout bien et tout honneur, cependant; circonstance à noter car, lorsque messieurs les Sikes sont amoureux, c'est en général d'une manière bien peu vertueuse)'[31] Europeans enjoyed chronicling the erotic pleasures of the Sikhs, which were real. But we should not forget Sir Lepel Griffin's caution 'the bazaars of Lahore [. . .] were not so shameless as Piccadilly'.[32]

On 16 August 1831 Burnes and Wade were given an audience of leave by Ranjit Singh, who was fulsome in his tribute to his visitors. He was also very generous. Burnes reported, 'Previous to my departure His H invested me with a string of pearls, and seven other jewels – also a sword, with a horse richly caparisoned in gold besides a handsome *khilat*, or robe of honour. He gave a like token of friendship to Mr Leckie. Three natives of my establishment received presents and he ordered 2,100 rupees to be distributed among my servants.'[33] The horse Ranjit Singh gave Burnes was to have an exciting history.

Wade left immediately for Ludhiana by dak – the express porterage service of British communication routes – leaving Burnes and Murray to follow by normal stages.[34] This would enable Wade to get his reports off first to the Governor-General.

The narrative account of his Indus journey, which Burnes submitted to Bentinck on 12 September 1831 became the third volume of his *Travels into Bokhara*. All of Burnes' publications were drawn from official reports, after removal of survey results, particularly those relating to military logistics, and of political content. In publishing, Burnes was at pains to downplay danger. A shipwreck and a flash flood are much more graphically portrayed in his official reports than in his books.

Burnes' great skill was political insight; he was able to understand complex situations and grasp the salient points. The following observation about Ranjit Singh's Sikh Empire was in his official report but deleted from his published travels:

> It cannot, however, be disguised that he stands alone and unequalled in his kingdom, and that the power he has consolidated must fall dismembered at his death [. . .] he has no successor in his own family; his eldest sun, Hurruk Sing, is a man of no energy [. . .] and without fitness to rule. Among the Seik Sirdars of the Punjab, we find no-one that possesses much political influence – most of those about the person of Runjeet are unpopular, and have been raised by himself [. . .] The Maharaja himself bids fair, before his demise, to shake the power he has so diligently acquired, for his troops have ceased to be the object of his primary solicitude, and his increasing avarice keeps their pay in arrears [. . .]

Burnes seems to have been the only relevant British official who took full account of the personal and precarious nature of Ranjit's empire.

He wished to obtain permission from Bentinck for his proposed expedition to Kabul and Bokhara, but relations there were Wade's responsibility. To have Burnes take away his mantle as the Afghan expert was a career threat. Wade therefore threw up an objection, in a letter written to Bentinck on 3 August 1831:

> Lieutt Burnes informed me [. . .] he has submitted a proposal thro' his Government to visit Afghanistan; and explore the countries which lie along the Oxus [. . .] with reference to the important interest which we are supposed to have in that part of Asia from the recent extension of the Russian arms in Persia, and the ambitious view which the former nation is believed to entertain toward India [. . .] considering the ostensible motive of Lieutenant Burnes' mission to Lahore, I put it to him that he could not, in my opinion, prosecute his scheme without exciting the suspicions of Maha Rajah Runjeet Singh, and that if Government approved of a plan [. . .] it would be better to commence it after his return to Bhooj.[35]

In Simla, Burnes now met Macnaghten for the first time. Macnaghten had a commanding personality and tremendous capacity for work. He was the second son of Sir Francis Macnaghten, and his ancestors were chiefs of the clan. Born in Ulster, he had been sent to Charterhouse and was at ease with the aristocracy. In 1809, aged sixteen, he came to India with a cadetship in a Madras cavalry regiment. Bentinck was then Governor of Madras. Macnaghten was appointed to his bodyguard and lived in the Residence as one of the family.[36] He was a phenomenal linguist, and in 1814 gained a coveted transfer to the lucrative Bengal Civil Service.

He was appointed interpreter to the Diwan Adalat or Court of Appeal. He stayed with the judicial branch, eventually rising to be a judge of the Supreme Court in Calcutta. Once Bentinck became Governor-General, Macnaghten obtained enormous influence. In late 1830 Bentinck had departed on a tour of the upper and western provinces including the first ever summer retreat to Simla. As there existed no mechanism for taking the government with him, and indeed the Charter was deemed to forbid the Council leaving Calcutta, Bentinck had chosen Macnaghten to travel as Secretary, with no other policy advisers.

Burnes had succeeded wonderfully in his mission to Lahore, He had surveyed the entire river system and produced maps and charts of high quality. His diplomatic goals, with all the native rulers, had been accomplished with a flair that could hardly have been expected. His detailed reports on the countries, peoples and military topography were brilliant. Burnes was highly conscientious; en route to Simla to present his reports, he called on his old surveying and mapping tutor Major Jervis in the Nilgiri Hills, so that Jervis could quickly check his work.

Bentinck was impressed by Burnes when he met him, and even more impressed by the quality of Burnes' written reporting. He had been reluctant to approve any forward exploration, but was sufficiently swayed by Burnes – and his instructions from the Secret Committee in London – to agree now that he should continue his exploration to Kabul, Bokhara and the Caspian. Burnes' description of Sikh power also led Bentinck to push ahead with his plan for a meeting, in replying to Ranjit's complimentary letter:

> details of the excellent administration of all his officers and of the discipline and efficiency of his troops, have been made known to the Governor-General by the verbal communication of Lieut Burnes and Mr John Leckie [. . .] If it pleases the Almighty the Governor-General will quit Simla on the 19th October and arrive at Rooper [. . .] on the 26th of the aforesaid month, where an interview will take place in the manner and the conditions agreed upon through the medium of Captain Wade [. . .] the friendship and union which has been established [. . .] will thereby be publickly manifested to the whole country.[37]

To make copies by hand of Burnes' voluminous reports was a long task. Drawing up the maps from the survey data required skill in mathematics and draughtsmanship, and this Burnes undertook himself. The reports and surveys were in great demand. It was with perhaps a feeling of self-importance that he wrote to his home Presidency of Bombay, in a letter marked 'Govr. Genl.'s Camp Simla 16th Sept 1831' that: 'I take this opportunity to mention that the Rt Hon the Gov General has called on me for a copy of the papers on the Indus for transmission to England [. . .] I regret that it is not in my power to comply instantly with His Lordship's request.'[38] Lord Clare in Bombay would have to wait. Alexander was in demand in higher places.

On 28 September 1831 Burnes formally submitted his full portfolio. In addition to the Report, which was constructed in sixteen chapters,[39] there was a Personal Narrative, a further 171 large, closely-written pages, giving all the picturesque colour and political discussion. He explained that he was still drawing up the maps.[40]

The Report begins triumphantly. 'There is an uninterrupted navigation from the Sea to Lahore. The distance by the course of the river amounts to about 1,000 British miles. The following papers detail its practicality with minuteness, but not more, I trust, than the great importance of the subject deserves. They also describe the state of the countries and the people'. Burnes described the Indus as having below Uch a depth of never less than fifteen feet in the dry season, and a width seldom more than half a mile. He gives the Chenab depth at twelve feet and the Rani at six, stressing these are minima. But he adds the important proviso:

> This extensive inland navigation, open as I have stated it to be, can only be considered traversable to the boats of the country, which are flat bottomed [. . .] The largest of these carry about 75 tons [. . .] steam vessels could ply if constructed in this manner, but no vessel with a keel could be safely navigated.[41]

This was a sober appraisal; Burnes made it quite clear that ocean-going vessels could not do it and specially constructed steamers would be needed. Burnes went on to state that while there were no physical obstacles, traders on the Indus were robbed by the people and over-taxed by the rulers, so trade to the Punjab and Central Asia went by circuitous land routes instead.

But what commanded most interest in Calcutta and London was Burnes' view on the strategic defence of India. These parts of his Report are not reproduced in his published work:

> The military advantages of the Indus are great. It is navigable for a fleet from Attock to the sea, and conducts an invader to the central portions of India. The insulated Fortress of Bukkur is a most important position [. . .] By securing it

we arrest the invader and retain command of the navigation in a most fertile country.

Chapter 8 of this Report is entitled 'On the Invasion of India from the Indus and Countries Westward.' It charts the scenes of his future career:

> Bukkur is the key of Sinde, and the most important military position on the Indus. With the fort of Attock higher up, it must at all times engage the attention of the invaders and the invaded, in any operation conducted on India from that river [. . .]
>
> It is not the strength of the works which constitutes the importance of Bukkur, but it lies on a most important line of route from Persia to India, and may be approached from Candahar, a distance of 450 miles, with the heaviest artillery. This road crosses the mountains of the long and narrow pass of Bolan [. . .] across the plains of Cutch Gandava, on to Sinde and Shikarpoor [. . .] I know it to have been travelled by a force of 6,000 Afghans, with a train of artillery, this very month [May 1831] [. . .]
>
> I need not say that the pass of Bolan is to be considered as one of the strongest mountain roads in the world, and might be defended by a handful of men. It runs through the country of the Brahvoors, who are a type of Beloochee mountaineers.[42]

In the final chapter of his Report on the Punjab, Burnes tramples all over Claude Wade's patch in trying to bring the Governor-General's attention to the imminent dissolution of the Sikh Empire:

> But the successful compulsion of the political power by one man seems destined to be transient. Runjeet Singh is in his 51st year, of a weakly frame of body – his habits of dissipation are at variance with hopes of longevity. With his dissolution ends the dynasty, his only son Kurruck Sing, is an imbecile, and it is doubtful if any of his spurious offspring could mount a claim with a chance of success. The Maharaja himself gained the throne by art and conquest, and he has carefully neutralized the power of the Sirdars who were once his equals. The elements of discord are therefore at hand and on his death we may see a relapse to it.[43]

In Ludhiana Burnes called on the exiled Shah Shuja, a pensioner of the British. Burnes' impression was that Shuja was not a strong enough ruler to control Kabul. From his official Narrative he was permitted to publish in *Travels into Bokhara*, 'From what I learn, I do not believe the Shah possesses sufficient energy to again seat himself on the throne of Cabool [. . .]' Nevertheless, Burnes had personal sympathy for Shuja. The following passages were deleted by the Company before publication:

> our sympathies are kindled in his favor, when we consider that he lost his crown from a humanity unheard of among his nation, in not blinding the brother, who at last dethroned him, when in his power [. . .]

At Lodeeana, I had an opportunity [...] of perusing the memoirs of Shah Shooja in Persian [...] One page of his history contains a sad detail of inhospitality and unkindness which he experienced from Runjeet Sing, and which did not even terminate with his forcefully possessing himself of the Koh-i-Noor [...] The Shah at length fled from the Seik capital by the assistance of his Queen, who had previously affected her escape in the disguise as a courtezan; he cut his way through 7 walls, and reached the exterior of the city by creeping thro the common sewer [...] he and a few followers betook themselves to the mountainous country of Histwar, preparatory to an attack on Cashmere, where he had powerful partizans. Fate, as he says, seems to have decreed against him for a snowstorm that fell as early as August, proved destructive to his hopes, many of the troops which he had gathered together perished, and his partizans in Cashmere, unsupported, were massacred. The Shah and a few supporters crossed the Hemilaya by an untrodden path, and [...] arrived at the British post of Subattoo [...] His description of having reached in safety this friendly spot is pathetic and touching.[44]

Burnes empathised with Shuja to an extent the Company considered unwise for publication.

CHAPTER TEN

# Rupar, the Field of the Cloth of Cashmere

Given his recent success it is not surprising that Alexander was invited to join Lord William and Lady Bentinck's party to meet Ranjit Singh at Rupar in October. This meeting of the two most powerful men in India, on the border of their respective empires, had been a feat of some diplomatic skill to put together. Burnes' mission had been a part of this.

He had already come far from the mundane duties of Assistant to the Resident at Cutch, still his official position. Though a humble Lieutenant, at Rupar he was in the Bentincks' inner circle.

There he met James Skinner, the founder of Skinner's Horse – another of the astonishing contributions to India of the small town of Montrose, whence his father Hercules had emigrated. Like Burnes, Skinner's grandfather had been Provost.[1]

Burnes gave a detailed account of the events at Rupar in a letter to Major-General Ramsay, of the family of the Burnes' Angus patrons, the Earls of Dalhousie. Burnes arrived at Rupar with Bentinck on 22 October. That evening Bentinck wrote to Clare, reminding him that the Court of Directors in London had directed them 'to secure the full navigation of the Indus for purposes of political and commercial communication, in case the mission of Lieut Burnes should give reason to believe the facilities afforded by this river to be as great as were supposed'. Bentinck suggested the first step was to send Pottinger as Resident to Sind to conclude a treaty with the Amirs for free navigation, and ensure that its provisions were kept and appropriate transport infrastructure built.[2]

On 23 October the bulk of the British military escort formed camp on the eastern bank of the Sutlej. This included both Royal and Company regiments, with lancers and horse artillery polished to their parade ground best. Burnes tells us that when Ranjit Singh did not arrive on 24 October, 'politicians' around the Governor-General were quick to allege bad faith, but on 25 October the Maharaja appeared, riding to his camp on the western bank through a lane of irregular cavalry two miles long.

In fact Ranjit had taken alarm at the thought of proceeding into the British camp. He had only been persuaded to go ahead by Allard, and by his astronomers, who told him that he must present an apple to Bentinck. If Bentinck accepted it, all would be well.

The next day another Dalhousie, General Ramsay, led a delegation mounted on elephants over a bridge of boats to conduct the Maharaja to meet the Governor-General. Considering the equipage of the British elephants to be inferior, Ranjit Singh remounted the British officers on his larger beasts, with glittering gold and silver howdahs, for the return crossing. Ranjit Singh was flanked by 4,000 regular cavalry, resplendent in bright yellow uniform.

The display was meant to impress, and it succeeded:

> His Highness himself with his son [. . .] occupied the Centre. His chiefs in Gold and Silver Howdas preceded and followed. His Generals and Commanders seated on highly caparisoned horses arranged the Troops – a body of 4,000 cavalry, uniformly dressed in yellow, formed the wings of this magnificent procession. The Maharajah himself directed every movement with the eye and Confidence of a Soldier [. . .] and was forthwith obeyed. His every word seemed talismanic [. . .] The coup d'oeil, as the troops debarked from the bridge of Boats was the most picturesque and striking; his body guard spread on each side to swell the pageant of their King.[3]

Bentinck mounted his own elephant to meet Ranjit. As the elephants drew alongside each other, the howdah doors were opened. First an apple was passed across, and accepted by Bentinck, who had been forewarned of this test by spies. Then the old Maharaja leapt 'with some agility into His Lordship's arms', somewhat to Bentinck's surprise. It was an auspicious start to festivities which were to be remarkably cordial.

Lord William had taken care to ensure that the presents given to Ranjit were of the highest quality. Fifty-one trays of them were placed before the Maharaja. Ranjit Singh got up and examined every single present, then oversaw their packing away. They included products of British technology such as clocks, telescopes, sextants, broadcloth, knives and needles, but Lord William had also made sure that Ranjit's taste for fine jewels was not ignored.

On 27 October it was the turn of the British party to cross the Sutlej and be received by Ranjit Singh, captured most vividly by Burnes:

> There were seventy elephants advancing with Sikh Chiefs and European Gentlemen in full dress [. . .] The procession was preceded by a band of music, and the Lancers and Bodyguards closed it [. . .] Two Regiments of Infantry were drawn up at right angles to one another, and at the end of the triangle was

a spacious triumphal arch, covered with red cloth and gold ornaments lined with yellow silk. Another Arch more splendid than the first was erected a short distance in advance, and proceeding through there we reached the Courtyard [. . .] There was a silence [. . .] that made the spectacle more than imposing [. . .]

Runjeet conducted the Governor-General to [. . .] where the durbar was to be held, and seated his Lordship between himself and his Son [. . .] The durbar, thus formed, was shaded over by a lofty arcade covered with yellow Silk: on the floor were spread out the richest Carpets and Shawls of Cashmere, and behind the Maharajah stood a spacious tent glittering with every ornament; it was composed partly of crimson velvet, yellow French satin, and Cashmere shawls. [. . .] But the Maharaja himself was a greater object of attraction than even this magnificence. He was robed in green satin; on his right arm he wore that splendid diamond, the 'Koh-i-noor', and his wrist and neck were encircled by the most superb pearls [. . .] There were about three hundred chiefs introduced, some of them wore chain armour; and one individual, Soojet Sing, a Raja [. . .], wore a casque surmounted by a white plume, and splendidly adorned with pearls and diamonds [. . .]

The Maharaja gave a signal, which brought his Regiment of Amazons, about 70 in number. They were richly attired in yellow silk and [. . .] drew up in front of Runjeet and the Governor-General under the command of a favorite Commandant, who commanded the multitude with a long Cane. Some of the ladies were very beautiful; nor did they seem to regret that, on such an occasion, so many eyes should·be turned towards them. Many of them had stained their lips with roseate red [. . .] The ladies succeeded in making an impression and were desired to withdraw, after chanting a few Persian odes on love and beauty [. . .]

Burnes was delighted to see his friends Allard and Court given the honours of allied generals and invited to Lady Bentinck's table. There were two days of field manoeuvres, with each army closely observing the other. But the highlight was the party Ranjit gave on 29 October, at which everyone got drunk, covered in gold dust and played around with the Koh-i-Noor. These were unrepeatable events, and the twenty-six-year-old Burnes was plainly dazzled, as were even the Bentincks, themselves fabulously wealthy:

His Highness' Tents were splendidly illuminated and the continued succession of fireworks gave his whole camp an appearance as bright as day [. . .] the Regiment of Amazons, with their bewitching figures, each armed with a Bow and Arrow, flattered and sung the hours away. Runjeet amused his guests by displaying his jewels: the invaluable diamond was handed round to every individual with a confidence that deserves remark
[. . .] It formed at one time a gem in the crown of descendants of Timour [. . .] and now the property of a once predatory and plundering chief; it was exposed to the gaze, and shall I say, the covetousness of a British Assembly. But the Maharaja [. . .] desired an Amazon to chant the Song of the Hooly: he ordered the goblet, and with it the vessels filled with gold-leaf-dust [. . .] assisted by his

regiment of females, he scattered the dust around. No one escaped not even the Governor-General and Lady William; and one Lady indeed nearly blinded the one-eyed Maharaja in the scuffle – the little man then quaffed his wine, talked lowly in its praise, drank freely of it and endeavored to prevail on many of the gentlemen to imitate his example [...] the party broke up and for two days afterwards most of those, who composed it, might be distinguished by their glittering and bespangled faces: there was no ridding oneself of the gold dust [...]

The small group around Bentinck included a Burnes, two Ramsays and a Skinner: much of that gold dust fell on Montrose. Victor Jacquemont complained that British accounts toned down the real Ranjit: for example 'Rendjit pissa fort gravement dans un coin de la superbe tente ou il se trouvait avec Lord William et tout le cour du gouverneur general.'[4] Beneath the show, serious diplomacy was in process. Bentinck tackled Ranjit Singh over his annexation of northern districts of Bhawalpur; he made plain that Britain was entering treaty relations with Sind and other states of its north-western frontier. All must respect each other's borders.

Burnes had a stark reminder of his rank when he received letters from the Amirs of Sind, asking him to convey their respects, and desire for good relations, to the Governor-General. Burnes translated these letters and gave them to Bentinck's Private Secretary. He was instructed to thank the Amirs but inform them that their correct channel of communication was through Colonel Pottinger.[5] This was humiliating.

After Rupar, Burnes again was Wade's guest at Ludhiana while he wrote up yet more reports. He produced a lengthy comparison of the Indus and Ganges. The Ganges was the main artery of British India, and by stressing to those who had never seen the Indus that it was even larger than the Ganges, Burnes hoped to increase the impact of his mission.[6]

Bentinck, once sceptical, was now fulsome:

> The Governor-General [...] desires me to convey to you, his high approbation of the manner in which you have acquitted yourself [...] and his acknowledgement for the full and satisfactory details furnished [...]
>
> In like manner His Lordship considers you to be entitled for commendation for the extent of geographical and general information collected in the voyage [...] The map submitted by you forms an addition to the geography of India of the first utility and importance [...][7]

The presents Burnes and Leckie had received had to be handed in to the Company. The Governor-General's office wrote to Captain Robert, Acting Resident in Bhuj (Pottinger being in Haidarabad) that 'considering the eminent success which has attended this interesting expedition, and which is attributable [...] to the good conduct of those concerned, Government will be quite prepared to take into its favourable consideration the question of their suitable remuneration.'[8] Unfortunately the remuneration was worth much less than the presents. Burnes was with Wade for Christmas, but on Boxing Day rather than receiving gifts he was giving them back. This is the packing list for the consignment to the Paymaster General:[9]

(From Ranjit Singh)
A sword ornamented with gold and pearls
A sword ornamented with emeralds
Two Cashmere carpets
A bed and curtains of Cashmere shawls
A bow and quiver of arrows
A Dagger
Two Heron's Plumes
A Matchlock with velvet pouch
A bottle ornamented with silver

A sword with gold mountings (from Nuseer Khan)
A sword with gold mountings (from Roostum Khan)
A sword with gold mountings (from Roostum's brother)
A Scindian Matchlock (From Bhawul Khan)

Signed A Burnes Lodeana 26th December 1831

The gold and jewel encrusted Damascus sword he received from Murad Ali Khan does not appear on the list of presents he handed in, nor the string of pearls from Ranjit. There may be an innocent explanation.

Burnes was also told that, whereas he had drawn a bill for Rs20,000 to cover expenses, his receipts only amounted to Rs17,568. On top of which the government calculated he had made an exchange rate gain of a further Rs593. He was therefore asked to repay over Rs3,000, approximately £300. The days of fortune-making in British India were over.

By the time the extra pay for his mission to Lahore was worked out, it was March 1832, and Burnes was in Afghanistan. The Governor-General granted an additional monthly allowance of Rs1,500 for nine months. That was a bonus of £1,350, which though not a fortune, was a good sum. Leckie received a meagre bonus of £225.[10]

While waiting final permission from Bentinck to travel to Bokhara Alex paid a visit to Delhi, where he stayed with Charles Trevelyan and D'Arcy Todd, who shared a house. Todd found Burnes 'a very intelligent and pleasant man'.[11] Burnes paid a call on the Mughal Emperor amid the decaying splendour of the great Red Fort, and reflected: 'The mummery of the ceremony was absurd, and I could not suppress a smile as the officers mouthed, in loud

# ALEXANDER BURNES' GREAT JOURNEY

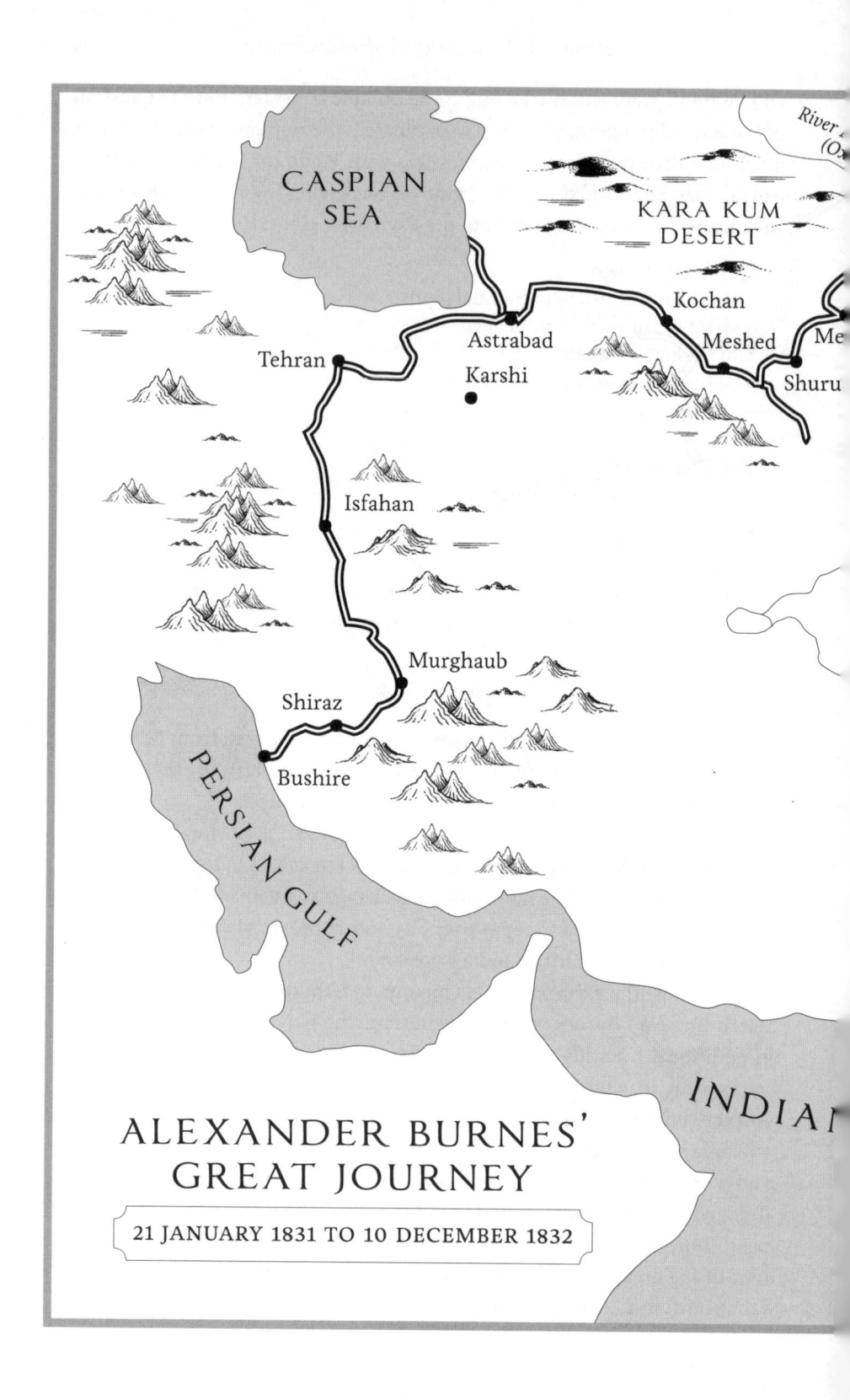

21 JANUARY 1831 TO 10 DECEMBER 1832

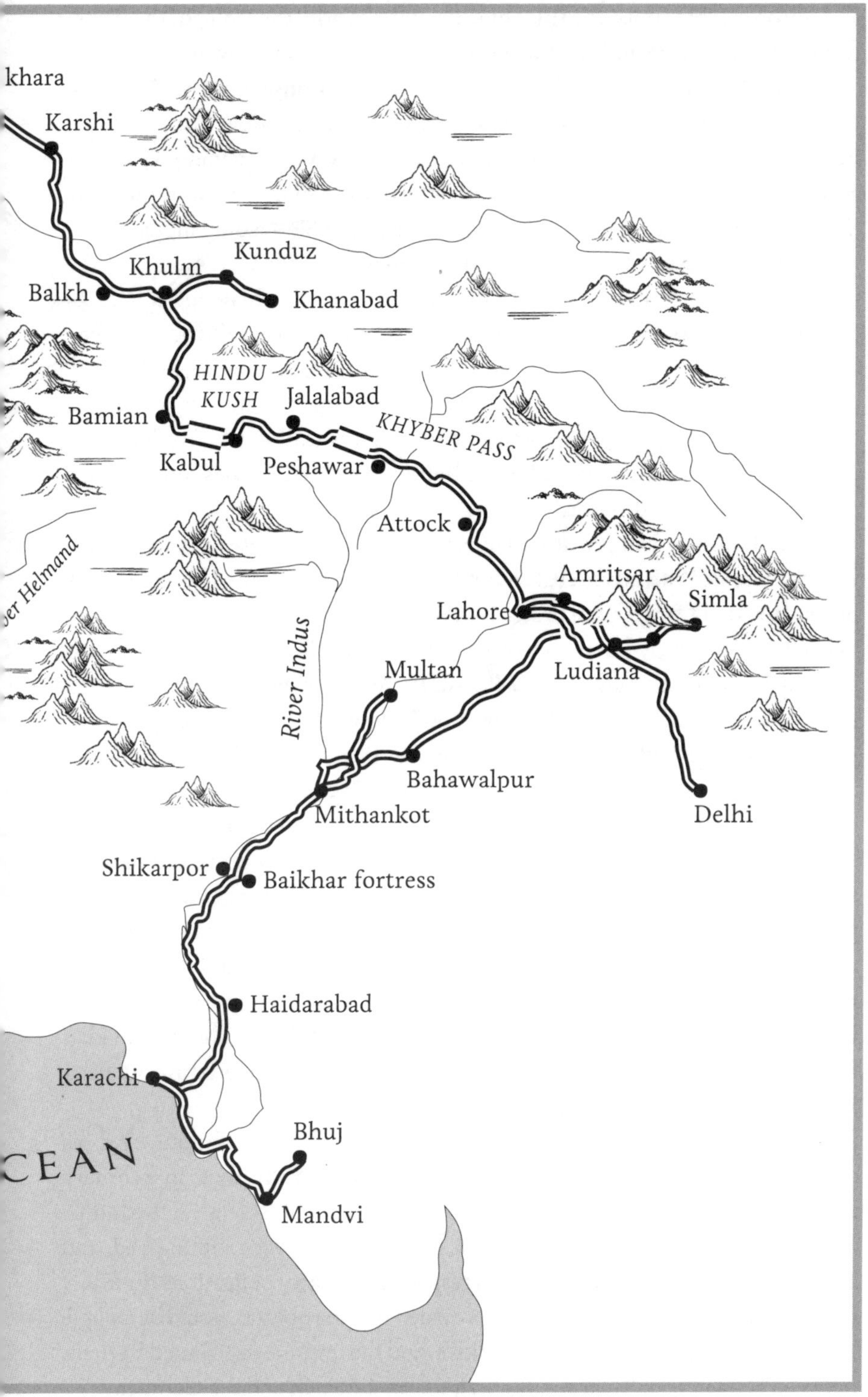
khara
Karshi
Kunduz
Khulm
Balkh
Khanabad
HINDU
KUSH
Jalalabad
Bamian
KHYBER PASS
Kabul
Peshawar
Attock
ver Helmand
Amritsar
Lahore
Simla
River Indus
Multan
Ludiana
Bahawalpur
Mithankot
Delhi
Shikarpor
Baikhar fortress
Haidarabad
Karachi
Bhuj
CEAN
Mandvi

and sonorous solemnity, the titles of King of the World, the Ruler of the Earth, to a monarch now realmless, and a prince without the shadow of power.'[12]

On 19 December Bentinck sent a long report to the Court of Directors, examining the policy consequences of Burnes' Indus mission. He noted that Burnes had won the Amirs of Sind round, and they now had a genuine desire for good relations. Their fears of encroachment from the Sikhs were well-founded. If the British could restrain Ranjit Singh, influence in Sind would increase.

Bentinck stressed that Burnes had shown that the Indus was essential to the military defence of India. Britain must therefore establish alliances with all the adjacent rulers. Burnes had reported a possible marriage alliance between the Talpur Dynasty of Sind, and Persia. Britain must head this off, and indeed prevent any external alliances of all Indus states. Finally, Bentinck noted that he had granted Burnes permission to continue his exploration to the Oxus, returning to his Residency via Persia. Bentinck praised Burnes' professional abilities in the highest terms.[13]

Henry Pottinger had proceeded to Haidarabad to negotiate the Indus treaty with the Amirs. With all his customary aggression he threatened both an attack on Sind by Ranjit Singh and a British punitive expedition because of Khosa raids. What the Amirs really wanted was a guarantee against Ranjit; Pottinger saw this as an opportunity to make Sind a British protectorate and control its foreign policy. But Bentinck turned these proposals down flat; his Rupar agreement with Ranjit Singh had stipulated both Sind and Punjab should be independent.

On 4 April 1832 Pottinger signed a treaty with the Amir of Khairpur and on 20 April with the Amir of Haidarabad which opened the Indus to trade at a fixed rate of tolls and duties, but forbade the passage of arms and military supplies, and banned the British from living in Sind. Pottinger had failed to get agreement to British Residencies in Khairpur and Haidarabad. A separate treaty dealt with the suppression of raiders from Thar and Parkar. The following December Claude Wade agreed with Ranjit Singh a similar treaty to open the commercial navigation of the Indus and Sutlej. The British plan for the Indus had been achieved on paper. Pottinger remained Resident at Bhuj and non-resident Envoy to Sind.

Wade also reached an agreement with the Nawab of Bhawalpur over his stretch of the Indus, including a British Resident at Mithankot. In February 1833 Lieutenant Mackeson was given the grand title of 'Resident on the Indus', and continued the never-ending task of surveying the river's shifting bed, and attempting to make the various rulers respect their treaty obligations. In 1834 a further treaty with all the Indus rulers provided that the only tax would be a single toll per vessel to be collected by the British, and the revenue distributed by them between Haidarabad, Khairpur, Bhawalpur, Ranjit Singh and the Company.

CHAPTER ELEVEN

## Journey through Afghanistan

Burnes wrote to his sister Anne in Bhuj, 'The home government have got frightened at the designs of Russia, and desired that some intelligent officer should be sent to acquire information in the countries bordering on the Oxus and the Caspian; and I, knowing nothing of all this, come forward and volunteer for precisely what they want. Lord Bentinck jumps at it [...]'[1]

It was becoming standard to send a doctor with every small party, to try to reduce the appalling mortality rate. The Aberdonian Dr James Gerard of the Bengal Service had already explored the Himalayas more widely than any European, had experience of surveying, and was a natural choice.[2] Mohammad Ali, who had done so much of the work on the Indus, stayed with Burnes.

While Burnes and Charles Trevelyan got on well, they had different viewpoints. Trevelyan argued with evangelising zeal from his desk. With Thomas Babington Macaulay, Calcutta's Legal Officer, he was at the core of a new Anglicising movement in British Indian administration. He published tracts on the advantages of English language education, and the superiority of Christianity. While achieving some good, such as Bentinck's suppression of Thuggi and Sutti, this movement heralded a new arrogant cultural superiority, a creed from which Burnes largely appeared immune.

Charles Grant, President of the Board of Control, had appointed Macaulay to the Supreme Council in Calcutta precisely to carry out Anglicising reform. Macaulay's father Zachary had made his fortune in the EIC. There was a public alliance between Macaulay and Trevelyan – and a private closer one. Macaulay had an overwhelming attachment to his two sisters that was possibly incestuous. His letters to his elder sister Margaret are at least very strange, and one directly compares their love with Byron's 'troubles' with his sister – and everyone knew what that meant. The younger sister Hannah had always been included in this emotional bond, and after Margaret married, Macaulay took Hannah with him to India. When Hannah got engaged to Trevelyan, Macaulay wrote to Margaret: 'Since you left me, she was everything to me. I loved her, I adored her [...] I am to be henceforth nothing to her.' This is not a normal reaction to a sister getting engaged.[3]

Trevelyan had not socialised much with British colleagues other than in field sports. He had no conversation other than work, and nothing in common with his wife. He 'was indeed much perplexed by the conversation of his wife and her brother.'[4] Extraordinarily, Trevelyan made it a condition of marrying Hannah that Macaulay move in with them – and they lived together in India and later London. Incest possibly continued: in 1839 Hannah wrote about her brother, 'I cannot endure the thought that I will ever love him less than I do now, though I feel how criminal it is.' The relationship was strange in every way. The joint household had already been going for three years when Burnes wrote to Masson that Trevelyan travelled with four (presumably Indian) wives.

The new English College at Delhi was central to the reformers' initiative, and Trevelyan was a Governor. He grandiloquently declared it 'destined to change the moral aspect of the whole of Upper India'. Mohan Lal was a student in its first English medium class. Not the best scholar, but the most charming and active, Lal came from a high caste Kashmiri Pandit family, which had fallen on hard times after the Court of the Mughal Emperors declined. His father had switched his allegiance to the British and been Mountstuart Elphinstone's munshi in his mission to Peshawar. Trevelyan became fond of Mohan. He had secured him a scholarship and sometimes helped further with money.[5] In 1828 the religious authorities in Delhi outlawed the English class. Mohan Lal had assisted Trevelyan in resolution talks,[6] and recorded that 'he gave me a document in which he promised to promote my prosperity in the world'. On 18 December 1831, Burnes met the eighteen-year-old Lal in the home of the Residence Secretary Mr Fitzgerald, and was instantly won over. He applied for permission to appoint Lal as munshi to the expedition at an annual salary of Rs1,000.

Lal later untruthfully stated that Mohammed Ali was the munshi and he a diplomat. In fact, Ali was assistant deputy surveyor, on a salary almost twice Lal's.[7] Burnes had left Delhi to return to Ludhiana as guest of Wade over Christmas, and there the small party made rendezvous, Mohan Lal the last to arrive by pony on 2 January. By the following nightfall they had reached the border of Ranjit Singh's realm, where a cavalry escort awaited. Their route involved regular Sikh presents of bows, purses and too much food, with increasingly large escorts and entertainment by local sirdars. Just outside

Lahore on 16 January 1832 they were met by General Allard and escorted into Lahore amidst a cloud of yellow robed cavalry. Ranjit Singh gave audience to Burnes and Gerard in a magnificent crimson pavilion, where they were seated on golden chairs on a velvet-covered dais. There followed a fortnight of Ranjit's magnificent entertainment, including two boar hunts. One tent was completely encrusted in pearls, with a border of precious stones, and worth in itself several lakhs of rupees. Burnes noted that Ranjit cannily did not drink much, while pressing his guests. Ranjit and Alexander conversed for hours. Sohan Lal Suri recorded of Burnes and Gerard 'the glorious sahibs indulged in drinking wine with the dancing girls and were lost in the ocean of intoxication'.[8] Lal felt that Ranjit's open familiarity with the dancing girls was 'improper'. At their final night's carousing with Ranjit the entertainment consisted of highly sexualised fighting between girls in which they tore at each other, and winners were richly rewarded.

On 11 February they left Lahore, and adopted native dress. Young Mohan was astonished to see Burnes and Gerard in turbans, shifts, loose trousers and slippers, sitting cross-legged on the ground, eating rice with their fingers from a communal camp dish. On 7 March 1832 at Rawalpindi they stayed in a house of Shah Shuja, which Burnes described as a 'miserable hovel'. Here they reduced their equipment much further to just two mule-loads, shaved their heads and assumed the appearance of poverty.

Burnes was not only taking the advice of General Court but also of Mountstuart Elphinstone: 'In most parts of the country, a poor stranger would be received with hospitality and kindness; but a wealthy traveller [...] might lay his account with being plundered.'[9] They now went into full disguise, the first time Burnes had ever done this. He became 'Sikunder Khan' while Mohan Lal became 'Hasan Jan', an identity he kept for most of their subsequent journey. Burnes generally used disguise only on the road and abandoned it when dealing with local rulers.

Having visited several centres of the salt-mining industry, which brought an annual revenue of 30 lakhs, they became the first Britons to be admitted to the great stronghold of Rotas. Burnes made a comprehensive plan of its defences and found it to be very strong, but with the obvious weakness of no internal supply of fresh water. It contained 400 houses, of which Mohan Lal claimed fifty were inhabited by dancing girls. On 9 March at Rawalpindi Gerard was struck down with a severe fever, probably malarial. He struggled on. Two days later at Magala, Burnes was able to talk about the route for two hours with a Hindu goldsmith recently returned from Bokhara.

On 14 March they were entertained by the great Sikh General Hari Singh at

Sirkika Bela on the Indus. Mohan Lal noted that Hari's personal morality was on the same level as Ranjit's. The next day they were forced to skirt Attock as Sikh regiments were in mutiny over pay arrears. Attempting to ford the Indus with their Sikh escort, three men were swept away and drowned. The party were therefore mounted on elephants, and even then the crossing was nerve-racking. On 19 March they stayed the night at Pirpai, where Syed Ahmed had been defeated and killed and his remaining supporters massacred. They were put up in a single, crowded hovel, but that evening noble envoys arrived from Peshawar and next morning they were conducted to the city, where they were greeted by the Sirdar, Sultan Mohammed Khan Barakzai, whom Burnes had met briefly at Lahore.

In Chapter 2 we introduced the background of the feud between the Saduzais and the Barakzais. Dost Mohammed Khan Barakzai had raped a daughter of Shah Mahmoud Saduzai, the King of Afghanistan who had displaced Shah Shuja. Dost Mohammed's act had repelled his own family; but when in retaliation Crown Prince Kamran Saduzai first blinded then tortured to death the vizier Futth Khan Barakzai, the Barakzais united in a vicious struggle.

Over a decade of civil war ensued, until in 1825 Dost Mohammed had established himself as ruler in Kabul, while other Barakzai family members ruled in Kandahar, Jallalabad and Peshawar. The Saduzais clung on only in Herat.

Both the Saduzais and Barakzais were members of the Dourani tribal confederacy. The Barakzais were a khail, or group of families, whereas the Saduzais were an ulus, or single family, within the Popalzai khail. The Saduzai ulus were the royal family, a status that the leading Mohammedzai ulus of the Barakzais did not claim.[10] Dost Mohammed ruled in Kabul without the title of Shah. The Barakzais were the largest and most warlike of the Dourani khails, a major power base.

There had never been a state with the borders of Afghanistan today. Afghanistan had been part of the wide Safavid and Mughal Empires; its manifestation as a single political unit is traced to the empire founded by Ahmed Shah Dourani from 1747. That also included Sind, Baluchistan, Peshawar and Kashmir. The nineteenth-century British concept of Afghanistan was more ethnically homogeneous than the modern state, in that it was based on the Pashtun homeland. Modern Afghanistan has little homogeneity; all its major ethnic groups have most of their population over the borders in Afghanistan's neighbours.[11] Current northern Afghanistan between the Hindu Kush and the Amu Darya, including Balkh and Mazar-i-Sharif, was not considered by the British in 1832 as part of Afghanistan, though Herat was. Afghanistan's northern border was Bamian.

The Afghans themselves seldom referred to Afghanistan at all. They knew the word and did have a concept of being Afghan, though this was much less important than tribal identity. They generally thought of Kabulistan, stretching from Bamian to Attock, and of Zabulistan or Khorasan, which included Kandahar and Herat.

Afghanistan was a country of bitter feud. However it would be wrong to characterise the regions into which Burnes was venturing as uncivilised. In the Middle Ages it had outshone Europe in intellectual achievement. Despite decline, there still existed a high culture. Patterns of trade were well established. In Bokhara, Kunduz, Kabul or Shirkapur, Burnes could exchange for gold with local merchant banking networks promissory notes written in the British mission in Bhuj and redeemable in Bombay, at a premium that seldom varied from 6 per cent. That argues a high degree of sophistication, also found in other activities. Mountstuart Elphinstone noted that 'The smallpox carries off many persons, though inoculation has long been practised by the Moollahs and Sayyids in the remote parts of the kingdom.'

The British Residency at Delhi had, since 1809, maintained native agents in Kabul, Kunduz and Bokhara, who reported on political and commercial matters. Recent British travellers into Afghanistan included an adventurer named Durie, son of a Scottish father and Indian mother, who had travelled to Kabul and Kandahar in 1808–9 disguised as a pilgrim to Mecca. Durie lived entirely off hospitality, and though several times discovered as a Christian encountered no personal violence. The more celebrated travels of Moorcroft and Trebeck from 1820 to 1825 were epic and tragic, and underlined the risks that Burnes was taking.

From February 1828 to April 1829 another Company civil servant, Edward Stirling from Port of Menteith, had travelled through Persia and the Uzbek lands beyond the Hindu Kush in full disguise as a Muslim merchant before returning via Kabul. He was suspended by the Company for eighteen months for returning three weeks late from leave.[12] He bemoaned, 'The members of Government could not be roused to take an interest in the subject. The knowledge I had been in these interesting countries produced no desire for intelligence regarding them.'[13]

There had been earlier British travellers. At the siege of Kandahar in 1649 the artillery bombardment was supervised by Peter Miller and David Chester, under Captain Dowlett, who served Shahs Jehan and Aurungzeb. Another officer, William Hicks, had a grave in Kabul dated 1666.[14]

Peshawar had been the winter capital of the Afghan kingdom until a decade earlier, but was now tributary to Ranjit Singh. Sultan Mohammed Barakzai, brother to Dost Mohammed, was Governor. Peshawar's wealth came from its position as an entrepot between Central Asia and India, and its fertile agricultural valley, while government monopolies of hemp and saffron boosted state revenues.

The party stayed in a house adjoining that of Sultan Mohammed. Sultan was fond of Westerners and had previously hosted Moorcroft and Josiah Harlan. He arrived most evenings with servants bearing a sumptuous meal, and ate with Gerard and Burnes from a common platter, although Gerard found Afghan food greasy. There was a stream of supplicants for medical services, especially after Gerard performed some eye cataract operations. Afghan nobles invited the party to breakfast, held as mid-day picnics in beautiful gardens of flowers and fruit trees. Gerard complained that heat and sun made it impossible to enjoy these occasions, and was ill with fever. But Burnes' iron constitution seemed immune.

Burnes enjoyed Sultan Mohammed's company enormously, and this sojourn at Peshawar was an idyll which left a lasting impression. Sultan was secretly urging Burnes that the British should take over Peshawar. Although Sikh suzerainty was nominal, Sultan feared more effective Sikh annexation, and also was worried about the designs of his half brothers at Kabul and Kandahar. He felt that his position would best be secured by a British protectorate.[15]

Alexander wrote warmly about Sultan Mohammed. Yet Mohan Lal said that Sultan: 'is fond of pleasure. He is notorious for lewdness, and is always surrounded by females, both married and unmarried. He is careless of his country and employed in adorning himself'.[16] Burnes was drawn to this sybaritic existence. Peshawar occupied a vital strategic position, but it is difficult not to conclude Burnes was spinning out his time there. He was indignant to find Russian goods on sale in the bazaar. He bought distinctive blue-tinged Russian paper, and pointedly used it for reports back to India.[17]

Both Burnes and Lal recount an incident where a tailor brought to Sultan Mohammed the bodies of his wife and her lover, a maulvi or learned man. He had killed them with a sword after catching them in bed together. Burnes records that Sultan praised the tailor; Lal adds that Gerard and Burnes concurred. Another amorous maulvi had seen Mohan Lal riding through the town. He invented a medical complaint in order to meet with Mohan. He recited love poetry and fervently requested that he be allowed to visit Mohan daily, and Lal primly records 'I did not think proper to refuse his request.'

Burnes and Gerard made a short expedition to Kohat, reputedly rich in minerals. They discovered anthracite, which proved to burn satisfactorily. Gerard surmised correctly that high quality coal might underlay this. They reported the discovery as important for steam navigation of the Indus.

Nawab Jabbar Khan, half brother to Dost and Sultan had heard they they were en route to Kabul, and invited them to stay as his guest there, and also on his estate at Gandamak. Sultan was anxious that they should not go to Kabul, as he did not want the British to form a relationship with Dost Mohammed. He suggested that they instead pass through Kandahar and Herat to Bokhara. As that route had already been travelled by Arthur Conolly, Burnes did not take his advice.

The British authorities had sponsored another investigation. Arthur Conolly and Charles Trevelyan had organised the finance of an Afghan merchant, Sayid Muhin Shah,[18] to take up British goods – mostly cloth – with the great Lohani annual migration caravans to sell in Kabul and Bokhara.[19] The route proved viable, and a good profit – over 100 per cent – was made on the speculation. They appeared to confirm a serious market for British cloth. Muhin Shah had previously traded from Herat to Bombay, taking horses, dried fruit and nuts south and returning with Indian and British manufactured goods, and slaves (an illegal traffic in Africans through Bombay and Mandvi was brisk). Many of the British goods Muhin Shah sold at Herat were taken on to Bokhara and further by other merchants.

Burnes now met Muhin Shah in Peshawar and discussed with him the possibility of the Burnes mission travelling as part of his caravan. Muhin demurred on the grounds that their presence might endanger his own success.

On 19 April 1832 Burnes left Peshawar after staying exactly one month. They were in company with a Kabul merchant, Mohammed Sharif Khan, a Qizilbash or Central Asian Persian. Burnes found the urbane and educated Sharif good company. In view of recent fighting between Sikhs and Afghans, they did not penetrate the disturbed Khyber pass, but took a more circuitous route being used by caravans, via Chor. They had a strong escort sent to them from Kabul. In the first few days the temperature reached 100°F, or 38°C, while Gerard's fever was still higher. They used pathways where they had to lead their horses alongside dizzying precipices, and crossed the Kabul river in spate on a raft of inflated skins. Gerard wrote: 'the party were carried into an eddy, and "wheeled round" several times; the raft was laden to the edge, and [...] the people started calling to their "Ali" [...] the travellers were naturally rather alarmed, but extricated themselves at last'.[20]

They would set off at dead of night, and stop at mid-morning. They were very much at the mercy of their guides, who would frequently stop to smoke, or break into a gallop for no discernible reason. As they ascended, they switched to travelling in daylight.

Arriving at Kabul on 1 May, Burnes quickly sent a letter to reassure his mother:

> My journey has been more prosperous than my most sanguine expectations could have anticipated [...] we have hitherto been feasted and caressed by the chiefs of the country. I though Peshawur a delightful place, till we came to Caubul [...] The people here know me by the name of Sikunder, which is the Persian for Alexander, and a magnanimous name it is. I am living with a most amiable man [...] by the name of Jubbur Khan, brother to the chief of Caubul.

Jabbar was the eldest brother, though his mother had been a slave girl, and was a highly cultivated man with a wide reputation for assisting Europeans. He had also fought bravely at the battle of Shupaiyan, where the Afghans, devastated by Sikh artillery, had lost Kashmir to Ranjit Singh. He gave Burnes much information about mineral deposits in Afghanistan and one evening told Alexander of his alchemical researches. He then suggested that Burnes reciprocate and tell some western secrets. Alexander launched into an explanation of freemasonry, which he said 'was an institution where, though we did not attempt to change the baser metals into gold, we attempted to change the baser and blacker passions of men into philanthropy and charity'. Jabbar asked to join, but Burnes replied that the initiation ceremony required 'the number of the Pleiades', presumably seven members.[21]

The day after Burnes' party arrived, the eccentric Joseph Wolff stumbled into the city. Wolff was a clergyman, a convert from Judaism, and married to Lady Georgina Walpole, who was related to Lady Bentinck. He had travelled through the Middle East and Central Asia preaching the Gospel. Robbed in Afghanistan, by his own account he arrived in the city naked. There may be an element of truth in this. Wandering naked holy men known as malang were protected in Afghan society, viewed as touched by Allah. Burnes sent him clothes and money, but was somewhat perplexed to find himself associated with this disputatious fellow, who was a disruptive presence at meetings with Dost Mohammed and his ministers. Burnes was extremely kind to the destitute Wolff, but formed a contempt for him.

Wolff joined the party in Jabbar Khan's house, and his passion for religious debate attracted numbers of curious Afghans. As their interest was at least partly mocking, Burnes got frustrated. As he and Wolff were from the same country, arrived at the same time and stayed in the same house, it is natural Afghans would believe them connected. Gerard noted that the house 'became a perfect congregation of Jews' to whom Wolff preached.[22] Wolff claimed to have had an ecstatic vision of Elijah.

Dost Mohammed had emerged as ruler in Kabul after twenty-five years of civil war following the death of Timur Shah, son of the great Ahmad Shah Dourani. Four of Timur Shah's sons had briefly ruled – Zeman, Mahmud, Shuja and Habibulla. Mahmud had blinded Zeman, Shuja had imprisoned

Mahmud. Zeman had briefly shown enterprise and skill and threatened to restore greatness, aided by the Barakzais who also aided Mahmud. That alliance had been broken by the Herat rape, and the consequent murder of Futth Khan Barakzai. Habibulla's brief reign was the final use of a puppet Saduzai king by the Barakzais.

The second youngest of the twenty-one acknowledged sons of Sarafraz Paydanah Khan, and by a junior wife, the daughter of one of his Qizilbash bodyguard, the child Dost was looked down upon by purer blood elder brothers, and was repeatedly sodomised by one, Semund Khan.[23] For protection he attached himself as a page to the eldest, the soldierly Futth Khan, and aged fourteen gained Futth's approval by shooting a man with whom Futth had a blood feud.

Dost had organised the looting and massacre of a number of large trade caravans in acts of simple banditry. He had a reputation for debauchery. He was fully embroiled in the labyrinthine civil wars, and was not only brave in battle but also murdered Mirza Ali Khan by stabbing him in the back. Dost was given the government of Kohistan and brought this unruly district to order by wholescale executions. He conspired with Ranjit Singh to foil his brother Mohammed Azim Khan's attempt to retake Peshawar. There really is nothing admirable in his early career.

He gained Kabul in 1825, ousting his brother Sultan, after lengthy fraternal conflict that had seen eight different Barakzais control Kabul in nine years.[24] But on coming to power he produced a remarkable personal transformation. He undertook the Toba, a kind of religiously motivated cold turkey. After a period of ritual cleansing, he forswore alcohol, tobacco and other drugs. From then on he attended religious duties unstintingly, and lived a life of comparative austerity. Not all pleasure was forbidden, and his zenana swelled with young women.

Of his official wives, the senior was Aga Taj who had been captured at Kabul, a Saduzai, niece of Shuja and granddaughter of Timur Shah. But his favourite was Khadija, a Popalzai, whose sister was a wife of Shuja. His favoured son, Mohammed Akbar, was the eldest by this wife, and her next was Haidar Khan, also in high favour. His eldest son, Mohammed Afzul, was by a Qizilbash wife who died young. Another son, Akram Khan, by a wife taken hostage from her Kohistani father, had been given command of a military expedition against Kunduz the previous year. There were over twenty other official sons, and nine other acknowledged wives, plus many daughters nobody ever listed, and a cloud of concubines.

Dost invited Burnes, Wolff and Gerard to dinner on 11 May in the royal apartments of the great fortress of Kabul, the Bala Hissar. They were struck by the austerity of surroundings and meal. Burnes had now met the Mughal and Sikh Emperors and the rulers of Jodhpur, Jaysulmir, Cutch, Sind, Bhawalpur and Peshawar. Dost Mohammed was alone in making no attempt to impress by regal show. Burnes admired Dost's straightforward manner, and reported back to Calcutta that he was 'unquestionably the most influential and talented man of these days in Afghanistan'.[25] However there remained a stand-offishness about Dost Mohammed, and Burnes never approached the degree of informality and sheer fun he had experienced with Sultan Mohammed.

Gerard's description of Dost is acute:

> he shows off to advantage as far as intelligence and shrewd conversation go. As to his dress, it is very humble [...] He wants Sultan Mahomed's attention and condescension, but considering that he was rising into power, and views with suspicion our friendship with Runjeet Singh on the one hand, and Russian and Persian influence on the other, it is no wonder that he keeps a little aloof from us [...][26]

Historians have tended to treat the Russo-Persian threat as a British imaginary construct foisted upon Afghanistan. In fact it was already a main concern of the ruler of Kabul, even before meeting the British.

While Dost's welcome was gratifying, there were signs that he wished to push this new friendship further. He offered Burnes the command of his army of 12,000 cavalry and twenty cannon. When Burnes declined, he asked him to recommend someone and suggested that the British combine with him to crush Ranjit Singh. Burnes pointed out that Britain had a treaty of alliance with Ranjit, and added he was but an officer returning home on leave.

Alexander was heartened to find that a number of British manufactures were in the Kabul markets, and British chintzes more popular than Russian cloth.[27] Kabul was a cosmopolitan entrepot where trade was picking up under Dost Mohammed's encouragement. The inhabitants included Pashtuns, Lohanis, Hazaras, Tajiks, Qizilbash, Armenians and Georgians. Many of the shopkeepers and bankers were Indian Hindus, and there was a small Jewish community.

Gerard described the bustling life of Kabul:

> when the bazar opens, one is amply gratified by a scene, which for [...] activity of business, variety of objects and foreign physiognomy, has no living model in India. The fruits which we had seen out of season at Peshawar loaded every shop; the masses of snow for sale threw out a refreshing chill, and sparkled by the sun's heat: the many strange faces and strange figures, each speaking in the dialect of his nation [...]
>
> The covered part of the bazar, which is entered by lofty portals, dazzled my sight [...] when reflected against the setting sun. In these stately corridors, the

stores rise in benches above each other, the various articles with their buyers and sellers, regularly arranged in tiers, representing so many living strata.[28]

Gerard appreciated the achievement of Dost Mohammed:

> Kabul is rising into power under his Republican system of government, and [...] is destined to an importance in spite of itself, for it is the key to India. It is astonishing how much the country is relieved by the overthrow of the royal dynasty [...] In Shah Shuja's haughty career here, robberies and bloodshed disgraced the precincts of his court. Dost Mahommed's citizen-like demeanour and resolute simplicity have suited the people's understanding.[29]

Among the many Afghans who came to the house was one whose features struck the mission as European. They were suspicious of his 'knowledge of Russian and Polish affairs' and Gerard believed he betrayed signs of understanding English. Wolff directly challenged the man, in German, and he fled. Who he was is unclear.[30] On 12 May Wolff left for Peshawar, with money which Burnes gave him for the journey.

Their last meeting with Dost Mohammed lasted until well after midnight, and Burnes clearly enjoyed these occasions, despite the lack of alcohol, tobacco or dancing girls. As he prepared to continue his journey, he wrote back to Montrose of his travelling style:

> Never was there a more humble being seen. No tent, no chair or table, no bed, and my clothes altogether amount to the value of one pound sterling [...] My dress is purely Asiatic, and since I came to Caubul [...] [m]y head is shaved of its brown locks, and my beard dyed black [...] I now eat my meals with my hands, and greasy digits they are, though I must say, in justification, that I wash my hands before and after meals. I frequently sleep under a tree, but if a villager will take compassion upon me I enter his house. I never conceal that I am a European [...] With all my assumed poverty, I have a belt of ducats around my waist, and bills for as much money as I choose to draw. I gird my loins and tie on my sword on all occasions, though I freely admit I would make more use of gold and silver than of cold steel. When I go into company, I [...] say in all humility to the master of the house 'peace be unto thee', according to custom, and then I squat myself down on the ground. This familiarity has given me an insight into the people of the country which I never otherwise could have acquired [...] The people of this country are kind-hearted and hospitable; they have no prejudices against a Christian, and none against our nation. When they ask me if I eat pork, I of course shudder, and reply it is only outcasts who commit such outrages. God forgive me, for I am very fond of bacon, and my mouth waters as I write the word! [...]
> Our breakfast consists of <u>pillaw</u> (rice and meat), vegetables, stews and preserves, and finishes with fruit [...] Apples, pears, quinces [...] and as for the grapes, they are delicious. They are kept in small boxes in cotton, and are

preserved throughout the year [...] I am too much of a politician to drink wine in a Mahomedan country [...] I never was in better spirits.[31]

This first visit by Burnes to Kabul lasted just seventeen days. His conclusions were that Dost Mohammed was a rising man worth backing, and that Russian influence in Kabul was a real danger.

As Gerard put it, 'Everybody at Caubul speaks in praise of the Russians, and if India is ever threatened by them, the Afghans will be their friends, if we are not sharp. The fate of India must be decided in Caubul.'[32]

Burnes left Kabul on 18 May 1832 to continue to Bokhara. That same month another traveller arrived in the city, as Karamat Ali, the British newswriter in Kabul appointed by Wade, was to report:

> A European arrived here in the month of May, and resided some four months [...] He describes himself as an Englishman, by name Masson, and of the sect of priests. He had been absent from his country 12 years [...] had lately come from Karachi Bunder through Sindh and Kandahar, and had with him two or three books in a foreign character, a compass, a map and an astrolabe. He was shabbily dressed, and his outward appearance denoted distress [...][33]

Masson was a deserter, an educated private soldier of the Bengal Artillery named James Lewis. He had slipped away from the siege of Baratpur in 1824.

Something had gone wrong in Burnes' relationship with Henry Pottinger. In June, Pottinger wrote to Bentinck that the Indus was much more navigable than Burnes' survey had claimed. The usual depth of the stream Pottinger had found to be four to six fathoms and in places ten. Burnes gave significantly lower figures. Pottinger added he had found a boatman who had accompanied Burnes, who assured him the river was no lower then. Pottinger concluded that Burnes' surveying was inaccurate, adding that Burnes' commercial information was wrong on the availability and price of goods in local markets. He concluded with a disingenuous disclaimer:

> I am certain His Lordship will not imagine from any of the remarks contained in this letter that it is my wish to criticise or detract from the information which Lieutenant Burnes's journals contain [...][34]

Burnes was unaware of this attack. He was trying to find a route to Bokhara which avoided the Kunduz territory of the notorious Uzbek ruler, Murad Beg. Beg's evil reputation was deserved. He had taken Badakshan in 1829 and deported 20,000 inhabitants into slavery. His tax assessment on Saigan and Khamard was one slave per every three households – annually. Murad had a reputation for enslaving travellers, particularly non-Muslims. Delays, detentions and fines he had imposed on Moorcroft and Trebeck had contributed to their deaths. Beg had expanded his territories by conquest and owed part of his military success to an artilleryman deserter from the 24th Bombay NI known as 'Jemadar Sahib'.[35] But he had also expanded his revenues by encouraging caravans to pass through his territories with safe escort, and only levying the sharia-ordained duty of one-fortieth.

The only way to avoid his territory was to skirt the Hindu Kush to Herat, a circuitous route to Bokhara which Burnes eschewed. Jabbar Khan organised a passage for them with a small caravan that was going via Khulm, traversing the territory but not the capital of Murad Beg, led by an experienced kafilbashi named Hyat. Burnes and Gerard now became Armenian merchants, Sikunder Armeni and Gerard Armeni, while Mohan Lal was going to work in one of the Indian banking houses in Bokhara. The surveyor Mohammed Ali became an Indian merchant. Jabbar insisted on riding with them for several miles and Burnes wrote, 'I do not think I ever took leave of an Asiatic with more regret than I left this worthy man.'[36]

The high passes of the Hindu Kush were dangerous. At 12,000 feet they rode with boots frozen to their stirrups and eyes snowblind. They crossed a series of ravines on weak snowbridges.[37] As usual, Burnes' published account downplayed the danger, but he wrote privately:

> Our journey across the Hindoo Koosh was [...] a fearful undertaking. We wound for days among hills and ravines, which hid the sun from our view, and rose over us to a perpendicular height of two and three thousand feet [...] I had my nose frost-bitten [...] and nearly lost my sight from the glare [...] I shall indeed be sorry when our journey draws to a close, for I have never spent a happier time in my life [...][38]

Burnes was not merely conforming to an archetype of the dauntless British explorer: he was helping to create that archetype. Gerard wrote to his brother that the Hindu Kush was nothing compared to the Himalayas proper.[39] But he wrote to a fellow officer that, entering the fatal territory of Khulm and Bokhara, he expected they would be 'martyred'.[40]

On 26 May the small party were surrounded by a large force of raiders. Fortunately, the chief of Kamard, Rahmatulla Khan, had sent his son to guide them on this stage and the band, owing some allegiance to the father, were persuaded to let them go. But it had been a close call.

At Bamian, they paused to study the famous giant statues, which Burnes correctly identified as Buddhist. The valley of Bamian was hauntingly desolate, and studded with low remains of habitations. These were deserted, but the caves pockmarking the cliff face around the Buddhas were inhabited. One of the giant figures itself contained caves where people were living, and at night the glimpses of torchlight in the recesses, combined with the odd human shout, were unnerving. Gerard wrote 'one dwells in the contemplation of the scene, till it actually appears of an infernal kind [...]'.[41] From Bamian they had an escort provided by the Governor, Haji Khan Kakar, until they reached the territories of Murad Beg.

Burnes and Gerard now wound their turban cloths close around their faces, but arriving at Khulm, it was plain that their disguise was far from foolproof. They were detained in the town until word could be received from Murad Beg as to whether they were allowed to proceed. On 1 June 1832 Mohan Lal was invited to dinner by Chiman Das, a prominent Hindu merchant, who told him that he realised that he was a munshi travelling with farangis. Chiman Das suggested to Mohan that, if the British really were spies, he extort money from them and split it with him, but Lal stoutly maintained they were just poor men returning home.

The customs official who detained them was sympathetic, but in fear of his own life if he allowed them to pass without express permission of Murad Beg. He had seen through their disguise, but Burnes bribed him with twenty gold tillars. Eventually, he agreed to take Burnes to Murad, while the rest of the party waited at Khulm. Burnes was genuinely worried about his appearance before the notorious Murad Beg. As he departed for the seventy miles to Kunduz, Mohan Lal noted: 'perseverance appeared to vie with the anxiety and melancholy which appeared on his face'.

At Kunduz they discovered that Murad was in Khanabad, and on 5 June they were escorted there to meet him. Murad Beg accepted his officer's description of Burnes as Armenian without close scrutiny. Burnes wrote home that he 'quite humbugged Moorad Khan and all his court, and got a dress of honour and an escort out of the country', though he did add that it was the customs officer who did the talking.[42] Appearing before Murad Beg in disguise, Burnes had been in very great danger, and was not out of it yet. His account of an 'escort out of the country' was untrue. He galloped all the way back from Kunduz to Khulm in a single stage, and Gerard and he then dashed out of Khulm without even stopping to collect food and their clothes, leaving Mohan Lal and the rest of the party to pay, pack and follow. Burnes reported that Murad Beg was 'a cruel and unrelenting man'.[43] Mohan Lal noted that Beg had sex with every little boy he saw, either by payment or by force.[44]

On 10 June 1832 Mohan and the party with an escort of horsemen provided by Chiman Das rejoined Burnes and Gerard at Mazar i Sharif. They stayed at the same lodging house where Trebeck had died of fever. Burnes, who had a sentimental side, was very affected. They learnt that it was in Mazar that most of Moorcroft's effects had been plundered on his way towards Bokhara, and the chief was believed to possess many of his papers. But warned that the city was full of Islamic fanaticism, they reluctantly decided it was best not to pursue this.

On 11 June they reached Balkh, where they were subjected to search by customs officials. The chief officer attempted to seduce Mohan Lal, offering him Rs400 and reciting to him a Pashtun verse which Lal translated as 'If you sit on my head and my eyes, I will bear you pleasantly because you are agreeable'! Gerard misses this incident and specifically commends the customs officer as helpful, taking 10 per cent of their declared gold coin as duty but not troubling them further.[45]

For Burnes, Balkh had more innocent pleasures than those requested by the customs officer. He noted the climate was delightful, despite the area's reputation as unhealthy. The apricots were as big as apples, while Burnes was happy to have cherries for the first time since arriving in India.[46] He spent time wandering around the ancient ruins, making sketches and scratching for coins and artefacts.

In the early hours of a moonlit night, their little party wound out of the town for a simple but moving ceremony. Led by an aged haji who had taken part in the burial, they paid their respects to the graves of Moorcroft and Guthrie, buried at the margin of the foetid marshland. As unbelievers, Moorcroft and Guthrie had been consigned to this desolate spot and their graves unmarked. The haji advised them against erecting a grave marker, lest it become a focus for desecration.

By comparison, at least young Trebeck's lonely grave in Mazar had received some respect, lying in a garden in the shade of a mulberry tree: 'A whole party, buried within twelve miles of each other, held out small encouragement to us who were pursuing the same track and were led on by nearly similar motives.'[47]

On 15 June, after a twelve-hour ride in temperatures that peeled skin from their faces, they reached the banks of the Amu or Oxus. They were unable to resist galloping straight to the river and throwing themselves in. Their work now went into overdrive, as the practicability of a Russian invasion through Balkh and Kabul, after coming down the Oxus from the Aral Sea, was the priority subject set for them to investigate. They had been surveying the route all the way from Kabul; they now needed information on the Oxus itself, its navigability and the availability of boats, its fords and ferries, and the capacity of the countryside to provision an army, plus the allegiances and views of local chiefs and the capability of their forces. Very little of this was to be published by Burnes, but rather was provided in reports to the Secret Department. The two carefully surveyed the river, marking the precise co-ordinates, altitude, width, depth and flow at this strategic crossing place, concluding that the river was a little smaller in all respects than the Indus at Attock.

On 17 June they crossed the Amu at Termez in a ferry pulled by swimming horses, a method Burnes thought might usefully be adopted in India. Their crossing point was slightly to the west of where the Soviet 'Friendship bridge' stands today. Gerard noticed that the ferry looked more capable than anything on an Indian river, of a construction similar to a British sloop. They continued their journey by camel, slung one each side in panniers four feet long, a stifling and sickening method of travel. Karshi in June is over 100°F and not even pleasant in a LandRover. As usual, Burnes is reticent about the hardships, but Mohan Lal not so: 'People who have not been in the desert, and have not undergone the torment of thirst, can scarcely believe our sufferings [...] my tongue stuck to my palate, my parched lips burned with the heat of fire, and my throat was so dry that I could not speak.'

Burnes, as a product of the Scottish Enlightenment, had a wide range of intellectual interest, which fortunately included medicine. He and Gerard had both caught malaria in Balkh or Termez – where it is still endemic today. Alexander went down first with severe fever – the only time he is recorded as getting ill. Gerard, who had been suffering bad health for months, followed a few days later.

Burnes had taken a revolutionary new treatment with him – quinine – and taking large doses at the first sign of fever he used this successfully to combat the illness, which had killed both Moorcroft and Trebeck. Gerard, a Company surgeon, refused Burnes' quinine and treated himself with calomel. Calomel, or mercury chloride, is a naturally occurring, mildly toxic, laxative mineral widely used by the British at this period. It was normally stored in cedar boxes; exposure to sunlight changes it to highly poisonous mercury bichloride.

Only once extremely weak did Gerard agree to try quinine. Company surgeons were still treating malaria with bleeding. Emily Eden in 1838 had hers treated with leeches, and then with morphine. The Transylvanian physician to the Sikh Court, John Honigberger, was frustrated: 'As for the deadly poisons calomel and opium! These glitter as brightly on the East Indian medical horizon as they do amongst English physicians.'[48] Eventual acceptance of quinine in the British Empire is generally attributed to the success of Baikie's Benue expedition in 1857.[49] Burnes' adoption of cutting-edge medicine – presumably advised by James – was a generation ahead of his time.

CHAPTER TWELVE

## To Bokhara and Back

It was not that difficult to reach Bokhara. The hard part was to get back again. Moorcroft, Trebeck, Stoddart, Conolly and arguably Gerard all died in the attempt. Burnes succeeded. He was not unique. Joseph Wolff was a successful contemporary, Witkiewicz and other Russian envoys were known there. A formal Russian mission in 1820 was associated with a brave German doctor, Eversmann, who spent three months living in disguise gaining covert intelligence.

The merchant Anthony Jenkinson of the Royal English Muscovy Company had reached Bokhara in 1558. Jenkinson found little interest in English broadcloth, and was unable due to local wars to proceed to Tashkent, Khokand and China as planned. But he did succeed in freeing twenty slaves and making friends with the Emir of Bokhara.[1] The journey was probably safer in Jenkinson's time, during the great flowering of Islamic culture in Central Asia, which had since narrowed to a more obscurantist view.

Bokhara remained the most prosperous trading centre of Central Asia, at the hub of routes from Kabul, India, Russia, Persia and Western China. Its population of 150,000 included a large merchant community, over 800 Hindu bankers from Shikarpur and Multan, and some 3,000 Jews. It was not a closed Muslim city, merely a paranoid one. Merchants of all nationalities thronged the streets, but had first to establish their bona fides as genuine traders. Many who failed this test were summarily executed.

Bokhara had been in decline for centuries from its central position in Muslim theology, but a mild revival had been undertaken in the 1820s by a reforming Emir, who reinvigorated the state with religious underpinning, just as Dost Mohammed was doing in Kabul. The next young Emir, Nasrullah Khan, had inherited something of the religious mystique of his predecessor but was a bad character. He had beheaded three of his full brothers and twenty-eight half brothers or first cousins. and became notorious in Britain for the execution of Stoddart and Conolly, by no means his only European victims. Burnes was in extreme danger while in Bokhara.

Disease was perhaps a still greater risk. Bokhara was recovering from a cholera epidemic. The most immediate result for Russia of attempts to boost trade with Bokhara was the arrival, via merchants, of cholera in Moscow in 1830; 9,000 people were infected and 5,000 died.[2]

Cholera is a marker of trade flows from Central Asia in this period. The first cholera pandemic originated in Calcutta in 1817 and spread through the Punjab, Afghanistan and Bokhara to southern Russia. The second originated in Bokhara in 1828 and spread through Russia to Western Europe, and thence to Great Britain, Ireland and the USA. Cholera was a new horror outside Asia and its spread a direct result of trade globalisation. The widespread revolutionary outbreaks in European cities in 1830–1 and 1848–9 coincided with cholera pandemics travelling from Bokhara.

Bokhara faced severe water shortages. It stood six miles from the river and was fed by a canal which was only opened one day in fifteen, to conserve water, and also served as a sewer. Burnes reported a major drought; the canals had been dry for 60 days. People existed on a rationed supply from the city's tanks, filled from the sewerage-laden canal.[3] This lack of clean water contributed to the cholera.

Once Burnes reached Bokhara, he felt sufficiently secure in his achievement to send back a report to Bentinck himself. He reported hopefully that the twenty-seven-year-old Emir was entirely dependent upon his minister, the Kush-Begi 'an elderly man, partial to Europeans and from whom we received much civility.'[4] Burnes had been summoned to see the Kush-Begi or 'Lord of Chiefs' the very day they arrived, 27 June 1832. Gerard had been put to bed, still delirious. Burnes had changed into good quality native clothes and walked into the Ark or Citadel of Bokhara, where it was forbidden to non-Muslims to ride. He had carefully observed etiquette, and had got on well with the Kush-Begi following a two-hour interrogation. The Kush-Begi was an imposing man, well-dressed and well-spoken, who wore fine clothes and the high-heeled long leather boots favoured by Uzbek nobility of both sexes.

The Kush-Begi agreed that they might reside in a private house rather than the public caravanserai. They had to wear 'infidel' dress – a black gown fastened with a simple rope, and a black cap. Burnes rather skates over this, perhaps he saw it as degrading, but Gerard is quite explicit. They were never allowed to ride in the city, and did all their writing secretly by hooded lights. Gerard notes that Moorcroft had suffered none of these restrictions, but he had declared himself a British Envoy, whereas Burnes and Gerard appeared as officers travelling home privately. They never felt any hostility.[5] Burnes asked the Kush-Begi whether he might meet the Emir. This alarmed the minister, who replied: 'I am as good as the Emir [...] what have travellers to do with Courts?'[6] Only years later did Burnes realise 'it seems he feared the King doing us an injury [...].'[7]

The Kush-Begi's son committed a rape while the party were in Bokhara. He was tried before the Qazi, and the brutal sentence of seventy-five lashes carried out, then he was led around the town tied to a scrawny camel, subject to the abuse of the mob. His father officiated at the punishment. Bokharan justice was fierce but impartial. Burnes noted that the women of Bokhara were attractive and the men were not jealous, adding in Latin that they were more interested in young boys.[8]

Alexander sent the alarming information to Bentinck that the Russians had applied to Bokhara for permission to bring an army through their territories to invade India, but that the Emir had declined.[9] This was a fiction invented by the Kush-Begi to curry favour with the British. He played the same game with Russian envoys.

Burnes went outside the city to visit the tomb of Bahaudin Naqshbandi, a Sufi divine whose followers still constitute an important sect, and whose descendants settled in Jerusalem, where they live today under increasing pressure from a government which covets their district. Burnes enjoyed the festive atmosphere of the Bokharans galloping out to the tomb on donkeys, and noted that the locals considered two visits to this tomb the equivalent to performing the Haj.[10]

In Bokhara Burnes met Sarwar Khan and his brother Omar. Sarwar Khan was the paramount chief of the Lohanis, the great nomadic tribe which ranged annually deep into India and as far north as Bokhara. The Lohanis were the principal carriers of goods between India and Central Asia, trading as individuals, and operating as financiers too. Their caravans could consist of 30,000 camels, and groups divided and reunited as they wandered a network of traditional routes, varying according to climate, grazing, wars and available merchandise. Burnes immediately realised that the Lohanis were the essential conduit for the penetration of Central Asia by British goods.

He befriended the Lohani brothers, who as traders already knew about British India. Sarwar Khan had united the disparate Lohani groupings under his leadership. He could reputedly bring 20,000 cavalry into the field, and though he shunned war he had his own cannon foundry, as well as a zenana of 200 wives and concubines. His extensive lands lay across the main Lohani migration route into India, and he collected transit duties from his own people.

The party had given some quinine to the Kush-Begi, who among his many duties was the Emir's physician. This helped gain permission to depart and they left Bokhara on 21 July, not without relief, heading north-west. Their caravan halted at Mirabad, because of news that the Khan of Khiva and his army at Merv were out despoiling any passing caravan. They also heard rumours that the Emir of Bokhara, having discovered they were spies, was sending men to kill them. They were stuck nearly a month in a hamlet of just twenty houses, but made good friends with the local Turkmen.

On 14 August they received letters and newspapers forwarded by Allard, their first contact with India for months. A Russian Embassy was apparently approaching Bokhara. On 17 August their caravan recrossed the Oxus on the ferry at Betik. Their route to Merv and Meshed now led through fierce desert of high dunes of soft sand, through which even camels' splayed feet could plunge up to the knee. At Khaju on the banks of the river Murghab they met the camp of the Khan of Khiva. The senior merchants went to do obeisance: The caravan was charged the sharia fortieth, and Burnes and Gerard survived yet another inspection by officials, this time passing as Hindus. All counted themselves very fortunate the caravan had not been seized.

Since the Hindu Kush they had frequently encountered the slave trade, from victims in chains stumbling along behind caravans, to market places with slave-pens. On 21 August in the Kara Kum desert they came across seven weeping Persian boys in iron neck collars, pulled behind the horses of Turkmen slavers. Their bare feet were blistered from the very hot sand. Burnes gave them a melon, which was all he could do. At the oasis of Sarakhs they entered a Turkmen encampment of 3,000 tents. Besides the Turkmen there were fifty Jews, 1,500 male Persian slaves and 1,000 slave girls, who were used casually for sex. Whilst there, Burnes witnessed a particularly beautiful girl sold to a merchant for seventy-seven gold tillas. 'She had changed her character from slave to wife' Burnes noted, indicating ironically that she had more freedom as a slave. Burnes' pony was stolen: 'The sturdy little creature had followed me from Pune [...] had borne me in many a weary journey, and I cannot tell how much it vexed me [...]'[11] He was shocked one morning to find a huge camel spider, bigger than his hand and with mandibles like the claws of a scorpion, clinging to his leg, but managed to strike it off with his inkwell without being bitten.

Burnes found a nobility in the Turkmen hospitality, and was surprised by the kindness shown him by these notorious plunderers. But their commitment to raiding the Persians was inveterate; one Turkmen quoted him a poem:

> The Kuzzilbashes have ten towers,
> In each tower there is only a Georgian slave,
> Let us attack them.[12]

The caravan proceeded through these lawless regions in constant fear of attack by Turkmen or Alaman raiders. It was with relief that on 14 September 1832 they reached the Persian city of Meshed. Here they were entertained by the beautiful Armenian wife of Captain Shee of the British army, who was campaigning with the Crown Prince Abbas Mirza. After a week of recuperation, ditching their vermin-ridden robes, they joined the Crown Prince's camp at Qochan. There Alex enjoyed the company of Colonel Borowski, a Polish Jewish adventurer in the service of Abbas Mirza. He had just taken the fort of Qochan after a hard battle, in which Russian and Polish troops had been prominent and formed the new garrison. Burnes met the Wazir of Herat, Yar Mahommed, who was both trying to avert the Crown Prince's ambition towards his own city state, whilst seeking to ensure his own position should Persia take it.

Burnes had still not completed the tasks set by the Secret Committee. He needed to reconnoitre the Russian presence on the Caspian Sea and possible routes of advance for a Russian army from its eastern shores. Gerard still had malaria, and could scarcely ride. Leaving Mohan Lal to take care of Gerard at Qochan on 29 September, Burnes accompanied by Mohammed Ali and his valet Ghulam Ali, struck out north-west for the Caspian. Alex parted from Mohan with a joking 'Adieu, Mohan Lal, and take care of your head', but the munshi was shocked, as Burnes had not warned him they were splitting.

Burnes had a safe conduct from the Crown Prince in his pocket, and was travelling with the regional Governor and an escort of 300. He had however returned to Muslim disguise, with long beard and shaven head, quite comfortable in this identity. The escort was not under his command, and Burnes was unable to prevent them looting and raping in every settlement they passed.

Eventually Burnes was able to leave his escort and proceed to Astrabad, but remained outside the town because of plague. He reached the Caspian after travelling through the empty forests of Mazanderan and immediately observed Russian shipping on the east coast of the Caspian. He was even taken out to sea by one captain and fed caviar and boiled sturgeon, washed down with Russian champagne.

Alexander made straight for Tehran and reported to James Campbell, the British minister there. Campbell arranged for him to meet the Shah of Persia and recount his journey. Burnes did this in entertaining fashion, answering detailed questions on the cities he had passed through and their rulers. Asked what had impressed him most, Burnes replied it was the sight of the Shah himself; Burnes always performed courtly diplomacy with aplomb.

Gerard and Lal recuperated for two months at Meshed, and Mohan was of some assistance to the Secretary of the British Legation, John McNeill, who persuaded Abbas Mirza not immediately to march on Herat after taking Qochan. Gerard and Lal also were on good terms in Meshed with Yar Mohammed Khan, Wazir of Herat. They left for Herat, arriving on 30 December. Here Gerard remained a further six months, with Mohan Lal making occasional trips to Meshed for money and medicine. Gerard was in correspondence with McNeill and both were working to prevent a Persian attack on Herat. Lal reported that the ruler of Herat, Shah Kamran Saduzai, was a drunken debauchee addicted to opium.

On 25 July 1833 Gerard was well enough to leave; Lal and he were suspected by Kamran of being Russian spies. They reached Kandahar on 25 August 1833, where again they remained two months, making friendships with the reigning Dil Khan Barakzai family. Passing through Ghazni, they reached Kabul on 5 November 1833, where Gerard met Charles Masson and gave him some funds, introducing him to Jabbar Khan, who was able to offer patronage for the archaeological investigations Masson had begun. Gerard held discussion with Dost Mohammed about Russo-Persian intentions. Together with Masson and John Martin Honigberger, who was gradually returning from Lahore to Transylvania overland, he spent twelve days in archaeological investigation around Kabul of various topes or stupas, discovering coins, sculptures and inscriptions.

Karamat Ali had reported back to Wade that in September 1832 Masson set out for Bamian at the invitation of its Governor, Haji Khan Kakar. Masson had been conducting extensive archaeological investigations there and in these Honigsberger, who had already opened several ancient tombs around Kabul, now joined him. Together they were pioneers in uncovering the Greek-influenced early Buddhist kingdoms of Central Asia. Honigberger sent Wade 'a long account of his excavations'. On reaching Ludhiana, Gerard convinced Wade of 'their value and importance'. Based on this, on 9 April 1834 Wade wrote to Macnaghten informing him that Masson was a deserter, but that he had initiated correspondence with him. In fact, it had been public knowledge that Masson was a deserter for over a year.[13]

Wade acknowledged that 'Desertion is a crime viewed by our government with a degree of rigour which scarcely admits of pardon', but suggested that Masson be employed by the British government, taking over the job of newswriter in Kabul:

Campbell would quickly be recalled and Burnes succeed him as Ambassador.

From 10 December 1834 to 8 April 1835 Whig rule was interrupted by a short-lived Tory administration, in which Lord Ellenborough was President of the Board of Control. Ellenborough, a fierce partisan, regarded Burnes as too close to the Whigs, and was seeking to block the promised preferment.[5] But in any event Burnes turned the offer down. This was extraordinary – he remained Assistant Resident in Cutch, and was still a Lieutenant. Ambassador to Persia was a huge promotion, with the additional attraction of working jointly for the Company and the Foreign Office, opening up a new career path. But Burnes felt he had become a figure of influence in India, and that the top appointments were there to be reached for.

Burnes did not take the decision lightly – he consulted widely, including with Mountstuart Elphinstone and John Stuart Mill. He justified his decision to turn down Persia boldly: 'What are a colonelcy and a KLS[6] to me? I look far higher, and shall either die or be so.' Burnes had become firm friends with McNeill, whose book *The Progress and Present Position of Russia in the East* (1836) was the most influential of all the publications representing the Russian threat to India. In England the two advised on each other's manuscripts. Although McNeill's book was anonymous, all of official London knew the author.

For Burnes to have accepted would have been to block McNeill's career. On Burnes declining, McNeill was appointed, with Burnes' commendation: 'He is an able fellow, and by far the fittest person in England for the situation.'[7] They remained firm friends.

Burnes was also close with Mountstuart Elphinstone, who lived a solitary, syphilis-blighted life in England but had warmed to the fellow Scot who in many ways was following in his footsteps. Burnes outlined to Elphinstone his wish to become Envoy to Kabul. But Elphinstone, who was well aware that such appointments frequently led to military entanglement, was against further British involvement in Afghanistan.[8] So was Henry Tucker, Chairman of the Court of Directors. Alex lobbied to be appointed to head a commercial mission. Tucker 'declined then to propose or concur in the appointment [. . .] feeling pretty sure that it must soon degenerate into a political agency, and that we should [. . .] be involved in [. . .] the entanglements of Afghan politics'.[9]

Burnes had financial security for a while. He had received £840 from John Murray for his book,[10] and a healthy bank balance must have contributed to his optimism.

He was travelling back on the Company's new fast steamer route, including overland via Suez. From there, Burnes joined the *Hugh Lindsay* to sail down the Red Sea and on to Bombay. This pioneering steam vessel had been built by the Company in Bombay in 1828, but was very uncomfortable. Built with insufficient space for coal for her inefficient steam engines, it started voyages with coal stored even in the saloon and passenger cabins, and had to put in to port to refuel every five days.[11] It is nonetheless astonishing that just sixteen years after the world's first commercial steamship service on the Clyde, a locally-built oceangoing steamship was sailing out of Bombay. Putting in for coals at Jeddah, Burnes met a French government official, M. Fontanier.

Fontanier wrote that Burnes was overrated as a traveller. A number of Frenchmen, including Court, Ventura and Allard, had also travelled in Central Asia without becoming so famous, and Court's command of the Persian language was better than Burnes'. He also felt that *Travels into Bokhara* was not all Burnes' own work:

> Sir Alexander's work had been taken up by the East India Company, and was revised and corrected by Mr Elphinstone [. . .] not only did he add his own observations, but caused the officer to suppress certain passages which he considered prejudicial to the interests of the British Government.

This was of course true, but no more so than of any book published by a Company officer. Elphinstone's revisions do not appear substantive.[12] Fontanier's determination to be unimpressed wilted when invited to dinner with Burnes:

> He had a quick, penetrating mind, and his society was very agreeable [. . .] he was very unassuming and natural in his manners, and showed proof of much frankness in his conversation [. . .] we conversed a great deal about Persia and Eastern policy.[13]

Fontanier surmised correctly that Burnes' views on Persian policy came from McNeill. He found Burnes angry that the slave trade was active in Jeddah. He also found Burnes determined to continue his feud with Wolff. The latter claimed to have preached Christianity at the Mecca Gate in Jeddah which, as Fontanier put it drily, 'appeared rather strange to those who are acquainted with Mahometans'.

Burnes was determined to prove Wolff a liar. He therefore led a curious little party, consisting of Captain Wilson of the *Hugh Lindsay*, a Lieutenant Buckle and Mr Frazer, fellow passengers, and M. Fontanier, in search of Malam Yusuf, with whom Wolff had lodged, to ask if the story were true. Malam Yusuf replied that nobody could ever tell what language Wolff was speaking. Sometimes it seemed to be Persian or Arabic, but the pronunciation was terrible. One day he had indeed gone to the Mecca Gate with a Bible under his arm; but when there 'if he had spoken or gesticulated, nobody had noticed it'. Fontanier concluded that Wolff was sincere but 'I had met that missionary, and know the strange delusion into which he had fallen, as to his oratorical abilities.' Fontanier himself had tried to converse with Wolff in French, Italian, Persian and Turkish, without success, even though Wolff seemed to believe he was fluent in all those languages.

CHAPTER SEVENTEEN

## While Alex was Away

Even as Burnes had been taking ship in 1833 on his triumphant way to England, Shah Shuja had been setting off to recapture his throne in Kabul. He did so with the active connivance of Claude Wade, who had obtained for him four months' advance on his pension, and the right to purchase weapons in Delhi tax free. By a treaty of 17 February 1833 he had financial assistance and Muslim levies from Ranjit Singh, in exchange for which Shuja made over his claim on Peshawar, Derajat and Kashmir to the Sikh.

While the Amirs of Sind were negotiating permanent release from any fealty to Kabul in return for one-off assistance to Shuja, Shuja moved with his force through Bhawalpur and occupied Shikarpur, where he extracted loans from the merchants and financiers. After a lengthy stand-off in which more followers rallied to Shuja, boosted by the universal belief he had British support, Shuja defeated the Amirs in battle near Sukkur on 18 January 1834. He then marched on Kandahar with an army of 40,000.

The Barakzais were divided. The Kandahar sirdars urged their brother Dost Mohammed to come to Kandahar to battle Shuja, with the secret intent that Sultan Mohammed Khan from Peshawar would then take Kabul. Dost Mohammed was too wily and instead seized Jalalabad. He then turned back towards Kandahar, arriving just in time to defeat Shah Shuja before its walls, in a battle in which 90,000 troops were theoretically involved but few actually fought, with most chiefs waiting to see who had the advantage. Shuja fled prematurely and decided the battle.

Shuja fled virtually alone, as fast as possible – which happened to mean on Alexander Burnes' horse, given him by Ranjit Singh. Burnes had ridden it to Ludhiana, Simla, Delhi and Peshawar, and there he had parted with it before his journey to Bokhara, as he did not want an expensive horse to draw attention in Afghanistan. He donated it to two mullahs who had helped him with letters of introduction. They had given it to their father, residing at Shuja's court-in-exile in Ludhiana. Shuja had seized it, and its speed and endurance now saved his life as he fled to the fortress of Kelat, hotly pursued for over a week. At Kelat the ruler, Mehrab Khan, explained to the pursuers that the law of hospitality obliged him to defend his guest. Kelat being a strong citadel, they gave up.

Going through the wreck of Shuja's camp, Dost Mohammed discovered letters from Claude Wade, advising various chiefs that support for Shah Shuja would be appreciated by the British government.[1] Dost Mohammed had received Burnes' protestations of friendship only two years before, and his faith in the British must have been severely shaken.

Shortly after, in March 1834, the British extended their intelligence network by sending their newswriter, Mir Karamat Ali, to Kandahar. He had a monthly salary of Rs250, plus Rs50 per month for qasids, writing materials and travel.[2] His postion must have been difficult and dangerous. In accordance with the secret agreement with Shuja, the Sikh general Hari Singh 'seized' Peshawar from Sultan Mohammed Khan, (who was in on the plot), a terrible blow to the Afghan state. Dost Mohammed must have regarded the British as implicated in the loss of Peshawar. Indeed, the bilateral treaty of 1834 between Ranjit Singh and Shah Shuja contained an open reference to British involvement:

> Regarding Shikarpore and the territory of Scinde [...] the Shah agrees to abide by whatever may be settled as right and proper, in conformity with the happy relations of friendship subsisting between the British Government and the Maharajah through Captain Wade.[3]

The British subsequently denied it; but Wade had assisted Shuja's attempt. One result was that Dost Mohammed sent an Ambassador to Russia, requesting assistance over Peshawar. If the British were hostile, perhaps help might come from their rivals.

The authorities in London took a dim view, rebuking Bentinck:

> We think that this indulgence ought not to have been granted to Shah Shoojah ool Moolk. The arms, though stated by you to be intended 'for the protection of his person on his intended journey', must to all intents and purposes be regarded as purchased for the purpose of invading Caubul with a view to the recovery of his throne. And the exemption of these arms from the ordinary duties constitutes, so far, a virtual breach of the neutrality [...] the British Government ought, and professes to, observe.[4]

At Kandahar one mercenary corps had fought hard for Shuja, under a soldier of Scots and Indian parentage named William Campbell. Campbell had fought against the British at the siege of Baratpur, and in 1826 had entered

Ranjit Singh's service, but been dismissed in a dispute over women. Campbell had raised a regiment of Hindu infantry for Shuja. At Kandahar, he was seriously wounded and captured, but Dost had him treated and engaged in his own service, together with his regiment; they were to feature in the final act of this story.

Dost returned to Kabul. On 4 September 1834 he took part in a solemn ceremony to legitimise his rule. With a stern escort of irregular cavalry including none of his Shia Qizilbash bodyguard, without feasting or show, Dost Mohammed rode out from Kabul. Alongside him rode the hereditary head of the Sunni clergy of Afghanistan, Mir Waiz, to the Sufi shrine of Siah Sung. There, Mir Waiz delicately placed a few blades of grass into the turban[5] of a stooping Dost Mohammed.

The ruler of Kabul thus became the Emir al-Muminin – the Commander of the Faithful, Dost Mohammed Ghazi. Dost was now ruler rather than Governor, but with the religious title of Emir rather than the secular one of Shah. He was declaring jihad against the Sikhs of Ranjit Singh, a holy war to win back Peshawar.[6] His religious asceticism appeared genuine, his dress and diet became still plainer, his pomp still less, access for complainants still easier.

Dost now had coins struck in his own name, and was referred to as the ruler in Friday prayers in all his lands' mosques. These were the traditional marks of a ruler in Muslim lands. He never made a claim to hereditary Kingship, or took the title of Shah. But he was staking a stronger claim, that of leadership in holy war. The Qazi having ruled it was legal to force infidels to pay for jihad, Shikarpuri bankers throughout Afghanistan were tortured and extorted into making contributions. There was a tremendous response to Dost's call of jihad and on 2 January 1835 he left Kabul at the head of a vast army for Peshawar.

On 4 May 1835 at Noushera, the Emir lost Peshawar without a blow being struck. Sultan Mohammed, with all his troops, deserted to Ranjit Singh after days of negotiation. The numbers on each side now roughly equal, Dost Mohammed realised he had no chance against the Sikh artillery and made an ignominious retreat back to Kabul. Sultan became again Sirdar of Peshawar – his agreement with Ranjit Singh renounced all family claims and accepted that he and his Peshawar levies would fight with the Sikhs if they attacked Jalalabad, Kandahar or Kabul. It was the ultimate treachery to his family, his faith and his country. As the Emir retreated without a fight, his ghazi supporters pillaged the baggage and deserted in disgust.

A curious Russian counter to Burnes' visit to Bokhara had occurred while Alex was enjoying London. Claude Wade had reported to Macnaghten information received from Bokhara.[7] Dr Martin Honigberger in May 1834 reached Bokhara in a caravan conducted by kafilbashi Hyat, the same man who had led Burnes. Honigberger reported to Wade that a Russian Ambassador, a Muslim Russian subject named Mirza Jafer, was in Bokhara. His purpose was to obtain the Emir's agreement to a Russian military expedition against the Khanate of Khiva. Jafer also revealed that Persia, with Russian aid, would soon attack Herat.

The Bokharan authorities arranged for Honigberger to depart for Russia with Jafer. Honigberger noted, 'Besides Persian and Arabic he speaks Italian very fluently and is a good-looking and intelligent man. I shall have an agreeable companion on my journey to Russia.'[8]

Honigberger realised 'Mirza Jafer' was not really a Muslim, and to Honigberger he represented himself as a Frenchman, Baron Demaison, in disguise in the service of Russia. He had been denounced by Tartar merchants in Bokhara, who were themselves Russian subjects but resentful of their overlords. He had responded by producing written testaments of theological credentials from Kazakh mullahs, and Honigberger was present when they were examined by the Kush-Begi. Jafer was a hair's breadth from execution; rather peculiarly Honigberger suggested to the Kush-Begi that an examination of his skin and hair colouring might give the answer. Jafer escaped this test because he had given 'large presents' to the Kush-Begi.

Who Demaison was remains a mystery. Years later, after dining with Witkiewicz, Burnes reported that the Pole definitely 'is not that Mirza Jaffir who was at Bokhara some years ago [. . .] The true name of that person is Maizon and he is Arabic.'[9] Rumours of the mysterious Russian agent Maison or Demaison had been picked up a few years earlier by British intelligence.[10]

Honigberger discovered that Burnes' visit to Bokhara had damaged the Kush-Begi's view of Britain substantially:

> His first inquiry was, whether I knew Jussuff Wolff and Alexander Burnes? 'Wolff' continued he, 'was a very good-hearted man, but as for Burnes he was a deceiver, because he told me [. . .] that his intention was to go to England, via Russia, whereas he returned to Hindostan, via Khiva.' He was convinced that Burnes was a spy [. . .][11]

Burnes' deceit had an impact on the later Bokharan treatment of Stoddart and Conolly.

Masson's appointment as newswriter would have enhanced his local standing. It also meant that Wade had an alternative expert to Burnes to put forward in policy battles. However Wade's relationship with Masson was stormy, and he did not pass on the originals of Masson's reports to Macnaghten and Auckland, but rather summaries which often distorted Masson's views.

Masson had been in correspondence with British officials before Wade appointed him. He had then held no official position and supposedly was interested only in antiquarian research, yet was continually pumping Pottinger for diplomatic information. For example on 3 October 1833, plainly in response to a request from Masson, Pottinger had replied:

> I have not been at Bombay since I left it this time two years [...] I am not able to tell you how the Vakeels from Kabul were treated, or whether they succeeded with their object.[12]

Honigberger, Masson and Gerard had sent back reports and drawings to the Asiatic Society in Calcutta along with numerous coins and artefacts. This occasioned great excitement. It was the first understanding that a Hellenic civilisation had flourished in Central Asia for centuries after the passing of Alexander. A grant of Rs1,500 and annual stipend of Rs1,000 had been sent to Kabul by the Asiatic Society; Honigberger and Gerard having quit the scene, it all went to Masson. Pottinger obtained a further grant of Rs1500 for Masson from the Government of Bombay.[13] He also noted he had sent Masson another Rs300 as a personal donation. He was still not aware of Masson's true identity, as he wrote to Lord Clare recommending Masson as an 'American gentleman'. Masson's archaeological excavations were not only well-financed by the British but also by Dost Mohammed's son Akbar Khan, a fact worth bearing in mind when reading British accounts of 'Afghan savages'. In April 1834 Masson bagged a further Rs500 as a personal donation from Sir James Campbell, departing British Envoy to Persia.[14]

According to government historians: 'Though Honigberger mentions Masson only casually, it appears that the latter accompanied him as far as Orenburg.'[15]

I hesitate to mention the possibility that Maison was Masson, lest this long shot devalues much more definite evidence of Masson's Russian connections. It would require collusion by Honigberger – not impossible as he worked for Ranjit Singh. The Doctor mentions only Maison/Jaffer going with him to Orenburg, and Masson is very peculiarly absent from his memoir in general. Masson was fluent in French – how is unknown – and appears in a nineteenth-century Paris 'Biographie Nationale' as a Frenchman.[16]

Through their correspondence on antiquarian studies, Pottinger had become enthralled by Masson. In September 1834 Pottinger was offering to organise publication of his works. At this stage the British authorities had officially been aware who Masson/Lewis was for a year, as Pottinger gushed:

I beg to assure you, that if I can be the medium of making your most interesting discoveries known to the world [...] my sole object will be obtained.

On the subject of your MSS I told you in my last, that if you would entrust them to me, I would undertake that they should be published either under the auspices of the Bombay Government, or by one of the learned societies of Great Britain, any of which would gladly snatch at such a prize.[17]

The authorities now moved to regularise communication with Masson. Not only had Pottinger been informing Masson continually of the movements and views of Company officials, but also Masson had started to draw large sums of extra cash on bills of exchange he was signing off in Kabul as redeemable on a variety of British officials. On 27 February 1835 Pottinger wrote to Masson to say that if one substantial bill for Rs500 on Claude Wade were not honoured, then Pottinger himself would pay it. In the same letter Pottinger encloses for Masson a copy of an instruction from the Governor-General's office, forbidding Pottinger to continue his correspondence with Masson. In future all contact between Masson and the British government was to be through Claude Wade. Pottinger denied the authority of the Governor-General to prevent non-official correspondence:

I have no idea that the Supreme Government will offer the smallest objection to my continuing to correspond with you on antiquarian and literary subjects which would in truth be an interference with our private actions.[18]

It seems that Calcutta was unhappy about the amount of intelligence Pottinger was giving Masson; Pottinger told Masson he had replied that 'my correspondence with you has been, and is, of a purely literary nature'. This was a downright lie; Pottinger had told Masson of British naval movements, of views on Russia and the prospects of war, of the detailed affairs of the British mission to Persia, and other sensitive subjects. Pottinger enclosed a hundi for yet another Rs1,000 from the government of Bombay for Masson's researches.

In January 1836, two years after 'Mirza Jafer', Witkiewicz had ridden to Bokhara on an open mission,[19] to negotiate the release of detained Russian merchants. But like Burnes, he was in secret studying armed forces and fortifications, and surveying possible routes for a Russian army, as well as looking for evidence of British activity. Witkiewicz reported back to St Petersburg:

The British have their man in Bukhara. He is a Kashmiri called Nizamuddin and has been living in Bukhara for four years now under the pretext of trade [...] He is a very clever man [...] and entertains the Bukharan noblemen; at least once a week he sends letters with secret messengers to Kabul, to the Englishman Masson [...] The most curious thing is that Dost Mohammed is aware of Masson's activities [...] but leaves the spy alone, saying; one man

> cannot harm me [...] This man lives in Kabul under the pretext of looking for ancient coins.

Nizamuddin was doing a good job:

> Nizamuddin sought my acquaintance as soon as I arrived and asked me [...] about Novo-Alexandrovsk, the New Line, our relations with Khiva etc. Having been forewarned, I did not give him any definite answers. All the same he sent a letter to Kabul the very next day.[20]

The arrival of a Russian envoy in Bokhara was vital strategic news. But Masson did not pass on Nizamuddin's letter to Wade or to Calcutta. It is possible that Masson had never received the letter from Nizamuddin, but the qasids were a distinct profession who were trained from childhood and could trot fifty miles a day. It was fundamental to their working practice that they must return with a reply or acknowledgement.[21]

Shortly after this, Masson came under suspicion from Claude Wade. I have not discovered precisely of what Masson was accused. According to Burnes, Pottinger was also amongst Masson's accusers.[22] It led to an official investigation, and it appears that Masson's defence was that he had been tricked or misrepresented into a false position. Burnes submitted a testimonial in Masson's support, and on 9 March 1836 Burnes, in his first direct communication with Masson, wrote:

> from the moment I heard of the difference I was satisfied that you had been undeservedly compromised to promote views and ends which it was not part of your own desire to promote – Your exculpation is complete but it is humiliating to me even to think that exculpation ever was necessary.[23]

Burnes was here unwise; firstly in vouching for a man he had never met, and secondly criticising Claude Wade in correspondence with Masson:

> Captain Wade – To that gentleman I owe something for hospitality and kindness [...] but I fear that poor Gerard's opinion of him in his public character is very much my own – My journey is [...] happily terminated but, however much I feel Captain Wade's <u>private</u> kindness, I owe him nothing publicly indeed much the reverse – All this I am bound to state to someone whose feelings have been trifled with as yours.

In fact, Wade had judged Masson's character much better than Burnes.

CHAPTER EIGHTEEN

## Return to the Indus

Burnes found himself kicking his heels at Bhuj. After turning down Persia, he had been offered nothing else. One reason for this was the inopportune promotion away from Indian affairs of Charles Grant, after a brief Tory hiatus.

In May 1835 Burnes was despatched on a diplomatic mission to Sind over an Indian cargo vessel wrecked on the coast. Local custom was that any wrecked vessel and its cargo became the property of the rulers. Burnes now found the Amirs anxious to co-operate. They were preoccupied with the threat of invasion by Ranjit Singh. Burnes found it impossible to confine discussion to the narrow case of commercial compensation. Rather the Amirs were offering a complete opening of the Indus to free trade, British control of their foreign policy, and the stationing of a British Resident at Shikarpur. What they wanted in exchange was a guarantee of British protection.[4]

Burnes and Pottinger strongly recommended a treaty to establish these arrangements and achieve longstanding policy goals. But the Acting Governor-General, Charles Metcalfe, loathed the idea of military commitments beyond existing frontiers and rejected the idea.

A farcical turf battle between the British occurred in Haidarabad. Nur Mohammed, who had succeeded his father as principal Amir in 1832, requested a British physician to attend him. Pottinger sent Dr Hathorn of the 15th Regiment, stationed in Cutch, to join Burnes. Lord Clare also sent a physician, Dr J F Heddle, on a steamer under Lt Corless. This was another British attempt to use a pretext – delivering the physician – to forward the survey of the Indus.

Although as Resident in Bhuj, Pottinger was subject to Lord Clare, as Envoy to Sind he had been appointed by Calcutta. Pottinger now argued that Clare had no right to send Dr Heddle as Calcutta was responsible for relations with Sind. This was the precise opposite of Pottinger's position when he had been despatching Burnes to Sind, and a direct insult to Clare who was, in all normal circumstances, Pottinger's boss. Pottinger instructed Burnes to stop Heddle from seeing the Amirs. Burnes complied, adding the breathtakingly hypocritical observation that to send a boat with Heddle was an unworthy ruse for spying. The Amirs refused to see Heddle and he left affronted, though Lt Corless' steam survey was to continue for two years. There now occurred a monumental disagreement between Burnes and Pottinger. It involved Pottinger's role as head of the Cutch Durbar, or Council of State, and seems to have concerned control over the port of Mandvi, which was important to British troop movements and where the Resident at Bhuj and the Rao of Cutch, had their summer residences. Burnes believed that Pottinger was abusing his authority against the interests of the Rao. By his own account, Pottinger was devastated by the blazing row. Four years later he was to write to the Governor-General:

> I am unwillingly obliged here to trouble Your Lordship by reverting to Sir Alexander Burnes' conduct to me [...] and to the long series of indignities and reprehension I suffered through the support his unfounded misrepresentations met with from the then Governor of Bombay, the late Sir Robert Grant
> [...] they were such as many persons would have sunk under [...] they bid fair for a time to blacken and ruin my public character [...] and [...] plunged me in a state of such misery and anxiety as I cannot at all describe[1]

Burnes had the opposite view, that Sir Robert Grant had not done enough:

> he was a good man but an execrable Governor, he meant well but did nothing [...] Is it true that the court have reversed the Mandavee decision? I cannot believe it. I do think however that they might leave the sovereignty (but only that) with the Rao. Nothing showed Grant's incapacity more, than his allowing Pottinger to bully as he did [...][2]

Life at Bhuj must have been very difficult. As Burnes was taking the side of the local ruler against the British Resident, it is unlikely that he was supported by the officers of the garrison. The rift, however, is not surprising. Burnes' description of Pottinger as bullying seems accurate, while Burnes' liberal views on Indian government would not have endeared him to Pottinger. Burnes believed that locals should be given much more responsibility. He wrote 'Men will say, "wait till they are ready." I can only say that, if you wait till men are fit for liberty, you will wait forever [...] Will a man ever learn to swim without going into the water?' Burnes doubted the entire Imperial venture: 'Instead of raising up a glorious monument to our memory, we shall impoverish India more thoroughly than Nadir, and become a greater curse to it than were the hordes of Timour.'[3]

Once the expansionist Lord Auckland arrived to take over as Governor-General, Pottinger was despatched to Sind to take up the Amirs' offer. Furthermore the Bombay Presidency was authorised to send troops into Sind if needed to deter the Sikhs from Shikarpur.

Wade gave the message to Ranjit Singh that the British Government 'could not but view with regret and disapprobation the prosecution of plans of unprovoked hostility, injurious to native states with whom that Government is connected'. It was enough, and Ranjit Singh cancelled his project against Shikarpur.[5]

The reinvigoration of Burnes' career was prompted by events in Persia. In Kandahar, the Dil Khans were alarmed by the ambition for eastward expansion of Mohammed, the new Shah of Persia, and by the continuing desire of Kamran Saduzai in Herat to attack them. They had therefore sent an Envoy, Aziz Muhammad Khan, to persuade the Persian Shah to enter an alliance for the removal of the Saduzais from Herat. The Ambassador's message finished with a rhetorical flourish that the Muslims of Afghanistan were ready to put themselves in the Shah's service for a united march to free Delhi from the infidel.

There was no chance of the mostly Sunni Afghans marching under the Shia Shah of Persia anywhere, but nonetheless the event was picked up by the British Ambassador in Tehran, Henry Ellis. He was getting nowhere in trying to conclude a new commercial treaty, while at the same time seeking an annulment of Britain's guarantees of defending Persia against European attack. Ellis reported that the Shah intended to invade Herat in the spring and press his claim to Kandahar and Ghazni as well, with Russian support.

Ellis suggested Britain needed an entirely new regional strategy:

> since, in such an event, Persia will not or dare not place herself in a condition of close alliance with Great Britain, our policy must be to consider her no longer an outwork for the defence of India, but as the first parallel from which the attack may be commenced or threatened.[6]

In response, on 25 June 1836 the President of the Board of Control, John Cam Hobhouse wrote to Lord Auckland, instructing him to act:

> whether by despatching a confidential agent to Dost Muhammad of Kabul merely to watch the progress of events, or to enter into relations with this chief, either of a political or merely, in the first instance, of a commercial character, we leave to your discretion, as well as the adoption of any other measures [. . .] in order to counteract Russian influence in that quarter, should you be satisfied [. . .] that the time has arrived [. . .] to interfere in the affairs of Afghanistan.[7]

There was never any real doubt who the confidential agent would be. Alexander Burnes was back in play. Auckland had already prepared a despatch to London outlining Burnes' mission and added in a postscript that he had anticipated Hobhouse's instructions.[8]

Auckland considered from the start the Burnes mission as a political one; it was never a purely commercial undertaking. Auckland gave private instructions to Burnes:

> I am unwilling to give the alarming colour of political speculation to a mission, the main object of which is commercial, but it is impossible to divest of political interest any observation of the Countries on the Indus and to the West of the river. It is difficult to see without some anxiety the exertions made on every occasion by the ruler of the Punjab to extend his power [. . .][9]

So Burnes' initial instruction was that his mission was not political, but that it was understood that this was 'impossible'. At this time Auckland saw Ranjit as the aggressor.

Alarm at Russian expansion caused a flurry of British intelligence activity which is the context of Burnes' mission. Russia was fighting spirited resistance in its newly-conquered Caucasus territories. Palmerston sent a British ship, the *Vixen*, into the Black Sea in 1836 to run arms to Dagestani rebels, under cover of a cargo of salt. It caused a diplomatic incident when the ship was intercepted by Russian forces, but Palmerston sent an assurance to the Russian Foreign Minister Nesselrode that the British government had no knowledge of the venture. Palmerston was an accomplished liar. The *Vixen* was part of widespread activity by the British secret service in sending arms and advisers to the Chechen, Dagestani and Circassian rebels, which has modern echoes. The operation had been organised by David Urquhart 'who had brought all the scattered mujahedin units together and even created a single command structure for them to direct their military action against the Russian army'.[10] Urquhart then took up his appointment as First Secretary at the British Embassy in Constantinople. Four years earlier Palmerston had organised secret smuggling of arms for the Polish uprising. Colin Mackenzie, who served in Kabul with Burnes, had taken part.[11] The anti-Russian mood of the British establishment went well beyond rhetoric.

Burnes' second navigation of the Indus is darkened by the shadow of looming disaster, and attention has naturally focused on events in Kabul at its conclusion. Burnes recounts this journey in his posthumously published *Cabool*. He was obliged to omit any reference to the diplomatic negotiations. But as a story of travel and adventure *Cabool* is a delightful book.

Alexander commanded a party of four British officers, the other three being Lieutenant Robert Leech of the Bombay Engineers, Lieutenant John Wood of the Indian (Company) Navy and Dr Percival Lord of the Bombay Medical Service and his instructions from the Government of India were:

to work out its policy of opening the River Indus to commerce, and establishing on its banks, and in the countries beyond it, such relations as should contribute to the desired end [...] to prosecute the commercial inquiries with extreme caution, [...] and in all to act so as to mark the anxious desire of the British Government for the restitution of tranquillity and for the establishment of friendly relations.[12]

Burnes was expected thoroughly to survey the rivers for steam navigation, to locate sources of wood, coal and other fuel, to explore the market for British manufactured goods, to report on possible trade routes and make commercial contacts, to outline the current agricultural and manufacturing output and prospects for future economic growth, to explore for mineral deposits capable of commercial exploitation, to find the best site to hold an annual trade fair on the Indus, and to negotiate with the various governments from Sind to Kabul for trade access, reduction of tariffs and protection of goods and merchants.

It is a tribute to the spirit of the age that scientific investigation of the geology and natural history of the region, including the collection of a large number of specimens of both flora and fauna, were considered part of the official activities of the mission and supported with public funds. Archaeological investigation and collection of ancient coins, artefacts and inscriptions held a kind of semi-official status, but were certainly approved activities. It went without saying that the mission was also to report on military forces and fortifications, the practicability of roads for artillery and the availability of food, fodder and shelter for armies.

The commercial mission was not simply a front for espionage. The British wanted to make money from new markets for what was still the world's most efficient manufacturing industry. They also believed that such trade would enrich the Afghans, stabilise their government, and bind them to Britain through commercial ties, all of which would increase their value as a buffer state to the Empire.

Accordingly the group carried manufacturers' samples to show Afghan merchants, and Burnes' instructions on security and tax immunity of British merchants and duties for British goods, were real business. I spent some of my own diplomatic career engaged in this kind of work. The pressure from taxpayers for diplomats to earn their keep by bringing a flow of wealth back to the home country is a constant political reality. Burnes' reports[13] on manufactures, commodities, raw materials, trading routes, distributors, retail outlets, financial networks and credit availability, prices, tariffs and tolls were painstaking. The British merchants to whom they were made available commented that you would think that Burnes had been nothing but a trader himself his whole life.[14]

Burnes' plan of establishing trade fairs to coincide with the Lohani tribal migrations made sense. These Afghan nomadic migrations were as much about trade as pasture. The maldar or wealthy nomad could be a merchant and financier on a large scale. Louis Dupree found this still to be true in the 1960s:

> the search for grass has its commercial side. In fact, several nomads told me that they consider herding secondary to trading. The system involves both cash and barter, with barter more important than cash in some areas. Items brought in by nomads include kerosene, matches, cloth, sugar, tea, spices, peppers, guns, ammunition, iron tools, milk and milk products, livestock, hides, leather, rugs, carpets.[15]

The Russian government had established an annual fair at Nizhni Novgorod to boost the trade with Central Asia which had been flowing through that city since at least the fourteenth century.[16] This had proved attractive to merchants from Central Asia and even India. It had been a huge investment – a then astonishing £1m in the trade grounds and warehouses, including flood containment works on the river. By 1836 40 per cent of all Russia's imports flowed through Nizhni Novgorod. Unfortunately, then as now, the Russian economy was not well developed for the production of consumer goods, and imports much exceeded exports. The annual caravan from Bokhara to Orenburg had 5,000 laden camels going out, but only 600 returning. Russia became alarmed at the outflow of bullion through the fair and tried from the 1820s to ban the export of ingots and coin, with little practical effect.

Burnes divided the work among his little mission – he took on most of the commercial, economic and political reporting, Lt John Wood as a naval man was naturally in charge of surveying the rivers, Lt Leech was tasked with noting the military features, and Dr Lord was asked to focus on geology and natural history. There was a fifth European with the party, a Goan Portuguese draughtsman named Jose Goncalves. Burnes had a new secretary, a young Parsi named Nourozji Fourdonji, a graduate of Elphinstone College, Bombay. Burnes had deliberately sought another young Indian to promote: 'I hope only that Nawazjee may do as well as Mohan Lal & I am sure of his being cherished by Government & of his deserving to be so – Having been instrumental in bringing forward a native of Delhi, I now feel anxious to do what I can for one of the Bombay Presidency that both may run the race fairly.'[17] The professional ranks of the mission were completed by Dr Mahomed Ali of the Bombay Medical Service, one of the first local doctors trained, again Burnes' deliberate choice.

The expedition set out from Bombay at midnight on 26 November 1836, after dinner hosted by the Governor on Malabar Point.[18] After a five-day halt in Mandvi, they sailed westward towards the Indus Delta, where they disembarked into Sind on 13 December. They were minus Dr Lord, who would be joining them further up river.

Burnes was delighted that many of the boatmen who had taken him up to Lahore on his previous trip were anxious to serve with him again. He noticed that the hostility towards the British which had been so dangerous six years earlier had almost disappeared. He also witnessed the extraordinary movement of channels and silt in the Indus Delta; he could now ride his horse for two miles up what had been the main channel last time. Twenty-three-year-old Lieutenant Wood from Perth had already spent two seasons exploring the lower Indus on a specially constructed steam boat. The British had put the first steamer on the Indus, under the command of twenty-one-year-old Lieutenant Corless, only three years after Burnes' pioneering voyage up it.

Sailing up the Indus, the mission met Corless and Pottinger sailing down, after the latter had concluded negotiations with the Amirs. Pottinger briefed Burnes on his success, which included further free trade provisions and a permanent British Resident at Shikarpur.[19] Burnes noted that all this only formalised what he had been offered by the Amirs on 5 December 1835 but Metcalfe had vetoed. He also briefed in detail Sayyid Azimal Din, who had been appointed British Agent at Karachi, finding Din 'a highly qualified public servant'.

On 27 December, proceeding slowly up river in luxurious state jumtis supplied by the Amirs, Burnes received instructions from Auckland to establish communication direct with John McNeill, and co-ordinate their positions. Burnes wrote, 'the state of Persia and her designs backed by Russia already engage attention & before I reach Tatta on my commercial mission I find the seeds to be sown for important political concerns. I shall give this subject my most anxious consideration.'[20]

Lieutenant Wood was continually out in small boats conducting detailed measurement. Burnes agreed that Wood should dictate the pace of their progress, as his work was at this stage the most important, characterising this trip as a 'survey' compared to which his first voyage was a 'reconaissance'.

At Tatta Burnes noted the very large numbers of African slaves. 'They were shipped from Muscat via Karachi but also through British held Cutch. Every Mahomedan who can afford it purchases them [...] All people who have shops of the better order have slaves.'[21]

Burnes' instructions from Macnaghten included a demand on the Amirs of Sind to stop the raids on Indus traffic by the Mazari tribes, who inhabited the northern limit of the Amirs' territories. The instructions were based on a report on Mazari depredations by Mohan Lal. Before Burnes could take action, Ranjit Singh seized on this excuse for further aggrandisement. He annexed the Mazari capital of Roghan and then razed a frontier fort garrisoned by Shikarpur itself, and mobilised Sikh forces on the frontier. It became plain that the efforts of Burnes' mission to open the commerce of the Indus could be jeopardised by the start of a major war along its banks.

In Haidarabad they were enthusiastically received by the Amirs, who offered to accompany them as far as Shikarpur, with the intention of deterring any move by the Sikh army on Mithankot.[22] Burnes reported that the Amirs could field 32,000 men between them, but none of their artillery was serviceable. He noted the extensive links between the Shia Amirs in Sind, and religious shrines in Persia, and constant communications between the Sind and Persian religious hierarchy and ruling families. He saw danger in this if Persia gained ground in Afghanistan: 'if the King of Persia were successful in his present expedition, the religious commerce that exists between Sinde & Persia might avail the enemies of India.'[23]

On 2 February 1837 Burnes wrote a letter from Haidarabad to Masson in Kabul, explaining his mission:

Hydrabad in Sinde
2 February 1837

My Dear Sir,
You will doubtless have heard rumours [...] of my having been deputed by Lord Auckland to conduct a Mission up the Indus to Attock and thence by Peshawar to Cabool, Candahar and Shikapoor [...]

the main and great aim of Government is to open the Indus and to inform the Chiefs in Afghanistan and the merchants [...] of the arrangements that have been entered into – Runjeet Sing threatened Sinde and was alone prevented by British influence from attacking it – the Government said justly that if the balance of power on the Indus is destroyed our commercial hopes are ruined and we therefore concluded a Treaty with the Ameers taking them under our protection and fixing a British Agent in Sinde.

We have no wish to extend our political relations beyond the River but a great one to enter into friendly commercial ones [...] I shall travel with as little parade as possible [...] unsuited particularly for the duty which I am executing –

I go to Mittun to be present at a Congress [...] of the Vakeels of Lahore, Bhawulpore and I hope Sinde who with Cap. Wade, Mr Mackison and myself are to fix upon a site for a bazar and arrangements similar to Nijni Novogorod [...]

We hardly know what is the object of this invasion of Herat and here I can scarcely find out if the King has advanced on it or not – if he has [...] I would not be surprised at the British Government withdrawing their Ambassador from his Court –

To Dost Mahomed Khan I should feel obliged by your expressing my remembrance of his kindness [...] Tell the Nawab [...] that he lives always in my remembrance and I have some hundreds of kinds of seed for him [...]

My Dear Sir
Yours sincerely and faithfully
Alex Burnes[24]

Mohan Lal joined the party at Haidarabad, having been sent, not now as munshi but as an agent on Rs250 a month. Burnes was delighted at their reunion.

Pottinger, who detested the Amirs and their capital, was less than delighted to be appointed to the Residency at Haidarabad. However he remained also Resident in Bhuj. An Assistant, Lieutenant Eastwick, was appointed in Haidarabad on the substantial monthly salary of Rs1,000, on the understanding Pottinger would be much of the time away. The Court of Directors declared itself delighted with the results of Pottinger's diplomacy. They were, however, disappointed that he had not been able to sell the Amirs an iron steam boat for the Indus which the Company had speculatively sent to Haidarabad.[25]

Since Burnes' first river mission, the work of surveying the Indus had proceeded apace.[26] Claude Wade had set out with Mohan Lal, Lieutenant Mackeson and a Mr Hodge, and conducted a survey sailing down the Sutlej and then the Indus as far as Bhawalpur,[27] where Mackeson moved his station. In January 1836, Charles Hugel noted Mackeson an excellent linguist and 'a most intelligent young officer, who has accepted a place in a desert, 300 miles from Ludhiana, where he will have to superintend and protect the English vessels in the navigation of the Indus [...]'[28] In both 1836 and 1837 surveying missions under Lieutenant Corless drew up charts and maps of the river from the sea to Mithankot.[29]

The British had also taken practical steps to encourage Afghan merchants to participate in the Indus trade. In Kabul, Karamat Ali was instructed by Wade to

> tell all the merchants [...] of the establishment of a mart at Mithenkote and the advantage of their finding a market at that place for the fruits of Cabul [...] whatever quantity of fruits they may bring [...] they will find purchase for it among the merchants of Hindustan and other parts who will supply them with any kinds of goods they may require. By this means they will be saved the trouble and inconvenience to which they are exposed on a long journey through the Punjab to Hindustan.[30]

After Masson replaced Karamat, he took up the promotion of the Mithankot market with renewed zeal, working with the major Kabuli merchant Mullah

Khair al-Din. Masson drew up a list of those British articles for which he believed a ready market existed in Kabul and beyond, replacing Russian items of inferior quality:

> Chintzes, fine calicos, muslins, shawls [. . .] broad-cloth, velvet, paper, cutlery, china, gold and silver lace, gold thread, buttons, needles, sewing silks and cotton thread, iron bars, copper, tin, brass, quicksilver, iron and steel wire, looking glasses [. . .]

The notion was not fantastic. In 1835 Central Asia had not yet slipped from regional trading hub to backwater, and was not economically far behind Iran and India. Khiva, Bokhara and Khokand were undergoing a period of economic resurgence. Afghanistan was recovering from the years of civil war. Incorporating Central Asia into the economic system of the British Empire was not judged unprofitable by those who studied it closely. The impracticality lay in creating the political conditions for the incorporation.

Ranjit Singh proved keen on opening up the Indus to commerce. He was persuaded to invest in sending a cargo of opium and Cashmere shawls by boat down the Sutlej and Indus, to be trans-shipped at Karachi, and on to Bombay. The Company provided a Dr Gardner to accompany Ranjit's goods safely through Sind. The speculation was deemed a success.[31]

All Burnes' missions appear to have been remarkably free of friction between the participants, and fast friendships were formed. Admiral Charles Malcolm (John's brother) had in 1836 instructed Lieutenant Wood to carry out the survey work on the lower Indus. He now wrote on 4 May to Wood approving his proposed surveying techniques for the Burnes mission, adding 'I am very happy to find that you continue to be so well pleased with the chief of the expedition.'[32] This larger mission gave Burnes more chance to exhibit his talent as a leader. Malcolm also notes that he had advised Burnes to take an additional midshipman to help with soundings and sextant readings, but Burnes had declined as he was under instructions to keep down expenses.

Alexander was anxious to further Mohan Lal's prospects and get others to accept that an Indian could be a competent officer, given responsibility. While the mission was in progress, he sent reports by Mohan Lal direct to the Governor-General, pointing out that this was not because they were prepared by 'an Asiatic', but because they were 'a very useful public document'.[33]

The mission, in addition to the four British officers, consisted of sixty people, quite a substantial camp. In addition to two surveyors, there were various categories of servant, cook, groom, grasscutter, and an escort of irregular cavalry. Before reaching the Khyber they had been augmented by a harem of Kashmiri concubines and six Arab bodyguards.[34] In addition qasids were continually arriving and being despatched again, with McNeill in Persia, Pottinger in Sind, Masson in Kabul, Mackeson on the Indus, Wade in Ludhiana, Macnaghten in Calcutta and the Court of Directors in London, not to mention personal mail. Burnes paid the qasids Rs40 to carry mail from Dera Ghazi Khan on the Indus to Kabul, with a promise of a further Rs40 when they returned with confirmation of delivery. The parsimonious Masson paid Rs25 for the same journey.[35]

This was a time of financial strain for the Company. Trade was depressed, the great Calcutta banking houses had collapsed, and there had been major falls in the prices of tea, opium and cotton.

The 'Great Panic' of 1837 was the first truly global banking crisis as confidence evaporated in New York, London, Moscow, Calcutta and Beijing. The drive to open up the Indus as a new area of commercial opportunity should be seen against this background. Britain was in the turmoil of the greatest economic collapse of the nineteenth century, from 1836 to 1843, when the textile industries in particular, after a period of massive expansion of factory production, found the home market unable to absorb their products. In summer of 1837 there were 50,000 unemployed workers in Manchester.[36] The numerous reports Burnes sent back on the prospects of selling British woollen cloth to Central Asia, continued a quest for elusive markets for broadcloth that runs as a woollen thread through the history of the EIC, but also reflected an urgent national priority in 1837.

CHAPTER NINETEEN

## The Gathering Storm

Back in London the Court of Directors were therefore keeping a close eye on Indus policy. John Stuart Mill wrote to Auckland with a comprehensive clarification of the Company's views.

1. The communications with Runjeet Sing on [Sind] were very skilfully conducted by Captain Wade [...] Though [the Maharaja] has not renounced his claims on Shirkapoor he has recalled his troops [...] and has apparently abandoned all serious thought of prosecuting an enterprize by which he now knows he would forfeit the friendship of the British Government.
2. Meanwhile your reasonable demonstration of a determination to preserve the integrity of the Sinde state has had a most beneficial effect upon our relationship with the Ameers [...] Every request of Colonel Pottinger with regard to the navigation of the river, is now granted as soon as made, and no facilities for commerce [...] are likely to be refused [...] The survey of the river is in progress [...] The Ameers have consented that a British Officer should be stationed in their country [...]
3. Both Runjeet Sing and the Ameers have given a favorable reception to the suggestions which you have made to them, for the establishment of Fairs (resembling those on the Russian Frontier) [...] one of these fairs to be held at Tatta, or Shirkapore, and the other at Mithenkote. The commercial Mission of Captain Burnes, by the Indus and Attock, to Cabul and Candahar, will tend to supply information from which you may better judge of the expediency of establishing these fairs [...]
4. The intelligence we have received of the progress of Captain Burnes as far as Attock is satisfactory [...]
5. The state of Afghanistan is apparently becoming more and more unsettled, but any observations which it may be thought proper to make on this subject will be addressed to you by the Secret Committee. We approve however of the intimation you have made to Shah Shooja, that if he makes any further attempts to recover his throne by means of an armed force, he will forfeit his Asylum in the British Territories.[1]

## The Gathering Storm

On 10 April 1837 Auckland therefore wrote to Burnes instructing that he inform Dost Mohammed that 'The circumstance of the British Government having resolved decidedly to discourage the prosecution by the Ex-King, Shah Shooja-ool-Moolk [. . .] from further schemes of hostility'[2] was proof of Britain's friendly intent.

John McNeill, now British Ambassador in Persia, had also in January 1837 advised Auckland against backing Shuja, sending him a lengthy memorandum which concluded: 'I cannot venture to affirm that [. . .] it would be wise to identify our interests with those of the Suddozais.'[3] When Auckland was invited at the beginning of 1837 to attend the spectacular wedding ceremonies of Ranjit Singh's favourite grandson, Nao Nehal Singh, Auckland declined precisely to avoid giving offence to Dost Mohammed and causing problems for Burnes' mission.[4] Sir Henry Fane, Commander-in-Chief, represented him.

The events of 1837 were to make the commercial aspects of Burnes' mission irrelevant. Suddenly Afghanistan became the scene of warfare above the normal border skirmishes and tribal disputes. Dost Mohammed's informants in Peshawar noted the withdrawal of most of the occupying Sikh forces to participate in the wedding in Lahore and Amritsar, and the tardiness of those forces in returning (due to conflicts over pay arrears).[5] Seizing the moment, Dost Mohammed declared jihad and launched an army towards Peshawar, and in May 1837 the Afghans, under Dost Mohammed's valiant sons Afzul and Akbar, inflicted a close but bloody defeat on the Sikhs at Jamrud.

Ranjit Singh's best general, Hari Singh, was killed, leading a charge of cavalry in an attempt to secure captured guns. He was felled by cannon fire, alongside the cavalry commander, a Colonel Gordon (known to the Sikhs as Carron). These were staggering blows to the dangerously ill Ranjit. Hari had been the driving force behind the occupation of Peshawar, about which Ranjit Singh had entertained serious doubts. Jamrud marked the end of the extraordinary expansion of the Sikh Empire.

It now became certain that the new Shah of Persia, Mohammed Mirza, was determined to launch a major assault on Herat, the western key to Afghanistan and last territory of the Saduzai dynasty. This in the face of strenuous objections to the Shah from McNeill, who believed the war was being urged on by his Russian counterpart – something Nesselrode constantly denied to Palmerston.

Burnes not only faced a war ahead of him, but also sniping from the rear. Pottinger used his longer experience to discredit Burnes' reports. On 15 April 1837, he wrote to Charles Metcalfe:

I have nothing to do with Capt. Burnes' reports other than to pass them on [...] I have seen enough of them to satisfy me that his information is incorrect. He asserts in one of them that Karachee had been [...] 'for ages' the sea port of Scinde and dwells on the 'beaten path' thence to Tattah as the desirable one for a passage – so far from this being the case, Karachee was only taken from the Khan of Kelat (Beloochistan) by the present Emirs in 1795 [...][6]

Pottinger was being pedantic;[7] Burnes' point was simply that Karachi would be the best site to develop a commercial port. Today one of the busiest areas of Karachi is Burnes Road.[8]

After leaving Haidarabad Burnes started to encounter discipline problems with his growing party,. Some of their servants got drunk and robbed and beat a shopkeeper, and he noted 'we have had great difficulty in keeping our people in order & a scuffle followed by abuse left me no remedy but to sober the offenders by cold water and a few stripes which latter I abhor as a punishment.'[9] As the Amirs were relaxed about it, Wood was detached to spend his time surveying the river. Burnes was now travelling up river with the Amirs, who were on a hunting expedition. The hunting consisted of shooting from hides at penned animals driven towards them. Burnes found it very dull: 'The weather seems to have no influence on the Ameer – it rains – it blows – he goes to hunt notwithstanding – his passion seems almost a disease.' After enduring a fortnight of this, they finally had an audience of dismissal from Amir Nur Mahommed Khan at Nasri on 16 February 1837.

Burnes declared the meeting 'shewed the Ameer in a light truly favourable'. He fully supported British proposals for Indus commerce, and said he would send a vakeel (advocate) to the meeting at Mithankot. Moreover, he stated that he understood that the recent agreement concluded with Henry Pottinger meant the British would be taking control of the country. He stated his trust that the Amirs would receive the kind of 'munificent treatment' accorded the Emperor at Delhi.[10] They were to be greatly disappointed.

On 25 February the party were sent a present of cooked fowl by a local Sayyid. Burnes found the bird's feet unusual, and sent out bearers to capture some live specimens to be recorded.[11] He bemoaned in his diary the absence of a qualified naturalist on the expedition, but himself catalogued the longtailed grass warbler, *Prinia* or *Laticilla Burnesii*, among hundreds of samples sent back.

Burnes had received letters of welcome from his friend Rustam Khan of Khairpur, and as promised a fleet of vessels awaited his mission at the frontier when they arrived on 1 March.

Alexander had suggested Dera Ghazi Khan as the site for the proposed Indus inland port and trade fair. Wade proposed Mithankot as an alternative, and requested the meeting of British Agents and local vakeels there. Wade also believed their display at Mithankot would be a deterrent to Ranjit's designs in that direction. Ranjit accepted the invitation to send a vakeel to the meeting, and cautioned the Amirs through Burnes that it was in their interest to follow suit.[12] Burnes wrote to Wade

> I have notified to all the chiefs and merchants [. . .] that such a meeting was to take place at Mithankote; and as it has naturally excited the greatest interest at Shikarpoor and other marts, and has been to them a solid proof that the British Government has in earnest taken up the subject of the Indus trade, it is of the first importance to keep our faith and word on this point.

On 16 March they reached Khairpur, where they were entertained by Rustam Khan enthusiastically for sixteen days. Rustam repeatedly pressed Burnes for a separate treaty of friendship, which Burnes was not empowered to give. Here they were joined by their surgeon, Percival Lord. A graduate of both Dublin and Edinburgh universities, Lord had been selected for his strong linguistic skills. They became the first Europeans to be admitted to the famous fortress of Baikhar.[13] When Burnes asked Rustam to act to prevent depredations on the Indus trade by the Mazari tribe, Rustam threw all the nearest Mazari leaders and their families into the dungeons of Baikhar, and Burnes had to persuade him to be more gentle.

Mazari raids had been the pretext for a move of Sikh troops into the area around Mithankot, and on 23 March Burnes received news that Ranjit Singh had agreed to withdraw forces and leave Burnes to settle the question.[14] This pre-empted a vakeel from the Khan of Kelat, the Baluch and Brahui kingdom ruled from the mountains west of Sind, who reached Khairpur on 28 March offering Kelati forces to help expel the Sikhs.[15] The Envoy pointed out that Burnes' proposed return route through the Bolan Pass to Shikarpur ran through the territory of the Khan of Kelat, and asked that he pay a courtesy visit.[16] Burnes wrote to Macnaghten requesting permission to do so.[17]

The party were entertained to a nautch by Jewan Baksh, a wealthy courtesan who built mosques and funded charity work among the poor. Burnes found her 'a girl with delicate fey melancholy features. Her troupe danced into the small hours, portraying tales of soldiers, lovers and jealous husbands', until they collapsed in alcoholic stupour.[18]

To Alexander, Rustam already 'seemed to have an excellent idea of the designs of Russia – He talked of their strategy & their designs on India, their power in Persia, their large army'. Burnes replied that Russia lacked financial muscle.[19] The fear of Russian designs towards India was not a purely British preoccupation.

From 2 to 9 April the mission stayed at Shikarpur, collecting much information from the great commercial and financial market, where Burnes found many merchants who had connections to people he knew in Kabul and Bokhara. The town was large, prosperous and 90 per cent Hindu. Burnes noted that the women were attractive. He found some caution towards the Mithankot fair from merchants who wished to protect local monopolies. British ironware was on sale in the market, and Burnes noticed: 'our camp is pitched near a field of [poppy] – The smell near the fields is very sickening & the people employed in collecting the opium say that they are half intoxicated at night – They split the head of the top with a three pronged knife & collect the juice which exudes in a clam shell.'

On 10 April the mission moved on to Mulaman where Burnes lectured the refractory Bundi chief, Sher Mohamed Khan, about the advantages of peace and trade. Here Burnes hired six Arab bodyguards 'to keep away thieves and robbers', who became closely attached to him.[20] Emily Eden met these men and noted they were of Arab descent rather than from Arab lands.[21] After two days' excellent progress, they reached Gandava where Burnes sent a musical box and a map to the thirteen-year-old Nassir Khan, heir to Kelat, who was being educated there, and collected mineral samples from the Gandava Hills. Burnes noted in his journal that all the treaties Britain made about the Indus were as little known to the officials and rulers on its banks as they were in Timbuktu. He was also concerned that he had invited a great gathering of chiefs, vakeels and merchants to Mithankot to discuss the trade fair, but had still heard nothing from Wade. He learnt that Henry's nephew, Lieutenant Eldred Pottinger, who had passed through Shikarpur ahead of him, was with a caravan detained by a local war at the entrance to the Bolan Pass, which Eldred was charged with surveying. Eldred was escorted by Edul Khan of the Sind Irregular Horse, who was instructed to get him to Herat then rejoin Burnes in Kabul.[22] Pottinger was travelling in the stock disguise of a horse dealer.

Burnes himself was vexed that he had not been given the power to settle the Mazari border dispute, which he felt he could have done in 'a couple of days', but instead had to refer it back to Macnaghten.[23] He found that no chief believed his mission was purely commercial 'some laugh, some are silent', and confided to his journal that history showed they were right to distrust the British.

On 18 April they arrived at the frontier of Bhawal Khan and transferred into luxurious state barges, with an escort of forty scarlet uniformed soldiers 'we found all the usual kindness [. . .] and we gladly exchanged our comfortless boats for these – I must not forget to state that among the supplies for us is one boat literally full of bedsteads!!' Scores of people were provided to haul the boats against the current. Burnes again wrote praising Bhawal Khan's assistance and lavish hospitality, and suggesting some reciprocation from the Governor-General.[24] This time the purse strings of the Raj were opened, and the Governor-General sent Bhawal Khan a small wooden orrery, an astronomical device.[25]

Burnes was very happy with the progress of young Nourozji Fourdonji, who was becoming 'a useful public servant' quicker than expected, while Mohan Lal was 'all I could wish [. . .] the very person I could select to communicate with the chiefs and people I meet', but he was becoming a little careworn. He added 'I find a good deal of trouble in managing the details of this little mission & journey.'[26]

On reaching Ahmedpur, they much enjoyed Bhawal Khan's company, and met the commander of his regular infantry Hamish McGregor McPherson, a British officer cashiered duelling, who Burnes had helped back in 1831 (probably financially).[27] Bhawal Khan sent what Burnes called the corps de ballet to keep his guests company, as noted in Burnes' diary 'in a big house where every whisper was re-echoed'. Presumably there were many hushed endearments.

They proceeded with Bhawal Khan to Bhawalpur where Burnes received a 'very friendly' letter from Ranjit, complaining however about the border settlements. Burnes noted, 'The Haidarabad Ameers, who deserved little, have got everything & in this we have managed to offend Roostum Khan, Bhawal Khan and Runjeet, the great, greater & greatest of our friends.'

Burnes, Leech, Lord and Wood were at dinner in Bhawal Khan's guest lodging with McPherson, when Benoit Argoud first arrived. Alex went out to greet him, insisting that he join their meal. Argoud had started as a drummer boy in the Napoleonic service, and worked his way up to officer rank. After Napoleon's fall, he had served in the Turkish army before enlisting with Ranjit Singh as a Colonel in 1836. An extremely brave individual, though alcoholic, he had been the only one of Singh's European officers to confront the Maharaja about his salary arrears. He had obtained his back pay, but also his dismissal. He was now heading for the Bolan Pass and Kandahar, to seek employment with Dost Mohammed in Kabul.

There followed a drunken evening. Argoud in his cups liked to show his prowess as a drummer by beating out rhythms on the table, 'and as a tenor accompaniment, made a knife vibrate between its under surface and his thumb' to loud applause. Argoud however 'knew not when to desist', but fortunately soon drank himself into a stupor and they put him to bed.

The next morning Burnes slept in, hungover. Argoud woke up, and passed Percival Lord, who was sitting in the hall performing taxidermy on a duck. Argoud, still not sober, then crashed into Burnes' room:

That officer was not yet dressed, on which M. Argoud called out: 'Why sare, the battle of Wagram was fought before this hour, and you are still in deshabille? Will you take wine with me?' 'No,' said Captain Burnes, 'I never take wine before breakfast.' 'Then sare,' said Argoud, 'You insult me and I demand satisfaction.' He ran out and soon reappeared with his small sword and asked Burnes to send for his rapier. But the latter, thinking he had humoured the fiery little Frenchman quite enough, politely requested him to continue his journey.[28]

This amusing interlude could have gone horribly wrong. Argoud eventually did reach Kabul through Bolan. Burnes kept a friendly eye on him through Masson, and continued correspondence with the Frenchman, though noting, 'poor creature he is I fear both insane and drunk'. Dost Mohammed, though he allowed Argoud to remain in Kabul, did not offer him employment.

But Burnes now received disappointing news:

> I have heard from Cap. Wade who is not coming to Mittuncote – How is our faith & word to be kept with the merchants & chiefs of Sinde if this meeting does not take place – I confess I do not see how and I have written so to Wade – We must await his answer – I have had a mesh of intricacies in this journey already.[29]

The mission had not been idle. On 11 May Burnes sent back Lord's reports on the mineral resources of the Gandava Hills, and on the trade of Shikarpur and Upper Sind by himself, the latest section of Indus survey by Wood, and a basic grammar of the Brahui language and a survey of Mandvi's port by Leech. They were now progressing up river with following winds (why they had not been given the use of an Indus steam boat is unclear). At Mithankot, Burnes had been very disappointed to receive a letter from Wade proposing that Burnes continue straight up the Indus, without calling in to Lahore or seeing Ranjit Singh, in view of 'the peculiar disposition of his Highness and his advisers', following both Jamrud and British pressure on Ranjit not to attack Sind.[30]

Burnes found Mithankot itself 'a mean town' of about 3,000 inhabitants, two miles from the Indus, and so prone to inundation that any fair site would need to be three miles from the river. He thought it was the wrong site. It appears from his journal the grand meeting planned with merchants and vakeels did not happen.

The mission pushed on into Derajat. Since Burnes' last Indus mission, the Sikhs had taken firmer control of this district. Bhawal Khan had held it as tributary of Ranjit Singh, but his forces had been pushed out and General Ventura installed as Sikh Governor. In consequence annual Sikh revenues there had increased from two and a half to eleven and a half lakhs. 'The town of Multan has a prosperous appearance, which is altogether attributable to M.

Ventura, who was until lately in charge of it. Under Bahawal Khan the officers were guilty of the greatest extortion, but since 1832, when the Sikhs recovered it, the place has greatly recovered.'[31] Unlike other areas under direct Sikh control, Ventura had not suppressed Muslim religious practice or committed random atrocities.

Burnes now received urgent news from John McNeill, written from Teheran on 13 March. McNeill told Burnes that the Shah was absolutely set on taking Herat, and that given constant Herati raids – including one in October 1834 when the Heratis took 10,000 slaves – the Persians were justified. Nonetheless, McNeill viewed this as a dangerous development given Russian influence in Persia. Representatives of Persia, Russia and Herat were all gathered at Kabul. One of the parties in Russian pay, Mir Mohammed Khan, was also in McNeill's pay, and he had in consequence obtained copies of the entire correspondence. All the Afghan factions were vying with each other in expressing allegiance to Persia, each hoping to further their own ambitions.

The letter which Dost Mohammed had written to the Shah of Persia is a key document. Burnes, McNeill and Masson all argued that the Emir was merely insuring himself against the expected Persian move, and reacting to the absence of offers from the British, with whom Dost would prefer an alliance. Who, they argued, could possibly prefer an alliance with Persia to one with Britain? But Dost Mohammed's appraisal of the dangers of British alliance has a ring of sincerity:

> I have been long engaged in war with 100,000 horse and foot of the wicked infidels [Sikhs] and 300 guns, but [...] I have not yet been subdued by the faithless enemy, and have been able to preserve the true faith. But how long shall I be able to oppose this detestable tribe and [...] resist their aggression? [...] As [...] Kandahar, and the capital Kabul, and the countries bordering on Khorosan [...] form part of the Persian territory and are among the Kingdoms of the King of Kings, the misery and welfare of these dominions cannot be separated from the interests of the Persian Government [...] I shall persist in contending with the Seiks as long as I am able, but [...] [if] I am unable to resist that diabolical tribe, then I [...] must commit myself with the English, who will then obtain complete authority over the whole of Afghanistan, and it remains to be seen hereafter to what places and to what extent the flame of the violence of that nation will be carried.[32]

McNeill's own view of the policy Britain should adopt was clear: actively to promote a strong and united Afghanistan under Dost Mohammed. He urged that Britain should finance Dost to take both Herat and Kandahar and that current British policy was mistaken as 'we cannot make Persia [...] [both] strong against Russia and powerless against Afghanistan [...]'[33]

Burnes was buoyed that McNeill's opinion was identical to his own. He felt he had been thrust into the centre of events in a way that justified his decision to turn down the offer of the Persia mission. He also felt that this was the time to cash in on his fame and his London contacts – including the influence with Auckland he had gained at Bowood House. On 12 May 1837, camped outside the town of Uch, Burnes wrote a letter to Auckland, not as usual through Macnaghten, the Political Secretary, but rather through Colvin, the Private Secretary. In later sending Masson a copy, Burnes stressed this was not an official letter.

Burnes first gave Auckland the news that Dost had opened diplomatic correspondence with Persia. Burnes attributes this to British neglect of Dost and the latter's desire for Persian aid to recover Peshawar, and to deflect any Persian attack on Kabul via Herat. Burnes then gets to the crux. He suggests Britain should promise to assist Dost to recover Peshawar and the right bank of the Indus down to Shikarpur – but only on the death of Ranjit Singh. The Emir would be a stable and commerce-friendly ruler, and if supported by Britain, a bulwark against Persian and Russian intrigue.

Having set out his policy recommendation, the still-inexperienced Burnes overplayed his hand. He pointed out that he had discussed the matter with Charles Grant and with then Prime Minister Earl Grey. This name-dropping would scarcely awe Auckland, and was too obvious an attempt by a mere Captain to impose on the Governor-General.[34]

On 6 June, from Multan, Burnes wrote his reply to McNeill, more fully than to Auckland,[35] explaining his own strategy for the north-west frontier. Alexander accepted the alliance with Ranjit Singh and that it would be wrong to act contrary to his interests. But Burnes pointed out that Ranjit Singh was going to die soon.

Burnes reasoned that Dost's stable administration would be the best lynchpin for British commerce. His proposal was not outlandish: restore to Kabul the Indus territories down to and including Shikarpur. These had all been a part of the Dourani Empire recently, and all had a largely Muslim indigenous population. For Ranjit Singh: 'let him keep Peshawar while he lives and meantime [let us] turn Dost Mahomed Khan's attention towards Candahar and Herat'. This fitted with McNeill's proposal. Burnes continued, 'As for Suddozye ascendancy in Cabool, I consider that quite hopeless, either from Kamran, or Shoojah ool Moolk; the former, by the way, is said to be dying of dropsy, and the latter has not the head to manage anything.'

He concluded: 'On all these points I hope soon to be better informed, and before I get to Cabool to find myself invested with other authority than what I now hold.' He explained to Masson, 'As yet I have no authority beyond that of conducting a commercial Mission, but various hints [...] have served to convince me that a stirring time of political action has arrived and I shall have to shew what my Govt. is made of as well as myself.'

Letters from both McNeill and Burnes passed through Wade on the way to Auckland. Wade added comments, and on 27 June forwarded McNeill's letter with a lengthy one from himself, arguing strenuously against the consolidation of Afghanistan. Wade argued that the division of Afghanistan made its weak rulers more susceptible to British influence, Dost's rule would never be accepted, and if he moved against Herat then Kamran would turn to Persia.

Burnes sent Masson copies of all the British secret correspondence; the letters to him from McNeill and the Governor-General, Wade's report of the consequences of the battle of Jamrud, and the reports of his agents in Afghanistan and Bokhara, together with copies of all his replies. He asked Masson for his advice, 'well assured as I am that in putting you in possession of these important documents, I am but advancing the interests of Government.'[36]

He realised that sending Masson all this diplomatic correspondence was irregular. Burnes also forwarded two letters for Masson from Pottinger, who was carrying out his promise of defying the Calcutta prohibition on his communication with Masson.

When Burnes did receive further instructions, they told him to wait at the Indus, as active war had again broken out over Peshawar, right on Burnes' route. But a few days later he received a letter from John Colvin in which Auckland gave him permission to go on if it appeared safe.[37] Burnes wrote to James Holland from the Indus on 5 July 1837:

> another express still cries pause, but places a vast latitude in my hands and 'forward' is my motto; forward to the scene of carnage where, instead of embarrassing my Government, I feel myself in a situation to do good [...] I can hardly say how grateful I feel to Lord Auckland. I have not as yet got the replies to my recommendations on our line of policy[38]

Burnes sent letters to Dost, to Jabbar Khan and to the religious leader Mirza Sarwar Khan urging them to come to terms with Ranjit Singh over Peshawar lest they hamstring relations with Britain. In asking Masson to deliver these letters, he said 'it will never do to offend Runjeet Sing whose alliance we court and must cherish.'[39]

Conventional accounts of the Great Game have tended to stress the role of the Imperial powers, but to ignore the existence as independent players of states like Kabul, Persia, Lahore, Kelat and Sind. While Burnes was leaving Sind, a Persian Envoy and Agent, Qambar Ali, was arriving at Kandahar for a mission there and to Kabul. His instructions were very detailed, and in many ways mirror those of Burnes, including on intelligence gathering:

When you pass by the boundary of Kerman [...] you will detail the following particulars [...] namely the state of the towns and villages [...] an estimate of the population and strength of the tribes at such places, Seistanees, Beloochees, Afghans and Kuzzilbashes, an account of the revenue and expenditure of these countries, their produce, their principal cultivation, & from what kind of cultivation most profit is made: and an account of the taxes [...] and of the impact of commerce; finally whether there is water on the road and whether the latter is level or mountainous [...]

passing through Beloochistan, you must raise great expectations of the munificence of His Majesty in the minds of the Khans of Beloochistan and Seeistan [...] All these Khans should [...] prepare their troops [...] they are to join the Royal Stirrup.

At Kandahar he will deliver the firman and robes of honour to Kohundil Khan [...] and excite his hopes of the generosity of His Majesty [...] Kohundil Khan must undertake to send one of his brothers in advance to the Court while he himself will [...] await the arrival of the Royal Army. He will get his troops in readiness and prepare as much cavalry as is practicable for please God the campaign of Herat will be entrusted to him [...] Kumber Ali Khan will form an acquaintance with all the persons in authority and with the Afghan and Kuzzilbash Khans as well as with the Kuzzilbashes in general. The object will be to excite their hopes of generosity [...]

When he has finished his affairs in Candahar he will proceed to Kabul and deliver a dagger as a mark of His Majesty's favor to Dost Mohammed Khan, and he will convey the auspicious robes of honour to Nawab Jubber Khan. He [...] will give them the strongest assurances that after the arrival of the royal army in those countries, favors of every description shall be unceasingly lavished on them [...] and he will declare that, please God, Dost Mohammed Khan shall enjoy the royal favor to such an extent that these countries shall be placed completely in his possession, and he shall have entire control over them [...][40]

Persian diplomacy was no less sophisticated than British. The Persians thought Dost the best man to rule all Afghanistan as a Persian tributary, but this was to be kept from other Afghan rulers. Burnes recognised that Qambar Ali was engaged in the same game as himself. He commented to McNeill on seeing these intercepted instructions: 'Why the Government of India in despatching me to Bokhara gave me nothing so perfect, and in my present journey, tho' they are as anxious for accurate information as it is possible, they do not put forward so accurate an outline [...]'[41]

Poor Dr Gerard had died of malaria shortly before Burnes reached India. His final months, at the small post of Subatu, had been miserable. He had spent a year travelling back from Persia due to long halts to recover his health. In consequence he had been absent from duty, and the Company caused

Campbell would quickly be recalled and Burnes succeed him as Ambassador.

From 10 December 1834 to 8 April 1835 Whig rule was interrupted by a short-lived Tory administration, in which Lord Ellenborough was President of the Board of Control. Ellenborough, a fierce partisan, regarded Burnes as too close to the Whigs, and was seeking to block the promised preferment.[5] But in any event Burnes turned the offer down. This was extraordinary – he remained Assistant Resident in Cutch, and was still a Lieutenant. Ambassador to Persia was a huge promotion, with the additional attraction of working jointly for the Company and the Foreign Office, opening up a new career path. But Burnes felt he had become a figure of influence in India, and that the top appointments were there to be reached for.

Burnes did not take the decision lightly – he consulted widely, including with Mountstuart Elphinstone and John Stuart Mill. He justified his decision to turn down Persia boldly: 'What are a colonelcy and a KLS[6] to me? I look far higher, and shall either die or be so.' Burnes had become firm friends with McNeill, whose book *The Progress and Present Position of Russia in the East* (1836) was the most influential of all the publications representing the Russian threat to India. In England the two advised on each other's manuscripts. Although McNeill's book was anonymous, all of official London knew the author.

For Burnes to have accepted would have been to block McNeill's career. On Burnes declining, McNeill was appointed, with Burnes' commendation: 'He is an able fellow, and by far the fittest person in England for the situation.'[7] They remained firm friends.

Burnes was also close with Mountstuart Elphinstone, who lived a solitary, syphilis-blighted life in England but had warmed to the fellow Scot who in many ways was following in his footsteps. Burnes outlined to Elphinstone his wish to become Envoy to Kabul. But Elphinstone, who was well aware that such appointments frequently led to military entanglement, was against further British involvement in Afghanistan.[8] So was Henry Tucker, Chairman of the Court of Directors. Alex lobbied to be appointed to head a commercial mission. Tucker 'declined then to propose or concur in the appointment [. . .] feeling pretty sure that it must soon degenerate into a political agency, and that we should [. . .] be involved in [. . .] the entanglements of Afghan politics'.[9]

Burnes had financial security for a while. He had received £840 from John Murray for his book,[10] and a healthy bank balance must have contributed to his optimism.

He was travelling back on the Company's new fast steamer route, including overland via Suez. From there, Burnes joined the *Hugh Lindsay* to sail down the Red Sea and on to Bombay. This pioneering steam vessel had been built by the Company in Bombay in 1828, but was very uncomfortable. Built with insufficient space for coal for her inefficient steam engines, it started voyages with coal stored even in the saloon and passenger cabins, and had to put in to port to refuel every five days.[11] It is nonetheless astonishing that just sixteen years after the world's first commercial steamship service on the Clyde, a locally-built oceangoing steamship was sailing out of Bombay. Putting in for coals at Jeddah, Burnes met a French government official, M. Fontanier.

Fontanier wrote that Burnes was overrated as a traveller. A number of Frenchmen, including Court, Ventura and Allard, had also travelled in Central Asia without becoming so famous, and Court's command of the Persian language was better than Burnes'. He also felt that *Travels into Bokhara* was not all Burnes' own work:

> Sir Alexander's work had been taken up by the East India Company, and was revised and corrected by Mr Elphinstone [. . .] not only did he add his own observations, but caused the officer to suppress certain passages which he considered prejudicial to the interests of the British Government.

This was of course true, but no more so than of any book published by a Company officer. Elphinstone's revisions do not appear substantive.[12] Fontanier's determination to be unimpressed wilted when invited to dinner with Burnes:

> He had a quick, penetrating mind, and his society was very agreeable [. . .] he was very unassuming and natural in his manners, and showed proof of much frankness in his conversation [. . .] we conversed a great deal about Persia and Eastern policy.[13]

Fontanier surmised correctly that Burnes' views on Persian policy came from McNeill. He found Burnes angry that the slave trade was active in Jeddah. He also found Burnes determined to continue his feud with Wolff. The latter claimed to have preached Christianity at the Mecca Gate in Jeddah which, as Fontanier put it drily, 'appeared rather strange to those who are acquainted with Mahometans'.

Burnes was determined to prove Wolff a liar. He therefore led a curious little party, consisting of Captain Wilson of the *Hugh Lindsay*, a Lieutenant Buckle and Mr Frazer, fellow passengers, and M. Fontanier, in search of Malam Yusuf, with whom Wolff had lodged, to ask if the story were true. Malam Yusuf replied that nobody could ever tell what language Wolff was speaking. Sometimes it seemed to be Persian or Arabic, but the pronunciation was terrible. One day he had indeed gone to the Mecca Gate with a Bible under his arm; but when there 'if he had spoken or gesticulated, nobody had noticed it'. Fontanier concluded that Wolff was sincere but 'I had met that missionary, and know the strange delusion into which he had fallen, as to his oratorical abilities.' Fontanier himself had tried to converse with Wolff in French, Italian, Persian and Turkish, without success, even though Wolff seemed to believe he was fluent in all those languages.

CHAPTER SEVENTEEN

# While Alex was Away

Even as Burnes had been taking ship in 1833 on his triumphant way to England, Shah Shuja had been setting off to recapture his throne in Kabul. He did so with the active connivance of Claude Wade, who had obtained for him four months' advance on his pension, and the right to purchase weapons in Delhi tax free. By a treaty of 17 February 1833 he had financial assistance and Muslim levies from Ranjit Singh, in exchange for which Shuja made over his claim on Peshawar, Derajat and Kashmir to the Sikh.

While the Amirs of Sind were negotiating permanent release from any fealty to Kabul in return for one-off assistance to Shuja, Shuja moved with his force through Bhawalpur and occupied Shikarpur, where he extracted loans from the merchants and financiers. After a lengthy stand-off in which more followers rallied to Shuja, boosted by the universal belief he had British support, Shuja defeated the Amirs in battle near Sukkur on 18 January 1834. He then marched on Kandahar with an army of 40,000.

The Barakzais were divided. The Kandahar sirdars urged their brother Dost Mohammed to come to Kandahar to battle Shuja, with the secret intent that Sultan Mohammed Khan from Peshawar would then take Kabul. Dost Mohammed was too wily and instead seized Jalalabad. He then turned back towards Kandahar, arriving just in time to defeat Shah Shuja before its walls, in a battle in which 90,000 troops were theoretically involved but few actually fought, with most chiefs waiting to see who had the advantage. Shuja fled prematurely and decided the battle.

Shuja fled virtually alone, as fast as possible – which happened to mean on Alexander Burnes' horse, given him by Ranjit Singh. Burnes had ridden it to Ludhiana, Simla, Delhi and Peshawar, and there he had parted with it before his journey to Bokhara, as he did not want an expensive horse to draw attention in Afghanistan. He donated it to two mullahs who had helped him with letters of introduction. They had given it to their father, residing at Shuja's court-in-exile in Ludhiana. Shuja had seized it, and its speed and endurance now saved his life as he fled to the fortress of Kelat, hotly pursued for over a week. At Kelat the ruler, Mehrab Khan, explained to the pursuers that the law of hospitality obliged him to defend his guest. Kelat being a strong citadel, they gave up.

Going through the wreck of Shuja's camp, Dost Mohammed discovered letters from Claude Wade, advising various chiefs that support for Shah Shuja would be appreciated by the British government.[1] Dost Mohammed had received Burnes' protestations of friendship only two years before, and his faith in the British must have been severely shaken.

Shortly after, in March 1834, the British extended their intelligence network by sending their newswriter, Mir Karamat Ali, to Kandahar. He had a monthly salary of Rs250, plus Rs50 per month for qasids, writing materials and travel.[2] His postion must have been difficult and dangerous. In accordance with the secret agreement with Shuja, the Sikh general Hari Singh 'seized' Peshawar from Sultan Mohammed Khan, (who was in on the plot), a terrible blow to the Afghan state. Dost Mohammed must have regarded the British as implicated in the loss of Peshawar. Indeed, the bilateral treaty of 1834 between Ranjit Singh and Shah Shuja contained an open reference to British involvement:

> Regarding Shikarpore and the territory of Scinde [. . .] the Shah agrees to abide by whatever may be settled as right and proper, in conformity with the happy relations of friendship subsisting between the British Government and the Maharajah through Captain Wade.[3]

The British subsequently denied it; but Wade had assisted Shuja's attempt. One result was that Dost Mohammed sent an Ambassador to Russia, requesting assistance over Peshawar. If the British were hostile, perhaps help might come from their rivals.

The authorities in London took a dim view, rebuking Bentinck:

> We think that this indulgence ought not to have been granted to Shah Shoojah ool Moolk. The arms, though stated by you to be intended 'for the protection of his person on his intended journey', must to all intents and purposes be regarded as purchased for the purpose of invading Caubul with a view to the recovery of his throne. And the exemption of these arms from the ordinary duties constitutes, so far, a virtual breach of the neutrality [. . .] the British Government ought, and professes to, observe.[4]

At Kandahar one mercenary corps had fought hard for Shuja, under a soldier of Scots and Indian parentage named William Campbell. Campbell had fought against the British at the siege of Baratpur, and in 1826 had entered

Ranjit Singh's service, but been dismissed in a dispute over women. Campbell had raised a regiment of Hindu infantry for Shuja. At Kandahar, he was seriously wounded and captured, but Dost had him treated and engaged in his own service, together with his regiment; they were to feature in the final act of this story.

Dost returned to Kabul. On 4 September 1834 he took part in a solemn ceremony to legitimise his rule. With a stern escort of irregular cavalry including none of his Shia Qizilbash bodyguard, without feasting or show, Dost Mohammed rode out from Kabul. Alongside him rode the hereditary head of the Sunni clergy of Afghanistan, Mir Waiz, to the Sufi shrine of Siah Sung. There, Mir Waiz delicately placed a few blades of grass into the turban[5] of a stooping Dost Mohammed.

The ruler of Kabul thus became the Emir al-Muminin – the Commander of the Faithful, Dost Mohammed Ghazi. Dost was now ruler rather than Governor, but with the religious title of Emir rather than the secular one of Shah. He was declaring jihad against the Sikhs of Ranjit Singh, a holy war to win back Peshawar.[6] His religious asceticism appeared genuine, his dress and diet became still plainer, his pomp still less, access for complainants still easier.

Dost now had coins struck in his own name, and was referred to as the ruler in Friday prayers in all his lands' mosques. These were the traditional marks of a ruler in Muslim lands. He never made a claim to hereditary Kingship, or took the title of Shah. But he was staking a stronger claim, that of leadership in holy war. The Qazi having ruled it was legal to force infidels to pay for jihad, Shikarpuri bankers throughout Afghanistan were tortured and extorted into making contributions. There was a tremendous response to Dost's call of jihad and on 2 January 1835 he left Kabul at the head of a vast army for Peshawar.

On 4 May 1835 at Noushera, the Emir lost Peshawar without a blow being struck. Sultan Mohammed, with all his troops, deserted to Ranjit Singh after days of negotiation. The numbers on each side now roughly equal, Dost Mohammed realised he had no chance against the Sikh artillery and made an ignominious retreat back to Kabul. Sultan became again Sirdar of Peshawar – his agreement with Ranjit Singh renounced all family claims and accepted that he and his Peshawar levies would fight with the Sikhs if they attacked Jalalabad, Kandahar or Kabul. It was the ultimate treachery to his family, his faith and his country. As the Emir retreated without a fight, his ghazi supporters pillaged the baggage and deserted in disgust.

A curious Russian counter to Burnes' visit to Bokhara had occurred while Alex was enjoying London. Claude Wade had reported to Macnaghten information received from Bokhara.⁷ Dr Martin Honigberger in May 1834 reached Bokhara in a caravan conducted by kafilbashi Hyat, the same man who had led Burnes. Honigberger reported to Wade that a Russian Ambassador, a Muslim Russian subject named Mirza Jafer, was in Bokhara. His purpose was to obtain the Emir's agreement to a Russian military expedition against the Khanate of Khiva. Jafer also revealed that Persia, with Russian aid, would soon attack Herat.

The Bokharan authorities arranged for Honigberger to depart for Russia with Jafer. Honigberger noted, 'Besides Persian and Arabic he speaks Italian very fluently and is a good-looking and intelligent man. I shall have an agreeable companion on my journey to Russia.'⁸

Honigberger realised 'Mirza Jafer' was not really a Muslim, and to Honigberger he represented himself as a Frenchman, Baron Demaison, in disguise in the service of Russia. He had been denounced by Tartar merchants in Bokhara, who were themselves Russian subjects but resentful of their overlords. He had responded by producing written testaments of theological credentials from Kazakh mullahs, and Honigberger was present when they were examined by the Kush-Begi. Jafer was a hair's breadth from execution; rather peculiarly Honigberger suggested to the Kush-Begi that an examination of his skin and hair colouring might give the answer. Jafer escaped this test because he had given 'large presents' to the Kush-Begi.

Who Demaison was remains a mystery. Years later, after dining with Witkiewicz, Burnes reported that the Pole definitely 'is not that Mirza Jaffir who was at Bokhara some years ago [...] The true name of that person is Maizon and he is Arabic.'⁹ Rumours of the mysterious Russian agent Maison or Demaison had been picked up a few years earlier by British intelligence.¹⁰

Honigberger discovered that Burnes' visit to Bokhara had damaged the Kush-Begi's view of Britain substantially:

> His first inquiry was, whether I knew Jussuff Wolff and Alexander Burnes? 'Wolff' continued he, 'was a very good-hearted man, but as for Burnes he was a deceiver, because he told me [...] that his intention was to go to England, via Russia, whereas he returned to Hindostan, via Khiva.' He was convinced that Burnes was a spy [...]¹¹

Burnes' deceit had an impact on the later Bokharan treatment of Stoddart and Conolly.

Masson's appointment as newswriter would have enhanced his local standing. It also meant that Wade had an alternative expert to Burnes to put forward in policy battles. However Wade's relationship with Masson was stormy, and he did not pass on the originals of Masson's reports to Macnaghten and Auckland, but rather summaries which often distorted Masson's views.

Masson had been in correspondence with British officials before Wade appointed him. He had then held no official position and supposedly was interested only in antiquarian research, yet was continually pumping Pottinger for diplomatic information. For example on 3 October 1833, plainly in response to a request from Masson, Pottinger had replied:

> I have not been at Bombay since I left it this time two years [...] I am not able to tell you how the Vakeels from Kabul were treated, or whether they succeeded with their object.[12]

Honigberger, Masson and Gerard had sent back reports and drawings to the Asiatic Society in Calcutta along with numerous coins and artefacts. This occasioned great excitement. It was the first understanding that a Hellenic civilisation had flourished in Central Asia for centuries after the passing of Alexander. A grant of Rs1,500 and annual stipend of Rs1,000 had been sent to Kabul by the Asiatic Society; Honigberger and Gerard having quit the scene, it all went to Masson. Pottinger obtained a further grant of Rs1500 for Masson from the Government of Bombay.[13] He also noted he had sent Masson another Rs300 as a personal donation. He was still not aware of Masson's true identity, as he wrote to Lord Clare recommending Masson as an 'American gentleman'. Masson's archaeological excavations were not only well-financed by the British but also by Dost Mohammed's son Akbar Khan, a fact worth bearing in mind when reading British accounts of 'Afghan savages'. In April 1834 Masson bagged a further Rs500 as a personal donation from Sir James Campbell, departing British Envoy to Persia.[14]

According to government historians: 'Though Honigberger mentions Masson only casually, it appears that the latter accompanied him as far as Orenburg.'[15]

I hesitate to mention the possibility that Maison was Masson, lest this long shot devalues much more definite evidence of Masson's Russian connections. It would require collusion by Honigberger – not impossible as he worked for Ranjit Singh. The Doctor mentions only Maison/Jaffer going with him to Orenburg, and Masson is very peculiarly absent from his memoir in general. Masson was fluent in French – how is unknown – and appears in a nineteenth-century Paris 'Biographie Nationale' as a Frenchman.[16]

Through their correspondence on antiquarian studies, Pottinger had become enthralled by Masson. In September 1834 Pottinger was offering to organise publication of his works. At this stage the British authorities had officially been aware who Masson/Lewis was for a year, as Pottinger gushed:

I beg to assure you, that if I can be the medium of making your most interesting discoveries known to the world [...] my sole object will be obtained.

On the subject of your MSS I told you in my last, that if you would entrust them to me, I would undertake that they should be published either under the auspices of the Bombay Government, or by one of the learned societies of Great Britain, any of which would gladly snatch at such a prize.[17]

The authorities now moved to regularise communication with Masson. Not only had Pottinger been informing Masson continually of the movements and views of Company officials, but also Masson had started to draw large sums of extra cash on bills of exchange he was signing off in Kabul as redeemable on a variety of British officials. On 27 February 1835 Pottinger wrote to Masson to say that if one substantial bill for Rs500 on Claude Wade were not honoured, then Pottinger himself would pay it. In the same letter Pottinger encloses for Masson a copy of an instruction from the Governor-General's office, forbidding Pottinger to continue his correspondence with Masson. In future all contact between Masson and the British government was to be through Claude Wade. Pottinger denied the authority of the Governor-General to prevent non-official correspondence:

> I have no idea that the Supreme Government will offer the smallest objection to my continuing to correspond with you on antiquarian and literary subjects which would in truth be an interference with our private actions.[18]

It seems that Calcutta was unhappy about the amount of intelligence Pottinger was giving Masson; Pottinger told Masson he had replied that 'my correspondence with you has been, and is, of a purely literary nature'. This was a downright lie; Pottinger had told Masson of British naval movements, of views on Russia and the prospects of war, of the detailed affairs of the British mission to Persia, and other sensitive subjects. Pottinger enclosed a hundi for yet another Rs1,000 from the government of Bombay for Masson's researches.

In January 1836, two years after 'Mirza Jafer', Witkiewicz had ridden to Bokhara on an open mission,[19] to negotiate the release of detained Russian merchants. But like Burnes, he was in secret studying armed forces and fortifications, and surveying possible routes for a Russian army, as well as looking for evidence of British activity. Witkiewicz reported back to St Petersburg:

> The British have their man in Bukhara. He is a Kashmiri called Nizamuddin and has been living in Bukhara for four years now under the pretext of trade [...] He is a very clever man [...] and entertains the Bukharan noblemen; at least once a week he sends letters with secret messengers to Kabul, to the Englishman Masson [...] The most curious thing is that Dost Mohammed is aware of Masson's activities [...] but leaves the spy alone, saying; one man

cannot harm me [...] This man lives in Kabul under the pretext of looking for ancient coins.

Nizamuddin was doing a good job:

> Nizamuddin sought my acquaintance as soon as I arrived and asked me [...] about Novo-Alexandrovsk, the New Line, our relations with Khiva etc. Having been forewarned, I did not give him any definite answers. All the same he sent a letter to Kabul the very next day.[20]

The arrival of a Russian envoy in Bokhara was vital strategic news. But Masson did not pass on Nizamuddin's letter to Wade or to Calcutta. It is possible that Masson had never received the letter from Nizamuddin, but the qasids were a distinct profession who were trained from childhood and could trot fifty miles a day. It was fundamental to their working practice that they must return with a reply or acknowledgement.[21]

Shortly after this, Masson came under suspicion from Claude Wade. I have not discovered precisely of what Masson was accused. According to Burnes, Pottinger was also amongst Masson's accusers.[22] It led to an official investigation, and it appears that Masson's defence was that he had been tricked or misrepresented into a false position. Burnes submitted a testimonial in Masson's support, and on 9 March 1836 Burnes, in his first direct communication with Masson, wrote:

> from the moment I heard of the difference I was satisfied that you had been undeservedly compromised to promote views and ends which it was not part of your own desire to promote – Your exculpation is complete but it is humiliating to me even to think that exculpation ever was necessary.[23]

Burnes was here unwise; firstly in vouching for a man he had never met, and secondly criticising Claude Wade in correspondence with Masson:

> Captain Wade – To that gentleman I owe something for hospitality and kindness [...] but I fear that poor Gerard's opinion of him in his public character is very much my own – My journey is [...] happily terminated but, however much I feel Captain Wade's private kindness, I owe him nothing publicly indeed much the reverse – All this I am bound to state to someone whose feelings have been trifled with as yours.

In fact, Wade had judged Masson's character much better than Burnes.

CHAPTER EIGHTEEN

## Return to the Indus

Burnes found himself kicking his heels at Bhuj. After turning down Persia, he had been offered nothing else. One reason for this was the inopportune promotion away from Indian affairs of Charles Grant, after a brief Tory hiatus.

In May 1835 Burnes was despatched on a diplomatic mission to Sind over an Indian cargo vessel wrecked on the coast. Local custom was that any wrecked vessel and its cargo became the property of the rulers. Burnes now found the Amirs anxious to co-operate. They were preoccupied with the threat of invasion by Ranjit Singh. Burnes found it impossible to confine discussion to the narrow case of commercial compensation. Rather the Amirs were offering a complete opening of the Indus to free trade, British control of their foreign policy, and the stationing of a British Resident at Shikarpur. What they wanted in exchange was a guarantee of British protection.[4]

Burnes and Pottinger strongly recommended a treaty to establish these arrangements and achieve longstanding policy goals. But the Acting Governor-General, Charles Metcalfe, loathed the idea of military commitments beyond existing frontiers and rejected the idea.

A farcical turf battle between the British occurred in Haidarabad. Nur Mohammed, who had succeeded his father as principal Amir in 1832, requested a British physician to attend him. Pottinger sent Dr Hathorn of the 15th Regiment, stationed in Cutch, to join Burnes. Lord Clare also sent a physician, Dr J F Heddle, on a steamer under Lt Corless. This was another British attempt to use a pretext – delivering the physician – to forward the survey of the Indus.

Although as Resident in Bhuj, Pottinger was subject to Lord Clare, as Envoy to Sind he had been appointed by Calcutta. Pottinger now argued that Clare had no right to send Dr Heddle as Calcutta was responsible for relations with Sind. This was the precise opposite of Pottinger's position when he had been despatching Burnes to Sind, and a direct insult to Clare who was, in all normal circumstances, Pottinger's boss. Pottinger instructed Burnes to stop Heddle from seeing the Amirs. Burnes complied, adding the breathtakingly hypocritical observation that to send a boat with Heddle was an unworthy ruse for spying. The Amirs refused to see Heddle and he left affronted, though Lt Corless' steam survey was to continue for two years. There now occurred a monumental disagreement between Burnes and Pottinger. It involved Pottinger's role as head of the Cutch Durbar, or Council of State, and seems to have concerned control over the port of Mandvi, which was important to British troop movements and where the Resident at Bhuj and the Rao of Cutch, had their summer residences. Burnes believed that Pottinger was abusing his authority against the interests of the Rao. By his own account, Pottinger was devastated by the blazing row. Four years later he was to write to the Governor-General:

> I am unwillingly obliged here to trouble Your Lordship by reverting to Sir Alexander Burnes' conduct to me [...] and to the long series of indignities and reprehension I suffered through the support his unfounded misrepresentations met with from the then Governor of Bombay, the late Sir Robert Grant [...] they were such as many persons would have sunk under [...] they bid fair for a time to blacken and ruin my public character [...] and [...] plunged me in a state of such misery and anxiety as I cannot at all describe[1]

Burnes had the opposite view, that Sir Robert Grant had not done enough:

> he was a good man but an execrable Governor, he meant well but did nothing [...] Is it true that the court have reversed the Mandavee decision? I cannot believe it. I do think however that they might leave the sovereignty (but only that) with the Rao. Nothing showed Grant's incapacity more, than his allowing Pottinger to bully as he did [...][2]

Life at Bhuj must have been very difficult. As Burnes was taking the side of the local ruler against the British Resident, it is unlikely that he was supported by the officers of the garrison. The rift, however, is not surprising. Burnes' description of Pottinger as bullying seems accurate, while Burnes' liberal views on Indian government would not have endeared him to Pottinger. Burnes believed that locals should be given much more responsibility. He wrote 'Men will say, "wait till they are ready." I can only say that, if you wait till men are fit for liberty, you will wait forever [...] Will a man ever learn to swim without going into the water?' Burnes doubted the entire Imperial venture: 'Instead of raising up a glorious monument to our memory, we shall impoverish India more thoroughly than Nadir, and become a greater curse to it than were the hordes of Timour.'[3]

Once the expansionist Lord Auckland arrived to take over as Governor-General, Pottinger was despatched to Sind to take up the Amirs' offer. Furthermore the Bombay Presidency was authorised to send troops into Sind if needed to deter the Sikhs from Shikarpur.

Wade gave the message to Ranjit Singh that the British Government 'could not but view with regret and disapprobation the prosecution of plans of unprovoked hostility, injurious to native states with whom that Government is connected'. It was enough, and Ranjit Singh cancelled his project against Shikarpur.[5]

The reinvigoration of Burnes' career was prompted by events in Persia. In Kandahar, the Dil Khans were alarmed by the ambition for eastward expansion of Mohammed, the new Shah of Persia, and by the continuing desire of Kamran Saduzai in Herat to attack them. They had therefore sent an Envoy, Aziz Muhammad Khan, to persuade the Persian Shah to enter an alliance for the removal of the Saduzais from Herat. The Ambassador's message finished with a rhetorical flourish that the Muslims of Afghanistan were ready to put themselves in the Shah's service for a united march to free Delhi from the infidel.

There was no chance of the mostly Sunni Afghans marching under the Shia Shah of Persia anywhere, but nonetheless the event was picked up by the British Ambassador in Tehran, Henry Ellis. He was getting nowhere in trying to conclude a new commercial treaty, while at the same time seeking an annulment of Britain's guarantees of defending Persia against European attack. Ellis reported that the Shah intended to invade Herat in the spring and press his claim to Kandahar and Ghazni as well, with Russian support.

Ellis suggested Britain needed an entirely new regional strategy:

> since, in such an event, Persia will not or dare not place herself in a condition of close alliance with Great Britain, our policy must be to consider her no longer an outwork for the defence of India, but as the first parallel from which the attack may be commenced or threatened.[6]

In response, on 25 June 1836 the President of the Board of Control, John Cam Hobhouse wrote to Lord Auckland, instructing him to act:

> whether by despatching a confidential agent to Dost Muhammad of Kabul merely to watch the progress of events, or to enter into relations with this chief, either of a political or merely, in the first instance, of a commercial character, we leave to your discretion, as well as the adoption of any other measures [. . .] in order to counteract Russian influence in that quarter, should you be satisfied [. . .] that the time has arrived [. . .] to interfere in the affairs of Afghanistan.[7]

There was never any real doubt who the confidential agent would be. Alexander Burnes was back in play. Auckland had already prepared a despatch to London outlining Burnes' mission and added in a postscript that he had anticipated Hobhouse's instructions.[8]

Auckland considered from the start the Burnes mission as a political one; it was never a purely commercial undertaking. Auckland gave private instructions to Burnes:

> I am unwilling to give the alarming colour of political speculation to a mission, the main object of which is commercial, but it is impossible to divest of political interest any observation of the Countries on the Indus and to the West of the river. It is difficult to see without some anxiety the exertions made on every occasion by the ruler of the Punjab to extend his power [. . .][9]

So Burnes' initial instruction was that his mission was not political, but that it was understood that this was 'impossible'. At this time Auckland saw Ranjit as the aggressor.

Alarm at Russian expansion caused a flurry of British intelligence activity which is the context of Burnes' mission. Russia was fighting spirited resistance in its newly-conquered Caucasus territories. Palmerston sent a British ship, the *Vixen*, into the Black Sea in 1836 to run arms to Dagestani rebels, under cover of a cargo of salt. It caused a diplomatic incident when the ship was intercepted by Russian forces, but Palmerston sent an assurance to the Russian Foreign Minister Nesselrode that the British government had no knowledge of the venture. Palmerston was an accomplished liar. The *Vixen* was part of widespread activity by the British secret service in sending arms and advisers to the Chechen, Dagestani and Circassian rebels, which has modern echoes. The operation had been organised by David Urquhart 'who had brought all the scattered mujahedin units together and even created a single command structure for them to direct their military action against the Russian army'.[10] Urquhart then took up his appointment as First Secretary at the British Embassy in Constantinople. Four years earlier Palmerston had organised secret smuggling of arms for the Polish uprising. Colin Mackenzie, who served in Kabul with Burnes, had taken part.[11] The anti-Russian mood of the British establishment went well beyond rhetoric.

Burnes' second navigation of the Indus is darkened by the shadow of looming disaster, and attention has naturally focused on events in Kabul at its conclusion. Burnes recounts this journey in his posthumously published *Cabool*. He was obliged to omit any reference to the diplomatic negotiations. But as a story of travel and adventure *Cabool* is a delightful book.

Alexander commanded a party of four British officers, the other three being Lieutenant Robert Leech of the Bombay Engineers, Lieutenant John Wood of the Indian (Company) Navy and Dr Percival Lord of the Bombay Medical Service and his instructions from the Government of India were:

to work out its policy of opening the River Indus to commerce, and establishing on its banks, and in the countries beyond it, such relations as should contribute to the desired end [...] to prosecute the commercial inquiries with extreme caution, [...] and in all to act so as to mark the anxious desire of the British Government for the restitution of tranquillity and for the establishment of friendly relations.[12]

Burnes was expected thoroughly to survey the rivers for steam navigation, to locate sources of wood, coal and other fuel, to explore the market for British manufactured goods, to report on possible trade routes and make commercial contacts, to outline the current agricultural and manufacturing output and prospects for future economic growth, to explore for mineral deposits capable of commercial exploitation, to find the best site to hold an annual trade fair on the Indus, and to negotiate with the various governments from Sind to Kabul for trade access, reduction of tariffs and protection of goods and merchants.

It is a tribute to the spirit of the age that scientific investigation of the geology and natural history of the region, including the collection of a large number of specimens of both flora and fauna, were considered part of the official activities of the mission and supported with public funds. Archaeological investigation and collection of ancient coins, artefacts and inscriptions held a kind of semi-official status, but were certainly approved activities. It went without saying that the mission was also to report on military forces and fortifications, the practicability of roads for artillery and the availability of food, fodder and shelter for armies.

The commercial mission was not simply a front for espionage. The British wanted to make money from new markets for what was still the world's most efficient manufacturing industry. They also believed that such trade would enrich the Afghans, stabilise their government, and bind them to Britain through commercial ties, all of which would increase their value as a buffer state to the Empire.

Accordingly the group carried manufacturers' samples to show Afghan merchants, and Burnes' instructions on security and tax immunity of British merchants and duties for British goods, were real business. I spent some of my own diplomatic career engaged in this kind of work. The pressure from taxpayers for diplomats to earn their keep by bringing a flow of wealth back to the home country is a constant political reality. Burnes' reports[13] on manufactures, commodities, raw materials, trading routes, distributors, retail outlets, financial networks and credit availability, prices, tariffs and tolls were painstaking. The British merchants to whom they were made available commented that you would think that Burnes had been nothing but a trader himself his whole life.[14]

Burnes' plan of establishing trade fairs to coincide with the Lohani tribal migrations made sense. These Afghan nomadic migrations were as much about trade as pasture. The maldar or wealthy nomad could be a merchant and financier on a large scale. Louis Dupree found this still to be true in the 1960s:

> the search for grass has its commercial side. In fact, several nomads told me that they consider herding secondary to trading. The system involves both cash and barter, with barter more important than cash in some areas. Items brought in by nomads include kerosene, matches, cloth, sugar, tea, spices, peppers, guns, ammunition, iron tools, milk and milk products, livestock, hides, leather, rugs, carpets.[15]

The Russian government had established an annual fair at Nizhni Novgorod to boost the trade with Central Asia which had been flowing through that city since at least the fourteenth century.[16] This had proved attractive to merchants from Central Asia and even India. It had been a huge investment – a then astonishing £1m in the trade grounds and warehouses, including flood containment works on the river. By 1836 40 per cent of all Russia's imports flowed through Nizhni Novgorod. Unfortunately, then as now, the Russian economy was not well developed for the production of consumer goods, and imports much exceeded exports. The annual caravan from Bokhara to Orenburg had 5,000 laden camels going out, but only 600 returning. Russia became alarmed at the outflow of bullion through the fair and tried from the 1820s to ban the export of ingots and coin, with little practical effect.

Burnes divided the work among his little mission – he took on most of the commercial, economic and political reporting, Lt John Wood as a naval man was naturally in charge of surveying the rivers, Lt Leech was tasked with noting the military features, and Dr Lord was asked to focus on geology and natural history. There was a fifth European with the party, a Goan Portuguese draughtsman named Jose Goncalves. Burnes had a new secretary, a young Parsi named Nourozji Fourdonji, a graduate of Elphinstone College, Bombay. Burnes had deliberately sought another young Indian to promote: 'I hope only that Nawazjee may do as well as Mohan Lal & I am sure of his being cherished by Government & of his deserving to be so – Having been instrumental in bringing forward a native of Delhi, I now feel anxious to do what I can for one of the Bombay Presidency that both may run the race fairly.'[17] The professional ranks of the mission were completed by Dr Mahomed Ali of the Bombay Medical Service, one of the first local doctors trained, again Burnes' deliberate choice.

The expedition set out from Bombay at midnight on 26 November 1836, after dinner hosted by the Governor on Malabar Point.[18] After a five-day halt in Mandvi, they sailed westward towards the Indus Delta, where they disembarked into Sind on 13 December. They were minus Dr Lord, who would be joining them further up river.

Burnes was delighted that many of the boatmen who had taken him up to Lahore on his previous trip were anxious to serve with him again. He noticed that the hostility towards the British which had been so dangerous six years earlier had almost disappeared. He also witnessed the extraordinary movement of channels and silt in the Indus Delta; he could now ride his horse for two miles up what had been the main channel last time. Twenty-three-year-old Lieutenant Wood from Perth had already spent two seasons exploring the lower Indus on a specially constructed steam boat. The British had put the first steamer on the Indus, under the command of twenty-one-year-old Lieutenant Corless, only three years after Burnes' pioneering voyage up it.

Sailing up the Indus, the mission met Corless and Pottinger sailing down, after the latter had concluded negotiations with the Amirs. Pottinger briefed Burnes on his success, which included further free trade provisions and a permanent British Resident at Shikarpur.[19] Burnes noted that all this only formalised what he had been offered by the Amirs on 5 December 1835 but Metcalfe had vetoed. He also briefed in detail Sayyid Azimal Din, who had been appointed British Agent at Karachi, finding Din 'a highly qualified public servant'.

On 27 December, proceeding slowly up river in luxurious state jumtis supplied by the Amirs, Burnes received instructions from Auckland to establish communication direct with John McNeill, and co-ordinate their positions. Burnes wrote, 'the state of Persia and her designs backed by Russia already engage attention & before I reach Tatta on my commercial mission I find the seeds to be sown for important political concerns. I shall give this subject my most anxious consideration.'[20]

Lieutenant Wood was continually out in small boats conducting detailed measurement. Burnes agreed that Wood should dictate the pace of their progress, as his work was at this stage the most important, characterising this trip as a 'survey' compared to which his first voyage was a 'reconaissance'.

At Tatta Burnes noted the very large numbers of African slaves. 'They were shipped from Muscat via Karachi but also through British held Cutch. Every Mahomedan who can afford it purchases them [...] All people who have shops of the better order have slaves.'[21]

Burnes' instructions from Macnaghten included a demand on the Amirs of Sind to stop the raids on Indus traffic by the Mazari tribes, who inhabited the northern limit of the Amirs' territories. The instructions were based on a report on Mazari depredations by Mohan Lal. Before Burnes could take action, Ranjit Singh seized on this excuse for further aggrandisement. He annexed the Mazari capital of Roghan and then razed a frontier fort garrisoned by Shikarpur itself, and mobilised Sikh forces on the frontier. It became plain that the efforts of Burnes' mission to open the commerce of the Indus could be jeopardised by the start of a major war along its banks.

In Haidarabad they were enthusiastically received by the Amirs, who offered to accompany them as far as Shikarpur, with the intention of deterring any move by the Sikh army on Mithankot.[22] Burnes reported that the Amirs could field 32,000 men between them, but none of their artillery was serviceable. He noted the extensive links between the Shia Amirs in Sind, and religious shrines in Persia, and constant communications between the Sind and Persian religious hierarchy and ruling families. He saw danger in this if Persia gained ground in Afghanistan: 'if the King of Persia were successful in his present expedition, the religious commerce that exists between Sinde & Persia might avail the enemies of India'.[23]

On 2 February 1837 Burnes wrote a letter from Haidarabad to Masson in Kabul, explaining his mission:

Hydrabad in Sinde
2 February 1837

My Dear Sir,
You will doubtless have heard rumours [...] of my having been deputed by Lord Auckland to conduct a Mission up the Indus to Attock and thence by Peshawar to Cabool, Candahar and Shikapoor [...]

the main and great aim of Government is to open the Indus and to inform the Chiefs in Afghanistan and the merchants [...] of the arrangements that have been entered into – Runjeet Sing threatened Sinde and was alone prevented by British influence from attacking it – the Government said justly that if the balance of power on the Indus is destroyed our commercial hopes are ruined and we therefore concluded a Treaty with the Ameers taking them under our protection and fixing a British Agent in Sinde.

We have no wish to extend our political relations beyond the River but a great one to enter into friendly commercial ones [...] I shall travel with as little parade as possible [...] unsuited particularly for the duty which I am executing –

I go to Mittun to be present at a Congress [...] of the Vakeels of Lahore, Bhawulpore and I hope Sinde who with Cap. Wade, Mr Mackison and myself are to fix upon a site for a bazar and arrangements similar to Nijni Novogorod [...]

We hardly know what is the object of this invasion of Herat and here I can scarcely find out if the King has advanced on it or not – if he has [...] I would not be surprised at the British Government withdrawing their Ambassador from his Court –

To Dost Mahomed Khan I should feel obliged by your expressing my remembrance of his kindness [...] Tell the Nawab [...] that he lives always in my remembrance and I have some hundreds of kinds of seed for him [...]

My Dear Sir
Yours sincerely and faithfully
Alex Burnes[24]

Mohan Lal joined the party at Haidarabad, having been sent, not now as munshi but as an agent on Rs250 a month. Burnes was delighted at their reunion.

Pottinger, who detested the Amirs and their capital, was less than delighted to be appointed to the Residency at Haidarabad. However he remained also Resident in Bhuj. An Assistant, Lieutenant Eastwick, was appointed in Haidarabad on the substantial monthly salary of Rs1,000, on the understanding Pottinger would be much of the time away. The Court of Directors declared itself delighted with the results of Pottinger's diplomacy. They were, however, disappointed that he had not been able to sell the Amirs an iron steam boat for the Indus which the Company had speculatively sent to Haidarabad.[25]

Since Burnes' first river mission, the work of surveying the Indus had proceeded apace.[26] Claude Wade had set out with Mohan Lal, Lieutenant Mackeson and a Mr Hodge, and conducted a survey sailing down the Sutlej and then the Indus as far as Bhawalpur,[27] where Mackeson moved his station. In January 1836, Charles Hugel noted Mackeson an excellent linguist and 'a most intelligent young officer, who has accepted a place in a desert, 300 miles from Ludhiana, where he will have to superintend and protect the English vessels in the navigation of the Indus [...]'[28] In both 1836 and 1837 surveying missions under Lieutenant Corless drew up charts and maps of the river from the sea to Mithankot.[29]

The British had also taken practical steps to encourage Afghan merchants to participate in the Indus trade. In Kabul, Karamat Ali was instructed by Wade to

> tell all the merchants [...] of the establishment of a mart at Mithenkote and the advantage of their finding a market at that place for the fruits of Cabul [...] whatever quantity of fruits they may bring [...] they will find purchase for it among the merchants of Hindustan and other parts who will supply them with any kinds of goods they may require. By this means they will be saved the trouble and inconvenience to which they are exposed on a long journey through the Punjab to Hindustan.[30]

After Masson replaced Karamat, he took up the promotion of the Mithankot market with renewed zeal, working with the major Kabuli merchant Mullah

Khair al-Din. Masson drew up a list of those British articles for which he believed a ready market existed in Kabul and beyond, replacing Russian items of inferior quality:

> Chintzes, fine calicos, muslins, shawls [...] broad-cloth, velvet, paper, cutlery, china, gold and silver lace, gold thread, buttons, needles, sewing silks and cotton thread, iron bars, copper, tin, brass, quicksilver, iron and steel wire, looking glasses [...]

The notion was not fantastic. In 1835 Central Asia had not yet slipped from regional trading hub to backwater, and was not economically far behind Iran and India. Khiva, Bokhara and Khokand were undergoing a period of economic resurgence. Afghanistan was recovering from the years of civil war. Incorporating Central Asia into the economic system of the British Empire was not judged unprofitable by those who studied it closely. The impracticality lay in creating the political conditions for the incorporation.

Ranjit Singh proved keen on opening up the Indus to commerce. He was persuaded to invest in sending a cargo of opium and Cashmere shawls by boat down the Sutlej and Indus, to be trans-shipped at Karachi, and on to Bombay. The Company provided a Dr Gardner to accompany Ranjit's goods safely through Sind. The speculation was deemed a success.[31]

All Burnes' missions appear to have been remarkably free of friction between the participants, and fast friendships were formed. Admiral Charles Malcolm (John's brother) had in 1836 instructed Lieutenant Wood to carry out the survey work on the lower Indus. He now wrote on 4 May to Wood approving his proposed surveying techniques for the Burnes mission, adding 'I am very happy to find that you continue to be so well pleased with the chief of the expedition.'[32] This larger mission gave Burnes more chance to exhibit his talent as a leader. Malcolm also notes that he had advised Burnes to take an additional midshipman to help with soundings and sextant readings, but Burnes had declined as he was under instructions to keep down expenses.

Alexander was anxious to further Mohan Lal's prospects and get others to accept that an Indian could be a competent officer, given responsibility. While the mission was in progress, he sent reports by Mohan Lal direct to the Governor-General, pointing out that this was not because they were prepared by 'an Asiatic', but because they were 'a very useful public document'.[33]

The mission, in addition to the four British officers, consisted of sixty people, quite a substantial camp. In addition to two surveyors, there were various categories of servant, cook, groom, grasscutter, and an escort of irregular cavalry. Before reaching the Khyber they had been augmented by a harem of Kashmiri concubines and six Arab bodyguards.[34] In addition qasids were continually arriving and being despatched again, with McNeill in Persia, Pottinger in Sind, Masson in Kabul, Mackeson on the Indus, Wade in Ludhiana, Macnaghten in Calcutta and the Court of Directors in London, not to mention personal mail. Burnes paid the qasids Rs40 to carry mail from Dera Ghazi Khan on the Indus to Kabul, with a promise of a further Rs40 when they returned with confirmation of delivery. The parsimonious Masson paid Rs25 for the same journey.[35]

This was a time of financial strain for the Company. Trade was depressed, the great Calcutta banking houses had collapsed, and there had been major falls in the prices of tea, opium and cotton.

The 'Great Panic' of 1837 was the first truly global banking crisis as confidence evaporated in New York, London, Moscow, Calcutta and Beijing. The drive to open up the Indus as a new area of commercial opportunity should be seen against this background. Britain was in the turmoil of the greatest economic collapse of the nineteenth century, from 1836 to 1843, when the textile industries in particular, after a period of massive expansion of factory production, found the home market unable to absorb their products. In summer of 1837 there were 50,000 unemployed workers in Manchester.[36] The numerous reports Burnes sent back on the prospects of selling British woollen cloth to Central Asia, continued a quest for elusive markets for broadcloth that runs as a woollen thread through the history of the EIC, but also reflected an urgent national priority in 1837.

CHAPTER NINETEEN

## The Gathering Storm

Back in London the Court of Directors were therefore keeping a close eye on Indus policy. John Stuart Mill wrote to Auckland with a comprehensive clarification of the Company's views.

1. The communications with Runjeet Sing on [Sind] were very skilfully conducted by Captain Wade [...] Though [the Maharaja] has not renounced his claims on Shirkapoor he has recalled his troops [...] and has apparently abandoned all serious thought of prosecuting an enterprize by which he now knows he would forfeit the friendship of the British Government.

2. Meanwhile your reasonable demonstration of a determination to preserve the integrity of the Sinde state has had a most beneficial effect upon our relationship with the Ameers [...] Every request of Colonel Pottinger with regard to the navigation of the river, is now granted as soon as made, and no facilities for commerce [...] are likely to be refused [...] The survey of the river is in progress [...] The Ameers have consented that a British Officer should be stationed in their country [...]

3. Both Runjeet Sing and the Ameers have given a favorable reception to the suggestions which you have made to them, for the establishment of Fairs (resembling those on the Russian Frontier) [...] one of these fairs to be held at Tatta, or Shirkapore, and the other at Mithenkote. The commercial Mission of Captain Burnes, by the Indus and Attock, to Cabul and Candahar, will tend to supply information from which you may better judge of the expediency of establishing these fairs [...]

4. The intelligence we have received of the progress of Captain Burnes as far as Attock is satisfactory [...]

5. The state of Afghanistan is apparently becoming more and more unsettled, but any observations which it may be thought proper to make on this subject will be addressed to you by the Secret Committee. We approve however of the intimation you have made to Shah Shooja, that if he makes any further attempts to recover his throne by means of an armed force, he will forfeit his Asylum in the British Territories.[1]

On 10 April 1837 Auckland therefore wrote to Burnes instructing that he inform Dost Mohammed that 'The circumstance of the British Government having resolved decidedly to discourage the prosecution by the Ex-King, Shah Shooja-ool-Moolk [. . .] from further schemes of hostility'[2] was proof of Britain's friendly intent.

John McNeill, now British Ambassador in Persia, had also in January 1837 advised Auckland against backing Shuja, sending him a lengthy memorandum which concluded: 'I cannot venture to affirm that [. . .] it would be wise to identify our interests with those of the Suddozais.'[3] When Auckland was invited at the beginning of 1837 to attend the spectacular wedding ceremonies of Ranjit Singh's favourite grandson, Nao Nehal Singh, Auckland declined precisely to avoid giving offence to Dost Mohammed and causing problems for Burnes' mission.[4] Sir Henry Fane, Commander-in-Chief, represented him.

The events of 1837 were to make the commercial aspects of Burnes' mission irrelevant. Suddenly Afghanistan became the scene of warfare above the normal border skirmishes and tribal disputes. Dost Mohammed's informants in Peshawar noted the withdrawal of most of the occupying Sikh forces to participate in the wedding in Lahore and Amritsar, and the tardiness of those forces in returning (due to conflicts over pay arrears).[5] Seizing the moment, Dost Mohammed declared jihad and launched an army towards Peshawar, and in May 1837 the Afghans, under Dost Mohammed's valiant sons Afzul and Akbar, inflicted a close but bloody defeat on the Sikhs at Jamrud.

Ranjit Singh's best general, Hari Singh, was killed, leading a charge of cavalry in an attempt to secure captured guns. He was felled by cannon fire, alongside the cavalry commander, a Colonel Gordon (known to the Sikhs as Carron). These were staggering blows to the dangerously ill Ranjit. Hari had been the driving force behind the occupation of Peshawar, about which Ranjit Singh had entertained serious doubts. Jamrud marked the end of the extraordinary expansion of the Sikh Empire.

It now became certain that the new Shah of Persia, Mohammed Mirza, was determined to launch a major assault on Herat, the western key to Afghanistan and last territory of the Saduzai dynasty. This in the face of strenuous objections to the Shah from McNeill, who believed the war was being urged on by his Russian counterpart – something Nesselrode constantly denied to Palmerston.

Burnes not only faced a war ahead of him, but also sniping from the rear. Pottinger used his longer experience to discredit Burnes' reports. On 15 April 1837, he wrote to Charles Metcalfe:

I have nothing to do with Capt. Burnes' reports other than to pass them on [...] I have seen enough of them to satisfy me that his information is incorrect. He asserts in one of them that Karachee had been [...] 'for ages' the sea port of Scinde and dwells on the 'beaten path' thence to Tattah as the desirable one for a passage – so far from this being the case, Karachee was only taken from the Khan of Kelat (Beloochistan) by the present Emirs in 1795 [...][6]

Pottinger was being pedantic;[7] Burnes' point was simply that Karachi would be the best site to develop a commercial port. Today one of the busiest areas of Karachi is Burnes Road.[8]

After leaving Haidarabad Burnes started to encounter discipline problems with his growing party,. Some of their servants got drunk and robbed and beat a shopkeeper, and he noted 'we have had great difficulty in keeping our people in order & a scuffle followed by abuse left me no remedy but to sober the offenders by cold water and a few stripes which latter I abhor as a punishment.'[9] As the Amirs were relaxed about it, Wood was detached to spend his time surveying the river. Burnes was now travelling up river with the Amirs, who were on a hunting expedition. The hunting consisted of shooting from hides at penned animals driven towards them. Burnes found it very dull: 'The weather seems to have no influence on the Ameer – it rains – it blows – he goes to hunt notwithstanding – his passion seems almost a disease.' After enduring a fortnight of this, they finally had an audience of dismissal from Amir Nur Mahommed Khan at Nasri on 16 February 1837.

Burnes declared the meeting 'shewed the Ameer in a light truly favourable'. He fully supported British proposals for Indus commerce, and said he would send a vakeel (advocate) to the meeting at Mithankot. Moreover, he stated that he understood that the recent agreement concluded with Henry Pottinger meant the British would be taking control of the country. He stated his trust that the Amirs would receive the kind of 'munificent treatment' accorded the Emperor at Delhi.[10] They were to be greatly disappointed.

On 25 February the party were sent a present of cooked fowl by a local Sayyid. Burnes found the bird's feet unusual, and sent out bearers to capture some live specimens to be recorded.[11] He bemoaned in his diary the absence of a qualified naturalist on the expedition, but himself catalogued the longtailed grass warbler, *Prinia* or *Laticilla Burnesii*, among hundreds of samples sent back.

Burnes had received letters of welcome from his friend Rustam Khan of Khairpur, and as promised a fleet of vessels awaited his mission at the frontier when they arrived on 1 March.

Alexander had suggested Dera Ghazi Khan as the site for the proposed Indus inland port and trade fair. Wade proposed Mithankot as an alternative, and requested the meeting of British Agents and local vakeels there. Wade also believed their display at Mithankot would be a deterrent to Ranjit's designs in that direction. Ranjit accepted the invitation to send a vakeel to the meeting, and cautioned the Amirs through Burnes that it was in their interest to follow suit.[12] Burnes wrote to Wade

> I have notified to all the chiefs and merchants [. . .] that such a meeting was to take place at Mithankote; and as it has naturally excited the greatest interest at Shikarpoor and other marts, and has been to them a solid proof that the British Government has in earnest taken up the subject of the Indus trade, it is of the first importance to keep our faith and word on this point.

On 16 March they reached Khairpur, where they were entertained by Rustam Khan enthusiastically for sixteen days. Rustam repeatedly pressed Burnes for a separate treaty of friendship, which Burnes was not empowered to give. Here they were joined by their surgeon, Percival Lord. A graduate of both Dublin and Edinburgh universities, Lord had been selected for his strong linguistic skills. They became the first Europeans to be admitted to the famous fortress of Baikhar.[13] When Burnes asked Rustam to act to prevent depredations on the Indus trade by the Mazari tribe, Rustam threw all the nearest Mazari leaders and their families into the dungeons of Baikhar, and Burnes had to persuade him to be more gentle.

Mazari raids had been the pretext for a move of Sikh troops into the area around Mithankot, and on 23 March Burnes received news that Ranjit Singh had agreed to withdraw forces and leave Burnes to settle the question.[14] This pre-empted a vakeel from the Khan of Kelat, the Baluch and Brahui kingdom ruled from the mountains west of Sind, who reached Khairpur on 28 March offering Kelati forces to help expel the Sikhs.[15] The Envoy pointed out that Burnes' proposed return route through the Bolan Pass to Shikarpur ran through the territory of the Khan of Kelat, and asked that he pay a courtesy visit.[16] Burnes wrote to Macnaghten requesting permission to do so.[17]

The party were entertained to a nautch by Jewan Baksh, a wealthy courtesan who built mosques and funded charity work among the poor. Burnes found her 'a girl with delicate fey melancholy features. Her troupe danced into the small hours, portraying tales of soldiers, lovers and jealous husbands', until they collapsed in alcoholic stupour.[18]

To Alexander, Rustam already 'seemed to have an excellent idea of the designs of Russia – He talked of their strategy & their designs on India, their power in Persia, their large army'. Burnes replied that Russia lacked financial muscle.[19] The fear of Russian designs towards India was not a purely British preoccupation.

From 2 to 9 April the mission stayed at Shikarpur, collecting much information from the great commercial and financial market, where Burnes found many merchants who had connections to people he knew in Kabul and Bokhara. The town was large, prosperous and 90 per cent Hindu. Burnes noted that the women were attractive. He found some caution towards the Mithankot fair from merchants who wished to protect local monopolies. British ironware was on sale in the market, and Burnes noticed: 'our camp is pitched near a field of [poppy] – The smell near the fields is very sickening & the people employed in collecting the opium say that they are half intoxicated at night – They split the head of the top with a three pronged knife & collect the juice which exudes in a clam shell.'

On 10 April the mission moved on to Mulaman where Burnes lectured the refractory Bundi chief, Sher Mohamed Khan, about the advantages of peace and trade. Here Burnes hired six Arab bodyguards 'to keep away thieves and robbers', who became closely attached to him.[20] Emily Eden met these men and noted they were of Arab descent rather than from Arab lands.[21] After two days' excellent progress, they reached Gandava where Burnes sent a musical box and a map to the thirteen-year-old Nassir Khan, heir to Kelat, who was being educated there, and collected mineral samples from the Gandava Hills. Burnes noted in his journal that all the treaties Britain made about the Indus were as little known to the officials and rulers on its banks as they were in Timbuktu. He was also concerned that he had invited a great gathering of chiefs, vakeels and merchants to Mithankot to discuss the trade fair, but had still heard nothing from Wade. He learnt that Henry's nephew, Lieutenant Eldred Pottinger, who had passed through Shikarpur ahead of him, was with a caravan detained by a local war at the entrance to the Bolan Pass, which Eldred was charged with surveying. Eldred was escorted by Edul Khan of the Sind Irregular Horse, who was instructed to get him to Herat then rejoin Burnes in Kabul.[22] Pottinger was travelling in the stock disguise of a horse dealer.

Burnes himself was vexed that he had not been given the power to settle the Mazari border dispute, which he felt he could have done in 'a couple of days', but instead had to refer it back to Macnaghten.[23] He found that no chief believed his mission was purely commercial 'some laugh, some are silent', and confided to his journal that history showed they were right to distrust the British.

On 18 April they arrived at the frontier of Bhawal Khan and transferred into luxurious state barges, with an escort of forty scarlet uniformed soldiers 'we found all the usual kindness [. . .] and we gladly exchanged our comfortless boats for these – I must not forget to state that among the supplies for us is one boat literally full of bedsteads!!' Scores of people were provided to haul the boats against the current. Burnes again wrote praising Bhawal Khan's assistance and lavish hospitality, and suggesting some reciprocation from the Governor-General.[24] This time the purse strings of the Raj were opened, and the Governor-General sent Bhawal Khan a small wooden orrery, an astronomical device.[25]

Burnes was very happy with the progress of young Nourozji Fourdonji, who was becoming 'a useful public servant' quicker than expected, while Mohan Lal was 'all I could wish [...] the very person I could select to communicate with the chiefs and people I meet', but he was becoming a little careworn. He added 'I find a good deal of trouble in managing the details of this little mission & journey.'[26]

On reaching Ahmedpur, they much enjoyed Bhawal Khan's company, and met the commander of his regular infantry Hamish McGregor McPherson, a British officer cashiered duelling, who Burnes had helped back in 1831 (probably financially).[27] Bhawal Khan sent what Burnes called the corps de ballet to keep his guests company, as noted in Burnes' diary 'in a big house where every whisper was re-echoed'. Presumably there were many hushed endearments.

They proceeded with Bhawal Khan to Bhawalpur where Burnes received a 'very friendly' letter from Ranjit, complaining however about the border settlements. Burnes noted, 'The Haidarabad Ameers, who deserved little, have got everything & in this we have managed to offend Roostum Khan, Bhawal Khan and Runjeet, the great, greater & greatest of our friends.'

Burnes, Leech, Lord and Wood were at dinner in Bhawal Khan's guest lodging with McPherson, when Benoit Argoud first arrived. Alex went out to greet him, insisting that he join their meal. Argoud had started as a drummer boy in the Napoleonic service, and worked his way up to officer rank. After Napoleon's fall, he had served in the Turkish army before enlisting with Ranjit Singh as a Colonel in 1836. An extremely brave individual, though alcoholic, he had been the only one of Singh's European officers to confront the Maharaja about his salary arrears. He had obtained his back pay, but also his dismissal. He was now heading for the Bolan Pass and Kandahar, to seek employment with Dost Mohammed in Kabul.

There followed a drunken evening. Argoud in his cups liked to show his prowess as a drummer by beating out rhythms on the table, 'and as a tenor accompaniment, made a knife vibrate between its under surface and his thumb' to loud applause. Argoud however 'knew not when to desist', but fortunately soon drank himself into a stupor and they put him to bed.

The next morning Burnes slept in, hungover. Argoud woke up, and passed Percival Lord, who was sitting in the hall performing taxidermy on a duck. Argoud, still not sober, then crashed into Burnes' room:

> That officer was not yet dressed, on which M. Argoud called out: 'Why sare, the battle of Wagram was fought before this hour, and you are still in deshabille? Will you take wine with me?' 'No,' said Captain Burnes, 'I never take wine before breakfast.' 'Then sare,' said Argoud, 'You insult me and I demand satisfaction.' He ran out and soon reappeared with his small sword and asked Burnes to send for his rapier. But the latter, thinking he had humoured the fiery little Frenchman quite enough, politely requested him to continue his journey.[28]

This amusing interlude could have gone horribly wrong. Argoud eventually did reach Kabul through Bolan. Burnes kept a friendly eye on him through Masson, and continued correspondence with the Frenchman, though noting, 'poor creature he is I fear both insane and drunk'. Dost Mohammed, though he allowed Argoud to remain in Kabul, did not offer him employment.

But Burnes now received disappointing news:

> I have heard from Cap. Wade who is not coming to Mittuncote – How is our faith & word to be kept with the merchants & chiefs of Sinde if this meeting does not take place – I confess I do not see how and I have written so to Wade – We must await his answer – I have had a mesh of intricacies in this journey already.[29]

The mission had not been idle. On 11 May Burnes sent back Lord's reports on the mineral resources of the Gandava Hills, and on the trade of Shikarpur and Upper Sind by himself, the latest section of Indus survey by Wood, and a basic grammar of the Brahui language and a survey of Mandvi's port by Leech. They were now progressing up river with following winds (why they had not been given the use of an Indus steam boat is unclear). At Mithankot, Burnes had been very disappointed to receive a letter from Wade proposing that Burnes continue straight up the Indus, without calling in to Lahore or seeing Ranjit Singh, in view of 'the peculiar disposition of his Highness and his advisers', following both Jamrud and British pressure on Ranjit not to attack Sind.[30]

Burnes found Mithankot itself 'a mean town' of about 3,000 inhabitants, two miles from the Indus, and so prone to inundation that any fair site would need to be three miles from the river. He thought it was the wrong site. It appears from his journal the grand meeting planned with merchants and vakeels did not happen.

The mission pushed on into Derajat. Since Burnes' last Indus mission, the Sikhs had taken firmer control of this district. Bhawal Khan had held it as tributary of Ranjit Singh, but his forces had been pushed out and General Ventura installed as Sikh Governor. In consequence annual Sikh revenues there had increased from two and a half to eleven and a half lakhs. 'The town of Multan has a prosperous appearance, which is altogether attributable to M.

Ventura, who was until lately in charge of it. Under Bahawal Khan the officers were guilty of the greatest extortion, but since 1832, when the Sikhs recovered it, the place has greatly recovered.'[31] Unlike other areas under direct Sikh control, Ventura had not suppressed Muslim religious practice or committed random atrocities.

Burnes now received urgent news from John McNeill, written from Teheran on 13 March. McNeill told Burnes that the Shah was absolutely set on taking Herat, and that given constant Herati raids – including one in October 1834 when the Heratis took 10,000 slaves – the Persians were justified. Nonetheless, McNeill viewed this as a dangerous development given Russian influence in Persia. Representatives of Persia, Russia and Herat were all gathered at Kabul. One of the parties in Russian pay, Mir Mohammed Khan, was also in McNeill's pay, and he had in consequence obtained copies of the entire correspondence. All the Afghan factions were vying with each other in expressing allegiance to Persia, each hoping to further their own ambitions.

The letter which Dost Mohammed had written to the Shah of Persia is a key document. Burnes, McNeill and Masson all argued that the Emir was merely insuring himself against the expected Persian move, and reacting to the absence of offers from the British, with whom Dost would prefer an alliance. Who, they argued, could possibly prefer an alliance with Persia to one with Britain? But Dost Mohammed's appraisal of the dangers of British alliance has a ring of sincerity:

> I have been long engaged in war with 100,000 horse and foot of the wicked infidels [Sikhs] and 300 guns, but [...] I have not yet been subdued by the faithless enemy, and have been able to preserve the true faith. But how long shall I be able to oppose this detestable tribe and [...] resist their aggression? [...] As [...] Kandahar, and the capital Kabul, and the countries bordering on Khorosan [...] form part of the Persian territory and are among the Kingdoms of the King of Kings, the misery and welfare of these dominions cannot be separated from the interests of the Persian Government [...] I shall persist in contending with the Seiks as long as I am able, but [...] [if] I am unable to resist that diabolical tribe, then I [...] must commit myself with the English, who will then obtain complete authority over the whole of Afghanistan, and it remains to be seen hereafter to what places and to what extent the flame of the violence of that nation will be carried.[32]

McNeill's own view of the policy Britain should adopt was clear: actively to promote a strong and united Afghanistan under Dost Mohammed. He urged that Britain should finance Dost to take both Herat and Kandahar and that current British policy was mistaken as 'we cannot make Persia [...] [both] strong against Russia and powerless against Afghanistan [...]'[33]

Burnes was buoyed that McNeill's opinion was identical to his own. He felt he had been thrust into the centre of events in a way that justified his decision to turn down the offer of the Persia mission. He also felt that this was the time to cash in on his fame and his London contacts – including the influence with Auckland he had gained at Bowood House. On 12 May 1837, camped outside the town of Uch, Burnes wrote a letter to Auckland, not as usual through Macnaghten, the Political Secretary, but rather through Colvin, the Private Secretary. In later sending Masson a copy, Burnes stressed this was not an official letter.

Burnes first gave Auckland the news that Dost had opened diplomatic correspondence with Persia. Burnes attributes this to British neglect of Dost and the latter's desire for Persian aid to recover Peshawar, and to deflect any Persian attack on Kabul via Herat. Burnes then gets to the crux. He suggests Britain should promise to assist Dost to recover Peshawar and the right bank of the Indus down to Shikarpur – but only on the death of Ranjit Singh. The Emir would be a stable and commerce-friendly ruler, and if supported by Britain, a bulwark against Persian and Russian intrigue.

Having set out his policy recommendation, the still-inexperienced Burnes overplayed his hand. He pointed out that he had discussed the matter with Charles Grant and with then Prime Minister Earl Grey. This name-dropping would scarcely awe Auckland, and was too obvious an attempt by a mere Captain to impose on the Governor-General.[34]

On 6 June, from Multan, Burnes wrote his reply to McNeill, more fully than to Auckland,[35] explaining his own strategy for the north-west frontier. Alexander accepted the alliance with Ranjit Singh and that it would be wrong to act contrary to his interests. But Burnes pointed out that Ranjit Singh was going to die soon.

Burnes reasoned that Dost's stable administration would be the best lynchpin for British commerce. His proposal was not outlandish: restore to Kabul the Indus territories down to and including Shikarpur. These had all been a part of the Dourani Empire recently, and all had a largely Muslim indigenous population. For Ranjit Singh: 'let him keep Peshawar while he lives and meantime [let us] turn Dost Mahomed Khan's attention towards Candahar and Herat'. This fitted with McNeill's proposal. Burnes continued, 'As for Suddozye ascendancy in Cabool, I consider that quite hopeless, either from Kamran, or Shoojah ool Moolk; the former, by the way, is said to be dying of dropsy, and the latter has not the head to manage anything.'

He concluded: 'On all these points I hope soon to be better informed, and before I get to Cabool to find myself invested with other authority than what I now hold.' He explained to Masson, 'As yet I have no authority beyond that of conducting a commercial Mission, but various hints [...] have served to convince me that a stirring time of political action has arrived and I shall have to shew what my Govt. is made of as well as myself.'

Letters from both McNeill and Burnes passed through Wade on the way to Auckland. Wade added comments, and on 27 June forwarded McNeill's letter with a lengthy one from himself, arguing strenuously against the consolidation of Afghanistan. Wade argued that the division of Afghanistan made its weak rulers more susceptible to British influence, Dost's rule would never be accepted, and if he moved against Herat then Kamran would turn to Persia.

Burnes sent Masson copies of all the British secret correspondence; the letters to him from McNeill and the Governor-General, Wade's report of the consequences of the battle of Jamrud, and the reports of his agents in Afghanistan and Bokhara, together with copies of all his replies. He asked Masson for his advice, 'well assured as I am that in putting you in possession of these important documents, I am but advancing the interests of Government'.[36]

He realised that sending Masson all this diplomatic correspondence was irregular. Burnes also forwarded two letters for Masson from Pottinger, who was carrying out his promise of defying the Calcutta prohibition on his communication with Masson.

When Burnes did receive further instructions, they told him to wait at the Indus, as active war had again broken out over Peshawar, right on Burnes' route. But a few days later he received a letter from John Colvin in which Auckland gave him permission to go on if it appeared safe.[37] Burnes wrote to James Holland from the Indus on 5 July 1837:

> another express still cries pause, but places a vast latitude in my hands and 'forward' is my motto; forward to the scene of carnage where, instead of embarrassing my Government, I feel myself in a situation to do good [...] I can hardly say how grateful I feel to Lord Auckland. I have not as yet got the replies to my recommendations on our line of policy[38]

Burnes sent letters to Dost, to Jabbar Khan and to the religious leader Mirza Sarwar Khan urging them to come to terms with Ranjit Singh over Peshawar lest they hamstring relations with Britain. In asking Masson to deliver these letters, he said 'it will never do to offend Runjeet Sing whose alliance we court and must cherish'.[39]

Conventional accounts of the Great Game have tended to stress the role of the Imperial powers, but to ignore the existence as independent players of states like Kabul, Persia, Lahore, Kelat and Sind. While Burnes was leaving Sind, a Persian Envoy and Agent, Qambar Ali, was arriving at Kandahar for a mission there and to Kabul. His instructions were very detailed, and in many ways mirror those of Burnes, including on intelligence gathering:

When you pass by the boundary of Kerman [...] you will detail the following particulars [...] namely the state of the towns and villages [...] an estimate of the population and strength of the tribes at such places, Seistanees, Beloochees, Afghans and Kuzzilbashes, an account of the revenue and expenditure of these countries, their produce, their principal cultivation, & from what kind of cultivation most profit is made: and an account of the taxes [...] and of the impact of commerce; finally whether there is water on the road and whether the latter is level or mountainous [...]

passing through Beloochistan, you must raise great expectations of the munificence of His Majesty in the minds of the Khans of Beloochistan and Seeistan [...] All these Khans should [...] prepare their troops [...] they are to join the Royal Stirrup.

At Kandahar he will deliver the firman and robes of honour to Kohundil Khan [...] and excite his hopes of the generosity of His Majesty [...] Kohundil Khan must undertake to send one of his brothers in advance to the Court while he himself will [...] await the arrival of the Royal Army. He will get his troops in readiness and prepare as much cavalry as is practicable for please God the campaign of Herat will be entrusted to him [...] Kumber Ali Khan will form an acquaintance with all the persons in authority and with the Afghan and Kuzzilbash Khans as well as with the Kuzzilbashes in general. The object will be to excite their hopes of generosity [...]

When he has finished his affairs in Candahar he will proceed to Kabul and deliver a dagger as a mark of His Majesty's favor to Dost Mohammed Khan, and he will convey the auspicious robes of honour to Nawab Jubber Khan. He [...] will give them the strongest assurances that after the arrival of the royal army in those countries, favors of every description shall be unceasingly lavished on them [...] and he will declare that, please God, Dost Mohammed Khan shall enjoy the royal favor to such an extent that these countries shall be placed completely in his possession, and he shall have entire control over them [...][40]

Persian diplomacy was no less sophisticated than British. The Persians thought Dost the best man to rule all Afghanistan as a Persian tributary, but this was to be kept from other Afghan rulers. Burnes recognised that Qambar Ali was engaged in the same game as himself. He commented to McNeill on seeing these intercepted instructions: 'Why the Government of India in despatching me to Bokhara gave me nothing so perfect, and in my present journey, tho' they are as anxious for accurate information as it is possible, they do not put forward so accurate an outline [...]'[41]

Poor Dr Gerard had died of malaria shortly before Burnes reached India. His final months, at the small post of Subatu, had been miserable. He had spent a year travelling back from Persia due to long halts to recover his health. In consequence he had been absent from duty, and the Company caused problems over his pay and expenses. While Burnes received both an allowance and a substantial bonus, all Gerard got was eventual agreement that he would receive the same money for the entire period of his travels as he would have got on normal duty with the engineering corps.[42] The government refused to accept most of his expenses and his bills were repudiated.

Burnes was pursued everywhere by creditors bearing bills for Gerard. He received some which he had no doubt were genuine, and was exasperated at the attitude of the Company, advised by Claude Wade, in refusing to meet them. From Dera Ghazi Khan on 2 June 1837 Burnes wrote to Masson:

> I have come to the resolution of paying those of Dr Gerard from my own pocket if I cannot move Government and [. . .] have already advanced 2300 Rs at Shikapore – but national honor is too dear at present to be swapped for a few thousand rupees and if poor Gerard himself were alive I know he would have lived on bread and water to avoid it. I have [. . .] no doubt of the justice of many demands that have been challenged [. . .] Dr G's seal and signature and a detail of expenditure supercede contradiction tho' Cap. Wade may hesitate.[43]

In thus redeeming the credit of his fellow Scot, Burnes was taking a personal risk, as the Company had already repudiated Gerard's claims. Burnes wrote to Macnaghten that Gerard had needed the money to make payments and gifts to chiefs and their servants, and to kafila bashis, qasids and guides. The claims amounted to Rs7,188.[44] The Court of Directors eventually repaid Burnes Rs2,306 'on account of alleged debts of the late Dr Gerard, directing him at the same time to exert extreme caution in the admission of such claims.'[45] Burnes paid out a considerably greater amount. In the correspondence on Gerard's debts, Masson had evidently complained of some wrongdoing in Kabul by Mohan Lal. We have only Burnes' reply, which suggests that Lal 'as an inexperienced youth had been betrayed into much that was blameable', and should be forgiven. This may refer to payments which had been made by Burnes through Masson and Mulla Rahim to the family of 'Mohan Lal's girl'.[46] Alexander was loyal to his friends.

On 9 June, a petty theft had taken place on Burnes' boat, and he intervened to prevent a trial by ordeal. The suspects were being forced to pick copper coins from a cauldron of boiling oil; if they were burnt they were guilty. In the afternoon he collected many crocodile eggs, but could not try eating them as all he broke contained young.[47]

On 20 June at Dera Ismael Khan the mission was met by Mackeson. Here Burnes received another friendly letter from Ranjit Singh, anxious for support in the dispute over possession of the fort of Roghan.

On 14 July 1837 Burnes' flotilla arrived at Kala Bagh. The Indus was fierce with monsoon rains. Sails, oars, bullocks and tow-ropes all strained to make progress. The attempt was futile. 'The scene is wild, picturesque and striking,' wrote Burnes, 'but I fear it is the end of our grand voyage.'[48] However Lt Wood was left with two small boats to make headway against the current. Burnes and his party continued by land. They had now acquired a Sikh escort, and to Burnes' frustration they insisted it was not safe to take the direct route through Tutun Dera, but rather they must continue up the Indus' eastern bank.[49] Burnes was however pleased to receive a letter from Dost Mohammed's secretary explaining that Mohammed Akbar had arranged an escort for him through the Khyber pass.[50]

The battle of Jamrud had sparked renewed resistance among the Muslim populations ruled by Ranjit, and the flotilla sailed right through a force of 10,000 men and eighteen guns under Sujit Singh, which was sent against Ahmad Khan, chief of the Isa Khail. At night, they heard the war drums of both parties, and the next day saw the remarkable situation that the Sikhs were escorting part of Burnes' party up the left bank and the opposing Pathans the remainder up the right.[51]

On 22 July the party were proceeding along an 'execrable road', but buoyed by the news that Eldred Pottinger had finally made it safely to Kabul. Their progress was further impeded by being jumbled with a regiment of Sikh irregular cavalry on its way to join Ranjit, which was commanded by an Englishman, Captain Fawkes. It was dawning on Burnes that Ranjit did not approve of this mission – little assistance was forthcoming and 'we have not a single individual of consequence with us' as they passed through Sikh territory.[52] On 30 July Wood reappeared, having been prevented from sailing to Attock as nobody would crew for him.

On 1 August they were joined by Hugh Falconer and his collaborator Captain Proby Cautley. Burnes heard from Dost Mohammed that he was receiving proposals and diplomatic representatives were being sent from both Persia and Russia, but he would do nothing until Burnes arrived. Burnes immediately wrote to Colvin and Macnaghten insisting that he needed more powers and discretion to act, noting in his diary, 'I am to talk, they [the Persians and Russians] are to act. They had better recall me than act thus.' He was to repeat often a belief that Auckland was placing him in an impossible situation.

But that same evening there was time for enjoyment amid the gloom. They dined al fresco in the beautiful but decaying Mughal garden, flooded with roses, the Bagh-i-Wah. 'We pitched our camp by the crystal rivulet, filled our glasses with Burgundy, and drank to the memory of the fame of Noor Muhal and her immortal poet Thomas Moore.'

Burnes frequently quotes Moore and his 'Mughal' poetry, especially *Lalla*

Rook. He had met Moore in London, and Burnes' own works are acco[...] an influence on Moore. Undoubtedly this poetic sensibility affec[...] attitudes, particularly his partiality for Islamic culture. Moore's [...] not proved 'immortal', but he was enormously popular at this [...] all of Europe. His poetry inspired music by Schumann and Ber[...] countless artists and writers. Tsar Nicholas and his Tsarina played roles [...] Moore in sumptuous tableaux.[53] The passage Burnes is here referencing – an[...] presumes his readers will get the reference – is

> The mask is off – the charm is wrought –
> And Selim to his heart has caught,
> In blushes, more than ever bright
> His Nourmahal, his Haram's light!
> And well do vanish'd frowns enhance
> The charm of every brighten'd glance;
> And dearer seems each dawning smile
> For having lost its light awhile;
> And happier now, for all its sighs,
> As on his arm her head reposes,
> She whispers him, with laughing eyes,
> 'Remember, love, the Feast of Roses!'[54]

That was a wonderful evening under the stars in Hasan Abdal – the rivulet, the roses, the burgundy, Goncalves' guitar, the poetry and added to Burnes' mission of already very remarkable men, the great paleontologists Falconer and Cautley, who much influenced Darwin. Cautley also was the genius who designed and constructed the great Ganges canal.

By the time Burnes reached Attock on 6 August the news was alarming. The Russian-officered Persians were marching on Herat; Qambar Ali was in Kandahar; Dost Mohammed was in correspondence with the Russians and had written to the Governor-General threatening a Russian alliance if Britain did not assist him over Peshawar. Burnes was heading straight into the eye of this diplomatic storm. Alexander wrote to Masson of Auckland's indecision:

> I much fear with such a haver I shall yet be involved in great embarrassments. I have only one sheet anchor left which is that they will be moved in Calcutta to make some decided exertion at variance with our late sleepy policy and if they act not then I even question the propriety of their having ever deputed me to Cabool.[55]

CHAPTER TWENTY

## Peshawar Perverted

On 12 August 1837 Burnes, Leech and Lord arrived at Peshawar. Burnes' previous stay had been idyllic, before the Sikh conquest. He was now a guest of the new Governor, Avitabile, the most extraordinary of Ranjit's European officers. Burnes had met him in Lahore, and was pleased to see a friendly face. There were letters of welcome waiting from Allard and Court.

Avitabile was a forty-five-year-old Neapolitan, who had been a Sergeant-Major in the Napoleonic artillery and eventually entered Sikh service via Turkey and Persia. He had been appointed by the Shah to govern turbulent Persian provinces, where he had succeeded through utmost brutality. In Ranjit Singh's service since 1826, he had become Governor of Wazirabad in 1829, where he greatly increased revenues by similar tactics, and became Governor in April 1835 of Peshawar, newly conquered and unreconciled.

His words were not empty bragging:

> When I marched into Peshawar I sent on in advance a number of wooden posts, which my men erected around the walls of the city. The men [. . .] laughed at the madness of the Feringhi, and louder still when my men came in and laid coils of rope at the foot of the posts. Guns and swords, they said, were the arms to rule the city, and not sticks and ropes. However, when my preparations were completed, they found one fine morning dangling from these posts, fifty of the worst characters in Peshawar, and I repeated the exhibition every day till I had made a scarcity of brigands and murderers.
> 
> Then I had to deal with the liars and tale-bearers. My method with them was to cut out their tongues [. . .] And then a surgeon appeared and professed to be able to restore their speech. I sent for him, and cut out his tongue also.[1]

For variation, Avitabile liked to hang people in rows, alternately by the neck and the feet. He introduced skinning alive on a large scale; it took two hours for the victim to die. He was a psychotic sadist. Dr Honigberger recorded:

> He was afflicted with a frequent contraction of the muscles of his face [...] this disease I attributed to his immoderate consumption of champagne [...] The pleasure which he took in seeing people hung in dozens must be attributed to the affection of his brain [...] Living in his house for three years, I had the opportunity of knowing him well.[2]

Avitabile also had an ill-controlled sexuality. Masson in Lahore, Wolff in Wazirabad and Barr in Peshawar all refer to pornographic paintings in Avitabile's bedrooms. He insisted on taking visitors to see them. He was 'unscrupulous in gratifying his lust', and British Indian historians in 1929 could only say that: 'Avitabile's moral delinquencies and fiendish cruelties are even now remembered in the districts he once governed, by legends or grim stories, some of which we dare not publish.'[3] They did publish the skinning alive.

These unpublishable moral delinquencies included paedophilia. Several British officers noted the children around Avitabile. Lieutenant William Barr was entertained to a nautch in 1839:

> Amongst the number were a few children, varying from seven to ten years of age, who [...] are gradually being initiated into the mysteries of a craft most derogatory in its nature, as carried on in the East [...]
>
> Behind the governor stood two of his servants, a pair of diminutive Afghan boys [...] one of whom [...] would have made a remarkably pretty girl; he, however, looked quite out of place in attendance upon a masculine individual like Avitabile, and would have been better suited for the occupation of a lady's page.[4]

Surgeon-General Atkinson noted of Avitabile the same year:

> he lives in good style, and is distinguished for his hospitality, which has been amply experienced and acknowledged by the British officers [...] On every occasion, his table has been crowded with guests, and, according to oriental custom, the sumptuous entertainments always concluded with a grand nautch, his figurante-company of Cashmeer women consisting of about thirty, singers and dancers, from the age of twelve to twenty-five.[5]

By 1840, Avitabile was entertaining so many British officers that he obtained a monthly allowance of Rs1000 towards the expense. Here we have one of those rare glimpses behind the curtain that reveals the truth about the 'nautches' which were such a frequent feature of the lives of British officials:

> At the same time the Government of India, who had heard of the disgraceful orgies which attended some of the entertainments, directed that none but the most senior officers were to be entertained by him, and gave the political officer an allowance of 500Rs a month, on behalf of the younger ones.[6]

So the senior officers got the disgraceful orgies, and the junior officers got dinner with Mackeson.

Yet Burnes is more reticent than other British sources about Avitabile. He states in *Cabool* that the hospitality was 'princely' but gives no detail; and of the mutilated corpses displayed in scores all around the city, Burnes makes no mention, beyond noting the existence of gallows and that 'the General did not pretend to be guided by European ideas', and 'his measures appeared to us to be somewhat oppressive'.

Burnes stayed a full nineteen days in Peshawar, living with his mission in the beautiful gardens of the Wazir Bagh, where he had been so happy on his previous stay. He was regularly entertained by Avitabile. One explanation of Burnes' discretion is that the epicurean food – Avitabile kept eight excellent chefs – unlimited champagne and 'disgraceful orgies' were much to Burnes' taste. It was not diplomatic reticence: the heir to the Sikh throne, Khurruck Singh, was also in Peshawar, and Burnes had no hesitation in publishing that 'His imbecility is such that he can scarcely return an answer to the most simple question.'[7]

Khurruck invited Burnes to a review of the Sikh army, where Burnes met senior Sikh nobles including Lena Singh, who asked on Ranjit's behalf what was the object of his mission to Dost Mohammed. Burnes replied that it was purely commercial, and that Britain would never act against the interests of Ranjit Singh.[8] Lena replied that only the friendship of the British restrained Ranjit from taking Jalalabad and Kabul. Burnes was then asked directly about British designs on Shikarpur, which they had prevented Ranjit from annexing. Burnes assured Khurruck Singh that the British had no desire to take Shikarpur, but merely wished to prevent war. Wade inserted a marginal comment on Burnes' report of this meeting, that Burnes should not have been so categorical in ruling out British annexation of Shikarpur.[9] The taking of Sind was already on the British agenda.

Burnes found the Sikh occupation of Peshawar distressing. Orchards had been uprooted, gardens destroyed and mosques turned over to stables. 'Mohammedan usages had disappeared – the sounds of dancing and music were heard at all hours and all places.' He was especially saddened by a visit from the Barakzai brothers in whose company he had been so happy, and by the official constraints which prevented him from sympathising with them.[10]

He was forced to keep professional distance with Sultan: 'I drew before him a broad line of distinction between the feelings of a friend and of a public servant.' But he also expressed to Masson his disgust that Sultan Mohammed had betrayed his religion in helping Ranjit Singh take Peshawar and that 'it yet appears to me conduct outraging to every Moslem [. . .] The Moslems will not view it in the light of a gratification of private enmity but as a breach of faith.' Local Muslims called him 'Sultan Singh'.[11]

The great paleontologist Hugh Falconer was still with the mission. Exploratory work continued, and Falconer and Lord set out for Kohat on a geological investigation of the tectonic depression there.

There was an element of pure science in the remit of Burnes' mission, although of course the Company was interested in the commercial benefit of anything discovered. But you cannot study this period without being impressed at the amount of official time, money and resources put into geological, paleontological, astronomical, meteorological, historical, literary, ethnographic, and archaeological investigation, and the varied interests and wide education of the military officers involved.

The time of Lord and Falconer in Kohat was truncated, as they met mounting threats from the local population, and were forced to ride for their lives with shots ringing out behind them. A rendezvous was abandoned with the indefatigable Lieutenant Wood, who was making his way to Kohat by boat to gauge the prospects of river transport of Kohat coal. But they were only able to find bituminous shale, not suitable for powering steamers. Leech meantime was heading further up the Indus to Swat in full disguise as 'a fakeer'.[12]

Burnes was relieved to receive at Peshawar a further, more conciliatory letter from Dost to Auckland. He wrote to Masson, 'In fact if Dost Mahomed Khan continues to contemplate attacks on the Sikhs and to increase his duties on the merchants then we may very well ask the utility of holding any communication with him.'[13]

There is no evidence Burnes had any predisposition to favour Dost's interest. In Peshawar he was forming a clear idea of the diplomatic parameters of a possible settlement which would enable British influence to be pre-eminent, and Russian influence discounted, in Kabul. On 25 July when travelling from Kala Bagh he had written to Masson that the Sikhs were much reducing their troop levels in that region.[14] In Peshawar this impression was confirmed. Avitabile told Burnes that Ranjit 'has every disposition to withdraw from this unprofitable [. . .] place.'[15] Crucially Burnes now learnt from Wade that Ranjit Singh had written to Dost offering negotiations over Peshawar, with the possibility of it being given to Sultan as a Sikh tributary.[16] Burnes wrote to Macnaghten on 22 August that 'Peshawar is a complete drain on the finances of the Maharaja from which [. . .] his Highness would now willingly withdraw.'[17] The same day Burnes wrote to Masson that the actions of Ranjit Singh:

> I really begin to interpret into a disposition to withdraw his troops altogether [. . .] but if it is to end as I anticipate is yet doubtful – If Sooltan Mahomed Khan got Peshawar would Dost Mahomed Khan let him alone – there is the rub – and if Sooltan Mahomed were again installed would he rest without injuring the Ameer?[18]

Burnes had identified the precise nub of the ensuing crisis. On 22 August he noted: 'there are difficulties in dealing with this subject [. . .] If the Maharaja would surrender Peshawar to Sooltan Mahomed & his family would they cease to intrigue against Cabool – if not it would be giving fangs to those deprived of them.'[19]

On 30 August 1837 the mission quit Peshawar surrounded by an escort of 2,000 Sikh troops. They camped at Jamrud on the ground of the recent battle, surrounded by thousands of unburied corpses. Burnes wrote, 'although some months had elapsed since the battle, the effluvia from the dead bodies [. . .] were quite revolting'. Despite their huge escort, the situation seemed ominous. Some of the mission's camels were stolen by local Afridi tribesmen, and the headless corpses of two Sikh foragers were brought back into camp.

This was not good for morale just before attempting the notorious Khyber pass. There had been almost continual warfare for four years between the Sikhs and Afghans. The Khyber pass, dangerous at any time, had never been more so. Burnes had been daily expecting the strong escort under Mirza Agha Jan which had been promised by Akbar Khan. When on 1 September there was still no news, Burnes decided, against the strong urging of Avitabile, that the party must push on as news of Persian moves against Herat precluded further delay.[20]

Burnes reported back to Calcutta:

> I entered the defile without any protection but the Khyberees themselves. They escorted us safely and even, in the confusion which ensued in the pass (which runs in the bed of a river) when unexpectedly overflowed by a torrent, they resisted all temptations to plunder.
>
> From enquiries instituted on the spot, I do not doubt that this great commercial road could be thrown open by an arrangement with the different Khyber chiefs. In the time of the Moghul Emperors they were kept in regular pay, and the scale of transit duties, which they now produced to me [. . .] was by no means exorbitant.[21]

Burnes understood both the necessity and traditional basis of paying the tribes for keeping the passes open. He added that it was Ranjit Singh, not the Afghans, who was most hostile to trade.

As Burnes and his mission – now about 120 people – left behind their Sikh escort at Jamrud, it was not quite true that he had no protection bar the Khyber tribes. He now came in contact with a Scottish deserter from the Company's service named Rattray, alias Leslie, who had taken service with Ranjit. In 1836 he deserted Ranjit and took service with Dost. He converted to Islam and became Fida Mohammed Khan, to Dost's annoyance, who commented there were enough Muslim crooks already.[22] Appointed Lieutenant Colonel, Rattray's forces swept all before them at Jamrud, until finally forced back by the disciplined battalions of Allard. Akbar Khan had left Rattray in charge of the garrison of Ali Musjid, in the mouth of the Khyber, but he had taken up residence in a cave overlooking Jamrud. Here he could watch the Sikh forces constructing their new fortress, and he had the ability to cut off their water supply. This he only did intermittently, letting the water flow in exchange for bribes.

Burnes seemed to like this rogue, though Rattray continually tried to fleece the mission. Wood records that Rattray borrowed Burnes' copy of Elphinstone's *Account of the Kingdom of Caubul* and then offered separately to sell to Wood, Leech and Lord 'intelligence' culled directly from it. Rattray was evidently no fool as he had identified the division of labour. Wood noted: 'To Dr Lord he promised an account of the rivers of Khorassan, and the site of all the valuable ores between Indus and Kabul. To Lieut Leech the military resources of kingdoms and states from Lahore to Meshed and from Sindh to Kashmir; to me a map of half the continent of Asia, in which should be delineated every river and mountain chain, and every town and route.'[23]

Rattray accompanied the mission to Kabul.[24] Burnes persuaded him to write his memoirs, and undertook to seek a publisher. In December 1838 he deserted Dost and went to seek employment in Bajour, but vanished forever.

Burnes entered into correspondence with chiefs of the seven major Khyber tribes. On 2 September the mission nervously set off into the pass with a large escort of the local Kaki khail under their chief Ullah Dad Khan. Burnes also had his faithful Arab bodyguard, and they regularly encountered checkpoints at the territory of different khails, where sometimes tense negotiations were undertaken. He was acutely aware that they were carrying trade goods, presents and gold. He noted laconically, in his journal 'Our march was not without a degree of nervous excitement.'

The flash flood was terrifying. The river rose from a trickle to a devastating torrent in a matter of minutes. These events are frequent in Afghanistan, and are often caused not by precipitation but by strong sunlight hitting snow in high mountains. Alexander the Great's army had been caught by such a flood with substantial loss. Burnes wrote to Masson that 'a tremendous storm came on and we only saved our baggage by dragging it bodily up hill where we sat all day wet and shivering gazing at the grandeur of the torrent [...]'

He noted that the event had left the mission totally helpless but nothing had been plundered by the faithful Khyberis, who had rescued the party and all of their goods.[25]

The tribes were not so hostile as reputed. All they requested from traders was the sharia ordained transit toll of two and a half per cent of the value of goods carried. Burnes therefore believed the route viable for trade caravans from the Indus. His report was however despatched to Macnaghten through Wade, who added comments to the effect that there was no possibility of trade resuming through the Khyber in the present state of Sikh–Afghan hostility.[26] Wade was routinely hostile to the notion of British trade with Central Asia. He continually tried to cast doubt on the methodology used by Trevelyan and Conolly employing Muhin Shah.[27] The truth was that Wade persistently denigrated any initiatives by British officials other than Wade.

The key to the stabilisation of Britain's north-west frontier was the ending of the conflict over Peshawar. Alexander already had a clear view, and on 8 September he sent back from his camp near Jalalabad an analysis of all thirteen Sikh territories west of the Indus,[28] together with this observation:

> The policy of conquest [...] has been throughout a source of much anxiety and latterly a cause of disaster [...] Peshawar is a drain on the finances of the Lahore state with the additional disadvantage of being so situated as to lead the Sikhs into constant collision with desperate enemies.[29]

He added that the Sikh hold on all their lands west of the Indus was weak. Their suppression of Muslim religious practice caused resentment, so that the inhabitants were ready to rise up at the first sign of faltering of the Sikh empire.[30]

Burnes had in place a group of native agents sending him intelligence. He was alarmed at correspondence between the Dil Khan sirdars and Count Simonicz, Russian Ambassador in Tehran, who had sent them presents including guns, cloth, watches and jewellery.[31] The British Agent Karamat Ali[32] was particularly efficient at procuring all the Dil Khan brothers' correspondence. This was viewed by Burnes as clearly indicating Russian intent to extend influence through Kandahar after taking Herat.[33] The Dil Khans had also received a proposal from Ranjit Singh that he would restore Sultan in Peshawar and they should combine to attack Dost Mohammed.

Burnes' caravan had swollen and become rowdy. It now included a troupe of Kashmiri musicians, under a leader called Qadirju, in the employ of Mohan Lal,[34] and Kashmiri women, presumably dancers, who Lal specifies were hired to cater for the sexual needs of Burnes and his assistants. There were also many unconnected to Burnes who had joined the caravan at Peshawar.

Burnes was concerned that some men from Peshawar were Sikh spies, and some loyal to Sultan Mohammed and the Dil Khans. He wanted Masson to explain to Dost that he could not vouch for everybody in his camp.[35] It had become an incongruous scene of revelry, with the abundant hospitality of local chiefs being augmented by a small cloud of pedlars, entertainers and prostitutes. Word even reached the religious authorities in Kabul of the sinful practices, as Masson wrote to warn Burnes, who replied on 13 September:

> we have I fear a precious set of roues with us [. . .] they have been fed at the public expense ever since we left by the bounty of our hosts and have besides had large pay so that the necessary consequence is debauchery and revel at every place we go to. Punishment, flogging have had no effect [. . .] nor even I hope for amendment till the 'supplies are stopped' [. . .] You will think after this that we have a very disorderly suite of persons but such is really not the case – in all we have but 80 mules and 35 camels which in India would be nothing [. . .][36]

On 16 September, 'from Tezin', Burnes wrote full of optimism to Masson, affirming that the Dil Khans would expel Qambar Ali from Kandahar, and that if Ranjit kept his word there now seemed a definite prospect of settling Peshawar. He also urged Masson to send them some good quality tea.[37] The situation did not appear too menacing. Burnes wrote that they were all very much enjoying the change to a cool climate. Masson arrived with the tea at Butkhak, twelve miles out of Kabul, and they discussed the political situation. Among their topics was Eldred Pottinger, who had quit Kabul out of unfounded concern that Dost would detain him.[38] He had managed to offend the entire British influence in the city, as Burnes noted:

> Sayyid Muhin Shah who behaved so kindly to Conolly came out to meet me here & brought a letter from Eldred Pottinger to whom he has been equally kind – I hope to return this in some way. Pottinger has gone to Herat and never told the Nawab – Mr Masson – Mr Harlan or Hyat Cafila Bashee.[39]

Burnes told Masson this was a mistake by Eldred, but was comforted that Eldred was accompanied by two of Burnes' best agents, Alidad Khan and Edul Khan, armed with letters of credit Burnes had provided.

CHAPTER TWENTY-ONE

## The Kabul Negotiations

On 20 September 1837, as the party neared Kabul, they were met by a splendid body of Afghan irregular cavalry, preceded on an elephant by Akbar Khan Barakzai, now a fine-looking man of twenty. Greeting Burnes warmly, he mounted him on his elephant and accompanied him back into Kabul. Here the mission was given a fine residence in spacious gardens, just under the great fortress of the Bala Hissar.

The next day the Emir received them. He was warm in his welcome and in his approbation of Lord Auckland's letter. Told he had been brought 'some of the rarities of Europe' as presents, he replied that the rarities which most delighted him were Burnes and his friends.

Unfortunately, the presents from the Company were meagre: a pistol, a telescope, and some pins and needles were viewed by the Court as an insult. Thirty years before, Mountstuart Elphinstone had brought magnificent gifts to Shah Shuja, to the extraordinary value of £29,000. Even these had drawn complaints from the Afghans, which Elphinstone found infuriating. He noted in his journal that the presents were 'a mark of friendship [. . .] they were the best procurable. Nothing could exceed the meanness of this complaint.'[1]

That mission had arrived with sixteen British officers escorted by 400 British troops. Elphinstone said, 'As the court of Kaubul was [. . .] supposed to entertain a mean opinion of the European nations, it was determined that the mission should be in a style of great magnificence.'[2] Burnes' cheap presents were a stark contrast,[3] and in Afghan eyes reflected poorly on his status and intentions. Burnes failed to notice that Dost Mohammed's observation that the visitors delighted him more than the gifts was two-edged. In private the Emir exclaimed, 'Behold! I have feasted and honoured this Feringee to the extent of six thousand rupees, and have a lot of pins and needles and sundry petty toys to show for my folly!'[4]

They were warmly received by the people, making a fine show in luxuriously braided dress uniforms as they passed through Kabul with an Afghan cavalry escort. Crowds called out, 'Take care of Kabul' and – perhaps with more foresight – 'Don't destroy Kabul.' Burnes was delighted with Dost's attitude. He recorded in *Cabool*, 'Power frequently spoils men, but with Dost Mahomed, neither the increase of it, nor his new title of Ameer, seems to have done him any harm. He seemed even more alert and full of intelligence than when I last saw him.'[5]

In 1835 Dost's reaction to his discovery of the letters from Wade urging Afghan chiefs to support Shuja had been, not to quarrel, but rather to try to secure Britain's friendship, and he had opened correspondence with Lord Auckland to this effect. He reasoned that if the British could deter Ranjit from seizing the riches of Shikarpur, surely they could secure the return of the less wealthy Peshawar to Kabul?

Burnes noted that 'Dost Mahomed Khan treats me as an old friend.'[6] Their first interview was most satisfactory. He met the Emir inside the harem of the Bala Hissar,[7] accompanied only by Akbar, and the three talked over dinner. Dost declared himself enthusiastically in favour of opening up trade via the Indus. He said he had protected merchants both from attack and from excessive duties, and that as a result he had seen a large increase in his customs revenues. He was therefore convinced that trade led to prosperity. He seemed just what Britain needed.

Dost now addressed the subject of Peshawar. He said that he had been mortified to discover documents that proved Shuja had turned Peshawar over to the infidel Sikhs. Either the Emir did not mention he had also found Wade's letters, or Burnes left it out of his report. Dost went on to say that it was his religious duty to recover Peshawar for Islam, and that of course war was detrimental to commerce, both from violence and from the high taxes required. All Asia knew the British had saved Shikarpur from Ranjit – could they not do the same for Peshawar?

Burnes cautioned the Emir against taking on Ranjit Singh's powerful army, saying that he understood Ranjit intended to devolve more authority in Peshawar to Dost's brothers there. The well-informed Emir then asked whether Peshawar were not a large drain on the Sikh treasury. With this sketching out of what would be the substance of future negotiations, this first meeting concluded. Burnes reported to Macnaghten in great detail.[8] He also remarked that Jabbar Khan had told him that Simonicz was sending offers of Russian money to attack Peshawar in return for assisting Persia to take Herat.

On 11 September 1837 Macnaghten sent Burnes from Calcutta more detailed, if not internally consistent, instructions. Burnes received them on 21 October.

The quiet and unassuming character given at the outset [...] will, owing to recent events, be very much changed [...] it is evident that you cannot confine yourself, in the existing state of excitement, to matters of a commercial nature [...]

It is not the intention [...] to invest you with any direct political power beyond that of transmitting any proposition which may appear to you reasonable through Captain Wade to your own Government.

You are authorised, however [...] to communicate without reserve with Dost Mohammed [...] that under any circumstances our first feeling must be that of regard for the honour and just wishes of our old and firm ally Runjit Singh [...]

You will [...] discourage all extravagant pretensions on the part of Dost Mohammed [...] His Lordship in Council would be inclined to think that, if Peshawar were restored to any members of the Barukzye family on the condition of tribute to Runjit Singh the terms would be as favourable as any that could be expected; and if Dost Mohammed rejecting all attempts at drawing him into an alliance with Persia should consent to the restoration of permanent tranquillity on this basis [...] you are authorised to state that you will recommend to your government the support of such an arrangement [...]

You have full authority to proceed to Candahar and Herat should you be of opinion that your presence in those countries would have the effect of counteracting Persian intrigues and of promoting the general tranquility of the countries bordering on the Indus.[9]

At least Burnes now had clear instructions to enter political negotiation and to discuss sympathetically an arrangement for Peshawar. A further letter of 20 October from Macnaghten reiterated agreement with the proposal to restore Peshawar to one of the Barakzai brothers.[10]

Dost was given to calling in on Burnes to chat. An example of 27 September gives a good illustration of the Emir's character and of their relationship:

In the afternoon the Amir dropped in without ceremony and sat till 8 o'clock his son & all his court having followed him [...] He told us of the utility of cavalry in war which he rated far below infantry if the infantry stood – he explained the bridging of the Indus – he told us of the beasts and birds of Kabul – of the grapes & gardens [...] of the lineage of his race from the children of Israel – of the law preventing customs of giving a daughter no inheritance & marrying a brother's wife which is not Mohammedan but I have neither time nor inclination to record all [...][11]

Even for such a dedicated ethnographer as Burnes, the Emir could be exhausting. The next day Jabbar Khan visited, but his talk was much more directly political, on his desire to reconcile his brothers Dost and Sultan.

On 5 October a London paper reached the mission bearing news of the death of William IV and the accession of Queen Victoria. They drank the young Queen's health with Jabbar and Akbar Khan and commissioned the decoration of a Kabul fountain in her honour.[12]

On 24 October the Emir and Jabbar came to see Burnes, and declared their regret at having entered into discussions with Persia, and desire to ally with Britain. They pledged to refuse to receive Qambar Ali, and Dost wrote to the Dil Khans, 'We have an enemy like Runjeet Sing in our neighbourhood, and the English may get the affair of Peshawar settled. How then can we enter into an alliance with others [...] I see nothing for the Mussulmans, in their wars against the Sikhs, but to be friendly with the English government.' [13]

The Emir also turned down a proposal from Sobdar Khan, one of the Amirs of Sind, canvassing a wider alliance with Persia against the Sikhs. Burnes' diplomacy was going well, but he worried about the lack of clarity in his intructions. He wrote to James Holland on 30 October 1837, 'I hardly know what the Government of India will make of my measures, for my line of conduct is only indicated by them, not marked out.'[14]

That was certainly fair comment as his most recent relevant instructions ran:

> If you believe that the Sikhs and Afghan Amirs should have but little disposition to advance [...] and that the desire has been evinced by both the contending parties rather for political adjustment than for conflict and that without committing your Government to the exercise of direct influence, you may either safely act on your original instructions or perhaps contribute something to the restoration of peace.[15]

This is typical of the stream of back-covering faux-wisdom with which Burnes was bombarded by Macnaghten and Auckland. But Burnes was able to report that he had made remarkable progress in squaring the circle of achieving agreement with Dost Mohammed, while at the same time persuading him to acknowledge Sikh overlordship of Peshawar.

Burnes was correct that Ranjit Singh was prepared to compromise over Peshawar. The occupation of the province was costing more than the revenue raised. The Sikh troops stationed west of Attock, essential to defend Peshawar, were continually mutinous, in part because the location broke a religious taboo. As Henry Durand observed, the consequence was that: 'These considerations had disposed Runjeet Singh [...] to assent to any arrangement which might relieve him of his troublesome conquest, without compromising his own position.'[16]

Alexander had talked Dost round to what might be a reasonable solution. The Emir would send Akbar to Lahore to acknowledge Ranjit's sovereignty over Peshawar, and apologise for Afghan aggression (sic). Ranjit would then give Peshawar back to the Barakzais as a fiefdom; they would pay him a symbolic tribute. Burnes' view was that this would be in practice a temporary arrangement until Ranjit Singh died, when he expected the Sikh Empire to disintegrate. Dost would declare himself a firm British ally and renounce any contact with Russia or Persia. The Emir accepted this proposal in full.

Burnes reported, 'I have [. . .] offered to stand as mediator between the parties, and Dost Mahomed has cut asunder all his connection with Russia and Persia, and refused to receive the ambassador from the Shah now at Kandahar.'

One of very few men on good personal terms with both Ranjit Singh and Dost Mohammed, Burnes had discussed Peshawar with each. If he could not broker peace, then who could? At the end of October 1837 Burnes certainly believed he had achieved agreement, writing that Dost

> met me as an old friend [. . .] instead of putting forward extravagant demands, urged his views in such a reasonable manner that I am sure I only await answers to my dispatches to enter on a negotiation for peace between him and Runjeet [. . .] It is probable the Sikh will withdraw from Peshawar, and Dost Mahomed Khan agrees to pay him tribute for it. How delightful it is to be the humble instrument of calming a nation's fury![17]

Burnes viewed Wade as the main obstacle to a settlement, mocking him in a private letter: 'Runjeet will accede to this plan I am certain, but Wade is a great little man [. . .] and while he is looking to the horizon (to use his own words) of politics, events crowd on, and spoil his speculations.'

On 12 July 1837, while Burnes was still in Peshawar, Wade had already written to Macnaghten warning against any agreement with Dost, on the grounds that this would negate the possible British use of Shah Shuja, a key British asset. Wade went so far as to withhold from Auckland at least one of the letters Dost Mohammed sent about Peshawar.[18] He was at or beyond the limit of professionally acceptable behaviour in his selective summaries of Masson's reports, in his heavy commentary on, and sometimes delay of, the dispatches of Burnes, and his handling of the Emir's letters. Henry Durand, who knew both men, wrote

> The correspondence, having to pass through Wade's hands, was always forwarded to the Governor-General with his opinions and surmises; and, there being no inconsiderable jealousy between the two men, Wade was ever inclined to frustrate rather than to adopt Burnes' views [. . .]

It appears that Wade was reprimanded for excessive interference with Burnes' despatches. Burnes wrote in a note to Masson, 'You will see Wade had got it again from Government for "commenting" on my letters.'[19]

## The Kabul Negotiations

But Burnes and Wade did not enjoy a bad personal relationship. Burnes always stayed with Wade in Ludhiana, sometimes for several weeks. On 7 September 1838 Burnes wrote to James asking him to accommodate Wade's nephew, arriving at Bombay, as 'it is the only mode which I am ever likely to have of returning much civility from Wade'.[20]

Close contact with Shuja led all the British[21] to be contemptuous of him, except Wade, who had the closest and longest contact of all. Henry Durand said, 'Wade had been won to the Shah's interest by flattering [. . .] attention, and by the skill with which the ex-monarch had [. . .] engaged Wade in his confidence.' Malcolm Yapp describes Wade as 'probably' corrupt, but offers no evidence. The institutional model seems to me a more likely explanation; the more important Shuja was, the more important Wade was. If Shuja were merely a bypassed failure, nursemaiding him would hardly be career-enhancing.

Durand, who was eventually Lieutenant Governor of the Punjab, states that the British government had a Machiavellian motive against peace, which was to tie up Sikh forces towards Afghanistan, and thus away from their border with the British.[22] Auckland Colvin, whose father was Lord Auckland's Private Secretary, confirms this.[23] The Russians were playing exactly the same game, encouraging the Persian Shah to attack Herat to draw his forces away from the border with Russia.

But a vital internal policy memo from Auckland to his Secret Committee dated 9 September 1837, is not looking to push Ranjit to war with Kabul. Auckland states that both Kandahar and Kabul have 'proffered submission to Tehran', but argues that this is understandable as 'the declared motive has been the alarm of Sikh invasion'. Auckland continues:

> I have, on these grounds, seen with uneasiness the continuance of acrimonious and violent differences in the vicinity of Peshawar. I am thoroughly convinced that it is for the best interests of Runjeet Singh himself that he should come to terms of proper accommodation with the Afghans.[24]

While Auckland gives no precise formula, there is no doubt that in the early winter of 1837 Burnes' proposals in Kabul were entirely consistent with both the letter and spirit of the policy as set out at that time by Auckland. The accepted view of historians, that Burnes was acting contrary to policy, is a nonsense. Burnes cannot have been expected to predict that Auckland was to change his mind.

Burnes felt grateful to Masson for the briefings he had sent him and the support he offered in Kabul. On 9 October he wrote to Auckland: 'I shall owe much to Mr Masson, whose [. . .] accurate knowledge of people and events afford me [. . .] the means of coming to a judgement, more correct than, in an abrupt transition to Cabool, I could have possibly formed.'[25] In passing this letter on, Wade added his own warm commendation. The only result was a letter to Masson conveying the thanks of Lord Auckland. Masson wrote on the bottom of this, plainly in sarcasm, 'Oh be joyful in the Lords all ye lands, come before their presence with thanksgivings, and shew yourselves glad in them with psalms.'[26]

The following day Burnes sent Macnaghten a substantial paper on the Qizilbash of Kabul. Shia Persians, they had been brought to Kabul by Nadir Shah around 1740 as loyal central troops. Literate, they had come to dominate the state bureaucracy. Around 5,000 families in Kabul, inhabiting a substantially walled quarter, they were in sporadic conflict with their Sunni neighbours. Originally loyal to Dost Mohammed, whose mother was a Qizilbash, they had become alienated when he transformed into a fiercely Sunni Emir. If Persia conquered Herat and marched on Kabul, they would be very significant. Otherwise, Burnes concluded that long term they faced extermination.[27]

He spent some pleasant evenings at a country estate outside Kabul with his old Qizilbash friend, Mohammed Sharif Khan, who had travelled from Peshawar to Kabul with Burnes and Gerard in 1832.[28] The Qizilbash were under suspicion of Persian loyalties, so their leader Khan Shirin Khan was not able to communicate with Burnes direct; but he opened friendly communication through Sharif.[29]

Things seemed to be going so well that the mission felt able to make an excursion for a few days, north of Kabul, into the Kohistani countryside. Burnes urged Masson to join them, but he declined.[30] Alex waxed lyrical in his diary:

> In a day exactly as one finds in Autumn in Europe we worked our way through gardens to the commencement of the famed gardens of Thukundurra – Famed they might well be for the landscape is at once glorious and mellow – The gardens are in terraces over each other and [. . .] the very hills are clad with gardens high up [. . .] overlooking the King's Gardens we had a delightful prospect.[31]

Here, they celebrated the anniversary of the start of their mission. After four more days of delight, Burnes declared himself speechless by 16 October when they reached the most famous beauty spot of Istalif. On 20 October Burnes returned to Kabul with Don Goncalves and Leech, while Lord and Wood with kafilbashi Hyat headed into the Hindu Kush.[32]

Burnes remained very popular in London, where the President of the Board of Control, John Cam Hobhouse, consistently supported building a strong Afghan buffer state under the Barakzais; but a dispatch from India to London took three months, and vice versa. Hobhouse was too distant to have any practical effect on Burnes' negotiations. Alex wrote to Holland that he still had no clear indication from Calcutta of support for his proposed Peshawar settlement, but felt confident: 'I am inspirited by their free use of laudatory adjectives regarding my proceedings hitherto.'[33] Those adjectives were about to come to a screeching stop.

Alex seemed to be making good progress. On 28 October 1837, at Burnes' urging, Dost wrote to his half-brothers in Kandahar rebuking them for seeking to accommodate Persia: 'What fruits do you hope to reap by sending your son to Persia? If the British would not be friendly then you might make friends with others. The former are near to us and famous for preserving their word. The latter are nothing in power compared to them.'[34]

Every day Alex had sent painstaking letters and long reports on every detail of the economy, commerce, politics and geography of the towns and country through which he passed. It was beginning to take its toll. On 29 October 1837 he wrote from Kabul to George Jacob:

> I find I have ceased to be my own master, or rather become a slave of the public [...] The very hours of rest are passed in thinking, and the very mechanical labour of writing is such that my eyes and hands alike suffer.[35]

He was feeling the strain of responsibility and wished there was somebody else on the mission with political experience. However:

> The party accompanying me is all I could wish. Lord is a very superior man in every way – a gentleman and a companion without Indianization in his head, and consequently I drink with him fresh from the spring [...] Wood and Lord are everything I could wish, and if we do not give satisfaction the fault may be my own.[36]

On 26 November Burnes sent a detailed analysis of the politics of Kabul to Macnaghten, remarking that the Afghan people are motivated by a 'Republican genius' and that no central authority could impinge on the traditional tribal rights. But Dost's limited territories, and his continual maintenance of a war footing against the Sikhs, had forced him to exact taxes from tribes never subject to central authority, particularly in Kohistan. He praised Dost's trade policies, but said he maintained an army larger than the country could sustain, which was building up political problems.[37]

The mission's work continued. Robert Leech had been in charge of surveying the route and collating information, although all the party contributed. In Kabul, Leech finished drawing up his survey and sent it to Calcutta.

He gave physical descriptions of the Khyber pass with altitudes, rates of incline, width of gorge and several alternative trackways. He described defensive strongpoints and barriers where transit dues were collected. He outlined the distribution, numerical strength, arms and allegiances of the various tribes. He then listed the subsidies they received from central government for keeping the passes open. In the time of Ahmed Shah Dourani the tribes received an annual total of Rs130,000, divided between seven tribal chiefs. Now annual subsidies paid by Dost amounted to Rs19,500 divided between eight chiefs, who between them mustered 28,000 fighting men.

Leech's conclusions were that the geography of the pass and number of warriors made it very difficult to force, but that the tribes were co-operative if paid a modest stipend (the equivalent of £2,000 a year), while the earlier, much higher subsidies showed the potential value of trade given peaceful conditions.[38] Leech is credited as being the first to identify the Mughals around Ghor as a distinctive ethnic group and to chronicle their culture.[39] This report was followed by one from Wood detailing the practicality of the Khyber pass and the route of the Kabul river for an army and guns.[40]

Burnes continued to oversee the work of the mission in its original purpose. Exhaustive studies were made of the shops, merchants, warehouses, manufactures, bankers, taxes, prices and trade volumes of Kabul. Burnes became more than ever convinced of the centrality of the annual Lohani caravan migrations. He was happy to meet his old friends, the brothers Sarwar and Omar Khan Lohani. Dost Mohammed – who had never quite lost his taste for brigandage – had seized the very large sum of 20,000 ducats, about £9,000, from them and Burnes repeatedly lobbied the Emir on their behalf, pleading for the sanctity of trade. He eventually achieved partial restitution, which cemented their friendship. Burnes wrote to Macnaghten that the Governor-General should receive the Lohanis, and noted that in 1836 the Central Asian merchants visiting the Nizhni Novgorod fair had all been introduced to Tsar Nicholas, with great impact.[41] Burnes also arranged for the brothers to take 300 sheep and twelve rams to Mithankot as breeding stock for the government of Bombay.

Writing privately, Burnes reviewed the irritable history of European communication with Murad Beg of Kunduz and came to a remarkably liberal conclusion: 'it would seem that the Europeans have hitherto behaved as ill to Murad Beg as he to them.'[42] He therefore sent a friendly message, and received greetings in return, with a present of a horse and request that Dr Lord come to Kunduz and treat Murad's brother, who was suffering from blindness. In return Murad offered to hand over papers and books of Moorcroft.[43] Burnes seized this opportunity to send Lord and Wood to extend their survey, telling

Jacob that 'while I hope the cure may be affected, I am certain of a geographical section through these mountains, with chronometrically fixed positions [. . .] which will be sinking a geographical mine in Asia'. He added gleefully that Murad Beg 'does not know that I am the man who was dragged to his door in 1832, nor shall he know'.

Lord and Wood were caught in a blizzard on the Saraulang pass in the Hindu Kush. They were travelling with an envoy from Dost Mohammed to Murad Beg, who insisted on pressing on when Lord and Wood turned back. The envoy and all his party perished in the snow.[44] Once they were able to get through, with Murad Beg's favour Lord gathered much intelligence, particularly on the transit trade between Kabul and Bokhara. Murad Beg encouraged caravans and charged duty only at the Koranic two and a half per cent. On high value items like Cashmere shawls he charged no duty at all, to encourage wealthy merchants. Despite his vicious reputation, he was a shrewd ruler. Kunduz stood not just on the main route between Kabul and Bokhara, but on a route to Kashgar in China. Lord reported that Murad's annual income from taxes on Kafilas amounted to Rs60,000.

Before returning to Burnes' Kabul negotiations we should note that the other members of the mission had successes in their designated tasks. On 10 January 1838 Burnes was able to report Lord's initial success in recovering Moorcroft's papers,[45] and while this first batch proved to be printed volumes from Moorcroft's library, it was not long before manuscript notes and journals started to come in. The haul included material from an unknown and unidentifiable early British traveller.

Wood travelled among the Hazara people and produced one of the first accounts, in which he correctly identified them as Shia and of Central Asian origin, in contrast to later more romantic British conjectures. He noted they were pacific and much subject to slave-raiding by the Sunni Uzbeks.[46] Wood surveyed and outlined the high passes of the Hindu Kush.

Burnes was concerned about the lack of reliable information on Russian progress in the Uzbek Khanates of Bokhara, Khiva and Kokhand. He suggested to Macnaghten that they send secret agents disguised as merchants to the Russian trade fair at Nizhni Novgorod. Burnes feared that Russian intelligence on Central Asia was better than Britain's.[47] He submitted an intelligence digest including the observation that in Bokhara the Emir had become erratic, and less inclined to pay attention to the moderate Kush-Begi. The report detailed slave-raiding by Khiva, and concluded that both Russians and Persians had legitimate grievances against that Khanate, which it was in the British interest to neutralise lest they become excuses for Russian conquest.[48]

On 20 October Burnes sent Macnaghten a lengthy account of Russian activity in Central Asia since his journey to Bokhara, starting with the visit of 'Mirza Jafer' in 1832, who Burnes identifies not by name but as a Russian officer posing as a Muslim. In 1835 Russia had established the fortified port of Mungusluk on the eastern shore of the Caspian, and a 'hunting party' from there had set out towards Bokhara. The whole party of 120 had been captured and all but the two Russian officers – who remained hostages – sold into slavery. In retaliation Khivan merchants at Nizhni Novgorod had been incarcerated, and the standoff continued. Burnes' sympathies were with Russia against Khiva.[49]

In Kabul, Burnes was in continual contact with Masson, who became effectively a member of the mission. The two usually met daily, and often exchanged short notes. Those Burnes sent to Masson are preserved and they show that Burnes wrote to Masson on average more than once a day throughout his stay. Any day they were not able to meet, they sent an explanation. They shared journals and books. The notes show that Jabbar Khan and Akbar Khan were part of Burnes' daily social life, and that he regularly invited Masson to join them for a meal or a picnic. A few quotes give the tenor of Burnes' relationship with the Kabul rulers: 'I have had Mahomed Akbar Khan here for a long time and have had much general conversation';[50] 'I am going out to dinner tonight to meet the Nawab taking a soiree at Burr u Deen';[51] 'I was just coming over to you [. . .] when the Ameer dropped in – Today I am writing as hard as I can for the packet just starting which will also prevent my coming over but I hope to bring you over to have a chat with us at dinner.'[52] All the senior Afghans took an interest in discussing Burnes' and Masson's antiquarian researches, including Dost Mohammed, who sent them sketches of artefacts at Bamian.[53] Burnes also maintained a relationship with senior clergy, including Mulla Rahim, to whom he made several payments.[54] Alex felt that Masson was poorly treated by Wade, particularly over salary and expenses. On 27 October Burnes wrote to Masson offering to advance him all outstanding payments and criticising Wade's 'prevarication'.[55]

Apart from Rattray and Campbell, there was a further European in Dost's service commanding a regiment, an American doctor named Josiah Harlan. Like so many of the flotsam and jetsam of white mercenaries, Harlan had previously served the Company and then held minor commands under Ranjit Singh and Shah Shuja. Harlan repeatedly tried to insinuate himself into Burnes' negotiations with the Emir, which Burnes resisted, returning Harlan's letters unopened.[56] Harlan was a braggart, but there appears some truth in his claim that he played an important role, as an agent of Ranjit, in exacerbating the distrust between Dost Mohammed and his half-brother Sultan at Peshawar, which was a major obstacle to Burnes' negotiations, to which we now return.

On 13 November Dost sent for Burnes and showed him a copy of an agreement between Kandahar and Persia. Burnes already knew from his agents that this was genuine, and that in return for the alliance Qambar Ali had cancelled his further mission to Kabul and was returning to Persia with senior Dil Khan children as hostages. Kandahar had agreed to supply troops for the siege of Herat.[57] Dost now suggested to Burnes that Britain and Kabul were on the same side in the face of a Persian/Russian advance:

> It was very evident there was some crisis at hand in the affairs of the West and that Herat certainly and Kandahar probably would fall into the hands of Persia if some arrangement were not speedily entered upon [...] [as] Persia could not of herself act in this manner she must be assisted by Russia. His motive in having sought this private interview was to assure me he was entirely English in his views [...] and that his [...] power [was] at our disposal [...][58]

This was a clear offer of alliance against Russia. Burnes had, however, no instructions to make such an alliance and he temporised, pointing out that the authenticity of the Kandahar/Persian treaty was dubious.[59] He also said Herat was not yet under attack and the danger was not immediate. The Emir must have been disappointed by this lukewarm response.

Burnes had recruited paid spies in the Afghan court, and the next day he received a copy of a letter to Dost from his Ambassador to Persia, Haji Ibrahim, enclosing one from Count Simonicz. Simonicz's letter was carefully bland, but he had given a spoken gloss to Ibrahim:

> The Shah directed me to inform you, that he will shortly send an ambassador, who [...] will proceed to Ranjit Singh, to explain to him [...] that if he will not restore all the Affghan countries to you, he must be prepared to receive the Russian army. When the Shah takes Herat, he has promised to send you money and any troops you want.
>
> The Russian Ambassador who is always with the Shah, has sent you a letter which I enclose. The substance of his verbal messages to you is, that if the Shah does everything you want, so much the better, and if not, the Russian Government will furnish you with everything wanting. The object of the Russian Ambassador, by his message is to have a road to the English, and for this they are very anxious.[60]

Four days after sending back this evidence of Simonicz's intentions, Burnes wrote on 19 November asking the Government to think ahead to what they should do if Herat fell, and requested instructions:

> It may perhaps therefore appear worthy of consideration [...] to decide how far Government can go in its offers, either of money, countenance or protection, to divert the chiefs of Afghanistan from a Persian alliance [...] when Herat is threatened from day to day and may fall it will not [...] be premature to consider what may be done in that event in Cabool and Candahar.

In fact, the great outlying fortress of Ghorian had already fallen to Persia, not without treachery by its commander, and the Persian siege of Herat began just three days after Burnes' letter was written.

The Persian forces included a regiment of Russian 'deserters', which the British regarded as a ruse to supply Tsarist troops. This was probably a wrong imputation. In 1830 Arthur Conolly had noted that some 7,000 Russian military absconders were resident in north-east Persia; that though most had become nominally Muslim, they were in general very drunken, and that 3,000 were in the Shah's military service.[61] Stoddart paints a more creditable picture, saying that many were Poles who had rebelled against Russian rule. They had performed well at Qochan but played little part in the siege of Herat and seemed 'but little indisposed towards the Heratees'. This 'regiment' refused an order to return to Russia once the siege was lifted.[62]

Dost Mohammed was concerned that Herat would fall. He was aware that Herat was more defensible than Kandahar, and also that Herat was a good base of supply for provisioning an army. A fall of Herat could lead very quickly to a situation in which either Kandahar would also fall, or would ally with Persia against Kabul.[63]

Burnes now received a letter from Eldred Pottinger who had been detained in Herat by the vizier Yar Mohammed Khan as a possible asset or hostage in the Persian siege, but was not being mistreated otherwise. The bumbling young man had lost his surveying instruments, and wrote that he had been trying to make a compass by striking iron.[64] Burnes sent Eldred his own spares.

Five weeks later, news of the attack on Herat had still not reached Auckland and Macnaghten as they wrote a reply to Burnes, following Christmas festivities in a splendid camp at Kanpur. They were dismissive of the threat to Herat, and made plain that Burnes' aim must be to maintain the status quo – something clearly now impossible. Burnes would not have received these infuriatingly obtuse and pompous instructions until February, when Herat had been under siege for ten weeks and a Russian envoy had been six weeks in Kabul offering alliance to Dost:

Captain A Burnes
On a Mission to Cabool

Sir,
1. I am desired [. . .] to acknowledge the receipt of your letters dated the 10th, 15th, 16th, 18th and 19th ultimo regarding the latest intelligence respecting the designs of Persia eastward, the probable result of an attack on Herat and the ulterior motives which has Russia to Herat [. . .]

2. In reply, I am directed to acquaint you that the information acknowledged is interesting, but it is not sufficiently authentic to admit of any satisfactory conclusion being formed as to the designs of Persia on Candahar, or to lead to any immediate apprehension that the integrity of Herat will be impaired [...]

3. It would be useful if the conviction could be impressed on the Herat and Candahar chiefs that by their mutual contests, they are furnishing the means of threatening and injuring both, to Persia [...] The same reasoning will apply [...] to any attempt on the part of the ruler of Cabool to found upon your presence at his court any pretensions of superiority, or to an undue influence over the chief of Candahar – and whilst His Lordship thinks that he can trace in some of your dispatches some such design on the part of Dost Mahomed, he relies [...] upon your strict attention to the instructions which have already been given to you [...] the most studious caution is indispensably necessary and [...] a visit of friendly intercourse from you or from some member of your mission, designed to mark our recognition of that independence to the courts of Candahar and Herat may become desirable at an earlier period than you seem to anticipate. In the precarious position in which Dost Mahomed is placed our good offices for the peace and security of his remaining territory should be thankfully accepted by him [...]

I have etc

Sir W H Macnaghten
Secty to the Govt of India
With the Governor-General
Camp at Cawnpore
The 27th Decr 1837[65]

So Burnes was to visit Kandahar and Herat to assure them of support, not against Persia, which was invading, but against Dost Mohammed who was not threatening them.

CHAPTER TWENTY-TWO

## Stand-off

Persia had begun the siege of Herat in earnest with a full assault on 22 November 1838. On 25 November Burnes received another letter from Ranjit Singh. Ranjit knew very well the course of the Kabul discussions from his own agents. After copious expressions of friendship, and a pointed reference to an assurance from Auckland that nothing would be done in Kabul against his interests, Ranjit turned to Peshawar which he stated was held by Sultan Mohammed and Pir Mohammed as chiefs under him in return for a tribute of 'horses of noble breed'. Ranjit ignores the role of Avitabile and stationing of Sikh forces. He concludes that he hopes that Burnes will 'not do any injury to the countries under me'. The letter is a warning off, but does not close the door on a revised tributary arrangement for Sultan Mohammed.

In the evening of 11 December Charles Masson came to see Burnes. He talked long of his antiquarian researches and his health, and suggested that he leave Kabul for three months to recuperate. The next day Burnes wrote giving his permission for Masson to take three months' leave on full pay and offering to pay outstanding expenses claims. He criticised Wade for niggardliness, adding:

> These are all public matters but in private – if my own purse can avail you [. . .] the use of it will always be to me a very gratifying proof of your confidence – I know that you have friends to do such service for you, but they are absent and I am present.[1]

As usual, the Emir simply turned up at Burnes' house to tell him startling news from his son at Ghazni. The Russian agent, Witkiewicz, was on his way from Ghazni to Kabul. Burnes immediately sent a note to Masson:

> I should feel very much obliged if you could come over as I wish to speak particularly with you – the Russian has arrived here!!! & the Ameer has been with me to know what to do – I would come over to you but I am not certain the Ameer will not call me to him.[2]

Witkiewicz had ridden from St Petersburg as far as Moscow with Dost Mohammed's Envoy, Haji Hussain Ali, who had delivered the Emir's letter to the Tsar. Witkiewicz was bringing the reply. The Haji had been taken ill, and Witkiewicz had left him at Moscow. Witkiewicz had been spotted en route, travelling by night, by Henry Rawlinson in a famously romantic encounter in the deserts of north Persia. Rawlinson was himself an astonishing character, with heroic achievements as archaeologist and military adventurer. At school, I copied diagrams of his death-defying acrobatics, which involved using ladders to bridge gaps in ledges over dizzying chasms, as he noted down rock-cut cuneiform inscriptions. He became the first to decipher the ancient Mesopotamian and Persian languages.

Witkiewicz had pretended not to have any common language with Rawlinson, though in truth they had several. He had then gone on to join the Shah's camp at Mishapur, en route to Herat. Colonel Stoddart, British Military Attache with the camp reported that Witkiewicz had told the Shah that a large Russian force was to arrive at Astrabad to support the Persian attack.[3] This was an untruth, probably fed to Stoddart. But certainly Witkiewicz conveyed from St Petersburg further encouragement of the Shah's attack. Burnes shared with Masson: 'The Elchee is from Moscow but last from Count Simonitch from him he has letters to say his word is my word and his doings are my doings.'[4]

Dost was acutely aware of the problems this unsought visitor might bring him with the British. As Burnes reported to Auckland:

> Dost Mohammed Khan said [. . .] that he wished to have nothing to do with any other power than the British, that he did not wish to receive any agent from any other power whatever, so long as he had a hope for any sympathy from us; and that he would order the Russian agent to be turned out, detained on the road, or act in any other way I desired him.

Burnes replied that the Emir should receive Witkiewicz, but report everything that transpired. This is precisely the response that an MI6 officer today would give. Burnes was confident he could intercept all Witkiewicz' communications and gather intelligence on Russian intentions.[5]

The clash of Burnes and Witkiewicz, pushing the British and Russian interests in Kabul, encapsulates the romance and intrigue of the Great Game. Witkiewicz was long viewed in Britain as splendidly mysterious. Historians were baffled by Masson's claims that Witkiewicz was not really a Russian agent, combined with the fact that he was strenuously disowned by Nesselrode, who keen to avert a clash with Britain, wrote to Palmerston on 20 October 1838 that Witkiewicz was merely a local appointment by Count Simonicz, the Russian Ambassador in Persia, and his remit was purely commercial. This was untrue – prior to his embassy to Kabul, Witkiewicz was on the staff of the Governor-General of Orenburg, and the letters of credence he carried were from the Tsar himself. But it suited the British to pretend to believe Nesselrode.

Burnes had no doubt that Witkiewicz was who he said he was, an Envoy of the Imperial Russian court. Witkiewicz had already been received in Kandahar, where he had attempted to persuade the Dil Khans to join the Persian forces attacking Herat. He flourished the Tsar's commission. He wore spectacular Cossack uniform, and wore it well. He promised presents, spoke of large subsidies, and let it be known that a major Imperial army was assembling at Astrabad, ready to combine with the Persian army.

In short, Witkiewicz was the nightmare of the British Raj personified. His instructions from St Petersburg were almost an exact mirror of Burnes'. In addition to the usual surveying and intelligence gathering, he was to persuade Kabul and Kandahar that an alliance with Russia offered them the best protection from aggression. He was to induce Afghan merchants to go directly to buy goods at Nizhni Novgorod. And 'he was to indicate to Dost Mohammed and Kohan Dil Khan that Russia would not assist them to expand their respective domains, but that Russia would intercede as a friend on their behalf through Persia.'[6]

To make matters worse, Burnes now received intelligence that Herat would soon fall and Kandahar was committing to an alliance with Russia and Persia. He had no reply yet to his letter of 19 November asking whether finance might be offered to Kandahar to take the British side, but felt obliged to act. On 21 December he confided to his diary:

> I received such messages from Candahar that I resolved to offer the Chiefs there pecuniary assistance if they would not join Persia [. . .] how else can I uphold British Interests [. . .] My despatches explain my reasons & they may bring on me high satisfaction or high disapprobation so wide are my instructions.

He was right in imagining that this decision would be pivotal to his career. On 22 December Burnes made a careful facsimile of the Pole's credentials and the Tsar's letter and sent them to Macnaghten, noting in his journal, 'This is a very serious affair. The promises of the Emperor and the calligraphy of his letter are equally splendid which are saying a great deal.'[7] The next morning he addressed a long personal letter to Auckland, in which he directly disabused Auckland of the notion that the Sikhs posed a direct threat to Kabul, explained the need to aid Kandahar against a Russian-inspired Persian advance; and pleaded that the proposals for Peshawar be discussed with Ranjit Singh.[8]

On Christmas Eve Burnes sent Masson a note: 'We have seen the Russian & a very gentlemanly good sort of fellow – he is to dine with us tomorrow

– he was in full tog & belongs to the Cossacks!'⁹ And on 27 December he recorded:

> The Russian agent Mr Vitkiewitsch gives one room for a great deal of curious reflection and consideration – If his private history is to be relied upon he is in the service of Russia as an Officer in the Cossacks at Orenburg – he is about 28 or 30 years of age – he speaks and writes French fluently – he also knows Toorkee and Persian [. . .] he has been three times to Bokhara, twice on government business and once on his own [. . .] he has been all round the Northern part [the Aral] and as high up the Sir [. . .] as Tashkent. All that country he says has been examined by Russian officers but the Govt of that country does not allow officers to publish what reseignments they make – he had examined the unfrequented road by Lash and Seistan from which he travelled to Candahar and Cabool.¹⁰

Good personal relations apart, Witkiewicz alarmed Burnes by letting it be known that he had come as a result of Dost's letter telling the Tsar that he feared the British intended to back Shuja against him, and suggested that Afghanistan be taken under Russian protection.

Witkiewicz' report back to Simonicz of his first meeting with Dost was not entirely positive:

> The reception of Dost Mohammed Khan [. . .] was sufficiently marked, polite and kind.
> I was lodged in the house of the first minister [. . .] and after three days, I demanded an audience, when I delivered the Imperial credentials and the letter of your lordship [. . .] I added verbally, that the object of my coming was [. . .] to declare that His Majesty the Emperor [. . .] vouchsafed to him protection and friendly alliance; that the rulers of Afghanistan [. . .] should acknowledge, or place themselves, under the dominion of Persia, with whom Russia is connected by truly friendly relations.

It is unsurprising that Dost did not leap at the Russian offer, when the first point was Persian suzerainty. In fact the Russians were constrained in their offers by their relationship with Persia, just as the British were by their relationship with the Sikhs. Dost replied:

> that a friendly treaty of the Affghans with the Persians could not be because an English envoy, Captain Burnes [. . .] was concluding a mutual treaty. That Dost Mahomed Khan, having collected as large an Affghan army as possible, would go to the assistance of Kamran, against the Persians besieging Herat, and by the treaty the English bound themselves [. . .] to make over the possession of Affghan Peshawar and the other conquests of Runjeet on the right bank of the Indus [. . .]¹¹

This account by Dost Mohammed is a wild exaggeration of anything Burnes had said. It was invented to persuade the Russians to match this fictitious British offer. The Emir wrote to Simonicz, thanking him for his offers of support but noting that: 'Before the arrival of your agent the English government had deputed Alexander Burnes, who is now with me in Kabul. That officer is sowing the seeds of friendship between Ranjit Singh and myself; nothing is yet settled, however, but let me wait the result.'

Burnes' informants told him that Witkiewicz had offered Dost large funding for war against Ranjit.[12] Witkiewicz makes no mention of any such offer. The sophisticated Afghans were feeding both Burnes and Witkiewicz with false reports of offers, in order to bid up the rival powers. Kohan Dil Khan had written to Dost suggesting this strategy.[13] This is confirmed by Josiah Harlan, who was present in the Afghan counsels, and wrote 'every subterfuge that duplicity could devise, and every pretext that cunning could suggest, were used to work upon the English agent. The imaginary terrors of a Russian invasion were prominently displayed to him.'[14] Harlan fails to note the Afghans were similarly playing on Witkiewicz.

Dost had himself given Burnes an account of Witkiewicz' audience. He also showed Burnes the letter he had written to the Tsar in 1836, stating 'The British Government exhibit no favorable opinions towards me,'[15] explaining that he had sent it after his friendly advance to Auckland had been rebuffed. Burnes reported to Auckland that

> Mr Vickovich informed Dost Mahomed Khan, that the Russian Government had desired him to state his sincere sympathy with the difficulty under which he labored; and that it would afford great pleasure to assist him in repelling the attacks of Runjeet Singh on his dominions; that it was ready to furnish him with a sum of money for the purpose, and to continue the supply annually, expecting in return the Ameer's good offices.[16]

The Emir had much more frequent and direct contact with Burnes than Witkiewicz, who could, however, negotiate through his host the Mirza. Witkiewicz blamed his lack of direct access on Burnes.

Masson tried repeatedly to persuade Burnes that Witkiewicz was an impostor. He produced a conical loaf of sugar from the market, and suggested that the wax seal affixed to Witkiewicz' credentials was created from the Russian export duty stamp on the bottom of the cone. Burnes was in fact already aware of these stamps, having noted them on 27 September.[17] He believed the sugar loaves to be of British manufacture and re-exported through Russia.

As we have seen Nizamuddin had written to Masson from Bokhara in 1836 that Witkiewicz was a Russian diplomat. So why had Masson been at such pains to deny Witkiewicz' identity, even going through the charade with a loaf of sugar? Years later Burnes acquired compelling evidence that Masson had been deceiving him. On 22 November 1840 Burnes wrote to Lord from Kabul:

> A couple of years before our mission arrived at Cabul, Vicovitch (the true Vicovitch) came to Bokhara, called at Ruheem Shah's relative's house, and asked him to send letters to Masson at Caubul for MM. Allard and Ventura. The King of Bokhara took offence at Vicovitch's presence, and the Koosh-Begee sent him off sharp. So the letters were never sent. This shows an earlier intention to intrigue on the part of Russia; but how came Masson not to report this, and if he reported it, how came he to give, years afterwards, twenty-one reasons for Vicovitch not being what he was? I cannot unravel this. I once spoke of this before to you, and to no other man [. . .][18]

As Burnes realised, Witkiewicz would hardly have been seeking to forward letters through the British newswriter at Kabul without some prior arrangement with Masson. Masson had separately suppressed reports about Witkiewicz from Nizamuddin; it is not plain if Burnes also eventually discovered this. But what is certain is that Masson was faking lack of knowledge of Witkiewicz and trying to plant false doubts about the Pole's authenticity.

Allard and Ventura, to whom Masson had been supposed to forward letters from Witkiewicz, were both originally sent into Sikh service by the Russian Ambassador in Persia,[19] after the British government had pressured the Shah to dismiss his French officers. The British had also stipulated that Persia should prevent the French officers from joining Ranjit Singh, so Allard and Ventura had to travel in disguise.[20] On arrival in Lahore in 1822, their first act had been to inquire as to Moorcroft's progress into Central Asia, and what force accompanied him. Moorcroft had intercepted at Yarkand a message from Nesselrode to Ranjit, (the Russians believed Moorcroft killed their messenger).[21]

The Frenchmen maintained their own intelligence contacts in Kabul, independent of Ranjit particularly through Jabbar Khan.[22] As the British had forced them from Persia, it would be surprising if their network did not include some contact with Russian intelligence. The evidence that Masson was part of the Russian intelligence network seems strong. The obvious possibility is that Witkiewicz, 'Mirza Jafer', or Allard and Ventura had recruited Masson to supply intelligence to Russia.

Correspondence between Pottinger, Wade and Masson was routinely sent via Allard and Ventura, who forwarded it through qasid exchanges at Peshawar.[23] Given that the British were avowedly engaged in an intelligence battle with Russia, their communication security appears naive. They were more concerned with internecine dispute. With the advantage of seeing communications in both directions, Wade could time his internal policy intervention to maximum effect. In January 1838, Wade suggested to Auckland that the solution to the problem of Afghanistan lay in 'facilitating the return of Shah Shoojah':[24]

> Runjeet Singh would be brought with difficulty to acknowledge the elevation of Dost Mahomed Khan to the sovereignty of the Afghans, while, should the consolidation of that people become a measure of indispensable necessity to the establishment of security on the frontier of the Indus, the election of Shah Shooja, would only be in fulfilment of the compact which was formerly made with him, and would exact no new concessions.[25]

The same week Burnes was bemoaning to his diary, 'It is proper that all governments should be difficult to move and that much scrutiny should be used before acting, but Captain Wade offers his opinions which are not grounded in experience and these seem to confuse government.'[26]

There was another influence undermining Burnes' position with Auckland.[27] As the gubernatorial procession reached Patna, and as Witkiewicz approached Kabul, a visitor for Auckland arrived 'warning him against Burnes' loquacity'. That visitor was General Ventura. While Ventura was acting in the Sikh interest in countering Burnes' proposals for Peshawar, he was also promoting the Russian interest in undermining Burnes in Kabul. Count Simonicz, the pro-active Russian Ambassador in Teheran, had himself been a Napoleonic officer, and was reputed to know some of Ranjit's officers from that time.[28]

Burnes was receiving reports from McNeill that Persia planned to march on Kandahar, but also that the Dil Khan sirdars there were considering a separate alliance with Persia. On 22 December Burnes received a letter from the Dil Khans, representing to him that he had led them into a position of hostility to Persia, which placed them in danger, but had provided no security. On Christmas Eve Burnes received another visit from the Emir, who told him that Witkiewicz had claimed that a Russian army 4,000 strong had moved east of the Caspian Sea to tie up the Turkmen in support of the Shah's siege of Herat.[29]

On 26 December, at Macnaghten's direct instruction,[30] Burnes sent Leech to bolster the chiefs of Kandahar. Leech also carried Burnes' unauthorised offer of three lakhs of rupees to finance the defence. Burnes wrote to George Jacob:

> Herat has been besieged fifty days, and if the Persians move on Candahar, I am off there with the Ameer [. . .] We have good stuff, forty-six guns and stout

*Above*. Bow Butts, Montrose, the now derelict Burnes house.

*Left*. James Burnes senior, Alex' father and Provost of Montrose.
By permission of Angus Council.

Montrose Academy, where Burnes was schooled.

Eighteenth-century masonic sign over the Royal Arch bar, Montrose.

Map of Montrose 1824 with the Burnes house clearly marked, just south of the Bowling Green.

Joseph Hume of Montrose, radical MP and Burnes' assiduous patron. Copyright National Portrait Gallery

*Above.* Mumbai Old Town Hall, centre of the social and intellectual life of the community. Here Burnes presented papers to the Asiatic, Geographical and Geological Societies.

*Left.* The Governor's ballroom at Sans Pareil is a pale reflection of its former glory.

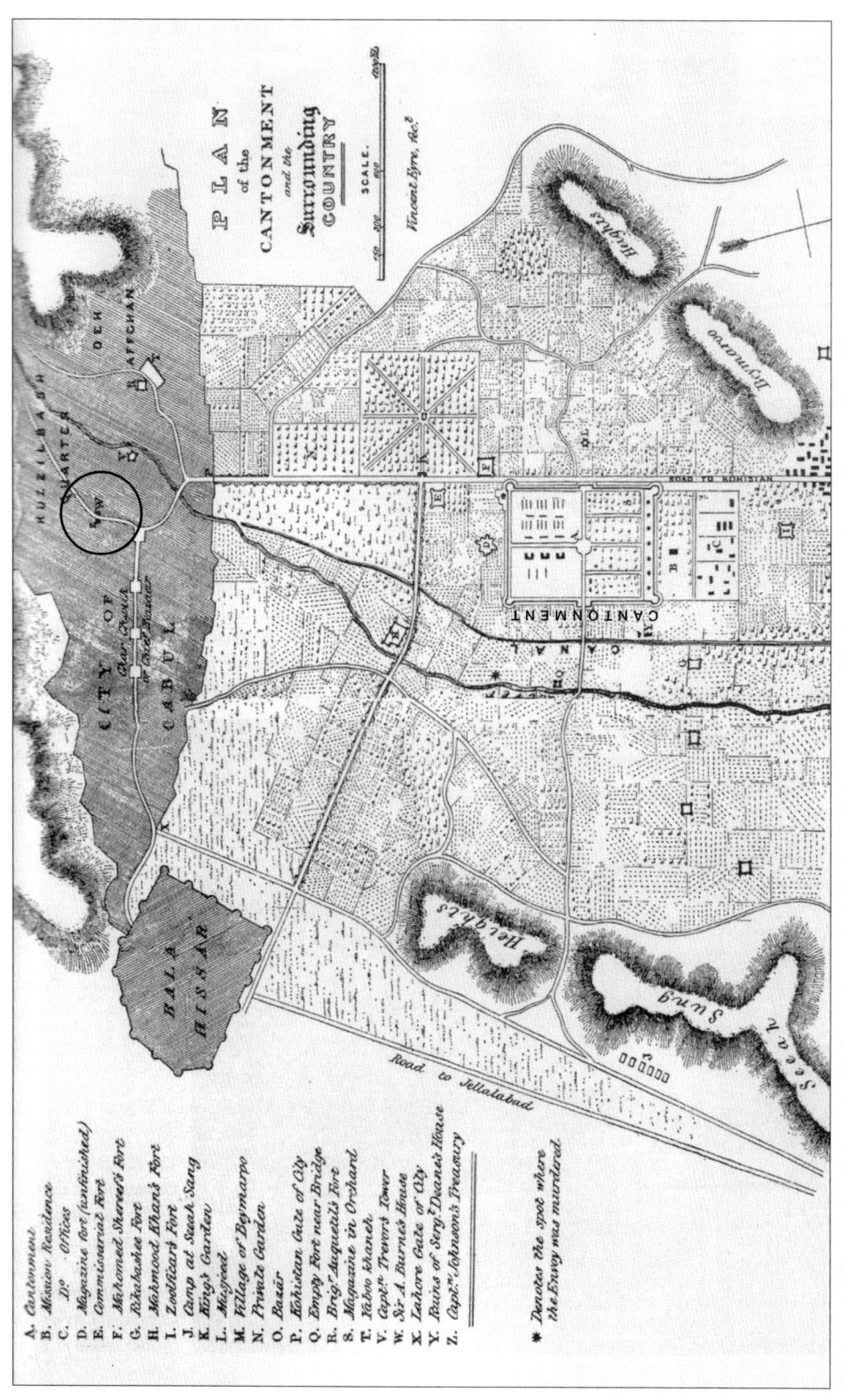

Kabul 1841 by Vincent Eyre (pub 1843) with Burnes house (W) clearly marked at centre top. This shows its position relative to the British cantonment.

Many of the Mandvi boatbuilders still know of Burnes, and claim their ancestors sailed with him.

Large wooden boats are still built in Mandvi, where Burnes' flotilla was specially constructed.

The British military cemetery at Bhuj consists predominantly of graves from the Burnes' period, and reflects the unhealthy climate reported by James.

The Rao of Cutch's bedchamber.

The hall of mirrors in the palace at Bhuj, where Burnes was frequently received by the Rao of Cutch.

The irascible Sir Henry Pottinger, who came to hate Burnes. Painted here as the first Governor of Hong Kong after satisfying his bellicosity in the Opium War. Copyright the Government Art Collection

Sans Pareil, the Governor's Residence and seat of administration at Bombay, now the Cholera Institute.

An eighteenth-century painting of Sans Pareil still on the wall of the Cholera Institute, Mumbai.

Maharaja Ranjit Singh, the brilliant creator of the Sikh Empire, which Burnes foresaw could not outlive him. Wikimedia licence

The hall of audience in the Red Fort at Delhi where Burnes met the Moghul Emperor.

The accepted 'image' of Burnes is not him at all. The engraving was expressly altered so it is not his face.

This portrait of Burnes by William Brockedon shows him in the act of removing his red-lined Bokharan robe, and revealing the British uniform underneath. Copyright Mumbai Asiatic Society

Lodge Canongate Kilwinning, the oldest purpose-built Masonic building in the world. Adjoining is the Scottish HQ of the Order of St John. Copyright Historic Environment Scotland

*Inset top left*. The Order of the Dourrani Empire, a St John's Cross.

*The Man Who Would Be King*. Alex claimed to have found the masonic inscription of the square and compasses on ruins in Central Asia. THE MAN WHO WOULD BE KING © 1975, renewed 2003 Columbia Pictures Industries, Inc. All Rights Reserved. Courtesy of Columbia Pictures.

The Russian Trade Fair at Nizhni Novgorod by Augustin de Betancourt 1824. Burnes and Auckland planned to replicate on the Indus this great mart for Central Asian goods.

The Chinese Pavilions at the Nizhni Novgorod Trade Fair.

*Above.* The fortress of Baikhar on the Indus sketched by James Atkinson, 1839, from the British camp just after Burnes negotiated its surrender.

*Left.* James Rattray 1841, *Kabul Women in Indoor and Outdoor Dress.*

James Rattray 1841, *Kohistani Warriors*.

Emily Eden's sketch of Dost Mohammed in exile surrounded by three of his sons. Haidar Khan, Governor of Ghazni, is top left.

Three sketched portraits by Dr James Atkinson on the expedition, which show how the British leaders dressed in Afghanistan. Copyright the National Portrait Gallery.

(a) William Hay Macnaghten, Burnes' pompous and overbearing boss

(b) Macnaghten's nephew Arthur Conolly, whom Burnes considered a Christian fanatic

(c) Burnes' friend the highly clubbable General Sir Willoughby Cotton

Mohan Lal journeyed to Scotland in 1843 to return Burnes' papers to his family. This calotype, or early photograph, was taken in Edinburgh. Copyright Scottish National Portrait Gallery.

Afghans, as brave as irregular troops need be. I am on stirring ground, and I am glad to say I am up to it in health and all that, and was never more braced in my life.[31]

Burnes established a regular messenger service to Leech at Kandahar, and soon was feeding hopeful reports to Dost that the Persians had been defeated before Herat, which was true, and had fallen back on Meshed, which was not. Witkiewicz complained to Simonicz 'all this has occasioned Dost Mohammed to behave very coldly towards me'. Burnes seemed to be winning again.

Lieutenant Mackeson had now been moved from Peshawar to be Resident at Lahore. This infuriated Wade, who was still Resident at Ludhiana but, although Mackeson reported through him, was now cut off from direct contact with Ranjit. The Maharaja had a letter from the Qazi of Kabul read out to Mackeson:

> That the Russian envoy and Captain Burnes occasionally meet in durbar before Sirdar Dost Mohammed Khan and have warm discussions [. . .] That lately in presence of Captain Burnes the Russian Envoy had remarked in a loud tone to the Amir that [. . .] [he] would not do well to rely on the promises of the English nation who had come so far from their own country to make conquests in the east and who would succeed [. . .] if the Amir allowed himself to be cajoled by their soft words. On hearing this remark both Dost Mohammed and Captain Burnes remained silent.[32]

Neither Burnes nor Witkiewicz give any account of joint meetings with the Emir. But plainly the Qazi believed Ranjit's sympathies to be with Russia. He also reported that Burnes had sent Witkiewicz wine and fruit, showing that Britain was tributary to Russia – an unfortunate interpretation of Burnes' well-meaning welcome. But it does seem that Witkiewicz and Burnes continued some friendly communication in Kabul – for example they updated each other on their reports from Herat.[33]

Witkiewicz now attempted to push Russian diplomacy right to the frontier of British India by proceeding to Lahore for discussions with Ranjit Singh. He wrote to Avitabile in Peshawar to inform him.[34] Avitabile asked Ranjit for instructions, and Ranjit asked Mackeson for advice. Mackeson, a cynic about the 'Russian threat', appeared unconcerned. This attitude was reinforced by the fact that Ranjit had just given him news of the Persian defeat before Herat.[35] There were senior Sikhs who argued that a Russian agent should be welcome to counter the demands of the British.[36]

Mackeson received instructions from Macnaghten to give Ranjit Singh a different reply:

Regarding the supposed intention of the Russian agent [...] to proceed to Lahore [...] the Governor-General would strongly discourage the reception of that individual by the Maharajah. Captain Vicowitch is [...] reported to be the minister of Persian intrigue and his objects must be regarded with suspicion. To Lahore he has no accredited mission, and his reception by the Ruler of the Punjab would be open to misconstruction [...][37]

By 6 January 1838 Auckland felt confounded, and he blamed Dost, writing to Hobhouse:

> Burnes is well established at Kabul, with only this disadvantage, that he can hardly hope that Dost Muhammad will be satisfied with anything that would not be offensive to Ranjit Singh; and yet he ought to be satisfied that he is allowed to remain at peace, and is saved from actual invasion. But he is reckless, and intriguing, and will be difficult to keep quiet [...][38]

Auckland was still under the misapprehension that a Sikh invasion of Afghanistan was realistic, and that Dost feared it. Auckland, like Burnes, believed the conflict between Russia and Britain would more likely be resolved between the principals: 'It is in Europe and Persia,' wrote Colvin to Burnes 'that the battle of Afghanistan must probably be ultimately fought.'

In Kabul Burnes was still attempting to construct an acceptable compromise over Peshawar on the basis of Auckland's pronouncements. Then on 20 January 1838 a messenger arrived from India bearing two letters, finally giving Burnes clear instructions. Macnaghten declared it impossible that Ranjit Singh should be asked to cede control of Peshawar to Dost Mohammed. But he might agree to hand it to Sultan Mohammed.

This was not incompatible with Burnes' own plan, tentatively agreed with Dost. But of all his half-brothers, Dost Mohammed was on the worst terms with Sultan, who had designs on heading the family himself. Sultan had betrayed Dost's original jihad for Peshawar. The Emir regarded Sultan as a traitor and a collaborator. Sultan viewed Dost as having treacherously seized the throne of Kabul from him. There was also a personal hatred. Sultan had been promised a Saduzai princess, Aga Taj, in marriage. As she prepared to leave Kabul for Peshawar, 'The Amir also had lost his heart for her beauty, and got hold of her by force and married her immediately. This at once created [...] a fatal animosity between the brothers.'[39] So a second rape of a Saduzai princess by Dost was to have fatal consequences.

Burnes sought an immediate meeting with Dost to put forward Macnaghten's plan. The Emir saw him straightaway, with Nawab Jabbar Khan, whose advice Dost relied on very heavily; they conferred every morning. The meeting lasted nearly five hours,[40] and Burnes wrote a detailed account to Macnaghten[41]. With trifling differences of language, this could have been a note of a meeting sent back by an Ambassador during my diplomatic career, right down to format.

Dost noted that he had agreed to Burnes' previous idea of sending 'tribute, horses and apology' to Ranjit Singh, and holding Peshawar under him. He said in doing so, he had intended to continue to allow Sultan Mohammed his jaghir, or revenues, from Peshawar uninterrupted. But while he did not doubt the good intentions of the British, they must not understand that Sultan had sought to overthrow him before in league with Ranjit, and might do so again. The Emir concluded that he understood why the British did not want Kabul or Kandahar allied with Persia; but to set up Sultan at Peshawar would be to invite his own destruction.[42]

Burnes replied that the British government had proposed friendly intervention with the Sikhs to help the Emir, because he had agreed to renounce an alliance with Persia. But Dost should consider the boost to his reputation from putting the Sikhs back across the Indus, and thus allowing the Muslims of Peshawar to practise their religion. If war with the Sikhs were ended, the Emir would save much expenditure. The Barakzai family would control Kabul, Peshawar and Kandahar. The British government may take further measures to restrain any possible attack on Kabul.

Dost countered that he was currently under no threat from Ranjit's possession of Peshawar, but would be so if Sultan were there. Rather to Burnes' surprise, Jabbar Khan joined in and said it was true that the bad blood between Sultan and Dost would make it unsafe to set up Sultan in Peshawar.

Burnes had believed that Dost Mohammed was committed to recovering Peshawar for Islam. This conversation proved that Dost was, rather, interested in recovering Peshawar for himself. To explain this apparent selfishness, the Emir now reluctantly revealed to Burnes that he had new intelligence. Sultan had just sent a message to Shuja, offering with Sikh support to help restore Shuja in Kabul, thus reinstating the alliance against Dost of 1834. Sultan was to be Shuja's wazir in Kabul.

Jabbar Khan suggested a solution. Peshawar's revenues should be split equally between Dost and Sultan; both would pay an annual tribute to Ranjit. This was a reinstatement of the arrangement when Ranjit had first briefly taken Peshawar, in 1823. The Emir agreed to this, adding that Jabbar should govern the city, on behalf of the co-proprietors.

Burnes undertook that the British government would consider this proposal. That ended the meeting, and Burnes concluded his report with the recommendation that Jabbar Khan's proposal deserved serious consideration. It would meet British objectives of keeping a powerful buffer in Afghanistan by cementing an alliance with the Emir, while the proposal on

Peshawar should meet the needs of Ranjit Singh.

It is typical of Alexander Burnes that, at this crucial moment, with issues of war and peace at stake, he still managed to pursue scientific interests. And it is typical of that equally remarkable man, Jabbar Khan, that he was enthusiastically co-operating with Burnes in a scheme to introduce the potato and other crops into Afghanistan, from seed Burnes had brought. Burnes had discussed horticulture with the Nawab, who was an enthusiast, at their first meeting in 1833 and had written to Jabbar ahead of his return that he was bringing 'hundreds of seeds'.[43] Jabbar had already begun agricultural improvements on his Afghan estates, on European lines, and had shown his work to Josiah Harlan. Dr Wallich of Calcutta Botanic Garden had supplied Burnes with 356 different types of seed, and Dr Lush of the Bombay Botanical Garden had contributed more.[44] Burnes had a serious intent to introduce useful new crops and varieties into Afghanistan, with active Afghan coadjutors.

The Sikh Empire was very much Ranjit's personal creation, and started a spectacular implosion immediately on his death. Yet Burnes is the only one who seems to have factored Ranjit's imminent demise seriously into his policy thinking – he was unable to get Macnaghten to do so, despite explicitly arguing the point with him.[45] In fact Macnaghten had somehow convinced himself that on Ranjit's death the Company would acquire the Sikh Empire peacefully. He had advised Bentinck that 'after his death I look upon it as certain that his supremacy will devolve upon us by the national consent'.[46]

Burnes therefore was trying to find a peaceful resolution over Peshawar, while his superiors were itching to annex it. Burnes waited anxiously for the reply to his proposal. What he got was a bombshell.

On 22 February 1838 he received a letter from Macnaghten dated 20 January, covering another from Auckland addressed to Dost Mohammed. Macnaghten told Burnes that the Governor-General rebuked him strongly for exceeding his authority, in offering to provide subsidies to help defend Kandahar from any Persian advance.

> These promises are entirely unauthorized [. . .] They are most unnecessarily made in unqualified terms and they would [. . .] commit the government upon the gravest questions of general policy [. . .] But the rulers of Candahar must not be allowed to rest in confidence on promises so given [. . .] you will endeavor to set yourself right with the chiefs [. . .] his Lordship feels he could not enlarge upon his strict injunction that you in the future conform punctually on all points to the orders issued for your guidance.
>
> Positive engagements to assist opposition to actual invasion from the westward, by arms or subsidies, have not been contemplated by his Lordship – Not to speak of the exceeding inconvenience of political engagements at a

distance so great from our own resources, these measures might raise questions of serious national difficulty, which ought, if possible, to be reserved for the unfettered consideration of the Government of England.[47]

Macnaghten instructed Burnes to speak to Dost in a way that was insulting and designed to provoke conflict between Britain and Kabul, admonishing the Emir 'to behave in a less mistaken manner' to Ranjit Singh, and 'That, in the precarious position in which he was now placed, our good offices for the peace and security of his remaining territory should be thankfully accepted by him'.

In fact, Dost's position at Kabul was secure; the main threat to him was from the British – something he was coming to understand. These instructions had been sent before Macnaghten received Burnes' account of his recent major meeting with the Emir. Burnes might have used that fact to delay acting on these highly unpalatable instructions. But he went ahead to act precisely as instructed.

Burnes was further instructed to insist that Dost dismiss Witkiewicz immediately – and to state that if the Emir would not do so, then he would himself leave and 'the act will be regarded as a direct breach of friendship with the British government'.[48]

Burnes delivered this message, tantamount to a threat of war, to Dost the very next day, as he reported back to Macnaghten on 23 February. Josiah Harlan was in the Emir's council when Auckland's insulting letter was handed round, and wrote that there followed an 'embarrassed silence' before the storm of indignation broke.[49] On 5 March Burnes sent a further report, saying that the Emir was holding nightly counsels in the Bala Hissar, and powerful nobles were pressing him to 'take the British at their word' and send Burnes away. The Emir himself had 'given vent to very strong expressions'.

At this stage, Masson claims, Burnes had a nervous breakdown, hiding his head in towels and closeting himself from the world. Certainly his prestige had taken a severe knock – for example Auckland wrote to John McNeill informing him that Burnes had been reprimanded.[50] But there is no evidence to support Masson's account that Burnes disintegrated. Burnes' notes to Masson continue at least once a day. His journal continues, and notes the setback quite phlegmatically. The flow of correspondence with Calcutta and with Wade, McNeill, Lord and Leech is unbroken.

Masson was becoming less attached to the mission. Burnes' notes to him are increasingly about Masson's failures to turn up, generally on a plea of illness. Masson claimed to be in constant pain, and Burnes is continually sending him medicine for his unspecified illness – and money, with polite hopes that the pain was bearable. Also books, articles, pens and paper, brandy, wine and numerous other considerations, and always more money. Burnes does betray some impatience: 'I hope nothing will prevent you joining us tomorrow [. . .] but however glad we shall be to have you it will be very wrong if we do not leave you a free agent.'[51]

Witkiewicz was now led, preening in his Cossack uniform, through the streets of Kabul with a large cavalry escort. He was for the first time received by Dost Mohammed in full durbar.

Witkiewicz was delighted. He reported to Simonicz:

> On the 21st February was received from Lord Auckland a reply decidedly to refuse all that Burnes had negotiated [. . .] Dost Mahomed Khan, abandoning his hopes of assistance on the part of the English, has sent to Candahar the letter received from Lord Auckland, and requested for cooperation and consultation one of the Sirdars of that place. Burnes has written to Lieutenant Leech at Candahar, that he should by all means endeavor to dissuade the Sirdars from coming to Cabool [. . .] But the ill-conducted intrigues of Leech have been disclosed [. . .] and led the Affghans to adopt the opposite course, to join Dost Mohammed Khan and break off all connection with the English, and place themselves under the sway of Persia, with the guarantee of Russia [. . .] and that after the taking of Herat, the Shah himself, with his troops, should advance into Affghanistan for the recovery of provinces occupied by Runjeet.[52]

Auckland had scored an own goal. Witkiewicz reported that 'Burnes declares' that Auckland himself rejected the Peshawar compromise which Ranjit would have accepted. It is interesting to speculate who told Witkiewicz this. Masson?

CHAPTER TWENTY-THREE

## 'Izzat wa Ikram'

Jabbar Khan had returned to his country estate, but on hearing of these developments rushed back to Kabul. He called on Burnes on 3 March. Burnes did not attempt to soften the line:

> in regard to Maharaja Runjeet Sing, that we could tender our good offices, which consisted in an endeavour to use our influence at Lahore to put a stop to future aggression on the part of the Ruler there on the Affghan dominions [. . .] I further told the Nawab of the views of Government regarding Peshawur, of its restoration being in the hands of Runjeet Sing, but most certainly it would not be given to the Ameer.

The Nawab replied that this was a misunderstanding; Kabul was in no danger from Ranjit Singh. Britain was insisting that Kabul cut all communication with Russia, Persia and Turkestan, in return for nothing except a pledge to advise Ranjit Singh against attacks he was not going to make.

Burnes said that if Kabul wanted more, he had not been told of it. What precisely did the Emir want? *'Izzat wa Ikram'*, replied the Nawab. Dignity and respect. It was a devastating reply, and it touched precisely on what British diplomacy was trying to take from the Afghans. Jabbar continued 'and to be looked upon in the light of being able to do something for the British Government, and for such service to receive its real friendship and not a proffer of its sympathy'. Afghanistan wanted the dignity of a nation, not British condescension.

He then asked Burnes a perceptive question. What were Auckland's real intentions – to break with the Afghans, or to ally with them? Burnes replied that he could not say more than was in Auckland's letter. At which point these men, who greatly liked each other, realised they would soon be at war. The Nawab then proposed – in a last ditch effort – that if the British plan was, as originally stated, to install Sultan Jan in Peshawar, Kabul would not interfere.

The next day the Emir's Secretary visited Burnes and told him Dost Mohammed was extremely depressed. In seeking friendship with the British, he had brought their enmity upon himself. The Emir's chief nobles were urging him that the formal concession of Peshawar to Ranjit Singh would disgrace him in this world and damn him in the next. The Emir thought that the hostility of the British may have come from a misunderstanding of the nature of his dealings with Witkiewicz, who they had ordered to quit Kabul after Navruz (21 March). Burnes said the delay was not acceptable, and demanded the originals of correspondence with the Russians. The Secretary did not agree to this humiliating demand.

On 5 March Burnes received a letter from Stoddart with the Shah of Persia's camp at Herat, enclosing another from Eldred Pottinger. The Persian forces were baffled. This changed perceptions in Kabul, where the fall of Herat had seemed imminent and Dost had been more and more identifying with the Qizilbash and other Shia factions.

Burnes' communications with Eldred had been cut by the siege, but Stoddart had got his message through, shielded by his diplomatic status in the Shah's camp. Burnes had been sending advice, instructions and money which had all been intercepted, leaving Eldred feeling abandoned.[1] Stoddart was himself in dire financial straits and Burnes promised to get Rs10,000 to him.

By 15 March Burnes realised he had been firmly displaced in Kabul by Witkiewicz, who was now receiving musical entertainments from Jabbar Khan. Burnes noted 'they are off with the old love and on with the new'. He refers to Witkiewicz as 'the Pole', so evidently had learnt something of his antecedents.[2]

For the first time, in reporting to Auckland, Burnes did not argue against policy. His report stiffly concludes: 'I am aware that the views of Government are decided, and it would be highly presumptuous in me to make any observations [. . .]' He now requested permission to leave Kabul.

Extraordinarily, throughout Burnes' negotiations, the British never asked Ranjit Singh if any of the proposed compromises over Peshawar was acceptable to him. Wade thought the proposal for the Barakzais to hold Peshawar from Ranjit and pay tribute was 'reasonable' and in line with Ranjit's own proposal the previous August. On 3 March 1838 Wade had written to Macnaghten that:

> I am ready [. . .] to communicate the proposition now made to Ranjit Singh, and to support by every argument that I can use the expediency of its acceptance by him.[3]

Macnaghten instructed Wade not to put Dost's proposal to Ranjit. Burnes wrote to Masson: 'I am astonished at his not having told R Sing a word of what has passed here.'[4] Burnes wrote to Macnaghten asking directly for Ranjit's reaction. Macnaghten's reply, dated 22 May 1838, was a mixture of sophistry and petulance:

> You dwell on the long silence as to the feelings of Ranjit Singh regarding Peshawar [. . .] it was distinctly stated in the instructions of the 20th January and 7th of March that Dost Mohammed must first disclaim all intention of making a *sine qua non* of the restoration [. . .] to him [. . .] of Peshawar, before we could enter. [. . .] on the subject with Ranjit Singh. That disclaimer [. . .] he has never made [. . .] he has insisted on pretensions in a spirit directly the reverse, so that for the result he has only to accuse himself.[5]

Only four months previously Auckland had written, 'I am thoroughly convinced that it is for the best interests of Runjeet Singh himself that he should come to terms of proper accommodation with the Afghans'. Auckland's views had changed completely, and rendered Burnes' mission impossible.

At the celebration of Navruz the Emir's minister Mirza Sami Khan held a dinner for Witkiewicz. During the evening it was decided that Burnes had better also be invited. He, however, declined; Mohan Lal would represent him. Seated next to Witkiewicz, Mohan was pumped for information. How many British troops were stationed at Ludhiana? How far apart were the garrisons of Karnal, Merat and Kanpur? What percentage of Company troops were Muslim? How much residual loyalty remained towards the old Mughal emperor?

On 25 March 1838 Dost wrote to Auckland, attempting one last direct appeal:

> I have no [. . .] inclination to enter into any [. . .] alliance but with the British. The Russians are publicly assisting the Persians & have made a breach in the treaty which has long forbidden them & the British stepping into the country of the Afghans. If such things do take place what then prevents yr Ldshp remedying our grievances [. . .]?[6]

On 29 March, Burnes met a new arrival in Kabul, a French adventurer named Cerron, a connection of Ventura. Burnes found him 'really a good fellow', and invited him to dinner. Cerron claimed to be on the way to Bokhara.[7] On 1 April, Dost visited Burnes and stayed a full three hours but found him sulky and unhelpful. Burnes had convinced himself that it was Dost's inflexibility over Peshawar which had caused the failure of his negotiations. He wrote to Masson:

> This brings the Ameer to ask in which way he has not met the wishes of Govt. I might have asked in which way <u>has</u> he but I am sick of the matter [. . .] never touched on business – Why should I – Vitkievitch is here and has no intention

of moving – the good Ameer declines all preliminaries for peace with Runjeet and writes to Candahar –[8]

Burnes had lost sympathy with Dost's hostility to Sultan, which he believed was having disproportionate effects: 'But all what the Ameer has done about Peshawar by his abuse of Sooltan Md Khan – he deserves it.'[9] Burnes' warm personal friendship with Sultan perhaps affected this mood. He began to adopt an openly antagonistic attitude to the Emir and satirised Dost's pleas: 'He gave the old story – no benefit – no one cares for a falling nation – I offered my wares for sale & you would not buy', while equally boasting of how robust he had been in response: 'I gave it fearfully & left him in a furious rage but not a word was forgotten of what I purposed for him.'[10]

In the first week of April, Burnes' position in Kabul became still more impossible. Witkiewicz had sent further messages to the Sirdars of Kandahar, and Leech was able to obtain these and send them on to Burnes. The message purported to be from the Tsar, and promised that if they united with Dost Mohammed against the Sikhs, Russia would send them arms and Persia money. Russia would then assist them to take Multan, Derajat and Sind. In return Russia asked them to accept a Russian Agent at Kandahar who would control their foreign policy: 'they were to make war when desired and make peace when desired.'[11]

Mehir Dil Khan arrived from Kandahar to firm up Burnes' offers of support against Persian attack, and weigh up the British against the Russian offers. This put Burnes in a difficult position. He had offered subsidy and his own presence if Kandahar were attacked. He had been reprimanded by Auckland for doing so. Burnes received Mehir Dil Khan in the humiliating position of having to withdraw, face to face, his offers of assistance. Burnes tried to argue that the presence of Leech in Kandahar was already sufficient evidence of British government support. He reported: '[T]he Sirdar [. . .] declared that neither he nor his brothers could accept such general promises'.

There are few positions more embarrassing than that of the repudiated Envoy. I have been there myself. My stringent public criticisms of the Uzbek dictatorship had won me a measure of influence with the Uzbek government. In Central Asia, strength and forthrightness are respected – diplomatic politeness is viewed as weakness. But when the British government took fright at my criticisms of our ally, they signalled to the Uzbek authorities that I did not have my government's support.[12] My influence evaporated immediately. A repudiated Envoy is in a position of stinging personal humiliation. Burnes wrote to Auckland on 25 April 1838 informing that he was leaving Kabul straightaway, 'The immediate cause of such a step being necessary, is the arrival of Sirdar Mehir Dil Khan [...] and the demands in consequence made by him [...] for a direct promise of protection from Persia, should Herat fall.'[13]

On 15 April Burnes received a large delegation representing both the Kabul and Kandahar Barakzais, headed by Jabbar Khan and Mehir Dil Khan. They offered to break off relations with Persia and Russia and place both Kabul and Kandahar under British protection in return for two mildly worded demands:

> First, a direct promise of its good offices to establish peace at Peshawar; and second, a promise to protect them from Persia, in whatever way the British judged it best for their interests.

Burnes had been warned so strongly to stick to his instructions, that even this offer, worded to be face-saving for the Afghans rather than binding on the British, had to be turned down flat. Witkiewicz was supported by a Cossack escort and staff from the Russian Legation in Teheran. It was the Legation's Secretary, M. Goutt, who delivered to Dost the further promises – including financial and military support for the recovery of Peshawar – which had sealed the failure of Burnes' mission.[14]

Dost viewed with horror the looming conflict with Britain. With Mehir Dil Khan, he now made one final offer, accepting all British demands. He would agree to Sultan Jan Mohammed having Peshawar as tributary to Ranjit Singh. Kabul and Kandahar would both agree to cease all diplomatic and trade relations with Persia and Russia. In return they asked for a British guarantee against military attack from Persia. This Burnes was specifically precluded from giving, so this last attempt at conciliation also failed. Dost wrote to Auckland, offering to accept almost any terms:

> If Herat falls into the hands of the Persians, it will cause serious loss and damage to the whole country of Affghanistan [...] I hope [...] that your lordship will apply an immediate cure to my pains, for the Russians are publicly assisting the Persians.
>
> If your lordship is pleased to bestow a little trouble to adjust affairs between this country and the Maharajah Runjeet Sing, who is the great and old ally of the British, how is it possible that we should make objections to it, or to suitable arrangements for peace.[15]

He went on to quote the defensive treaty signed by Shuja and Mountstuart Elphinstone in 1809, an excellent point which showed that he regarded Kabul as a continuing state. The British stance was to ignore Kabul's rights as a state and treat it as some kind of second order tribal chieftaincy. There was one last Afghan attempt to re-open negotiations through the agency of Josiah Harlan. Again Burnes refused to involve the American.

Burnes had delayed in Kabul, awaiting the return of Lord and Wood from Kunduz once the passes cleared of snow; but found his position impossible and quit on 26 April. Burnes had one last, mutually sorrowful, meeting with the Emir. There was a flash of temper from the Emir when Burnes referred to Britain's willingness to restrain Ranjit Singh; the Emir replied 'that if the Governor General believed it was protection of Cabool he had sued for, it was a mistake'. Dost still supplied free provisions and carriage for all of Burnes' party. Burnes rode out alongside Masson, with high marks of honour, accompanied for several miles by three of the Emir's sons. Burnes had sent Leech in Kandahar a message to return to Shikarpur via the Bolan pass.

Another professional Ambassador – Afzal Khan – made a detailed study of Burnes' proceedings in Kabul, and refutes the notion that Burnes did anything wrong.[16] Burnes' professional conduct as a diplomat was impeccable. The First Afghan War happened despite Burnes, not because of him, because his superiors were determined that it would happen.

As Burnes was leaving Kabul, Eldred Pottinger in Herat was having to eat the same wormwood, and tell Yar Mohammed and his ministers that the offers of financial assistance made to the defenders would not now be honoured, and that he had exceeded his instructions in making them. This instruction from Macnaghten had come to Eldred via John McNeill, who like Burnes then closed his mission and withdrew from the Shah's camp after copious insults. British diplomacy appeared in collapse throughout the region.

Burnes rode quickly from Kabul, spurred by the bitterness of failure. He offered the Frenchman Cerron the position of newswriter in Kabul on Rs250 a month, and gave him an immediate advance of Rs 1,000. Cerron fulfilled his role conscientiously, though Wood discovered that his travelling tales had been inventions.[17] Cerron, like all Great Game players on the British side, was to run into accounting difficulties after cashing bills to the tune of Rs6,000, to pay informants. This was still unresolved when he died on a mission for the British government in Bajour in 1839.

The mission now returned down the river. In Jalalabad they waited while rafts were built, and then shot down the Kabul water to Peshawar. The river tumbles down beneath walls of stone so high that often there is no point from which any sky is visible and nowhere that a person tossed from a boat could get a footing. Speed was not the only attraction – the route avoided the different but still very real dangers of a journey through the Khyber pass. Burnes employed characteristic understatement in his journal: 'the excitement in passing down the river of Cabool was very great and great care is required [. . .]' One of their rafts was churned round the Fuzul whirlpool for three hours. He described the worst rapid:

> I shall never forget in my life the approach to it. We had dropped down for half an hour under heavy clouds and with precipitous rocks of some hundreds of feet on either side. As we approached the famed spot we could see the water boiling [. . .] and nearing it thunder rolled and lightning flashed, the wind lifted the water upon us but we passed all in safety.

Burnes reached Peshawar late on 4 May 1838, and was joined by Lord and Wood twelve days later.[18] There he vented his anger at Auckland in a letter to James:

> The game is up. The Russians gave me the coup de grace & I could hold on no longer at Cabool so I have fallen back upon Peshawar [. . .] the Secretary of the Russian legation Mr Goutt came down with [. . .] offers of assistance and money, and as I had no powers to counteract him by a similar offer, and got wigged for talking of it [. . .] we must now do something and that too rapidly for Herat is on the eve of falling and Russia promises to aid Cabool in fighting Runjeet Sing!! – I am not so much chagrined at my retrograde movements as you would expect [. . .] only save me from ever again working under a 'safe man' as my Chief is designated by his party in England [. . .] I [. . .] shall either be ordered to Simla or Sinde, or to await the fall of Herat, or to lead the ex-King against the Barukzyes, this last I will not do – The Barukzyes consigned themselves to us, and merely asked for Persia to be warned off and we would not do it![19]

Burnes was to allow his mind to be changed on leading Shuja against the Barakzais.

He had left before he received a reply from Auckland explicitly approving his departure. He was highly relieved to receive an instruction from Auckland to quit, dated the day after they had left Kabul.[20]

Other news reached him in Peshawar. Holland's sister Cecilia was now on the way out to India.[21] It appears highly probable that her brother's in-law, the famous Alexander Burnes, was high on her list of targets. Sadly the two were never to meet.

CHAPTER TWENTY-FOUR

## Regime Change

Burnes' recall from Kabul coincided with despatches from Palmerston to Auckland, urging him to counteract the growing threat from Russia.[1] The network of Burnes' agents was still active, and Alex in Peshawar received copies of Witkiewicz' reporting. Auckland therefore soon saw Witkiewicz' proposal for the Russian-backed Persian army to come through the Khyber pass to Peshawar.

This makes the British invasion of Afghanistan less inexplicable. The decision was facilitated by a constitutional quirk. When physically separated from his Supreme Council, the Governor-General could take decisions alone. This was sensible as government could not be paralysed when the Governor-General was travelling, but it had not been envisaged that he would abandon his capital for a lengthy period. Lord Auckland was absent from Calcutta on a 'progress' which lasted from January 1837 to February 1840. The Company's government became, by default, an autocracy. The Council were almost entirely cut out of decision making. Letters from London were sent first to the Governor-General in his camp, and only then copied on by him to the Council in Calcutta together with his replies and decisions.[2]

Lord Auckland on tour had a retinue of 12,000. But the only ones who counted were William Macnaghten, John Colvin and Henry Torrens, respectively the Political, Private and Deputy Secretaries. Do not be confused by terminology. These were extremely powerful men. The influence of this clique was understood – and resented – throughout British India. In the remote southern station of Rajamundri, the wife of the district judge could write home in 1838:

> India is, in fact, governed by the Private Secretaries, who [. . .] are often intent only on feathering their own nests and promoting their young relations. Half the experienced men in the country who really understand matters are kept in subordinate situations.[3]

Auckland was a vacillating character, easily influenced. John Colvin was haughty and arrogant. Colvin and Macnaghten had the primary influence in launching the invasion of Afghanistan.

Henry Torrens was the most junior and consistently denied any involvement in decision-making, saying his role was purely administrative. There is no compelling evidence otherwise. Torrens was a minor poet of some merit, who composed a verse address to James Burnes on his Masonic tour of Calcutta in 1840.[4] Macnaghten and Torrens had been charged by the Asiatic Society with producing a translation of *The Thousand and One Nights*, which shows another side to the Imperial administrators, though they sadly bowdlerised their effort.

Colvin was second son of the proprietor of a major Scottish merchant house in Calcutta; he had been educated in St Andrews and became an accomplished golfer. St Andrews University was then a corrupt and intellectually moribund institution of 150 students. It has of course changed – it now has more students. Leaving the university at fourteen he went on to the EIC college at Haileybury, in the same year with Charles Trevelyan. He was the very stuff of the Raj: related to Charles Metcalfe, John Kaye, Henry Lawrence and Sam Browne.[5] On arrival in Calcutta in 1826 the nineteen-year-old Colvin became Assistant to Macnaghten at the Court of Appeal, and then in various Residencies until 1830, when Macnaghten secured him a job in Calcutta in the Revenue and Judicial Department.

Colvin and Macnaghten were at the heart of the tight Calcutta social circle which included Trevelyan and Macaulay. When Auckland arrived in 1836, Macnaghten recommended Colvin to be the Governor-General's Private Secretary. Colvin was very much Macnaghten's man.

Auckland's 'Progress' was nearly scuppered. The year 1837 was one of drought along the north-west frontier, in which 500,000 died. After the Governor-General's column reached Cawnpore, Macnaghten tried to convince him to turn back because of the strain that 12,000 men and 30,000 baggage animals would put on the devastated area. But Auckland and his sisters were anxious for a cooler climate, so the progress continued. The Edens had been thrown together with his staff in the intense companionship of camp life, an intimacy otherwise impossible in their society. As Emily Eden noted:

> besides the odd native groups our friends catch us up in their *deshabille* – Mrs A [Colvin] carrying the baby in an open carriage, Mrs C [Torrens] with hers fast asleep in a tonjaun [...]Mrs B [Macnaghten] carrying Mr B's pet cat in her palanquin carriage, with her ayah opposite guarding the parroquet from the cat.[6]

In this poor atmosphere for decision-making, Auckland's views assimilated to those of his companions.

Auckland finally made a firm commitment to the restoration of Shah Shuja in a minute of 12 May 1838, drafted in his own hand. His minute[7] opens with a review of historic British policy, and blames the weak state of Afghanistan on internal Barakzai feuding. It then details minutely the reasons for war:

> The rapid and successful advance of Persia [...] the presence of a Russian agent at Cabool, and his own restless and unaccommodating spirit, have led Dost Mohammed to reject the terms which are held out to him of security in his actual possessions [...] since [...] my despatch of the 8th February to the Honorable Secret Committee, in which I stated that it was not then my intention to oppose the hostile move of Persian forces upon Candahar and Cabool [...] circumstances have occurred which may materially alter my views. For now Russian agents have prominently put themselves forward in support of the designs of Persia [...] The extraordinary excitement which has been produced in the public mind [...] in consequence of the approach of the Persian power, is also a signal to me of the mischief that might arise were that power to attain a settled influence of authority over all the Afghan countries [...]
>
> Dost Mahommed Khan has shown himself to be so disaffected and ambitious that, with him at least, we could form no satisfactory connection [...]
>
> It is clear to me that, upon the departure of Captain Burnes [...] a declaration should be made to Runjeet Singh [...] He may be invited to state the measures [...] which, by himself or in concert with us, he may be inclined to pursue, for the security of his Western frontier, and we may tender our cooperation [...] it may be remarked to him, that any endeavour on his part, exclusively to establish his authority in Cabool, would combine against him all national and religious feeling and would almost ensure failure. But as [...] he is not likely to take this course, he would rather [...] like to assure to himself a friendly Afghan influence at Cabool, by enabling Shah Shoojah ool Moolk to proceed, with better arms and equipment, on a second expedition to recover his throne.
>
> Some degree of concert on his part with us will probably be felt by him, in every event, to be expedient [...]
>
> Should Herat fall [...] we must prepare to see the most rapid advance of Persian influence, if not her arms, towards India [...] we may take the course of resistance to Persia without [...] hampering ourselves by the additional embarrassment of reference to the Russian connection [...] giving our aid and countenance in concert with Runjeet Singh to enable Shah Shuja ool Moolk to re-establish his sovereignty in the Eastern division of Afghanistan under engagements which shall conciliate the feelings of the Sikh ruler, and bind the restored monarch to the support of our interest appears to me that,

which is decidedly the most deserving of attention [...] Runjeet Singh would assist by the employment of a portion of his troops and we by some contribution in money and the presence of an accredited agent of the government and of a sufficient number of officers for the direction of the Shah's army [...] Shah Shooja [...] so attended might be expected rapidly to disperse or break down all formidable elements of opposition [...] in such a scheme of defensive alliance [...] the Scindians must be [...] made to contribute to the general safety [...] The occupation of Shikapore by an efficient force, and the skilful improvement of its defences would be prominent objects [...]

Sgd Auckland
Simla
May 12th 1838

A decision to go to war can seldom have been communicated less incisively. But you can dig out the key points from what is in full a very long document. Dost Mohammed is portrayed as an irredeemable enemy. Auckland orders the military occupation of Sind almost casually. Ranjit Singh is to be encouraged to invade Afghanistan to restore Shuja with British help, firstly if Herat falls, and secondly if Herat does not fall. A permanent British military advisory presence in Afghanistan is mooted. Divisions between Shia and Sunni are to be consciously exploited. Macnaghten will negotiate all this with Ranjit Singh, and nobody is to mention Russia.

Auckland's views had changed completely since his minute of 9 October 1837 when he had written:

> I am thoroughly convinced that it is for the best interests of Runjeet Singh himself that he should come to terms of proper accommodation with the Afghans.[8]

There had been another key influence acting on Auckland – the Sikhs. On 1 May a large deputation, headed by Ranjit's nephew Ajit Singh, had arrived at Simla and entered into intense negotiations over ten days with Auckland; Macnaghten was interpreter and adviser. The Sikhs departed on 11 May and on the 12th Auckland signed off his fateful minute setting the policy of deposing Dost Mohammed.[9] Wade, Macnaghten and Colvin were present with Auckland as he drafted.

Macnaghten was to negotiate with Ranjit Singh to turn the invasion of Afghanistan into reality. Macnaghten thought restoring Shah Shuja was the correct policy, in blunt contradiction of reports and arguments from Burnes. Why?

Undoubtedly Wade was influential. Masson was also advising Macnaghten to replace Dost Mohammed with Shah Shuja.[10] But there was another British officer with expertise on Afghanistan, who had been there before Burnes – Arthur Conolly.

Conolly, like Burnes, thought highly of Dost. In his *Journey to the North of India Overland* he wrote:

> In bright contrast to these is Dost Mohummud Khan [...] Albeit not formerly of a very good character, he is now widely famed for the excellence of his rule; and the inhabitants of Caubul [...] would probably be sorry to see him supplanted [...] [He] has followed a liberal line of policy, endeavouring to conciliate the nobles and all classes of the people; he enlists Dorraunees, and has brought under subjection the disaffected Ghilgies within his district. He affects the strictest forms of the Soonnee creed, while he is most tolerant to the many Sheeahs of Caubul [...]

Conolly put great stress on the Persian threat to Afghanistan. But his idea of how to strengthen Afghanistan against Persia was precisely opposite to that of Burnes. He argues:

> The Affghauns generally have in every way suffered so much from the revolution that they would hail the resumption of the royal authority, whether by Kamraun or by any other man of the family [...] The rulers of petty Affghaun states cannot have the motives to oppose foreign invasion of India that would be felt by a monarch whose dignity and interests would in many way be associated with ours.[11]

He wrote a lengthy paper on 'The Overland Invasion of India', carried in the influential *Calcutta Courier* on 1 and 2 July 1831. Conolly, working together with Trevelyan, played a key role in establishing Afghan policy. While Burnes was in England, Mohan Lal had re-attached himself to Trevelyan and had input into Conolly and Trevelyan's work.[12]

Conolly's friends and family resented that he had not received the hero's reception that awaited Burnes, whose journey was arguably less arduous than Conolly's overland trek from St Petersburg to Calcutta. Conolly had not been to Kabul or Bokhara, but then Burnes had not been to Herat or Meshed.

Arthur Conolly was William Hay Macnaghten's nephew. Macnaghten took his nephew's line in every respect, and particularly that the Afghans were eager to welcome a Saduzai restoration, on which an official paper by Conolly and Trevelyan of 15 March 1831 had concluded:

> It is gratifying to reflect that while we shall consolidate the Afghan empire for our own interests we shall [...] establish a lasting claim upon the gratitude of that people and our name will become associated with all the blessings [...] from the restoration of security and good order.[13]

Macaulay was another key influence behind the armed restoration of Shuja. In an *Edinburgh Review* justification of the invasion he quoted Conolly at length,[14] and argued that advances by Persia had 'combined to unsettle the mind and resuscitate the dormant enmity, of the Mahomedan population throughout the Peninsula. Their hopes of recovered dominion were strengthened by the expectation that our power would be simultaneously assailed in other quarters.' An offensive move was the only way to counter the dangerous perception of British vulnerability.

Auckland shared Macaulay's concern about internal unrest. The Company's most recent martial performances – in Burma and Nepal – had been less than glorious, and rumours and portents abounded. As the *Calcutta Review* later recalled:

> The year 1838 was marked by a deplorable change in the feelings of our own subjects, and of the princes of India, towards our authority. The confidence [...] in the permanence of our supremacy was displaced by a feverish anxiety [...] A general opinion began to be formed in the minds of our own subjects that the empire was about to be assailed [...][15]

Crucially this mood affected the Company's own sepoys. Naik Sita Ram recollected:

> The Mahommedans said that a large army was coming to invade India and tried [...] to excite the feelings of the people. They gave out that this invading army was supported by a large force of Russians; when it made its appearance on this side of the passes, it would be a signal for the entire Mahommedan population to rise against the Sirkar and drive the foreigners out of India. These reports daily gathered strength until fear filled the mind of the whole Native Army.[16]

There was nothing unusual in the replacement of an existing ruler by British military force, installing a rival family member as a puppet. This was the standard EIC mode of operation from its displacement of Chanda Sahib by Muhammad Ali as Nawab of the Carnatic in 1752. Some of the worst imperialist aggressions, such as the destruction of Tipu Sultan and his Court at Mysore, are still written of by historians as though they were desirable steps on the road to progress, and as though a very rich and complex culture were barbarian. Indeed, had the British occupation of Afghanistan been a military success, condemnation of Auckland by historians would have been muted. Immorality was clearest perceived when it failed to advance British interests.

Sir Penderel Moon's monumental *The British Conquest and Dominion of India* details twenty-seven usurpations by the British in India before we get to Dost Mohammed. The most recent had been the annexation of Oudh in

1837, involving the installation by armed force of a puppet monarch. During the occupation of Kabul, the British also deposed the ruler of Kurnal and took Aden. Historians of the First Afghan War have in general neglected the connected usurpation of Mehrab Khan of the vast territory of Kelat.

In short, the invasion of Afghanistan was no more morally reprehensible than general British policy in India, merely less successful.

On 29 May Burnes received a letter asking him to report to Macnaghten at Adinagar. Macnaghten also asked Burnes to produce a paper of options for policy in Afghanistan. On 2 June 1838 Burnes replied with a 3,000-word study.[17] This stated that the problem was not Afghanistan, but Persia and Russia. The best thing Auckland could do was to write strongly to the Shah of Persia threatening severe consequences if he persisted in attacking Herat or other parts of Afghanistan. A divided and weak Afghanistan was not in British interests; a strong, united buffer state was.

He continued, 'If it is the object of government to destroy the present chief of Caubul', then the options were to replace him with Sikh rule, with Sultan Mohammed, or with Shah Shuja. The Afghans would never accept Sikh rule, Ranjit Singh would not live long, and his empire would implode. Sultan Mohammed did not have the ability to rule Kabul. That left Shuja.

Burnes started his analysis of the Shuja option by saying that he had 'no very high opinion' of Shuja, but then crossed this out. He had already published that unequivocally in a bestselling book. He continued:

> As for Shah Shuja the British Government has only to send him to Peshawar with an agent and two of its own regiments as an honorary escort, with an avowal to the Afghans that we have taken up his cause, to ensure his being fixed forever on his throne. The present time is perhaps better [. . .] for the Afghans, as a nation, detest Persia; and Dost Muhammed Khan's having gone over to the Court of Teheran, though he believes it to be from dire necessity, converts many a doubting Afghan into a bitter enemy. The Maharaja's permission has only to be asked for the ex-King's advance to Peshawar, granting him [. . .] some four or five of his regiments which have no Sikhs in their ranks, and Shuja becomes King. He need not move from Peshawar, but [. . .] [announce] from that city, that he has the co-operation of the British and the Maharaja; and with but a little distribution of ready money [. . .] he will find himself the real king of the Afghans in a couple of months.[18]

It was this option which Macnaghten seized upon. But Burnes ended that his preferred option was still to support Dost. His conclusion was a plea to Macnaghten:

> But it remains to be considered why we cannot act with Dost Muhammad. He is a man of undoubted ability, and has at heart high opinions of the British

nation: and if half what you must do for others were done for him [...] he would abandon Persia and Russia tomorrow [...] opportunity has been given to him, but I would rather discuss this in person with you, for I think there is much to be said for him. [...] it should not be forgotten that we promised nothing, and Persia and Russia held out a great deal [...] The man has something in him.[19]

Burnes then yet again displayed the remarkable multi-faceted nature of his intellect. He immediately wrote to Masson in Peshawar, giving detailed instructions on particular samples of skulls and horns he wished to send on to Hugh Falconer.[20] He also that day wrote a paper for the Bombay Geographical Society, giving a brief account of the Kabul mission and the various studies which would be forthcoming. He modestly claimed he had simply co-ordinated the excellent work of Lord, Leech and Wood.[21] Burnes then set off to join Macnaghten.

Even now Auckland was still prevaricating; as his sister Emily noted in her journal on 14 June, he changed his mind from morning to afternoon, depending on who was with him.[22] His dilemma was further increased by a letter from Thoby Prinsep, Secretary to the Supreme Council in Calcutta, warning him Shuja was believed incapable of governing Kabul.

On 1 June 1838 Macnaghten entered Ranjit Singh's magnificent audience chamber at the summer palace of Adinagar, dressed in cravat, yellow waistcoat, striped trousers and tails, leaving his top hat with the doorkeeper. As for his hosts, as Ranjit's court circular put it, 'the troops of the Maharajah, covered from head to foot with silver, jewels and all manner of beautiful clothes, were drawn up before his doors, and such was their appearance that the jewel-mine, out of envy, drew a stone upon its head, the river sat upon the sand of shame, and the manufacturers of the handsome cloth of Rum [Istanbul] pulled down their workshops.'

Ranjit Singh, on his last legs, tottered the entire length of the audience chamber to hug Macnaghten. The British delegation included Wade, Mackeson, William Osborne (Auckland's nephew and Military Secretary), Captains Murray and MacGregor and Dr Drummond. The Maharaja delightedly examined for some time the trays of jewellery and clocks Macnaghten had brought. This habit was often interpreted by his British guests as cupidity. In fact Ranjit was paying them a compliment. Indian princely etiquette was that tribute gifts should not even be looked at; those from equals and superiors should be ostensibly appreciated.

After an exchange of lavish compliments, Ranjit asked Macnaghten about his capacity for drinking strong alcohol and his hunting exploits. Neither was Macnaghten's strong suit. Ranjit resisted Macnaghten's attempts to move on to business, but suggested they meet again the next day. So on 2 June a business meeting took place. Ranjit was flanked by Dhian Singh, who had led the mission to Auckland at Simla, and his minister Aziz al Din. With Macnaghten were Wade and Osborne.

Macnaghten explained that Burnes' mission to Kabul had failed to reach a commercial agreement because Dost Mohammed was deviously negotiating with other powers. Britain had no fear of Russia or Persia as 200,000 professional troops could be mobilised at short notice. But unrest and rumour could 'unsettle the minds of men', and it would be better to concert measures for a more stable situation in Afghanistan. Macnaghten suggested Ranjit Singh's treaty of 1833 with Shah Shuja be revived, with Britain added as an extra party.

'That,' replied Ranjit, 'would be adding sugar to milk.' However the large majority of the Sikh court, led by Dhian Singh, were strenuously opposed to any alliance with the British. Only Aziz al Din was in favour. The outcome was by no means a foregone conclusion. Ranjit had been secretly negotiating a potential anti-British alliance with Nepal.

In March 1837 General Allard, returning from leave, had presented Ranjit credentials as Agent of France. Palmerston asked the French government to revoke this, and illegally intercepted French diplomatic bags for Lahore. Burnes had noted with regret he was no longer allowed to communicate with Allard.[23] France had retaliated against British diplomatic bags traversing France.[24] The British forces on the Sutlej had long had instructions to prevent potential mercenaries from crossing to join Ranjit Singh; Calcutta now issued specific orders to arrest any suspected Frenchmen, and British missions in Alexandria and Bushire were ordered to intercept French officers. Ventura was refused a passport to travel through British India on his way to leave in France. So relationships were strained.

Auckland's instructions to Macnaghten were clear. Kabul could be taken directly by the Sikhs or by Shuja. In neither case would British troops be used. Finance, supplies, trainers and advisers yes; boots on the ground no. Macnaghten, Wade and Mackeson believed this policy mistaken, that Sikh aggrandisement was also a danger to British India, and that Britain should restore Shuja directly. If the Sikhs were involved, it must only be as junior partners to a major British force. In three weeks Macnaghten wrote no fewer than thirteen letters to Auckland putting forward this view, but Auckland resisted sending a British force which might come into conflict with Russia, with unknown ramifications in Europe.

Adinagar in June was oppressively hot, and both Macnaghten and Murray became so ill that Dr Drummond wanted to evacuate them. Soon Wade too was sick, so seriously that he did not expect to survive. Given Ranjit Singh's

## Regime Change 237

health, there can never have been such a vital diplomatic conference of invalids. Much of the negotiation was carried out by Mackeson and Aziz al Din. Ranjit pressed his claims to Sind and settled for an agreement that the Amirs would again be made to pay tribute to Shuja, and half of that tribute would go to Ranjit. He also made an entirely speculative claim to Jalalabad, which Macnaghten bought off with another two lakhs of rupees per year from Shuja.

On 4 June Burnes wrote to Masson that Auckland had made it plain that Shuja was to be imposed, and that Burnes would be expected to take part. Lord Auckland declared himself 'perfectly assured also that you will now apply yourself to the fulfilment of any new post [. . .] with the same assiduity [. . .] which you have always manifested [. . .]'[25]

Burnes had lost the policy battle, but was excited at the prospect of action. On 8 June he described 'stirring times [. . .] It is all settled that Shooja is to be set up, the Maharaja having agreed to everything'. He was still in daily communication with Masson at Peshawar and actively lobbying for his employment, telling him, ' The feeling towards you I have got hold of is decidedly good and I hope at Simla to have your mind set at rest.'[26] In the meantime Burnes succeeded in getting Macnaghten to double Masson's salary as newswriter to Rs500 monthly. Burnes was also receiving direct reports from Eldred Pottinger. He found the Indian newspapers full of the British expedition to Kharg in the Persian Gulf, and a general cry for war set up in in the press.[27]

Ranjit Singh had moved his court from Adinagar to Lahore, and Macnaghten was forced to follow. On 17 June Burnes arrived, paid a call on Ranjit Singh in the Shalimar Gardens, and had an enthusiastic social reception, but was excluded by Macnaghten from the negotiations. However Sikh sources credit Burnes at Shalimar with finally goading Ranjit to commit to the invasion, by repeating insults he claimed Dost Mohammed had uttered.[28] Ranjit valued Burnes' opinion, and although he could not include Burnes if Macnaghten did not, he sent Aziz al Din to have three lengthy meetings with him. Aziz had been with Ranjit for over thirty years and was integral to his rule. He asked Burnes for his candid opinion as to whether it would advantage Ranjit to set up Shuja. Burnes replied that it would benefit Ranjit, but whether it would benefit Afghanistan was a different question.

Alex spent his time otherwise writing up his recent mission. A selection of this material, concentrating on the commercial and ethnographic and excluding the military and political, was published by government.[29] On 18 June he wrote a further paper for Macnaghten on the modalities of installing Shuja. In this he argued that, as Dost Mohammed had never claimed the Kingship, installing Shuja did not mean deposing the Emir. The original mistake of Shuja's Kingship had been not to conciliate the Barakzai, whose support he needed to be secure. A position of honour and responsibility should therefore be found for Dost 'and we escape the odium of being privy to his entire destruction'.[30]

Reading the full eighteen articles of the treaty Macnaghten eventually agreed with Ranjit, it is remarkably lopsided. Ten operative points place a burthen exclusively on Shuja, while the British and Ranjit are put under exclusive obligation by only two each. There are six operative points where obligations are mutual. Among the exclusive obligations on Shuja are the acknowledgement of Sikh sovereignty over no fewer than thirty-two of his own former territories, including Kashmir, Attock and Peshawar. Not only must he pay twenty-two lakhs upfront plus two lakhs annually to Ranjit, but also agree to joint Sikh and British control of Afghan foreign policy. The major Sikh obligation was to provide Muslim troops to assist Shah Shuja's British-financed forces.

On 21 June Burnes wrote to Masson from Lahore that all was virtually settled:

> I feel our relationship with the Punjab on the verge of being materially altered and Shooja ool Moolk close to ascending the throne of his ancestors – You may remember the treaty between the Shah and Runjeet – that is the basis of everything and it only now remains to decide whether he is to go by Peshawar or by Candahar to his throne [. . .] The Shah is to have an Agent on our part with him – English officers and English money but it is not yet settled whether he is to have any of our troops – I am keen for a Regiment or two but there seems to be some form of objections to the thing on the part of Runjeet Sing – the treaty to be formed is tripartite.[31]

Burnes asked Masson which he wished canvassed with Auckland for his employment – a roving commission throughout Afghanistan, or Assistant to the Resident in Kabul. Masson was with Allard in Peshawar, and Burnes told him he might as well inform the Frenchman what was happening, as the network of munshis on all sides shared everything anyway. As usual Burnes sent money to Masson, and also gave details of money he was managing with the Bombay banks on behalf of Avitabile. A few days later Burnes was writing to Masson again, urging him to forward on some of Wood's collection of Central Asian trade goods, including wool samples and tea-cups.[32]

The tripartite agreement to restore Shuja was signed by Macnaghten and sealed in wax with Ranjit's signet ring on 26 June. There was no provision for the British to send troops to Afghanistan, but they were to supply a division to garrison Shikarpur as an advance base – which Ranjit Singh saw as a further move to block him in that direction. On 13 July Macnaghten left Lahore with Burnes, Mackeson and Wade and rode on to Amritsar, from where on 14 July

Burnes wrote to Masson how lopsided the treaty was: 'Runjeet we left greatly delighted – Never was a man so pleased and so he may be [. . .] all its articles are in his favor – To this we are a guarantee and also to 2 lacs of rupees a year.'[33]

On 15 July they rode on to Ludhiana where Macnaghten met Shuja and communicated that Britain was to restore him to his throne. Shuja – who had not been consulted – would not immediately agree to the annual payment of two lakhs for Jalalabad, but was cajoled by Macnaghten. Shuja also baulked at the stipulation that he would pay over to Ranjit Singh twenty-two lakhs of the alleged tribute arrears from the Amirs of Sind, and eventually this was reduced to fifteen – but the remainder was to go to the British, and none to Shuja.

The Shah was unhappy at the territories to be annexed by Ranjit, stressing that he had received assurances from Ranjit that Peshawar would be returned if he were restored in Kabul. But Shuja's Minister, Mullah Shukhr, pointed out that the territorial concessions merely repeated the 1833 treaty, and the Sikh held the land already. Shuja conceded. He also wished to increase the force under his own name, though raised, paid and officered by the British. To this Macnaghten agreed. Shuja emphasised that the revenues of Kabul and Kandahar could not support a central government, but agreed to add his seal. At the last moment he produced a new objection – the British must not free slave girls and must hand back runaways. Macnaghten was taken aback by this, but replied he was sure the Governor-General wished to honour local customs. Shuja added his seal, and Macnaghten left Ludhiana.

A stream of news had reached Auckland in Simla, before Macnaghten's return on 19 July, which cast the Afghan situation in a dark light. McNeill had been repudiated by the Shah before Herat, and the siege was going ahead under the active direction of Russian officers. Palmerston had authorised McNeill to withdraw his Embassy following the assault of a diplomatic messenger and the ransacking of his documents in Teheran. There were rumours of a Russian expeditionary force from Orenburg preparing to march on Khiva. Auckland instructed that the plan negotiated with Ranjit Singh be put into immediate effect.

On 16 July Auckland received a long despatch from Hobhouse and the Secret Committee of the EIC, dated 10 May – it had arrived remarkably quickly by the new steam packet and Suez route. This despatch supported Auckland in ordering Burnes' withdrawal from Kabul. It also gave an update on events in Persia. But it did not even mention the possibility of a British invasion of Afghanistan.

Furthermore there was a separate despatch from the Political Committee dated 9 May 1838, signed by John Stuart Mill. The Committee made an emphatic point:

> The state of Afghanistan is apparently becoming more and more unsettled, but any observations which it may be thought proper to make on this subject will be addressed to you by the Secret Committee. We approve however of the intimation you have made to Shah Shooja, that if he makes any further attempts to recover his throne by means of an armed force, he will forfeit his Asylum in the British Territories.[34]

The 9 and 10 May despatches, Political and Secret respectively, were based on information from Simla no later then February. On 24 October 1838 Hobhouse sent another despatch, approved by both the Secret Committee and the Cabinet, based on Simla's information up until May. In this October despatch, Auckland was instructed to invade Afghanistan on lines extremely similar to those he was actually undertaking. So, allowing for the time lag, there was no real difference in decision-making between Auckland and the British authorities, once they had the same papers before them.

Palmerston was thoroughly of the opinion that the invasion was his policy, not Auckland's. He wrote to brief the British Ambassador in St Petersburg: 'Auckland has been told to take Afghanistan in hand and make it a British dependency [. . .] we have long declined to meddle with the Afghans, but if the Russians try to make them Russian we must take care that they become British.'[35]

Burnes arrived in Simla with Lord and Mohan Lal on 20 July. Masson reports that Burnes told him that he was accosted by Colvin and Torrens, who urged him not to try and talk Auckland out of the invasion 'and prayed him to say nothing to unsettle his Lordship; that they had all the trouble in the world to get him into the business, and that even now he would be glad to retire from it'. This account has been much disputed, but it is consistent with evidence of Auckland's state of mind. It is also normal for a Private Secretary to try to pre-determine the smooth outcome of a meeting.

A difficult meeting with Auckland was recounted to James. Burnes had offered to resign:

> I first gave opinions, and then asked leave to withdraw, but Lord A proved to me that it would be desertion at a critical moment & I saw so myself, but I entered on support of his policy, not as what was best, but as what was best under the circumstances which a series of blunders had produced [. . .] I saw that I had a duty to my country, ill as the representative of that country in India had behaved to me.[36]

This is broadly consistent with Colvin's account that Burnes asked for long leave but was talked out of it by Auckland.[37] So ultimately Burnes agreed to assist the invasion. Why? He could not stop the invasion. He had made his opinion clear. He was still only a junior officer. In order to maintain his opposition, he would have had to resign the service, or at best return to an obscure Assistant Residency.

Burnes was a member of a disciplined service, and it was his duty to follow policy. I faced exactly the same dilemma when ordered as Ambassador to give my support to a vicious dictatorship in Uzbekistan, and downplay human rights' abuses. In particular I had protested, twice, in formal diplomatic telegrams to the Secretary of State about our use of 'intelligence' passed to our security services by the CIA, but originating in the murderous torture chambers of the Karimov regime.

At meetings with the Foreign Office I was told that my intervention was regarded as 'unpatriotic' at a time when our country was at war, and the most intense pressure was put on me. The Foreign Office had developed a kind of collective war mentality. To voice doubt about either the existence of Iraqi weapons of mass destruction, or about the value of intelligence material from the extraordinary rendition programme, was simply not tolerated.

Burnes faced precisely the same pressures from precisely the same institution. George Buist, editor of the *Bombay Times*, wrote:

> This was the political mania of the Foreign Office for the time. And anyone demanding an explanation of the words 'Russian influence', or daring to doubt the potency and malignancy of its effects, must have run the risk of having his sanity, sincerity or patriotism called into question.[38]

I found my sanity, sincerity and patriotism all subject to official investigation and government leaks to the media. I know exactly how Burnes felt. To turn your back on the country you serve is not easy, above all in time of war. To throw away a hard-won position, from a non-privileged background, is not easy. Burnes said privately, 'I was afraid of being thought a deserter in the day of trial. What more could I say, when he [Auckland] tells me I am a man he cannot spare?'[39] The answer to 'why did he do it?' is, from a sense of patriotic duty in response to a personal appeal by the Governor-General. We must also not forget that he did not come from a monied background, and was dependent on his income to support himself and subsidise his family in Montrose. He could not lightly give up his career.

But the prospect of active service perked Burnes up substantially. He was promised a major role. Burnes' stay in Simla provided him with the opportunity to get close to the Edens and rub shoulders with the most powerful men in India. His expertise on Afghanistan was invaluable, and his charm brought easy acceptance. Alex was now part of the inner circle planning the invasion, and so was Percival. Torrens recorded, 'I well recollect the subsequent discussions and difficulties as to execution, and in these Clerk, Wade,

Colvin, Mackeson, Burnes, D'Arcy Todd, Lord and others had a share.'[40] Burnes wrote he was in 'hourly consultation' with Auckland. Lieutenant Henry Fane, ADC to his father, General Sir Henry Fane, Commander-in-Chief, declared Burnes the most decent fellow he had ever met, and his father shared the opinion.

Auckland's flattery had led Burnes to expect political charge of the expedition. He wrote so in a private letter on 22 August and declared that it must be *'aut Caesar aut nullus'*. The next day he had evidently learnt he would be serving under Macnaghten, as he was writing:

> Of myself I cannot tell you what is to become. The commander-in-chief wants to go and to take me – but this will not be, and I believe the chief [Fane] and Macnaghten will be made a commission – Wade and myself political agents under them. I plainly told Lord Auckland that [. . .] I am disappointed. He replied that I could scarcely be appointed with the chief in equality, and pledged himself to leave me independent quickly, and in the highest position [. . .] It is an honour, not a disgrace, to go under Sir Henry; and as for Macnaghten, he is Secretary for all India, and goes *pro tem*. Besides, I am not sorry to see Dost Mohammed ousted by another hand but mine.[41]

General Fane wanted undivided control of the expedition, with Burnes as the senior political officer. Auckland, however, wished to have the expedition under joint civilian and military command. Macnaghten, who carried no military rank, was his choice. This scheme of divided command was an error.

Macnaghten had very little field experience, had never seen Afghanistan, and had himself recommended Henry Pottinger for the post. Auckland turned this down on the grounds of Pottinger's notorious bad temper. In fact, Colvin had written to Macnaghten before Burnes even arrived in Simla, telling him he was to be Envoy Plenipotentiary and British Minister at Kabul:

> The stake is so important that Lord Auckland feels that it may not become him to withhold his best card [. . .] There must be free and confidential communication with the Government, and besides this, influence at Lahore, influence at Peshawar, over Wade, over Burnes, over every officer engaged, as well as thorough cordiality in Lord Auckland's views regarding Sind. All this is not easy to see how to combine except in yourself.

In the same letter, Auckland stated that he had changed his mind about the British role in the invasion: 5,000 British troops might be required as there must be 'no chance of failure'.[42] Auckland delayed telling both Burnes and Fane about Macnaghten's appointment. When he did, he kept Burnes on board by a direct assurance that Macnaghten's role was temporary and Burnes would take over in Kabul once Shuja was established.

## Regime Change 243

Like many, Burnes wondered at Auckland's conversion from being sceptical about the 'Russian threat', to being so horrified that an immediate invasion was necessary. But Burnes' habitual optimism bubbled through. He wrote to James on 7 August 1838:

> I am to have a highly honorable appointment in the approaching campaign with Sir Henry Fane [...] We have had a hard struggle west of the Indus & it affords me no small gratification that I saw so far into futurity long ago as to predict the current crisis – Letter after letter told me that the Governor General thought I exhibited too much of the gloomy side of the picture but times are changed! My side is now even too cheerful – Alas! To be behind the scenes & see how little Wisdom governs the world makes one wonder.[43]

The next day he wrote to George Jacob. Though lighthearted, this is probably the best explanation of Burnes' thought process:

> Well, next came the next act – they ask me what is to be done. I replied you have behaved infamously to Dost Mahomed Khan, but self-defence is the first law of nature, up with the Suddozyes! You will have to maintain them by the sword, and by your treasure, but Russia is at your door![44]

Burnes felt a huge mistake had been made and the consequence was an alliance between Russia, Persia and the Barakzais. So forward defence was required. He was happy to be working with Fane. In Simla he was now very active in writing and despatching letters through the network of paid agents he had so assiduously cultivated, to numerous Afghan chiefs of his acquaintance. He was starting that 'little distribution of ready money' which he believed could ensure the restoration of Shah Shuja with little bloodshed.

Sir Henry Fane viewed invading Afghanistan as a gross strategic error. But Auckland had received a letter from John McNeill advising that Herat was most likely to fall, which would 'destroy our position in Afghanistan and place all that country under the influence [...] of Russia and Persia.'[45] McNeill thought it essential to send a British force to relieve Herat. Auckland, being Auckland, had not quite agreed or disagreed. Fane therefore advised that, as potentially the army would have to face not just the Afghans but a large Russian-backed Persian force, then British regiments, both Queen's and Company, were essential. Five brigades of infantry, one of cavalry and one of artillery were told off for the invasion. The troops were drawn from both the Bombay and Bengal Presidencies.

It was now the rainy season; the British were suffering a debilitating flea infestation, and their houses' flat mud roofs leaked. Burnes and Lord spent eight weeks in Simla, leaving around 10 September. Infuriatingly Emily Eden's journals for precisely this period disappeared; we do not know what she made of Burnes. Her only pen picture is of Burnes and Percival Lord in the dining room of their leaking bungalow, eating dinner 'every day' under umbrellas held over their heads by servants.[46] This is a delightful picture of their companionship and must have been undertaken in a spirit of fun, as some more practical arrangement was surely possible.

To Percival and Alex's delight, Auckland agreed to transfer Lord from the medical to the political service. He was ordered to report to Wade at Ludhiana, and given the vital task of persuading the tribes of the Khyber pass to come to Shuja. From September 1838 Lord began the dangerous work of riding the Khyber hills to meet with the chiefs. He received a hopeless instruction from Wade that he should only use money in the last resort but instead appeal to their patriotism.[47] Thankfully he was also provided with the not insubstantial sum of Rs50,000.[48]

Alex did not forget Masson, and persuaded Auckland that he should be offered a formal position. Masson was treated as part of the team, with Burnes writing to him to arrange baggage mules to be sent down from Peshawar to Ludhiana.[49] On 13 September Burnes wrote to Masson that Sir Henry Fane 'would place the intelligence department under yourself from your great local knowledge and acknowledged fitness but all this we can now settle at Shirkapoor'. They corresponded frequently on sending payments to Cerron and others, and arranging publication of various of Masson's archaeological reports.[50]

However, all this was not to be. Macnaghten intervened and had Masson's appointment cancelled.[51] At this, Masson resigned his position as newswriter. He thanked Burnes and claimed to be happy to concentrate on publishing antiquarian research. Burnes replied: 'I am right glad you are so satisfied with what I endeavoured to do and I now see that you will even be free now to prosecute your researches [. . .] No one will rejoice more in your increase of fame than myself'.[52]

Auckland had resolved on a way to keep Burnes motivated; on 1 September Alex wrote to a friend:

> 'I mean therefore', continued [Auckland] [. . .] 'to gazette you as a political commissioner to Kelat, and when the army crosses [the Indus] to regard you as an independent political officer to cooperate with Macnaghten.' Nothing could be more delicately kind. I have permission, if I like, to send an assistant to Kelat. I start in a week, and drop down the Indus to Shikarpoor, where, with the assistance of a brace of commissaries, I prepare for the advancement of the army [. . .] I think you will hear the result of my negotiation to be, that the British flag flies at Bukkur.[53]

## Regime Change

There was enormous excitement among the army gathered for the invasion. Colonel Dennie of the 13th Light Infantry wrote home on 22 August 1838:

> We are on the eve of something momentous. A great army from our northern provinces is forming [...] They say we are going to fight the Persians or Russians, the latter of whom are now besieging Herat in concert with the former; and are actually not further from our frontier than these stations of Kurnaul, Meerut etc. are from Calcutta. The Russians have long conceived this gigantic design [...] They have conquered Persia [...] and have really stolen across this immense extent of country, without our almost being aware of their insidious advance [...]⁵⁴

Burnes had been sent into Sind to make preparations for the army. At Ferozepore in September 1838 he received a letter addressed to 'Lt Col Sir Alexander Burnes' and found official notification that he had been knighted on 6 August 1838 and raised to Lieutenant Colonel in the Company's army.⁵⁵ Most sweetly of all, the awards came as a result of the approval of the Court of Directors for his Kabul negotiations, and particularly his stance over Peshawar and offer of support for Kandahar – the very issues on which he had been reprimanded by Auckland.

Inundated with letters of congratulation, he found time to reply to his friend George Jacob:

> Thanks for the gratulations! [...] The Governor-General and I were at issue on the politics of Cabool, and His Lordship favored me with a wig[ging] [...] of six sheets for my presuming to offer money to Candahar [...] Hah! The home authorities have knighted me for it, and made me a Lieutenant-Colonel, and to the honor of the Governor-General [...] His Lordship is the first man to 'cordially congratulate me' and 'to say that I may in candour mention that, upon the one point where there was some difference between us, opinions for which I have the highest respect are in your favor'.⁵⁶

Burnes replied to Auckland that his frank letter meant more to Burnes than the honours themselves, and 'they are to me truly acceptable, not as empty honours, but as setting my mind at rest that my conduct in Afghanistan has been approved'.⁵⁷ Burnes plainly was still troubled by his decision to support the invasion, and he explained again to Jacob:

> I entirely disapproved of their overthrowing Dost Mahomed, but when they could not act with him, I told them they had no hope but to counteract him [...] I would have backed out of the business if I durst, but that would have shown me to be but a sorry public servant [...] so after a little demur I gave in my adhesion to the policy – it was only the best because we had lost other opportunities. I believe that is the reason I am not <u>the</u> Envoy. I am <u>an</u> Envoy, which is the highest compliment they have paid me.

Burnes believed it was his interception of Witkiewicz' reports which had tipped the balance in favour of an invasion.

> Russia was at us in every court between India and Persia, and they would not believe until secret service money had made it as plain as the sun – be it so, we have not taken the field a moment too soon – I have no fear of the result, but I tremble for our political consistency.

There had been typically thunderous Palmerstonian instructions on dealing with Persia over Herat. A small Company force was landed from the steamers *Semiramis* and *Hugh Lindsay* on the Gulf island of Kharg to threaten Persia. Colonel Stoddart was given instructions to inform the Shah of this and demand he immediately end the siege of Herat.[58] The Shah had been sickened by repeated repulses, especially the bloody affair of 24 June 1838, while his troops were starving and many deserting.[59] He immediately agreed, replying that

> we accede to the demands of the British Government [...] our desire was that the Affghan tribes should be prevented from plundering and ravaging our dominions – Please God we shall make an arrangement with the people of Herrat, and return speedily.[60]

There were three weeks before the Shah actually withdrew, during which the Russians tried to change his mind (though the Shah refused to receive Witkiewicz),[61] and Prince Kamran of Herat asked the Shah to help him assassinate his minister Yar Mohammed before he left.[62] Finally, in a letter to Auckland dated '9 September 1838, 26 minutes past 10 o'clock AM', Stoddart wrote 'The Shah has now mounted his horse and is gone.'[63]

With tragic consequences, Stoddart concluded that bullying was the best way to deal with oriental rulers. But the threat which had prompted the British invasion of Afghanistan had dissipated. Eldred Pottinger became a hero, credited with single-handedly stiffening the resistance of feckless Afghans, fighting off Russian attacks, and driving with the flat of his sword the evil and skulking wazir of Herat to fight on the ramparts. He was a prototype of muscular Christianity.

This should be taken with a pinch of salt. It is improbable that a single Christian would have a profound effect on morale, especially when there was no shortage of Europeans on the other side. Pottinger was not even the only European in the Herat durbar. The Persian army was never able fully to invest Herat, and had powder and shot only infrequently, while provisions were much cheaper in the city than in the Persian camp.[64] The siege was in general a desultory affair.

The only evidence for Pottinger's heroics was allegedly in his journals, which were the basis of the account of 'The Hero of Herat' by the doyen of British Indian historians Sir John Kaye. But this evidence disappeared in one of those infamous Victorian study fires, in which papers potentially embarrassing to the Imperial narrative were apt to vanish.[65] It seems likely that this fire is where Alexander Burnes' private diaries disappeared too, with their evidence of religious scepticism (and perhaps sexual adventure). Kaye published that 'the journals and correspondence of Sir Alexander Burnes were given to me by his brother, the late Dr James Burnes',[66] but there, to my extreme frustration, the trail ends. The same conflagration took private papers of those martyr icons of Victorian India, Henry Lawrence and John Nicholson. It is very probable Kaye was deliberately destroying evidence of sexual and religious unorthodoxy.[67]

While modern historians have not echoed the adulation of Eldred Pottinger, they have repeated the improbable story that Pottinger just happened to be in Herat when the Persians attacked, tootling around on leave. Even the meticulous M E Yapp described his presence in Herat as 'fortuitous' and 'accidental'.[68] This had been the cover story put out by the British, in the same way the Russians disavowed Witkiewicz.

In fact, Eldred had been surveying the western passes and had proceeded to Herat in disguise on Burnes' direct orders, who once the siege was under way wrote to Herat's vizier certifying Eldred's true identity, but did not formally attach him to his mission (giving diplomatic status) as 'I do not wish to commit the government.' Burnes ordered Eldred 'to inspirit them in any way'.[69] Burnes explained to Stoddart that the reason Pottinger had not been openly declared as a British agent, was that his role in Herat would breach the treaty obligation of non-interference in any conflict between Afghanistan and Persia.[70]

The lands of Herat had been devastated, ravaged by soldiers and camp-followers. Eldred Pottinger remained under Burnes' direct command. British agents in Kandahar had reported a new plan by Witkiewicz for the Dil Khan sirdars to take Herat, and Burnes considered this a more substantial danger than Persia, as the weakened Herat would be less inclined to resist a Sunni Afghan force. Burnes therefore, with Auckland's authority, authorised Eldred Pottinger to plough in a lakh of rupees to repairing Herat's defences.[71]

Burnes had to swallow the unpleasant distinction of being cited by name as the man whose mission was the cause of war, in the manifesto published by Auckland to justify the invasion.

**Simla Declaration 1 October 1838**

> Captain Burnes was deputed, towards the close of the year 1836, on a mission to Dost Mohammed Khan, the Chief of Cabool. The original objects of that officer's mission were purely of a commercial nature. Whilst Captain Burnes, however, was on his journey to Cabool, information was received by the Governor General, that the troops of Dost Mohammed Khan had made a sudden and unprovoked attack upon those of our ancient ally, Maha Raja Runjeet Singh [. . .] it was to be feared that the flames of war once kindled in the very regions into which we were endeavouring to extend our commerce, the peaceful and beneficial purposes of the British government would be altogether frustrated. In order to avert a result so calamitous, the Governor General resolved in authorising Captain Burnes to intimate to Dost Mohammed Khan that, if he should evince a disposition to come to just and reasonable terms with the Maha Raja, His Lordship would exert his good offices with His Highness for the restoration of an amicable understanding between the two powers [. . .]
>
> Shah Shoojah-ul-Moolk will enter Afghanistan, surrounded by his own troops, and will be supported against foreign interference and factitious opposition by a British army. The Governor General confidently hopes, that the Shah will be speedily replaced on the throne by his own subjects and adherents, and when once he shall be secure in power, and the independence and integrity of Afghanistan established, the British Army will be withdrawn.
>
> The Governor General has been led to these measures by the duty which is imposed upon him, of providing for the security of the possessions of the British crown; but he rejoices that in the discharge of his duty he will be enabled to assist in restoring the union and property of the Afghan people [. . .]

This proclamation was tendentious. Peshawar had only been annexed for the Sikhs definitively (after a sacking in 1819) by Hari Singh in 1833. The Sikhs had no claim to Peshawar, which had been part of the Empire of Nadir Shah and then part of the Dourani Empire from 1747. Peshawar's almost entirely Muslim population was engaged in continuing resistance. To characterise Dost's attempt to recover Peshawar as an act of aggression was sheer distortion. Burnes was incensed by the hypocrisy of the British position, noting acerbically that we had not objected to Ranjit Singh's attacks on the Afghans, and that 'we had no desire to the flames of war in the abstract – it depended entirely on the party who kindled them whether we should fan or quench them.'[72] What Burnes wanted was an ethical foreign policy that dealt fairly with the various parties. What he served was naked Imperial aggression.

Mundane worries intruded. There is always an irresoluble conflict between the exigencies of spying and the needs of public accountancy. Payments for information, informal messengers, gifts, payments for supplies of provisions from locals who may be illiterate – all had somehow to be accounted for. A significant proportion of the manuscripts indexed under 'Alexander Burnes' in the National Archives of India consist of detailed querying of his accounts.

To give but one example, in the midst of his vital negotiations with Dost, on 4 December 1837, Burnes sat down to submit his mission accounts for the period when his mission had been living largely on boats and travelling from Karachi to Sukkur. Burnes made no attempt to provide receipts, and instead wrote:

> Cabool
> 4th December 1837
>
> Sir,
> I have the honour to forward statements of my actual receipts and disbursements for the months of January, February and March 1837, which I declare upon honour to be correct and according to the best of my knowledge.
>
> I have etc
> Alexr. Burnes
> On a Mission to Cabool
>
> To The Accountant General
> Fort William[73]

On 10 October 1838 this was forwarded from Accountant General Charles Morley to the Secretary in Bombay, with a sniffy note:

> Sir,
> The Civil Authority having returned the accounts (noted in the margin) of the receipts and charges connected to Captain Burnes' Mission to Cabool – unaudited, from the circumstance of their not having been approved [...] I have the honor to forward them for the orders of His Honor the President in Council, together with a copy of a letter from Captain Burnes to my address [...] which accompanied them.
>
> It will be observed that the charges exhibited in the accounts are unsupported by original receipts, or any other document than the declaration furnished in the conclusion of Captain Burnes' communication before adverted to, and that the funds have been raised by Bills upon Presentation under the Bombay Presidency.[74]

Bombay batted them straight back to Calcutta advising that they would need to be considered by Auckland himself:

> I have been directed [...] to [...] point out that the accounts having been rendered by Captain Burnes without vouchers it will be necessary if the Governor-General considers the charges to be moderate and warranted that His Lordship should authorize their being passed to Captain Burnes in account leaving receipts to be adjusted and checked by comparison with the accounts of the Treasury on which his bills were drawn.[75]

It is not a small point. Empires live on their accounting – some of the oldest documents in the world are surviving accounts of Mesopotamian empires, indelibly inscribed on clay tablets. The commercial origins of the EIC made accounting even more central to its culture. The pressure on Burnes over accounts was a major worry; if the government repudiated his bills he could be ruined.

Moorcroft and Gerard both died penniless for this very reason. Burnes had already lost money redeeming Gerard's bills. Mohan Lal's life was devastated by government refusing to refund payments made in the last days of the Kabul garrison. Edward Stirling's expenses were turned down entirely. Stoddart's Herat accounts were repudiated and many of Arthur Conolly's bills remained unhonoured at his death. The entire story of the Great Game on the British side has this strange undercurrent.

Back in high policy, Auckland wrote to Hobhouse on 15 November:

> The magnitude of the measure on which I am embarked is alarming even to myself, and it will be for others to pronounce whether I am attempting at too great a hazard and at too great an expense to establish and to maintain a British influence throughout the nations of Central Asia; or whether it would have been safer to leave Herat, Khiva, Cabul and Candahar either to the occupation of Russia or to the exercise of the political agency of that power, combined with Persia against us. I have looked upon my course to be strictly one of self-defence. I embarked in it most painfully and unwillingly, but having embarked I will, please God, manfully go through with it.[76]

Auckland's prediction of 'too great a hazard and too great an expense' was right on both counts. It is as though Auckland realised he was doing something stupid, but could not stop himself. He was implementing a policy strongly urged on him by Palmerston. The majority of the British Cabinet at the time were convinced of the reality of the Russian threat. Queen Victoria's diary entry of a conversation with her Prime Minister is revealing:

> We were seated much as usual; Lord Melbourne sitting near me. He said 'You should see those Indian papers, to see what Auckland's about' [...] he said [...] there was going to be a great war [...] a struggle between Russia and England, which is to have possession in the East. We depend upon Runjeet Singh, who has always been our friend, and who he says we have no reason to

doubt; but he is very old; 'he has an army of 70,000 disciplined troops,' Lord M. said; 'he is a Hindoo and not a Mahomedan, and won't allow any cows to be killed [...]' 'One can understand the origin of it,' said Lord M., 'the Cow being the mother of the Calf and giving milk; I have no doubt that's the origin, and with the Egyptians the same'[...]

Lord M. then talked again of these Indian papers which he said I couldn't read through [...] 'There'll be an immense crisis; it's coming to a crash in Central Asia; I dare say it'll be staved off for the present,' but must come to something hereafter, to be decided whether England or Russia should reign there [...]'[77]

Melbourne immediately went on to flirt with Victoria, saying that young men might go for blondes but more mature men like himself preferred black hair. Making every allowance for age, Victoria's lack of curiosity at being told the country she ruled was about to go to war with Russia is startling: she accepted advice not to read the papers.

The portion of the army designated as being Shah Shuja's own forces were in composition not significantly different from the Company's regiments, from which the officers were seconded. The men were recruited during 1838 in Bengal and Oude from the same classes as the Bengal Native troops, with the addition of a battalion of Gurkhas.

The British officers viewed Shah Shuja's regiments as weak. Recruitment was hardly an attractive proposition, as an officer wrote:

> Time did not allow the selection to be very good and [...] I fear it will be many a day before the troops will be much use [...] firstly [...] only a couple of months being given to raise so large a body in; secondly the knowledge that they were destined to fight against a race celebrated throughout the East for bravery and fanaticism; and thirdly and above all their being immediately marched into a country where [...] the snow was known to lie some four months in the year.[78]

Company sepoys normally underwent a full year of hard drill before even being allowed to join the ranks.[79] The Shah's forces were given just six weeks' training.

On 27 November Auckland and Ranjit Singh met at Ferozepore to review the troops, and again the lavish spectacle of a meeting between the Maharaja and a Governor-General was played out, amid tented splendour. There were manoeuvres, salvoes, jewels, fireworks, presents and dancing girls. The baptist Henry Havelock did not approve:

> The time will [...] come in India when national custom will be no longer pleaded as an excuse for the introduction [...] of groups of dancing and choral prostitutes [...] into the presence of the ladies of the family of the British Governor-General.[80]

His solicitude was misplaced. Emily Eden enjoyed seeing prostitutes, and complained on occasions when they were cleared away.

There should have been stark reason to worry about their Sikh ally's stability, and thus the possibility of the supply chain collapsing behind them. With Ranjit visibly failing, claimants to the Sikh throne were lobbying senior British officers for support in the coming succession struggle. On Christmas Eve, Ranjit collapsed with a stroke; he was never able to speak clearly again.

Burnes now wrote a long letter to John Cam Hobhouse arguing that the spread of Russian influence was a real danger. The best and cheapest way to counter this would once have been to back Dost Mohammed. The only way forward now was a wholehearted commitment to imposing Shuja. Hobhouse had throughout supported Burnes; there was no change now.

# FIRST AFGHAN WAR TO DEATH OF BURNES

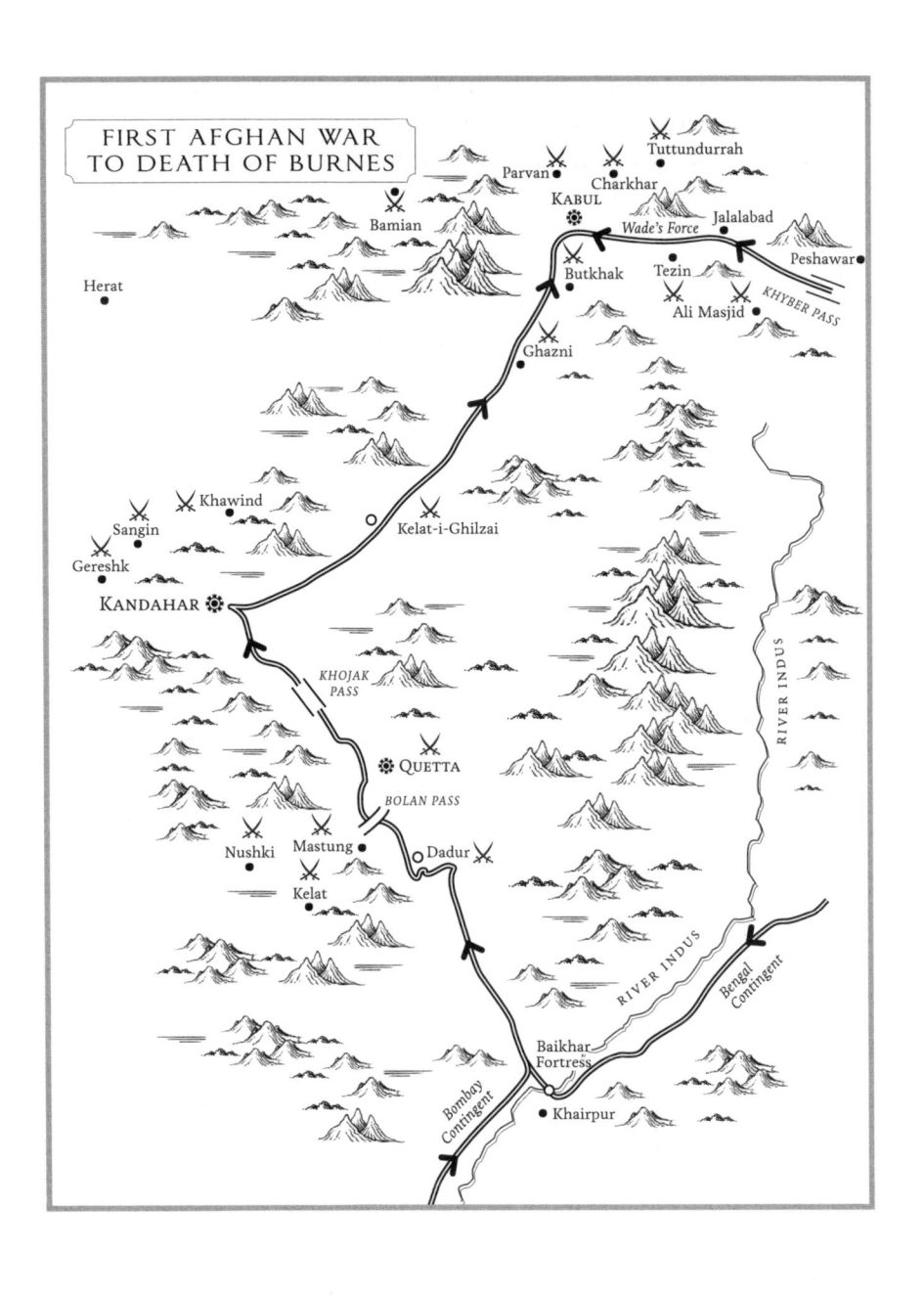

CHAPTER TWENTY-FIVE

## Securing Sind

Henry Pottinger was now Resident in Haidarabad, and was deeply concerned about the tribute to Shah Shuja demanded from Sind. The Amirs told him that, in return for their financial contribution towards his campaign of 1833/4, Shuja had renounced all future claims. Pottinger expostulated to Auckland:

> The question of money-payment by the Amirs of Sindh to Shah Soojah-ool-Moolk is [. . .] rendered very puzzling by two releases written in Korans, and sealed and signed by His Majesty [. . .] Their argument now is, that they are sure the Governor-General does not intend to make them pay again for what they have already bought.

The reply to Pottinger was blunt: the Amirs must pay up or be deposed, plus a British subsidiary force would be garrisoned upon them for which the Amirs must annually pay the British 3 lakhs. This was the usual means in British India of initiating the takeover of a new state – 'subsidiary' meaning that the British force was subsidised by the host rulers.

The Amirs would be permanently barred from communication with other states – i.e. Britain would control foreign policy. Again this was usual in British takeover of new territory. The failure of the ruler to pay the subsidy in a bad harvest year, or 'treasonous' correspondence with other rulers, became the pretext for full annexation. The Amirs were acutely aware of this repeating pattern.

The Amirs were Shias, and therefore Calcutta feared a possible Persian alliance. The British now worked on the Shia/Sunni divide. One of the Amirs, Sobdar, was a Sunni and Macnaghten instructed Pottinger that Sobdar should be excused his share of the 'tribute': Britain should retain the policy option of deposing all the other Amirs and replacing them with Sobdar.

Auckland wrote to the Amirs specifying his demands, citing Article 4 of the bilateral treaty of 1834 between Singh and Shuja as the legal basis of

British intervention:

> Regarding Shikarpore and the territory of Scinde lying on the right bank of the Indus, the Shah will agree to abide by whatever may be settled as right and proper, in conformity with the happy relations of friendship subsisting between the British Government and the Maharajah, through Captain Wade.

After Shuja's defeat at Kandahar, Lord Bentinck had specifically repudiated this clause as unauthorised. Britain now depended on it for its legal 'right' to take over Shikarpur. Burnes delegated Mohan Lal to arrange with the Lohanis for money and provisions to be taken to Shikarpur.

Burnes was negotiating in Upper Sind with his old friend Rustam Khan of Khairpur, having arrived there by boat on 25 October 1838.[1] By 6 November he had already sent six despatches to Auckland and received approval in principle of treaty outlines.[2] The vital objective was to secure the fortress at Baikhar; the major part of the allied army was to cross the Indus here. Rustam Khan's demands for money were comparatively slight. But he, like his Talpur cousins at Haidarabad and Bhawalpur, was smarting from Britain's cursory notification that it was abrogating the provision of the April 1832 treaty which said the Indus would not be used for military transport.

Since his first meeting with Burnes seven years previously, Rustam had wanted Khairpur to become a British protectorate. Burnes could finally grant this. However, it became obvious to Rustam that Haidarabad was contemplating armed resistance, and he sought to temporise. To surrender the famous fortress of Baikhar might bring him obloquy throughout the Islamic world. The British plan of invasion was dependent upon the convergence of the Bengal and Bombay contingents at Sukkur, and that meant obtaining the fortress. If agreement could not be reached with Rustam, then full-scale war with a united Sind would follow.

War brought out a new side of Burnes' personality. Rustam had previously seen only the affable traveller and envoy. Burnes could also threaten. He sent a message to the Bengal Division which was on the way from Ferozepore to Sukkur, stating that Rustam may not cede the fortress 'in which case you must attack and take it [. . .]'[3] Rustam gave numerous reasons that the British Army should not pass through. The harvest had been poor, the time of year was wrong, crops would be destroyed by the army before they could be harvested.

Burnes stood with Rustam on the banks of the Indus and pointed to the mighty river rolling by. The British army was coming, he said. They had as much chance of damming the great Indus as of stopping it. The Amir believed him. Still there was much opposition from Rustam's court; Burnes and Mohan Lal hit on a stratagem. Burnes left Khairpur under the pretext of looking for alternative crossing points, taking the vizier and Rustam's brothers with him. In his absence Mohan Lal browbeat Rustam into signing in a dramatic all-night session into the morning of 24 December.

Burnes was riven by internal conflict. He wrote privately of his anguish at mistreating his friend Rustam.[4] At the same time, he gloried in his success. He missed his gung-ho friend Lord, and on 1 January 1839 wrote to him: 'I have been travelling to Khyrpore, treaty-making on a grand scale, and [...] I have got the fortress of Bukkur ceded to us on our own terms [...] the Khyrpore State to place itself under British protection [...] All these great doings happened at Christmas, and I only wanted your hilarious tones to make the enjoyment of the day complete.'

Auckland had spent Christmas with Ranjit at Firozepore, Lahore and Amritsar. Burnes sent a message announcing success at Khairpur to Willoughby Cotton commanding the Bengal Contingent, and Henry Fane who was travelling alongside it with his suite on seven large river barges. The river party included Wood and Masson, though the latter had no official capacity. The Bengal Contingent pressed on through Ahmedpur and Khanpur to join Burnes, who met them on the boundary of the Khairpur territory. He warned Cotton and Fane that there may still be resistance to ceding the crossing.

At Sabzalkot Burnes mentioned to Masson that Leech had not made much progress in securing provisions from Kelat. Masson asked to be appointed to serve in Kelat. He recorded, 'Sir Alexander held down his head, and made no reply.'[5] Burnes had made great efforts to get Masson employment, but had been blocked. Masson wrongly suspected Burnes of thwarting him and railed against Burnes to anybody who would listen. This common hatred helped cement his friendship with Henry Pottinger, with whom he went to stay for several months.

They received the first communication from the Bombay force under Sir John Keane. It had landed by sea near Vikkur, and was stuck until baggage animals could be brought up from Cutch, while the Haidarabad Amirs had refused to give any help, and had called up their levies of 25,000 men.

Better news was that Shuja and his newly-raised forces had already crossed the Indus by boats and were establishing themselves at Shikarpur. Having briefed the commanders, Burnes galloped back to Rustam. The engineers were already building the bridge of boats across the river, but Rustam insisted nobody could cross until he had received the treaty ratified by Auckland. There was still concern Rustam might change his mind.

The Bengal contingent encamped near Rustam Khan and his force of 8,000 men. Burnes with Mohan Lal and his attendants had a separate camp by the river. The next morning, a delegation led by Rustam Khan's wazir – a fierce anti-British nationalist – called on Sir Henry Fane, and 'Sir A. Burnes acted as interpreter, and conducted the negotiation and ceremonial, and displayed admirable tact [. . .] by which he contrived to inspire with confidence.'[6] Burnes now started a close friendship with an aide de camp of Cotton, the teetotal, tactless and much passed-over Henry Havelock, a Lieutenant for fifteen years, and hidden military genius.

Burnes was also on excellent terms with both Fane and Cotton. Sir Willoughby Cotton was perfectly fitted to his name. A fat trencherman, he was very popular with the Sikhs for his drinking abilities. In his youth he had led the famous 'Rugby mutiny', blowing up the Headmaster's study with gunpowder.[7] But Cotton was no fool and had fought through the entire Peninsular campaign.

Burnes now joined Shuja's force at Shikarpur, spending two weeks with Lord, who had established a foundry and was engaged in 'casting cannon, forging muskets, raising troops, horse and foot, talking, persuading, bullying, threatening and bribing'.[8] Burnes recruited several hundred Afghan irregular cavalry – mercenaries were beginning to arrive at the prospect of employment. These irregulars did not form part of the disciplined force. On 25 January Burnes left Lord and rode back to join Cotton at Baikhar.[9]

On 26 January 1839 the ratified treaty arrived. On 27 January Burnes put on the uniform of a British Colonel. With Mohan Lal, he rode out to Rustam's camp, to escort him to hand over the keys. Fane and Cotton seated themselves in a great scarlet and gold tented pavilion to receive Rustam, with an avenue of cavalry drawn up along the approach. Facing them rose groves of date palms through which Burnes and the Sindian delegation were expected to emerge. But hours dragged by with no rustling in the palms. Eventually a huge Sindian crowd on horseback started to filter out, with Burnes, Mohan Lal and a grave, grey-bearded Rustam Khan at the front. No sooner had they come in sight than they stopped, and were engaged in visible altercation. Then the cavalcade started forward again, stopping several more times before finally arriving at the pavilion. In fact Burnes had been involved in heated discussion for many hours with Rustam, cajoling him into handing over the fortress as the only safe way to secure his rule, while the vizier and others argued forcefully against such treachery to Sind.

Once they arrived, things were not made easier by Fane's abrupt manner: he simply handed over the treaty to Rustam and demanded the keys. His receipt of Rustam's presents was 'perfunctory' and Fane baldly told him that 'I have wasted enough time in treating. I will now march down and attack [Haidarabad]; and if you like I shall show you the troops I shall send to do it.'[10] He then took a rather shell-shocked Rustam, 'a man of portly, rather comely, and very venerable appearance, and soft and courteous manners' on a review of the troops.

It took a further two days of cajoling for Burnes to get physical possession of the castle keys. Armed with these, Burnes, Fane and Cotton, with a small cloud of staff officers and a sepoy escort of the 35th NI, crammed into eight small boats commanded by John Wood and crossed to the fortress. They were aware that Rustam's move was unpopular with many of his nobles, and were unsure if all would pass peacefully, but on approach saw the bulk of the garrison leave the island fortress by boat. Burnes 'sprung ashore' and opened the door of the fortress with the great key.[11]

A troop of Rustam's men remained with the British garrison; but from the keep was unfurled a large Union Jack, to the cheers of the sepoys. Burnes wrote of his unabashed national pride; he had years earlier identified Baikhar as 'the key to the Indus', and now he had its key in his hands. The union flag flew there for over a hundred years. Havelock's judgement is correct: 'The negotiations of Sir Alexander Burnes which ended in the surrender of Fort Bukkur without a shot, deserve to be classed with the ablest efforts of British diplomacy.'

Getting an army across the river was no easy feat. James Broadfoot, a young engineer officer from Kirkwall, gave a vivid description:

> We were on the bank of a river 1,100 yards wide, with a torrent like a mill stream [. . .] First we seized, by great exertion, about 120 boats, then cut down lots of trees; these we made into strong beams [. . .] we made 500 cables out of a peculiar kind of grass which grows 100 miles from here; the anchors were made of small trees joined and loaded with stone. Out nails were all made on the spot. We then anchored the boats in the middle of the stream [. . .] leaving twelve feet between each; strong beams were laid across the boats, and planks nailed on these for a roadway. This is the largest military bridge which has ever been made.[12]

Remarkably this was completed between 26 January and 8 February 1839, despite the timber having to be felled at Ferozepore and drifted downstream. Lieutenant Wood played a major part, identifying and seizing every boat on 120 miles of river and advising on the construction. After completion Wood was appointed in charge of the bridge.[13]

Burnes' achievement at Sukkur stirred up renewed enmity from Henry Pottinger. Pottinger argued that Khairpur must be treated as subordinate to Haidarabad. It followed that Burnes' position as Envoy to Khairpur should be subordinate to Pottinger as Envoy to Haidarabad. Auckland did not support Pottinger in this view.

Pottinger's ex-assistant had moved, in a few weeks, from brevet Captain to Lieutenant Colonel Sir Alexander Burnes, and had then taken away some of Pottinger's territorial responsibility. Pottinger chose to believe that Burnes had not gained control of the crossing at Sukkur, but was being duped and wrote gleefully to Burnes, copying in Auckland, that Rustam Khan was in secret correspondence with his cousin Nur Mohammed at Haidarabad.[14] In fact Burnes was well aware that Rustam was playing a double game, but was confident that he would come down on the British side. It was Nur Mohammed, not Burnes, who was being played along by Rustam.

Burnes and Pottinger were forced to consult closely over the negotiations in Upper and Lower Sind respectively, with periods of sending daily letters. Pottinger remained bitterly opposed to separate discussions at Khairpur. His letter to Burnes of 29 October 1838 said: 'I have given the chief topic of your three letters the most mature and full consideration [. . .] I am unable to concur in the view you take on the advisability of confirming [. . .] the treaty which you have sent to me.'[15]

Pottinger wrote again to Auckland arguing that Khairpur was subordinate to Haidarabad; as Resident in Sind, he could fix an assistant at Khairpur any time he pleased, and offer a treaty. Rustam Khan and his court 'were assuming a tone of equality and dignity totally opposed to their relative stations to the British government'. Pottinger was unable mentally to process the fact that Burnes was no longer junior to him. The treaty Burnes had negotiated was initiated in the Governor-General's office. So Pottinger was effectively criticising Auckland.

The Governor-General now instructed Pottinger to step up the pressure on the Amirs at Haidarabad. Their continued correspondence with Persia (little more than routine diplomatic compliments), their failure to provide supplies and carriage to Keane, and their refusal to acknowledge the suzerainty of Shah Shuja, proved them to be 'disloyal'; a peculiar adjective as they had no loyalty to the British. Pottinger was to broadcast that the British had a candidate for the Sind throne, from the old Kalora dynasty, overthrown two generations previously. Pottinger was soon suggesting that it was already time to depose the principal Amir. Auckland replied in the pained tone he adopted with Pottinger:

> The Governor General is hardly disposed to concur entirely in [your] opinion [. . .] that the circumstances specified [. . .] however clearly they demonstrate the want of all honor and honesty in [. . .] Noor Mahomed Khan, are such as to place that chief at our mercy. Should [. . .] he evince a disposition to meet our just and necessary views, the Governor General would be unwilling to proceed to extremities.[16]

Nur Mohammed would avoid deposition only if he complied with all British demands, including supply of transport and provisions for Keane's corps, payment of a subsidy to maintain a permanent British force at Ferozepore, and the massive payment of thirty-three lakhs (over £300,000), supposedly arrears of tribute to Shuja, but to be divided between the British and Ranjit. On the 1834 agreement to end the tribute, Auckland's reply was Machiavellian:

> The Governor General refrained for the present from recording any opinion relative to the releases which His Majesty Shah Shuja is said to have executed. Admitting the documents [...] imply a relinquishment of all claim to tribute, still they would hardly appear to be applicable to present circumstances [...] His Majesty would [not] have foregone so valuable a claim without that some counterpart agreement should have been taken the unfulfilment of the terms of which, may have rendered null and void His Majesty's engagement.

Pottinger was much affronted by an 'impertinent' Khairpur envoy who queried the tribute demand, stating: 'it is a joke talking of it as the demand of the King, you have given him bread for the last five and twenty years, and any strength he has now, and may hereafter have, proceeds from you, so the demand is literally yours'.[17] But Rustam Khan had already sold the crossing, and the Haidarabad Amirs were also betrayed by Mehrab Khan of Kelat. Burnes was Envoy to Kelat, and he despatched Robert Leech there to negotiate for passage of British forces, and supply of provisions and transport. Mehrab Khan had received a letter from the Haidarabad Amirs, inviting him to join their armies to resist the coming British invasion. Instead he gave the Haidarabad letter to Leech, who sent it to Burnes. Pottinger raised it with Nur Mohammed, who denied its authenticity.

Although Mehrab was willing to warn the British against his rivals, he was not willing to assist the British invasion of Afghanistan, with which Kelat had a treaty of mutual defence. Eventually Burnes reached a deal with the wazir of Kelat, Muhammad Hussan, at Shikarpur, that the Khanate would sell provisions to the British and make route preparations. It was a sign of impending trouble that this man of intrigue warned Burnes of the alleged bad faith of his ruler, Mehrab Khan.

Pottinger was now writing sanguinely to Auckland about the possibility of war, and travelled to arrange provisions for Keane's force in a march upon Haidarabad. He felt, however, that the Amirs would surrender: 'The decided and unvaried language I have held to them has satisfied them that we will *take*, if they will not *give*, a passage through their country.'[18]

He worried that the taking of Baikhar fortress would infuriate Haidarabad and lead to his own murder. His party had been subject to stone-throwing and Pottinger now refused to leave his house.

## Securing Sind

Auckland rebuked both Pottinger and Burnes for their disputes:

> the Governor-General deeply regrets the tone which pervades your letter to the address of Lieutenant Colonel Sir A Burnes dated the 2nd Inst., and that officer's reply dated the 5th. His Lordship feels satisfied, that you will both on reflection, regret the use of expressions having the remotest tendency to irritation, and that at a crisis like the present when interests of such magnitude are entrusted to your charge, you will recognize the necessity of acting with cordial concert.[19]

Overwrought, Pottinger sent a quite extraordinary complaint to Auckland in which all his pent-up hatred of Burnes came tumbling out in a rant against the Khairpur treaty. It consists of eleven large pages, closely written. It was a bad misjudgement of Pottinger to believe that, with a war just starting, Auckland would welcome this. Pottinger opens by a lengthy reference to his historic disagreements with Burnes in Bhuj, and bitterly attacks Sir Robert Grant, former Governor of Bombay – a deceased friend of Auckland.

This letter was written at precisely the time Pottinger was refusing to leave his Residence for fear of assassination: he had probably suffered some kind of breakdown. A few paragraphs will give the general tone:

> When your Lordship did me the honor to nominate me to be Resident in Sinde, I neither anticipated that I was to be colleagued with Lt Colonel Sir Alexander Burnes, nor that that officer was to criticise [. . .] my dispatches, still less did I imagine that he [. . .] was to avail himself of his Lordship's instructions <u>to me</u>, as one of the means of carrying his own objects, even before these instructions could reach me [. . .]
>
> [W]hen Sir Alexander Burnes was appointed to go as Envoy to Kabool, he was placed [. . .] under my guidance so far as Sinde was concerned [. . .] he waited until he had just crossed the frontier of this province, and then addressed <u>direct</u> to government a dispatch, impugning all my measures [. . .] It was an easy task for me to refute what he then set forth [. . .]
>
> Again, Sir Alexander Burnes [. . .] talked of the facility I must have in negotiating his Bills, in the face of all I had so frequently written to him to the contrary. In another, he [. . .] asserted that I could get as many pack bullocks as might be required for the force from certain villages in Kutch [. . .] I [. . .] ask myself, what Your Lordship would have thought of me if I had not explained the unsoundness of the statements. Surely Your Lordship would have remarked 'Colonel Pottinger must be strangely apathetical, and neglectful [. . .]' [. . .]
>
> If Sir Alexander Burnes really thought his opinions were likely to weigh with me, he laboured under a sad mistake. They never did so [. . .] Had the highest and oldest political functionary in India addressed this letter to me [. . .] I would deem it a piece of presumptuous and uncalled-for vanity, and I have no milder term to apply, when I think of the author of it [. . .][20]

The reply from Auckland was drafted and signed by his Assistant Secretary, T H Maddock, and while not exonerating Burnes, plainly shows a preference to him:

> it is with exceeding pain that Auckland has learnt that such feelings have been excited on your part [. . .] He has to tender to you the warmest acknowledgements and thanks for the result of your recent negotiations [. . .]
>
> At the same time, His Lordship does not feel that it would be just or proper to mark with any extreme censure the part taken by Sir Alexander Burnes in pressing his own opinions for the consideration of government [. . .] He regards the letter addressed to you by Sir Alexr. Burnes on 27 December to have been certainly unsuitable and uncalled for. Yet it related to a topic of a very emergent nature, affecting the success of all His Lordship's plans, and the Governor-General cannot ascribe it to any other source than a pure, even though over-ardent, sense of public duty [. . .]

Then Auckland strikes:

> In compliance with what he believes to be your present wish, he grants to you leave to proceed to Bombay for the recovery of your health [. . .] He has sincerely regretted to hear that your health has been impaired by the weight of the labours and cares [. . .] imposed upon you. You will make over charge of the Residency to Lieut Eastwick [. . .][21]

All the correspondence had been copied to the Secret Committee in London, and further censure for Pottinger's behaviour was initiated by Hobhouse. Thomas Love Peacock wrote to Auckland that 'We do not therefore see with what propriety Coll Pottinger could censure Sir A Burnes on the 18th December, for an act which he had suggested to him on the 23rd November, and in terms we regret but ill-calculated to maintain [. . .] cordiality and good feeling between our functionaries.'[22]

The Bombay Government formally notified Hobhouse that: 'On the 29th of January, Colonel Pottinger tendered his resignation as Resident in Sinde, in consequence of Sir Alexander Burnes's proceedings.'[23] But Henry Pottinger was to pop up in Sind again just a few months later.[24]

Burnes had a further enemy in Charles Masson. Masson now blackened Burnes' name with the officers of the Army of the Indus. On 31 January 1839 Henry Durand noted in his diary at the camp at Shikarpur:

> [Masson] gave us a very amusing account of Burnes's rencontre with Captain Vicovich at Cabul. This Russian officer reached Cabul 'with a pair of black kid gloves, a French translation of Burnes' travels, and a long Persian epistle, well powdered with gold leaf, purporting to be from the Emperor of Russia.' The Afghans, of whom Mr Masson speaks highly, laughed at this *soi-distant* envoy, and discredited him *in toto*. Had Burnes had the sense to laugh too, all would

have gone well; but he took the thing seriously, lost his head, and was himself the person who induced the Afghans to consider Captain Vicovich in the light of an accredited envoy.²⁵

In his subsequent book, Durand alleges that Burnes, in his Kabul mission, had not behaved with the 'decorum, which in a Muslim country is seldom departed from', and that this had caused loss of influence. Masson was the source of Durand's information. Durand's account has been crucial in the established historical view of Burnes' womanising in Kabul. But all such allegations seem credibly to be traced back to Masson as a single source.

We might also consider Masson's curious movements after Burnes left him at Peshawar in May 1838. After hearing that Burnes had failed to gain him a political post, Masson sent in his resignation as newswriter and headed deep into Afghanistan, north over the Hindu Kush to Bamian. He claimed he was returning to his excavations. Even for Masson this was eccentric when the imminence of the invasion was well-known to the Afghans, but Bamian was the obvious place to go if he needed to communicate with Russian agents through Bokhara. Thereafter, he returned to Ferozepore and joined the Army of the Indus, despite holding no position. There he spread negative stories about Burnes and again sought to cast doubt that Witkiewicz really was a Russian Envoy. Masson travelled with the Governor-General's camp, and then on Fane's barge – with no obvious reason for either – until leaving for several months' residence with Pottinger. A spy could not have placed himself better.

Still worse for Burnes, in January 1839 the following article was published in London in the *Oriental Intelligencer*:

SIR ALEXANDER BURNES AND THE GOVERNMENT

Much umbrage it is said has been taken by the Government at the recusancy of Sir Alexander Burnes, who will insist on taking the views his ample experience and natural ability present to him, of the proposed restoration of Shah Shooja. Captain B affirms that of all the race, His Lordship's protege is the vilest, most despised and most hated by the Affghan tribes; the most tyrannical, indolent and useless; a coward and a fool. In every point of view [Dost Mohammed] offers the most favourable contrast to the Company's protege. He is brave, honest, frank and beloved [. . .] and it is said that the Captain is not very reserved on it or his general views of our proceedings.²⁶

Similar articles had been appearing in the Indian papers, and may have contributed to a cooling of Auckland's regard for Burnes. Alex's enemies sought to pounce using these publications. These anonymous letters were sent to John Cam Hobhouse:

Portland Place Jan 1 1839

Sir,
[...] If Captain Burnes [...] could be guilty of such rashness and insubordination what an example – I am not aware that Lieutt Burnes, Assistant to Col. Pottinger, performed any great military or civil service. He made researches in Cabul and Bohara was liberally rewarded – made a Captain – sent home on full pay never examined and his Brother given a Cadetship. Upon being appointed on a special mission to Cabul - and which by the way wholly failed and hence this disastrous and ruinous war! – he was by the Whig Government given the Brevet rank of Lieutt Colonel and a Knighthood [...]
What has been done for Mr Macnaghten [...] and what will be done for the gallant and intrepid young Lieutt. Pottinger surely he will be made a Lieut Coll and receive a Knighthood if Burnes has [...] Is it becoming in this crisis that one as young untried and apparently conceited as Captain Burnes should publish opinions which may be of incalculable mischief both in India and at home? He is said to be a 'leetle' hot and hasty [...] a most ambitious young man [...]

I have the Honour to be
Your very obedt. Servant
Zeta[27]

Two months later another was sent, in a different handwriting but evidently from the same interest:

Whig Justice!

Lieutt Burnes sent home his notes and [...] a Book of his Travels was brought out. No one could gainsay it for it was a new country to us – He was made a Captain sent home on full pay but never examined, given a cadetship for his Brother [...] by anticipation of what he was to do but which proved a failure was gazetted brevet Lieutt Colonel and given a Knighthood. What was the feeling erected amongst all old officers who have fought and bled to see Lt Burnes get so much and they all passed over – contrast this with Lieut Eldred Pottinger [...] He is Lieutt still whilst a book which [...] may or may not have been written by Burnes, and may or may not be true, has raised him above all old officers – and [...] Alexander Burnes does not scruple to publish his opinions as being directly opposed to the determination of Government and the Governor-General [...] neglect of the long service of Colonel Pottinger and of the ability of Mr Macnaghten the Government Secretary none of whom receive honour or reward [...]

An Old Indian
Oriental Club
Hanover Square Febr 27 1839.[28]

Surely these letters originated with the Pottingers? Hobhouse also the same month received open campaigning for honours by the Pottinger family:

Feb 7 1839

Sir,
I have the honour to enclose [...] statements of the services of my brother Colonel Pottinger and my son Lieutenant Eldred Pottinger [...] as a further claim of my family to the distinctions I have requested I beg to state that I lost four brothers on service in the last war [...] and that I have two brothers [...] [in] Her Majesty's 6th Foot and four sons [...] still in the service. I also served for fifteen years in H.M.s 8th Hussars [...] all my family for the last two hundred years have been either soldiers or sailors in the service of their country.

Under all these circumstances I look with confidence to Her Majesty's Government to confer the rank of Baronet on Colonel Pottinger and on Eldred Pottinger the defender of Herat [...]

I have the honor to be
Your Most Obedient Servant
Thomas Pottinger[29]

But Burnes' securing of the crossing of the Indus brought him a further commendation from the Court of Directors.[30] Then at Shikarpur Burnes again faced a crisis of conscience about the deposition of Dost Mohammed 'with whom we have dined, and who has treated us as private friends'.[31] He told Macnaghten that he did not wish to accompany the army into Afghanistan, but would rather remain at Shikarpur to oversee relations with Sind and the army's supply lines, with Mohan Lal as his assistant. Macnaghten agreed. The 1,800-mile Karachi to Kabul supply line, none of which was in British territory although the British seized key military points, would be vital to the prospects of the Army of the Indus. In December 1839 the Secret Committee ordered the urgent construction in Bombay of six more specially designed Indus steamers, to support the army and later for use in the expected Indus trade. Key parts were sent out from the UK.[32]

Burnes was talked into accompanying the invasion by Fane, who persuaded him that the army needed him. It appears that Burnes' conscience was sufficient to overcome his ambition, but not when reinforced by personal appeals to his patriotism. So the *Bombay Gazette* of 3 April 1833 reported: 'Lieutenant Eastwick has been appointed to the political charge of upper Scinde in place of Sir Alexander Burnes, who seems determined to push on with Sir Willoughby Cotton.' Eastwick in turn was replaced at Haidarabad by Burnes' carthorse companion Leckie – and the Residence clerk was their old assistant Pitumba.

Burnes' agents in Afghanistan were sending him reports on Dost's preparations to resist the invasion. The Emir was concentrating on the strengthening of the fortress of Ghazni, indicating that Dost knew the British were coming via Kandahar and not Jalalabad. Burnes also reported that Mehrab Khan of Kelat was a firm ally, but rather wished British protection than to become a vassal of Shah Shuja.[33]

In the Khyber pass, Lord wrote to Burnes for assistance and advice. The tribal leaders wanted both to hedge their bets and increase their price. Typical was Bahadur Khan, who had helped escort Burnes and Lord through the pass in 1837 and to whom Lord now gave a letter from Burnes. Bahadur congratulated the British on their role in turning back the Persians before Herat, but added that he had received a message from Dost saying: 'I hear you are in communication with Shah Shuja and Sikunder Burnes. What harm have I done you? If you want more money, say so. But remember that you are an Afghan and a Musulman, and that the Shah is now the servant of the Kafirs.'

Bahadur continued that he received Rs8,000 annually from Dost. What were the British offering? Lord added that Bahadur in truth received about half this. Negotiations with the Khyber chiefs were rich in goodwill expressions, but centred on cash.[34] Burnes provided Lord with briefing notes on how to deal with each of the chiefs, for example:

> Qutab-Alam [...] is a clever, shrewd fellow; and his father being with the Shah gives him an interest in doing good. He is, however, very thick with Avitabile. That has its advantages and its disadvantages.[35]

To secure the army supply route from Bombay, the British annexed the port of Karachi, which remained British territory for the next 107 years. Their excuse was that the harbour fort had fired on the Company warship *Wellesley*. The Karachi authorities claimed it was a single shot salute with no ball, and Henry Pottinger travelled to investigate, reporting that the Sindi explanation was true and there were no guns in the fort capable of firing in anger. Despite Pottinger,[36] Auckland insisted on the annexation of coastal Sind in spring 1839.[37]

With the news that the Persians had abandoned the siege of Herat, the British realised they would not be fighting the Russian-officered Persian Army, still less the Russians themselves. The size of the Bengal contingent was therefore reduced, and Fane, in poor health, decided not to go. He now drew lots to decide which two of the five Bengal Divisions should be left behind. Fane did not want to be blamed by eager officers left out. The results were foolish: for example, of the Royal regiments the 13th, which had lost 180 men to cholera, was selected, while the fresh Buffs were stood down.

Sir John Keane, commanding the Bombay Division, had arrived in Sind on 25 November on the Company's new paddle steamer, the *Semiramis*. At 1,000 tons against the *Hugh Lindsay*'s 400, and with twin 180-horsepower engines, it was a major improvement.[38] Pottinger had been put in charge of the disembarkation of Bombay troops by the acting Governor of Bombay, James Farish. This had a strange consequence. Pottinger was obsessed with proving Burnes wrong about the potential of Karachi, and insisted the force land at Sanda instead. Here men, stores, guns and horses had to be transshipped into small boats and brought over the sandbar and surf. The dangerous process took weeks and brought losses. The force's chief surgeon, Edinburgh's Richard Kennedy, noted:

> Sir Alexander Burnes, who knew more of Sind and the Indus than any other person [...] had recommended Kurachy as the point that should have been first occupied. But his superior knowledge [...] [was] overruled [...] The subsequent events most fully demonstrated that Kurachy should have been the point selected [...] Lord Keane himself expressed the same opinion.[39]

They had limited supplies and almost no baggage animals. For two months no part of this force was capable of moving, and would have been endangered by any attack.

On 30 November 1838 Fane handed overall command to Keane. Under him Sir Willoughby Cotton commanded the Bengal infantry, and General Wilshire the Bombay infantry. The Bombay and Bengal cavalry were combined under General Thackwell and the artillery likewise under Brigadier Stevenson. The Chief Engineer was Major Thomson. This was the Army of the Indus proper. The Shah's contingent under Brigadier Simpson and the Sikh contingent under Sheikh Basawan, and assorted Afghan irregulars, were not formally part of the Army, though under Keane's operational command. Lt Col Sir Alexander Burnes was not on the Army's roll, being present as a diplomatic Envoy.

The final composition of the force was 21,100 men. There were 9,500 of the Bengal Army, 5,600 of the Bombay Army, and 6,000 of Shah Shuja's contingent. Approximately 19,000 marched through the Bolan pass into Afghanistan. In addition Claude Wade was to invade through the Khyber pass with an allied army of 10,800, consisting of 4,800 irregulars under Shazada Timour, Shuja's Crown Prince, and 6,000 Sikh troops. There were reserves of 4,500 Bengal troops at Ferozepore and Ludhiana and 3,000 Bombay troops in Sind.

It was a small army with which to attempt to subjugate Afghanistan – though any larger an army could not have been fed. The Army of the Indus was tiny compared to the 81,000 regular foot, 10,000 regular and 23,000 irregular cavalry which the British had mobilised as the Grand Army of Hindustan in 1817 to finish Mahratta resistance and Pindari brigandage. The Army of the Indus was also substantially smaller than the forces used in the contemporary invasions of Nepal and Burma.

Rather than starting immediately through the Bolan for Afghanistan, Cotton with Fane's concurrence, advanced on Haidarabad with the bulk of his Division, to support Keane. Cotton's and Keane's Divisions were unable to communicate with each other. On 6 February 1839 Macnaghten wrote to John Colvin, Auckland's private secretary:

> The state of our intelligence department is lamentable in the extreme. We are utterly ignorant of Sir John Keane's movements and motives, whether he is at Jurruck or Tatta, whether he has retreated, and if he has, whether from deficiency of means, or to lead the enemy on; and we know nothing as to what the Ameers are doing, where they are, or what terms have been offered them.[40]

Macnaghten was furious at Cotton's moving on Haidarabad. He feared the campaign in Sind might delay the expedition an entire year. The Amirs of Sind had a reputation for vast wealth and Macnaghten suspected that the soldiers were motivated by prize money. He also had doubts about Cotton: 'Sir Willoughby is clearly gone on a wild goose chase. He cannot possibly, I think, be at Hydrabad under twenty five days from this date, and he seems to be travelling by a route which has no road. He will soon, I fear, find himself in the jungle.'

Sir Willoughby did precisely that. Macnaghten wrote imploring him to invade Afghanistan. This had no effect, particularly as Cotton was supported by Fane, who was drifting on a 'magnificent boat'[41] down the Indus alongside Cotton's troops, in a sickbed. Fane continued to issue detailed advice on logistical and strategic arrangements. Burnes and Pottinger had both advised the move on Haidarabad. They and Fane were right, and Macnaghten was wrong. For Cotton to have marched off, leaving the unsubdued 25,000 strong army of Sind blocking Keane would have been irresponsible. It was unknown if the Amirs would comply with British demands or attack Keane.

News arrived from London that the Government were not inclined to agree to Fane's request to resign. He was lifted from his bed and placed on his horse to march on Haidarabad. At the head of the advancing column rode Alexander Burnes and Mohan Lal.[42] Prize money was a very real consideration. Even the sack of the minor city of Kittur in 1824 brought £100,000 in prize money of which the customary one-eighth share, a fortune, went to the Commanding Officer, Colonel Deacon.[43]

Macnaghten had crossed the bridge of boats with the artillery on 9

February[44] to get the march into Afghanistan underway. Fuming at the delay, he wrote a peremptory letter to Cotton:

> I [...] require you to furnish me with such a force as shall be sufficient to enable me to give effect to His Lordship's plans in Afghanistan. I have already urged in the strongest terms your crossing over to this side of the river with your whole force. Of Sir John Keane's army there can be no apprehension.

This caused fury from Fane, which resulted in Macnaghten being rebuked by Auckland. Joint civilian and military operational command in war was a recipe for disaster. This lesson was not taken. The Amirs' intelligence was rather better than the British, and they knew Cotton was coming and that Khairpur had capitulated. Facing combined British armies of 13,400 men against their own feudal forces of 25,000, virtually without artillery, Sind surrendered. Keane had accepted the submission of the Amirs just as Cotton had set off for Haidarabad.

The Army of the Indus had been extremely keen to sack Haidarabad, and had anticipated treasure to the value of eight crores of rupees, or £8m. When news of the surrender reached them on 7 February, the officers of the Bengal column were most disappointed.[45]

The existence of the famed riches was proven when the massive sum of ten lakhs in tribute were paid over to Pottinger in coin over the space of just three days, from 7 to 9 February 1839. This was the first instalment of twenty-five lakhs collected altogether. The British were bound by treaty to hand over fifteen lakhs to Ranjit Singh; they never did. Finding provisions and carriage to buy proved much more problematic than getting the money.

CHAPTER TWENTY-SIX

## The Dodgy Dossier

In England, many old India hands could not understand why an expensive war was being undertaken so far from British borders. In February 1839 the Court of Directors demanded to see all the correspondence leading to declaration of war. Hobhouse high-handedly replied that they would have to wait until the Government placed documents before Parliament – which secretly he was delaying.[1]

In presenting the case for war to Parliament, Hobhouse and Palmerston faced two major difficulties. The first was Russia. The real motive for war was the desire to counter Russia in Central Asia. But Russia had backed down, disowned and removed Simonicz and Witkiewicz. On 31 October 1838 Witkiewicz had been in Kandahar, distributing 10,000 gold ducats to the Dil Khans and promising 40,000 more to help resist the British. But on 11 November Count Nesselrode, the Russian Foreign Minister, wrote to Palmerston deprecating Witkiewicz and avowing that

> there has not existed the smallest design hostile to the English government, nor the smallest idea of endangering the tranquillity of the British possession in India.

to which Palmerston replied

> Her Majesty's government accept as entirely satisfactory the declaration of the Russian Government that it does not harbour any designs hostile to the interests of Great Britain in India.[2]

The next month Palmerston was pursuing further complaints about Simonicz. He asked the British Ambassador in St Petersburg, Lord Durham, to discover whether Simonicz had acted on instructions in promoting the attack on Herat. Nesselrode replied:

> that if count Simonicz had acted in the manner mentioned by Mr McNeill

he had done what was in direct opposition to his instructions. The count had been distinctly ordered to dissuade the Shah from prosecuting the present war [. . .] in any circumstances.[3]

Palmerston's pressing priority was to persuade Russia to accept an international system of guarantee for Turkey against the encroachment of the Egyptian Pasha, Mehmet Ali. This would mean Russia surrendering some of the diplomatic gains made in the Treaty of Unkiar Skelessi, particularly control of the Dardanelles. Palmerston was concerned about Russian threat towards India, but had no means other than conciliation to cause a Russian withdrawal from the Bosphorus.

So Hobhouse and Palmerston had to present a case for war in Afghanistan to avert a withdrawn threat, from a Russia they now wished to placate. They were working with Russia towards the treaty of July 1840 which contained Great Power agreement to coerce Mehmet Ali into giving back Syria to the Ottomans. This negotiation had caused great tension with Mehmet Ali's backers in Paris. Palmerston had obtained agreement of his own Government only by threat of resignation. The Cabinet had been baffled by the sudden transition of Russia from enemy to ally against Louis-Philippe. They viewed the French King as an important liberal figure. It seemed to many leading Whig politicians not to make sense, especially when they were still heading for war in Afghanistan to thwart the Russians.

By comparison, Palmerston and Hobhouse's second problem must have seemed a minor annoyance – they had to account for the fact that the war was being launched against the advice of the only Afghanistan 'celebrity' whose name carried public weight, Alexander Burnes.

The answer was twofold: to overwhelm parliamentarians with material; nine dense volumes of blue book were published, much of it tangentially relevant; and rigorous editing was employed. References to the Russian threat were largely excised. Burnes' despatches were redacted to remove reference to Dost's pro-British sentiments, or his agreement to reasonable terms. Burnes' own policy recommendations were cut out, up to the time where he had been ordered that the policy was to install Shuja, and had started making recommendations on how to implement this.

Nobody reading only these blue books would know Burnes had argued for alliance with Dost Mohammed. The editing was undoubtedly tendentious; they made a false prospectus for war by eliminating the alternative. There is a respectable argument for omitting passages which might offend Russia, but the systematic misrepresentation to Parliament of Burnes' views is not defensible.

The actual editing was carried out by William Cabell, Chief Clerk of the Foreign Office, with both Hobhouse and Palmerston then making further emendations. Under Palmerston, the entire staff of the Foreign Office in London was only about three dozen people. This was therefore a major task for overstretched officials. Two volumes dealt with Burnes' correspondence, one anent Witkiewicz, the second Dost Mohammed. The second was the more heavily edited. The sting was drawn from the first by separate publication by the FO of correspondence with Russia in which Witkiewicz had been disowned.[4]

Revisionist historians[5] have portrayed the distortion of Burnes' views as myth. But Burnes was always convinced he had been deliberately misrepresented. Writing to his friend George Jacob from Kabul in December 1839:

> I hardly thought, when writing my dispatches, that they were so soon destined to form a part of history. I would much have preferred that the whole of my views had been published rather than serving up to the public as a report only so much as the Government could digest. You would then have seen that their policy towards Dost Mohammed had been very questionable.[6]

On 14 February Cabell wrote to Palmerston and Hobhouse giving the genesis of the publication strategy.[7] Stating the problem as how to justify the 'decision of the Governor-General', without offending Russia, Cabell suggests they should initially publish nothing except the trilateral treaty with Shuja and Ranjit. The opposition would demand more, and the Government would be able to tell Russia its hand was forced. They should then publish McNeill's letters about Persian designs on Herat and Simonicz' role, and extracts of Burne's letters about Witkiewicz, but also Nesselrode's letters denying they acted on instructions. In this plan, the only material published from Burnes would relate to Witkiewicz.

Cabell stated the aim as to demonstrate that 'no other course was open', while not endangering relations with Russia. He simply presumes that the Government will only publish those papers supporting its case: that this is an exercise in self-justification, not in providing material to Parliament. The editing of Burnes' despatches was only a part of a campaign of tendentious Government handling of Parliament in the run-up to war, which cannot fail to evoke comparison with Blair's misleading of Parliament to promote the invasion of Iraq.

A studiously unhelpful minute[8] is written by Hobhouse to Cabell instructing a response to requests from Hobhouse's Tory shadow Ellenborough. In reply to Ellenborough's request for any treaty with Bhawalpur, Hobhouse replied that there was no treaty that had 'yet arrived in England'. But Hobhouse knew the treaty for the 'loan' of Baikhar fortress had been signed on 26 December – that the ratified copy had not yet arrived was true, but hardly a full answer. Similarly in respect of a request for any treaty with the Amirs of Sind, Hobhouse replied there was 'no treaty yet that we are aware of', but he had copies of the draft, and knew that three months earlier it was on the point of signature. It was in fact already signed.

Hobhouse's simple blanking of Ellenborough was not a legitimate way to treat Parliament. This is vital context to the editing of Burnes' despatches, which was part of a wider distortion. To the current generation it is irresistible to note the parallels with the work of John Scarlett and Alistair Campbell in filleting and filtering disparate intelligence to give the entirely false picture in the 'dodgy dossier', on the threat from Iraq's (non-existent) Weapons of Mass Destruction. Imperialist resource grabs, in whatever century, entail duplicity at the centre of government. This dishonesty was as shocking in 1838 as in 2003.

Mountstuart Elphinstone was among the many in Britain who had severe doubts about the invasion. He wrote presciently to Burnes, in an undated letter which Burnes marked 'received Cabool 25 August 1839':

> You will guess what I think of affairs in Cabool, you remember when I used to dispute with you against having even an Agent in Cabool, and now we have assumed the protection of the state, as much as if it were one of the Subsidiary Allies in India – If you send 27000 men [...] to Candahar [...] <u>and can feed them</u> I have no doubt you will take Candahar and Cabool, and get up Shoojah – but for maintaining him in such a poor, cold, strong and remote country, among a turbulent people like the Afghans, I own it seems to me to be hopeless [...] If the disgrace of a close connection with us were not enough to make it unpopular, the connection with Runjeet and our guarantee of his conquests must make us detested.[9]

The Company administration was divided. The Court of Directors and the Political Committee remained very sceptical. The Government-dominated Board of Control and Secret Committee not only supported the invasion, but were planning to advance British influence another thousand miles north, not just to the Oxus (Amu) but the Jaxartes (Syr). A document approved by Hobhouse and the Secret Committee on 12 February 1839 stated that Russia aimed to conquer Khiva and Bokhara. Remarkably the paper states of Russia:

> it is her [...] duty to make herself mistress of those territories, for the triple purpose of preventing the slavery of her own subjects, of giving the blessings of European civilisation to extensive tracts of great natural fertility, beauty and almost unequalled salubrity, and of diverting a great part of the more valuable commerce of India into the channel of those countries and European Russia.

But the paper then argues that Britain equally has this right, and must do it first. As with the Indus, the spread of preponderant British influence was to be won peacefully through trade penetration using the rivers. The aim was:

> opening to commercial navigation the Oxus and Jaxartes rivers, which appear to offer an uninterrupted natural navigation of nearly 2000 miles between Kalif on the Oxus and Kokaun on the Jaxartes. The question is not whether this shall be done, but whether England or Russia shall do it. Steam vessels [. . .] may be conveyed in frame from the Indus to the Oxus. In this way we may establish a commercial intercourse mutually beneficial, preoccupying this important navigation, and tending to ensure the friendship of those states on its borders.[10]

This project to encompass the territory of modern Uzbekistan was not meant to be a distant dream, but a step which the Board of Control was instructing Auckland to take as soon as the British Army had control of Kabul. Burnes had surveyed parts of the Amu, but there was no reliable information on the Syr. That accounts for the wildly optimistic view that it was navigable from the Aral Sea to Kokhand. Equally ill-informed was the description 'of unequalled salubrity'. I have experienced +52°C in summer and -32°C in winter in the countryside between Karshi and Samarkand.

The EIC offices in Leadenhall Street must have been an extraordinary place to work. The correspondence of the Political Committee was drafted by John Stuart Mill. The correspondence of the Secret Committee – including this scheme – was drafted by the major novelist Thomas Love Peacock.

Hobhouse was as actively engaged in war preparations as the communications delay would allow. He ordered that the 13th Dragoons remain indefinitely in India while the 15th Dragoons were to be sent out urgently to Bombay. Every Queen's regiment in India was to be expanded by ten men, while 4,000 new bayonets were to be supplied.[11] Hobhouse tried to speed up the mails to allow him a more direct influence. The overland route by Suez, allied with the advent of steam, had revolutionised communication and letters now took ten weeks not six months, but a twenty-week turnaround still effectively took him out of the war. Cabell organised speed trials of the official mail versus Mr Waghorn's steam-packet service via Malta, but the results were similar.[12] Mr Waghorn got the contract and Hobhouse wrote to the Egypt Office emphasising that mails must be sent on to Malta the moment they arrived.[13] By 1840 Hobhouse had achieved seven weeks to Bombay and nine to Calcutta.

CHAPTER TWENTY-SEVEN

## Kelat

Mehrab Khan of Kelat was widely believed to be sympathetic to restoring the Saduzai monarchy in Afghanistan. He had sheltered Shuja following his defeat before Kandahar in 1834, and had refused to surrender him. In fact, Mehrab had a deep sense of honour, and was acting more in accordance with his obligations to a guest than out of regard for Shuja.

The route from Ferozepore to Kabul through the Bolan pass is long and circuitous. But Fane was initially tasked to march to Herat, not Kabul. Fane consulted, among others, Arthur Conolly and the chosen route was that which Conolly had travelled from Herat. By the time news of the raising of the siege of Herat had arrived, the army was already collected at Ferozepore for the Bolan pass.

Most of the long march was through Kelat, which started at the Indus and continued either side of the mountain barrier they would cross, encompassing Quetta in the district of Shawl, which was to become the campaign's forward base. Before the mountains it was sand and scrub; the mountains were bleak, and Shawl was sparsely populated. Furthermore, 1838 had brought a third successive drought year. Quetta often struggled to feed its own population.

Even in good times, the route was ill-suited to an army, with its accompanying mass of camp followers. But this was during a disaster. The failure of rains was widespread. Kanpur was 'in many places like a charnel house, and the river has become disgusting from the flocks of vultures tearing the starved corpses to pieces'.[1]

Burnes' career had taken off when, as a young Deputy Quartermaster-General, he had taken on the functions of a political officer. Now as a senior political officer, he found himself instructed to undertake the functions of a Quartermaster-General for the provisioning, transport and logistics of the army. Burnes' contacts with local chiefs were essential, and he was authorised to draw an enormous sum of money – nineteen lakhs or £190,000 – on the Shikarpur bankers to procure supplies.[2] He had already concluded agreements with Sarwar Khan Lohani over carriage and with Rustam Khan of Khairpur and Mehrab Khan of Kelat over provisions. He had now had to make these work, despite failed harvests.

He found he was obliged to micro-manage. On 20 February he rode into Shikarpur alongside Willoughby Cotton at the head of the Bengal contingent. A British officer wrote home:

> Every impediment has been thrown in the way of our procuring supplies in this territory [...] And it was only by Sir Alexander Burnes telling the chiefs hereabouts, that if they interfered with or impeded in his endeavours the man who had contracted to supply grain, they should answer for it most heavily, that we have managed to get grain at reasonable prices.[3]

Burnes' duties were many and various. James Atkinson, Bengal's Surgeon-General, was travelling with the horse artillery through Sind, accompanied by Delawar Khan who was handling their logistics 'in the employ of Sir Alexander Burnes'. At the town of Goetki the local mullah implored Atkinson's intercession on behalf of two villagers, one of them wounded, who had been arrested for stealing baggage camels. The mullah protested their innocence, and was assured 'that the culprits would be handed over to Sikunder Burnes, who would act in the case according to the evidence advanced'.[4] The name evidently carried public confidence in Sind. Burnes consistently intervened to prevent executions.

The Army of the Indus had about three camp followers to every soldier, fewer than usual in India. There was one driver for every three camels, of which there were tens of thousands. Each horse had two attendants – a groom, and a grass-cutter who had the dangerous job of going out for forage. There was a driver for every two draught bullocks, of which there were numbers for each cannon, tumbril and cart. There were drovers for load bullocks and mules. There were messengers, and palanquin and dhoolie bearers for carrying the sick and wounded, at least two relays of four for each casualty. There were hundreds of lascars who pitched and struck the tents and vast numbers of personal servants. The rank and file slept ten or twelve to a tent; each tent had a cook, dhobi and water carrier. There were herdsmen who supplied the army with mutton, and mobile chicken farms. There were merchants who set up camp bazaars, selling victuals, fabrics, weapons, jewellery, bed linen, shawls, medicines, aphrodisiacs, firewood, brassware, earthenware and furniture. Bankers and moneylenders had their stall with private doctors, barbers, letter-writers, fortune-tellers and entertainers. There were also the women, attached and unattached, and dancing boys for those so inclined.[5]

Macnaghten, Burnes, D'Arcy Todd and Cotton on 21 February 1839 discussed the available intelligence. Eldred Pottinger and Colonel Stoddart had been forced to quit Herat after continuing quarrels with the wazir, Yar Mohammed, despite the lavish sums Pottinger had given him. Burnes had heard from McNeill that the Shah, who still had not evacuated Ghorian, might again attack Herat; he had also heard from Kandahar that Witkiewicz was in the city. Another agent had informed Burnes that Baluch tribesmen were planning to block the Bolan pass.

Cotton was still furious at Macnaghten's criticism of his move on Haidarabad. It was a bad time for Macnaghten now to suggest that 1,000 of his contingent's camels be given to the Shah's force. Cotton exploded. Macnaghten recorded: 'I was distinctly told that I wanted to assume the command of the army; and that he, Sir Willoughby, knew no superior but Sir John Keane, and that he would not be interfered with etc. etc.' Burnes managed to reconcile the two over a hearty dinner. Macnaghten acknowledged that 'we parted at a late hour last night very good friends.'[6]

Keane and the Bombay contingent had still not arrived. Cotton, under pressure from Macnaghten and Burnes, without reference to Keane, set off with the Bengal contingent for the Bolan pass on 23 February with 85 per cent of the total available carriage, leaving Shah Shuja's levies marooned at Shikarpur. The Bengal column found very little food on the march and the following Bombay force, virtually none. The latter had never had sufficient baggage animals, and partly depended on boats for carrying its equipment up the Indus. Their camels were delayed by another extraordinary interference by Pottinger in Burnes' arrangements, again noted by Dr Kennedy: 'Colonel Pottinger prohibited the camels for the Bombay Division collected at Deesa from crossing half the distance of the same [Thar desert] route, and compelled them to march seven hundred miles round by Arrysir, and Bhooj, and Luckput, and through Sind, instead of three hundred miles across, via Balmeer!'[7] As with Karachi, so in the Thar desert, Pottinger intervened to prevent the army using supply routes Burnes had personally surveyed.

As Cotton led the Bengal contingent into Cutch Gandava, it was travelling along roads freshly cut by Baluch levies of the Khan of Kelat under the supervision of Robert Leech. Burnes himself was ahead of the force. At Rojihan, he oversaw the construction of a deep well, faced with brick. From this point they were in desert; by the time they got to the Bolan pass, the army had already come close to disaster. Wrote Colonel Dennie:

> Desert will hardly describe the aspect of that fearful tract, where no sign of animal or vegetable life is to be found; and as for the heat you [...] can form

no conception of it [...] I shudder to look back at what I and those with me underwent. The tract of country above described is by the nations of India considered as the hottest in the world. The Persians [...] [say]: 'Oh Allah! Wherefore make hell when thou hast made Dadur?' Colonel Thompson [...] died instantly in his tent, and Lieutenant Brady fell dead in the same manner, their bodies turning as black as charcoal.[8]

After four days, at Bushor, the cavalry commander urgently consulted Major Thomson; the horses were already suffering due to lack of forage and water and he suggested the cavalry turn back. A hay store at Jandira, collected by Burnes and Sayyid Mahommed Sherif, the Governor of Gundava, had been attacked by marauders. Thomson persuaded the commander they should press on, as a retrograde movement would inspire resistance.

In the eighty miles between Jandira and the Ustar, the only water of any use to the army was at Rojihan. It was Burnes' efforts, riding with the Adjutant-General Major Craigie, Mohan Lal and Mahommed Sherif, which somehow bought enough water and provisions to get the army across, suffering but not destroyed. This was extremely exerting and very dangerous, with long rides in a small party ahead of the main force while active bands of local resistance were already harassing the British. Burnes usually rode by night, preceded by meshalchis who held in one hand a roll of flaming flax and in the other a skin bottle of oil to pour on the torch.

Burnes instructed Leech to ride on to Sebi and cut the dam there, releasing water into the Nari river in the path of the British forces, but also devastating the agricultural economy of the region. It should be stated in fairness that the British were meticulous in paying out agricultural compensation for damages down to payments to individual farmers. The growing cereal crops were destroyed for forage; the British Army advanced like a plague of locusts. In every field of green grain, an officer of the Quartermaster-General's department marked off specific portions for named corps of the army. Each regimental Quartermaster issued duplicate chits to the farmer and to Headquarters for the crops consumed. The farmer was then paid in coin by the Executive Commissariat officer of Brigade. Every day these officers would face disputes over entitlement to compensation, and the British showed a systematic bias towards the peasant against his landlord. But as surprisingly well-motivated as this was, a few coins were not going to assist the farmer when all food and water reserves had been destroyed over a wide area. The passing army brought starvation, disease and ruin.

Leech had constructed offshoot canals from the Nari around Bushori, and though the water did not reach Cotton and the first brigade of the Bengal division on time, it did trickle down to assist the rest of the army. Burnes instructed over 100 new wells dug between Bushori and Mirpore. Arriving at Mirpore the army found him encamped in a stupa, snatching a few hours of archaeological excavation. He informed Cotton that 100 Jokrani tribesmen were on a maraud to attack baggage. Such raiding parties, splitting into smaller units and lying in ambush, were difficult to combat.

Isolated detachments or supplies were now picked off. An attack on a hospital wagon provoked fury, and orders were given to take pre-emptive action. This led to attacks on locals whose probable hostility had not taken any active form, and Burnes became alarmed this could prompt general resistance; he remonstrated with Cotton that his orders were 'bloodthirsty and calculated to bring about a blood feud'.[9] Burnes still hoped that the invasion might pass without much violence. He believed his distribution of bribes meant that it would be 'a triumph without bloodshed' providing the British maintained their discipline.[10]

By the time the hungry army reached Dadur at the entrance to the Bolan pass on 6 March 1839, not 10 per cent of the supplies expected from Mehrab had arrived, despite Mehrab's brother, now assisting Burnes, writing Mehrab a remonstrance. This was by chance delivered with a missive from Shuja containing a threat to depose Mehrab Khan and replace him with a rival, Nawaz Khan, in Shuja's camp.

Leech recruited 200 Baluch cavalry as a flying column, to protect the baggage and stem the flood of desertions. As supplies grew scarce and the situation more dangerous, drovers, dhoolie bearers, grooms, grass cutters and others were deserting, many taking animals or loot with them. Flogging was prescribed for salaried non-combatants who tried to leave, and Leech was authorised to pay his men Rs5 for every deserter captured. Leech was obliged to tell Cotton there were no new supplies of grain for the next march, through the Bolan pass itself.

He persuaded Cotton to promulgate a declaration, requiring all troops and followers to 'be careful not to interfere with, or insult the prejudices of, the people of the country through which we are about to pass'. The order specified that only Muslims may enter a mosque and that wayside flags and other objects of religious significance must not be touched. Fruit trees must not be used for forage, nor the women of the country 'interfered with'. Officers were to ensure that these instructions were explained to all troops, and given out in all bazaars and civilian lines.[11] Sadly, the British did not live up to these standards.

Arthur Conolly had noted that the Bolan streams were fed only by autumn rainfall, and became foetid pools: 'In summer the sun acting upon these pent-up waters, causes a pestilent air, and the road between Quetta and Dadur is shut. Native cossids are indeed to be found whose poverty will tempt them to carry letters, but they often remain on the road as food for hyenas.'[12]

The road was precisely that along which the British now marched 19,000 troops, 40,000 camp followers and 40,000 animals, from March to late May, in a drought and famine. The consequences were predictably hideous.

Before a fortnight was through, troops were on half rations and eventually quarter rations, even as they struggled to cross high mountain passes with artillery, baggage and equipment. By the time they won through to Quetta, three-quarters of the 40,000 baggage animals were rotting corpses stretching a gruesome path across Baluchistan. The soldiers' sufferings were made worse as, owing to the shortage of carriage, each infantryman was carrying thirteen pounds more than usual.

Colonel Alexander Burnes was the first member of the Army of the Indus to enter the Bolan pass, riding alongside Major Cureton of the 16th Lancers, who commanded one troop of lancers and three companies of native infantry, plus all of the sappers, miners and engineers. The British expected the pass to be defended, especially by snipers – Burnes was at the position of maximum danger.

It was inevitable that the army passing would bring conflict with Mehrab. Burnes was Envoy to Kelat. It was a sign of Burnes' still rising standing with Auckland and the military establishment that on 11 February 1839 a young officer was 'placed at the disposal of the Envoy to Kelat'[13] – Alex's youngest brother Charlie, who thus left the 17th Bombay NI to join the more remunerative Political Service.

Nepotism was the norm in British India – Henry Pottinger had his nephew Eldred assisting him, Auckland's nephew William Osborne was his aide-de-camp and Macnaghten was reported to by three Conolly nephews. The Commander-in-Chief, General Sir Henry Fane, had both Lieutenant Colonel Henry Fane and Lieutenant Henry Fane as aides-de-camp. Sir John Keane had his son Lieutenant E A W Keane. One of Major-General Willoughby Cotton's aides was Captain Willoughby Cotton. But to exercise this patronage required a certain standing, which Lieutenant-Colonel Sir Alexander Burnes had now achieved. His arrangement for Charlie gave him great pleasure. Charlie received the very substantial annual salary of £720.

Alex had secured Charlie's career. He had brought his sisters out to India, and found them husbands. It is probable that he had himself paid for their passages, trousseaux and possibly dowries. He noted in his will that he was not leaving anything to his married sisters as he had given them over Rs15,000 each already.[14] He left his unmarried sister Cecilia £1,000, or half that if she meantime married. He had also given a substantial sum to his brother Davie to set up his private medical practice in London.[15]

Burnes was constantly receiving reports from his agents, and when the Bengal division finally struggled to the head of the Bolan pass, he was able to relay that the Dil Khan brothers at Kandahar had not raised any force to defend the Shawl or Pishin valleys, and so far taken no measures to defend Kandahar, rather concentrating on removing their personal fortunes. At the very summit of the Bolan, the engineers with Burnes in advance blasted out an old animal track with gunpowder, increasing the width from three to twelve feet. They thus cut out the last steep incline of an ascent that had already killed thousands of baggage animals, and reduced the distance by three miles. The blasting continued right up to the passing of the first column.

The largest population centre on the route through Kelat – Quetta – had just 500 houses.[16] The entire population of the province of Shawl – the most fertile through which the army passed – did not exceed 20,000. The land was incapable of sustaining the pressure placed on it by the British army. The region between Bolan and Quetta was named Dasht-i bi Daulat, 'poverty-stricken plain'. Eighteen months after the British army first passed along the route, this is Masson's description:

> So entirely had the country been devastated that I could no longer recognise it [...] Villages, then flourishing, had ceased to exist; those remaining were destitute of their attendant groves of trees and even the very waste had been denuded of the jangal of small trees and shrubs [...] the road [...] was now well marked by the skeletons of camels [...] whose bleached [...] bones too well described it.[17]

Macnaghten wrote to Auckland:

> They had good cause for dissatisfaction [...] their crops have been destroyed, and the water intended for the irrigation of their fields has been diverted to the use of our armies [...] little [...] effort seems to have been made either to [...] appease the discontent [...] Sir A Burnes may be led, by vague rumours of the Khan's unfriendly disposition, to recommend offensive operations against him. In what difficulties we may be involved [...] it would be impossible to foretell [...] considerable sums must be expended, not only in compensating the people for their losses but in bribing the authorities [...] damage [...] done to the crops [...] is grievous [...][18]

Macnaghten wrote of the Bolan pass on 23 March 1839, 'The Bombay force is nearly on the point of starvation – this is a wretched country [...] It may be said to produce nothing but plunderers; but with the knowledge we now have of it, we may bid defiance to the Russian hordes as far as this route is concerned.'[19] It was rather late to be concluding that a Russian attack on British India was impractical.

On 19 March, Cotton with 'Fighting Bob' Sale's brigade arrived at Sir-i-Ab, ten miles from Quetta, where Burnes, Cureton and the vanguard were waiting. Brigadier Arnold's brigade arrived on the 23rd and General Nott's on the 24th. Cotton had orders to wait for Keane and the Bombay division, which would take weeks. The lack of supplies was critical. Burnes tried to convince the British staff that Mehrab Khan was genuine, even if he had limited control over his nominal subjects. There was scepticism in the army, and rumour that grain, stores and carriage had been removed by Mehrab to Kelat. Burnes left on 24 March with Lieutenants Simpson and Pattison, Mohan Lal and the Governor of Quetta, and an escort of only one NCO and fifteen yellow-jacketed irregulars of Skinner's Horse to ride the eighty-eight mountainous miles to the fortress of Kelat. The half-starving army awaited the outcome anxiously.

Cotton moved forward on 27 March to make camp at Quetta proper. There Leech had found but two days' supply of grain. Arriving at Mustung, between Quetta and Kelat, Burnes was able to find no grain or forage; the inhabitants pled the poor harvests. He sent back a negative report to Cotton, who despatched Major Craigie back through the Bolan pass to Keane at Dadur, to impress on Keane the urgent necessity for Cotton to move his forces on to more fertile regions on the road to Kabul. Craigie returned with the news that Keane had refused permission, as Macnaghten insisted the British must not enter Afghanistan before Shuja, who was with Keane. Keane intimated he would press on and reach Cotton in a week.

Burnes was met a day's ride from Kelat by the Khan's fifteen-year-old son, Nassir, and escorted in by him. Alex wished to tie Mehrab Khan down to a new treaty, and persuade him to come to Quetta and do obeisance to Shah Shuja. Burnes found Mehrab afraid of assassination by Shuja, or exile by the British. Burnes informed him that the British proposed that he should hold his territory as tributary to Shuja, on the same terms as in the reign of Ahmed Shah. Supplies for the army would be paid for.

On 30 March 1839 Burnes wrote to Auckland reporting Mehrab's observations of Dost Mohammed:

> a man of resource and ability; and though we could easily put him down through the Shah Soojah [. . .] we could never win over the Affghan nation by it [. . .]
>
> 'Wait,' said he, 'till sickness overtakes your troops – till they are exhausted with fatigue from long and harassing marches, and from the total want of supplies; wait till they have drank of many waters; and wait, too, till they feel the sharpness of the Affghan swords.'[20]

These trenchant views echoed Burnes' own forebodings, and he described Mehrab as 'a man of no ordinary shrewdness and vigour of mind'.[21] In their next conversation he told Burnes:

> Shah Shoojah ought to have trusted the Afghans to restore him; whereas he is essaying to deluge the land with Hindoostanees, an insult which his own people will never forgive him [. . .] You English may keep him by force upon the musnud, but as soon as you leave the Kingdom [. . .] he will never be able to resist the storm of national and religious animosity which is already raised against him in the breasts of Afghans.[22]

Mehrab could offer nothing more for the army's immediate needs than 10,000 sheep. Burnes wrote to Macnaghten: 'my inquiries have served to convince me that there is but a small supply of grain [. . .] and none, certainly, to be given to us, without aggravating the present distress of the inhabitants – some of whom are feeding on herbs and grasses [. . .] This scarcity is corroborated by a blight in last year's harvest.'[23] Lieutenant Simpson was with Burnes and in charge of a large sum of money; he attempted to buy stores between Kelat to Quetta, but none was to be had at any price. Simpson was inclined to believe the rumours that Mehrab was stockpiling somewhere.

A treaty was agreed by Burnes and Mehrab in Kelat on 28 March 1839.

> Article 1
> As Naseer Khan and his descendants [. . .] held possession of the country of Khelat, Kutchee, Khurasan, Mekran, Kedge, Bea, and the port of Soumeeanee in the time of the lamented Ahmed Shah Dooranee, they will in future be masters of their country in the same manner.
> Article 2
> The English Government will never interfere between the Khan, his dependants, and subjects, particularly lend no assistance to Shah Newaz [. . .]
> Article 3
> As long as the British army continues in the country of Khurasan, the British Government agrees to pay to Mehrab Khan the sum of one and a half lakhs of Company's Rupees [. . .]
> Article 4
> In return for this sum the Khan, while he pays homage to the Shah and continues in friendship with the British nation, agrees to use his best efforts to procure supplies, carriage and stores [. . .][24]

Burnes left to return to the army, leaving Mohan Lal to finalise matters with Mehrab and escort him in to Shuja. Masson thought Burnes had miscalculated, as Mehrab was insulted at being dealt with by a munshi, and claimed that Mohan made himself ridiculous by pretending influence with Auckland, and attempting to purchase a high-class slave girl. Masson viewed Burnes' respect for Mohan Lal as 'indulgent', while Burnes valued and trusted Lal: it is doubtful anyone could have overcome Mehrab's distrust of Shuja.

The new treaty broke down immediately. What actually happened is a mystery. During Burnes' return to Quetta, his party was possibly attacked. Masson stated that he read a letter by Burnes to a friend, in which Burnes said that Mehrab had the party waylaid, in order to steal back the treaty. He added that Burnes told him that two or three of his party were wounded.[25] Lal contradicted Masson, stating Burnes did not have the treaty in his possession.

William Hough quotes Burnes' companion Simpson as saying that they had to leave Kelat precipitately as they had discovered a plot to murder their party.[26] Mohan Lal says that 'apparently' a group had come to Kelat to murder them, but that Mehrab's involvement was uncertain.[27] A few months later Lieutenant Loveday, Agent at Kelat, had never heard of the incident, and put down Burnes' repudiation of the treaty to anger that Mehrab Khan had refused to come in to Quetta. Havelock met Burnes immediately on his return and does not mention any actual attack.

The current Khan of Kelat[28] has told me that there was an attack made on Burnes' party, but the Khan was not involved. That accords with Henry Durand that the attack was by plunderers who had heard of the money Simpson was carrying.[29] Baluch historians attribute the incident to Wazir Muhammad Hassan as part of his plot to have the British remove Mehrab Khan.[30] This was also the final assessment of Masson, and of the British intelligence services.[31] If so it worked – the British decided the treaty was a dead letter. They were immediately to break all of its provisions.

In fact Mehrab, though he had reigned for over twenty years, had never enjoyed authority over all his large territories, and had been embroiled in civil war. He had executed or assassinated five cousins, two wazirs and scores of tribal chiefs. He had no effective control of Shawl or Mustung from 1835, and also none over the Murri and Bugti tribes of Brahuis in the north-east, who raided British columns in the hills. Macnaghten was presented with copies of letters from Mehrab Khan to them, but the source, Mehrab's wazir Muhammad Hussan, was playing a double game. It is impossible to know if the letters were genuine. Baluch tradition is that Hussan wrote the letters himself to incriminate Mehrab.[32] As both Hussan's father and brother were executed by Mehrab, it is not unlikely.

The British consistently overestimated the control chiefs had over their followers, from Mehrab Khan during the advance to Akbar Khan at the retreat. They assumed Afghan tribes were similar to Scottish Highland clans, a comparison first drawn by Mountstuart Elphinstone. In fact a Scottish clan chief had much more control. Afghan Khanships were less simply hereditary. Tribesmen had no sense of unconditional attachment. Allegiances competed with other obligations like blood feuds, and events like pastoral migrations. Sometimes significant groups might disagree with the Khan and withdraw allegiance. In Scotland rebellion against a chief was rare, indeed tragically so in the Clearances. In Afghanistan rebellion was frequent. The British expected Khans to exercise control well beyond their power. As the Khans were happy to accept British subsidies for keeping the peace, they seldom explained their inadequacy.

Burnes achieved one intelligence coup in Kelat, by subverting Abdul Wahhab Khan Popalzai, agent of the Dil Khans of Kandahar. Alex obtained from him copies of the extensive correspondence on resistance between Persia, Russia, Kabul, Kandahar, Kelat and Haidarabad. Having turned him, Burnes then sent him back to Kandahar to convert other senior Dourani nobles to Shuja's cause.

At Quetta, the British army continued to suffer severe food shortage, exacerbated once Keane, Macnaghten and the Shah's contingent arrived. Macnaghten wrote, '[T]he troops and followers are nearly in a state of mutiny for food.' He still suspected that Mehrab was hiding food and blamed Burnes for being soft. He was, moreover, frustrated by the pessimism around him, and lacked confidence in the military commanders. On 4 April 1839 he wrote to Auckland, 'Sir Willoughby is a sad croaker; not content with telling me we must all assuredly be starved, he assured me that Shah Shuja is very unpopular in Afghanistan.'

He did not think through the consequences of what he reported:

> The Shah is in good health and spirits; but he says he never had so much trouble and bother in his lifetime [. . .] on previous occasions [. . .] no complaint was ever allowed to reach the sacred person of His Majesty. His opinion of the Afghans as a nation is [. . .] extremely low. He says that they are a pack of dogs.[33]

A few days later Macnaghten was writing again:

> The whole of the force, from Sir W. Cotton downwards, are infected with exaggerated fears relating to the character of the King, and the prospects of the campaign. They fancy they see an enemy in every bush. The Khan of Khelat is our implacable enemy, and Sir J. Keane is burning with revenge. There never was such treatment [. . .] as we have been subjected to in our progress through the Khan's country. I will say nothing of Burnes's negociations. His instructions were to conciliate, but I think he adhered too strictly to the letter of them. The Commander in Chief is very angry[34]

On Macnaghten's instructions, Leech forced open the grain stores of Quetta and conducted aggressive searches, but the total amount of food they found – from private kitchens – did not amount to a single day's supply. Shuja announced that he had deposed the qasi, or chief Islamic judge, of Quetta and confiscated his lands. The qasi's unripe crops were devastated as the army's animals were sent to graze on them. While this measure saved some of the army's little carriage, it was also an early sign of Shuja's alienation of the religious establishment.

To be with a starving army that blames you cannot be pleasant. Army rumour was very much against Burnes, with contemporary reports that, 'Sir Alexander Burnes had been severely remonstrated with by the Governor-General [. . .] for not making better provision for the army.'[35] This must have been mortifying for Burnes, who had made heroic efforts to fulfil the impossible task of feeding the 40,000 who eventually assembled at Quetta in a drought. He had again demonstrated his work rate and endurance on his long rides, covering hundreds more miles than the army, as he scouted for supplies and conducted negotiations in all directions. On return to Quetta from Kelat, one of Burnes' party, young Lieutenant Pattison, collapsed in 'a high fever brought on by excessive fatigue'. Burnes just kept on going.

Blame must attach to Burnes, not for failing to work miracles with food, but for failing forcefully to explain to his superiors that Mehrab Khan had very little control and very limited provisions. Perhaps the failures of supply left him feeling vulnerable. He must have been physically tired. For whatever reason, Burnes bowed to Keane and Macnaghten and agreed that Mehrab Khan should be deposed.

CHAPTER TWENTY-EIGHT

## A King in Kandahar

With the campaign under way, Auckland wrote to Macnaghten on 8 December 1838 outlining a new treaty to establish Britain's relations with Shuja. The key provisions were a permanent British Resident in Kabul, and a subsidiary force, paid for by the Shah, under the command of British officers and answerable only to the Resident. Non-British Europeans would be banned, and taxation light. The Resident would approve all policies 'conducive to peace and commerce'.

Ministers in London were unimpressed. John Cam Hobhouse commented, 'this is perpetual interference and control'. Melbourne wrote with disapprobation on his copy, 'Mr Macnaghten is King of Affghanistan.' On 17 February 1839 Hobhouse wrote warning Auckland that 'People at home would look upon such an engagement as indicating an intention to extend our actual military control over parts of Central Asia, and would be alarmed lest some scheme of indefinite aggrandizement should result [. . .]'[1]

On 7 April 1839 the army moved out for Kandahar, preceded by sappers, engineers and the 1st European regiment of the Bengal Army, who carried out the back-breaking work of making the road over the Khojuk pass practicable for wheeled carriage. The entire force was still on half rations. The land through which they were passing produced grain, but the crop was unripe. The British had timed their advance to the period of greatest dearth. There was no opposition, other than the usual plunder of isolated baggage. It took from 11 to 21 April to get through Khojuk, and losses included 27,400 musket rounds and much powder. A peculiar loss was the capture of two of Macnaghten's elephants.

Macnaghten adopted a munificent style. Aside from his personal elephants, his chaprasis or messengers had caused amusement to the Bombay contingent when they had first arrived with letters:

> They were clad in scarlet, well armed, and mounted on camels very elegantly caparisoned. Their appearance and appointments gave us some idea of the retinue [...] of the envoy and minister; and the liberality with which the Bengal government adorns the tail of its official.[2]

A few Afghan adherents of Shuja started to come in, the most notable being Haji Khan Kakar, a serial traitor who acted as an agent for Ranjit Singh,[3] and had been involved in the desertion of Afghan forces that enabled the Sikhs to take Peshawar. Burnes had got to know him as Governor of Bamian in 1832, and in 1838 had sent him from Simla a bribe of Rs10,000.[4] In return the Haji, who Kohan Dil Khan had charged with Kandahar's forward defence, now defected with his tribesmen and rode into the British camp. Less spectacular but equally effective was Mohan Lal's subversion of the Dil Khans' minister, Mullah Nasu, who helped induce them to flee without resistance.

The British marched into Kandahar on 25 April 1839 amidst what Macnaghten believed genuine popular enthusiasm.[5] He wrote privately to Auckland that 'The Shah made a grand public entry in the city this morning, and was received with feelings nearly amounting to adoration.'[6] Macnaghten's account was sent to all Residents and political agents throughout India and beyond, with instructions to impress on local rulers the complete success of British arms.

Lieutenant Fane made a critical observation: '[T]he king was surrounded by his loving subjects and ragamuffin soldiers,' he wrote, 'but by very few men of rank and consequence.' Crowds will turn out for victory parades; it might prove prudent. There is also the draw of spectacle in hard lives. Henry Havelock is probably close to the truth: '[T]he population, if not in ecstasies of enthusiasm on occasion of the revolution which they had witnessed, were at least tranquil, and disposed to be civil.'[7]

The royal Saduzai family were part of the Popalzai khail of the Dourani tribe. Originally Pashtun, the tribe emigrated west to the borderlands and became largely Persian speaking. Ahmad Shah, the founder of the royal dynasty, considered it tribal and Kandahar-centred, but his son Shah Timur moved to Kabul in order to try to increase his influence with other key groups, notably the Ghilzais and the Qizilbash. Kandahar remained the revered ancestral home.

Shuja immediately processed to the Friday mosque, escorted by Macnaghten, Burnes and Keane, to drape himself in the reputed gown of the Prophet. He was following in the footsteps of Ahmad Shah, but also of Dost Mohammed after his victory five years earlier. In 1995 Mullah Omar of the Taliban donned the same gown.[8]

While Macnaghten felt triumphant, he had seen enough of Afghanistan. He complained to Auckland of overwork – he was not getting breakfast until three in the afternoon. He was indignant that the Dil Khans had retreated on his own stolen elephants. He suggested that he now needed urgently to return to Lahore and then Simla, for policy consultations. Alexander Burnes could take over as Envoy to Kabul. 'In case of my return' Burnes could be posted to Kandahar, but it was plain Macnaghten preferred not to return.

The army had reached Kandahar with only two days' half rations left, and the cavalry non-functional; fifty-eight of their horses had died in a single day (22 April 1839) and hundreds over the course of the march. At Kandahar several horses drowned in the river as they rushed to drink and fell exhausted. The draught animals fared still worse. The army lost 33,000 animals on its march to Kabul. The infantry was exhausted. Diarrhoea was rife. The British troops were in somewhat better shape than the mostly vegetarian sepoys, as some mutton had been available, whereas grain was almost non-existent. But the British soon started dying in numbers as grain and meat remained scarce but abundant fruit exacerbated diarrhoea. The army needed more tailors to take in uniforms, and soldiers were having to make extra holes in their belts.[9] The Dil Khans were allowed to flee to their castle at Girishk because the British were too debilitated to pursue.

The arrival of the army caused a steep rise in food prices, for everybody, and any enthusiasm for Shuja soon waned under the pressure of occupation. On 27 April Burnes moved into a grand mansion built by a Dourani noble for his wife. 'It has an air of magnificence and grandeur. The walls had a novelty of decoration never so well done [...] the chunan or plaster being [...] worked into a pattern over which a varnish of powdered talc is spread, which [...] resembles the [...] hue of new and unfrosted silver plate [...]'[10] In his polished rooms the maximum temperature averaged 84°F and the minimum 74°F, compared to 104°F and 64°F in the tents.

On 5 May the Bombay contingent under Wilshire finally marched into Kandahar. Alex immediately invited his friend Dr Kennedy to breakfast: 'Sir Alexander Burnes received me [...] with all that unaffected goodness, simplicity of manner, and warmth of heart which mark his character.' Kennedy was to publish: 'Of the great minds which I have been allowed to study, the distinguishing characteristic was their simplicity and naked truth; and in this essentiality of greatness Sir Alexander is most especially modelled.' Robert Leech and D'Arcy Todd were also at breakfast and Kennedy was startled that Burnes, Leech and Todd had all grown 'bushy beards'.

The Army of the Indus was for the first time united, bar the brigade left under General Nott to hold Quetta, and detachments garrisoning Baikhar,

Shikarpur and Dadur. Those posts remained British for 107 years, as did Karachi and Mithankot, whose garrisons were not officially part of the Army of the Indus.

The precariousness of British supply lines became obvious. A convoy of 2,000 camels carrying grain was sent from Shikarpur: less than a quarter got through the Bolan and Khojuk passes to Kandahar. The attempt to set up a regular dak service from Kandahar to Dera Ismael Khan failed.[11]

Yar Mohammed Khan sent a Herati Envoy to Kandahar to do homage to Shuja and assure the British of his support, and also sent an Envoy to Persia to canvass an anti-British alliance. Eldred Pottinger had been seeking to reduce the misrule of Yar Mohammed, who made income from enslaving local Shias, and by extortion under torture from wealthy citizens. Pottinger also insisted on British control of Herat's foreign policy, and in return for much money was permitted to farm Herat's taxes. Auckland was horrified by the British involvement in the government of Herat this implied, but the cash advance had already been given. Tax revenue raised never exceeded 10 per cent of the yield Yar Mohammed had indicated.

In truth Prince Kamran and Yar had ruined Herat by bad government. Their looting and enslaving had reduced the population from 100,000 in 1819 to 50,000 in 1840. Minorities, including Hindu bankers vital to the city's trade, had been driven out by relentless exactions. Pottinger tried to make British money conditional on reform. But the view in Simla was that the attempt to enforce good governance was mistaken, and Colvin wrote to Burnes on 17 January 1839: 'Why is it that Englishmen everywhere are [. . .] without tact and address and more disliked by foreigners than any other people?' Auckland decided that Eldred had to be replaced.

Macnaghten asked Burnes to replace Eldred in Herat. Burnes refused. Both he and Macnaghten supported annexing fertile Herat to Kabul to make the state more economically viable; Auckland turned down the idea. Burnes reasoned there was only trouble in Herat now. He would face the same problems as Pottinger in dealing with Yar, and would be away from Kabul where he hoped to succeed Macnaghten as Envoy.

Instead, Major D'Arcy Todd was appointed. Having been Military Secretary to McNeill in Persia, he had then been part of the invasion planning group in Simla with Burnes, who liked and respected Todd. Macnaghten still regarded Herat as the great bastion against Russian advance and therefore agreed Todd would be accompanied by a party of engineers to repair and strengthen Herat's defences, and Britain would pay a regular subsidy to Kamran.

Percival Lord was impatient in Peshawar, where the Sikh and irregular forces had still not set off through the Khyber pass. He was again living in the beautiful gardens of the Wazir Bagh where the mission had stayed in August 1837. Now he converted it into an armaments workshop, where Lieutenant Barr visited him: 'It is indeed better known to us as "Lord's workshop" than by its proper name. Cannon, rifles, bullets [...] were progressing towards completion [...] in a place evidently dedicated to peace, and where all ought to have been lovely, soft and beautiful.'[12]

Lord was receiving messengers from the agents recruited in Kunduz. It was he who in March 1839 first heard that Stoddart was effectively under arrest.[13] Lord connected this to news that Bokhara was in discussions with the Russians; it all fuelled continued anxiety about an imminent Russian advance.[14]

On 14 May 1839, Macnaghten forwarded to Auckland a letter received from Stoddart, got out through Nazir Hyraldghir, one of Burnes' Bokhara agents.[15] Stoddart had written on 14 March 1839 that he had been imprisoned for eighty-four days in the zindan or state jail, but was in good health.[16] He had been arrested on orders of the Kush-Begi who alleged that he had 'come to seize the country'. Macnaghten was sanguine; he sought Auckland's advice on measures to 'chastise' Bokhara, and suggested that they might subsidise an attack by Murad Beg.[17] The reply from Auckland dated 17 June – Stoddart had now been imprisoned six months – cautioned Macnaghten to await developments, but to send an Envoy to Murad Beg.[18]

On 8 May a coronation was held for Shuja in Kandahar in an attempt to use pageantry to garner support. It did not work. British officers made fun of the programme's provision of a stand for 'the populace restrained by the Shah's troops', which remained virtually empty. It was a great spectacle, with cannon roaring and cavalry galloping. The citizenry displayed 'mortifying indifference'.[19] The one person still enamoured of Shuja was Macnaghten. He reported to Hobhouse that 'he is a mild, humane, just and intelligent man – not deficient in energy or resolution. His faults are pride and parsimony.'[20]

On 12 May, Brigadier Sale with 1,000 men including artillery and cavalry set out towards the Helmund to take the Barakzai fortress of Girishk. The force crossed the Helmund by firing across a rope attached to a howitzer shell. The crossing was made on a raft of empty rum casks – the strong grog ration still being part of the pay of British troops: the daily free alcohol intake per soldier was the equivalent of five pints of standard lager today. The Dil Khan Barakzais fled further towards Persia, while Girishk was garrisoned by the Shah's contingent under Macnaghten's nephew, Edward Conolly. Girishk was the centre of conflict for British forces in 2002–14, where scores of British troops died fighting the Douranis. The false appellation 'Taliban' was part of the propaganda of the 'War on Terror'. They were just locals fighting British invaders, yet again.

CHAPTER TWENTY-NINE

## Death in St Petersburg

On the morning of 9 May 1839 the body of Jan Prosper Witkiewicz was discovered in his room at the Paris boarding house in St Petersburg, his brains blown out, apparently by his own revolver. His superior L G Sinyavin, Director of the Asiatic Department, wrote to Count Perovsky, Governor at Orenburg: '[W]ith him perished all the information about Afghanistan which would now be particularly [. . .] useful to us. Only what he managed to relate to me about it is known.'[1]

Witkiewicz had left a businesslike suicide note:

> Not knowing anyone who would care about my destiny in any way I find it sufficient to explain that I am taking my own life voluntarily. As I am currently employed by the Asian Department of the Ministry of Foreign Affairs, I humbly beseech the said Department to dispose of the 2 years' wages due to me [. . .] in the following way: 1. Settle the bill for officer's uniform articles, for the total sum of about 300 roubles; 2. Give 500 roubles to the tailor Markevitch for the dress I ordered from him but haven't collected; 3. Allow my man Dmitry the use of all my belongings that I have with me at the moment. I have burnt all the papers relating to my last journey [. . .] I have settled the bill with the landlord of the Paris Inn up until May 7, but should he have any other requests I humbly beseech the Department to satisfy him from the above-mentioned sum. May 8, 1839, 3a.m. Vitkevitch.[2]

So it appears that Jan's last thoughts were about his accounts. There is nothing for his family. There is nothing about the Polish nationalist cause he was once prepared to die for.

Sinyavin does not mention the possibility of foul play in his letter though he notes, 'He burned our papers without handing them over. Those papers constituted various observations to assist him in drawing up a report on the affairs of Afghanistan and copies of the despatches of British agents to various individuals in Afghanistan.' Witkiewicz specifies in his note that the papers he had burned were those relating to Afghanistan – why burn them?

There is a divergence between British accounts of Witkiewicz' death, which claim that he was in official disfavour, and Russian accounts which state that he was in high favour. Burnes received this account of 15 September 1839 from Nazir Khan Ullah, his Bokhara newswriter.

> The Russian agent here [. . .] said that when Vicovitch returned from Cabool to Russia, he told the Russian authorities that he had sent them many letters soliciting Military and Pecuniary assistance [for Dost Mohammed Khan] and that they never sent him any reply [. . .] and that this neglect had made him out a liar in the country of Cabool and Candahar, and therefore he felt disgraced, and on hearing of the answer of the Cabinet of St Petersburgh, he shot himself.[3]

This sounds plausible, and ironic because Burnes himself had seen his own tenders to Dost Mohammed rejected by his superiors. It is also consistent with what the British Ambassador in St Petersburg, Lord Clanricarde, wrote to Palmerston, that 'the cause is said to be the disapprobation & disavowal of his conduct in Afghanistan by the Russian Government instead of the reward and promotion he expected'.

This, however, is flatly contradicted by Senyavin's letter to Perovsky, written the day before Clanricarde's letter:

> He was extremely well received by the Ministry and on the very day of his death the report came through authorising his transfer to the guards, and on top of that, rewards of promotion, honours and money [. . .] I recounted [. . .] how before your departure you had especially recommended that I organise a decent reward for him for such a difficult expedition. He seemed very satisfied and merry, and a day before his death I saw him at the theatre, where he sat the whole evening and chatted with Prince Saltykov. On the eve of his suicide they saw him again [. . .] and again he was merry; in the evening he visited Count Simonitch [. . .] It is all very strange.

If official disapprobation had caused Witkiewicz' death, the Russian government may have wished to hide the truth from the wider world; but it seems far-fetched for Sinyavin to lie to Perovsky about it, as Perovsky would be bound to find out.

Nesselrode told Palmerston that Simonicz' and Witkiewicz' actions in Persia had been unauthorised. From the same motive, he would have ensured that Clanricarde believed that Witkiewicz had been spurned. We can take Sinyavin's account of Witkiewicz' rewards as a true one. Indeed the transfer to be a guards officer necessarily implies that his titles of nobility, stripped from him at fifteen, were being returned to him. There is further evidence for Sinyavin's version, in that Nesselrode had agreed to the request of Shah Mohammed to invest Witkiewicz with the Persian Order of the Lion and the Sun. They would not have agreed if he had been in disfavour.

I do not lay great weight upon the story that Witkiewicz was visited by an old Polish revolutionary comrade, Tiszkiewicz, and killed himself in shame following reproaches for serving Imperial Russia. This was not first recorded until fifty years after the event, and then at second-hand by Tiszkiewicz' brother.[4]

The last person, other than staff or servants, we know Witkiewicz saw before his death was Simonicz, whom he met that evening after the theatre, so presumably quite late. Witkiewicz had been under Simonicz' direct orders in Afghanistan. After meeting him he apparently burnt his Afghanistan papers and shot himself – six weeks after the British Parliament had published the correspondence with the Russian government[5] in which Nesselrode had brusquely disowned Witkiewicz. This diplomatic climbdown had not been published in Russia, and it is plausible that news would reach Witkiewicz of this public humiliation around the time of his suicide – possibly from Simonicz.

I F Blaramberg, who had ridden with Witkiewicz from Tiflis to Tabriz, said he found him continually depressed on that journey and he had stated that one day he would blow out his brains. This would have been more convincing had Blaramberg written it up before the suicide.

There is one further element to the mystery. Some sources state that a Kirghiz servant died with him.[6] If that is true, it could be either murder suicide, or suicide pact. More likely is that both were murdered by a third party. Whether or not the valet was killed, in accepting that we do not know the answers, we should acknowledge the possibility that Witkiewicz was murdered by a Russian, Polish or British agent. The Witkiewicz family tradition is that Jan Prosper was all along a Polish nationalist agent code-named Wallenrod and was killed by the Russians. Alternatively the Tiszkiewicz story may indicate the Poles killed him as a turncoat serving the Russian Empire. As for the British, it is plausible that news of the impending Russian attack on Khiva would lead the secret service to assassinate Witkiewicz, a key Russian asset. As the British were willing to launch an invasion of Afghanistan to counteract Russia in Central Asia, a single assassination to the same end is not improbable. The British secret service, for example, were running arms to anti-Russian fighters in Dagestan. One assassination in a boarding house in St Petersburg was a simpler operation. For now, Witkiewicz' strange death remains a mystery. One thing is certain; as with Burnes, a proper biography is long overdue.

CHAPTER THIRTY

## Ghazni

The condition of the British Army at Kandahar had been slowly improving. Both basic foods and luxuries became available, though prices escalated, and there was plenty of pasturage. There was still much dysentery. British officers were concerned that, while Shuja set up in state, no great nobles were coming in. Attempts to bribe the Ghilzai tribes into tendering submission failed. Haji Khan Kakar was created by Shuja 'Nasir-ud-Dowlut', or 'Defender of the State' and granted the jaghir of Pishin, but was rumoured to have higher ambitions.

Mohan Lal complained that the British had made a great many promises to leading nobles, in letters organised by Burnes and sent by Leech and Lal, but once the British had secured Kandahar 'we commenced to fail in fulfilling them'. There were 'numerous instances of violating our engagements and deceiving the people in our political proceedings'.[1] Mullah Nasu and Abdul Wahhab Popalzai were among those who did not receive promised rewards.

Burnes was enjoying life. On 25 May he received a consignment of champagne, burgundy and preserved foods from Forbes and Company in Bombay, and went on a two-day bacchanal on the banks of the Argandab with Colonel Arnold, Commander of the Bengal cavalry. The veteran had been shot through the lungs at Waterloo, and was a famous drinker. He died of liver disease a few weeks later.[2]

In May 1839 Macnaghten proposed that Mehrab Khan be punished by the annexation to Kabul of his provinces of Kacchi, Shawl and Mustung, giving the British control of their entire route of march. Macnaghten argued that Kelat was historically subject to Kabul and therefore Shuja was Mehrab Khan's sovereign, and could dispose of his provinces as he wished. That was a whole series of highly disputable assertions.[3] Furthermore the land grab ignored the tribal migrations of the Baluch pastoralists who spent summer on the Kelat plateau, and winter in the lowland pastures it was now proposed to annex. Kelat was the closest entity in the region to a nation state, so its dismembering provoked fierce resistance from the Baluch and Brahuis.

Auckland's reply queried why Mehrab Khan should not be deposed and the whole of Kelat annexed to Afghanistan. Macnaghten responded that the Brahuis had for centuries been autonomous and would rebel against direct rule; and suggested that Mehrab Khan be replaced with Nawaz Khan.[4]

The political officer for Upper Sind, Ross Bell, requested substantial troop reinforcements to act against the 'Doomkies, Jakranees and Boogtees and other plundering tribes subject to Mehrab Khan'.[5] Auckland suggested that Bell rather try to persuade these tribes to accept permanent British rule: 'the Governor-General [. . .] is anxious to see these turbulent and semi-barbarous tribes induced by a conviction of our justice and moderation to place themselves in willing dependence on our power'.

But the Baluch showed no interest in British rule, and in August Bell wrote again: 'there is the clearest evidence [. . .] of marauders acting under instructions received direct from Mehrab Khan'.[6] In fact, these were more of the wazir's 'planted' letters, for which Bell enthusiastically fell:

> it would be inexpedient to leave him in possession of any portion of Kelat [. . .] Mihrab Khan [. . .] is not entitled to any consideration from the British Government. He did not oppose us as a fair and open enemy. On the contrary he avowed his desire of entering into friendly relations with us [. . .] at the very time he was encouraging his half-savage tribes to attack our convoys. The system [. . .] has led to such [. . .] cold-blooded atrocity, that he has fully merited the fate of a felon.[7]

On 21 June D'Arcy Todd set out for Herat, accompanied by Richmond Shakespear and James Abbott. They carried with them £20,000 in gold to repair the defences, and hopes of a Saduzai federation between Kamran and Shuja under British protection.

Burnes was still trying to mitigate the horrors of war. Having caught two raiders who had murdered camel guards, the British 'decided to make a terrible example [. . .] in the hope that it would have some effect on their comrades'. The men were sentenced to be blown from the mouth of a gun. In Kandahar's central square, in front of Shuja and his court, serried British troops and a large crowd, one teenaged prisoner disdained the drawing of lots to see who went first, and calmly walked up to embrace the cannon's mouth; he was instantly executed. The second prisoner, a bearded elder, had been equally stoical, and sat smoking a hookah while his colleague was obliterated. Then, with no apparent fear, he was strapped to the cannon; the execution was stopped at the last second, 'the Shah influenced, it is said, by the entreaties of Sir Alexander Burnes, having granted his pardon'.[8]

Food price increases were becoming serious. Major William Hough noted bluntly, 'We nearly starved the inhabitants of Candahar.'[9] British popularity was plummeting.[10] Distress ended on 23 June when a Lohani caravan swept into camp carrying a vast quantity of grain and other supplies from Shikarpur, led by Burnes' friend Sarwar Khan Lohani. Wartime proved the good sense of what Burnes had proposed in peace. This caravan had been arranged by Mohan Lal at a meeting at Multan in September 1838. Sarwar received just over one lakh for the carriage, paid in advance by Lieutenant Eastwick. The convoy had been harassed by the Ghilzai, but Sarwar Khan had won through, aided by a dashing yellow-jacketed squadron of Skinner's Horse under Rissaldar Azim Khan.

Unfortunately the Lohanis, who were continuing on their pastoral migration, could not be induced to act as transport with the army to Kabul. They explained their families were at the mercy of Ghilzai raids. Therefore the advance continued on half rations, with most stores left at Kandahar.

The division of command resulted in an unseemly row between Macnaghten and Keane. The General wished to leave a large garrison in Kandahar; Macnaghten wanted almost the full force to march on Kabul. Keane was infuriated. This row may have sparked Keane's decision to leave his siege train with the garrison in Kandahar, though lack of draught animals was a genuine problem.[11]

The army marched by columns, the Bengal division on 27 June, Shah Shuja's contingent on 28 June and the Bombay division on 29 June, following the same path. It arrived, with just two days' half rations remaining, before the great fortress of Ghazni, exactly three weeks after leaving Kandahar.

Minor attacks on baggage by Ghilzai tribesmen had increased. On 12 July an important Ghilzai chief Abdul Rahman requested a parley, which was refused by Shuja, who declared him deposed. On 18 July a body of Qizilbash horse came in, having deserted Dost Mohammed. They were followed two days later by representatives of Hazara tribes; the Shia communities were taking the lead in switching allegiance.

As the army marched from Kandahar to Ghazni, two regular columns of Ghilzais had been tracking parallel on each side for a fortnight, under Abdul Rahman and Gul Mohammed. As the British Army defiled onto the plain before Ghazni, large groups began to gather on surrounding hilltops beneath green and black silken banners of jihad.

Alexander was riding in uniform in the vanguard.[12] Approaching Ghazni he was joined by Willoughby Cotton and the staff officers of the Bengal division, eager to see the famous fortress, when they came under fire from the fortress' cannon, and jezzails from surrounding gardens. There was sharp fighting with

British light companies clearing the vineyards, gardens and outlying forts. The engineers carried out a reconnaissance and declared the fortress stronger than they had supposed. They were in a dangerous position, with no siege guns. Horse artillery and howitzers would not be effective against the walls; the moat was too deep and the walls too high for escalade. Several thousand Ghilzais were shadowing the army, The British could not leave Ghazni controlling their line of communications, yet had no food to stop and besiege.

Colonel Dennie wrote home scathingly, 'Our leader had left his battering train behind him at Kandahar, after dragging those guns over rivers, mountains, and awful passes, by manual labour in great part, for one thousand eight hundred miles; and when within two hundred miles of the object for which they had been carried from Indostan, they were left behind.'[13]

Ghazni was reputed the strongest fortress of Asia. The British Army deployed to surround Ghazni on 21 July, but ravines and strong streams led to their being strung out. Several hundred of the Suleiman khail, sworn to holy war against this infidel invasion, swept down and headed straight for Shuja's tents, led by Sayyids holding the Koran. They were repelled by the disciplined cavalry of the Shah's contingent. Several senior Ghilzai chiefs were killed, including a father-in-law of Dost Mohammed. About sixty prisoners were taken into Shuja's camp and, refusing to recant, were all beheaded after one of their number wounded an attendant of Shuja. There was no effort by the British command to stop this atrocity.

Nineteen-year-old Ghulam Haidar Khan, Dost's younger son and Governor of Ghazni, was exasperated. He had called a meeting to suggest that all the town's women be moved into the inner citadel, the Bala Hissar, for protection. Today, 23 July 1839, the British force had sent columns round both sides of the fortress town, meeting at the Kabul road. Haidar Khan had spent all day on the battlements observing them through his telescope – a present from his friend Alexander Burnes, whom he had accompanied for miles on Burnes' ignominious departure from Kabul. His communications with the capital through the Kabul Gate – the only one not built across in preparation for this siege – were now cut.

He was not, however, greatly worried. He had 4,000 troops, provisions for three months and the strongest fortress in Central Asia. He had seen the Ghazi banners flying, and though the British had driven them back, they would return. His brother, the great fighter Sher Afzul, was only two days' march away with 6,000 men and an artillery train. His father Dost Mohammed was gathering a great host at Kabul, and could arrive within a fortnight.

At the same time, he had heard about British military prowess; the encircling army had already killed a few dozen of his men with artillery fire of astonishing rapidity and accuracy. Everyone knew what happened when a defended city was taken. That was why he had ordered all the women brought into the inner citadel. But this had caused an outcry. There were, of course, many soldiers within the citadel, and he could understand the reluctance to send the burqa-clad womenfolk. He had called this council to reassure the elders about arrangements to protect honour and decency. Some of the interminable speakers even seemed to doubt his own motives, and he did not receive the deference he felt was due. He was not quite sure what to do about it. Now the wind was howling so that he could not hear what the old men were saying, shutters kept banging, and some of the oil lamps were guttering, creating even more smoke than usual. But he could not enforce his will on these proud tribesmen without hearing them first; it was their right.[14]

The council lasted right through to the early hours. Suddenly there was a huge rumble, followed by a sharp increase in the previously sporadic firing. At first the chiefs were silent, looking at each other, then one or two started to leave, and there was a panicked rush and wild shouting. The British were in the fortress!

The injustice of a war exists alongside individual heroism. The capture of Ghazni within forty-eight hours of arrival, in two hours of assault, was a major achievement by the British Indian Army. Ghazni had twenty-five-foot walls built on a steep thirty-foot mound, the whole surrounded by a wet ditch, with numerous bastions, and additional walls to screen from artillery, plus strategically placed high towers and an inner citadel.

The day before the army reached Ghazni, a nephew of Dost Mohammed, Abdul Rashid Khan Barakzai, had come over to the British camp. Abdul Rashid had been sent with his younger brother by Dost ostensibly to join the defenders of Ghazni, but also as a species of hostage. Haidar Khan swiftly executed the younger of his two cousins. Abdul Rashid had been in written contact with Mohan Lal, though one of the latter's messengers had been caught and executed in Ghazni. Abdul Rashid now made good his escape disguised as a Ghazi. He arrived in the British camp with a dozen followers and was taken to Burnes, who was struck by Abdul's physical resemblance to Dost.

Abdul explained that only the Kabul gate had not been built over. Burnes went to Keane with this vital intelligence. Keane was relieved, but sent engineers under Captain Thomson to assess the information – which could have been a trap – and do a thorough survey of the defences. This the party did at considerable risk, with shot kicking up dust all round them. Thomson confirmed Burnes' intelligence, seeing a horseman exit by the gate. The only practical way to attack without artillery was to blow in the Kabul gate with gunpowder.

This simple approach was fraught with difficulties. The approach to the fort's gate was down a narrow alley between two walls which projected out to defend it. Handling sacks of gunpowder in battlefield conditions was tricky; and even if the gate were blown, to assault a well-defended fortress through a single small entrance was a desperate undertaking.

The storm that evening was an unexpected piece of British luck. It confused sound and provided plenty of distraction. Captain Peat and Lieutenants Durand and McLeod, with three sergeants and eighteen sappers, crept up to the gates, passing right below the sentries twenty feet above them, who were lighting 'bluefire' illuminations but only on the parapets; if a single one had been thrown onto the road below, it would have been a disaster for the attack. The final few yards across the bridge, the stacking of the leather bags of powder and laying of the fuse, were conducted by Henry Durand, who was dizzy with fever, and the sergeants. They were finally spied and fired upon from the parapet, but nobody was hit. There were lower breastworks from which the little party would have been easily annihilated, but these were unoccupied. On reaching the gates, Durand saw, through chinks between the planks, guards smoking on the other side, just a yard from him as he started to lay down eighteen sacks of powder. Three minutes later, he lit the seventy-foot fuse – which failed and he had to return and light again after scraping it with his fingernails.

Concerned that the gates may have been reinforced, the engineers used too much powder, bringing down the entire bastion. They were only supposed to blow the bloody doors off. The assaulting party then had to scramble over a large mound of stone blocks and confused rubble. HM's 13th Foot led, white crossbelts removed so they did not show up in the dark. They were joined by the grenadier companies from HM's 2nd and 17th and the Bengal European Regiment.

The storming party was thus entirely British, in the nineteenth-century sense encompassing Ireland, which was well represented including by the heroic Colonel Dennie who led the forlorn hope. They met fierce resistance from equally heroic Afghans brandishing swords.

After desperate hand-to-hand fighting, the light companies found themselves in pitch dark inside the gate but with internal walls blocking further progress and increasing numbers of Afghans surging up to attack. Engineer Captain Peat had been dashing forward to check on the delay caused when the fuse went out, and had thus been caught by the explosion. He staggered back to the supporting column of the 2nd and 13th, commanded by 'Fighting Bob' Sale. As a result of Peat's muddled account, which indicated the light companies had been repulsed, a bugler sounded the retreat at Sale's instruction.[15]

So 200 men were progressing into the city, but nobody was following. In the ten minutes before the confusion cleared and Sale's column carried on, the breach became choked with Afghan swordsmen. Sale found himself pinned down by an Afghan, before Captain Kershaw ran him through. Once this melee resolved, resistance crumbled and the citadel was not defended. The sack of the city from house to house was not occasioned by fighting. The last fortified house surrendered after the demand was met for the trusted 'Sikunder Burnes' to take personal charge of the women and protect them from rape.[16]

Perhaps 1,000 Afghans were killed, while British casualties were light – seventeen dead and 171 wounded; 1,600 Afghans were taken prisoner, perhaps 1,000 escaped. Those numbers can only indicate a massacre by the British forces after the city was taken. Dennie described it as a '[d]isgusting slaughter'.[17] Other British accounts are more circumspect, but you can read atrocity between the lines:

> There was an upper-roomed house to the right [...] where a Company of H.M.'s 17th Foot killed 58 Affghans. There was a heap of straw here, some stray shot struck it, a movement was observed, a shower of balls was poured in, the straw fired, only one man escaped, and he was shot close to the burning mass.[18]

Alexander was present throughout the brief siege. He wrote of Keane: 'He and I get on well and I was under fire with him at Ghuznee for 3 days, and at least can vouch for him being a cool and steady soldier. What a grand affair that was [...]'[19] Keane had outraged the Afghans by setting up his headquarters in the tomb of Futth Khan Barakzai, Dost Mohammed's brother. Mohan Lal wrote 'Lord Keane and his staff, as well as Sir Alexander Burnes and myself, stood upon the steep hill, which was frequently fired upon from the garrison, and Colonel Parsons was slightly wounded by a ball which just missed me.'[20] Keane's despatch on the battle included a paragraph on Burnes, but this was removed because Burnes was a 'political' and therefore not officially part of the army.[21]

The next day, when Haidar Khan was found in the city, he was handed over to Burnes' custody, which Keane noted 'an arrangement very agreeable' to Haidar Khan.[22] He slept in Lal's tent next to Burnes' own, with armed guards, but was treated with courtesy. His dependants were kept separately in a house but also under Burnes' care. Haidar's wife reminded Alex that in 1832 in Kabul, when she was fourteen, he had come with Dr Gerard to treat her sore eyes. Eventually, Haidar Khan was sent back to India with Keane when the latter handed over command. Keane agreed his request to go to Bombay, where he lived on a handsome allowance, socialising in the highest circles, eventually returning to Afghanistan after the war.

Keane's triumph was celebrated in London; he became Lord Keane of Ghazni, and Ghazni medals were struck for all who had taken part. Richmond Shakespear wrote to James Outram, both having been there: 'I think Sir J Keane's making his fortune by blowing open the gates of Ghazni instead of receiving censure for leaving his siege guns at Candahar is one of the most amusing instances of good luck that can be found either in truth or fiction.'[23]

There were vital practical benefits to the British Army, who captured the large supplies stockpiled for the garrison plus 1,000 good horses. The Company's famed iqbal appeared irresistible. To reinforce this message, Auckland ordered twenty-one-gun salutes fired at every British post throughout India.

The advance guard of Afzul Khan's relieving column reached Ghazni just a few hours after the British had taken it. They were astonished that the 'impregnable' stronghold had fallen so quickly. Afzul panicked. At this stage the Afghans did not understand that three-quarters of the British horde moving upon them were non-combatants. Afzul Khan sped back towards Kabul, abandoning his guns, elephants and baggage at Urghundi, just six miles from Ghazni. Dost Mohammed was coming up behind with 6,000 Qizilbash. When it became plain that they were also planning to desert him, he fled north towards Bamian with 2,000 loyal horsemen.

Dost had a few years earlier brutally brought Kohistan under government control, and enforced taxes on the district. Kohistan had risen for Shuja behind Dost once he left Kabul. Burnes, through Mohan Lal, had sent the Kohistani chief Ghulam Khan Popalzai a bribe of Rs40,000. Ghulam had spread further British bribes around numerous Kohistani chiefs, and paid Rs8,000 to Kabul's Sunni religious leader, Hafiz Ji, son of the deceased Mir Waiz. Hafiz had been close to Burnes during the Kabul negotiations, where Burnes had tested the waters on using the Sunni leadership against Dost's Shia links.[24] Burnes had prepared for the British invasion throughout Afghanistan with carefully targeted bribes, secretly delivered on inch-square paper notes of hand, signed by Burnes, redeemable on the Bengal government through Shikarpur bankers. In Kabul the Hindu banker Pokur had been caught by the Emir dealing in them, but treated fairly leniently with a fine and imprisonment.

The British left the 16th NI to garrison Ghazni, with small detachments of artillery and cavalry in support, and prepared to march on Kabul. On 28 July Jabbar Khan rode to the British camp. Burnes – to whom dealings with the Barakzai family were always delegated – greeted his old friend and escorted him to camp. Their meeting in these new circumstances was 'painful to both' and there were tears in Jabbar's eyes.[25] The nawab had not come to surrender, but to offer terms which the two discussed as they rode in together. These were what Burnes had suggested to Macnaghten in April 1838 – that Dost would step down for Shuja to take the throne, but that Dost should be vizier, which he now claimed, with some justice, as his hereditary right.

With the road to Kabul open, there was no way that Macnaghten or Shuja would agree. But the meeting was memorable for the question which Jabbar boldly put to Shuja:

> If you are to be King, what use is the British army here? If the British are to rule over this country, what use are you?

The same question might have been asked of President Karzai in our generation – another Dourani ruler supported by Western occupiers, from the same Popalzai khail as Shuja.[26]

Shuja attempted to win over the nawab with estates and honours, but Jabbar replied that he must follow his brother's fortunes. The British considered his conduct 'noble'.[27] But Jabbar was incensed at Macnaghten's gratuitous refusal of a request that his niece, Haidar Khan's wife, should be handed over to him, and also at hearing the screams of an Afghan woman in a British tent.[28]

Deserted by his army, his realm lost, Dost Mohammed focused his fury on the enemy he knew best; Alexander Burnes. 'The greatest error in my life lay in this,' he exclaimed, 'that I allowed the English deceiver to escape with his head.'[29] James Outram was sent north in pursuit of the fleeing Emir, but was handicapped by his ally Haji Khan Kakar, who constantly delayed the pursuit, hedging his bets again. Dost, having eluded Outram, established himself in the ruined city of Balkh, nominally subject to the khan of Bokhara.

CHAPTER THIRTY-ONE

## Mission Accomplished

The British Army pushed forward from Ghazni to Kabul. Burnes rode with Cureton's reconnaissance party of 200 HM's 16th Lancers. They quickly secured the twenty-eight cannon abandoned by Afzul Khan and unchallenged cantered for three days until they entered Kabul through unguarded gates. As organised by Burnes, Ghulam Khan Popalzai had already entered the city with his Kohistani force and proclaimed Shuja. On arrival, Burnes procured a cartload of the best fruit, and with a block of 'clear bright ice as hard as flint and brilliant as diamond'; he sent it to his friends in the Bombay contingent who were still marching to Kabul. As Shuja progressed in more stately fashion, large bodies of the army of Dost Mohammed and Afzul Khan adhered to Shuja's ranks, including the Qizilbash en masse.

At 3pm on 7 August 1839, a grand procession entered Kabul's Kandahar gate and wended its way to the Bala Hissar. It was led by Shuja on a magnificent white horse, accompanied by a cloud of mounted courtiers. Then came General Keane, William Macnaghten and Sir Alexander Burnes, followed by other senior officers. Burnes was in diplomatic uniform, not the army colonel's uniform worn on the march, but 'a cocked hat fringed with ostrich feathers, a blue frock coat with raised gold buttons, richly embroidered on the collar and cuff, epaulettes not yielding in splendour to those of a field-marshal, and trowsers edged with very broad gold lace'. Just behind Mohan Lal rode in 'a new upper garment of very gay colours, and under a turban of very admirable fold and majestic dimensions, and was one of the gayest and most sagacious and successful persons in the whole cortege'.[1]

A squadron of dragoons, a troop of horse artillery and a squadron of lancers formed the imposing escort. Crowds had gathered to watch; but the onlookers were curiously silent. As they entered the Bala Hissar, Kabul's great fortress, the great drums above the gatehouse, a prerogative of Timurid and Mughal royalty, beat out a royal salute. Jinjals cracked in response from the backs of eighty kneeling camels in the courtyard. When they reached the palace, Shuja wept to see its dilapidation. His brother Zeman had earlier restored it to some of the glory it had enjoyed in the days of Shah Jahan. The more practical Dost Mohammed had improved the defences and removed features which impeded fire, including knocking down the Chehel Sihun, or 'pavilion of the forty pillars',[2] where Shuja had delighted with his wives and written poetry. Shuja's tears hardly endeared him to the accompanying British officers.

Burnes' informants in Central Asia had brought him the first definite news of the Russian expedition against Khiva. Danilevsky and Perovsky were to attack with 7,000 men, although departure was postponed three months as scouts found the oases dry on the long desert route. For Burnes and Macnaghten, the invasion of Afghanistan appeared the beginning of the scramble for Central Asia and they began to consider further British advances. Macnaghten longed to propel the Army of the Indus to the Oxus, but Burnes believed such an advance impossible with the existing forces. Privately he was sympathetic to the Russians, and opposed to British occupation in Afghanistan. He wrote to a friend on 19 November of the Russian advance on Khiva:

> She has the right to relieve her enslaved countrymen; and if she have the power, why should she have so long hesitated? But the time she has chosen for this blow is an awkward one. I hold, however, that the man who recommends the cantonment of a British or an Indian soldier west of the Indus is an enemy to his country.[3]

Macnaghten drafted a letter to Auckland, which he showed to Keane, stating that the Bombay brigade would return to India by Kelat, where they would depose Mehrab Khan. The Bengal brigade would meantime remain in Afghanistan, stationed chiefly at Kabul. An expeditionary force would be sent across the Hindu Kush to Balkh and Bokhara, with the object of freeing Stoddart, putting pressure on Dost and forestalling Russian influence along the Oxus. The draft apologised that it had been impossible to consult Auckland in advance due to the need to push on before winter set in. Keane was horrified at the proposal to extend British forces over 500 more miles of difficult terrain. He sent the letter back with regrets that he could not be party to it. This killed the draft, and the expedition into Turkestan.

The British invasion was supposed to be a pincer movement. But by mid-July Wade's Khyber force had still not moved, due to Sikh prevarication following Ranjit's demise, and difficulties in rendering the Shahzada Timur's troops effective. The Army of the Indus was in Kabul and Wade was still building defensive stockades to protect his unready force.[4]

The Afghans, too, were beginning to have their doubts about their invaders. They had not realised that non-combatants outnumbered soldiers by four to one, and the tonnage of books, wines, silver plate and porcelain outweighed the tonnage of cannon. But they learnt. George Lawrence, on his way to join Macnaghten as military secretary, was disconcerted to be told by an Afghan noble:

> you are an army of tents and camels; our army is one of men and horses. What could induce you to squander crores of rupees in coming to a poor rocky country like ours, without wood or water, and in order to force on us a Kumbukht (unlucky person) as a king, who the moment you turn your own backs will be upset by Dost Mahommed our own king?[5]

On 26 August a party of irregular Afghan horse cantered up to where Burnes was staying in Kabul. After a brief parley, Burnes' guard opened the gates and admitted them to the garden. His Arab bodyguard warily fanned out from the door, but then started clapping and embracing the horsemen's leader, an imposing bearded man in travel-stained robes with a large white turban and bright red cummerbund in which was stuck a heavy Afghan sword or tulwar. Dr Percival Lord had arrived, having galloped ahead of Wade and the Shahzada's contingent. After a wash and change, Burnes accompanied Lord to report to Keane and Macnaghten and that evening Burnes, Lord, Outram and Dr Kennedy sat down to one of Burnes' comradely dinners, and the wines flowed.[6]

On 3 September 1839 the Shahzada's force finally arrived. Willoughby Cotton and Burnes escorted Timur formally past honour guards into the Bala Hissar, where his father, Keane and Macnaghten were waiting to receive him.

The British had a clear understanding of potential tensions during an occupation. The army was camped outside the city, and soldiers were ordered not to enter Kabul, except with a pass signed by the regimental commanding officer. These must be issued sparingly and only to 'men on whose steadiness and sobriety dependence can be placed'.

This went wrong. On 13 September:

> a drunken European soldier struck an Affghan in the city [. . .] and is said to have defiled the dinner he was cooking. The Affghan [. . .] went to seek for Sir A Burnes; not finding him at home he returned, and clasping the European round the body [. . .] threw him down, and sitting on his body, beat out his brains with a stone.[7]

This is the first of a number of instances where individual Afghans sought out Burnes to give them justice against abuse. They were usually disappointed, as his authority in the British hierarchy was limited. The atmosphere was fraught. Captain James Douglas summed up the general British view: 'The city is beastly dirty and so are the people. They are cunning, avaricious, proud and filthy, notwithstanding the romantic descriptions of Burnes & Co.'[8] Relations were not improved on 23 September when Shah Shuja reviewed in public the despised Sikh troops under Sheikh Basawan. This should have been a Muslim force but included Sikhs as Ranjit's regiments were generally mixed. Burnes protested against Sikhs guarding the Bala Hissar itself.

William Barr was a young Scottish lieutenant of the Bengal Horse Artillery. His observations reveal some of the fantastical nature of the court of Shuja who

> was attended by a long train of servants, habited in the costume of the days of Baber and Timour, and a more outre apparel can scarcely be conceived; some wearing a species of horn growing out of each shoulder, and others, a head-piece not very unlike a fool's cap. His Majesty's Executioner was one of these.[9]

The British found the costumes and ceremony of the Dourani court risible and its punishments barbaric. But there was a high culture here: Shuja was a decent poet in the Persian language, as were his father and grandfather. Mehir Dil Khan, who had come to Kabul for the end of Burnes' negotiations, led an influential revival of classical Afghan poetry.[10]

Shuja's insistence on reinforcing his superiority to the nobles clearly caused important disaffection, as another munshi from the same school class as Mohan Lal, Shahamat Ali, witnessed. By Dost Mohammed the nobles had been 'treated [...] almost on equal terms, and enjoyed much influence, while now they were made to undergo many hard ceremonies' and stand in positions of obeisance for hours. The Qizilbash leader, Khan Shirin Khan, felt particularly insulted, while the chiefs were 'disgusted' when they presented grievances: 'Shah Shuja seemed to take very little notice of what was happening, he only cared about holding his darbar, and speaking in a very haughty way to the people.'[11]

The responsibility for the construction of British cantonments was first given to Henry Durand, who went, accompanied by Mohan Lal, to a position some miles outside Kabul recommended by Burnes where there were three small forts in close proximity, which Burnes thought might be joined to form a single fortified base. Durand rejected the location as providing 'neither cover, space, water nor any other convenience for the troops' and instead recommended strongly that the force occupy the Bala Hissar, the great old fortress looming above Kabul.

Macnaghten turned this down. Shuja objected that foreign occupation of the great national symbol would be anathema to Afghans. Durand then suggested converting and extending outerworks of the Bala Hissar; less blatant, but would still give the British effective control of it when they wished. Work actually started on this, but Shuja objected that the troops might see the ladies of his zenana. The true problem was that the Afghan nobles and the Qizilbash, who had traditional military dominance in Kabul, did not want the British in firm control of the city – and perhaps neither did Shuja.

Since Macnaghten was not prepared to risk this symbol of occupation itself sparking resistance, Durand came up with another suggestion. Macnaghten himself was occupying Dost's compound of two large houses connected by a series of walled gardens at the foot of the Bala Hissar. These gardens could be built upon and a good position established incorporating other adjoining buildings. Durand proposed to start this work as Macnaghten set off for winter quarters in Jalalabad. Macnaghten objected strongly to losing his house. Responsibility for the cantonments was then passed to another Engineer, Sturt, who also argued strongly for the Bala Hissar.

Who chose the eventual low-lying and indefensible site, with ammunition, food supplies and treasury all outside the cantonments? Sturt made the detailed plans, which were approved by both Macnaghten and Cotton, against written objection by Brigadier Roberts, commander of the Shah's forces. It is plain that the eventual site selected was not the one recommended by Burnes. The blame must lie with Macnaghten, who vetoed all the engineers' other plans.

On 17 September 1839 Shuja held a durbar to award decorations to those who had returned him to the throne. A new chivalric order had been created, the Order of the Dourani Empire, very much along British lines. The fabulous gold and jewelled insignia were made by Kabul goldsmiths and modelled on those of the Hanoverian Guelphic Order. An Islamic state issued decorations in the form of the cross of the knights of St John.

The ceremony had strong elements of farce. It took place in a courtyard of the ruined palace; workmen continued repair work throughout, ignoring Shuja. The King was seated on a cheap British camp chair, placed on a dais. Two fat eunuchs stood behind him, holding plates containing a small number of medals.

Keane dropped to his knees before Shuja – with some difficulty because he had become rather too stout for his dress uniform. The Shah stood up, and was handed a medal and ribbon by one of the eunuchs. Shuja, with some fumbling, pinned this to Sir John's coat. Then Keane, now a Knight Grand Cross of the Dourani Empire, struggled to his feet and made a speech 'in which there was a great deal about 'hurling a usurper from the throne'.[12]

The army's chief Persian interpreter, Major Potter, was a shy man. His effort to translate Keane's long oration into Persian was hesitant and quiet.

During a pause Shuja, visibly bored, interrupted. Burnes now intervened to prevent him stopping Keane's speech, whispering *'Digar ast'* – 'There is more' – so loudly it was widely heard. The Shah subsided and let Potter continue, but the next time Potter paused, again butted in.

The Shah thought that recipients of his awards should be grateful and quiet. The British felt that their CO's speech should be heard. Burnes therefore again hushed the Shah. Again the nervous Potter started up, and yet again the Shah interrupted him. This time Burnes gave up the struggle.

There were no more speeches, and Macnaghten then Cotton were called forward, and given their awards. The King then announced that Burnes and Wade were also created Knights Grand Cross, but unfortunately they had run out of medals, so these would follow.

The names were then read out of the lower orders, the Knights Commanders and the Companions of the Dourani Empire, but there were no medals for them, either. The scene erupted when those British officers who had not been given awards started to object loudly. The Army honours had been awarded on the basis of rank, and brevet or local rank had been ignored. As this excluded many of the best senior officers, they were most annoyed.

Colonel Dennie was particularly incensed. He had been both an acting brigadier and the first man into the breach at Ghazni, and found himself offered only the Order of the Dourani Empire Third Class. Dennie declined it, drawing a rebuke from Keane, who hated him. There followed a bitter correspondence between the two, which was referred all the way to the Secretary for War in London.

Every one of the initial recipients of the Order was British, despite the fact that a very large majority of those who had put Shuja on his throne – Afghans, Sikhs and sepoys – were not British. Once the British entered Kabul, they had an urgent need for gold coin, and Major Macgregor and Mohan Lal had obtained loans from the Kabul merchants. Macgregor had recommended Lal for the Order, but this had been vetoed by Macnaghten.[13] Burnes was able to secure the Order for Lal at a later date, by asking Shuja direct.

Macnaghten now received Auckland's instructions, written in Simla on 20 August, on the future conduct of the occupation. His request to leave Afghanistan was denied. Auckland accepted Macnaghten's recommendation that the Shah's contingent would be insufficient to enforce Shuja's power, and that a British presence was needed to counter Russian moves in Central Asia. Therefore while the Bombay contingent and one Bengal division should return home, the other Bengal division should remain in Afghanistan. The British officered Shuja's forces, now numbering about 13,000, and 3,500 Sikh troops would also remain.

Burnes thought the Shah's regiments incapable of the crucial role they had now to play. He wrote to Lord, now political officer at Bamian: 'Sheets of foolscap are written in praise of the Shah's contingent but [. . .] I tremble every time I hear of its being deployed [. . .] Shuja never can be left without a British army, for his own contingent will never be fit for anything.'[14]

Keane, anxious to enjoy the rewards of victory, which included a peerage, was departing with the returning portion of the Bengal contingent. Realising how fragile was his apparent success and how bitterly the British were resented, he remarked presciently to an officer leaving with him: 'I wished you to remain in Afghanistan for the good of the public service, but since circumstances have rendered that impossible, I cannot but congratulate you on quitting the country for, mark my words, it will not be long before there is here some signal catastrophe.'[15]

It was 30 October before news of the taking of Ghazni and Kabul reached London. T M Waterfield of the Political Committee forwarded the despatches on to Hobhouse, adding, 'Glorious news from India. Ghazni taken and Kabul in Shah Shuja's possession' before going on to detail Hobhouse's latest experiments in speeding up the mails. The speaking notes survive for Hobhouse's victory speech to the House of Commons. He appended his own introduction to the official text: 'Lord Auckland arrived in Simla early in April 1838. The first intelligence which reached him was of a most alarming character. Herat about to fall, Candahar in disarray and to face next – Lieutt Burnes retiring discomfited from Caubul, Sinde whose chiefs had opened communications with Persia and Russia [. . .]'[16] Hobhouse received hundreds of votes of thanks and loyal addresses from all over the UK. Basking in triumph, he meticulously copied down the details of the senders, in thirty-six closely-written pages.[17]

The Army of the Indus was rapidly broken up. On 16 September the Bombay Army under Colonel Wilshire marched out of the Kabul camp, with a mission to attack Kelat on their way back to Karachi. On 25 September Wade left for Ludhiana with the irregular forces which had accompanied Shahzada Timur, and two regiments of the Sikh contingent. Then on 15 October Keane finally left with part of the Bengal contingent on their long journey home, also taking the Peshawar route, marching where the snows were already thickening above them and their breath steamed in the frosty air.[18] William Hough noted that the Khoord Kabul pass wound sunlessly for six miles between high mountain walls, and the river had to be crossed twenty-three times. There followed the Tezin pass which was 'more difficult than the Bolan Pass'. Then the ascending three-and-a-half miles of the Jugdulluck pass, of which Hough wrote:

The Pass winds several times almost at right-angles. The average width is about 40 or 50 yards; but there are three places where it is less than 10 feet, indeed one only 6 feet [. . .] The almost perpendicular cliffs, on both sides, appear as if threatening the destruction of the traveller. A small party of armed men would stop the passage of any force which had entered it.[19]

The Bombay contingent attacked Kelat on its way back to Karachi. Mehrab Khan died in his citadel, superb sword in hand, shot through the neck, together with all his key chiefs. Emily Eden recorded the view she learnt from Auckland and Macnaghten:

> The Khan of Khelat was by way of being our ally and assistant, and professing friendship; did himself the pleasure of cutting off the supplies of the army when it was on its way to Cabul; set his followers on to rob the camp; corresponded with Dost Mohammed etc.
>
> There was no time to fight with him then, and I suppose he was beginning to think himself secure, But G [Auckland] directed the Bombay army [. . .] to settle this little Khelat trouble [. . .] It was all done in the Ghuznee manner – the gates blown in and the fort stormed [. . .] The Khan and his principal chiefs died sword in hand, which was rather too fine a death for such a double traitor as he had been [. . .] They found [. . .] a great many of our camels and much of the property that had been pillaged from the army. Also there will be a great deal of prize money. Another man has been put on the Khelat throne, so that business is finished.[20]

For once Emily was wrong, but meanwhile Nawaz Khan was installed in Kelat, and promised £5,000 a year subsidy.

Mehrab's jewels were valued at £60,000. They were carried from Karachi in the *Hannah*, but it was wrecked on 17 March 1840. Colonel Pennycuik saved the jewels, but mysteriously they sold at prize auction in Bombay for just £6,000. The premises of the sales agent were robbed before they could be delivered to their new owner. The sales agent went bankrupt with the compensation.[21] I like to imagine they went back to Kelat, but I am a hopeless romantic.

Cotton assumed the military command in Kabul. The remaining forces in Afghanistan were garrisoned between Kabul, Kandahar, Jalalabad, Ghazni, Quetta and Kelat-i-Ghilzai.

CHAPTER THIRTY-TWO

## Kabul in Winter

There was a major financial cloud gathering over the British forces in Kabul. Burnes was much more alert than Macnaghten to the pecuniary impossibility of sustaining the British occupation. On first arrival at Kabul he told Josiah Harlan that the invasion had so far cost two and a half crore of Rupees, or £2.5m, and expressed exasperation at the vast train of baggage and camp followers.

Despite this threat, there now followed a honeymoon period, where the British occupiers felt secure and the local elite appeared reconciled. The regimental chaplain of HM 13th Foot, George Robert Gleig, gave the most evocative description of that extraordinary autumn of 1839. Gleig, a Brechin cousin of Burnes' mother, had served through the bloody Peninsular Campaign.

> The Cabul river flowed with a clear and rapid stream [. . .] giving an air of gladness to the scenery. Inured to the climate [. . .] our countrymen seemed to regard the intense heat [. . .] as a trifle, and enjoyed the cool airs of early morning and the hour that followed sunset intensely [. . .] [T]hey lived under canvas, the officers passing to and fro with a confidence which [. . .] appeared to command a like degree of honesty among the people [. . .] Parties rode hither and thither [. . .] Baba Shah's tomb.. the obelisk [. . .] the magnificent scenery about Areksai, and as far into the mountains as it was deemed prudent to go [. . .]
>
> Wherever Englishmen go, they sooner or later introduce [. . .] a taste for manly sports. Horse-racing and cricket were both got up [. . .][1]

The Afghans enthusiastically took part in horse-racing, but contrary to later mythology: 'The game of cricket was not, however, so congenial [. . .] it does not appear that they were ever tempted to lay aside their flowing robes and huge turbans and enter the field as competitors.'

The British also took part in Afghan sports, including cock and quail fighting and, surprisingly, wrestling. Gleig was wrong that the British had introduced a taste for manly sports into Afghanistan. Horse-racing and wrestling were long-established Afghan obsessions. Gleig states that whenever a Briton wrestled an Afghan, the Briton won. That is highly improbable, especially in view of the Afghans' greater experience. I found traditional Central Asian wrestling a terrific sight.

The winter of 1839/40 was exceptionally severe; and initially fun, as the lakes froze over:

> Forthwith our young gentlemen set themselves to the fabrication of skates: the artificers soon shaped the wood-work according to models given; out of old iron, smelted, and hardened afterwards, the blades were formed; and in due time, a party of skaters [. . .] appeared upon the lake. The Afghans stared in mute amazement while the officers were fastening on their skates, but when they rose, dashed across the ice's surface [. . .] and cut all manner of figures upon the ice, there was an end at once to disbelief [. . .]

Gleig says the Afghans chillingly exclaimed, 'Now [. . .] we see that you are not like the infidel Hindoos that follow you: you are men, born and bred like ourselves, where the seasons vary . . . We wish that you had come among us as friends, and not as enemies, for you are fine fellows one by one; though as a body we hate you.'

That problem was faced most acutely by Burnes, once a treasured friend in Kabul, and now a leader of the enemy. But his ready wit and endearing manner still could captivate, and he regularly hosted Afghan friends.

> Mention has been made of the hospitalities which were dispensed by Afghan chiefs to British officers. The latter were not backward to return the civility. Not only the houses of such men as the envoy, the commander in chief, and Sir Alexander Burnes, were thrown open to them, but the mess of the 13th received its frequent guests, most of whom ate and drank with as much good will and indiscrimination as if there had been no prohibitory clauses in the Koran or elsewhere.
>
> Among other means adopted to entertain the aristocracy of Central Asia, the British officers got up a play: a theatre was constructed, scenery painted, dresses prepared, and excellent bands in attendance; and as the pieces [. . .] were chiefly broad comedies, such as *the Irish Ambassador* [. . .] great amusement was offered to the audience [. . .] [T]hey changed the titles of the dramatis personae, so as to bring them [. . .] to the level of the Afghan comprehension; while Burnes and the others skilled in the dialect of the country, translated the speeches as they were uttered. The Afghans [. . .] have a keen relish of the ludicrous and the satirical; and as the interpreter never failed to bring the jokes of the actors home to them, they marked their delight by bursting into frequent peals of laughter.

It was a remarkable achievement successfully to interpret a play like this – not just a linguistic feat, but one of storytelling, timing and wit. There is nothing more deadening than sequential translation. Burnes was interpreting heavy comedies, about drawing-room society, littered with ponderous double entendres, like *The Irish Ambassador*:

> A mighty accomplished petticoat politician; but whether she's in for foreign affairs, or for my home department, or what may be the nature of the document in question, are points for a future Congress, and to me the most interesting of all my complicated transactions![2]

Yet we are told that, 'the interpreter never failed to bring the jokes of the actors home to them . . .' Presumably Burnes was gloriously extemporising, which tells us something about his extraordinary gifts.

Alex also found time to keep up his wider intellectual interests, collecting geological specimens and antiquities. He was delighted to find that Jabbar Khan had succeeded in multiplying the potatoes. Burnes now had the experiment repeated in Ghazni, Kandahar and Jalalabad. It is an effort to recall that the potato was only introduced as a crop into Burnes' native Angus fifty years before his birth; he introduced it into Afghanistan. Burnes also made an extensive collection of ancient coins, particularly from the Bactrian civilisation founded by Alexander's Greek colonists. To get the coins back safely to Britain, he gave them to his departing friend Colonel Charles Fox, illegitimate son of Lord Holland of Holland House. Fox later sold Burnes' collection to the Royal Museum in Berlin, now the Altes Museum.

Willoughby Cotton was summoned back to be Acting Commander in Chief in Calcutta. Robert Sale was now in command in Kabul, and General Nott in Kandahar. The government in London was keen to capitalise on the popularity of a triumphant campaign. Lord Keane of Ghazni was ennobled, Sir William Hay Macnaghten made a baronet, and a shower of lesser awards rained down on the British camps. Burnes, however, was ignored. He took this as an indication of the hostility from Auckland which he believed to be the motive behind Macnaghten's retention in Kabul. Macnaghten wrote Burnes three sympathetic letters at Alex being overlooked. The snub added to Burnes' growing disillusionment. He wrote to Lord: 'I ought never to have come here, or allowed myself to be pleased with fair though false words.'

As the long winter wore on, snow and ice lost their charms. Complained Dennie, 'it continues to descend untiringly, and [. . .] every object is covered with a mantle some feet in thickness of this boundless white [. . .] we are absolutely prevented from moving out of our houses.'[3] For the common soldiers it was worse – twenty-seven soldiers of the 13th Foot died of pneumonia. By mid-February Dennie's thermometer, which had recorded 125°F (51.5°C) in the shade at Dadur nine months previously, had fallen to 0°F (−18°C), below which it could not measure. The 13th had only 200 men fit for duty, and all their camels died.

The Commissariat at Kabul had entered contracts with the small Armenian population for the supply of arrack in place of rum. Dost Mohammed had banned alcohol in Kabul with some effect; this must be seen in the context of a religious revivalism in Central Asia, bringing a much narrower form of Islam. Havelock deplored the return of alcohol to the city, commenting 'the Affghans, like other nations invaded by our armies, will soon be taught the difference between Britons drunk and Britons sober'.[4] Military drunkenness contributed to the unpopularity of the occupation.

Burnes had taken up residence close to the base of the hill of the Bala Hissar and not far from the gates of the Qizilbash quarter. From his roof Burnes could look over the orchards of the houses of Afghan nobility, including many old friends. He bought Russian mirrors in the bazaar and scraped off the silver backing, fixing the glass into wooden frames, and installing Kabul's first windows. In the freezing winter this made the house much cosier than the original wooden latticework, and lighter inside. Burnes kept open house for both Afghans and British officers. Neither did he bear grudges: among his guests was fellow Freemason Josiah Harlan. Dr Kennedy was astonished by Harlan's shiny pea-green satin blouse, maroon trousers, silver lace girdle and high leather boots; not having met many Americans. The little Frenchman Argoud also turned up, this time hoping to gain employment with Shuja, although again unlucky.

In October 1839 copies reached a furious Burnes in Kabul of the Parliamentary Papers containing the tendentiously edited versions of his despatches from Kabul.[5] He wrote to James Holland:

> The exposition of the Governor-General's views in the Parliamentary Papers is pure trickery [...] I however acquit Lord Auckland of the fraud [...] All my implorations to Government to act with promptitude and decision had reference to doing something when Dost Mohammed was King, and all this they have made to appear in favour of Shah Shoojah being set up! But again, I did advocate the setting up of Shah Shoojah, but when was this? When my advice had been rejected, and the Government were fairly stranded. I [...] asked leave to withdraw, but Lord Auckland proved to me that it would be desertion at a critical moment, and I saw so myself, but I entered upon the support of his policy not as what was best, but what was best under the circumstances which a series of blunders had produced.[6]

The British early became acutely aware that Shuja was less popular than Dost. Havelock noted 'the people of Cabool [. . .] contrasting the mild and frank manners of their ex-Ameer with the repulsive haughtiness of their Shah'.[7] Pashtun tribal organisation militates strongly against central leadership. Ethnographers have classified Pashtuns as having an 'explicit segmentary lineage organisation'[8] – meaning there are several competing families and tribal sub-sets, none of which have an overriding claim to dominance. In this analysis, rebellion was directed at any centralising authority, against the British as against Dost's own centralising efforts. But we must also take into account the undoubted religious element to the anti-British feeling.

It was now plain Shuja could not hope to meet the cost of his Disciplined Force. Burnes had repeatedly reported that the great problem of government was that, with the loss of Kashmir and Peshawar and of tribute from Sind, the government had insufficient money to meet its obligations without resorting to methods which caused great hostility among the tribes.

Burnes proposed financial reform of the kingdom, with emphasis on simplifying and reducing customs duties while making their collection more efficient, in pursuit of his long-standing schemes for stimulating trade. He attempted to centralise collection of duties on the customs house in Kabul, ending a complex web of local arrangements. This involved a constant battle against corrupt officials. Burnes concentrated on taxing the substantial quantity of coin and bullion that flowed through Afghanistan to India from Russia, China and Central Asia, and he increased central revenue from this source fivefold.

He acted as spymaster for the agents and newswriters throughout Central Asia. In addition, based on the knowledge carefully culled by Leech and himself, he negotiated agreements with the Ghilzais and the Khyber chiefs, fixing the payment levels for keeping the passes open. The rates were higher than those paid by Dost, but below the rates paid by Shuja prior to 1809.[9] While this broke promises that Shuja would restore historic rates, the tribal leaders accepted that the country had deteriorated meantime, but that rates would be improved once circumstances allowed. While the British paid, these agreements generally worked.

But Burnes was continually thwarted in his administrative efforts by the corrupt and incompetent wazir, Mullah Shukhr. The wazir's faculties had declined and he could no longer function effectively. Burnes noted 'so completely is this poor man's memory gone, that he never recognises a man he has once seen; so that the commonest business requires half a dozen notes'. A few weeks later and Burnes' sympathy had lessened; 'Bad ministers are in every government solid grounds for unpopularity; and I doubt if a King ever had a worse set than Shah Shoojah'.[10]

Alex was disappointed that Macnaghten was still Envoy. It had always been understood between them that Macnaghten would return to Calcutta as soon as Shuja was established. At the end of November 1839 Alex wrote caustically to Holland that Auckland seemed 'literally to believe that the whole of Afghan politics would stand still if Macnaghten left the country'.[11] Just before Christmas he vented the same frustration to George Jacob:

> I drive the coach while Macnaghten is with the King. On our arrival here, the Envoy made a bold push to get away [...] but the Governor-General beseeched him to stay a while longer, and appointed your humbler servant Resident in Candahar, but this I declined, and now I get Rs 2,500 for staying here. The obnoxious crime of being a young man is I suppose what keeps me a second so long, but I get on well with Macnaghten, and only want responsibility to be a happy man.[12]

Auckland himself had planned to quit the scene at this stage. Like Bentinck before him, he intended to appoint an acting Governor-General and to leave without awaiting a successor. But Thomas Robertson declined the acting appointment; and Auckland decided that, given the Russian threat to Khiva and chaos in the Punjab, he should remain in India a while longer.

It was a relief for Burnes when Macnaghten, Sale and Shuja left for winter quarters at Jalalabad three thousand feet lower. It was a poor replacement for Afghanistan's former winter capital of Peshawar, but enjoyed a significantly milder climate than Kabul. Jalalabad had much declined, through earthquakes and constant warfare. There was only one decent house, which Macnaghten commandeered, leaving Shuja to cobble together a collection of the best hovels. They took four regiments with them plus the bulk of the artillery and the sappers, leaving only HM 13th Foot, the 35th NI and three guns with Burnes and Dennie to hold Kabul.

Macnaghten chose Percival Lord, the man with most experience of the small states north of Kabul, to regularise relations between them and Shuja, and attempt to deal with Dost. The former Emir, with his customary energy and skill, had increased his force in Balkh and even made inroads into the territory of Murad Beg, taking the Saigan and Kamard valleys and forcing Murad to hand over caravan tolls on trade between Kabul and Central Asia. This gave the Emir money to pay his supporters and continue the struggle.

Lord, now based in Bamian, reported to Burnes and Macnaghten that a dangerous alliance was developing between Murad Beg, Mir Wali and Dost, which might raise all of Turkestan south of the Oxus (modern northern Afghanistan) to fight Shuja. Macnaghten planned to send a brigade over the Hindu Kush into Khulm when the passes reopened in the spring of 1840.

Meantime, leading a small force of Gurkhas, irregular cavalry and horse artillery, Lord conducted a winter campaign and annexed Saigan to Kabul. With outstanding officers in George Broadfoot and Colin Mackenzie, Lord, who was acquiring a taste for this kind of thing, suggested that annexation of Balkh and other northern territories would help provide increased revenues desperately needed in Kabul.

Alex had written to James Burnes that 'I had a grand mission to Cabool and a fine lot of fellows with me'[13] and he remained in close touch with Wood, Lord and Leech now; they frequently backed each other up in official correspondence. Burnes now strongly supported Lord, adding that the Russian advance on Khiva would be countered by such a move, and as always advocating the return of Peshawar to Kabul. Macnaghten, who was finally coming to realise that the paltry revenues of Kabul made his whole project unviable, was inclined to agree. But Auckland, concerned that he had already pushed British forces much too far from India, vetoed further territorial expansion, setting the northern frontier at Bajgah, which the enterprising Lord had just annexed.

The British had suffered several defeats in the Khyber pass. An outpost held by 300 Najibs, or Punjab Muslims, recruited by Mackeson, had been massacred. Two attempts to resupply the garrison at Ali Musjid had resulted in humiliating retreat. Sale and Macnaghten therefore came down through the Khyber pass in late November 1839, after Mackeson had reaffirmed the subsidies of the Khyber tribes. They continued to Peshawar, where Willoughby Cotton had been waiting as the guest of Avitabile, having learnt that Sir Jasper Nicholls had after all arrived to take command in Calcutta. At one of Avitabile's grand dinners on 3 December 1839, Cotton, Macnaghten and Sale received from Burnes a letter detailing the fall of Kelat to General Wilshire. Avitabile conjured up an impromptu yet magnificent firework display. The following morning another letter arrived, from Auckland, ordering Cotton back to command in Afghanistan. Before returning to Kabul they were joined in Peshawar by Edward Conolly, returning from bringing up the officers' wives to the army in Afghanistan, led by Mrs Macnaghten and Lady Sale.[14] Probably meeting their wives was the real reason Macnaghten and Sale had gone to Peshawar.

Burnes' ability to affect policy had not improved, but at least he now had no superior immediately to hand, and he assumed the social leadership of the British in Kabul. On 31 December 1839 he threw a Hogmanay party and presided over it in his kilt. Neville Chamberlain wrote:

> We had a very merry party though we had nothing to drink but brandy and gin. At about 2 in the morning we [. . .] commenced dancing reels, Captain Sinclair standing on the table, dressed in the Highland costume, playing the bagpipes.

> Burnes [. . .] is liked by everyone, as there is no political humbug in him unlike most persons in that employ [. . .] [He is] a general favourite, and very justly so as he is, I think, the most unaffected, gentlemanlike, pleasant and amusing man that I have had the good fortune to meet.[15]

Ironically, Palmerston toasted in that New Year at his Broadlands estate with the Tsar's special Envoy, Baron Ernst De Brunow, having the previous month hosted a glittering banquet at the Foreign Office for the Tsarevitch in honour of the new-found amity between Britain and Russia. The Tsar had despatched De Brunow to London to secure a joint policy towards the Ottoman Empire. Exactly two years after Burnes hosted Witkiewicz to Christmas dinner in Kabul and sparked Palmerston to start a war, Palmerston hosted De Brunow to pheasant shooting and demonstrated that war's utter futility.[16]

Palmerston overplayed his hand. De Brunow advocated restraint in Central Asia, noting bluntly 'if we go on at this rate the Cossack and the Sepoy will soon cross bayonets on the banks of the Oxus'.[17] Confident in the British conquest of Afghanistan, Palmerston rejected De Brunow's offer of mutual recognition of the independence of all states between the territories of Britain and Russia in Asia. Nesselrode had eaten humble pie by disavowing Witkiewicz and Simonicz, but Palmerston now rubbed his nose in it. The long-term outcome was Russian conquest of Central Asia.

Nesselrode had in fact personally approved Witkiewicz' Kabul mission, but not his detailed offers. He believed the schemes to assist Dost against Ranjit Singh not worth the conflict it would provoke with Britain. Crucially, Nesselrode had managed to convince Tsar Nicholas I, who had previously given personal backing to Simonicz. However, the blow to Russian prestige of the British invasion of Kabul was too great to go unanswered, particularly as contrasted with Russo-Persian failure before Herat.

The British consistently overestimated the threat posed by the Russian expedition to Khiva. They were conditioned to do so – the British invading force had set off under the impression they were countering a Russian advance, and the Khiva expedition fitted this rationale. But Burnes was responsible for the intelligence from Central Asia, and he failed adequately to filter the alarmist reports of his agents. Throughout the winter of 1839/40 Khiva dominated British strategic thinking and diverted their energies from the urgent tasks of government in Kabul. On 19 December 1839 Burnes wrote:

> But everything [. . .] has been cast into the shade by the expedition which the Russians have now pushed into Central Asia. I had [. . .] numerous reports respecting their wagons, their material etc all of which is on a grand scale, giving rise to serious apprehension that their plans are not confined to the chastisement of the petty Khan of Khiva [. . .]

However, Burnes still had a generous intellectual outlook:

> Her attack on Khiva is justified by all the laws of nations, and in a country like England where slave dealing is so odiously detested, liable to find favor in men's eyes [...] Yet the time chosen [...] leads to the assertion that Russia has put forth her forces merely to counteract our policy [...] England and Russia will divide Asia between them and the two Empires will enlarge like circles in the water, till they are lost to nothing, and future generations will search for both of us in these regions, as we now look for the remains of Alexander and his Greeks.[18]

Russian frontier authorities had been contemplating action against Khiva for thirty years, but it took Perovsky's special relationship with the Tsar to get permission to go ahead. Perovsky was genuinely outraged at Khiva's taking of Russian slaves, but he also wanted to counter British influence. He wrote to the Tsar that Russia had much more justification for the annexation of Khiva than the French had to take Algeria.[19]

Nesselrode was anxious to avoid a clash between British and Russian expeditionary forces. In March 1839 in St Petersburg a committee of Nesselrode, Perovsky and War Minister Chernyshev came to this conclusion:

> Beyond its stated principal aim [the freeing of slaves] it must have another still more important; to establish and consolidate the influence of Russia in Central Asia, weaken the long-standing impunity of the Khivans, and especially that constancy with which the English government, to the detriment of our industry and trade, strives to spread its supremacy in those parts [...] however [...] we consider it more convenient to postpone the mission to Khiva until the end of the expedition undertaken by the Governor-General of the British possessions in India against the ruler of Kabul, Dost Mohammed.

The committee proposed to depose the Khan of Khiva and replace him with a puppet ruler, noting that this was following British precedent in Afghanistan.

Burnes forwarded on to Simla reports from his agent Nazir Khan Ullah in Bokhara. The Russians had sent an envoy there in September 1839 to prepare the ground diplomatically for their attack on Khiva. They had attempted unsuccessfully to persuade Emir Nasrullah to release Stoddart, as Nasrullah viewed him as a hostage against a British advance on Bokhara. The Russian Envoy said that Witkiewicz' suicide had prompted a feeling at the Tsar's Court that a forward policy in Central Asia had indeed been neglected, and funds were now released for an expedition against Khiva. A supply depot at Mangilaluk was being stocked. The expedition would proceed by sea across the Caspian to Kir, and overland to Khiva.[20]

Alex explained that he had separate intelligence that indicated Russia was indeed heavily buying provisions at the Caspian port of Mangilaluk. Strangely,

Burnes does not correct Nazir Khan Ullah's estimate of the land march from the Caspian to Khiva at four days; he himself had explored this territory and knew it to be many weeks. His agent Nazir felt in danger from the Emir in Bokhara, and requested Burnes that future correspondence be sent through his cousin Mahomed Amin Khan, and be written in Hindu script. Alex also sent on a letter from another of his agents, Qazi Mahomed Said of Herat, with intelligence from merchants who had seen a large Russian army advancing towards Khiva.[21]

On 31 January 1840 Pahawar Mul, another of Burnes' Bokhara agents, sent him an account of Dost's arrival there with about 600 men.[22] Nasrullah had sent Dost a present of robes, shawls and other costly goods, which Dost had refused, to Nasrullah's annoyance. Nasrullah had suggested his fellow Emir await the arrival of the Russian army then marching on Khiva, and use it to reconquer Kabul. Dost disagreed, enfuriating further the short-tempered Nasrullah. The Afghan had actually decided to contact the Russians, but secretly. Then on 17 January 1840 he sent the two sons with him, Akbar Khan and Afzal Khan, to escape from what had become confinement in Bokhara and ride back into Afghanistan. Dost now had only about fifty men left with him.

Pahawar Mul's letter also contained the news that Colonel Stoddart, still imprisoned, had been forcibly converted to Islam, which would have included circumcision. Burnes also received a report from Balkh dated 14 January 1840 stating that according to eyewitness reports of Balkh merchants, the Russian army was encamped on the Syr Darya on the way to Khiva, and had sent messages to the Khan demanding immediate surrender.[23] In handling this secret correspondence Burnes was working closely with Mohan Lal and placed great trust and responsibility in the hands of his assistant.[24]

On 23 February 1840 Macnaghten wrote to Burnes reviving his proposal that they send an expedition against Bokhara to free Stoddart and counteract the Russian move. The money for it could be taken from Bokhara itself. This scheme was also vetoed by Auckland.

On 15 March Dennie wrote to a friend:

> How are your predictions fulfilled with regard to Russia! See her now, actually at Khiva with a large regular army, and seventy two pieces of cannon! Burnes [. . .] who is with me here at Cabool, gave this information so far back as October last, and renewed it incessantly [. . .] but none so deaf as those who won't hear. I am with him daily, and see and hear the men he employs, and the letters they bring him from his agents in Khiva and Bokhara.[25]

Burnes, Macnaghten and Dennie all feared a two-pronged Russian spring offensive, with the Khiva force pushing over the Hindu Kush to Bamian and Kabul, and the Persian army advancing through Herat on Kandahar. But Macnaghten had doubts. On 1 April 1840 he wrote:

> I am rather sceptical as to this power of the Autocrat to push [...] an army so far, in one or even in two campaigns. Burnes however is alarmed. He says we are altogether deceived by the strength of the Russian army; that it is now actually in possession of Khiva, and will shortly be in possession of Bokhara. You may imagine the anxiety with which I am looking for authentic information from the North.[26]

In fact, the Russian army advancing on Khiva had been just 5,200 men, smaller than Burnes' reports indicated, and had met with disaster. Like the British, they had experienced the unusually cruel winter of 1839/40, but unlike the British billeted in Kabul, the Russians were trying to struggle through the bitterly cold Kizyl Kum desert. Their Kazakh camel drivers had attempted to turn back saying the expedition was impossible, but Perovsky had shot two ringleaders and ascribed the opposition to Islamic fanaticism. Progress was pitiably slow, and eventually the death of virtually all their 10,000 camels caused the army to retreat, still 200 miles from Khiva. The emaciated troops reached Orenburg in March 1840; 1,000 had died in the snows and another 2,000 were crippled by frostbite.

Macnaghten now proposed Burnes go off on various political missions, suggesting Herat, Kandahar and Bokhara. It seems he wanted to get his deputy away from the centre of power. Burnes, however, was determined to stay, and turned down all these suggestions, including the offer Macnaghten now made of Special Envoy to the Russian camp in the Kizyl Kum. Burnes wrote to Macnaghten saying he would go if given plenipotentiary powers to negotiate, but not as a simple courier. Macnaghten was indignant.

Burnes gave too much credence to rumours sent by panic-stricken agents during this period. There was also a systemic failure which continues today. If your system of intelligence depends on paying informants, they will naturally invent something to tell you, particularly of any threat you want to believe in. Burnes had fallen victim to this common intelligence delusion.

Macnaghten still hankered to extend British influence to the Oxus and agreed with Arthur Conolly an ambitious plan to secure the formation of a friendly Uzbek confederation of Kokhand, Bokhara and Khiva – modern Uzbekistan. This was in effect the plan of Thomas Love Peacock and the Secret Committee in London. The aim was to present a united front to Russian aggression – though with no British security guarantee – and establish a strong trading block, plus abolish slavery in the region. Britain offered nothing in return but trade and goodwill. Conolly proposed to set off on mission with Henry Rawlinson to promote this plan.

Burnes viewed this as ill-conceived, believing that in interfering beyond the Oxus, Britain was exceeding her physical ability to influence events. He actively opposed all of Macnaghten's schemes for sending agents, including Abbot and Conolly, into Turkestan. 'Is England to become security for barbarous hordes some thousands of miles from her frontier?' he asked in a minute to Auckland: 'What are we to get from it? Nothing, I see, but to attach to ourselves just and deserved reproach for interfering with Russia on ground already occupied by her merchants, and far beyond our own line of operations.'[27]

In fact, Arthur Conolly's proposed adventure was driven by suicidal urges following a broken engagement.[28] Burnes distrusted Conolly's Christian evangelism and enthusiasm for cultural reform. To Lord, he gently mocked Conolly: 'He is flighty, though a very nice fellow: he is to regenerate Toorkistan, dismiss all the slaves, and looks upon our advent as a design of Providence to spread Christianity.'

Burnes argued to Auckland that Britain's only chance to prevent Russian advance into Central Asia was for Palmerston to negotiate a comprehensive treaty that included Russia's European and Black Sea interests, where concessions could be made. Although initially agreeing with Burnes, Auckland changed his mind under pressure from Macnaghten and Colvin, and in September 1840 Conolly started on his mission to the Uzbeks, though fortunately for archaeology Rawlinson remained in Kandahar.

In spring of 1840 the Ghilzais attacked the communication lines between Kandahar and Kabul. General Nott sent 800 infantry, 360 cavalry and horse artillery under Captain Anderson to clear the line of the Turnuk river valley, and at Tazin they defeated a large Ghilzai force. The artillery were crucial but the infantry, an untried Hindu corps of the Shah's contingent, performed creditably, repulsing two cavalry charges at bayonet point.

Nott had no doubt that Saduzai misrule was the root cause of the uprisings. He wrote:

> The fact is that the [...] cruel oppression committed by the servants [...] of [...] Prince Timour, have [...] outrage[d] the feelings of the natives [...] should an opportunity offer, these cruel and shameful proceedings will be retaliated against the troops left in the country. Never in all history have I read of such plunder, cruelty, and oppression [...] The houses and cornfields of the unfortunate inhabitants are entered, their property plundered, and the owners cut and wounded in the most cruel manner [...] it was under the immediate eye of Prince Timour [...][29]

Mohan Lal thought Shuja was playing a multiple game, and that he was encouraging uprisings in order to weaken the British. He reported, 'the jealous and different view by the Shah who by the secret messages and sometimes by personal speech advised the Chiefs of the country to disturb the peace and oppose the British arms'.[30] Lal was with Burnes overseeing a large number of agents and informers, but the country was so rife with rumour the intelligence was difficult to filter. Given the hard school of fratricidal conflict in which Shuja had been brought up, it would be surprising if he were not attempting to play all sides.

Burnes felt pressured to produce reports validating the policies of the occupation, complaining to Lord:

> They have been at me again to write 'on the prospects of the restored government' [...] if they really wanted truth, I would give it cordially, but it is a chiming-in, a coincidence of views, which they seek [...] my conscience has not so much stretch in it as to approve of this dynasty.[31]

In May, Alex rode out to visit Kohistan, whose beautiful valleys and orchards he had so much enjoyed when resident in Kabul. It was at its most delightful at this spring season in both climate and blossom. The Kohistanis had detested the firm rule of Dost Mohammed, who had brought them under royal control by expedients including the wholesale slaughter of their chiefs. They had therefore been amongst the first to rally to Shuja, and Burnes was anticipating a pleasant expedition.

He was disappointed. He found the country laid waste by the Dourani sirdar appointed by Shuja, who had been unrelenting in tax-gathering. Many had fled to the hills, but at Shikardarra a delegation met Burnes, and gravely informed him of instances of abuse, including the imposition of taxes from which Shuja had specifically confirmed exemptions.

A worried Burnes returned to Kabul, where he outlined the abuses he had found to Shuja. Mullah Shukhur, the vizier, denied the complaints. A Kohistani deputation, invited by Burnes, was imprisoned by royal troops. After Burnes remonstrated, they were released and obtained partial redress. This was more than the villagers had expected, and Burnes noted they 'returned to their homes, blessing His Majesty.'[32] However once they were home, the concessions were cancelled and further reprisals were taken. The truth was Burnes had almost no power to rectify bad government.

Darcy Todd had taken over in Herat, and under a treaty[33] of 13 August 1839, Britain took control of Herat's foreign policy in exchange for an immediate payment of £10,000 and annual subsidies of £20,000. Major Sanders of the Engineers, and the colossal sum of thirty lacs, were provided for the repair and improvement of Herat's defences.[34] But Todd was so appalled by Yar Mohammed's misgovernment that by October he was recommending that Herat be either annexed or garrisoned. He discovered that Yar was offering to acknowledge Persian sovereignty in alliance to drive the British from Afghanistan.

Both Burnes and Macnaghten favoured annexation, but this was resolutely vetoed by Auckland. Then in December 1840 Hobhouse, with Palmerston's support, urged Auckland to annex Herat to counter Russian moves against Khiva. Auckland replied to London that the expense would be ruinous; the occupation of Kabul and Kandahar had already drained the Indian treasury.

Auckland's alternative was to instruct Todd to offer Herat financial support to retake Ghorian. Todd handed over another £20,000; Yar pocketed the cash and did nothing.

By the spring of 1840 Macnaghten faced so much hostility to British occupation throughout Afghanistan that he could not spare the troops for Lord's planned expedition over the Hindu Kush. News of the disastrous Russian expedition to Khiva had removed some of the strategic urgency. On 14 May 1840 Macnaghten wrote to Lord, 'Our policy should still be to make it appear as if an advance at least as far as Khoolm were intended, though that such an advance should take place is now more than ever improbable.' Relying on this bluff, Lord secured a defensive alliance with Murad Ali. Mir Wali then agreed to accept Kabul sovereignty over Khulm and a British garrison, and to pay Shuja the caravan toll. In return Lord awarded Mir Wali the revenues of Saigan and Kamard, which Lord had taken. The doctor's performance as a political officer appeared masterful.

Dost was imprisoned in Bokhara, where Nasrullah insisted he bring his zenana, intending to extort the personal treasure carried with them. The zenana was in charge of Jabbar Khan with Mir Wali in Khulm, but hardly safe: they were squeezed between Bokhara to the north and the British to the south, and Wali's Uzbeks might not forever resist the fortune in their midst. With Dost's permission, Jabbar Khan therefore entered into negotiations with Lord for the surrender of the zenana, and 239 wives, daughters, concubines, children and domestic servants were handed over at Arghandi on 15 July 1840. Shuja refused to give them asylum or contribute to their maintenance – Macnaghten proposed that he be forced, but as the British were pouring in vast subsidies to Shuja the argument was a dead letter.

The family were sent, under escort of Charles Burnes, to replace the Saduzais in Ludhiana. At Peshawar, Charlie handed them over to Lieutenant Nicolson, and received a receipt for them.

Received from Lieutenant Charles Burnes:

| | |
|---|---|
| Wives of Dost Mohammed | 9 |
| Younger Sons of Ditto | 11 |
| Sirdar Mahomed Afzul Khan Grownup son | 1 |
| Sirdar Akram Khan Ditto | 1 |
| Wives of Afzul Khan | 1 |
| Ditto Akber Khan | 3 |
| Ditto Akram Khan | 1 |
| Ditto Azeem Khan | 2 |
| Ditto Sheer Ali Khan | 1 |
| Ditto Hyder Khan | 1 |
| Daughters of the Ameer | 7 |
| Grandsons Ditto | 4 |
| Granddaughters ditto | 4 |
| Sons of the late Mahomed Khan | 2 |
| Wives | 4 |
| Female slaves for the above | 102 |
| Male Slaves and attendants | 210 |
| Relations | 14 |

P Nicolson, Lieutenant
Peshawar Dec 18 1840[35]

On 6 June 1840 Burnes was created a Companion of the Order of the Bath.[36] He was now Lieut Col Sir Alexander Burnes, KB, CB, FRS and still just thirty-five years old. His prospects looked tremendous. On 23 July 1840 the Army held a grand dinner to celebrate the anniversary of the capture of Ghazni. They toasted the health of poor Stoddart. It was an uproarious occasion which Arthur Conolly found a 'vulgar outbreak', but Burnes was in his element. He gave the speech, lampooning fellow officers, which went down well, and suggesting that if Stoddart were not released there would soon be a 'Baron Bokhara' to match Baron Keane of Ghazni. Conolly wrote, 'You may imagine the accent and energy with which Burnes thundered out' this threat.

In the Baluch territories, British attempts to impose rule on the Murri tribe were disastrous. A force of 150 men and one gun under Captain Brown was besieged in Kahun, while a column of 160 infantry and fifty cavalry under Lieutenant Clerk was annihilated in the Nufusk pass. At Mustung, twenty-five sepoys from the garrison at Kelat were wiped out, and on 21 June 1840 the neighbouring Kakar tribe attacked the small British garrison at Quetta.

Robert Leech, now Captain, was back at Kandahar as Political Agent with Nott, and the two made a good team. Leech successfully negotiated with the Achakzai chief, Salu Khan, whom he paid a considerable sum to reinforce Quetta, arriving just before a considerable Brahui force rolled up to besiege on

9 July. On 16 July the arrival of a further large body of horsemen organised by Leech caused the Brahuis to lift the siege. However they proceeded to besiege Kelat, where the Political Officer Loveday and the British puppet Shah Nawaz Khan were unable to depend on the loyalty of their largely Kelati garrison.

The son of Mehrab Khan, Nassir Khan, had been at Noshki when his father was killed, and was in the field with his Baluch Brahuis. The British tried to capture Nassir, and in doing so devastated Miranzai and Punjgur. On 28 July 1840 after a three-day siege Kelat fell to Nassir Khan. Loveday was taken prisoner, mistreated and eventually murdered, while Nassir assumed his father's throne. Masson, who had been in Kelat, was released, by his account to carry a message.

The British Army then suffered a further disaster in the Nufusk pass, as a relief column for Kahun of 464 infantry under Major Clibborn crossed the boat bridge across the Indus on 12 August 1840. Arriving in the pass on 31 August weak from thirst, they were attacked by the Murris. Clibborn lost 271 men killed and wounded, the remainder retreating to Pulaji. A quarter of the survivors died of thirst and exhaustion. On 28 September Captain Brown surrendered Kahun; he and his men were kindly treated and allowed to march with their guns to Pulaji, after a fruitless nine-month occupation of the Murri capital in supporting which 500 British troops had died.

On 28 October the Baluch army crossed the Bolan pass and attacked the British base at Dadur in an effort to recover Kacchi, but was repulsed in a series of encounters. On 3 November 1840, while the Baluch army was still away, Colonel Stacey and a force from Quetta took Kalat again for the British. The Baluch and Brahui war continued with renewed vigour.

As reports filtered back, opinion among the British in India became increasingly alarmed. At the forefront of campaigning was George Buist of the *Bombay Times*, who was getting information from Alexander through James. On 16 July 1840 the *Bombay Times* printed that:

> the accounts of the conduct and condition of Shah Shoojah, continue the same as formerly; that his habits are those of a haughty, silly, sensual, confirmed reprobate, totally unworthy of British [. . .] protection; who, the moment that our forces were withdrawn [. . .] would become the deserved victim of his own outraged subjects, by whom he is held in equal hatred and derision.

Opinion in the UK was not behind the invasion. The *Edinburgh Review*, house journal of the ruling Whigs, supported the invasion but explicitly admitted that this was a minority opinion.[37] The *Monthly Review* saw one bright spot of hope: 'so long as Alexander Burnes is actively employed at Kandahar, or at any other residency in the East, we have a most vigilant and influential representative'.[38]

CHAPTER THIRTY-THREE

## Dost Mohammed

In Kabul, Burnes had become steadily more worried as the British position deteriorated. He saw resistance flaring up throughout the country, and believed it stemmed directly from bad government.

Burnes was not alone. The military command were increasingly alarmed by the spirit of Afghan resistance. Willoughby Cotton sent reports to Auckland critical of Shuja and contradicted the optimistic picture painted by Macnaghten. Brigadier Simpson, Commander of the Shah's forces, was even more outspoken. As he was supposed to remain in military command once British forces withdrew, his opinions had weight, and he viewed the situation as untenable.

Macnaghten was furious that Auckland would not agree to annex Peshawar and occupy the Punjab, where since Ranjit Singh's death the British had been much harassed, writing to Auckland, 'I have perceived [. . .] lately, a want of confidence in my proceedings, and a disposition to listen to every unfavourable report regarding proceedings in this quarter; whilst I do not receive the support to which the overwhelming difficulties of my position entitle me.' He was shocked at Auckland's reply strongly supporting Simpson: 'His Lordship can only express his approbation of the care which is exhibited by the Brigadier.' Macnaghten now responded, asking to resign, in favour of Burnes: 'I never yet have served in an office where I had not the confidence of my superiors.'[1]

His resignation was not accepted. It was in these circumstances that Macnaghten received Burnes' long formal memorandum, dated 7 August 1840,[2] making a fundamental critique of the occupation policies. His was not an isolated voice. Macnaghten had to pass this document up to Auckland, but took a much more optimistic view, rebutting Burnes' opinions, before sending on the memo. This is a vital document as it defines the divisions at the top, exonerates Burnes from the major mistakes of the occupation, and shows Macnaghten at once highly optimistic and extremely defensive.

Burnes' opening is combative:

> when you have deemed my opinion [...] worthy of being called for, I have conscientiously given it [...] where my own views differed from your own I have made it a point to give way [...] I have resolutely resisted being drawn into any kind of correspondence regarding this country with my official superiors tho' I have been repeatedly invited even by the highest authority to do so [...] had I acted otherwise [I] [...] would have largely added to the embarrassments both of yourself and Government by letting forth opinions on things different from your own [...]

Burnes then referred to his expectation of taking over Macnaghten's job, an arrangement frequently mentioned in correspondence by both men.

> It would be an easy task for me to sit down and do only what Government or yourself directed me to do till the time should come when the direction of this country fell to myself

Burnes felt Afghanistan was in such a parlous state he must now give his candid advice. He started with the loss of Kelat. Macnaghten annotated:

> too much has been made of the misfortune which elicited this paper. Similar misfortunes have very generally occurred to us in the first establishment of our influence in other parts of the East. W.M.

Alex details discontent among the Dourani nobles at Kandahar over Shah Shuja's tax impositions, and criticises the giving of large sums of money to Yar Mohammed at Herat. Here, Macnaghten makes no specific riposte. Burnes then elaborates on his attempts to ensure good governance for the Kohistanis in the spring, and his frustration by Shuja, concluding:

> At this time the feeling in Kohistan is feverish in the extreme [...] an insurrection may break out at a moment's warning

Macnaghten simply negates this:

> The Kohistanees certainly did flock in great numbers to Cabul, and were well received. I have no reason to believe that they are generally not well affected, though they are proverbial for their love of turbulence and rapine [...] W.M.

Burnes then notes similar discord in Jalalabad and the Khyber, and writes of the economic non-viability of Afghanistan minus Herat, Peshawar and Kashmir. Of Shuja:

> To me it would be very astonishing if any Afghan king who had allied himself to the Sikhs and English would be popular; it is not in the nature of things.

Macnaghten denies even this. It is worth reminding ourselves that Macnaghten's comments are written for Auckland:

> The present system is not popular with some classes. The causes of this feeling I have repeatedly enumerated. The Shah himself is, I believe, personally popular with all, though he may not be able, with his limited resources, to satisfy unreasonable representations. W.M.

Burnes then describes the incapacity of Mullah Shukhr as Vizier, and regrets that Usman Khan Bamizai, whom Burnes had sought to force on Shuja to improve the administration, had been given nothing to do but sort through old revenue records. Macnaghten again negates Burnes:

> the picture of Moolah Shikore is rather a caricature. His only fault [...] lies in his age. He is thoroughly honest, and devoted to his majesty's interests [...] he will not allow his majesty to be cheated by others. This is the secret of much of his unpopularity. W.M.

Alex addresses the expense and inefficiency of the royal household, the worthlessness of many of the royal troops, the iniquities of the tax system and of quartering troops on districts to enforce collection, and the popular discontent among the Muslim population from stationing Sikh troops in central Kabul, even guarding the entrance to the Bala Hissar. All these points are discounted by Macnaghten, the last with the impractical observation that the British should not give way to religious intolerance.

Burnes had produced a damning critique of Shuja, and of Macnaghten's governance of Afghanistan. He was correct not just in his perception of what was going wrong, but of why. His letter concluded:

> It is better I think to meet these boldly than to shut our eyes to them. - I cannot expect you to accept all my opinions [...] but if I have [...] discharged a conscientious duty in laying before you the conclusions at which I have arrived, I shall have gained the end I had in view
> Believe me yours sincerely,
> Sgd. Lt Col Alex. Burnes

Having annotated all over the margins, Macnaghten also added a covering letter arguing that Burnes was wrong:

> His Majesty is merciful and kind-hearted in the extreme, and if the personal qualities of a monarch could ensure popularity, Shah Shoojah could not fail to obtain it. My longer experience of his majesty's character more thoroughly convinces me of the truth [...] that there is not an abler or better man than himself in all his dominions.

Macnaghten met with Burnes and opined he was 'too gloomy'. The situation went from bad to worse. Burnes had evidently put a lot of effort into his memorandum, and it had been a big decision to set down his criticisms. He must have been disappointed at Macnaghten's brusque refusal to move towards his views. Macnaghten also wrote separately to Auckland:

> we are in as prosperous condition as could have been expected. Sir A. of course wishes to prove the contrary, since by doing so, when he succeeds me, his failures would thus find excuse and his success additional credit.[3]

Burnes sent a copy of his paper to James on 20 August, adding a postscript in which he appeared, falsely, to exult in British disasters. We should remember this PS was only to his brother:

> PS 22 August 1840
> The above paper was written on the 7th August [...] it has been deemed too gloomy. The following events have occurred since, and if the facts enumerated were insufficient, they may serve to indicate where the truth lies.
> 1. Captain Hay, beyond Bameean, where all was indeed quiet, was invited to occupy some forts ahead of his position, he accepted the offer; 29 of his 100 men were wounded, and 9 killed, the party only saved from destruction by Lieutenant Hart leading two companies to the rescue!
> 2. Captain Macgregor sent 1500 Afghans against a place north of Jellalabad; they were defeated, lost their gun, and 100 men – 200 went over to the enemy!!
> 3. The Shah was going to Koh-i-Duman, thirty miles from his capital; the chiefs objected to it; he is obliged to give up his trip, and return his tents into store!!!
> 4. Kelat has no sooner fallen, than Beloochees have moved against Shawl again, and troops have gone down to Candahar to the rescue!!!!
> 5. The chiefs of Khooloom and Khoondooz have joined in a confederacy against us, and prevented Dost Mahomed coming in!!!!!
> 6. A conspiracy has been discovered by myself, and believed by the king and the envoy, implicating almost all the first men in Cabul and the surrounding countries in a plan to subvert the country!!!!!!
> 7. Letters from the Sikhs to Dost Mahomed have been intercepted, sending money!!!!!!!
> With seven points of wonder I close the result of twice seven days. A.B.

Dost Mohammed had escaped from captivity in Bokhara and boldly ridden into the Uzbek lands across the Oxus. Mir Wali immediately switched allegiance to him, and on 30 August the two led an attack which caused the precipitate withdrawal of the Gurkha and Afghan irregular force holding Bajgah for the British. A recently raised Afghan infantry regiment under

Captain Hopkins at Saigan deserted to Dost, causing the officers and a few remaining men to fall back on Lord's force at Bamian.

However, Lord, through his local agents, had received intelligence of Dost's approach and already sent for reinforcements: Dennie had arrived with the 35th NI, and Gurkhas from the Shah's contingent. On the morning of 15 September Lord told Dennie that an advance party of Mir Wali's forces were capturing forts at the head of the Bamian valley. Dennie rode out with a third of the garrison, about 700 men. He sent Gurkha detachments to drive the enemy from the heights on either side, while Dennie led several charges up the valley head, despite being surprised to discover not merely an advance guard but Dost Mohammed, Afzal Khan and Mir Wali, with an army of 6,000. It was the small artillery force under Lieutenant Mackenzie that scattered the enemy, which Dennie followed up with his customary ferocity. Unaccustomed to effective artillery, with 500 killed and over 1,000 wounded, Mir Wali and the Uzbeks fled. Hopkins' former men were ridden down by the Shah's new janbaz cavalry and by Anderson's horse, with whom Arthur Conolly charged. The British lost 100 killed. Dost himself was wounded by a howitzer shell.

Dennie was now offered the Order of the Dourani Empire (Second Class), which he again refused. Macnaghten responded by stopping Dennie's allowance as an acting brigadier. Burnes and Dennie had become close during their winter in charge at Kabul, and Alex sympathised.

> Cabool, 20 September 1840
>
> My Dear Colonel
> Accept the [...] heart-felt congratulations of a friend and admirer of your [...] most glorious success against Dost Mahomed Khan [...] A victory over a man of the stamp of Dost Mahomed is no small honour; and it will [...] fully prove, that the man they so unjustly injured at Ghuznee, deserved other things; and, forgetting all past slights and injuries, did in the hour of duty gloriously maintain the arms and honour of his country.
>
> Farewell to-day, and believe me always very sincerely yours,
>
> Alexander Burnes

After Bamian, Lord immediately arranged honourable terms of surrender for Dost, who was offered a comfortable exile and pension for himself and family. Dost Mohammed's reply was memorable:

> I am but a wooden spoon which can be thrown hither and thither without injury, but the British are a glass which, once broken, cannot be mended.[4]

Burnes had lost confidence in both Shuja and Macnaghten. On 6 September 1840 he wrote to James Holland that 'there is nothing here but downright imbecility'. But suddenly Macnaghten was much less sure that Burnes was an alarmist. On 12 September 1840 he wrote to Auckland 'Affairs in this quarter have the worst possible appearance. The whole Kohistan is reported to be ripe for revolt, though possibly in this there may be some exaggeration: and we hear of resolutions to rise in other parts of the country.'

He endorsed a request from Cotton that another full brigade be urgently sent from Bengal. Macnaghten was still urging Auckland to annex Herat and to act against the Sikhs, who were encouraging and funding Afghan resistance. The British reaction to Dennie's victory at Bamian is telling. They abandoned Bamian, handed back his lands to the defeated Mir Wali, and pulled back until their most advanced post was at Charikar, just forty miles north of Kabul. Akbar Khan, Dost Mohammed's favoured son, immediately established himself at Khulm.

The British were losing belief. Living conditions hardly helped. In their second freezing Afghan winter, most of the Kabul garrison in cantonment were still under canvas. As for their officers, Colonel Dennie was living in a self-built mud hut, 'like most of my neighbours'.[5] Kabul was rife with intrigue as Afghan factions vied for power. Edward Conolly was brought correspondence purported to be between the Sikh Durbar, Sultan Mohammed and Jabbar Khan planning harassment and sabotage. Jabbar was held as a broadly neutral figure; the other two were supposed to be allies. After investigation, Burnes and Mohan Lal declared the letters forgeries.

Macnaghten had ordered guns mounted in the Bala Hissar and was preparing the contingency of moving into the citadel. He wrote to Auckland that they may need to 'submit to the disgrace of being shut up in Kabul for a time'.[6] Burnes had intercepted more letters in Kabul between disaffected Kohistani chiefs. Nobles were disgruntled by the abolition of old privileges and the creation of a central standing army, the janbaz and hazirbaz. In these policies the British were in fact following Dost's lead, who had created a 3,000 strong royal 'umlai' cavalry, to great resentment.[7] Whoever ruled Afghanistan faced the same resistance to central authority.

The Emir was attempting to consolidate Kohistani resistance, but Burnes now moved to Charikar and used a classic secret service ruse to disrupt him. Afghan chiefs used nishans (facts only the receiver and sender would know) for communications security. They had long been in use due to the constant intrigue in Afghan politics: in 1832 Ata Mohammed sent Dost one: 'When the late Wazir Futth Khan left you at Kandahar with Shazadah Kamran, our friendship was sealed by a secret oath.'[8] Ever since the Emir had fled Kabul, Burnes had been collecting nishans from chiefs by initiating correspondence with them, claiming to be from Dost Mohammed, and collating the replies.[9]

He now used these to forge letters from key chiefs to the Emir, warning him that the people of their district supported Shah Shuja and powerful British forces were roaming, so Dost should not approach Kabul.[10] Dost himself was extremely experienced in employing forged letters, a commonplace of Afghan politics, so whether he was taken in is doubtful.

Sending and receiving of secret messages was Burnes' stock-in-trade. These were written on small squares of paper, often hidden in plain sight, for example as a prayer amulet. At the other extreme these could be rolled up in a section of quill pushed into the anus. Other common methods were to bake the message in a chapati, which could be swallowed, or scrunch it into a pistol wad which could be quickly fired away. The messengers or chaprasis adopted various disguises 'beautifully', including as naked holy men.[11]

On 29 September 1840 Burnes, Robert Sale and Shahzada Timur rode out from the fort of Charikar at the head of HM 13th Infantry, two companies each of the 27th and 37th NI, two squadrons of the 2nd Bengal Light Cavalry and five guns. Their object was to subdue Kohistan, viewed as an easy task; there was talk of British ladies joining them as an excursion.[12] Edward Conolly volunteered for fun.

Climbing into the highlands, unopposed except by sporadic sniping, they established a base camp at Karabagh. On 29 September they captured the fortified hill village of Tutundera, the stronghold of Ali Khan, whose correspondence with the Emir Burnes had intercepted. The villagers put up some resistance. Edward Conolly died instantly, shot through the heart. Six privates were also killed, with many more deaths on the Afghan side. Ali Khan escaped. At Burnes' prompting, the entire defences of the village and surrounding countryside were levelled.

After the destruction of Tutundera, the force moved back to Charikar, where they received more reinforcements of janbaz and irregular cavalry and three more guns. On the night of 1 October, the cavalry were despatched to overwhelm Julga. This was against Burnes' advice, as he believed the local chief, Mir Masjidi Khan, was about to surrender. The rest of the force arrived two days later after dragging the guns over hills. The fort refusing to surrender, Sale opened fire with six cannon. However the ramparts were protected by wide turf banks, and the shot made little impact. The infantry then made three attempts to escalade the walls, all of which failed as the ladders were too short.

In frustration, the British force took to levelling the whole town. After nightfall, the janbaz assisted the garrison of, it transpired, only fifty men to escape. The attackers had taken fifty casualties in the failed escalade. The next day the fort too was razed. Burnes reported to Macnaghten that 'the country is in a very unsettled state'.

Given British brutality, submissions started to come in. Burnes was receiving much intelligence on Dost's whereabouts. On 8 October the force returned to Charikar to try to intercept him, then pursued him to Karabagh and Nijrow. This period when Dost Mohammed was a fugitive resistance leader naturally entered into Afghan lore. Burnes was the arch-villain. This is from the epic Jangnama of Ghulam Kohistani:

> At the Amir's order, those courageous rebels
> Rode their horses through the mountainous lands
> Nowhere was there a moment's respite or hesitation
> Dreading in their hearts a Firangi attack
> For fear that *he* would beat them to it
> That wretched Burnes at Charikar.[13]

Burnes was receiving intelligence from double-dealing Kohistanis, while the Emir was receiving intelligence from among the janbaz. On 11 October 1840 Burnes heard that Dost with a small band had entered Ghurband, just two marches from Kabul. Macnaghten immediately ordered Dennie from Bamian back to the capital, which he described as 'in a very weak and defenseless state'. Cannon were strategically placed and British troops moved into the Bala Hissar.

On the 13th Lieutenant Dowson was sent on with the cavalry to catch the Emir at Tutundera, who narrowly escaped them. On the 17th Burnes and Sale razed the town of Babukushkar, despite their being no resistance. They destroyed two miles of beautiful vineyards and gardens. This provoked the first serious attack on Sale's force the following night, but it was beaten off without difficulty. Macnaghten was scathing: 'Burnes and Sale, with nearly 2,000 good infantry, are sitting down before a fortified position about twenty miles distant, and are afraid to attack it. The enemy made an attack upon them the night before last – killed and wounded some of our people, and got off unscathed – all this is very bad.'[14]

On 19 October Burnes and Sale received substantial reinforcements of six companies of the 37th NI and two nine-pounder guns. Two days later they approached a large Kohistani force at Kardera, which dispersed without a fight. Kardera too was levelled. This systematic destruction of homes as well as fortifications, with winter fast approaching, amounted to a campaign of atrocity in which Burnes was deeply implicated. This is the more remarkable as Burnes had, just six months previously, gone to great lengths to intercede on behalf of the Kohistanis, believing their grievances genuine. The humane traveller and writer, the officer who had opposed the invasion, who had tried to stop British reprisals in the Bolan pass, appeared to have disappeared. Burnes had been captured by his metier and by the pressure on the beleaguered British force. When he had sacrificed his principles and gone along with the invasion, it was inevitable that his honour would end up deeply compromised and the bitterness of bad conscience start to curdle his personality.

The Emir had succeeded in slipping through to to Nijrow, where a Kohistani army of 4,000 foot and 400 horse had assembled to support him just three easy marches from Kabul, in which direction he now moved. He had reached Parwandera when Burnes and Sale finally caught up with him.

The vanguard was under Colonel Salter and Dr Lord, and consisted of two guns, seven companies of Native Infantry, the two squadrons of the Second Cavalry and 200 of the Shah's horse under Captain Anderson. Burnes and Sale were at the head of the main force a mile behind. It was a beautiful morning, the sun sparkling off the mountain streams and irrigation canals.

Lord had met with village elders at the valley entrance. The villagers represented themselves as Shuja loyalists, and complained that the Emir's forces had plundered them. They indicated a track skirting the hills to the right, and said that a quick move by this route would enable the British to cut off Dost's force. Lord pressed this idea on Salter, who despatched the two squadrons of the 2nd Cavalry by this route, while Anderson's horse deployed to the left. Lord and Broadfoot, who had built the boat-bridge at Sukkur, rode with the 2nd Cavalry, forcing the pace to cut off the Emir.

As they blindly raced around the track, they were unaware that this led them right underneath Dost Mohammed, on a hill above with his cavalry. Seizing the moment, the Emir with about 400 irregular cavalry swept down. The vast majority of the sepoys of the 2nd Cavalry turned and galloped away, leaving just twenty men and ten British officers, who spurred their horses uphill to meet the Afghan charge. Lord was killed by a jezzail shot before he got ten yards. Broadfoot was allegedly killed by sepoys he tried to stop from fleeing.[15] Burnes had spotted the disaster unfolding, and was racing up with the horse artillery under intense fire – he kept as a souvenir a ball which struck close to him. He wrote to Davie, 'How I escaped unscathed God only knows.' But typically he downplayed his personal danger and urged Davie to 'Make no parade of these facts.' Burnes had now seen three friends – Edward Conolly, James Broadfoot and Percival Lord – killed before his eyes in the space of a fortnight. He wrote that in Broadfoot and Lord he had lost 'two of my dearest friends'.[16]

The Emir's forces now turned back towards Nijrow, but Dost himself, with a single attendant, carefully skirted the British camp and headed for Kabul.

Following Parwan, Burnes wrote a detailed letter to Macnaghten on strategy, arguing that, in the face of growing resistance across Afghanistan, the British force was not strong enough to occupy the entire country, and its isolated garrisons might find themselves cut off. As a matter of survival, the British should now concentrate their forces. Macnaghten received Burnes' letter and had read it with George Lawrence just before they went out together for the evening ride. Macnaghten was indignant. On his ride, he was astonished to be approached by Dost Mohammed, who surrendered.

Burnes was right. The Army of the Indus was too small to occupy Afghanistan, and its dispersed contingents were in grave danger. Burnes argued this in two further memoranda to Macnaghten at four-month intervals. The concomitant of Burnes' analysis was that the British Army had not only to concentrate, but then to leave the country. Burnes said so privately and often, but not to Macnaghten as he knew it would be summarily rejected. Rather, he waited for Macnaghten's planned departure.

Dost was well treated in captivity, including by Macnaghten, who underwent a complete change of heart on meeting the Emir. Dost's first visitor, naturally, was Burnes, who wrote to Davie:

> My interview with Dost Mohammed was very interesting and very affectionate. He taunted me with nothing, said I was his best friend, and that he had come in on a letter I had written to him. This I disbelieve, for we followed him from house to house, and he was obliged to surrender. On that letter, however, I hope I shall have got for him a stipend of two lakhs of rupees instead of one. On our parting, I gave him an Arab horse, and what think you he gave me? His own, and only sword, and which is stained with blood.[17]

Dr Atkinson attended the Emir and liked him, noting 'the remarkable self-possession he displayed under circumstances certainly embarrassing'. Atkinson reckoned that Dost tricked Burnes, and that 'the sword presented by Burnes was of a superior description, while that presented by the Ameer was only worth a few rupees'. Dost told Burnes that he hoped they could be good friends again.[18]

One of Dost's wives had remained in Kabul, and Lady Macnaghten provided her with various feminine desirables and took her to stay with Dost. The Emir gave Macnaghten a remarkable bit of advice. It would be better for Afghanistan, he said, if the British took the government into their own hands rather than let Shuja decide internal policy. He also warned that many of Shuja's courtiers, growing fat on British gold, were at the same time plotting against the British.[19]

On 13 November 1840 Burnes wrote: 'The surrender of Dost Mohammed has made the country as tranquil as Vesuvius after an eruption. How long it will continue it is impossible to say.'[20] Alex felt they were sitting on an active volcano.

For a while, things went well. The very day Dost had surrendered Kabul, General Nott reoccupied Kelat unopposed. Two weeks later Colonel Marshall launched a surprise attack on the mountain camp of young Nassir Khan at Kotrah, massacring his followers and capturing or killing seventeen chiefs. Nassir, to whom Burnes once gave a music-box, fled almost alone into the hills. Communications through the Bolan pass now seemed secure. On 12 November 1840 Dost was escorted from Kabul to exile in India, leaving with Cotton, who this time succeeded in getting out of Afghanistan. Macnaghten and Shuja left for another winter in Jalalabad, leaving Burnes again in charge in Kabul.

CHAPTER THIRTY-FOUR

## Discontent

In the winter of 1840 Captain Henry Palmer, Persian interpreter to Cotton and friend of Burnes, was offered the chance to transfer to the new commander designate and remain in Kabul. Palmer refused:

> 'Why then won't you stay with General Elphinstone, and not give up 900 Rupees a month by returning to your regiment as a captain on 450?' 'Because, Sir' I replied 'it is impossible that the present arrangement of four European Officers to command and officer regiments of Afghans from 800 to 1,000 strong, can last more than a few months before every European officer is murdered.'[1]

Many officers with units returning to India were offered substantial financial inducements to transfer to the Shah's forces, with British official approval, and all refused. Morale was already terrible: 'the regret of those who were destined to remain behind in Afghanistan was [. . .] unanimous.'[2]

Shahamat Ali (a munshi with Wade, and a former classmate of Mohan Lal) had a feel for the discontents of Kabul and the currents of Afghan society. In his short time in Kabul, he identified that Shuja's autocratic manner was alienating the major chiefs whose support was vital to the British strategy. He also noted a dangerous phenomenon – the ridicule of Shuja by rhyming couplet.

These mocking little verses may be considered the social media of their day – a casual form of social communication, turned to awaken political consciousness. The Afghan historian Ghulam[3] has preserved one of these couplets for us. The verse on Shuja's coinage was:

> Coin struck in silver and gold brighter than the moon and sun.
> Light of the Eye, Pearl of Pearls, Shah Shuja al-Mulk Shah.

which was passed around the wits of Kabul as:

The Armenian Shah Shuja, the light of the eye of Lord Burnes,
The dust of the foot of the Company, put his stamp on silver and gold.[4]

The two versions have elements of wordplay in the Persian which cannot be captured in translation. 'Armenian' probably meant no more than Christian. 'Light of the eye' is a standard phrase in Persian love poetry, often translated in English as 'apple of the eye'. The homosexual imputation is deliberate. Such couplets, portraying Shuja as a puppet, Christian and catamite to the British, were an effective weapon in public opinion. To the Afghans it was Sikunder Burnes, not Keane or Macnaghten, who was the personification of the occupation. Burnes had indeed earned a great name; but it was becoming despised.

The acknowledged attributes of kingship in Islamic states were the issuing of coins and the recital of prayers in the mosque on Friday in the king's name. Burnes was concerned to learn that in the mosques of Kabul, prayers were not said in the name of Shuja. He despatched Lal to call on the religious authorities, who was met with brazen defiance: he was told that Shuja was brought in by the British and a mere nominal king; it would be unlawful to say prayers in Shuja's name.[5] Burnes decided not to seek a religious confrontation.

In January, Dennie was ordered to vacate the Brigadier's warm quarters in the Bala Hissar and return to his mud hut in the snows of the cantonments, as Shuja sought to recover more of palace grounds. Burnes was furious.[6] It is worth noting that officers were charged rent by the Company for their accommodation. Half of the surviving 13th Foot were that winter declared medically unfit through cold-related illness – often frostbite – by Dr Brydon, who was himself reprimanded for excessive leniency to the troops.

Burnes was interfering to an increasing degree in Kabul's administration, exercising his responsibility as Resident just as British Residents behaved toward their puppet princes throughout India. The situation led him into continual conflict with Mullah Shukhr. Lal believed that Shukhr was putting out the story that Shuja was only waiting for his family to return from Ludhiana before attacking the British. In Kohistan, Shuja was again playing all sides, conniving with Ghulam Khan to levy and steal excess taxes, while telling local chiefs that Ghulam's oppressions were the fault of the British. Almost all the Afghan nobility were contriving to have a foot in every camp, including Shuja.

The British and Shuja had very different ideas about how to govern. We are able to look at one particular argument, over the price of food in Kabul. Burnes wrote to Macnaghten:

## Discontent 341

> In the last winter, [Shuja's] notions of Political economy led him to seize all the granaries around Cabool [...] from which he drew forth the grain, and had it exposed for sale in the Bazaar [...] at a price fixed by himself [...] The next freak of this minister was to reduce the number of Butchers' shops [...] and to compel these to sell at his own price, thereby ensuring a monopoly of meat to a few, and injuring many. For days the loudest complaints were uttered, till free trade was at last established. As I write, the shops in which flour is sold are now shut, the minister having turned his views from meat to bread [...][7]

Compare this to the same events reported by Shuja's chronicler Mohammad Hussan Herati:

> if the price of wheat was fixed at a particular rate, any trader who flouted the rules would be punished by Mullah Shakur in his role as assistant governor of Kabul – but whenever Alexander Burnes sent his chaprasi to protest that the trader in question was under his protection, the offender would be released [...] Burnes and Macnaghten did not like to be contradicted in any way [...] and day by day they grew more hostile to the Mullah.[8]

This is ideological conflict. For Scottish intellectuals of Burnes' era, belief in the economic doctrines of Adam Smith, and in the science of political economy, was fundamental. The market would operate most efficiently, and reach the best balance of supply and price, if left well alone. Mullah Shukhr had attempted to force a reduction in bread prices, and in consequence the traders had simply shut up shop and caused a bread crisis. But the British military presence had led to a steep rise in food prices: farmers and grain merchants had started to benefit, but the urban poor to suffer serious hardship. Burnes was not insensible – he was distributing 1,000 free loaves daily to crowds around his house.[9] But he could not see past free market doctrine in a severely distorted market, and was writing just when when free trade was about to become the official doctrine of the British Empire.

Mullah Shukhr and Mohammad Hussain Herati were coming from the opposite direction. For them, one of the prime functions of paternalistic kingship was to regulate trade and supply; the balance between producers and consumers should not be left to chance. They were baffled by Burnes' insistence that Shuja be prevented from exercising what was in their view an essential kingly activity. It appeared a deliberate attempt to denigrate Shuja's position.

We can sympathise more fully with Burnes in another complaint:

> [Shukhr] conceived it would please His Majesty to adorn the royal Gardens [...] long neglected, a measure most laudable and [...] highly popular, but this was to be done *gratis*, and by conscription [...] The poor peasantry were dragged in [...] at seed time, when their lands required their care, and

compelled to labor without any reward. Discontent rose to such a height that I sent [...] plainly told [the minister] that he was disgracing his King and himself; and that I would no longer stand silent [...] unless he at least gave the poor wretches bread.

Burnes started to acquire a reputation for arrogance. Lal complained that he would keep even senior Afghan nobles waiting for hours, and then might send them away. Doubtless Burnes was busy, and also frustrated by his lack of executive authority to help petitioners. But his rudeness was uncharacteristic, and evidence of personality changes that were increasingly apparent.

One accusation is ubiquitous. 'Alexander Burnes seems to have been one of the leaders in lechery.'[10] Yet the evidence is scanty. Unlike many other British officers, there is nothing connecting Burnes with a named Afghan woman or incident. I find Lal's explanation that Burnes' sexual needs were catered for by Kashmiri women brought along for the purpose much more convincing than if Lal had declared Burnes a paragon of chastity.

Kashmir had long been famed for sexual pleasure and the beauty of its females. The people of Kashmir had a legend of two good angels, Harat and Marat, who had been sent by Allah to reform mankind, but been seduced from their purpose by the irresistible Kashmiri girls. We have noted Ranjit Singh displaying his Kashmiri women to William Osborne; a generation earlier Mountstuart Elphinstone had been regaled by Musa Khan Alikozai with praises of the 'licentious pleasures' of Kashmir.[11] Victor Jacquemont observed in Kashmir *'toutes les petites filles qui promettent de devenir jolies sont vendues a huit ans, et exportee dans le Penjab at dans l'Inde. Elles sont vendues, par leurs parents [...] Il se presente chaque jour aux portes de mon jardin des bandes innombrables de filles.'*[12] No fewer than twenty-three of those contemporaries of Burnes documented in Gray and Garrett's *European Adventurers* are listed as having Kashmiri wives or concubines. Burnes' Kashmiri women are very credible.

After the Kabul force met disaster, Shuja sent a self-justificatory letter to Auckland claiming that all the occupation's mistakes had been against his advice, and criticising British officers at length. Here Shuja includes Burnes for outraging Afghans over women, but again does not give detail, though he does in relation to others.[13]

The British government in India was crippled by the costs of the occupation. Meantime, the civil arm continued to implement the commercial policy on which Burnes had worked so hard. The port facilities at Karachi were substantially improved and a regular steamship service opened on the Indus, while all transit fees were abolished. Burnes' trade fair on the Indus was established at Sukkur in January 1841, and did show promise in attracting merchants from the Lohani migration. The Company fondly anticipated strong tea sales to Central Asia, and a supply of raw wool for export to Britain.[14]

But it was far from convinced that the maintenance of Shuja was necessary for trade, and the Secret Committee had an acutely accurate perception of the situation in Afghanistan. On 31 December 1840 John Stuart Mill wrote to Auckland that the current system was impossible. Either the British must withdraw from Afghanistan or greatly increase their occupying force. Anything else was to invite disaster. Two days later he sent a follow-up to say that news just received of the surrender of Dost Mohammed in no way changed this opinion.[15]

Charles Masson had been arrested when he had arrived at Quetta bearing messages from the Kelatis. Historians have been unanimous in condemning his arrest as unjust. I suspect they are wrong. Durand confirms that Captain Bean, political officer at Quetta, suspected Masson of being a Russian agent, based on a report from James Outram that he had intercepted messages from an anonymous Russian agent in Kelat, together with 'incriminating reports' about Masson which Bean had received from Loveday. These included information that Masson was translating for the Kelati forces the despatches captured from British qasids transiting the Bolan pass.[16] Bean did not believe Masson that he had been released with messages while Loveday was detained. On 10 October 1840 Macnaghten confirmed Masson's arrest.[17]

Burnes, of course, was with Macnaghten in Kabul. Macnaghten would have consulted him about Masson's arrest. But we also know that this was just after the penny had dropped with Burnes, as he had sent Lord proof that Masson had been deceiving them in Kabul about his knowledge of Witkiewicz' identity. Burnes had also received further apparently conclusive information from Jabbar Khan, who now told him that during the negotiations in Kabul, Masson had been holding his own communications with the Emir, which had helped thwart British efforts.[18]

After the war Loveday, Macnaghten, Lord and Burnes were all dead. Official record is there none.

> A curious feature concerning Masson's detention and connection with Loveday and the Kelat insurrection is that, nowhere is it mentioned, neither in the official records, nor books concerning Baluchistan at this period.[19]

Loveday's reports to Bean, along with the latter's account of the reason for detention and the official correspondence where Macnaghten sanctioned the detention, had all disappeared from the files before 1929. Some quotations from Bean's account appear in the *Asiatic Register* of May 1841, but in the context of a lengthy refutation from Masson. Subsequent correspondence between Mountstuart Elphinstone and David Burnes refers to Leech not believing Masson's story.[20]

Masson stated that Loveday was a psychotic maniac who executed needlessly and set his dogs on people, once killing a man, thus helping spark the war to reinstate Nassir Khan.[21] Yet Loveday had donated a costly bed-covering of his own to shroud the forsaken body of Mehrab Khan;[22] that does not square with Masson's portrayal. Lal states that Masson's account of Loveday does not coincide with what he himself witnessed, nor with accounts of local witnesses.[23] He also says he saw no dog with Loveday.[24]

There is no corroboration that Masson was taken prisoner and released to bear messages. The evidence from Kabul indicates that Bean was right; Masson may have been not only a deserter, but a double-agent and traitor.[25] On 22 April 1845 Mohan Lal in London wrote to John McNeill trying to ascertain whether 'the grateful Masson' had held communications with Nesselrode, Simonicz and Dost Mohammed.

Masson's only biographer, Gordon Whitteridge, rejects the allegations categorically – but all his footnotes on the subject reference only Masson's own account. Sir Gordon was a Foreign Office man educated at Cambridge in the 1930s, and thus congenitally unable to recognise a Russian spy.

General Nott continued to take effective military action against uprisings breaking out around his Kandahar command. Macnaghten had asked for Nott to be replaced, as he found him too outspoken, but Auckland refused. Macnaghten did not need permission to remove Robert Leech on the grounds that his accounts were overdue for expenses incurred when preparing the way for the initial march of the army. Leech was replaced by Henry Rawlinson; Burnes commiserated with his friend. The Burnes, Lord, Leech team was now gone.

Shahzada Timur had been sent as Governor to the Dourani capital, Kandahar, and initially the Douranis were enthusiastic about the return of one of their own. This quickly waned as it became clear that the British had the first say in governing, and the second lay with old exiles from Shuja's Ludhiana days. Timur proved vicious and rapacious. He beheaded three Ghilzai chiefs who came in under truce.[26] The elite of Kandahar did not gain the influence they hoped. They were also much affected by the creation of the janbaz and abolition of their levies and privileges. They began again to plot resistance and by January 1841 Henry Rawlinson was convinced Shuja was conniving with them. Macnaghten dismissed Rawlinson's evidence. Timur was replaced by his brother Sagdar Jang, but the latter's open homosexuality estranged him from the British, particularly as he conducted relationships with young British soldiers. One, alleging that he had been drugged with opium and raped by Sagdar, committed suicide.[27]

The Ghilzais rose against the British construction of a fort at Kelat-i-Ghilzai, a key position between Kandahar and Gazhni. A strong force under Colonel Wymer was sent out from Kandahar and defeated the Ghilzais in a major engagement on 9 May 1841, in which hard fighting lasted all day and evening.

For the Douranis Akhtar Khan was in the field with 6,000 men. On 3 July at Girishk, Akhtar was checked by Captain Woodburn in a fierce battle with no clear victor. In both Wymer's and Woodburn's actions, the artillery was vital to British success. There were almost no British soldiers involved other than officers. The Indian and Afghan forces under British command performed extremely creditably.

The janbaz performed effectively at Khawind on 17 August, when Akhtar Khan was decisively defeated by Major Griffin. Sagdar Jang charged with the janbaz. Considering all the actions of the First Afghan War as a whole, it is not the case that HM regiments or Company European regiments – to be blunt, white troops – fought better for the British than their Indian, Gurkha or Afghan counterparts, despite that being (still) the common portrayal in British histories.

The most important single factor in determining the fate of the British in the field was the presence or absence of artillery. Time and again the use of shells – balls which exploded in the air above their target and scattered deadly fragments over a twenty-yard radius – demoralised the Afghan forces, particularly cavalry. Where artillery was absent, the loss of firepower and range was crucially debilitating to British forces. The Afghan jezzail had twice the range of the standard British musket, and also outranged the Company force's small number of rifles. British military technology was seventy years out of date. One young officer observed:

> It is astonishing at what range the fire from their long heavy jezzails is effective. Our men were continually struck with the Afghan bullets, when we could reach the enemy with nothing under a six-pounder. Our muskets were useless when playing at long bowls. The fact is, our muskets are about as bad specimens of fire-arms as can be manufactured. The triggers are so stiff, that pulling them completely destroys any aim [. . .] and, when the machine does go off, the recoil [. . .] [can] knock a man backwards. Again, the ball is so much smaller than the bore of the barrell that accuracy in its flight, at any considerable distance is impossible. The clumsy flint locks, also, are constantly missing fire.[28]

The musket was not supposed to be individually accurate; its purpose was to pour a volley into the massed ranks of an enemy formation at close quarters. The Afghans had more sense than to fight that way, and there are few examples of engagements in this war in which musketry volleys took substantial effect.

General Nott at Kandahar, despite larger and more persistent resistance to deal with than did the British command at Kabul, was more militarily successful. He ensured that the field forces he sent out were large enough for the purpose and well balanced between infantry, cavalry and artillery, even at the expense of leaving Kandahar itself exposed. By contrast the Kabul command appeared more concerned to keep a large force in cantonments, and the field forces were often neither well balanced nor strong.

Nott viewed the position of the British as entirely false, writing:

> The conduct of the thousand and one politicals in the country has ruined our cause, and bared the throat of every European in this country to the sword and knife of the revengeful Afghan and bloody Belooch, and unless several regiments be quickly sent not a man will be left to note the fate of his comrades.

At the same time and reviewing precisely the same events, Macnaghten wrote:

> These people are perfect children, and must be treated as such. If we put our naughty boy in the corner the rest will be terrified. We have taken their plaything, power, out of the hands of the Douranee chiefs, and they are pouting a good deal in consequence.[29]

Nott was not alone in his presentiment of the annihilation of the British force. On 7 July 1841 Major Hamlet Wade, Sale's senior staff officer and not a fanciful man, despite his first name, noted in his diary his famous premonition:

> Sir Robert Sale inspected the 44th this morning. The colours of the regiment are very ragged, and when they passed in review I was suddenly startled by what I took to be a large funeral procession. What put such a thing in my head I know not, as I was thinking of very different subjects. I cannot help recording this, it made such an impression.

Of course, many such forebodings have been recorded elsewhere with no relevant result, and are thus ignored. Nonetheless Wade's entry has an evocative power and can still cause a frisson. He had a strong subconscious fear about the British position in Afghanistan.

In Herat, Todd was outraged by the conduct of the Herati government in precisely the same ways that I as Envoy was 160 years later by the government of neighbouring Uzbekistan. Here Todd is writing to Macnaghten of Yar Mohammed's use of torture to extract money from wealthy citizens:

> The commonest method being by roasting or boiling or baking over a slow fire. The horrible ingenuities practised on these occasions are too disgusting [. . .] The wretch, writhing in agony, gradually disgorged his wealth and learned before he died that his wives and daughters had been sold to the Turkomans, or divided among the sweepers and doorkeepers of his murderers. Of two

recent victims one was half roasted and then cut into very small pieces, the other parboiled and afterwards baked.[30]

Compare my description of a victim of the Uzbek regime in 2002:

> The victim had died of immersion in boiling liquid. It was immersion rather than splashing because there was a clear tidemark around the upper torso and upper arms, with 100 per cent scalding underneath. Before he was boiled to death, his fingernails had been ripped out and he had been severely beaten around the face. Reading the dispassionate language of the pathology report, I was struck with a cold horror.[31]

Todd was an active Christian[32] and his conscience could not allow him to carry out his instruction to support Yar Mahommed. He was also aware that the vizier and Kamran were progressing discussions with Persia over an anti-British alliance, and encouraging Douranis to rise in Kandahar. On instructions from Auckland, Todd cut the massive payments being handed over to the vizier, and in consequence was expelled from Herat on 9 February 1841. He was blamed by Macnaghten and Auckland for the breakdown in relations, and suffered the devastating blow of being ignominiously dismissed from the Political Department.

Burnes was open in his warm support for Todd – something that increased Auckland's resentment of Burnes. Perhaps Alex was pricked by his failure to follow his conscience over Dost Mohammed's deposition.

In Herat Todd had opened correspondence with the Khan of Khiva, who had sent a representative to meet him. Under direct military threat from Russia, a British alliance held some attractions for the Khan. He had also heard that the British were lavishing much money on the rulers of Herat. Lieutenant Abbott was despatched by Todd to Khiva, where he was informed smilingly by the Khan that the last two supposed Englishmen had been executed as Russian spies.[33] This spread of British activity all seemed to Yar Mohammed in Herat to encircle him. He was in correspondence with the Emir of Bokhara, warning him of British ambitions; this was a factor in Nasrullah's treatment of Stoddart.

At Kelat-i-Ghilzai the British were building a fort to command this key point between Kandahar and Ghazni. The surrounding tribes were outraged and continually harassed the occupiers. The political officer in charge, Lieutenant Lynch, was deemed to have unnecessarily exacerbated the situation when he directed a force to reduce a local fort, which became a bloody affair. Lynch's action in marrying the daughter of a local chief increased hostility. Burnes investigated and concluded Lynch had behaved unwisely but not badly, in difficult circumstances. Burnes' letter to him was kindly:

'I am [...] altogether opposed to any fighting in this country, and I consider that we shall never settle Afghanistan at the point of a bayonet [...] As regards the Ghilzyes, immense allowance ought to be made for them; they were till within three generations the Kings of Afghanistan': of Lynch's attack on the fort, Burnes rebuked mildly, '[H]ad I been by, I would have said 'Build Khelat-i-Ghilzye, and pardon all kinds of insolence, for those who win may laugh.'[34] Lynch was dismissed by Auckland anyway.

Burnes and Auckland were unaware that Lynch had deliberately provoked the violence. On 27 December 1840 Lynch had written to Macnaghten:

> I hope you will now approve of my adopting a new system, for the conciliatory one will not work in the Tokey land for the future. We can easily get themselves to commit themselves, and in lieu of their present pay give them a few more rounds of canister from Anderson's guns.[35]

Eldred Pottinger, now political officer at Charikar, found the whole population of Kohistan hostile; unsurprising following Burnes' and Sale's depredations the previous autumn. In May 1841 he reported alarmedly to Macnaghten, suggesting that his single Gurkha regiment and one troop of artillery was an inadequate garrison. Macnaghten dismissed his report as due to inexperience. Eldred also identified the centralising efforts of the new wazir, Usman Khan, as part of the problem. Usman had sacked the Governor and given the position to his own twelve-year-old son.[36]

The notional regime in Kabul was the Company's longstanding 'subsidiary alliance' system, where a client ruler paid the Company a subsidy to cover the costs of the Company troops in his dominions 'protecting' him from internal and external enemies, and from any thoughts of his own. But Burnes stated the most essential point – bereft of the revenues of Peshawar, Kashmir and Herat, Shuja's administration never raised more than £220,000 annually – about 6 per cent of the costs of occupation.

The Afghan monarchy placated its powerful nobles in a number of ways, the most important the grant of land revenues in return for the feudal obligation to provide armed horsemen for military service. In fact the quality of mounts, equipment and personnel given to the crown had steadily declined and the annual muster had become farcical, while the rents the nobles received remained valuable. Under the British occupation Captain R S Trevor was put in command of the feudal horse, totalling some 7,000 men, and explained it this way:

> We must not look on the Irregular Cavalry merely as a military body, in that light 3 regiments may annihilate it tomorrow, but as an instrument which enables H.M.'s principal subjects to appropriate the greater part of his revenues

without making any return [. . .] its destruction would certainly be considered an invasion of private property.³⁷

The British administrators wished to replace the feudal levies with two bodies of regular cavalry, the janbaz and the hazirbaz, and gradually abolish the payments to the nobility for it. This struck directly at both the financial and political interests of the tribal chiefs. A king with his own independent military could much more effectively impose his views on his nobles.

Even where traditional forms of government were retained, the imbalance brought by British aid to the royal authority caused problems. Revenue had always been raised by quartering troops on a district to extract it. The system had been tempered by the ability of tribes to resist if demands became too onerous. With British troops to squash any rebellions, the system was out of balance, as Burnes saw: 'Such a system must clearly alienate all the people of this country from Shah Shoojah and from us, and the force we give him ensures what, if left to himself, he could not otherwise command.'³⁸

But the real problem was simply lack of revenue. Only about 8 per cent of the land area was cultivable, and raising taxes from nomadic pastoralists was difficult.³⁹ Without Peshawar, Kashmir and Herat – or the regular plunder of Indian wealth on which the system of Ahmed Shah Dourani had depended⁴⁰ – it could not be a viable economy. On 1 April 1841 Alexander wrote a clear-sighted analysis to his father in Montrose:

> We had no sooner got Dost Mahomed Khan into our power than Herat breaks with us, and the Punjab becomes a scene of strife. Out of both contingencies we might extract good [. . .] we may restore the lost wings of Afghanistan, Herat and Peshawur, to Shah Shoojah, and thus enable him to support himself, free us from the expense of Afghanistan, and what would be better, withdraw our regular army within the Indus, leaving Caubul as an outpost.⁴¹

It must have been galling for Burnes that Macnaghten was now arguing strenuously with Auckland that Herat and Peshawar should be annexed to Kabul. Macnaghten's resistance to Kabul recovering Peshawar had caused the war in the first place. Too late, he proposed what Burnes had argued all along, that Kabul's territory needed to be expanded into a viable buffer state.

Auckland suggested that Peshawar might be returned to Muslim rule but as a British Protectorate. The civil war in the Punjab following the death of Ranjit Singh had already led the British to take military control. On 26 May 1841 Auckland wrote to London:

> It is not clear to me that we should hastily declare that whatever we hold, we hold strictly in trust for Maharaja Sher Singh and more particularly on the side of Peshawar [. . .] if the Sikh authority should be dissolved and expelled,

its restoration is not to be regarded as a thing practicable [...] there must I presume be Sikh or there must be Mahomedan supremacy and the latter I conceive must prevail. But it must do so under our care and management [...][42]

On 2 April 1841 Burnes wrote to George Jacob about his loyal Arab guards, indicating Jacob was in touch with their families. Rubica had joined one of Shuja's newly raised bodies, the Afghan Pioneer Corps, on Rs50 a month, but still attended Burnes. Abdullah remained in Burnes' service, and had a new Kabul wife, although Burnes was pleased he was still sending money back to his first family in India. Alex had been trying to persuade them to return to India, but they refused to leave him.[43]

On 19 April 1841, Burnes made his final attempt at influencing policy, in another detailed memorandum, 'Notes on Consolidating Afghanistan'.[44] He again listed the problems of the occupation, particularly regarding unjust taxation and the billeting of troops on villagers. But he also had a new target – the network of bellicose British political officers:

> wherever our political officers are, collision forthwith follows. A native temporizes, a European officer fights; we are thus on the high road to denationalize Affghanistan instead of contributing to its stability as a kingdom; we shall subvert all its institutions, and not succeed in fixing our own in their stead [...] we shall have alienated a people who were neutral [...] and have to meet them as enemies.

Again Macnaghten annotated Burnes' memorandum, but his comments, though still defensive, are markedly less pugnacious than the previous year. To the above he merely noted:

> I shall hope that a few years of tact and patience would make this a very respectable kingdom. The people will naturally appreciate the comfort of justice and quiet after a little experience. W.M.

Burnes suggested that Shuja be enjoined to make a more public display of piety and attachment to Islam, and take care to show even-handedness in matters of justice between his subjects and the foreigners. Alex argued that the enmity of the people was, failing fundamental reform of the administration and revenue, something the British would have to accept and guard against. His memorandum is not convincing as a solution to the problems of the occupation, which in truth could never have been made acceptable.

Many others were trying to awaken Macnaghten to the perilous situation, chief among them Henry Rawlinson who wrote several detailed analyses of the continuing uprisings among Dourani tribes. In reply, on 13 June 1841

Macnaghten admonished Rawlinson for 'your taking an unwarrantably gloomy view of our position [. . .] We have enough of difficulties and enough of croakers without adding to the number needlessly.' Again on 2 August he urged Rawlinson to 'regard matters a little more couleur de rose'.[45]

Having sacked Leech, Macnaghten was still more dissatisfied with Rawlinson and, furious that Nott distrusted and disparaged the janbaz, was still trying to get Auckland to remove Nott. On 5 September Macnaghten wrote to Rawlinson that Auckland had agreed to remove Nott: this was overtaken by events.

Burnes to his friends put on a face of cheerful resignation. He wrote to his brother Adam, 'I am now a highly paid idler having no less than 3500 rupees a month, as Resident at Caubul, and being, as the lawyers call it, only counsel, and that a dumb one too – by which I mean that I give out paper opinions, but do not work them out.' He told Adam that the British Army should annex Peshawar and Herat to Kabul by conquest, and then withdraw to the Indus, which should be the permanent frontier of British India. He concluded, 'all this common sense is however too simple for the great man [Auckland]'. Inside, Burnes was eaten by rancour, hinting to Adam that he knew dark secrets and that the war had been undertaken for the personal interests of the decision-makers. He considered himself, however, ethically bound not to turn whistleblower:

> war has the double scourge of being hateful in itself, and ruinous in its consequences. I am often half disposed [. . .] to write on the political events which brought us here, and if I cannot print in my life, leave my executors to do it, and thus furnish food for reflection on the wisdom of the world [. . .] but again, while a Government employee, I look on any breaches of confidence as dishonest, and I therefore hold my pen, but some day or other [. . .] I shall record a wrinkle or two as to our advance here, which will make politicians stare, and show that there are other than state secrets. In fact, Adam, I have seen so much in my short life, that what you will not credit is in fact true, that men look alone to their own advancement, and not to their government.[46]

Sadly his private papers have vanished.

Burnes now stood to become a very wealthy man – his annual income as Resident in Kabul was over £4,000, higher than many in the aristocracy, and before him was the prospect of taking over as Envoy from Macnaghten, with a salary three times greater. He assured his family he lived well; he used part of his income to maintain his popularity with the garrison; this reflected a love of socialising. He had breakfast set for eight every morning for any officer who wished to drop in – and many usually did – and 'discuss a rare Scotch breakfast of smoked fish, salmon grills, devils and jellies'. Burnes continually plays up his Scottish identity, and the image of him in Kabul offering Arbroath smokies to the officers is irresistible.

He gave a weekly dinner party. In recounting the treats he imported for his guests, he refers proudly to his work on opening up the Indus to British goods, and reducing the effect of transport costs, tolls and duties:

> I can place before my friends at one-third in excess of the Bombay price my champagne, hock, madeira, sherry, port, claret, sauterne, not forgetting a glass of curacao and maraschino, and the hermetically sealed salmon and hotch-potch (veritable hotch-potch, all the way frae Aberdeen), for deuced good it is, the peas as big as if they had been soaked for bristling.

On quiet evenings he would dine with his brother Charlie and his housemate and assistant, William Broadfoot, whose brother James had died before Alex's eyes at Parwan. At thirty-one William was a formidable Orcadian who had raised a regiment of Afghan pioneers, now under command of another brother, George. William was described as: 'Like a father to these men, in attention to their real wants, while he exacted from them the most implicit obedience to his orders, and punished their faults with a severity which many would have deemed ferocious.'[47] Broadfoot's sappers remained loyal to the British.

After dinner William, Charlie and Alex would drink port and talk on. Burnes always kept an eye on events in the *Montrose Review* and noticed the progress of James Duke, another Montrose Freemason and friend of Joseph Hume, who had become Liberal MP for Boston and now an alderman of London, which meant he would eventually be Lord Mayor. He told Charlie, 'I am glad of it, for he is a good fellow and deserves his prosperity.' That summer Britain was in the middle of an election campaign. Palmerston, campaigning in Tiverton, gloried in the successful invasion:

> We carried our armies into the centre of Afghanistan, and [. . .] rendered secure to us that vast empire which we possess in India, and the importance of which it is hardly possible to over-rate [. . .] We brought within British influence, in one campaign, a vast extent of country larger than France, almost as big as half of Europe.[48]

Despite such bombast, he was defeated and Sir Robert Peel formed a Tory adminstration.

Burnes spent a great deal of time reading. He much enjoyed Tacitus, describing him as timeless wisdom for governance. In summer 1841 he was also reading Byron, Guizot, Horace Walpole and Sidney Smith. His conscience continued to trouble him – he worried he had come to Kabul for the wrong reasons. He wrote to an old Montrose friend: 'That demon, ambition, makes us climb the high hill, as my great relative Burns said "Not for the laudable anxiety of viewing an extended landscape, but rather for the pride of looking down at our fellows." Yet I do feel also [. . .] that I am working for my country's good [. . .]"[49]

Alex and Charlie had another time-consuming occupation, started in summer 1841, assisted by another resident of the house, Pandit Gaurishankar, Alex's confidential clerk and book-keeper. Burnes was still furious at the editing of his despatches for publication by government. As it became plain how disastrous the war was, it was galling to be falsely portrayed as its author. Alex and Charlie therefore painstakingly wrote out full copies of hundreds of Burnes' despatches of 1836 to 1838, and sent batches back with every post to James in Bombay, and copies to be kept by his agents Forbes & Co. Alex also found time to write his book 'Cabool' and send it to John Murray.

Burnes' female Kashmirian companions had now been with him over four years, so there may have been tenderness or at least familiarity in the relationship. Lal specifies that there were women for Burnes, Charlie, Leech and Burnes' 'assistants' – so presumably at least Broadfoot. There were at least three living in the house. I find it reasonable to connect the professional musicians employed by Mohan Lal who lived two doors away and envisage nautch dancing. Whether the women ever dined with the men we do not know. There is an account of Allard and Ventura trying it with their Kashmiri wives, who found it too culturally uncomfortable. After four years there could have been children, but Lal does not refer to Burnes having a specific 'wife'.[50]

The new military commander at Kabul, General William Keith Elphinstone, is always described as a veteran of Waterloo. That is true, strictly speaking. But he spent the battle as a French prisoner, having been captured the evening before.[51] He told the US Navy captain Charles Samuel Stewart that he had been interrogated by Napoleon in person.

After years on the half-pay of a colonel and the declining income of his bleak Carstairs estates, Elphinstone had muddled his way into substantial debt, and had persuaded his friend Lord Raglan, Military Secretary at the War Office, to appoint him to India purely to make money. Raglan bears much of the blame for the later Charge of the Light Brigade. His appointment of Elphinstone was a still more costly error. Hobhouse tried to block it but Wellington insisted.[52] The Elphinstones had been central to the British administration for four generations, and the flagship of the Company fleet was the *Elphinstone Castle*. If a senior Elphinstone wanted something from India, it was in the natural order of things for it to be granted.

But Elphinstone's operational deployment was in Auckland' hands, and he had been placed in charge of the garrison at Meerut, an important station and key post for reinforcing Afghanistan. On 6 February 1840 Elphinstone called on Emily Eden en route to see Auckland. Elphinstone knew the Edens socially and was indignant that Auckland was his superior: 'It seems odd that I have never seen A. since we were shooting grouse together, and now I had to ask for an audience and for employment.' Emily Eden was appalled at his physical appearance. She 'never made out it was the same man till a sudden recollection came over me a week ago. He is in a shocking state of gout, poor man! – one arm in a sling and very lame [. . .]'[53]

Auckland appointed Elphinstone to Kabul after a personal interview and was aware of his physical disability. Auckland was concerned at the possibility of two other fronts opening, against the Sikhs in the Punjab and the Russians in the north. His appointment of the invalid Elphinstone in these circumstances is incomprehensible.[54]

Due to his continued battles with authority, in January 1841 Colonel Dennie was deprived of his brigade command and returned to command the 13th Foot. Colonel Shelton was appointed Brigadier, and started from India to Kabul. Thus the British garrison lost an extremely able second in command, in favour of a numbskull.

CHAPTER THIRTY-FIVE

## Dissent and Dysfunction

The spark that launched the revolt of the eastern Ghilzais was the reduction by Rs40,000 of their subsidy for keeping open the passes into Kabul. They had done this with efficiency. There were four staging posts over the Khoord Kabul route kept supplied with provisions and horses for the British; they policed casual banditry and cleared the paths in bad weather. The arbitrary reduction in the allowance was seen as bad faith. The practice of transit subsidy in the passes dated back at least to 350 BC, and is detailed by both Arrian and Strabo. Macnaghten claimed the chiefs 'acquiesced in the justice of the reduction'.[1] That was downright delusional.

Also cut were the sums paid to chiefs for provision of feudal cavalry. Here the cut was even larger: Rs300,000. This caused great resentment.

A rebalancing of the Afghan state to increase central authority was necessary after bloody anarchy, and Dost Mohammed had been engaged on just this. It was resentment of his centralising efforts that led many to desert him for Shuja. Reforms which from the Emir caused resentment were never going to be acceptable from infidels.

As British India went through its conquest cycles, the frequent wars had always been expensive. But they had paid off with revenues bringing a return on the investment. Afghanistan was a dead loss – there was no prospect even in the medium term of Afghanistan becoming profitable. The Secret Committee in London at the end of 1840 had suggested to Auckland that he consider pulling out. Auckland argued for more time time, and that expenditure could be reduced.

Who ordered the subsidy cut is disputed. Durand blames Burnes.[2] The cuts were supported by Burnes' ally, the wazir Usman Khan, who Afghan sources claim was playing a double game to provoke resistance.[3] Eldred Pottinger remonstrated with Macnaghten, who replied that 'He could not help the reduction, his orders were peremptory,'[4] and Macnaghten sent a report to Calcutta that 'the necessities of His Majesty [Shuja] and the frequent prohibitions I had received against further reliance on the resources of the British Government appeared to admit of no alternative'.[5] Calcutta had cut Macnaghten's budget, and he had decided the cuts should fall on payments to the chiefs rather than on the central expenditure of the Shah. Macnaghten never mentioned Burnes in this context and neither did Eldred Pottinger or George Lawrence.[6]

Macnaghten was cutting the wrong things. The Ghilzai subsidy reduction of £4,000 was a third of Macnaghten's annual salary, and a fraction of the money paid to maintain Shuja's zenana. Total annual salaries of the thirty-two British political officers in Afghanistan were £53,120. Payments of £200,000 had been made, fruitlessly, to Yar Mohammed in Herat. Mohan Lal was given the thankless task of trying to talk round the Ghilzai chiefs. They received him politely and listened carefully, then returned home and closed the passes.[7] Shuja despatched Hamza Khan, a Ghilzai noble, to placate the rebels. Hamza had himself lost money by the cut, and he simply stirred up resistance. On 1 September Usman Khan presented key nobles in Kabul with documents detailing the cuts and a new pledge of allegiance to Shuja. They refused to sign.[8]

Macnaghten now heard he was to be Governor of Bombay. He would occupy the beautiful mansion of Sans Pareil, become an extremely wealthy man, and he and his wife would rise a social level. In future he would be accepted in great homes not as a useful functionary but as a near equal.

On 8 September 1841, in reaction to this news, Burnes wrote bitterly in his journal:

> I have no responsibility, and why should I work, yet it is clear that if I had carried on a correspondence with Lord Auckland as he wished, I must have injured Macnaghten [. . .] he says he may go through Punjaub to settle affairs there. Why he has mismanaged all affairs [. . .] yet Sir William is Governor of Bombay [. . .] so I must change my standard of greatness and consider myself in total error.[9]

Out of misplaced loyalty, Burnes had suppressed his opinions about the conduct of the occupation, telling them only to his closest circle. He worried that he had damaged himself through association with failed policies by not telling influential friends his true views:

> I question myself how far I am right in avoiding correspondence with Mr Elphinstone, Lord Lansdowne, and all my numerous friends in England, or even with Lord Auckland; yet I believe I am acting an honest part to Macnaghten, and to Government, and yet I fear neither the one nor the other thank me.[10]

Burnes was excited to be rid of his tiresome boss. On 1 October he wrote home:

> Supreme at last – You have of course heard that Macnaghten is to be Governor of Bombay: I fear, however, that I shall be confirmed as Resident, and not as Envoy, which is a bore; but as long as I have power, and drive the coach, I do not much care. I hope I have prepared myself for the charge by hard study, and a knowledge of the country.[11]

There was potentially a huge difference – Macnaghten as Envoy had the colossal salary of £11,000, while Burnes as Resident earned the still very substantial £4,200. Envoys in theory had more discretion, being plenipotentiary – they did not have to refer agreements back for approval. But in practice, the difference was not great.

The *Bombay Times* under Buist thundered against the occupation, influencing opinion in India and London. However, James would not allow Buist to publish Alexander's copied despatches, to the editor's frustration. Alexander was not a whistleblower and said publication 'would be neither useful nor agreeable to him'. Buist in the *Bombay Times* of 9 October 1841 alluded to the correspondence but stated he was precluded from publication. Burnes' true opinions were not public before his death.

On 3 October 1841 at Quetta, a peace treaty was signed with Nassir Khan. The British finally recognised him as Khan of Kelat and agreed to restore almost all his territories. However he was to be nominally tributary to Shah Shuja, and to host a subsidiary force, while the British were to control his foreign relations and establish a Resident at Kelat. To cement the deal the British handed over their former puppet Nawaz Khan, to be gruesomely murdered.

Alex and William were joined on 7 October by Captain George Broadfoot, William's elder brother, now in charge of Broadfoot's sappers. They sat up debating and drinking, until 'near daylight'.[12] George had been in the city smithies that day, overseeing the manufacture of tools; he was perturbed to find all furnaces engaged in arms manufacture, but Alex assured him this was a normal preparation for the annual Lohani migration. They argued policy: George thought more stringent military action was needed, while Alex thought resistance could be discouraged with a display of confidence. George believed Burnes thought him a 'military pedant'.

Burnes loudly denounced the retrenchments which had caused the Ghilzai revolt, and said he had not been consulted, but believed the rising 'a tempest in a teapot'. George Broadfoot thought it much more dangerous, and believed Burnes was 'much shaken as to his own convictions'. Above all, 'Burnes was very anxious for the Envoy's departure, and thought he would easily quell the disturbances which had risen, and reign in his stead.' Broadfoot 'thought both Burnes and Macnaghten grievously wrong [. . .] though Burnes would have managed the bad system better than Macnaghten'.

While they argued, another Scottish officer, Captain Gray, also got no sleep. He was dashing from cover to cover along a goat path high above the Khoord Kabul pass, as jezzail fire splashed around him. Gray with a small sepoy escort was heading back to India, convoyed by 400 Afghans under one of Burnes' contacts, Azim Khan. Surrounded by the Ghilzais, the party was pinned down. A Ghilzai messenger offered Azim Rs3,000 for Gray, dead or alive. Azim had rather waited till nightfall and then broken clear, up into the hills where Gray, dressed as an Afghan, was now scrambling through the Ghilzai pickets in the dark. Gray (who escaped) was carrying papers from Burnes to India, and in the morning he sent back to Burnes a scribbled note, warning that the Ghilzais were out and the passes blocked, and that 'all Afghanistan were determined to [. . .] murder or drive out any Feringhee [. . .] that the whole country, and Cabul itself, was ready to break out [. . .]'

Alex, Charlie, George and William had been joined by Hamlet Wade for breakfast. Burnes read out the message and immediately sent it on to Macnaghten, who took no action.[13]

The British command structure in Afghanistan had become dysfunctional. George Broadfoot had been ordered to take 100 sappers and join a military force under Colonel Monteith to punish the Ghilzai tribes around Tezin, where Gray had just been attacked. The sappers were needed to destroy the Tezin forts. Monteith was then to continue to Jalalabad and quit Afghanistan through the Khyber pass. At Jalalabad he would be joined by Sale and Macnaghten, the force being split to ease supply. Broadfoot requested some basic information on the forts and whether resistance was expected.

Broadfoot visited Monteith, who 'complained bitterly' about his superiors, saying that expedition commanders were kept routinely 'in the dark' and his orders merely told him to proceed to Jalalabad. Broadfoot then called on General Elphinstone himself, who was so ill that getting out of bed required half an hour to recover. Elphinstone said he had no idea about Monteith's expedition, and wrote to Macnaghten requesting intelligence on the enemy's strength, sending Broadfoot with the note. Macnaghten was annoyed, and sent Broadfoot back with a curt reply that Elphinstone 'expected him to turn prophet'. The courtly Elphinstone was 'much pained' by the tone. He made Broadfoot outline the problem again, as he had forgotten everything, then sent him back to Macnaghten.

This time Macnaghten was 'peevish'. He said intelligence was needed from Usman Khan, and Broadfoot must wait. Eventually a messenger from the wazir stated that the forts and rebels were weak and they were about to abandon Tezin. Macnaghten said that Monteith was ordered to Butkhak 'as a demonstration' which would 'terrify the rebels', who would surrender, then Monteith would go on to Jalalabad.

Broadfoot asked what would happen if they did not surrender. Macnaghten said that then Monteith would remain at Butkhak until reinforced by the large punitive expedition which had been sent out to Zurmut. And if Monteith were attacked, asked Broadfoot. Macnaghten now

> became angry, said these were his orders, and the enemy were contemptible, the Eastern Ghilzis most cowardly of Afghans (a foolish notion he and Burnes had); that as for me and my sappers, twenty men with pickaxes were enough; it was a peaceable march to Jalalabad, and all that we were wanted for was to pick stones from under the gun wheels.

Macnaghten said Broadfoot must return to Elphinstone for orders. Broadfoot did so yet again. While there, Elphinstone received a note from Macnaghten 'ordering Monteith's immediate march' but 'declining all responsibility'. Broadfoot noted, 'The General was lost and perplexed, though he entirely agreed in the objections as to the move, yet he did not feel himself at liberty to prevent it.'

Elphinstone told Broadfoot he must decide what men and equipment he needed, but insisted on a written memorandum confirming these were Broadfoot's responsibility. Then suddenly Elphinstone rallied and sent Broadfoot to tell Macnaghten the Monteith expedition was a mistake. Macnaghten now accused Broadfoot of cowardice: 'He lost his temper [. . .] and said if I thought Col. Monteith's movement likely to bring on an attack, I need not go, there were others.'

Broadfoot made a low bow and left. He returned once-more to bed-ridden Elphinstone, who seemed glad to have company:

> He [. . .] told me once more how he had been tormented by Macnaghten [. . .] reduced, to use his own words, from the General to the Lord Lieutenant's head constable. He asked me to see him before I moved, but he said, 'If anything occur [. . .] for God's sake clear the passes quickly, that I may get away. For [. . .] I am unfit for it, done up body and mind, and I have told Lord Auckland so.' This he repeated two or three times, adding that he doubted very much if he ever would see home, even if he did get away.

So de facto control of the army lay firmly with the unqualified civilian Macnaghten. Elphinstone plainly should have been relieved of command by his officers. By early October 1841 the British command structure in Kabul was absolutely dysfunctional.[14]

On the 9th, Monteith marched to Butkhak and encamped with the 35th NI, a squadron of the 5th Cavalry, two guns and Broadfoot's sappers. The Ghilzais launched a determined night attack, which was beaten off by disciplined fire, but the British were now surrounded by a much larger force. Monteith, an excellent soldier, had been sent out with a force woefully inadequate, and the lack of effective action was crucial in giving momentum to the gathering of Ghilzai tribes.[15]

Bob Sale, with the Queen's 13th Light Infantry, came to reinforce Monteith on the 11th, and the next day the force battled its way into the Khoord Kabul. The Ghilzais fired from the heights and retired when pursued; Sale was injured as usual and Dennie took command. The pass was forced with only six killed and thirty-five wounded. Monteith remained in the pass while Sale and the 13th returned to Butkhak. Captain Macgregor joined Monteith as political officer and attempted to negotiate with the Ghilzais.

There followed a week of desultory fighting. On 20 October the litter-bound Sale again advanced into the Khoord Kabul to rejoin Monteith with the 13th Foot plus the 37th NI, a troop of the 2nd Cavalry, the rest of Broadfoot's sappers, the Shah's mountain train of artillery and 200 Jezalchais under Jan Fishan Khan. This amounted to 2,000 men, and there were over 3,000 baggage cattle.

The Ghilzais now agreed a settlement with Macgregor, who had ridden alone into the dark mountains to meet them. The deal was the return of their subsidies for the reopening of the passes. Macnaghten had intended Sale's force to attack rather than treat. But the Ghilzais delivered provisions to Sale as agreed, and on 26 October he moved forward towards Jalalabad with the bulk of the force. He left the 37th NI under Major Griffiths with three mountain guns and a detachment of sappers to hold Tezin and keep the pass clear for Elphinstone and Macnaghten, who were expected shortly with a further small force, to join the return to India.

At Jagdalak the main body of the force pressed on through the intimidating pass without waiting for the rearguard, which suffered heavy losses of men and baggage. Once through, they passed country controlled by the two British-officered Shah's regiments and irregular horse stationed at Gandamak. These Afghan levies, under Captain Burn, held out stubbornly after Sale passed, eventually making a fighting evacuation to Jalalabad. Again, Afghan troops in British service performed admirably. Likewise Sale's communications through the Khyber to India were kept intact by Mackeson with his corps of Yusufzais at Ali Musjid.

Meanwhile Burnes tried to convince Macnaghten that rebellion was brewing in Kabul itself. On 13 October Captain Henry Drummond came to see Burnes with vital intelligence from a Ghilzai friend. A number of senior chiefs in the capital were actively conspiring to enter rebellion in collaboration with the Ghilzais. They had sworn alliance, and fixed their seals to the Koran as a holy bond. Drummond had seen a consignment of powder and shot on its way to fuel the rebellion. His information coincided with intelligence reaching Mohan Lal from other sources. Lal believed he could obtain the Koran containing the seals. Burnes made a full report to Macnaghten – who advised him to do nothing.[16]

What was Macnaghten thinking? Possibly he did not wish to bring matters to a head. Such evidence would necessitate the chiefs' execution, which could itself spark an uprising. The British intelligence effort had become submerged in a welter of untrustworthy informants and forged documents. It was not even known whether widespread evidence that Shuja himself was inciting anti-British resistance was genuine or forged.

Macnaghten, continuing to hope that the rising discontent was a minor squall, had retreated into a psychological bubble that refused to admit bad news. Perhaps he was simply desperate to get out, and away to Sans Pareil. Macnaghten's secretary, Colin Mackenzie, was an unmitigated admirer, yet 'when Mackenzie reported to him that Akbar Khan had arrived at Bamian, he refused to believe it, though the merchant who brought the news had seen him with his own eyes'. Lady Sale wrote that Macnaghten 'is trying to deceive himself into an assurance that the country is in a quiescent state'.[17]

Burnes wrote in his diary on 16 October about the stress of still not knowing if he was to take over:

> Will they venture, after all that has been promised, and all that I have done, to pass over me? I doubt it much [...] I have been asking myself if I am altogether so well fitted for the supreme control here as I am disposed to believe. I sometimes think not, but I have never found myself fail in power when unshackled. On one point I am, however, fully convinced; I am not fit for the second place. In it my irritation would mar all business, and in supersession there is evidently no recourse but England. I wish this doubt were resolved, for anxiety is painful.[18]

On 21 October Macnaghten, believing Sale was about to overcome the Ghilzais, had written a private letter revealing his fondness of Alexander Burnes:

> I do not think I can get away from this before the 1st prox. The storm will speedily subside; but there will be a heaving of the billows for some time, and I should like to see everything right and tight before I quit the helm. Burnes is naturally in an agony of suspense about the succession to me. I think and hope he will get it. I know of no-one so fit for the office [...][19]

Alex did not share his colleagues' contempt for the Afghans and their asymmetrical warfare. On 23 October he wrote, 'I have often wondered at the hatred of the officers towards the Affghans [. . .] they are blamed because they fight at night, when in fact the poor wretches are at any other time unable to cope with disciplined armies; it was the same as the Scotch highlanders pursued a century since.'[20]

The next morning, George Lawrence joined Burnes for breakfast, and 'found him in high spirits at the prospect of [. . .] exercising *at last* the supreme authority in the country'.[21] On 29 October Macnaghten wrote to Bombay that he would be quitting Kabul on 2 November on the way to take up his post.

On 31 October 1831 it was the twentieth anniversary of Alexander's arrival in India as a sixteen- year-old cadet. He was superstitiously convinced that this auspicious day would decide his future. That morning he wrote in his diary:

> Ay! What will this day bring forth? [. . .] It will make or mar me, I suppose. Before the sun sets, I shall know whether I go to Europe, or succeed Macnaghten.[22]

But the sun set with no news. The next day Burnes reflected on all the criticism he had endured over Afghanistan. His last diary entry read, 'I grow very tired of praise, and I suppose I shall get tired of censure in time.'[23]

CHAPTER THIRTY-SIX

## Death in Kabul

Burnes was receiving a steady stream of intelligence about increased activity by resistance groups, and his intelligence operation had penetrated most of these. In a letter to the Rev. Piggott of St Columba's Church in Bombay, he noted, 'although the Afghan is less fierce in his bigotry than other Asiatics, I yet perceive from all their intercepted correspondence when caballing against us that their war cry is "jihad" or religion [. . .]'[1] It says a great deal about Burnes that in this same letter he agrees to Piggott's request to send him some specimens from the Hindu Kush for the Natural History Society.

The Akbarnama of Kashmiri tells what happened next:

> When night fell, all the Khans of Kabul came together
> At the House of Abdullah Khan Achakzai to sit and confer
> Now the remedy is in our hands, said they
> The bow is ready and the arrow is in our hands [. . .]
> Dying by the sword on the battlefield
> Is better than living in the prisons of Firang
> Like the very devil, all evil is the work of Burnes
> Concealed, he goes about whispering to every soul
> So this very night Mohammad Shah Khan Ghilzai must go forth
> With his tribesmen, brave and fierce
> They will ignite the fire of battle
> And throw brimstone upon the flames
> They will sit hidden between the mountain valleys
> And seize all the traders and travellers upon the roads
> So the Shah may send forth his army to make war
> Then, when the army leaves, we will deal with Burnes [. . .][2]

Ten years earlier Arthur Connolly had crossed the lands of the ringleader, Abdullah Khan Achakzai, a notorious character:

> Abdoolah Khan was a man-eater, who was not guided by a single just principle; who [. . .] evidently being altogether without religion, ought to be treated

worse than a kaufir [. . .] Some of his modes of torture were described, which were quite painful to think about. The lightest of his 'tender mercies' were [. . .] laying a man on his back and then placing weights upon his belly until money or life was squeezed out of him [. . .]

Abdoolah Khan [. . .] [had] as bad a name as could well be given to a man; his countrymen said that he must have been suckled by a devil.[3]

Conolly was told many stories of Abdullah's depradations against his own people, ten years before his actions against the British.[4] Still earlier, Mountstuart Elphinstone in 1816 wrote, 'The tribes most addicted to rapine in the West are the Atuchkye branch.'[5]

Abdullah had a particular grudge against Burnes. Firstly, Burnes had supported Kabul tradesmen recovering debts from Abdullah. Then one of his favourite slave-girls had eloped with a British officer. Abdullah appealed to Burnes, who asked the officer to return the girl, which he refused. When Abdullah returned to Burnes' house to follow up, Burnes threw him out angrily.

There are factors which should not be ignored. All sources agree the girl was an escaping slave. Abdullah was a well-attested sadist. When Abdullah first approached Burnes, he was courteously received, and Burnes appears to have tried to help him. It was only after speaking to the officer concerned that Burnes' attitude to Abdullah changed. What had he learnt?

Mohan Lal details three other instances of Afghan noblemen appealing to Burnes for assistance in recovering women from British officers and being rebuffed. Lal's view appears justified that in some cases Burnes was prejudiced in favour of the British officers: 'it was the partiality of Sir Alexander Burnes to his friends which made him obnoxious to dislike, and wounded the feelings of the chiefs, who formerly looked upon him as their old friend.'[6] There is no evidence that British sexual use of Afghan women fuelled popular discontent to the point of uprising. There is evidence it turned certain key Afghan nobles. Burnes was a focus of this discontent because he was seen as condoning and shielding the perpetrators.

George Gleig, as a regimental chaplain, was in a good position to know:

The Afghans are as open to jealousy as Orientals in general, and treating their wives often rudely, the latter could not but be pleased with the attention that the Feringhees showed them [. . .] our young countrymen did not always bear in mind that the domestic habits of any people ought to be sacred in the eyes of strangers. And hence arose, by degrees, distrust, alienation, and hostility, for which it were unfair to deny that there might be some cause.[7]

But there always is a lot of sex in military occupation, and it does not automatically cause an effective uprising. Bengal Surgeon-General Atkinson says there was much procured complicity from Afghan husbands, and doubtless this was sometimes true as well.[8]

Lal is firm that Burnes was not himself active with Afghan women. But Lal's general thesis about British officers became conflated with Masson's accusations, and the entire blame for sexual resentment became attached by historians to a single man. Peter Hopkirk's brilliant *The Great Game* states of Burnes: 'His blatant fraternisation with their womenfolk only served to deepen their hostility towards him.'[9] But there is a dearth of evidence.

The season was exactly right for an uprising. The fighting season started when the agricultural tasks of the year ended. As the ethnographer Louis Dupree put it, November marks the start of 'explosive violence':

> when the agricultural off-season occurs and the nomads are not moving, long hours of boredom result. Young men sitting idle [...] rapidly find suppressed hostilities, sublimated by work during the maximum work cycle, rising to the surface and violence easily erupts. How much better for group survival if this explosive violence can be channeled away from the village or camp, safely directed to outsiders.[10]

The harvest now over, Kohistani villagers had started to drift into Kabul. In May 1841 the British had taken over full control of the state revenues, and Captain Trevor had farmed the taxes. Around Kabul the rights to tax the productive fruit farms had been bought out by Indian banking houses.[11] The resulting squeeze on the farmers had caused much discontent. The people were taxed more heavily, and local dignitaries lost traditional revenues. The Kohistanis hated Burnes and Sale for their destructive campaign the previous year, and were heartened by Sale's discomfiture in the passes. It was Burnes' turn.

The climax to Alexander's story was tightly scripted. On the evening of 1 November 1841 Sir William and Lady Macnaghten had finished packing for the start of their arduous journey the next day, to Bombay and to splendour and riches. And Burnes would finally be in full political control of events in Kabul.

Burnes believed that Shah Shuja's only hope for a secure throne was for the hated British infidels, and their very expensive occupation, to be gone. He wanted the British to establish a firm line of strategic defence along the Indus, and now that Ranjit Singh was dead and his empire fallen to anarchy, Burnes wanted Peshawar and Kashmir returned to Afghan rule. A larger, richer Afghanistan without a British military presence might be a genuine buffer state.[12]

We can well imagine Burnes' mixture of impatience and satisfaction as the hour approached for Macnaghten to go. He called on Macnaghten at his home and '[c]ongratulated him on leaving the country in a state of profound tranquility'. I find it impossible to believe this line was not delivered with tongue firmly in cheek. Colin Mackenzie was an acute observer: 'Whether Burnes really believed in the tranquillity of the country it is difficult to say; he was certainly anxious for the departure of the Envoy, and he probably believed that he himself could put everything right.'[13]

But as Burnes spoke, a mile distant in Sirdar Alikozai's home Afghan chiefs were breathlessly discussing an urgent plan: to attack Burnes' house that very night, and to seize the house next door of Captain Johnson, paymaster to the Shah's force, and the treasure it contained.

Mirza Ata chronicled the events and Abdullah Khan's purported address to the nobles:

> Now we are justified in throwing off this English yoke: they stretch the hand of tyranny to dishonour private citizens great and small; fucking a slave girl isn't worth the ritual bath that follows it; but we have to put a stop [. . .] otherwise these English will ride the donkey of their desires into the field of stupidity, to the point of having all of us [. . .] deported into foreign imprisonment. I put my trust in God and raise the battle standard of our Prophet Muhammad, and thus go to fight; if success rewards us, then that is as we wished; and if we die in battle, that is still better than to live with degradation and dishonor! The other Sardars, his childhood friends, tightened their belts and girt their loins and prepared for Jihad – holy war.
>
> That very night before dawn had broken, they went to the house of Burnes, and with their pitiless swords killed the soldiers that were on guard there. The news of the fight spread [. . .] and the men of Kabul [. . .] welcomed it as a gift from God [. . .] They [. . .] took up arms and ran to the scene shouting '[. . .] O Four Friends, the rightly-guided Caliphs of Islam!' As dawn was breaking, locust like, they poured into the streets, and assembled around the house of Alexander Burnes.[14]

After a final handshake with Macnaghten, Burnes had ridden back the mile and a quarter up the Kohistan road from the cantonments to his own house. There he held a fine dinner with Charlie and William Broadfoot. We can imagine the toasts among these three young Scots – Alex, the eldest, was 36 – as he finally took political control of the British occupation.

William had repeatedly urged Burnes that they should move home to a safer location.[15] Presumably Burnes passed on to Charlie and William the warnings he received. Brigadier Anquetil, the new commander of the Shah's forces, and Captain Troup had been lodging with Captain Johnson in the house next door. All three decided to remain in the cantonments that night after they were warned.[16]

Burnes believed the only chance to survive in Afghanistan was to carry things with a high hand and rely on belief in the Company's iqbal. In other words, to bluff it out. As Charles Metcalfe put it, 'Our power does not rest on actual strength, but upon impression [. . .] Our greatest danger is not from a Russian army but the fading of our invincibility from the minds of the Native inhabitants [. . .]'[17] This involved the display of near superhuman levels of courage. Mohan Lal came to Burnes that evening and directly warned him of Abdullah Khan's plot, but Burnes refused Lal's suggestion to ask for a strong guard, as this would show fear. He understood this might prove fatal. However he remarked to Lal that 'the time is not far that we must leave this country'.[18]

Lal met with one of the conspirators and was taunted, so he returned to Burnes' house and warned him again. While they were talking an anonymous note in Persian was delivered, telling Burnes to leave quickly. Two other visitors arrived, Taj Mahomed Dourani and Burnes' Qizilbash friend Sherif, both with warnings. Burnes turned down Sherif's offer of a guard of 100 men. He told Lal to show no anxiety, and repeated that the time had come for the British to leave the country. These were the last remarks Lal was to hear from his friend.

After dinner the three comrades went to bed. Stationed in the courtyard house were Burnes' guard of twelve sepoys with their naik and havildar in charge, at least two of his Arab bodyguard, a few irregular soldiers including Edul Khan and a number of armed chaprasis. Various servants were around, and also the Kashmiri concubines. Next door in Captain Johnson's treasury, in a separately walled compound, a guard of thirty sepoys were watching over chests containing Rs170,000.

The conspirators were collecting men to begin the attack. Mohan Lal named the core group as Abdullah Khan Achakzai, Abdul Salam Khan Uzbek, Amir Ullah and Mir Afzul Khan. Rumour soon spread and noises were heard in the pitch black of the Kabul night. The Shah's officers were alarmed, and a mounted qasid was sent to Burnes' house, who gave one of Burnes' chaprasis named Bowe Singh a message: 'Go and inform your master immediately that there is a tumult in the city, and that the merchants are removing their goods and valuables from the shops.'

Bowe Singh replied that Burnes had already been warned and had no fear; he therefore declined to wake his master. When this news reached the Bala Hissar, Usman Khan headed with a strong escort towards Burnes' house.[19] He had attempted to dissuade some of the conspirators that evening, and been abused. In his view the attack was imminent.[20] He encountered Bowe Singh, who had repaired to a local tea-house for some early breakfast. Singh conducted the vizier to Burnes' house. Burnes was awoken and he dressed, and then spoke with the vizier, who urged him to leave for the cantonments or the Bala Hissar. Burnes levelly replied: 'If I do that, the Afghans will say that Sikunder Burnes was afraid, and ran away.'

Usman and Burnes conversed for some time. Shuja was now awake, and looking for his vizier. A messenger was sent, and Usman therefore made to leave, when he saw a group of Aminulla Khan's men already gathering in the street. He returned to Burnes and offered to bring a force to disperse them. Burnes advised him to return to the Shah as he had been urgently summoned. Lal thought it strange that Usman did not leave some of his escort of sixty men to help defend Burnes.[21]

Burnes now sent a qasid with an urgent message to Macnaghten requesting assistance. The initial attack on Burnes' house started just before dawn, and the shooting was heard in the cantonments by John Conolly, who was up early. He immediately warned Macnaghten; a few minutes later Burnes' message arrived; the situation was crystal clear.

Lal was awoken by his maidservant around 7am and informed of the gathering tumult in the city. He sent a message to Burnes to ask what he should do. Burnes replied he should stay inside, and that he had already sent to the cantonments for soldiers, who would soon arrive.[22] The principal attackers, only thirty strong, had not unsaddled so they might make a quick escape. Burnes sent out two of his staff to parley, one a Sayid. This man was hacked to pieces, the other mutilated and allowed to return. The assailants then occupied the surrounding rooftops and opened fire on Burnes' house, shooting out the Russian glass windows.

Burnes' house was a typical Kabul home, with buildings around an inner courtyard, and the exterior consisting of a series of stout mud walls, featuring few and small windows and set with heavy gates. At first there were desultory shots and stones were thrown. Several leading conspirators including Aminulla remained warily at the end of the street, horsed. Burnes was determined to resolve matters peacefully. Between sepoys, bodyguards, chaprasis and British officers, there were around twenty-eight armed men to defend the house, but he ordered them not to fire.

Opposite stood a hammam, or public bath; an official Burnes had dismissed organised fuel from there piled against the gates. Burnes stood in the garden and tried to reason, but was fired upon. While the gate was burning, the attackers broke into Johnson's house, massacring the sepoys there. The frenzied looting of coin brought a huge increase in the size of what had become a mob.

Shuja, urged by Usman Khan, acted decisively. Usman fought his way with Campbell's regiment and Prince Fatth Shah towards Burnes' house. But the dense central city was in uproar. They were engaged in fierce fighting down narrow alleyways, blocked at intervals by stout wooden gates with high sills; they could not use artillery. They had reached striking distance when an order was received from Shuja summoning them back because of the danger to Fatth Shah. Had Usman followed a slightly longer route he could have gone to Burnes' house across open ground at the curved base of the hill of the Bala Hissar, and not been held up in narrow streets.[23]

It was only a mile and a quarter from the British cantonments to Burnes' house, and 90 per cent of the route lay along the straight main Kohistan road. There were walled gardens to the side and four forts on the route, but no significant hostile forces. The British had both cavalry and horse artillery, and a strong party could have been at Burnes' house in minutes.

On receiving Burnes' message, Macnaghten passed it on to Elphinstone, with his opinion that the disturbance would 'speedily subside'. Around 8am Macnaghten, meeting with Elphinstone, dismissed George Lawrence's suggestion that a regiment be instantly despatched to rescue Burnes and arrest the ringleaders.[24] Elphinstone sent orders to Brigadier Shelton's force, which had returned from Zurmut and was encamped on the Siyah Sang heights, to march in to the Bala Hissar and assist Sir Alexander, but only once permission arrived from Shuja. Lawrence was sent to the Bala Hissar to ask for it. With an escort of only four he passed within 400 yards of Burnes' residence. Macnaghten and Elphinstone delayed their proposed departure.

At 8am Captain Trevor, who lived near Burnes, sent an urgent message to Macnaghten, reporting that Burnes' house was under attack and adding:

> I hope that it is all a lie, but I would earnestly recommend that the business be put an end to before night, at any risk [. . .] The plot is a party one now, but our slackness in driving these fellows out of their houses might make it serious.[25]

With the gates burning, Burnes' position had become desperate and he ordered the defenders to fire. This they did with some effect, but increased the rage of the growing mob. Once the gates fell, the mob surged in. William Broadfoot was shot in the stomach, and dragged into the house.

After Campbell's repulse, Prince Fatth Shah took more troops and made a more determined effort to cut his way through to Burnes.[26] This time the fighting was fierce and the Shah's troops suffered seventy killed and 100 wounded. Eventually they reached Burnes' street, but seeing the gates ablaze and the crowd surging through to the courtyard, they presumed it was too late.

Lawrence had inexplicably sent Shelton a message from the Bala Hissar that Fatth Shah had matters under control and he need not advance.[27] With the smoke from the Residence plainly visible, Shelton sent to ask again 'in view of the present emergency'. At the Residence, Broadfoot was dying in agony, and Burnes twice addressed the crowd from the balcony, offering to redress their wrongs and finally offering money. The fire spread from the gates to the room where Alex, Charlie and the wounded Broadfoot were barricaded, and Broadfoot was consumed by the flames. Bowe Singh described the desperate last moments:

> The jemadar of chuprassees told Sir A Burnes that there was a report of a regiment having come to assist him; he was going to the top of the house to look, and had got half way, when he met an Afghan, who said [...] there was not the least sign of a regiment.
>
> My master then turned back, and remarked, there was no chance of assistance coming from the cantonments or the king. A [...] Cashmeeree, came forward, and said 'If your brother and the chuprassees cease firing on the people, I swear by the Koran that I will take you safe through the kirkee of the garden to the fort of the Kuzzilbashes.'
>
> The firing ceased, and Sir A Burnes agreed to accompany him, and for the sake of disguise, put on a chogha and a longee.
>
> The moment he came out of the door [...] with the Cashmeeree, the wretch called out 'Here is Sikunder Burnes.' He was rushed on by hundreds, and cut to pieces with their knives. His brother Captain Burnes went out with him, and was killed dead before Sir Alexander.[28]

There are at least two people here inside the house, an Afghan and a Kashmiri, apparently unrecognised by Bowe Singh. Both played crucial roles. At one stage the Shah's troops had indeed approached the Residence. By contradicting the jemadar, the Afghan on the stairs may have prevented Burnes from signalling to his rescuers. And why did Burnes trust the equally mysterious Kashmiri? Who was he? One possibility must be that the Kashmiri was connected to Burnes' women, perhaps one of the musicians.

Mirza Ata recorded a quite different version of Burnes' last moments:

> it is said that Burnes at that moment was in the private quarters of the house, taking a bath with his mistress in the hot water of lust and pleasure [...] the guerilla Ghazis burst in and dragged them all from the changing room of life into the ashpit of death [...]

Mohan Lal watched from his rooftop.

> The houses of Sir Alexander Burnes and myself were surrounded [...] They were not accompanied with more than fifty men, but not a battalion was sent to our protection. After poor Sir Alexander Burnes was murdered and his house set on fire, I made a hole through the neighbouring house and was nearly cut to pieces, had I not been protected by the good-natured Nuwab Mohammed Zeman Khan.[29]

Lal says that he saw Prince Fatth Shah shouting, '[D]estroy the infidels and plunder their property' and was unsure which side Fatth was on: '[W]hether he said this to have safe escape back to the Bala Hissar or with the view to excite the people more against us is not known.'[30] It still is not known.

Lal contradicts Bowe Singh in the detail on Burnes' last moments. Rather than donning a disguise, Lal states that Burnes bound a black cloth over his eyes before entering the garden, so as not to see where the blows came from. The Russian historical tradition has Burnes trying to escape in a burqa.[31] All agree he put on something. A burqa makes more sense as a disguise than a chogha (tunic) and lunghi (turban).

The total number in the house was around forty. There were the three Europeans and a sepoy guard of twelve. Then there were some irregular troops, of whom we know that Mohammed Hussain Kasha and Edul Khan (who had escorted Eldred Pottinger to Herat) were both wounded but survived.[32] The ever-loyal Ghulam Ali, whom Princess Victoria had so admired, died with his employer,[33] as did the Arab bodyguard led by Abdullah, who had refused to leave him. Charlie and Broadfoot would also have had personal servants and of course there were the concubines. Bowe Singh was among the few survivors.

Burnes died about 10.30 to 11.00am. The cantonment road was not blocked; at least two messengers from Burnes, plus two servants of Captain Johnson and three unidentified chaprasis came down it, all while Burnes was still resisting. Johnson specifies that he received two reports after sunrise, at least an hour-and-a-half apart. Burnes was still alive at least two hours after Macnaghten's 8am meeting with Elphinstone. George Broadfoot wrote to James Burnes that: 'all accounts describe the resistance as desperate and prolonged [...]'[34] Mohan Lal said the attack started around 7am and lasted four hours.

Macnaghten and Elphinstone could easily have saved Burnes. Johnson had a better grasp than anyone of the timeline; his house was also under attack, so he was getting updates from his own servants. Waiting impatiently by his saddled horse, he was sure Burnes could be rescued:

> In the supposition that the General would immediately order down a detachment to suppress the tumult, as well as to save my Treasury and the life of [...] Burnes, from whom another letter had been received 'imploring immediate assistance', my horse was kept ready [...] Yet to our astonishment [...] [h]ours slipped by and no steps taken.[35]

There can be no mitigation. Macnaghten's behaviour had for weeks been delusional; he had refused to take on board evidence from Burnes, Drummond,

Pottinger, Lal, Mackenzie, Rawlinson and many others that national resistance had broken out. Now at the crisis, Macnaghten simply wished it away, with fatal consequences. His insistence on permission from Shuja before doing anything was ludicrous. Elphinstone was broken. Brigadier Shelton on Siyah Sang heard firing at 7am but did nothing for hours.

The total British forces at Kabul that morning were four regiments of infantry, one regiment of cavalry and three rissalahs of irregular cavalry, three companies of sappers, two batteries of field artillery and one of horse artillery plus various British officered bodies of the Shah's contingent. The initial attack against Burnes consisted of under 100 men.

Colin Mackenzie was convinced that Shuja had been secretly conspiring with the rebels. The leaders of the attack, Aminulla Khan Logari and Abdullah Khan Achakzai, were Saduzai loyalists whose allegiance to Shuja continued after Burnes' death. By sending troops to try to rescue Burnes, Shuja apparently did more than anybody else to help. But this was initiated by Usman Khan, and Shuja called off their efforts just when they appeared on the point of success.

Then there is Mohan Lal's witness of Fatth appearing to be fighting with the assailants. Mackeson was to take a deposition from Munshi Mohammed Bakhsh, an eye-witness from Shuja's administration who testified that Shuja had incited the attack and sent Fatth Shah to join in. Bakhsh stated that Shuja had realised that Burnes would now be in charge, and would not continue Macnaghten's policies. This detail lends credibility to Bakhsh's account. Bakhsh also said that Shuja expected to win either way, as if the attack failed it would rid him of some troublesome nobles who led it.[36] That Shuja was playing all sides seems probable. But soldiers with Fatth Shah testified that the rescue attempt had been genuine.

Macnaghten attempted justification in an official despatch found uncompleted on his desk after his own death. This said blandly, 'Before Brigadier Shelton could reach the Bala Hissar, the town had attained such a state of ferment that it was deemed impracticable to send aid to Sir Alexander Burnes' residence [. . .]'[37] But this ignores the failure to send aid from the cantonment, the delay in sending orders to Shelton and the wait for the Shah's permission.

Broadfoot is convincing as to why Burnes was attacked, listing six reasons. He was an easy target unprotected in the city; the symbolic blow would encourage general rebellion; he was hated as the man 'universally believed to have guided the Kaffirs into the country'; his abilities made him an asset to the enemy; he had advised the king against certain parties in petitions; he was known as a religious sceptic.[38] Broadfoot – who is not uncensorious, and knew Burnes well – makes no hint at sexual adventures as a motive. He misses one important point – Burnes was detested by the Kohistanis for his destructive campaign in their country.

Mohan Lal stated that he witnessed the Burnes brothers being hacked to pieces by 'Ghazis' in the garden. What became of them is unknown. Burnes' Qizilbash friend, Sherif Khan, who was deputy to Captain Johnson in the treasury, wrote to James Burnes to say he had collected the bodies two nights after the assassination and given them decent burial.[39] But if this is true, it is strange that the remains were not located by the returning British Army, as others were.

It was Burnes' consistent view that the best thing the British could do for Afghanistan, and for the security of India, was to leave. The most plausible explanation of Burnes' behaviour is that he was for months pretending to agree with Macnaghten that all was quiet, in order to get rid of the man without causing opposition to his own succession. Once himself in sole political charge, he could work on an urgent policy of getting the army out; a policy to which, in view of the alarming costs, Auckland might well have been amenable.

To have panicked about an insurrection on the night of 1 November would have led to cancellation of Macnaghten's departure the next day, and scuppered Burnes' chance to end the occupation. Alexander Burnes decided to brave it out, and paid for his courage. It was a gamble worth taking, and his death led to a much greater tragedy.

CHAPTER THIRTY-SEVEN

## Aftermath

Mohan Lal was rescued from the mob by one of Dost Mohammed's brothers, Mohammed Zaman. He was taken into the Qizilbash quarter and lived in the house of their leader, Shirin Khan. At some stage he was able to enter Burnes' looted house and rescue a substantial quantity of papers, including Burnes' private diaries.

Lal remained in Kabul, a vital asset to Macnaghten as the British position quickly deteriorated. With no effective action against a small uprising, there was a massive surge in the number of Afghan resistance fighters. Stupidly, the British had placed all their stores and provisions in buildings outside the cantonments, and these were all captured over the next few days. The British did not move into the Bala Hissar, and a number of sorties from the cantonment failed due to Shelton's poor tactics, quickly bringing a total collapse in morale.

For the Afghans, Burnes was the most prominent of the British and his death had a positive effect on their morale. The leaders in Kabul sent an appeal to join them to the Afridis of the Khyber:

> on the third Tuesday of the blessed month Ramzan in the morning time it occurred, that [. . .] we carried by storm the house of Sickender Burnes – by the grace of the most holy and omnipotent God the brave warriors [. . .] slew Sickender Burnes with various other Feringees of Consideration and nearly 500 Battalion men, putting them to the sword, and consigning them to perdition.[1]

Macnaghten entered negotiations for evacuation from Afghanistan – in effect capitulation – but concurrently sought ever more complex alliances with various chieftains, and by offering large bribes endeavoured to play the classic British game of divide and rule. Lal was the indispensable agent, in continuous communication with all parties and tolerated by the Afghan leadership groups, who were all still hedging their bets.

Soon Macnaghten was assassinated at a negotiation and the capitulating Kabul force wiped out in the passes of the Khoord Kabul as it attempted to reach Jalalabad. A number of senior officers had been given up as hostages. The story is beyond the scope of this biography, though I will say there were thousands more survivors than is generally acknowledged. Poor bewildered Elphinstone died of his illnesses a prisoner of Akbar Khan, who sent the body downriver to Jalalabad, where in May 1842 it was buried with full military honours. This from the *Delhi Gazette* seems a fitting encapsulation of the fate of the Afghan campaign:

> In the procession for the interment of Gen. E. a distinguished officer of the dragoons fainted from the dreadful effluvia omitted from the chinks of the coffin, made of rude wood [...] the pall bearers had a most unpleasant occupation.[2]

The campaign was riddled with military failings that cannot be laid at the door of one or two individuals. Rather the individuals were part of a rotten system. Properly regarded, the First Afghan War should be seen as an exposure of the fundamental failings in British military organisation and command structure that were to be revealed again in the Crimea.

This Afghan War was part of a century of policy when the British overthrew rulers and replaced them with puppet rival claimants, as the primary method of expansion of British dominance in India. The stationing of Company battalions at the host's expense, the raising of British-officered 'independent' regiments of the puppet ruler, the control of revenues and policy, had all been repeated dozens of times. This was how British rule *normally* expanded. The dissembling to disguise annexation was normal too. Afghanistan only seems exceptional to us because we know where the boundaries of British India eventually settled.

For later Victorian historians, in the grip of the religious frenzy of their period, the unique immorality of the First Afghan War could be portrayed as showing the Divine Hand of Providence because it resulted in unique punishment. The concomitant was that, as Britain's invasions of other places had not failed, they were subject to divine approval. That is how historians came to portray this episode as more immoral than the rest of the Empire. It fitted to add a Sodom and Gomorrah element – unique sexual rapacity had brought down divine justice.

British troops in Afghanistan indulged in sex and drinking, as all soldiers everywhere always have. This undoubtedly gave offence in a Muslim country. The primary resistance of the Afghans was nationalist. But it should also be noted that the British invasion coincided with a major shift of Islam in Afghanistan as the influence of Wahabbism first began to be felt there. Dost

Mohammed himself had undergone religious transformation around 1830, and changed from a carouser to a religious ascetic.

This was part of a wider transformation of Muslim society, but the Emir helped it along. Burnes in 1832 had noted the Jewish and Armenian communities were leaving because Dost had forbidden their trade in alcohol, overwhelmingly sold to Muslims. The Pushtunwall heroes had been hard drinking and womanising men, as had men in the Timurid and Mongol culture. A narrow religious obscurantism was now settling on Central Asia, and these events happened on the cusp of this change.

Those who believe the British Empire was beneficent might consider this account by a junior officer:

> Their wells, by which they irrigated the land, were blown up with gunpowder and rendered useless. These people lived, in great measure, on dried mulberries, as the land would not produce sufficient corn for their consumption. There were beautiful [. . .] mulberry trees around the forts. Every morning and evening two companies from each regiment were sent out to cut them down.
>
> We found out that by cutting rings through the bark into the heart of the tree, it was as effectively destroyed as if cut down; and it was [. . .] lighter work [. . .] we became quite adepts in the work of destruction, and a greater scene of devastation was perhaps never beheld.[3]

The deliberate starvation of the civilian population was an appalling crime. A rural economy dependent on tree crops could not survive the complete destruction of the trees, as there was nothing to live on until new trees grew. Some areas have never recovered from the deliberate devastation of the rural economy.

Nor was this the only atrocity. The attack on the tiny village of Ali Bagh on 18 June 1842 was not untypical. After British soldiers' effects were found there, the inhabitants were subjected to mass rape. A British officer wrote:

> The day before yesterday we burnt Ali Baghan to the ground. The event is one that was to be regretted, partly because it lay in the direct line of our communication, and partly because rapine to a horrible extent [. . .] is said to have preceded the other sort of violence.[4]

The *Delhi Gazette* felt this was justifiable:

> We can scarcely blame the troops for what has taken place, and very great allowance is to be made on discovering the property of their murdered comrades.

The *Hurkaru* took a better line:

> To ravage and burn villages, and to violate the women [. . .] are not precisely the best measures calculated to restore the honour of Great Britain. We talk about national disgrace, and begin ravaging villages and violating helpless women [. . .]

Mohan Lal had suffered capture and torture, and had been instrumental in negotiating the release of British hostages, but was disgracefully treated by the British after the war. They refused to pay bills of exchange he had raised for Macnaghten to provision the beleaguered garrison and to bribe chiefs, to the huge amount of almost £12,000. Then once the armies returned from Afghanistan they said there was no longer any job for him: his employment by Burnes was deemed irregular, and the question of permanent employment was referred to London, putting it on hold for years and still pending when Mohan Lal decided to go to London himself.

On 25 June 1843 he visited his old colleague from the Kabul mission, Nourozji Fourdonji in Bombay, and afterwards stayed with James Burnes there, and was much feted by Bombay's Freemasons. On 30 July he sailed on the *Sesostris* for Britain, via the Suez overland route. On 17 September he disembarked from the steamer *Cleopatra* in the Isle of Wight, where he was met by Claude Wade, and stayed with him there. A guest of many prominent people, including Lord Ashley, and then Charles Trevelyan in both Southampton and London, he was feted by the Court of Directors and given a dinner by Lord John Russell. He was presented to Queen Victoria at Buckingham Palace and then stayed as a guest of Mountstuart Elphinstone – it was as though the dramatis personae of Burnes' life were having a curtain call.

Finally on 23 October Lal arrived at Montrose, presented Burnes' papers to old James Burnes, and was embraced by Alex's mother. Returning to Edinburgh he stayed with John McNeill, was lionised by the Corporation and painted by Sir William Allan. He visited Glasgow and Dublin, and then at Liverpool was entertained by Henry Pottinger and Lord Stanley, before returning to London and the hospitality of Lord Auckland and Palmerston. He eventually returned to India via Germany and France. The Court of Directors granted him an annual pension of £1,000, but he was never given serious employment again, and lived beyond his means, addicted to champagne and dancing girls.

Mohan Lal had been received by British high society, but he was a reminder of a disaster people wished to forget. It became evident how much he had needed Burnes as his protector. Lal never again found a patron who valued him without racial prejudice. He was smeared with British stereotypes of the untrustworthy Asiatic: Sir John Kaye declared his espionage work showed him 'endowed with a genius for traitor-making'.[5] Nehru himself commented:

> In free India a man like Mohan Lal would have risen to the topmost rungs of the political ladder. Under early British rule, [. . .] he could not rise higher than the position of a Mir Munshi or at most Deputy Collector [. . .] There was apparently no place of activity suitable for him in India, and he must have lived largely in the past when he was the honoured guest of the Rulers of Asia and Europe.[6]

The papers Lal rescued were presumably among the collection James gave to John Kaye, and have vanished.

On 25 March 1842 the *Bombay United Services Gazette* published a selection of Burnes' original despatches, showing the excisions which had been made. Two months later these were widely reprinted in the British newspapers. But with the destruction of the Kabul force and uncertain outcome of the war, there was not the immediate political storm that might have been expected. The Conservatives under Sir Robert Peel were now in government, and Peel was anxious to avoid making the Afghan situation more difficult. The Whigs in opposition could hardly object as they had perpetrated the falsification.

Those pressing for the release of Burnes' original despatches were a group of radical liberals, including Joseph Hume, the small camp allied to John Stuart Mill (who had of course seen the originals) and the *Westminster Review*. They had strong support from a body of radical Conservatives.

On 23 June 1842 the Conservative MP for Inverness, Henry Baillie, put down a motion calling for full publication of Burnes' correspondence. His seconder was Alex's friend young Benjamin Disraeli. Baillie and Disraeli were opposed by their own government; Peel even arranged to have Baillie invited to dinner by the Duke of Buccleuch on the night of the motion, in the hope it would fall in the absence of its proposer. Baillie turned down the Duke and the plan failed. But neither Baillie nor Disraeli would accuse Hobhouse or Palmerston of misleading Parliament.

Hobhouse made a meticulous three-hour speech against the motion. He concluded by quoting Alexander Burnes' letter of 8 June 1838 on implementing the restoration of Shah Shuja, repeating the exact trick that Burnes had complained of in the first place. Hobhouse declared:

> There is no mistaking his words – two of our regiments as an honorary escort, a British agent, and an avowal to the Afghans that we had taken up [Shah Shuja's] cause, would ensure his being fixed for ever on his throne – and this is the authority which Lord Auckland is charged with having disregarded.

Peel backed Hobhouse, arguing that full disclosure would only harm relations with Russia. The motion was defeated by seventy-five votes to nine. The same year the radical MP Sir Frances Burdett, Hobhouse's former friend, made another attempt but was rebutted by the Conservative President of the Board of Control, Lord Fitzgerald, who said the government repudiated any suggestion that the previous government had indulged in misrepresentation.

This may ring bells with modern readers too. Once in power, Obama immediately withdrew election promises to pursue those in the Bush administration who were responsible for torture and extraordinary rendition. In the

UK the Chilcot Inquiry into the 2003 Iraq war – a very similar example to 1838 of the falsification of a government case for war – was simply pushed into the shadows until people had stopped caring. Governments almost always defend or excuse the crimes of their predecessors; this system secures their own future immunity.

Buist finally did a full publication in the *Bombay Times* of 30 July and 3 August 1842, which led to a much more widespread outcry in the British newspapers. On 1 March 1843 Thomas Roebuck, the radical MP for Bath, put forward a motion calling for a Select Committee inquiry. Peel argued explicitly that it is wrong for a government to investigate the wrongdoing of its predecessor:

> It has never been the usage for any government [. . .] to use all its power and influence [. . .] to bring under investigation the acts of its predecessors. It has never been the custom of the House and it would not be just now to establish such a precedent.[7]

Roebuck spoke well of 'palpable falsification' and, assisted by Disraeli, gained a very impressive seventy-five votes against both government and opposition whips, but 187 votes defeated him. Peel and Palmerston ostentatiously walked together into the division lobby.

The falsification of Burnes' despatches next arose in an extraordinary debate in the House of Commons over four early mornings between 8 February and 17 March 1848.[8] Thomas Anstey, another radical MP, brought a motion of impeachment against Palmerston. It was modelled on the impeachment of Warren Hastings, being a demand that the Crown produce documents on the basis of which the accusers could make out their case. That had led to one of Parliament's most famous debates, with contributions from Burke, Fox and Pitt. By contrast, Anstey's motion played out in the dim light of 3am Commons sessions, with the only people present the Speaker, Anstey, Palmerston and his second Shiel, and one Irish member, Smith O'Brien, who said nothing. Only at the very end of the final day did two other members come in, to talk the motion out for its last ten minutes, so no vote could be taken.

Anstey's speech would have lasted about six hours. Palmerston's reply must have taken about four hours. Anstey's motion listed thirty-six treaties or events concerning which he wished to see all papers. The invasion of Afghanistan was just one of these events. Anstey's general thesis, that Palmerston was culpably responsible for the growth of the Russian Empire over a thirty-year period, was ludicrous. This was unfortunate, because some of the complaints Anstey raised were worth a hearing. The gap between Palmerston's liberal rhetoric to attract popular support in a democratising Britain, and his actual foreign policy, would merit more concentrated attention from his biographers. But many of Anstey's assertions, like the claim that British Ambassadors to Persia had deliberately promoted Russian influence, were crazy.

Among the better points was a long passage on Alexander Burnes. That the editing of the despatches for publication had deliberately given a false impression of Burnes' views was ably demonstrated by Anstey though, depending on a great deal of exposition of texts, it must have made dull hearing.

Anstey correctly identified that, by editing out the words 'the sentiments of His Lordship upon them', the published version of Burnes' despatch of 26 January 1838 gives the impression that Lord Auckland's views are his own. Anstey also seized on Burnes' despatch announcing the arrival of Witkiewicz, of which the published version edits out that it was Dost Mohammed who told him of the arrival, and also that Dost had refused to receive Witkiewicz, had offered to be guided by Burnes, and had given Burnes a copy of Witkiewicz' letters. Anstey also pointed out that Burnes had sent a despatch (which Anstey does not specify) noting various allegations against Dost Mohammed, but saying on investigation they proved not to be true. The published version had omitted the fact that they were untrue.

In Palmerston's reply to the empty chamber, he made the blatantly false claim that:

> The passages omitted contained opinions on subjects irrelevant to the question at issue; and when the House remembers how much the Government is blamed for printing matters which do not bear upon the question
> [. . .] the House will be of the opinion that we were not wrong in striking out such matters which do not bear upon the question.

Anstey was allied with David Urquhart, now himself an MP, and was a member of Urquhart's band of Russophobes. This movement had taken an interesting turn, as Urquhart had allied with the Chartist movement, arguing that the working people of Britain should determine its foreign policy. For a period a network of Working Men's Foreign Affairs Committees flourished, and the injustice done to Alexander Burnes was among the subjects they discussed, and on which they petitioned for official redress. A key member of Urquhart's group, who wrote regularly for him, was Karl Marx, who also believed Palmerston was a Russian agent, which he expounded at length in a happily forgotten book, *The Story of the Life of Lord Palmerston*.[9] Marx was to refer to Palmerston's distortion of Burnes' views in his writings on colonialism.[10] The joining of Benjamin Disraeli and Karl Marx in seeking the release of the Burnes papers is a peculiar accident of history.

Sir John Kaye's *History of the War in Afghanistan*, published in 1851, defined the accepted view of the war for generations. His verdict on the misrepresentation of Burnes was damning:

> I cannot [...] suppress [...] my abhorrence of this system of garbling the official correspondence of public men – sending the letters of a statesman or diplomatist into the world mutilated, emasculated – the very pith and substance of them cut out by the unsparing hand of the state anatomist. The dishonesty by which lie upon lie is palmed upon the world has not one redeeming feature.[11]

The Whigs were now Liberals, and back in power. The President of the Board of Control was Fox Maule, a member of the Ramsay family. He asked Hobhouse if he would now object to full publication, who did object, and referred nastily to 'the rascallity of the Burnes family and their coadjutor in publishing confidential official papers for the sake of calumniating those who heaped rewards on their kinsman'.[12] Maule backed down.

But in 1858 the Conservatives were in office again, and their leader in the House of Commons was Benjamin Disraeli. The President of the Board of Control was Henry Baillie, MP for Inverness. The Company was in the process of abolition and the India Office of creation, and the new Secretary to the Secret Committee was Sir John Kaye. Disraeli was far too keen a street-fighter to ignore any chance of embarrassing the Liberals, and had never dropped a Quixotic attachment to Burnes' cause. Disraeli, Baillie and Kaye finally published as Parliamentary Papers 326 pages of Burnes' uncensored despatches and other previously edited documents, eighteen years after his death.

On 19 March 1861 Alex Dunlop, MP for Greenock, made the last parliamentary attempt to call for an inquiry into the falsification of Burnes' despatches. Dunlop made an excellent speech. Burnes

> was hacked to pieces by the Afghans [...] But his reputation was mangled still more cruelly by those who should have defended it [...] He had been falsely held out [...] as the instigator and advisor of that unjust and calamitous war, and this for the dastardly purpose of screening [the government] from a condemnation which they were conscious that they deserved, and laying on him the obloquy of a charge of which they knew him to be innocent.

John Bright seconded with a brilliant speech, asking:

> Who had so low a sense of honour and of right that he could offer to this house mutilated, false, forged opinions of a public servant who lost his life in the public service?

Bright pointed out that Palmerston's claims of Burnes' poor judgement were inconsistent with Palmerston's own actions. If Burnes' despatches had been censored because they were misguided and erroneous, why was Burnes not dismissed?

> although the noble Lord had these despatches before him, and knew all the feelings of Sir Alexander Burnes, he still continued Sir Alexander Burnes there. He was there two years after these despatches were written, in that most perilous year when not only himself but the whole Army [. . .] fell victims to the policy of the Noble Lord.[13]

But this time Disraeli argued that the truth had been established by the publication of full documents, and while he agreed with Bright and Dunlop, he did not see much to gain by a public inquiry. Palmerston, now seventy-six, made a spirited defence, aiming particularly at Burnes' change of mind, and criticising Burnes' 'confusion of ideas, misconceptions and over-credulity'.

It was the most direct attack on Burnes ever made in Parliament. Palmerston repeatedly stressed the 'Lieutenant' even though at the relevant period Burnes was a substantive captain. It was not a mistake. Palmerston's argument rested on authority – he did not deny that the government had edited out Burnes' opinions, but said it had the right to do it. Who rules India, after all, the Governor-General or some young lieutenant?[14]

Bright replied that Palmerston:

> [w]ent on to say that, after all [. . .] that what was in, or what was left out, was unimportant. But I should like to ask the noble Lord what was the object of the minute and ingenious, and [. . .] unmatched care which was taken in mutilating the despatches of a gentleman who was of no importance [. . .] The noble Lord has stooped so low as [. . .] to heap insult on the memory of a man who died in the execution of what he believed to be his public duty – a duty which was thrust upon him by the mad and obstinate policy of the noble Lord.[15]

Alexander was now dead twenty years, but his memory was still causing bitter debate between giants of parliamentary history. This last attempt failed like the others, by 159 votes to 49, with both party leaderships voting against. There was a sad little postscript. James, incensed by Palmerston's attack, started a lengthy and increasingly irascible correspondence with Palmerston, which he published. James wrote in a fine style:

> You were a party to the original falsification of my late brother's despatches. When taxed in the recent debate with the act, you attempted to cover it by traducing his memory, and when furnished by me with proof of the incorrectness of the assertions on which the calumnies were based, you remained silent.

But James' time was also coming to a close, and he died in Manchester, where he had been invited to address a Masonic gathering. The recurrent malaria he had picked up in Bhuj finally killed him.

# Notes

**Chapter 1 Montrose**
1. Robert Crawford: *The Bard; Robert Burns*, p. 26
2. James Burnes: *Notes on his Name and Family*, p. 22
3. T M Devine: *The Scottish Nation*, p. 33
4. Maggie Craig: *Bare-Arsed Banditti: The Men of the '45*
5. NLS/MF/MSS144/AC4647
6. http://www.burness.ca/ld42.htm#a0 Gleig also Glegg
7. Hugh Douglas: *Robert Burns: A Life*, p. 22
8. Charles Rogers: *Genealogical Memoirs*, p. 18
9. http://canmore.rcahms.gov.uk/en/site/224613/details/montrose+9+11+bow+butts+burness+house/
10. Report by L A L Rolland, Architect, 18 November 2008
11. In Scottish burghs when a person was elected Provost an ornamental lamp was placed outside their house and lit at public expense.
12. J W Kaye: *Lives of Indian Officers*, Vol. 2, p. 13
13. NLS/MF/MSS/144/Acc.4647
14. *The Gentleman's Magazine and Historical Review*, January to June 1863, p. 117
15. NLS/MSS/789/f.638
16. NLS/MSS/10688
17. R F Gould, 'The Chevalier Burnes', *Ars Quatuor Coronatorum*, Vol. 12, 1899
18. Norman Gash: *Aristocracy and People*, p. 10
19. Bruce Lenman: *Integration and Enlightenment*, p. 6
20. Bruce Lenman: *An Economic History*, p. 60
21. G Jackson and S G E Lythe (eds): *The Port of Montrose*, p. 82
22. NLS/MSS/789/ff.691–3
23. *The Gentleman's Magazine*, Vol. 17, Apr 1842, p. 434
24. J C Jessop: *Education in Angus*, p. 183
25. David Mitchell: *History of Montrose*, p. 44
26. Ibid., p. 128

**Chapter 2 A Rape in Herat**
1. Mountstuart Elphinstone: *An Account of the Kingdom of Caubul*, Vol. 2, p. 272

2 William Dalrymple: *Return of a King*, p. 13
3 Charles Hugel: *Travels in Kashmir and the Panjab*, p. 373
4 Mohan Lal: *Life of the Amir Dost Mohammed Khan*, Vol. I, p. 104
5 George Gleig: *Sale's Brigade in Afghanistan*, p. 20
6 T R Blackburn: *The Extermination of a British Army*, p. xvi

## Chapter 3  Scottish Patronage, Indian Career

1 David Gilmour: *The Ruling Caste*, p. 25
2 Penderel Moon: *The British Conquest and Dominion of India*, p. 370
3 T C Smout (ed.): *Scotland and the Sea*, p. 155
4 Writer to the Signet
5 John Rintoul taught reading and grammar at Montrose Academy, William Beattie writing and arithmetic.
6 NLS/MS/3813/f.112
7 NLS/MS/3813/f.113
8 John Greenwood: *The Campaign in Afghanistan*, p. 34
9 Charles Samuel Stewart: *Sketches of Society in Great Britain and Ireland*, Vol. 2, p. 119
10 William Dalrymple: *White Mughals*, p. 288.
11 A Lieutenant of the Bengal Establishment: *The Cadet's Guide to India*, p. 5
12 *Asiatic Journal and Monthly Register*, Vol. XI (Jan to Jun 1821) p. 409
13 Henry Durand: *The First Afghan War*, p. vii
14 BL/IOR/L/MIL/9/144/204-7
15 BL/IOR/L/MIL/9/373

## Chapter 4  A Griffin in India

1 W F B Laurie: *Sketches of Some Distinguished Anglo-Indians*, p. 3
2 David Mitchell: *History of Montrose*, p. 2
3 J W Kaye: *Lives of Indian Officers*, Vol. 2, p. 10
4 *Journal of the Royal Asiatic Society*, Vol. 1, 1834, pp. 193-9
5 Letter of June 1822 to George Jacob http://www.wayfarersbookshop.com/Russian InfluencePt2.php, item 37
6 William Dalrymple: *White Mughals*, p. 118
7 James Cotton: *Mountstuart Elphinstone*, p. 70
8 James Chambers: *Palmerston*, p. 53
9 Emily Eden: *Up the Country*, p. 271
10 'By a Lady': *Letters from Madras*, p. 82
11 William Dalrymple: *White Mughals*, p. 10
12 Emily Eden: *Up the Country*, p. 98
13 Thomas Williamson: *The East India Vade Mecum*, Vol 1, p. 412
14 J W Kaye: *The Life and Correspondence of Charles Lord Metcalfe*, Vol. 1, p. 118
15 J W Kaye: *Lives of Indian Officers*, Vol. 2, p. 13
16 James S Cotton: *Mountstuart Elphinstone*, p. 130
17 E M Collingham: *Imperial Bodies*, p. 29
18 J W Kaye: *Lives of Indian Officers*, Vol. II, p. 17
19 MAS Minute Book/CD1/p. 59
20 M M Kessler: *Ivan Viktorovich Vitkevich*, p. 7

21 *The Gentleman's Magazine*, Vol. 8, Apr 1842, p. 434
22 MM/CutPap/30Apr1825
23 J W Kaye: *Major-General Sir John Macolm*, Vol. 2, p. 209
24 Charles Hugel: *Travels in Kashmir and the Panjab*, p. 286
25 *Journal of the Royal Asiatic Society*, Vol. 1, 1834, pp. 193–9
26 Jack Harrington: *Sir John Malcolm*, p. 72
27 MAS/MinuteBook/CD1/p. 126
28 Martha McLaren: *British India and British Scotland*, p. 253
29 Robert Freke Gould: *Military Lodges*, p. 193
30 Charles Lyell: *Principles of Geology*, Vol.II pp306-11
31 RSA/EC/1834/11
32 K M Lyell: *Life, Letters and Journals of Sir Charles Lyell*, p. 454
33 Alexander Burnes: *Cabool*, p. 116
34 BL/IOR/MSS/EUR/E/161/3/f.74
35 BL/IOR/MSS/EUR/E/161/3/f.24
36 BL/EUR/MSS/B/28/f.40
37 Edward Ingram: *The Beginning of the Great Game in Asia*, p. 90
38 W F B Laurie: *Sketches of Some Distinguished Anglo-Indians*, p. 18
39 MM/OffCorr/15Dec1827
40 MAS/MinuteBook/CD1/p. 159
41 MM/OffCorr/31Jan1828
42 MAS/MinuteBook/CD1/p. 166
43 MAS/MinuteBook/CD1/p. 196

## Chapter 5  Dawn of the North-West Frontier

1 Demetrius C Boulger: *Lord William Bentinck*, p. 54
2 Afzal Iqbal: *Circumstances Leading to the First Afghan War*, p. 10
3 Edward Ingram: *The Beginning of the Great Game in Asia*, p. 43
4 Zalmay A Gulzad: *External Influences and the Development of the Afghan State*, p. 47
5 NAI/Pol/Sec/14October1830/Cons/Nos.3–8/f.59
6 MM/OffCorr/14Jul1828
7 MM/OffCorr/20Aug1828
8 MM/OffCorr/7Nov1828
9 MM/OffCorr/18Nov1828
10 MM/OffCorr/25Jan1829
11 MM/OffCorr/27Jul1829
12 MM/OffCorr/27Aug1829
13 RSA/EC/1834/11
14 NAI/For/Sec/Progs/14Jan–8Apr/ff.178–81
15 Emily Eden: *Up the Country*, p. 122
16 Http://www.dunsehistorysociety.co.uk/jamesgray.shtml
17 NLS/MSS/21241/f.47
18 E M Collingham: *Imperial Bodies*, p. 29
19 NLS/MF/MSS/144/Acc4647
20 Peter Hopkirk: *The Great Game*, p. 43
21 Durba Ghosh: *Sex and the Family in Colonial India*, p. 70

22 Frank Welsh: *A History of Hong Kong*, p. 150
23 Ronald Hyam: *Empire and Sexuality*, p. 26
24 G M Theal: *History of South Africa*, Vol. 4, p. 309
25 MM/OffCorr/26Sep1829
26 MM/Off Corr/18Oct1829
27 John Keay: *The Honourable Company*, p. 454
28 Robert A Huttenback: *British Relations with Sind 1799–1843*, p. 18
29 NAI/For/Pol/12February1830/Cons/No.7/ff.3–34
30 R H Kennedy: *Narrative of the Campaign of the Army of the Indus*, Vol. 1, p. 207
31 NAI/For/Pol/12Feb1830/Cons/No.7/f.3
32 NAI/For/Pol/12Feb1830/Cons/No.7/f.9
33 NAI/For/Pol/12Feb1830/Cons/No.7/f.35
34 NAI/For/Pol/12 Feb1830/Cons/No.6
35 MM/OffCorr/24Dec1829
36 A unit of distance, varying regionally
37 NAI/For/Sec/14Oct/1830/Cons/Nos.3–8/ff.65–6
38 NAI/For/Sec/14Oct1830/Cons/Nos.3–8/f.75
39 NAI/For/Pol/19Mar1830/Cons/No.1
40 NAI/For/Pol/5Mar1830/Cons/No.4/f.8
41 NAI/For/Pol/5Mar1830/Cons/No.4/f.1
42 NAI/For/Pol/5Mar1830/Cons/No.4/f.12
43 NAI/For/Sec/14Oct1830/Cons/Nos.3–8/ff.125–37
44 MM/OffCorr/3Feb1830
45 NAI/For/Pol/3Apr1830/Cons/No.3/f.3
46 NAI/For/Sec/14Oct1830/Cons/Nos.3–8/f.62
47 BL/EUR/MSS /F347
48 BL/Add/Mss/14382/f.47
49 NAI/For/Sec/14Oct1830/Cons/Nos.3–8/f.1
50 NAI/For/Sec/9August1830/Cons/Nos.3–8/ff.5–19
51 MM/OffCorr/10Mar1830
52 *The Spectator*, 17 April 1830, p. 7
53 BL/EUR/MSS/F347
54 James' original manuscript survives in Montrose Museum.

## Chapter 6   The Indus Scheme

1 MM/OffCorr/30Jun1830
2 MM/OffCorr/6Jul1830
3 NAI/For/Sec/14Oct1830/Nos. 3–8/f. 11
4 M E Yapp: *Strategies of British India*, p. 53
5 NAI/For/Sec/14October1830/Cons/Nos.3–8/f.8
6 David Gillard: *The Struggle for Asia 1828–1914*, p. 24
7 George De Lacey Evans, *On the Designs of Russia*, p. 23
8 George De Lacey Evans, *On the Practicability of an Invasion of British India*, pp. 96–8
9 NAI/For/Sec/19Feb1830/Nos.16–17
10 David Gillard: *The Struggle for Asia 1828–1914*, p. 30
11 Robert A Huttenback: *British Relations with Sind 1799–1843*, p. 19

12 J Abbott: *Sind: A Reinterpretation*, p. 69
13 Alice Albinia: *Empires of the Indus*, p. 32
14 David Gillard: *The Struggle for Asia 1828–1914*, p. 32
15 M E Yapp: *Strategies of British India*, p. 201
16 Edward Ingram: *The Beginning of the Great Game in Asia*, p. 64
17 NAI/For/Sec/23Apr1830/No.7
18 Jules Stewart: *Spying for the Raj*
19 MM/OffCorr/30Mar1831
20 BL/OIOC/L/PS/5/120/No.113
21 NAI/For/Sec/31Dec1830/Cons/No.7–9/f.7
22 Syad Muhammad Latif: *Ranjit Singh*, p. 44
23 NAI/For/Sec/31Dec1830/Cons/No.7–9/f.11

## Chapter 7  The Shipwreck of Young Hopes

1 NAI For/Sec/31Dec/1830/Nos.7–9/f.5
2 IOR/F/4/1264/50869
3 NAI/For/Sec/Progs/14Jan–8Apr1831/f.8
4 MAS/MinuteBook/CD1/p. 15
5 MM/OffCorr/30Dec1830
6 MM/OffCorr/20Jan1830
7 NAI/For/Sec/25Nov1831/Cons/Nos.22–4/f.8
8 Alice Albinia: *Empires of the Indus*, p. 29
9 *Transactions of the Bombay Geographical Society*, Vol. 16, p. 61
10 NAI/For/Sec/Progs.14Jan–8Apr1831/f.298
11 NAI/For/Sec/25Nov1831/Cons/Nos.22–4/f.6
12 MM/OffCorr/20Jan1831
13 Different currencies existed across India, many called Rupee. The three Presidencies each had their own Company Rupee, of varying values. Even within Company territories some subsumed native rulers still issued their own currency.
14 NAI/For/Sec/Progs/14Jan–8Apr1831/f.298
15 MM/OffCorr
16 NAI/For/Sec/ Progs/14Jan–8Apr183/f.299
17 NAI/For/Sec/Progs/14Jan–8Apr1831/f.12
18 NAI/For/Sec/Progs/14Jan–8Apr1831/f.14
19 NAI/For/Sec/14Jan–8Apr1831/Progs/f.314
20 NAI/For/Sec/14Jan–8Apr1831/Progs/f.313
21 NAI/For/Sec/14Jan–8Apr1831/Progs/f.320
22 NAI/For/Sec/14Jan–8Apr1831/Progs/f.321
23 NAI/For/Sec/8Apr1831/Cons/Nos.1–8/f.5
24 NAI/For/Sec/25Nov1831/Cons/Nos.22–4/f.11
25 Reaching the Indus in 1809, Mountstuart Elphinstone had recorded: 'They believe we carried certain great guns, packed up in trunks; and that we had certain small boxes, so contrived as to explode, and kill half a dozen men each, without hurting us.'
26 NAI/For/Sec/14Jan–8Apr1831/Progs/f.427
27 NAI/For/Sec/14Jan–8Apr1831/Progs/f.428
28 NAI/For/Sec/14 Jan–8Apr1831/Progs/f.324

29 NAI/For/Sec//14Jan–8Apr1831/Progs/f.323
30 NAI/For/Sec/14Jan–8Apr1831/Progs/f.325
31 NAI/For/Sec/14Jan–8Apr1831/Progs/f.430
32 MM/OffCorr/23Feb1831
33 NAI/For/Sec/14Jan–8Apr1831/Progs/f.435
34 NAI/For/Sec/14 Jan–8Apr1831/Progs/f.436
35 NAI/For/Sec/14Jan–8Apr1831/Progs/f.437
36 NAI/For/Sec/14Jan–8Apr183/ Progs/f.423
37 NAI/For/Sec//14Jan–8Apr1831/Progs/f.420
38 NAI/For/Sec/8Apr1831/Cons/Nos.1–8/f.8
39 NAI/For/Sec/14Jan–8Apr1831/Progs/f.448
40 NAI/For/Sec/14Jan–8Apr1831/Progs/f.446
41 NAI/For/Sec/14Jan–8Apr1831/Progs/f.444
42 NAI/For/Sec/14Jan–8Apr1831/Progs/f.442
43 NAI/For/Sec/14Jan–8Apr1831/Progs/f.457
44 NAI/For/Sec/14Jan–8Apr1831/Progs/f.458
45 NAI/For/Sec/14Jan–8Apr1831/Progs/f.440
46 NAI/For/Sec/14Jan–8Apr1831/Progs/f.448
47 MM/OffCorr/10Mar1833

**Chapter 8  The Dray Horse Mission**

1 Alexander Morrison: *Twin Imperial Disasters*, MS p. 25
2 M M Kessler: *Ivan Viktorovich Vitkevich*, p. 9
3 NAI/For/Sec/25Nov1831/Cons/Nos.22–4/ff.15–16
4 MM/Off/Corr/8Apr1831
5 MM/Off/Corr/4Apr1831
6 NAI/For/Sec/25Nov1831Cons/Nos.22–4/f.27
7 NAI/For/Sec/17Jun1831/Cons/Nos.8–10/f.9
8 NAI/For/Sec/17Jun1831/Cons/Nos.8–10/f.14
9 NAI/For/Sec/25Nov1831/Cons/Nos.22–4/f.37
10 NAI/For/Sec/17Jun1831/Cons/Nos.8–10/f.25
11 NAI/For/Sec/17Jun1831/Cons/Nos.8–10/f.26
12 NAI/For/Sec/17Jun1831/Cons/Nos.8–10/f.33
13 NAI/For/Sec/17Jun1831/Cons/Nos.8–10/f.35
14 NAI/For/Sec/25Nov1831/Cons/Nos.22–4/f.48
15 NAI/For/Sec/25Nov1831/Cons/Nos.22–4/f.49
16 NAI/For/Sec/25Nov1831/Cons/Nos.22–4/f.54
17 NAI/For/Sec/25Nov1831/Cons/Nos.22-4/f.57
18 NAI/For/Sec/25Nov1831/Cons/Nos.22-4/f.56
19 NAI/For/Sec/25Nov1831/Cons/Nos.22-4/f.59
20 MM/OffCorr/18May1831
21 NAI/For/Sec/9Sep1831/Cons/Nos.1–2/f.2
22 NAI/For/Sec/9Sep1831/Cons/No.3/f.4
23 NAI/For/Sec/8Jul–9Sep1831/f.1337
24 NAI/For/Sec/25Nov1831/Cons/Nos.22–4/f.77

**Chapter 9  The Dazzling Sikhs**

1 NAI/For/Sec/25Nov1831/Cons/Nos.22–4/ff.89–90
2 Khushwant Singh: *Ranjit Singh*, p. 167
3 NAI/For/Sec/25Nov1831/Cons/Nos.22–4/f.87
4 NAI/For/Sec/25Nov1831/Cons/Nos.22–4/f.124
5 NAI/For/Sec/Progs/8Jul–9Sep1831/f.1269
6 William Barr: *Journal of a March*, p. 101
7 M E Yapp: *Strategies of British India*, p. 191
8 NAI/For/Sec/25Nov1831/Cons/Nos.41–9/f.5
9 MM/Off/Corr/23Jan1831
10 NAI/For/Sec/Progs/8Jul–9 Sep1831/f.1166
11 Khushwant Singh: *Ranjit Singh*, p. 135
12 Grey and Garrett: *European Adventurers of Northern India*, p. 16
13 Jean-Marie Lafont: *Maharaja Ranjit Singh: The French Connections*, p. 154
14 NAI/For/Sec/25Nov1831/Cons/Nos.22–4/f.126
15 NAI/For/Sec/25Nov1831/Cons/Nos.22–4/f.126
16 NAI/For/Sec/25Nov1831/Cons/Nos.22-4/f.131
17 NAI/For/Sec/31Dec1830/Cons/Nos.7-9/f.19
18 NAI/For/Sec/25Nov1831/Cons/Nos.22–4/f.127
19 NAI/For/Sec/25Nov1831/Cons/Nos.41–9/f.9
20 J M Honigberger: *Thirty-Five Years in the East*, Vol. 1, p. 53
21 Charles Hugel: *Travels in Kashmir and the Panjab*, pp. 322–4
22 BL/IOR/MSS/EUR/E/161/3/f.23
23 NAI/For/Sec/16Apr1832/Cons/Nos.5–9
24 NAI/For/Sec/25Nov1831/Cons/Nos.22–4/f.131
25 NAI/For/Sec/8Jul–9Sep1831/Progs/f.1270
26 NAI/For/Sec/25Nov1831/Cons/Nos.22–4/f.134. 'Haramzada' means bastards.
27 E M Collingham: *Imperial Bodies*, p. 32
28 Victor Jacquemont: *Correspondance*, Vol. 2, p. 238
29 Carmichael Smith: *A History of the Reigning Family of Lahore*, p. 94
30 William Godolphin Osborne: *The Court and Camp of Runjeet Sing*, pp. 85–6
31 Victor Jacquemont: *Correspondence*, Vol. 2, p. 19
32 John Lawrence: *Lawrence of Lucknow*, p. 74
33 MM/OffCorr/20Aug1831
34 NAI/For/Sec/25Nov1831/Cons/Nos.41–9/f.1
35 NAI/For/Sec/8Jul-9Sep1831/f.1350
36 *Calcutta Review*, Vol. 2 (Oct–Dec 1844), p. 211
37 NAI/For/Sec/25Nov1831/Cons/Nos.41–9/f.33
38 MM/OffCorr/16Sep1831
39 NAS/GD45/5/80
40 NAI/For/Sec/25Nov1831/Cons/Nos.20–1/f.1
41 NAS/GD45/5/80/f.3
42 NAS/GD45/5/80/f.101
43 NAS/GD45/5/80/f.169
44 NAI/For/Sec/25Nov1831/Cons/Nos.22–4/f.163

## Chapter 10  Rupar, the Field of the Cloth of Cashmere

1  Dennis Holman: *Sikander Sahib*, p. 7
2  MM/OffCorr/22Oct1831
3  NAS/GD45/5/72
4  Victor Jacquemont: *Correspondance*, Vol. 2, p. 238
5  MM/OffCorr/31Oct1831
6  MM/OffCorr/14Nov1831
7  MM/Off/Corr/6Dec1831
8  MM/Off/Corr/25Nov1831
9  MM/Off/Corr/26Dec1831
10 MM/Off/Corr/15Mar1832
11 J W Kaye: *Lives of Indian Officers*, Vol. 2, p. 303
12 *The Gentleman's Magazine*, Vol. 17 (Apr 1842), p. 435
13 MM/Off/Corr/19 Dec1831

## Chapter 11  Journey through Afghanistan

1  James Lunt: *Bokhara Burnes*, p. 51
2  Alastair McKelvie: *Monarchs of All They Surveyed*, History Scotland, Vol. 7, No. 2, March–April 2007, pp. 45–52
3  Adam Kuper: *Incest and Influence*, pp. 172–8
4  W F B Laurie: *Sketches of Some Distinguished Anglo-Indians*, p. 385
5  Mohan Lal: *Travels in the Panjab, Afghanistan and Turkistan*, p. v
6  Shahamat Ali: *The Sikhs and Afghans*, p. vii
7  Hari Ram Gupta: *Mohan Lal Kashmiri*, p. 12
8  Khushwant Singh: *Ranjit Singh*, p. 181
9  Mountstuart Elphinstone: *An Account of the Kingdom of Caubul*, Vol. 1, p. 376
10 William H Dennie: *Personal Narrative of the Campaigns*, p. 8
11 Louis Dupree: *Afghanistan*, p. 65
12 Intelligence Branch, Indian Army: *Frontier and Overseas Expeditions from India*, Vol. 3, p. 287
13 J W Kaye: *History of the War in Afghanistan*, Vol. 1, p. 174
14 Charles Masson: *Travels in Baluchistan*, Vol. 2, p. 276
15 *The Asiatic Journal and Monthly Register*, Vol. 10, Jan–Apr 1833, p. 98
16 Hari Ram Gupta: *Mohan Lal Kashmiri*, p. 24
17 *The Asiatic Journal and Monthly Register*, Vol. 10, Jan–Apr 1833, p. 159
18 Muhin Shah had rescued Conolly in Herat when he was penniless, and accompanied him back to Delhi
19 Shah Mahmoud Hanifi: *Connecting Histories in Afghanistan*, p. 53
20 *The Asiatic Journal and Monthly Register*, Vol. 10, Jan–Apr 1833, p. 98
21 Robert Freke Gould: *Military Lodges*, p. 194
22 *The Asiatic Journal and Monthly Register*, Vol. 10, Jan–Apr 1833, p. 99
23 Josiah Harlan: *A Memoir of India and Afghanistan*, p. 120
24 Christine Noelle: *State and Tribe in Nineteenth-Century Afghanistan*, p. 13
25 NAI/For/Sec/24Dec1832/Cons/No.31/f.2
26 *The Asiatic Journal and Monthly Register*, Vol. 10, Jan–Apr 1833, p. 99
27 NAI/For/Sec/6Jun1833/no.8/f.2680

28  B D Hopkins: *The Making of Modern Afghanistan*, p. 145
29  *The Asiatic Journal and Monthly Register*, Vol. 12, Sep–Dec 1833, p. 113
30  *The Asiatic Journal and Monthly Register*, Vol. 10, Jan–Apr 1833, p. 100
31  J W Kaye: *Lives of Indian Officers*, Vol. 2, p. 31
32  *The Asiatic Journal and Monthly Register*, Vol. 10, Jan–Apr 1833, p. 100
33  Gray and Garrett: *European Adventurers of Northern India*, p. 189
34  MM/Off/Corr/11Jun1832
35  NAI/For/Sec/6Jun1833/Cons/Nos.1–10/f.2517
36  James Lunt: *Bokhara Burnes*, p. 89
37  Mohan Lal: *Travels in the Panjab, Afghanistan and Turkistan*, p. 82
38  *The Asiatic Journal and Monthly Register*, Vol. 10, Jan–Apr 1833, p. 159
39  *The Asiatic Journal and Monthly Register*, Vol. 12, Sep–Dec 1833, p. 115
40  Victor Jacquemont: *Correspondence*, Vol. 2, p. 359
41  *The Asiatic Journal and Monthly Register*, Vol. 12, Sep–Dec 1833, p. 116
42  *The Asiatic Journal and Monthly Register*, Vol. 10, Jan–Apr 1833, p. 159
43  NAI/For/Sec/12Feb1833/Cons/No.16/f.1
44  Hari Ram Gupta: *Life and Work of Mohan Lal Kashmiri*, p. 31
45  *The Asiatic Journal and Monthly Register*, Vol. 12, Sep–Dec 1833, p. 118
46  *The Asiatic Journal and Monthly Register*, Vol. 10, Jan–Apr 1833, p. 160
47  Peter Hopkirk: *The Great Game*, p. 145
48  John Martin Honigberger: *Thirty-Five Years in the East*, Vol. 1, p. xiii
49  Michael Fry: *The Scottish Empire*, p. 175

## Chapter 12  To Bokhara and Back

1  Kathleen Hopkirk: *Central Asia*, p. 15
2  Alexander M Martin: *Enlightened Metropolis*, p. 259
3  NAI/For/Sec/6Jun1833/Cons/Nos.1–10/f.2528
4  NAI/For/Sec/24Dec1832/Cons/No.31/f.3
5  *The Asiatic Journal and Monthly Register*, Vol. 12, Sep–Dec 1833, p. 115
6  NAI/For/Sec/6Jun183/ Nos.1–10/f.2521
7  WCL/*BurnesJournal*/1836–8/f.193
8  NAI/For/Sec/6Jun1833/Nos.1–10/f.2519
9  NAI/For/Sec/24Dec1832/No.31/f.4
10  NAI/For/Sec/6Jun1833/Nos.1–10/f.2539
11  Alexander Burnes: *Travels into Bokhara*, p. 43
12  NAI/For/Sec/6Jun1833/Nos.1–10/f.2553
13  *Asiatic Journal and Monthly Register*, Vol. 12, Sep–Dec 1833, p. 83
14  Gray and Garrett: *European Adventurers*, p. 194
15  BL/IOR/MSS/EUR/E/161/1/f.1
16  BL/IOR/E/4/743/f.75/para.171
17  MM/OffCorr/5Mar1833
18  NAI/For/Sec/6Jun1833/No.9/f.2691
19  NAI/For/Sec/6Jun1833/No.9/f.2692–3
20  Alastair McKelvie: *To Bokhara with Burnes*, History Scotland, Vol. 8, No. 2, p. 36
21  *The Asiatic Journal and Monthly Register*, Vol. 12, Sep–Dec 1833, p. 175
22  *The American Quarterly Observer*, April 1834, p. 392

23 BL/IOR/MSS/EUR/E/161/1/f.3
24 *The Asiatic Journal and Monthly Register*, Vol. 12, Sep–Dec 1833, p. 227
25 W F B Laurie: *Sketches of Some Distinguished Anglo-Indians*, p. 6
26 BL/IOR/MSS/EUR/E/161/1/f.3

## Chapter 13  The Object of Adulation

1 *Asiatic Journal*, Vol. 12, Nov 1833, p. 190
2 http://www.mandurahcommunitymuseum.org/downloads%5CThe%20Hooghly.pdf
3 J W Kaye: *Lives of Indian Officers*, Vol. 2, p. 36
4 Christopher Hibbert: *Queen Victoria*, p. 10
5 Viscount Esher: *The Girlhood of Queen Victoria*, Vol. 1, p. 89
6 *The Gentleman's Magazine*, Vol. 17, Apr 1842, p. 436
7 J W Kaye: *Lives of the Indian Officers*, Vol. 2, p. 37
8 NAS/GD45/5/72/2
9 G Buist: *A Memoir of Sir Alexander Burnes*, p. 21
10 A Adburgham: *Silver Fork Society*, p. 276
11 NLS/MSS/42048/f.27
12 Philip Guedalla: *Bonnet and Shawl*, p. 104
13 James Chambers: *Palmerston*, p. 88
14 A Adburgham: *Silver Fork Society*, p. 167
15 BL/EUR/MSS/F/88/92/ff.41–2
16 NLS/MSS/42048/f.3
17 BL/MSS/EUR/E/161/1/f.20
18 BL/IOR/L/AG/1/1/33/f.150
19 *Montrose, Arbroath and Brechin Review*, 17 January 1834
20 *Montrose, Arbroath and Brechin Review*, 21 February 1834
21 Robert Freke Gould: *Military Lodges*, p. 195
22 *Freemason's Quarterly Review*, March 1842, p. 65
23 NLS/MSS/19586/f.9
24 NLS/MSS/42048/f.1
25 BL/EUR/MSS/F/88/92/ff.41–2
26 NLS/MSS/42048/f.5
27 NLS/MSS/42048/f.3
28 NLS/MSS/42048/f.31
29 NLS/MSS/42049
30 NLS/MSS/42048/f.17
31 *Transactions of the Bombay Geographical Society*, Vol. 6, p. viii
32 NLS/MSS/42048/f.33
33 NLS/MSS/42048/f.35
34 *The Spectator*, Vol. 7, 1834, p. 160
35 J W Kaye: *Lives of Indian Officers*, Vol. 2, p. 36
36 W F B Laurie: *Sketches of Some Distinguished Anglo-Indians*, p. 12
37 BL/IOR/MSS/EUR/E/161/3/f.16
38 BL/MSS/EUR/E/161/1/f.28
39 BL/MSS/EUR/E/161/1/f.15

40 Norman Gash: *Aristocracy and People*, p. 36
41 PRO/Prob/11/1980/261
42 William Dalrymple: *White Mughals*, p. xlix
43 NAI/For/Sec/28Sep1842/Cons/Nos.33–42/p. 25
44 NLS/MSS/42048/f.23
45 NLS/MSS/42048/f.25
46 NLS/MSS/42048/f.31
47 BL/MSS/EUR/B256
48 NLS/MSS/42048/f.35
49 R F Gould : 'The Chevalier Burnes'
50 NLS/MSS/42048/f.40
51 NLS/MSS/42048/f.21
52 BL/Add/Mss/14382/f.47
53 Norman Gash: *Aristocracy and People*, p. 175
54 W Broadfoot: *The Career of Major George Broadfoot*, p. 123
55 J W Kaye: *Lives of Indian Officers*, Vol. 2, p. 85
56 NLS/MSS/42048/f.42

## Chapter 14  Castles – and Knights Templar – in the Air

1 James Burnes, *A Sketch of the History of the Knights Templar*, pp. 40 and 60–62
2 W A Laurie: *A Memoir of James Burnes*, p. 8
3 Nicholas Harris Nicolas: *History of the Orders of Knighthood*, Vol. 4, p. 72
4 Robert Freke Gould: 'The Chevalier Burnes'
5 John C Cunningham: *The Last Man*, p. 27
6 W A Laurie: *A Memoir of James Burnes*, p. 8
7 A G Mackey: *The History of Freemasonry*, Vol. 5, p. 1357
8 Robert Freke Gould: *Military Lodges*, p. 195
9 Robert Bigsby: *Memoir*, p. 206
10 Confirmed by the Lyon Office
11 *Court Circular*, 3 July 1858
12 Robert Bigsby: *Memoir of the Illustrious and Sovereign Order of St John of Jerusalem* p. 88
13 *The Gentleman's Magazine and Historical Review*, January to June 1863, p. 118
14 W A Laurie: *A Memoir of James Burnes*, p. 9
15 Maurice Lindsay: *Robert Burns*, p. 49
16 R F Gould: *The Chevalier Burnes* in Ars Quatuor Coranatorum, Vol.XII, 1899
17 Robert Freke Gould: *Military Lodges*, p. 197
18 D F Wadia: *History of Lodge Rising*, p. 2
19 R F Gould : 'The Chevalier Burnes'
20 Rudyard Kipling: *Something of Myself*, pp. 53, 42
21 Ben Macintyre: *Josiah the Great,*, p. 310. Unfortunately Macintyre makes the groundless claim that Kipling used Josiah Harlan as his model for Danny 'Sikander' Dravot.
22 David Gilmour: *The Long Recessional*, p. 37
23 Robert Freke Gould: *Military Lodges*, p. 195
24 Mountstuart Elphinstone: *An Account*, Vol. 1, p. 273
25 Ben Macintyre: *Josiah the Great*, p. 148
26 Robert L D Cooper: *Cracking the Freemason's* Code, p. 43

27  Alexander Burnes: *Travels into Bokhara*, p. 471
28  Alan Moorhead: *The White Nile*, p. 80
29  http://www.theislandwiki.org/index.php/Stirling_Castle
30  Robert Bigsby: *Memoir*, p. 34
31  Email from the Lyon Office, 24 April 2012
32  http://www.lck2.co.uk/Robert_Burns_and_The_Lodge.html
33  http://www.lck2.co.uk/Rudyard_Kipling.html
34  Sean Connery and Murray Grigor: *Being A Scot*, p. 117

## Chapter 15  To Meet upon the Level

1  D F Wadia: *History of Lodge Rising Star*, p. 3
2  Unpublished pamphlet: *District Grand Lodge of Bombay*, author's collection
3  C A Bayly: *Empire and Information*, p. 53
4  Michael H Fisher: *Counterflows to Colonialism*, p. 354

## Chapter 16  Imperial Rivalry in Asia

1  John C Griffiths: *Afghanistan*, p. 30
2  Alexander Morrison: 'Twin Imperial Disasters', MS, p. 23
3  BL/IOR/MSS EUR/E/161/1 f.28
4  Alexander Morrison: 'Twin Imperial Disasters', MS, p. 15
5  George Pottinger and Patrick Macrory, *The Ten-Rupee Jezail*, p. 37
6  Knight of the Lion and the Sun, a Persian honour.
7  W F B Laurie: *Sketches of Some Distinguished Anglo-Indians*, p. 8
8  NLS/MSS/14450/f.42
9  J W Kaye: *History of the War*, Vol. 1, p. 180
10  NLS/MS/42050
11  Howarth and Howarth: *The Story of P&O*, p. 29
12  NLS/MSS/42048/f.1
13  *Calcutta Review*, Vol. 2, Oct–Dec 1844, p. 290

## Chapter 17  While Alex was Away

1  Afzal Iqbal: *Circumstances Leading to the First Afghan War*, p. 5
2  BL/IOR/E/4/743 ff.69–77, para. 152
3  Henry Durand: *The First Afghan War*, p. 70
4  BL IOR/E/4/743/f.76
5  Mohan Lal: *Life of the Amir Dost Mohammed*, Vol. 1, p. 169
6  NAI/For/Sec/Cons/28Sept1842/Nos.33–42/p. 7
7  NAI/For/Sec/5Jun1834/No.5/f.1
8  NAI/For/Sec/5Jun1834/No.5/f.3
9  WCL/BurnesJournal/1836–8/f.248
10  Jean Marie Lafont: *Ranjit Singh*, p. 6
11  John Martin Honigberger: *Thirty-Five Years*, p. 63
12  BL/IOR MSS/EUR/E/161/1 ff.9
13  BL/IOR MSS/EUR/E/161/1 ff.9–12
14  BL/IOR MSS/EUR/E/161/1 f.13
15  Gray and Garrett: *European Adventurers in Northern India*, p. 236

16 Gordon Whitteridge: *Charles Masson of Afghanistan*, p. 11
17 BL/IOR/Eur Mss/ E/161/1/f.20
18 BL/IOR/Eur Mss/ E/161/1/f.38
19 M M Kessler: *Ivan Viktorovich Vitkevich*, p. 10
20 William Dalrymple: *Return of a King*, p. 87
21 C A Bayly: *Empire and Information*, p. 65
22 BL/IOR/MSS/EUR/E/161/3/f.24
23 BL/IOR/MSS EUR/ E/161/3/f.1

## Chapter 18  Return to the Indus

1 NAI/For/Sec/20Mar1839/Cons/No.190
2 NAI/For/Sec//28Sept1842/Cons/Nos. 33–42/f.13
3 J W Kaye: *Lives of Indian Officers*, Vol. 2, p. 45
4 BL/IOR/MSS/EUR/E/161/3/f.23
5 Auckland Colvin: *John Russell Colvin*, p. 60
6 *The Annual Register of the Year 1839*, Vol. 81, 1840, p. 321
7 Auckland Colvin: *John Russell Colvin*, p. 88
8 W K Fraser-Tytler: *Afghanistan*, p. 91
9 Robert A Huttenback: *British Relations with Sind*, p. 32
10 Gregory Bondarevsky: *The Great Game*, p. 32
11 George Pottinger and Patrick Macrory: *The Ten-Rupee Jezail*, p. 87
12 Afzal Iqbal: *Circumstances Leading to the First Afghan War*, p. 16
13 Burnes, Leech, Lord and Wood: *Reports and Papers Political*
14 W F B Laurie: *Distinguished Anglo-Indians*, p. 11
15 Louis Dupree: *Afghanistan*, p. 180
16 Gregory Bondarevsky: *The Great Game*, p. 14
17 WCL/*BurnesJournal*/1836–8/f.58
18 WCL/*BurnesJournal*/1836–8/f.1
19 WCL/*BurnesJournal*/1836–8/f.3
20 WCL/*BurnesJournal*/1836–8/f.12
21 WCL/*BurnesJournal*/1836–8/f.24
22 WCL/*BurnesJournal*/1836–8/f.44
23 WCL/*BurnesJournal*/1836–8/f.50
24 BL/IOR/Eur Mss/E/161/3/f.4
25 BL/IOR/E/4/758/ No.67/f.59–69/1838
26 BL/IOR/E/4/743/ff.69–77
27 NAI/For/Pol/23Oct1839/Progs./Nos.34–5
28 Charles Hugel: *Travels in Kashmir*, p. 260.
29 NLS/MSS/5899/f.151
30 Shah Mahmoud Hanifi: *Connecting Histories*, p. 62
31 BL/IOR/E/4/758/No.67/ff.59–69/1838
32 NLS/MSS/5899/f.157
33 Hari Ram Gupta: *Mohan Lal Kashmiri*, p. 100
34 BL/IOR/MSS/EUR/E/161/3/f.7
35 BL/IOR/MSS/EUR/E/161/3/f.32
36 Asa Briggs: *The Age of Improvement*, p. 294

## Chapter 19 The Gathering Storm

1. BL/IOR/E/755/ff.715–31
2. Henry Durand: *The First Afghan War*, p. 47
3. NAI/For/Sec/10Apr1837/No.8/f.27
4. John C Cunningham: *The Last Man*, p. 32
5. BL/IOR/MSS/EUR/E/161/3/f.23
6. NLS/MSS/5899/f.152
7. Naseer Dashti: *The Baloch and Balochistan*, p. 198
8. Renamed Bin Qasim, but still universally called 'Buns Road'.
9. WCL/*BurnesJournal*/1836–8/f.69
10. WCL/*BurnesJournal*/1836–8/f.73
11. WCL/*BurnesJournal*/1836–8/f.79
12. WCL/*BurnesJournal*/1836–8/f.54
13. *Parliamentary Papers*, Vol. 25, Session 2, 1859, p. 4
14. WCL/*BurnesJournal*/1836–8/f.94
15. WCL/*BurnesJournal*/1836–8/f.96
16. NAI/For/Pol/17Jul1837/Cons/Nos.41–7/f.1
17. NAI/For/Pol/17Jul1837/Cons/No.41
18. WCL/BurnesJournal/1836–8/f.91
19. WCL/*Burnes Journal*/1836–8/f.93
20. WCL/*Burnes Journal*/1836–8/f.107
21. Emily Eden: *Portraits*, Note to Plate 16
22. BL/IOR/E/4/798/f.1320
23. WCL/*BurnesJournal*/1836–8/f.108
24. NAI/For/Pol/17Jul1837/Cons/No.43
25. NAI/For/Pol/17Jul1837/Cons/No.47/f.21
26. WCL/*BurnesJournal*/1836–8/f.110
27. WCL/*BurnesJournal*/1836–8/f.116
28. John Wood, *Journey to the Source*, pp. 69–71
29. WCL/*BurnesJournal*/1836–8/f.115
30. NAI/For/Pol/17Jul1837/Cons/No.45
31. Alexander Burnes: *Cabool*, p. 182
32. BL/IOR/MSS/EUR/E/161/3/f.20
33. BL/IOR/MSS/EUR/E/161/3/f.19
34. BL/IOR/MSS/EUR/E/161/3/f.15
35. BL/IOR/MSS/EUR/E/161/3/f.23
36. BL/IOR/MSS/EUR/E/161/3/f.7
37. BL/IOR/MSS/EUR/E/161/3/f.34
38. W F B Laurie: *Sketches*, p. 12
39. BL/IOR/MSS/EUR/E/161/3/f.35
40. BL/IOR/MSS/EUR/E/161/3/f.22
41. BL/IOR/MSS/EUR/E/161/3/f.24
42. BL IOR/E/4/743/ff 69-77/para.153
43. BL/IOR/MSS/EUR/E/161/3/f.7
44. *Parliamentary Papers* Vol.XXV Session 2 1859 p. 5
45. BL/IOR/E/755/ff.715-31

46 BL/IOR/MSS/EUR/E/161/3/f.225
47 WCL/*BurnesJournal*/1836-8/f.136
48 WCL/*BurnesJournal*/1836–8/f.154
49 BL/IOR/MSS/EUR/E/161/3/f.28
50 *Parliamentary Papers*, Vol. 25, Session 2, 1859, p. 16
51 *Parliamentary Papers*, Vol. 25, Session 2, 1859, p. 11
52 WCL/*BurnesJournal*/1836–8/f.158
53 K Meyer and S Bryssac: *Tournament of Shadows*, p. 39
54 *The Poetical Works of Thomas Moore*, p. 58
55 BL/IOR/MSS/EUR/E/161/3/f.38

## Chapter 20  Peshawar Perverted

1 Gray and Garrett: *European Adventurers*, p. 131
2 J M Honigberger: *Thirty-Five Years*, Vol. 1, pp. 54–5
3 Gray and Garrett: *European Adventurers*, p. 118
4 William Barr, *Journal of a March*, pp. 236–49
5 James Atkinson, *The Expedition into Afghanistan*, p. 374
6 Grey and Garratt, *European Adventurers*, p. 135
7 Alexander Burnes: *Cabool*, p. 122
8 *Parliamentary Papers*, Vol. 25, Session 2, 1859, p. 17
9 NAI/For/Pol/20Oct1837/No.66/p. 277
10 Alexander Burnes: *Cabool*, p. 123
11 BL/IOR/MSS/EUR/E/161/3/f.45
12 WCL/*BurnesJournal*/1836–8/f.170
13 BL/IOR/MSS/EUR/E/161/3/f.42
14 BL/IOR/MSS/EUR/E/161/3/f.28
15 WCL/*BurnesJournal*/1836–8/f.163
16 J W Kaye: *History of the War*, Vol. 1, p. 357
17 *Parliamentary Papers*, Vol. 25, Session 2, 1859, p. 16
18 BL/IOR/MSS/EUR/E/161/3/f.42
19 WCL/*BurnesJournal*/1836–8/f.167
20 BL/IOR/MSS/EUR/E/161/3/f.45
21 NAI/For/Pol/20Oct1837/Cons/No.68/pp. 282–3
22 Gray and Garret: *European Adventurers*, p. 308
23 James Wood: *A Journey*, pp. 159–61
24 BL/IOR/MSS/EUR/E/161/3/f.48
25 BL/IOR/MSS/EUR/E/161/3/f.45
26 B D Hopkins: *The Making of Modern Afghanistan*, p. 84
27 Shah Mahmoud Hanifi: *Connecting Histories*, p. 58
28 *Parliamentary Papers*, Vol. 25, Session 2, 1859, pp. 19–24
29 NAI/For/Pol/20Oct1837/No.72/p. 304
30 NAI/For/Pol/20Oct1837/No.72/p. 309
31 *Parliamentary Papers*, Vol. 25, Session 2, 1859, p. 26
32 BL/IOR/E/4/743/ff.69–77/coll.2/para.308
33 NAI/For/Pol/20Oct1837/No.74/p. 315
34 Mohan Lal: *Life of the Amir*, Vol. 2, p. 326

35 BL/IOR/MSS/EUR/E/161/3/f.51
36 BL/IOR/MSS/EUR/E/161/3/f.53
37 BL/IOR/MSS/EUR/E/161/3/f.51
38 J W Kaye: *Lives of Indian Officers*, Vol. 2, p. 212
39 WCL/*BurnesJournal*/1836–8/f.190

## Chapter 21  The Kabul Negotiations

1 B D Hopkins: *Modern Afghanistan*, p. 131
2 Mountstuart Elphinstone: *Kingdom of Caubul*, Vol.1, p. 1
3 J C Marshman: *History of India*, p. 105
4 Josiah Harlan: *India and Afghanistan*, p. 139
5 Alexander Burnes: *Cabool*, p. 83
6 NAI/For/Sec//28Sept1842/Cons/Nos.33–42/p. 7
7 *Parliamentary Papers*, Vol. 25, Session 2, 1859, p. 30
8 NAI/For/Pol/27Dec1837/No.12/pp. 33–41
9 W K Fraser-Tytler: *Afghanistan*, pp. 330–2
10 *Parliamentary Papers*, Vol. 25, Session 2, 1859, p. 46
11 WCL/*BurnesJournal*/1836–8/f.194
12 WCL/*BurnesJournal*/1836–8/f.201
13 *Parliamentary Papers*, Vol. 25, Session 2, 1859, p. 50
14 James Burnes: *Notes,,* p. 61
15 Afzal Iqbal: *First Afghan War*, p. 15
16 Henry Durand, *The First Afghan War*, p. 37
17 NAI/For/Sec//28 Sept/1842/Cons/Nos. 33–42/f.5
18 B D Hopkins: *Modern Afghanistan*, p. 45
19 BL/IOR/MSS/EUR/E/161/3/f.137
20 NAI/For/Sec/28Sept1842/Cons/Nos.33–42/f.33
21 Including Macnaghten, though with him the process took longer
22 Henry Durand, *The First Afghan War*, pp. 37–8
23 Auckland Colvin: *John Russell Colvin*, p. 97
24 NAI/For/Sec/29Aug1838/Cons/Nos.5–6/f.29
25 BL/IOR/MSS/EUR/E/161/3/f.58
26 BL/IOR/MSS/EUR/E/161/3/f.65
27 *Parliamentary Papers*, Vol. 25, Session 2, 1859, pp. 39–42
28 WCL/*BurnesJournal*/1836–8/f.201
29 *Parliamentary Papers*, Vol. 25, Session 2, 1859, p. 75
30 BL/IOR/MSS/EUR/E/161/3/f.60
31 WCL/*BurnesJournal*/1836–8/f.204
32 BL/IOR/MSS/EUR/E/161/3/f.211
33 W F B Laurie: *Some Distinguished Anglo-Indians*, p. 18
34 NAS GD45/14/587/26x
35 NAI/For/Sec/28Sept1842/Cons/Nos.33–42/f.5
36 NAI/For/Sec/28Sept1842/Cons/Nos.33–42/f.10
37 *Parliamentary Papers*, Vol. 25, Session 2, 1859, pp. 66–71
38 NAI/For/Pol/27Dec1837/No.14/ff.43–57
39 Louis Dupree: *Afghanistan*, p. 74

40 NAI/For/Pol/27Dec1837/Cons/No.18/ff.61–5
41 *Parliamentary Papers*, Vol. 25, Session 2, 1859, p. 39
42 WCL/*BurnesJournal*/1836–8/f.193
43 *Parliamentary Papers*, Vol. 25, Session 2, 1859, p. 53
44 *Parliamentary Papers*, Vol. 25, Session 2, 1859, p. 76
45 NAI/For/Pol/14Mar1838/No.19
46 NAI/For/Pol/14Mar1838/No.21
47 NAI/For/Pol/11Apr1838/No.33
48 NAI/For/Pol/11Apr1838/No.34
49 WCL/*BurnesJournal*/1836–8/f.191
50 BL/IOR/MSS/EUR/E/161/3/f.166
51 BL/IOR/MSS/EUR/E/161/3/f.165
52 BL/IOR/MSS/EUR/E/161/3/f.159
53 BL/IOR/MSS/EUR/E/161/3/f.171
54 BL/IOR/MSS/EUR/E/161/3/f.221
55 BL/IOR/MSS/EUR/E/161/3/f.63
56 BL/IOR/MSS/EUR/E/161/3/f.72
57 *Parliamentary Papers*, Vol. 25, Session 2, 1859, p. 48
58 NAI/For/Sec//4Apr1839/Cons/Nos.47–9/f.1
59 NAI/For/Sec//4Apr1839/Cons/Nos.47–9/f.5
60 *The Annual Register of the Year 1839*, Vol. 81, 1840, p. 327
61 Arthur Conolly: *Journey to the North of India*, Vol. 1, p. n253
62 NAS/GD371/95/43
63 NAS/GD45/14/587/26x
64 BL/IOR/MSS/EUR/E/161/3/f.29
65 NAI/For/Sec//4Apr1839/Cons/Nos.47–9/f.9

## Chapter 22  Stand-off

1 BL/IOR/MSS/EUR/E/161/3/f.64
2 BL/IOR/MSS/EUR/E/161/3/f.125
3 *The Annual Register of the Year 1839*, Vol. 81, 1840, p. 325
4 BL/IOR/MSS/EUR/E/161/3/f.179
5 NAS/GD371/95/18
6 M M Kessler: *Vitkevich*, p. 12
7 WCL/*BurnesJournal*/1836–8/f.247
8 *Parliamentary Papers*, Vol. 25, Session 2, 1859, pp. 90–3
9 BL/IOR/MSS/EUR/E/161/3/f.191
10 WCL/*BurnesJournal*/1836–8/f.249
11 *The Monthly Chronicle*, Vol 3, May 1842, p. 207
12 *The Annual Register of the Year 1839*, Vol. 81, 1840, p. 328
13 *Parliamentary Papers*, Vol. 25, Session 2, 1859, p. 82
14 Josiah Harlan: *A Memoir*, p. 139
15 *Parliamentary Papers*, Vol. 25, Session 2, 1859, p. 85
16 *The Monthly Chronicle*, Boston, Vol. 3, May 1842, p. 200
17 WCL/*BurnesJournal*/1836–8/f.193
18 J W Kaye: *Indian Army Officers*, Vol 2, p. 65

19 Gray and Garrett: *European Adventurers*, p. 81
20 Jean-Marie Lafont: *Maharaja Ranjit Singh*, p. 23
21 B D Hopkins: *Modern Afghanistan*, p. 46
22 Jean-Marie Lafont: *Maharaja Ranjit Singh*, p. 83
23 BL/IOR/MSS EUR/E/161/1/f.30
24 Penderel Moon: *The British Conquest*, p. 502
25 Henry Durand: *The First Afghan War*, p. 44
26 WCL/BurnesJournal/1836–8/f.261
27 Auckland Colvin: *John Russell Colvin*, p. 71
28 B D Hopkins: *Modern Afghanistan*, p. 73, 197
29 BL/IOR/MSS EUR/E/161/3/f.147
30 *Parliamentary Papers*, Vol. 25, Session 2, 1859, p. 80
31 J W Kaye: *History of the War*, Vol. 1, p. 190
32 NAI/For/Sec/4Jul1838/Cons/No.19/p. 3
33 *Parliamentary Papers*, Vol. 25, Session 2, 1859, p. 99
34 NAI/For/Sec/4Jul1838/Cons/No.18/p. 8
35 NAI/For/Sec/4Jul1838/Cons/No.17
36 NAI/For/Sec/4 Jul1838/Cons/No.19/p. 4
37 NAI/For/Sec/4Jul1838/Cons/No.22
38 Auckland Colvin: *John Russell Colvin*, p. 94
39 Mohan Lal: *Dost Mohammed Khan*, Vol. 1, p. 222
40 WCL/BurnesJournal/1836–8/f.260
41 George Buist: *Operation of the British Troops*, pp. 49–56.
42 *Edinburgh Review*, Vol. 76, Apr–Jul 1840, p. 349
43 BL/IOR/Eur Mss/E/161/3/f.4
44 WCL/*BurnesJournal*/1836–8, f.46
45 Zalmay A Gulzad: *Development of the Afghan State*, p. 45
46 B D Hopkins: *Modern Afghanistan*, p. 53
47 *Calcutta Review*, Vol. 2, p. 220
48 *The Annual Register of the Year 1839*, Vol. 81, 1840, p. 328
49 Josiah Harlan: *India and Afghanistan*, p. 171
50 NAS/GD/371/147/1
51 BL/IOR/Eur/Mss/E/161/3/f.138
52 Mohan Lal: *Dost Mohammed Khan*, Vol.1, p. 329

## Chapter 23 'Izzat wa Ikram'

1 NAS/GD371/95/18
2 BL/IOR/MSS/EUR/E/161/3/f.210
3 J W Kaye: *War in Afghanistan*, Vol. 1, p. 357
4 BL/IOR/MSS/EUR/E/161/3/f.137
5 Auckland Colvin: *John Russell Colvin*, p. 99
6 NAS/GD45/14/587/25
7 BL/IOR/MSS/EUR/E/161/3/f.70
8 BL/IOR/MSS/EUR/E/161/3/f.72
9 BL/IOR/MSS/EUR/E/161/3/f.136
10 BL/IOR/MSS/EUR/E/161/3/f.229

11 NAI/For/Sec/1Aug1838/No.15/p. 14
12 Craig Murray: *Murder in Samarkand*
13 *The Monthly Chronicle*, Vol. 3, May 1842, p. 205
14 NAS/GD45/14/587/33x
15 *The Monthly Chronicle*, Vol. 3, May 1842, p. 202
16 Afzal Iqbal: *First Afghan War*
17 John Wood: *Source of the Oxus*, p. 423
18 WCL/BurnesJournal/1836-8/f.280
19 NAS GD45/14/587/33x
20 BL/IOR/MSS/EUR/E161/3/f.190
21 NAI/For/Sec//28Sept1842/Cons/Nos.33-42/f.33

## Chapter 24  Regime Change

1 *Calcutta Review*, Vol. 2, Oct–Dec 1844, p. 222
2 NAI/For/Sec//16Oct1839/Cons/No.5
3 'By a Lady': *Letters from Madras*, p. 107. This remarkable lady wrote in October 1838: 'The Affghans have not decided whether they will attempt to stand against us. I think they would win. The Indian Army is in a poor condition, especially the Bengal part of it, which would be sent.'
4 James Hume: *Writings of H W Torrens*, Vol. 1, p. 180
5 M M Kaye (ed): *The Golden Calm*, p. 62
6 Emily Eden: *Up The Country*, p. 33
7 NAI/For/Sec/29Aug1838/Cons/Nos.5-6
8 NAI/For/Sec/29Aug1838/Cons/Nos.5-6/f.29
9 Emily Eden: *Up The Country*, pp. 130-7
10 Henry Durand: *The First Afghan War*, p. 67
11 Arthur Conolly: *Journey to the North of India Overland*, Vol 2, p. 322
12 *Tait's Magazine*, Vol. 10, 1843, p. 382
13 M E Yapp: *Strategies of British India*, p. 204
14 *Edinburgh Review*, Vol. 71, Apr–Jul 1840, pp. 327–71
15 *Calcutta Review*, Vol. 2, Oct–Dec 1844, p. 216
16 Sita Ram: *From Sepoy to Subedar*, p. 86
17 BL/IOR/MSS/EUR/E/161/3/f.76
18 Auckland Colvin: *John Russell Colvin*, p. 103
19 W K Fraser-Tytler: *Afghanistan*, p. 99
20 BL/IOR/MSS/EUR/E/161/3/f.74
21 *Transactions of the Bombay Geographical Society*, Vol. 2, p. 73
22 Emily Eden: *Up The Country*, p. 145
23 WCL/BurnesJournal/1836-8/f.160
24 J A Lafont: *Maharaja Ranjit Singh*, p. 12
25 BL/IOR/MSS/EUR/E/161/3/f.78
26 BL/IOR/MSS/EUR/E/161/3/f.79
27 BL/IOR/MSS/EUR/E/161/3/f.81
28 Khushwant Singh: *Ranjit Singh*, p. 207
29 Burnes et al.: *Reports and Papers*
30 George Buist: *Outline of the Operation of the British Troops*, p. 69

31  BL/IOR/MSS/EUR/E/161/3/f.83
32  BL/IOR/MSS/EUR/E/161/3/f.85
33  BL/IOR/MSS/EUR/E/161/3/f.91
34  BL/IOR/E/755/ff.715–31
35  Peter Hopkirk: *The Great Game*, p. 190
36  NAS/GD45/14/587/34x
37  Auckland Colvin: *John Russell Colvin*, p. 133
38  George Buist: *Outline of the Operation*, p. 21
39  *Calcutta Review*, Vol. 2, Oct–Dec 1844, p. 458
40  James Hume: *Writings of H W Torrens*, Vol 1, p. xlvi
41  J W Kaye: *History of the War in Afghanistan*, Vol. 1, p. 367
42  Auckland Colvin: *John Russell Colvin*, p. 113
43  NAS/GD45/14/587/29
44  NAI/For/Sec//28Sept1842/Cons/Nos.33–42/f.13
45  W K Fraser-Tytler, *Afghanistan*, p. 100
46  Emily Eden, *Up The Country*, p. 157 My identification. Emily sometimes uses the real initial and sometimes a random letter. Captain B does not feature before Burnes' arrival, and Lord was one of only three doctors then at Simla. The following year a different Captain B features.
47  NAI/For/Sec/25Sep1839/Cons/Nos.30–1/f.15
48  NAI/For/Sec/25Sep1839/Cons/Nos.30–1/f.22
49  BL/IOR/MSS/EUR/E/161/3/f.93
50  BL/IOR/MSS/EUR/E/161/3/f.99
51  Gray and Garrett: *European Adventurers*, p. 200
52  BL/IOR/MSS/EUR/E/161/3/f.101
53  J W Kaye: *History of the War*, Vol. 1, p. 370
54  William H Dennie: *A Personal Narrative*, p. 31
55  Email from Court of the Lord Lyon King of Arms, Edinburgh, 8 May 2013
56  NAI/For/Sec/28Sep1842/Cons/Nos.33–42/f.19
57  W F B Laurie: *Distinguished Anglo-Indians*, p. 361
58  NAS/GD/371/95/28
59  NAS/GD/371/95/50
60  NAS/GD371/95/31/2
61  NAS/GD371/95/32
62  NAS/GD371/95/36
63  NAS/GD371/95/47
64  *Parliamentary Papers*, Vol. 25, Session 2, 1859, p. 84
65  Peter Hopkirk: *The Great Game*, p. 188
66  J W Kaye: *Lives of Indian Officers*, Vol. 1, p. ix
67  Ronald Hyam: *Empire and Sexuality*, pp. 29–30
68  M E Yapp: *Strategies of British India*, p. 361
69  BL/MSS/EUR/E/161/3/f.204
70  NAS/GD/371/95/18
71  J W Kaye: *Lives of Indian Officers*, Vol. 2, p. 53
72  George Buist: *Outline of the Operation*, p. 12
73  NAI/For/Sec/17Oct1838/Cons/No.184/f.3

74 NAI/For/Sec/17 Oct1838/Cons/No.184/f.1
75 NAI/For/Sec/17Oct1838/Cons/No.184/f.5
76 John C Cunningham: *The Last Man*, p. 40
77 Viscount Esher: *The Girlhood of Queen Victoria*, Vol. 2, p. 146
78 John C Cunningham: *The Last Man*, p. 40
79 Sita Ram: *From Sepoy to Subedar*, p. 16
80 Henry Havelock: *Narrative of the War*, Vol. 1, p. 78

## Chapter 25  Securing Sind

1 BL/IOR/MSS/EUR/E/161/3/f.101
2 NAI/For/Sec/6Mar1839/Cons/No.56/f.1
3 Henry Havelock: *Narrative of the War*, Vol. 1, p. 105
4 J W Kaye: *Lives of Indian Officers*, Vol. 1, p. 58
5 Charles Masson: *Narrative of a Journey*, p. 80
6 Henry Havelock: *Narrative of the War*, p. 122
7 George MacDonald Fraser: *Flashman*, p. 74
8 Shahamat Ali: *The Sikhs and Afghans*, p. 69
9 *Asiatic Journal and Monthly Register*, Vol. 24, May–Aug 1839, p. 23
10 William Hough: *A Narrative of the March*, p. 16
11 Henry Havelock: *Narrative of the War*, Vol. 1, p. 136
12 W Broadfoot: *Major George Broadfoot*, p. 7
13 William Hough: *A Narrative of the March*, p. 30
14 NAI/For/Sec/6Mar1839/Cons/No.54
15 NAI/For/Sec/6Mar1839/Cons/No.53
16 NAI/For/Sec/6Mar1839/Cons/No.5
17 NAI/For/Sec/6Mar1839/Cons/No.54
18 NAI/For/Sec/6Mar1839/Cons/No.52/a
19 NAI/For/Sec/6Mar1839/Cons/No.5
20 NAI/For/Sec/20Mar1839/Cons/No.190
21 NAI/For/Sec/20Mar1839/Cons/No.191
22 BL/ADD/MSS/36470/ff.118–25
23 BL/ADD/MSS/36470/f.128
24 BL/ADD/MSS/36470/f.347
25 Henry Durand: *The First Afghan War*, p. 42
26 *The Oriental Herald*, vol.III, Jan-Jun 1839 p. 42
27 BL/ADD/MSS/36470/ff.22-25
28 BL/ADD/MSS/36470/f.145
29 BL/ADD/MSS/36470/f.148
30 NAI/For/Sec/16Oct1839/Cons/No.5
31 Mohan Lal: *Travels in the Panjab*, p. 466
32 BL/ADD/MSS/36470/f.33
33 BL/ADD/MSS/36470/f.233
34 NAI/For/Sec/16Oct1839/Cons/No.70/ff.13–23
35 Mohan Lal: *Amir Dost Mohammed Khan*, Vol. 2, p. 252
36 NAI/For/Sec/4Sept1839/Cons/Nos.264–7
37 BL/ADD/MSS/36470/ff.118–25

38 *Asiatic Journal and Monthly Register*, Vol. 34, Jan–Mar 1841, p. 295
39 R H Kennedy: *Narrative of the Campaign*, Vol.1, p. 34
40 *Calcutta Review*, Vol. 2, 1833, p. 229
41 *Asiatic Journal and Monthly Register*, Vol. 24, May–Aug 1839, p. 23
42 Henry Havelock: *Narrative of the War*, Vol. 1, p. 149
43 Lawrence James: *Raj*, p. 74
44 The eighteen-pounder siege guns were too heavy for the bridge. Piers were constructed into the fast flowing river, and the guns floated across on attached platforms.
45 George Gleig: *Sale's Brigade*, p. 33

## Chapter 26 The Dodgy Dossier

1 G J Alder: 'The "Garbled" Blue Books', *The Historical Journal*, Vol. 15, No. 2, p. 231
2 John Bright: *Speeches on Public Policy*, Vol. 1, p. 116
3 *The Annual Register of the Year 1839*, Vol. 81, p. 322
4 BL/IOR/Add/Mss/46915/f.161
5 G J Alder, 'The "Garbled" Blue Books'; J A Norris, *The First Afghan War*
6 NAI/For/Sec/28Sept1842/Cons/Nos.33–42/f.19
7 BL/ADD/MSS/36470/ff.103–10
8 BL/ADD/MSS/36470/ff.151–3
9 NLS/MSS/14450/f.42
10 BL/ADD/MSS/36470/ff.87–90
11 BL/ADD/MSS/36470/f.156
12 BL/ADD/MSS/36470/f.160
13 BL/ADD/MSS/36470/f.167

## Chapter 27  Kelat

1 *Asiatic Journal and Monthly Register*, Vol 27, Sep–Dec 1838, p. 2
2 Shah Mahmoud Hanifi: *Connecting Histories*, p. 70
3 *Asiatic Journal and Monthly Register*, Vol. 29, May–Aug 1839, p. 99
4 James Atkinson: *The Expedition*, p. 91
5 I have drawn heavily here on Dennis Holman: *Sikander Sahib*, pp. 117–18
6 J W Kaye: *History of the War*, Vol. 1, p. 418
7 R H Kennedy: *Narrative of the Campaign*, Vol. 1, p. 187
8 William H Dennie: *Personal Narrative*, p. 57
9 Henry Durand: *The First Afghan War*, p. 132
10 George Buist: *Outline of the Operation*, p. 69
11 William Hough: *A Narrative*, p. 58
12 Arthur Conolly: *Journey to the North of India*, Vol. 2, p. 190
13 NAI/For/Sec/22May1839/Cons
14 PRO/Prob.11/1980/261
15 NAI/For/Sec/28Sept1842/Cons/Nos.33–42/f.5
16 George Lawrence: *Reminiscences*, p. 8
17 Charles Masson: *Journey to Kalat*, p. 272
18 Penderel Moon: *The British Conquest*, p. 512
19 *Calcutta Review*, Vol. 2, Oct–Dec 1844, p. 230
20 George Buist: *Outline of the Operations*, p. 91

21 Henry Havelock: *Narrative of the War*, Vol. 1, p. 261
22 T R Blackburn: *The Extermination of a British Army*, p. x
23 J W Kaye: *History of the War*, Vol. 1, p. 427
24 Naseer Dashti: *The Baloch and Balochistan*, p. 210
25 Charles Masson: *Narrative of a Journey*, pp. 81–8
26 William Hough: *A Narrative*, p. 74
27 Mohan Lal: *Dost Mohammed Khan*, Vol. 2, p. 194
28 The current Khan hosted me generously at his home in exile in Wales
29 Henry Durand: *The First Afghan War*, p. 144
30 Naseer Dashti: *The Baloch and Balochistan*, p. 215
31 Intelligence Branch, Indian Army: *Frontier and Overseas Expeditions*, Vol. 3, p. 38
32 Naseer Dashti: *The Baloch and Balochistan*, p. 202
33 J W Kaye: *History of the War*, p. 430
34 *Calcutta Review*, Vol. 2, Oct–Dec 1844, p. 232
35 *The Oriental Herald*, Vol. 4, Jul–Dec 1839, p. 144

## Chapter 28  A King in Kandahar

1 M E Yapp: *Strategies of British India*, p. 269
2 R H Kennedy: *Narrative of the Campaign*, Vol. 1, p. 176
3 NAI/For/Sec/4Jul1838/Cons/No.17/p. 3
4 Henry Havelock: *Narrative of the War*, Vol. 1, p. 318
5 BL/ADD/MSS/36470/f.322
6 *Calcutta Review*, Vol. 2, Oct–Dec 1844, p. 232
7 Henry Havelock: *Narrative of the War*, Vol. 2, p. 4
8 Ann Jones: *Kabul in Winter*, p. 28
9 *The Monthly Chronicle*, Vol. 3, May 1842, p. 212
10 R H Kennedy: *Narrative of the Campaign*, Vol. 1, p. 253
11 BL/ADD/MSS/36470/f.323
12 William Barr: *Journal of a March*, p. 264
13 NAI/For/Sec/26Jun1839/Progs/Nos.7–8/p. 6426
14 NAI/For/Sec/26Jun1839/Progs/Nos.129–30/p. 6297
15 NAI/For/Sec/21Aug1839/Cons/No.35/p. 11
16 NAI/For/Sec/21Aug1839/Cons/No.35/p. 13
17 NAI/For/Sec/21 Aug1839/Cons/No.35/p. 2
18 NAI/For/Sec/21Aug1839/Cons/No.39
19 John C Griffiths: *Afghanistan*, p. 31
20 BL/ADD/MSS/36470/f.323

## Chapter 29  Death in St Petersburg

1 Alexander Morrison, 'Twin Imperial Disasters', MS p. 27, awaiting publication in *Modern Asian Studies*
2 William Dalrymple, *Return of a King*, p. 199
3 NAI/For/Sec/18Dec1839/Cons/No.6/f.3
4 Mikhail Volodarsky, *The Russians in Afghanistan* (p. 83) states that Witkiewicz suffered psychological pressure from reproaches from Polish friends, in the plural.
5 BL/Add/Mss/46915/f.161

6 M M Kessler: *Ivan Viktorovich Vitkevich*, p. 26

## Chapter 30 Ghazni

1 Hari Ram Gupta: *Mohan Lal Kashmiri*, p. 126
2 R H Kennedy: *Narrative of the Campaign*, Vol. 2, p. 89
3 NAI/For/Sec/31Jul1839/Cons/No.29
4 NAI/For/Sec/13Nov1838/Cons/No.49/f.2
5 NAI/For/Sec/23Oct1839/Cons/Nos. 28–9/f.4
6 NAI/For/Sec/23Oct1839/No.31/f.2
7 NAI/For/Sec/23Oct1839/Cons/No.31/f.5
8 William Taylor: *Scenes and Adventures*, p. 98
9 William Hough: *A Narrative*, p. xvii
10 BL/ADD/MSS/36470/f.323
11 BL/ADD/MSS/36470/f.323
12 Henry Havelock: *Narrative of the War*, Vol. 2, p. 59
13 William H Dennie, *Personal Narrative*, p. 68
14 George Buist: *Outline of the Operation*, pp. 108–12
15 William H Dennie: *Personal Narrative*, p. 77
16 Hari Ram Gupta: *Mohan Lal Kashmiri*, p. 130
17 William H Dennie: *Personal Narrative*, p. 72
18 William Hough: *A Narrative*, p. 181
19 NAI/For/Sec/28 Sep 1842/Cons/Nos. 33–42/f.23
20 Mohan Lal: *Dost Mohammed Khan*, Vol. 2, p. 226
21 J W Kaye: *Lives of Indian Officers*, Vol. 2, p. 68
22 William Hough: *A Narrative*, p. 209
23 Penderel Moon: *The British Conquest*, p. 515
24 BL/IOR/MSS/EUR/E/161/3/f.227
25 R H Kennedy: *Narrative of the Campaign*, Vol. 2, p. 66
26 Ann Jones: *Kabul in Winter*, p. 39
27 William Hough: *A Narrative*, p. 224
28 Mohan Lal: *Dost Mohammed Khan*, Vol. 2, p. 237
29 Josiah Harlan: *A Memoir*, p. 194

## Chapter 31 Mission Accomplished

1 Henry Havelock: *Narrative of the War*, Vol. 2, p. 115
2 C W Woodburn: *The Bala Hissar*, p. 17
3 J W Kaye: *History of the War*, Vol. 2,, p. 36
4 NAI/For/Sec/25 Sep 1839/Cons/No.18
5 George Lawrence: *Reminiscences*, p. 12
6 R H Kennedy: *Narrative*, Vol. 2, p. 106
7 William Hough: *A Narrative*, p. 262
8 Ben Macintyre: *Josiah the Great*, p. 260
9 William Barr: *Journal of a March*, pp. 373–4
10 Louis Dupree: *Afghanistan*, p. 81
11 Shahamat Ali: *The Sikhs and Afghans*, pp. 478–84
12 R H Kennedy: *Narrative of the Campaign*, Vol. 2, pp. 113–18

13  Hari Ram Gupta: *Mohan Lal Kashmiri*, p. 133
14  John C Cunningham: *The Last Man*, p. 53
15  Henry Durand; *The First Afghan War*, p. 211
16  BL/ADD/MSS/36470/f.423
17  BL/ADD/MSS/36470/f.465–500
18  *Bombay Courier*, 26 Oct 1839
19  William Hough: *A Narrative*, p. 298
20  Penderel Moon: *The British Conquest*, p. 516
21  George Buist, *Outline of the Operation*, p. 131

## Chapter 32  Kabul in Winter

1  G R Gleig: *Sale's Brigade*, p. 69
2  CUL GB 012 MS.Add.4536. James Kenney: *The Irish Ambassador* (1838), Act II. The play was simultaneously running in Kabul, Cacutta and at the Haymarket Theatre in London.
3  William H Dennie: *A Personal Narrative*, p. 102
4  Henry Havelock: *Narrative of the War*, Vol. 2, p. 136
5  G J Allder: 'The "Garbled" Blue Books, p. 237
6  NAS/GD45/14/587/34x
7  Henry Havelock: *Narrative of the War*, Vol. 2, p. 149
8  Christine Noelle: *State and Tribe*, p. 135
9  NAI/For/Sec/28Sep1842/Cons/Nos.205–6/f.1
10  J W Kaye: *History of the War*, Vol. 2, p. 18
11  M E Yapp: *Strategies of British India*, p. 348
12  NAI/For/Sec/Cons/28Sep1842/Nos.33-42/f.23
13  NAI/For/Sec/28Sept1842/Cons/Nos.33-42/f.33
14  George Lawrence: *Reminiscences*, p. 34
15  William Dalrymple: *Return of a King*, p. 216
16  Tresham Lever (ed.): *Letters of Lady Palmerston*, p. 223
17  John Clark Marshman: *History of India*, p. 154
18  NAI/For/Sec/28Sept1842/Cons/Nos.33–42/f.23
19  Alexander Morrison: 'Twin Imperial Disasters', MS p. 37
20  NAI/For/Sec/18Dec1839/Cons/No.6/f.4
21  NAI/For/Sec/18Dec1839/Cons/No.6/f.14
22  NAI/For/Sec/30Mar1840/Cons/Nos.38–41/f.5
23  NAI/For/Sec/30Mar1840/Cons/Nos.42–3/f.5
24  NAI/For/Sec/28Dec1842/Cons/Nos.443–4
25  William H Dennie: *A Personal Narrative*, p. 113
26  *Calcutta Review*, Vol. 2, Oct–Dec 1844, p. 235
27  Peter Hopkirk: *The Great Game*, p. 235
28  J W Kaye: *Lives of Indian Officers*, Vol. 2, p. 131
29  T R Blackburn: *The Extermination*, p. xlv
30  NAI/For/Sec/28Dec1842/Progs/Nos.480–2/f.9762
31  J W Kaye: *Lives of Indian Officers*, Vol. 2, p. 69
32  NAS/GD45/14/587/31x
33  NAI/For/Sec/21Aug1839/No.37

34 *Calcutta Review*, Vol. 2, Oct–Dec 1844, p. 233
35 James Atkinson: *The Expedition*, p. 365
36 Email from Lyon Office, Edinburgh, 6 May 2013
37 *Edinburgh Review*, Vol. 71, Apr–Jul 1840, p. 331
38 *Monthly Review*,Vol 3, Sep–Dec 1840, p. 203

## Chapter 33  Dost Mohammed

1 J W Kaye: *History of the War*, Vol. 2, p. 66
2 NAS/GD45/14/587/31x
3 Penderel Moon: *The British Conquest*, p. 523
4 John C Cunningham: *The Last Man*, p. 53
5 W H Dennie: *Personal Narrative*, p. 117
6 Henry Durand:*The First Afghan War*, p. 293
7 *Parliamentary Papers*, Vol. 25, Session 2 1859, p. 66
8 Mohan Lal: *Dost Mohammed Khan*, Vol. 1, p. 109
9 James Atkinson: *The Expedition*, p. 344
10 George Gleig: *With Sale's Brigade*, p. 52
11 William Barr: *Journal*, p. 280
12 J W Kaye: *History of the War*, Vol. 2, p. 144
13 William Dalrymple: *Return of a King*, p. 245
14 J W Kaye: *History of the War*, Vol. 2, p. 92
15 George Buist, *Outline of the Operation*, p. 162
16 J W Kaye: *Lives of Indian Officers*, Vol. 2, p. 78
17 J W Kaye: *Lives of Indian Officers*, Vol. 2, p. 79
18 James Atkinson: *The Expedition*, p. 360
19 *Tait's Magazine*, Vol. 10, 1843, p. 372
20 George Buist: *Outline of the Operation*, p. 164

## Chapter 34  Discontent

1 W H Dennie: *Personal Narrative*, p. 55
2 William Barr: *Journal of a March*, p. 381
3 Christine Noelle: *State and Tribe*, pp. 47, 307
4 Jacob Seth Mesrov: *The Armenians in India*, p. 224
5 NAI/For/Sec/28Dec1842/Progs/Nos.480–2/f.9763
6 J W Kaye: *Lives of Indian Officers*, Vol. 2, p. 67
7 George Buist: *Outline of the Operation*, p. 165
8 William Dalrymple: *Return of a King*, p. 232
9 Mohan Lal: *Dost Mohammed Khan*, Vol. 2, p. 320
10 Patrick Macrory: *A Signal Catastrophe*, p. 122
11 Mountstuart Elphinstone: *An Account of the Kingdom of Caubul*, Vol. 1, p. 47
12 Victor Jacquemont: *Correspondance*, Vol. 2, p. 70
13 T R Blackburn: *The Extermination of a British Army*, p. 44
14 *Edinburgh Review*, Vol. 71, Apr–Jul 1840, p. 369
15 J W Kaye: *History of the War*, Vol. 2, p. 147
16 *Asiatic Journal* Vol. 35, May–Aug 1841, p. 182
17 George Buist: *Outline of the Operation*, p. 182

18 Mohan Lal: *Travels in the Panjab*, p. 335
19 Gray and Garratt: *European Adventurers*, p. 208
20 BL/MSS/EUR/F88/124/ff.139–40
21 Charles Masson: *Narrative of a Journey*, p. 117
22 J W Kaye: *The History of the War in Afghanistan*, Vol. 2, p. 28
23 Mohan Lal: *Dost Mohammed Khan*, Vol. 2, p. 202
24 Mohan Lal: *Travels in the Panjab*, p. 334
25 Henry Durand: *The First Afghan War*, p. 273
26 *Agra Ukhbar*, 23 June 1840, p. 1
27 George Buist: *Outline of the Operation*, p. 267
28 John Greenwood, *The Campaign in Afghanistan*, p. 76
29 Henry Durand: *The First Afghan War*, p. 315
30 M E Yapp: *Strategies of British India*, p. 371
31 Craig Murray: *Murder in Samarkand*, p. 27
32 John Lawrence: *Lawrence of Lucknow*, p. 36
33 Kathleen Hopkirk: *Central Asia*, p. 128
34 J W Kaye: *History of the War*, Vol. 2, p. 120
35 George Buist: *Outline of the Operation*, p. 271
36 NAI/For/Sec/28Dec1842/Cons/Nos.205–6
37 M E Yapp: *Strategies of British India*, p. 311
38 *Calcutta Review*, Vol. 2, Oct–Dec 1844, p. 247
39 Louis Dupree: *Afghanistan*, p. 45
40 Zalmay Gulzad: *External Influences and the Development of the Afghan State*, p. 16
41 J.W. Kaye: *Lives of Indian Officers*, Vol. 2, p. 80
42 B D Hopkins: *The Making of Modern Afghanistan*, p. 67
43 NAI/For/Sec/28Sep1842/Cons/Nos.33–42/p. 29
44 NAS GD45/14/587/31x
45 J W Kaye: *History of the War*, Vol. 2, p. 127
46 NAI/For/Sec/28Sept1842/Cons/Nos.29–32/pp. 5–6
47 W Broadfoot: *Major George Broadfoot*, p. 13
48 George Buist, *Outline of the Operation*, p. 294
49 David Mitchell: *History of Montrose*, p. 64
50 Mohan Lal: *Dost Mohammed Khan*, Vol. 2, p. 392
51 Charles Samuel Stewart: *Sketches of Society*, Vol. 2, p. 125
52 Tresham Lever (ed.): *Letters of Lady Palmerston*, p. 261
53 Emily Eden: *Up the Country*, p. 389
54 Extraordinarily, even after the disaster, Auckland insisted on appointing General Lumley to head the relieving force. Lumley was even more ill than Elphinstone, and Auckland only backed down after the Army sent him a medical report. J W Kaye: *History of the War*, Vol. 3, p. 20

## Chapter 35  Dissent and Dysfunction

1 Helen Mackenzie: *Storms and Sunshine*, Vol 1, p. 184
2 Henry Durand: *The First Afghan War*, p. 328
3 Christine Noelle, *State and Tribe*, pp. 49, 307
4 NAI/For/Sec/28Dec1842/Cons/Nos.205–6/f.20

5 NAI/For/Sec/28Dec1842/Cons/Nos.205–6/f.26
6 NAI/For/Sec/28Dec1842/Cons/Nos.205–6/f.2
7 NAI/For/Sec/28Dec1842/Progs/Nos.480–2/f.9770
8 Christine Noelle: *State and Tribe*, p. 51
9 NAI/For/Sec/28Dec1842/Progs/Nos.480–2/f.9805
10 J W Kaye: *Lives of Indian Officers*, Vol. 2, p. 85
11 *Calcutta Review*, Vol. 2, Oct–Dec 1844, p. 248
12 W Broadfoot: *Major G Broadfoot*, p. 23
13 NAI/For/Sec/28Sept1842/Cons/Nos.29–32/p. 12. On 8 April 1842 the *Bombay Courier* published a letter claiming Burnes suppressed this information. Hamlet Wade, the sole surviving witness, contradicted this
14 W Broadfoot: *Major George Broadfoot*, pp. 23–30
15 *Blackwood's Magazine*, Vol. 53, Jan–Jun 1843, p. 241
16 Helen Mackenzie: *Storms and Sunshine*, Vol. 1, p. 188
17 Margaret Kekewich: *Retreat and Retribution*, p. 18
18 J W Kaye: *Lives of Indian Officers*, Vol. 2, p. 86
19 Henry Durand: *The First Afghan War*, p. 338
20 George Buist: *Outline of the Operation*, p. xi
21 George Lawrence: *Reminiscences*, p. 59
22 J W Kaye: *Lives of Indian Officers*, Vol. 2, p. 86
23 James Lunt: *Bokhara Burnes*, p. 203

**Chapter 36  Death in Kabul**

1 NAI/For/Sec/28 Sep1842/Cons/Nos.29–32/f.9
2 William Dalrymple: *Return of a King*, p. 280
3 Arthur Conolly: *Journey to the North*, Vol 2, pp. 152–6.
4 Now a national hero http://www.pajhwok.com/en/2010/07/05/ghazi-abdullah-khan-achakzai-remembered
5 Mountstuart Elphinstone: *An Account*, Vol. 1, p. 299
6 Mohan Lal: *Dost Mohammed Khan*, Vol. 2, p. 398
7 George Gleig: *Sale's Brigade*, p. 67
8 James Atkinson: *The Expedition*, p. 282
9 Peter Hopkirk: *The Great Game*, p. 239
10 Louis Dupree: *The First Anglo Afghan War Folklore and History*, p. 8
11 Shah Mahmoud Hanifi: *Connecting Histories in Afghanistan*, p. 88
12 M E Yapp: *Strategies of British India*, p. 424
13 Helen Mackenzie: *Storms and Sunshine of a Soldier's Life*, Vol I, p. 194
14 William Dalrymple: *Return of a King*, pp. 292–3
15 W Broadfoot: *Major George Broadfoot*, p. 123
16 *The Monthly Chronicle*, Vol. 3, May 1842, p. 218
17 Penderel Moon: *The British Conquest*, p. 545
18 J W Kaye: *History of the War*, Vol. 2, p. 165
19 William Dalrymple: *Return of a King*, p. 276
20 Helen Mackenzie: *Storms and Sunshine*, Vol. 1, p. 195
21 NAI/For/Sec/28Dec1842/Progs/Nos.480–2/f.9972
22 Mohan Lal: *Dost Mohammed Khan*, Vol. 2, p. 402

23  Henry Durand: *The First Afghan War*, p. 352
24  George Lawrence: *Reminiscences*, p. 62
25  *Calcutta Review*, Vol. 2, Oct–Dec 1844, p. 251
26  NAS/GD45/14/587/31x
27  George Lawrence: *Forty-Three Years in India*, p. 64
28  *Bombay Times*, 23 April 1842
29  *Tait's Magazine*, Vol. 10, 1843, p. 382
30  NAI/For/Sec/28Dec1842/Progs/Nos.480–2/f.9972
31  Gregory Bondarevsky: *The Great Game: A Russian Perspective*, p. 39
32  BL/IOR/E/4/812/ f.1181
33  Burnes had left Ghulam Rs2,000 in his will.
34  NAS/GD45/14/587/31x
35  William Dalrymple: *Return of a King*, p. 295
36  T R Blackburn: *The Extermination of a British Army*, p. 10
37  *Calcutta Review*, Vol. 2, Oct–Dec 1844, p. 251
38  W Broadfoot: *Major George Broadfoot*, p. 123
39  *Transactions of the Bombay Geographical Society*, Vol. 6, p. ix

## Chapter 37  Aftermath

1  BL/ADD/MSS/37313/f.135
2  T R Blackburn: *The Extermination of a British Army*, p. 87
3  John Greenwood: *The Campaign in Afghanistan*, p. 127
4  T R Blackburn: *The Extermination of a British Army*, p. 165
5  Michael H Fisher: *Counterflows to Colonialism*, p. 358
6  Hari Ram Gupta: *Mohan Lal Kashmiri*, p. vi
7  G J Alder: 'The "Garbled" Blue Books', p. 245
8  William Cunningham: *The Debates on Motion (Palmerston)*
9  Isaiah Berlin: *Karl Marx*, pp. 147–50
10  K Marx and F Engels: *On Colonialism*, pp. 211, 332
11  J W Kaye, *History of the War*, Vol. 1, p. 204
12  G J Alder: 'The "Garbled" Blue Books', p. 247
13  *Hansard*, House of Commons, 19 March 1861
14  *The Spectator*, 23 March 1861, p. 294
15  John Bright: *Speeches*, Vol. 1, p. 114

# Bibliography

## MANUSCRIPT SOURCES

| | |
|---|---|
| BL | British Library |
| CUL | Cambridge University Library |
| FHM | Freemasons Hall, Mumbai |
| MAS | Mumbai Asiatic Society |
| ML | Montrose Library |
| MM | Montrose Museum |
| MSA | Maharastra State Archive, Mumbai |
| NAI | National Archives of India, Delhi |
| NAS | National Archives of Scotland, Edinburgh |
| NLS | National Library of Scotland, Edinburgh |
| PRO | Public Record Office, Kew |
| RSA | Royal Society Archives |
| WCL | Worcester College Library, Oxford |

## PUBLISHED PRIMARY SOURCES

Shahamat Ali: *The Sikhs and Afghans in Connection with India and Persia*, John Murray, London, 1847

James Atkinson: *The Expedition into Afghanistan: Notes and Sketches Descriptive of the Country*, W H Allen & Co, London, 1842

Lieut William Barr: *Journal of a March from Delhi to Peshawur, and from thence to Cabul, with the Mission of Lt Col C M Wade Kt CB*, James Madden, London, 1844

Robert Bigsby: *Memoir of the Illustrious and Sovereign Order of St John of Jerusalem, from the Capitulation of Malta in 1798, to the Present Period*, Richard Keene, Irongate, Derby, 1869

John Bright: *Speeches on Questions of Public Policy*, ed. J E Thorold Rogers, Macmillan & Co., Oxford, 1868

George Buist: *George Buist: Outline of the Operation of the British Troops in Scinde and Afghanistan betwixt November 1838 and November 1841, with Remarks on the Policy of the War*, The Times Office, Bombay, 1843

George Buist: *A Memoir of Sir Alexander Burnes, C.B.*, printed for private circulation, Edinburgh, 1851

Alexander Burnes: *Cabool: A Personal Narrative of a Journey to, and Residence in that City in the Years 1836, 7 and 8*, John Murray, London, 1842

Alexander Burnes: *Travels into Bokhara 1831–3: A Journey from India to Cabool Tartary and Persia and a Voyage on the Indus*, John Murray, London, 1834

Sir Alexander Burnes, Lieutenant Leech, Dr Lord and Lieutenant Wood: *Reports and Papers Political, Geographical, & Commercial Submitted to Government in the Years 1835–36–37 in Scinde, Affghanistan and Adjacent Countries*, Bengal Military Orphan Press, Calcutta, 1839

James Burnes: *Narrative of a Visit to the Court of the Ameers of Sinde*, Summachar Press, Bombay, 1829

James Burnes: *A Sketch of the History of Cutch*, John Stark, Edinburgh, 1839

James Burnes: *A Sketch of the History of the Knights Templar*, Blackwood, Edinburgh, 1840

James Burnes: *Notes on his Name and Family*, Printed for private circulation, Edinburgh, 1851

Arthur Conolly: *Journey to the North of India, Overland from England, through Russia, Persia and Affghaunistan*, Richard Bentley, London, 1834

William Cunningham: *The Debates on Motion for Papers with a View to the Impeachment of the Right Honourable Henry John Temple Viscount Palmerston*, Robert Hardwicke, London, 1860

William H Dennie (ed. William E Steele): *Personal Narrative of the Campaigns in Afghanistan, Sinde, Beloochistan, Etc.*, William Curry Jun. and Company, Dublin, 1843

Henry Durand: *The First Afghan War and its Causes*, 1879, Lancer Edition, New Delhi, 2008

Emily Eden: *Portraits of the Princes and Peoples of India*, J Dickinson & Co., London, 1844

Emily Eden: *Up the Country: Letters Written to Her Sister from the Upper Provinces of India*, 1866, Oxford University Press edition, Oxford, 1930

Mountstuart Elphinstone: *An Account of the Kingdom of Caubul and its Dependencies in Persia, Tartary and India*, 3rd edn, Richard Bentley, London, 1842

Viscount Esher (ed.): *The Girlhood of Queen Victoria: A Selection from Her Majesty's Diaries*, John Murray, London, 1912

George De Lacey Evans: *On the Designs of Russia*, John Murray, London, 1828

George De Lacey Evans: *On the Practicability of an Invasion of British India and of the Commercial and Financial Prospects of the Empire*, J M Richardson, London, 1829

George Robert Gleig: *Sale's Brigade in Afghanistan; With an Account of the Seizure and Defence of Jellalabad*, John Murray, London, 1846

John Greenwood: *The Campaign in Afghanistan*, 1844, Nonsuch edn, Stroud, 2005

Josiah Harlan: *A Memoir of India and Afghanistan*, J Dobson, Philadelphia, PA, 1842

Henry Havelock: *Narrative of the War in Affghanistan in 1838–39*, Henry Colburn, London, 1840

John Martin Honigberger: *Thirty-Five Years in the East: Adventures, Discoveries, Events and Historical Sketches*, H Bailliere, London, 1852

William Hough: *A Narrative of the March and Operations of the Army of the Indus in the Expedition to Affghanistan in the Years 1838–9*, W Tracker & Co., Calcutta, 1840

Charles Hugel: *Travels in Kashmir and the Panjab*, John Petheram, London, 1845

James Hume: *Writings of H W Torrens with a Memoir by James Hume*, R C Lepage & Co., Calcutta, 1854

Victor Jacquemont: *Correspondance avec sa famille et plusieurs de ses amis pendant son voyage dans l'Inde (1828–32)*, Garnier Frère, Paris, 1861

R H Kennedy: *Narrative of the Campaign of the Army of the Indus in Sind and Kaboul in 1838–9*, Richard Bentley, London, 1840

'By a Lady': *Letters from Madras during the Years 1836–39*, John Murray, London, 1846

Mohan Lal: *Life of the Amir Dost Mohammed Khan, of Kabul; with his Political Proceedings towards the English, Russian and Persian Governments, including the Victory and Disasters of the British Army in Afghanistan*, Longman, Brown, Green and Longmans, London, 1846

Mohan Lal: *Travels in the Panjab, Afghanistan and Turkistan to Balk Bokhara and Herat and a Visit to Great Britain and Germany*, W H Allen & Co., London, 1846

George Lawrence: *Reminiscences of Forty-Three Years in India*, John Murray, London, 1874

'A Lieutenant of the Bengal Establishment': *The Cadet's Guide to India, containing Information and Advice to Young Men about to Enter the Army of the Hon. East India Company*, Black, Kingsbury, Parbury and Allen, London, 1820Charles Lyell: *Principles of Geology or, the Modern Changes of the Earth and its Inhabitants Considered as Illustrative of Geology*, 6th edn, John Murray, London, 1840

K M Lyell (ed.): *Life, Letters & Journals of Sir Charles Lyell Bart.*, London, 1881, Cambridge University Press, reprint 2010

Tresham Lever (ed.): *Letters of Lady Palmerston*, Butler & Tanner Ltd, London, 1957

Helen Mackenzie: *Storms and Sunshine of a Soldier's Life, Lt Gen Colin Mackenzie CB 1825–81*, David Douglas, Edinburgh, 1884

Charles Masson: *Narrative of a Journey to Kalat; Including an Account of the Insurrection at that Place in 1840 and a Memoir on Eastern Balochistan*, Richard Bentley, London, 1843

Charles Masson, *Narrative of Various Journeys in Balochistan, Afghanistan, the Panjab and Kalat*, Richard Bentley, London, 1844

David Mitchell: *The History of Montrose*, George Walker, Montrose, 1866

Thomas Moore: *The Poetical Works of Thomas Moore*, A & W Galignani, Paris, 1827

William Godolphin Osborne: *The Court and Camp of Runjeet Sing*, Colburn, London, 1840

Parliamentary 'Blue Book': *Accounts and Papers, East India, Vol. XXV, Session 2 1859*, London, 1859

Richard Poole: *Memorandum regarding the Royal Lunatic Asylum, Infirmary and Dispensary of Montrose*, J & D Nichol, Montrose, 1841

Henry Pottinger: *Travels in Beloochistan and Sinde, Accompanied by a Geographical and Historical Account of those Countries*, Longman, Hurst, Rees, Orme and Brown, London, 1809

Sita Ram: *From Sepoy to Subedar*, Routledge & Kegan Paul, London, 1970

Charles Samuel Stewart: *Sketches of Society in Great Britain and Ireland*, Carey Lea and Blanchard, Philadelphia, 1834

J H Stocqueler (ed.): *Memoirs and Correspondence of Maj-Gen Sir William Nott*, Hurst & Blackett, London, 1854

J H Stocqueler (ed.): *Memorials of Affghanistan*, Ostell & Lepage, Calcutta, 1843

William Taylor: *Scenes and Adventures in Affghanistan*, T C Newby, London, 1842

Thomas Williamson: *The East India Vade Mecum; or, Complete Guide to Gentlemen Intended for the Civil, Military or Naval Service of the East India Company*, Black, Parry and Kingsbury, London, 1810

John Wilson: *Noctes Ambrosianae*, Redfield, New York, 1854

John Wood: *A Journey to the Source of the River Oxus*, John Murray, London, 1872

## SECONDARY SOURCES

J Abbott: *Sind: A Reinterpretation of the Unhappy Valley*, Oxford University Press, Oxford, 1924

Alison Adburgham: *Silver Fork Society*, Constable, London, 1983

Lesley Adkins: *Empires of the Plain: Henry Rawlinson and the Lost Languages of Babylon*, Harper Collins, London, 2003

Alice Albinia: *Empires of the Indus – The Story of a River*, John Murray, London, 2008

G J Alder: 'The "Garbled" Blue Books of 1839 – Myth or Reality?' *Historical Journal*, Vol. 15, No. 2, 1972

Anonymous Pamphlet: 'District Grand Lodge of Bombay Centenary Celebrations 1861–1961', unpublished

C A Bayly: *Empire and Information: Intelligence Gathering and Social Communication in India, 1780–1870*, Cambridge University Press, Cambridge, 1999

'Bengal Civilian': *Lord Auckland and Lord Ellenborough*, Smith Elder & Co., London, 1845

Isaiah Berlin: *Karl Marx, his Life and Environment*, Home University Library, New York, 1939

Terence R Blackburn: *The Extermination of a British Army: The Retreat from Kabul*, APH Publishing, New Delhi, 2008

Gregory Bondarevsky: *The Great Game: A Russian Perspective*, Christie Books, Hastings, 2002

Demetrius C Boulger: *Lord William Bentinck*, Clarendon Press, Oxford, 1987

Asa Briggs: *The Age of Improvement*, Longman, London, 1959

W Broadfoot: *The Career of Major George Broadfoot CB in Afghanistan and the Punjab*, John Murray, London, 1888

David Brown: *Palmerston: A Biography*, Yale University Press, New Haven, 2010

Henry Lytton Bulwer: *The Life of Henry John Temple Viscount Palmerston*, Bernard Tauchnitz, Leipzig, 1871

L R Burness: 'The Family of Burnes', unpublished MS, National Library of Scotland-
John Capper: *The Three Presidencies of India: A History of the Rise and Progress of the British Indian Possessions*, Ingram Cooke and Co., London, 1853

Major G. Carmichael Smith: *A History of the Reigning Family of Lahore with some Account of the Jumoo Rajahs, the Seik Soldiers and their Sirdars*, W. Thacker & Co., Calcutta, 1847

Suhash Chakravarty: *From Khyber to Oxus: A Study in Imperial Expansion*, Orient Longman Ltd, New Delhi, 1976

James Chambers: *Palmerston: The People's Darling*, John Murray, London, 2004

E M Collingham: *Imperial Bodies: The Physical Experience of the Raj c.1800–1947*, Polity, Cambridge, 2001

Peter Collister: *Hostage in Afghanistan*, Pentland Press Ltd, Bishop Auckland, 1999

Auckland Colvin: *John Russell Colvin: The Last Lieutenant Governor of the North-West under the Company*, Clarendon Press, Oxford, 1895

Sean Connery and Murray Grigor: *Being a Scot*, Weidenfeld & Nicolson, London, 2008

Robert L D Cooper: *Cracking the Freemason's Code*, Rider, London, 2006

James Cotton: *Mountstuart Elphinstone and the Making of South-Western India*, Clarendon Press, Oxford, 1896

Maggie Craig: *Bare-Arsed Banditti: The Men of the '45*, Mainstream, Edinburgh, 2009

Robert Crawford: *The Bard; Robert Burns. A Biography*, Princeton University Press, Princeton, NJ, 2009

John C Cunningham: *The Last Man: The Life and Times of Surgeon-General William Brydon CB*, New Cherwell Press, Oxford, 2003

William Dalrymple: *White Mughals*, Harper Collins, London, 2002

William Dalrymple: *Return of a King: The Battle for Afghanistan*, Bloomsbury, London, 2013

John Darwin: *After Tamerlane: The Global History of Empire since 1405*, Allen Lane, London, 2007

Naseer Dashti: *The Baloch and Balochistan*, Trafford Publishing, Bloomington, 2012

T M Devine: *The Scottish Nation: A History 1700–2000*, Viking, New York, 1999

Hugh Douglas: *Robert Burns: A Life*, Robert Hale, London, 1976

Louis Dupree: *Afghanistan*, Princeton University Press, Princeton, 1973

Louis Dupree: 'The First Afghan War: Folklore and History', *Afghanistan Historical and Cultural Quarterly*, Vol. 26, No. 4, March 1974

Michael H Fisher: *Counterflows to Colonialism: Indian Travellers and Settlers in Britain 1600–1857*, Permanent Black, Delhi, 2004

W K Fraser-Tytler, *Afghanistan*, Oxford University Press, Oxford, 1950, 3rd edn, 1967

Michael Fry: *The Scottish Empire*, Birlinn, Edinburgh, 2002

Norman Gash: *Aristocracy and People: Britain 1815–65*, Edward Arnold, London, 1979

Durba Ghosh: *Sex and the Family in Colonial India: The Making of Empire*, Cambridge University Press, Cambridge, 2006

David Gillard: *The Struggle for Asia 1828–1914: A Study in British and Russian Imperialism*, Methuen, London, 1977

David Gilmour: *The Long Recessional: The Imperial Life of Rudyard Kipling*, John Murray, London, 2002

David Gilmour: *The Ruling Caste: Imperial Lives in the Victorian Raj*, John Murray, London, 2005

R F Gould, 'The Chevalier Burnes', *Ars Quatuor Coranatorum*, Vol. 12, 1899
Robert Freke Gould: *Military Lodges: The Apron and the Sword or Freemasonry under Arms*, Gale & Polden Ltd, London, 1899
C Gray and H L O Garrett: *European Adventurers of Northern India 1785 to 1849*, Government Printing House, Lahore, 1929
John C Griffiths: *The Queen of Spades*, Andre Deutsch Ltd, London, 1983
John C Griffiths: *Afghanistan: Land of Conflict and Beauty*, 2nd edn, Andre Deutsch Ltd, London, 2009
Philip Guedalla: *Bonnet and Shawl: An Album*, Hodder and Stoughton, London, 1928
Zalmay A Gulzad: *External Influences and the Development of the Afghan State in the Nineteenth Century*, Peter Lang, New York, 1994
Hari Ram Gupta: *Life and Work of Mohan Lal Kashmiri 1812–77*, Minerva Book Shop, Lahore, 1943
Shah Mahmoud Hanifi: *Connecting Histories in Afghanistan: Market Relations and State Formation on a Colonial Frontier*, Stanford University Press, Stanford, CA, 2008
Jack Harrington: *Sir John Malcolm and the Creation of British India*, Palgrave Macmillan, New York, 2010
Philip Hensher: *The Mulberry Empire*, Flamingo, London, 2002
Christopher Hibbert: *Queen Victoria: A Personal History*, Harper Collins, London, 2000
Dennis Holman: *Sikander Sahib: The Life and Times of James Skinner 1778–1841*, Heinemann, London, 1961
B D Hopkins: *The Making of Modern Afghanistan*, Palgrave Macmillan, London, 2012
Kathleen Hopkirk: *Central Asia: A Traveller's Companion*, John Murray, London, 1993
Peter Hopkirk: *The Great Game: On Secret Service in High Asia*, Oxford University Press, Oxford, 1990
David Howarth and Stephen Howarth: *The Story of P&O*, Weidenfeld and Nicolson, London, 1986
Robert Huttenback: *British Relations with Sind 1799–1843: An Anatomy of Imperialism*, 1962, Oxford University Press edition, Oxford, 2007
Ronald Hyam: *Empire and Sexuality: The British Experience*, Manchester University Press, Manchester, 1990
H Montgomery Hyde: *A Tangled Web: Sex Scandals in British Politics and Society*, Constable, London, 1986
Edward Ingram: *The Beginning of the Great Game in Asia 1828–34*, Clarendon Press, Oxford, 1979
Intelligence Branch, Indian Army Headquarters: *Frontier and Overseas Expeditions from India; Baluchistan and the First Afghan War*, Vol. 3 (1910), Naval and Military Press, Uckfield, 2006
Afzal Iqbal: *Circumstances Leading to the First Afghan War*, Punjab Educational Press, Lahore, 1975
G Jackson and S G E Lythe: *The Port of Montrose: A History of its Harbour, Trade and Shipping*, Hutton Press Ltd, Tayport, 1993
Lawrence James: *Raj: The Making and Unmaking of British India*, Little, Brown and Company, London, 1997

J C Jessop: *Education in Angus*, University of London Press, London, 1931
Ann Jones: *Kabul in Winter: Life without Peace in Afghanistan*, Metropolitan Books, New York, 2006
J W Kaye: *The Life and Correspondence of Charles Lord Metcalfe*, Richard Bentley, London, 1854
J W Kaye: *The Life and Correspondence of Major-General Sir John Malcolm*, Smith Elder & Co., London, 1856
J W Kaye: *History of the War in Afghanistan*, 4th edn, W H Allen & Co., London, 1890
J W Kaye: *Lives of Indian Officers*, J J Kelliher & Co., London, 1905
M M Kaye: *The Golden Calm*, Webb and Bower, Exeter, 1980
John Keay: *The Honourable Company: A History of the English East India Company*, Harper Collins, London, 1991
Margaret Kekewich: *Retreat and Retribution in Afghanistan, 1842: Two Journals of the First Afghan War*, Pen and Sword, Barnsley, 2010
Melvin M Kessler: *Ivan Viktorovich Vitkevich 1806-39: A Tsarist Agent in Central Asia*, in Central Asian Collecteana, Washington, 1960
Rudyard Kipling: *The Man Who Would Be King*, Doubleday & McClure, London, 1899
Rudyard Kipling: *Something of Myself for My Friends Known and Unknown*, London, 1937, Asian Educational Services reprint, New Delhi, 1997
Adam Kuper: *Incest and Influence: The Private Life of Bourgeois England*, Boston, Harvard University Press, 2009
Jean-Marie Lafont: *Maharaja Ranjit Singh: The French Connections*, Guru Nana Dev University, Amritsar, 2001
Syad Muhammad Latif: *Ranjit Singh: Builder of a Commonwealth*, National Book Shop, Delhi, 2002
W A Laurie: *A Memoir of James Burnes, K.H., F.R.S.*, printed for private circulation, Edinburgh, 1851
W F B Laurie: *Sketches of Some Distinguished Anglo-Indians with an Account of Anglo-Indian Periodical Literature*, John B Day, London, 1875
John Lawrence: *Lawrence of Lucknow*, Hodder & Stoughton, London, 1990
Bruce Lenman: *An Economic History of Modern Scotland*, Batsford, London, 1977
Bruce Lenman: *Integration and Enlightenment: Scotland 1746–1832*, Edinburgh University Press, Edinburgh, 1981
Maurice Lindsay: *Robert Burns: The Man, his Work, the Legend*, 4th edn, Robert Hale, London, 1979
James Lunt: *Bokhara Burnes*, Faber & Faber, London, 1969
George MacDonald Fraser, *Flashman*, Harper Collins, London, 1969
Ben Macintyre: *Josiah the Great: The True Story of The Man Who Would Be King*, Harper Perennial, London, 2005
John M Mackenzie: *Orientalism: History, Theory and the Arts*, Manchester University Press, Manchester, 1995
Albert Gallatin Mackey: *The History of Freemasonry*, Vol. 5, Masonic History Company, New York, 1881
Patrick Macrory: *Signal Catastrophe*, Prion Books, London, 1966

John Clark Marshman: *The History of India from the Earliest Period to the Close of Lord Dalhousie's Administration*, Longmans Green Reader and Dyer, London, 1867

Alexander M Martin: *Enlightened Metropolis: Constructing Imperial Moscow 1762–1855*, Oxford University Press, Oxford, 2013

K Marx and F Engels: *On Colonialism*, Foreign Languages Publishing House, Moscow, 1967

Alastair McKelvie: 'Monarchs of All They Surveyed: The Himalayan Exploits of Alexander, James and Patrick Gerard', *History Scotland*, Vol. 7, No. 2 (March/April 2007), pp. 45–52

Alastair McKelvie: 'To Bukhara with Burnes; James Gerard's Last Expedition', *History Scotland*, Vol. 8, No. 2, March/April 2008, pp. 00–00

Martha McLaren: *British India and British Scotland 1780–1830*, University of Akron Press, 2001

Fitzroy Maclean: *A Person from England*, Century Publishing, London, 1958

Jacob Seth Mesrov: *Armenians in India from the Earliest Times to the Present*, Luzac & Co., London, 1897

Karl Meyer and Shereen Brysac: *Tournament of Shadows: The Great Game and the Race for Empire in Asia*, Abacus, London, 2001

Penderel Moon: *The British Conquest and Dominion of India*, Duckworth, London, 1989

Alan Moorhead: *The White Nile*, Hamish Hamilton, London, 1960

Alexander Morrison: 'Twin Imperial Disasters. The Invasions of Khiva and Afghanistan in the Russian and British Official Mind, 1839–42', MS awaiting publication in *Modern Asian Studies*

Sir Nicholas Harris Nicolas: *History of the Orders of Knighthood of the British Empire*, J. Hunter, London, 1842

Craig Murray: *Murder in Samarkand*, Mainstream Publishing, Edinburgh, 2007

Christine Noelle: *State and Tribe in Nineteenth-Century Afghanistan: The Reign of Amir Dost Muhammad (1826–63)*, Curzon, Richmond, 1997

J A Norris: *The First Afghan War 1838–42*, Cambridge University Press, Cambridge, 1967

George Pottinger: *Sir Henry Pottinger, First Governor of Hong Kong*, St Martins Press, New York, 1997

George Pottinger and Patrick Macrory: *The Ten-Rupee Jezail: Figures in the First Afghan War 1838–42*, Michael Russel Publishing Ltd, London, 1993

*Oxford Dictionary of National Biography*, Online Edition, Oxford University Press, 2004

Charles Rogers: *Genealogical Memoirs of the Family of Robert Burns*, W Paterson, Edinburgh, 1877

Khushwant Singh: *Ranjit Singh Maharaja of the Punjab*, George Allen Unwin Ltd, London, 1962

T C Smout (ed.): *Scotland and the Sea*, John Donald, Edinburgh, 1992

Jules Stewart: *Spying for the Raj: The Pundits and the Mapping of the Himalaya*, The History Press, London, 2007

Sir Percy Sykes: *A History of Afghanistan*, Macmillan, London, 1940

George McCall Theal, *History of South Africa, Vol. 4 (1834–54)*, Swan Sonnenschein & Co., London, 1893

Mikhail Volodarsky: 'The Russians in Afghanistan in the 1830s', *Central Asian Survey*, Vol. 3, No. 1, pp. 63–86

D F Wadia: *History of Lodge Rising Star of Western India*, British India Press, Bombay, 1912

Frank Welsh: *A History of Hong Kong*, Harper Collins, London, 1994

Gordon Whitteridge: *Charles Masson of Afghanistan*, 1986, Orchid Press Edition, Bangkok, 2002

C W Woodburn: *The Bala Hissar of Kabul*, Institution of Royal Engineers, Professional Papers 2009 No.1

M E Yapp: *Strategies of British India: Britain, Iran and Afghanistan 1798–1850*, Clarendon Press, Oxford, 1980

Henry Yule and A C Burnell: *Hobson-Jobson: The Anglo-Indian Dictionary: The Concise Edition*, 1886, Wordsworth Edition, Ware, 2008

Lynn Zastoupil: *John Stuart Mill and India*, Stanford University Press, Stanford, 1994

## LIST OF PERIODICALS

*Afghanistan Historical and Cultural Quarterly*, Kabul 1974
*Agra Ukhbar*, 1840–2
*Ars Quatuor Coronatorum*, London 1899
*The American Quarterly Observer*, Boston 1834
*The Annual Register*, London 1839–40
*The Asiatic Journal and Monthly Register*, London 1821–41
*Bengal Hurkaru*, Calcutta 1842
*Blackwood's Magazine*, Edinburgh 1843
*Bombay Courier*, 1839
*Bombay Gazette*, 1833
*Bombay Times*, 1840-4
*Bombay United Services Gazette*, 1842
*Calcutta Courier*, 1831-43
*Calcutta Journal*, 1843
*Calcutta Review*, 1844
*Central Asian Survey*, 1986
*Colburn's United Service Magazine*, London 1843
*Delhi Gazette*, 1842
*Edinburgh Review*, 1840
*Fraser's Magazine*, Edinburgh 1844
*Freemason's Quarterly Review*, London 1842
*The Gentleman's Magazine and Historical Review*, London 1842–63
*Hansard*, 1839–61
*The Historical Journal*, Cambridge 1972
*History Scotland*, Edinburgh 2007–8
*Journal of the Royal Asiatic Society*, London 1834

*The Monthly Chronicle*, Boston 1842
*The Monthly Review*, London 1840
*The Spectator*, London 1830–61
*Montrose Arbroath and Brechin Review*, 1818–43
*The Oriental Herald and Colonial Intelligencer*, London 1834–43
*Tait's Magazine*, Edinburgh 1840–3
*Transactions of the Bombay Geographical Society*, 1836–65

# Index

Abbas Mirza, Prince 117–19
Abbott, Lt James 296, 323, 347
Abdul Rahman 297
Abdul Rashid Khan 299
Abdul Wahhab Khan 285, 295
Abdullah (Burnes' servant) 350, 371
Achakzai, Abdullah Khan 132, 363, 364, 366, 367, 372
Aden 234
Adinagar 235, 236
Afghan Pioneer Corps 350
Afghanistan
   anneximg Kelat 296
   attacked by Shah Shujs 119, 120
   British invasion of 228
   British evacuation from 374
   Burnes' journey through 98
   crippling costs of 329, 342
   'a dead loss' 355
   history of 101–5
   increasingly unsettled 172
   invasion of 240–5, 267
   as a key buffer state 77
   lack of revenue 349
   low Army morale 339;
   native sports 312
   as part of Mughal and Safavid empires 100
   as a Persian tributary 182
   plans for united state 179–81
   in revolt 358–62
   Russian advance on Khiva 305
   wanting to be a nation 221
   at war 173
   weak state of 230
African slaves 167
Afzul Mohammed Khan (son of Dost) – *see* Barakzai
Aga Taj 105, 216
Ahmad Khan (Isa Khail chief) 184
Ahmad Shah Dourani 100, 104, 202, 288, 349
Ahmed, Jetta 62, 65, 67
Ahmed, Syed 77, 100
Ahmedpur 119, 177, 256
Ajit Singh 231
Akbar the Great 81
Akbar Khan (son of Dost) – *see* Barakzai
Akhtar Khan Dourani 345
Alaman people 117
Albinia, Alice 59, 60
Alexander the Great 63, 142, 158, 191, 314
Ali, Haji Hussain 209
Ali, Karamat 108, 118, 119, 155, 169, 192
Ali, Dr Mahomed 166
Ali, Mohammed (surveyor) 55, 65, 66, 97, 98, 109, 117, 271
Ali, Muhammad (Nawab of the Carnatic) 233
Ali, Qambar 181, 182, 185, 193, 197, 205
Ali, Shahamat 307, 339
Ali Bagh 376
Ali Khan (Tutundera) 334
Ali Musjid 191, 318, 360
Alidad Khan 193
Alikozai, Musa Khan 342, 366
Allard, General 77, 78, 90, 91, 98, 152,

185, 191, 213, 236, 238, 353
Altes Museum, Berlin 314
Aminulla Khan Logari 368, 372
Amritsar 239
Amu river 112
Anarkali, tomb of 81
Anderson, Capt 323, 332, 336
Anquetil, Brig 366
Anstey, Thomas 379, 380
Aral Sea 111, 125
Arbroath smokies 352
Argandab river 295
Argoud, Benoit 177, 178, 315
Arnold, Brig 282, 295
*Asiatic Journal* 122
*Asiatic Register* 343
Astrabad 209
Ata Mohammed 333
Athanaeum Club, London 130
Atkinson, Dr James 187, 276, 337, 364
Attock 100, 101, 168, 172, 185, 197
Auckland, Lord 134, 163, 172, 173, 180, 189, 194, 197, 208, 210, 214, 216, 218–69, 281, 282, 287–91, 296, 302, 305, 309–11, 315, 318, 321, 323, 325, 328, 330, 331, 333, 342–56, 377, 380
  agreement over Peshawar 199, 200
  backing Shuja 23
  deciding on war 231
  indecision of 184, 185
  instructed to invade 240
  insulting Dost 219
  ordered to annex Uzbekistan 274
  relieving Pottinger of duties 262
  sending Burnes to Kabul 164–71
  taking decisions alone 228
  taking over as Governor-General 162
Aurungzeb, Shah 101
Aushik, Mullah 9
Avitabile 186–90, 208, 215, 238, 266, 318
Azim Khan, Rissaldar 297, 358
Azimal Din, Sayyid 167
Aziz al Din 236, 237
Aziz Muhammad Khan 163

Babukushkar 335
Bactrian civilisation 314

Badakshan 108
Bagh, Wazir 291
Bahadur Khan 266
Bahawal Khan 179
Baikhar, fortress of 73, 175, 255–60, 273; in British hands 258–60
Baillie, Henry 378, 381
Bajgah 318, 331
Baji Rao (Peshwa of Pune) 21
Baksh, Jewan 175
Balkh 111, 125, 303, 305, 318, 321
Baluchi people 41, 72, 73, 279, 296, 327
Baluchistan 100, 182
Bamian 100, 101, 109, 110, 118, 263, 317, 321, 331, 332, 335, 361
Barakzai royal house 8, 100–05, 118, 154, 217, 225, 227, 238, 242, 291
Barakzai, Afzul Khan (son of Dost) 173, 226, 302, 304, 321, 332, 347
Barakzai, Akbar Khan (son of Dost) 158, 173, 190, 191, 194, 195, 197, 204, 284, 321, 333, 361, 375
Barakzai, Dost Mohammed Khan 74, 104, 118, 154, 155, 169, 178, 188–97, 202, 204, 210, 215, 222–7, 230–8, 242, 243, 245, 248, 249, 252, 265, 271, 272, 282, 293, 297, 303–8, 316, 321, 331–5, 343, 344, 347, 349, 355, 375, 376, 380
  agreement over Peshawar 197–200, 216–18
  alarm at conflict 225
  alliance against Russia 205–7
  alliance with Murad Beg 317
  annexing Kohistan 302
  attack at Nijrow 336, 337
  banning alcohol 315
  becoming an ascetic 376
  declaring jihad 156, 173
  double dealing 236
  escaping 331
  exile in India 338
  hostility to Sultan 224
  imprisoned in Bokhara 325
  insulted by Britain 219
  offer from Russia 211, 212
  plans to unite Afghanistan 179–82
  proposals from Russia 184, 185

rebuking his brothers 201
rape of princess in Herat 8, 9, 100
receives Witciewicz 220
reinforcing Ghazni 266, 298
ruler in Kabul 100, 105–8, 113
ruling Kohistan 324
under threat from Dil Khans 192
wounded at Bamian 332, 333
Barakzai, Futth Khan (brother of Dost) 8, 9, 100, 105, 301, 333
Barakzai, Ghulam Haidar Khan (son of Dost) 298–302, 304, 340
Barakzai, Haidar Khan 299, 301
Barakzai, Kohan Dil Khan 132, 210, 212, 288
Barakzai, Mehir Dil Khan 224, 225, 307
Barakzai, Sultan Mohammed Khan (aka Jan Mohammed) 100–2, 105, 106, 119, 154–6, 188, 190, 193, 206, 208, 216, 217, 221, 225, 234, 333, 363
Baratpur, siege of 155
Barr, Lt William 146, 187, 291, 307
Basawan, Sheikh 267, 307
Bean, Capt 343
Beckwith, General 59
Bell, Ross 296
Benevolent Lodge, Bombay 27
Benevolent Lodge, Kira 35
Bengal Army 78, 108, 256, 266–9, 276–78, 281, 287, 297, 305, 309, 334
Bengal Civil Service 85
Bengal Horse Artillery 307
Bentinck, Lord William 31, 32, 45, 50, 51, 53, 54, 58, 62, 64, 71, 74, 77, 81, 84, 85, 93, 96, 97, 108, 115, 119, 121, 124, 125, 155, 218, 255, 317
Bhawal Khan 73–5, 176–8
Bhawalpur 73, 75, 96, 169
Bhuj 24, 32, 34, 39, 47, 54, 92, 139, 144, 161, 162, 383
  size of garrison at 35, 36; Burnes family at 37
Bikaner state 73
Black Brothers 23
Blaramberg, I.F. 294
Bokhara 52, 54, 82, 84–7, 93, 101, 103, 108–10, 113–16, 119, 127, 128, 130, 143, 157, 159, 160, 166, 170, 204, 211, 273, 305, 320, 322, 331
  Ark or Citadel of 114
  Emir or Khan of 113, 116, 291, 303, 347
Bolan Pass 87, 175, 177, 267, 268, 275, 277, 279, 281, 282, 290, 310, 327, 335, 338
Bombay (Mumbai) 18, 24–30, 120, 377
Bombay Asiatic Society 26, 28, 29, 59, 129
Bombay Botanical Garden 218
Bombay Cholera Institute 24
*Bombay Gazette* 265
Bombay Geographical Society 26, 29, 235
Bombay Geological Society 26
Bombay Horse Artillery 27
Bombay Horticultural Society 121
Bombay Literary Society 23, 26, 27, 30
Bombay Natural History Society 363
*Bombay Times* 146, 148, 241, 327, 357, 379
*Bombay United Services Gazette* 378
Bonaparte, Joseph 77
Bonaparte, Napoleon 23, 353
Borowski, Col 117
Bow Butts, Montrose 3, 127
Bowe Singh 367, 370, 371
Bradford, General Sir Thomas 25, 29, 32–4
Bright, John 382
Broadfoot, George 318, 352, 357, 358, 371, 372
Broadfoot, James 258, 336, 352
Broadfoot, William 352, 353, 357–9, 366, 369, 370
Brockedon, William 129
Brougham, Lord 133, 134
Brown, Capt 326, 327
Browne, Dr 47
Browne, Sam 229
Bruce, James 143
Brunow, Baron Ernst de 319
Bryden, Dr 340
Buist, George 146, 148, 241, 327, 357, 379
Burdett, Sir Frances 378

# Index

Burn, Capt 360
Burnes, Adam (brother of AB) 48, 133, 351
Burnes, Alexander
  accused of lechery 342
  across the desert 116–18
  adjutant 22
  agreement over Peshawar 196–200, 217
  in Balkh 111
  on to Bokhara 113–15
  with Bhawal Khan 176, 177
  as a celebrity 123–35
  clash with Witkiewicz 209, 215
  created CB 326
  critiques of policy 328–31, 350
  death of 369–73
  detailed reports 120, 121
  exploring the north-west 32–5, 39–46
  failure of mission 224–7
  failures of intelligence network 322
  false portrait of 128
  Government publication of papers 272, 273
  'a highly paid idler' 351
  initiated as a mason 35
  insulting Dost 219
  interpreter in Bombay 23
  joining EIC 10–16
  journey into Afghanistan 98, 101–12
  in Kabul 105–7
  knighted and promoted to Lt Col 245
  leading advance to Haidarabad 268
  meeting Sikh leaders 75–83
  in Montrose 127
  negotiating with Rustam Khan 254–7
  negotiations over Kabul 203–7
  offered Ambassador to Persia 150
  in Peshawar 186–90
  plans to unite Afghanistan 179–85
  posted to Pune 19
  Pottinger's rant against 261
  proposing financial reform 316
  as Quartermaster-General 275–80
  religious beliefs 22
  return to India 134
  return to London 122, 123
  role in invasion 241, 242
  row with Pottinger 162
  sailing the Indus 70–4
  sailing to India 17, 18
  second survey of Indus 164–71
  seeking more power 184
  as 'Sikunder' 99, 109, 116
  skill at languages 19, 58
  stating policy options 234
  surveys of Cutch 24–8
  surveying techniques 42, 43
  survey of the Indus 50, 54–68
  success of mission 85
  at Tehran 118, 119
  through Khyber Pass 190, 191
  treaty with Mehrab Khan 283
  true portrait 129
  upbringing in Montrose 1–7
  views on strategic defence of India 86, 87
  writing book *Cabool* 353
Burnes, Charles (brother of AB) 1, 22, 132–4, 280, 325, 352, 353, 358, 370, 371
Burnes, David (brother of AB) 48, 123, 125, 128, 132–4, 336, 337, 344
Burnes, James (brother of AB) 2, 70, 119, 133, 229, 318, 331, 357, 373, 377, 378, 382
  at Bhuj 35
  in Bombay 23
  book on Sind 53
  children 37
  created Baron of Saxe-Coburg-Gotha 144
  death of 383
  and Freemasonry 136–40
  joining EIC 10–16
  marriage to Sophia Holmes 37
  posted to Malunga 18
  sailing to India 17, 18
  in Sind 25, 29
  Surgeon in Cutch 24
Burnes, James (father of AB) 3, 47, 48, 127, 133, 377
Burnes, James (grandfather of AB) 3
Burnes, Robert (great-great-grandfather of AB) 2
Burnes/Burns family tree 2

Burnes siblings 4; marriages of daughters 37, 39, 47, 122, 144
Burns, Robert 1, 2, 12, 30, 37, 129, 353; and Freemasonry 139–41, 145
Burnes, William (father of Robert) 3
Burns Clubs 140
Butkhak 193, 359, 360
Byron, Lord 59

Cabell, William 272, 274
Calcutta (Kolkata) 120, 229; collapse of banks in 171
  Asiatic Society 158, 229
  Botanic Garden 218
*Calcutta Courier* 232
*Calcutta Review* 233
*Caledonian Mercury* 47
camp routine 40
Campbell, Colonel 22
Campbell, Sir James 117, 150, 151, 158
Campbell, William 155, 204
Carnatic, Nawab of 233
Caroline, Queen 5
Cashmere shawls 74, 91, 93, 170, 203
Caspian Sea 117
Cassidy, Lt Col 125
caste system 21, 26, 40, 98, 119
Castelreagh, Lord 31
Cautley, Capt Proby 27, 184, 185
Cawnpore 229
Cerron, M. 223, 226
*Challenger*, HMS 63, 65
Chalmers, Patrick 127
Chamberlain, Neville 318
Chambers, W.J. 17
Chanda Sahib 233
Charge of the Light Brigade 353
Charikar 333–5, 348
Chernyshev (Russian War Minister) 320
cholera epidemics 24, 114, 267
Christie, Capt 37
Chunda, Rani 82
Clanricarde, Lord 293
Clare, Earl of (John Fitzgibbon) 58, 59, 62, 64, 67, 68, 71, 74, 81, 86, 89, 158, 161
Clarke, Stanley 11
*Cleopatra* (ship) 377

Clerk, Lt 326
Clibborn, Maj 327
*Clive* (EIC ship) 120
Clochnahill 2, 3
Colvin, Auckland 199
Colvin, John 36, 180, 181, 184, 199, 228, 231, 240, 241, 268, 291, 323
Congress Party of India 148
Connery, Sean 145
Conolly, Arthur 55, 56, 77, 103, 113, 114, 127, 157, 192, 206, 232–7, 250, 275, 279, 322, 323, 326, 332, 363, 364
Conolly, Edward 291, 318, 333, 334, 336
Conolly, John 368
Conroy, Sir John 123, 124
Cooper, Robert 143
Corless, Lt 167, 169
Corn Laws 123, 127
Cotasir 64, 65
Cotton, Maj-Gen Sir Willoughby 256–8, 265, 267–9, 276–9, 282, 285, 297, 306, 308–11, 314, 318, 328, 338, 339
Cotton, Capt Willoughby (son of above) 280
Court, M. 81, 82, 91, 99, 152, 186
Cowper, Lady Emily, liaisons of 126
Craigie, Maj 278, 282
Cureton, Maj 280, 282, 304
Cursetji, Maneckji 146
Cutch 24, 29, 33, 34, 37, 41, 51, 59, 64–6
  Burnes' surveys of 24–8
  Durbar 162
  Field Force 58, 130
  Gandava 277
  Runn of 27, 33, 38

Dadur 279, 290, 327
Dalhousie, Lord 125, 137
Dalrymple, William 20, 131
Danilevsky, General 305
Daraji, Reis of 65
Das, Chiman 110
Dasht-i bi Daulat 281
Daudputra 73, 74
Deacon, Col 268
Delawar Khan 276
Delhi 93, 98

English College 98
*Delhi Gazette* 375, 376
Demaison, Baron 157
Dennie, Col 245, 277, 298, 300, 301, 309, 315, 321, 332, 333, 335, 340, 354, 360
Dera Ghazi Khan 73, 174
Dera Ismael Khan 183, 290
Derajat 67, 178
Dhian Singh 236
Dil Khan brothers 192, 193, 210, 214, 270, 281, 285, 288, 289, 291
Din, Aziz al 76
Disraeli, Benjamin 125, 126, 378–82
*Dorah* (ship) 15
Dost Mohammed Khan – *see* Barakzai
Douglas, Capt James 307
Dourani royal house 8, 9, 100, 104, 180, 248, 289, 329, 344–9
Dowlett, Capt 101
Dowson, Lt 335
droughts 114, 229, 275, 280, 286
Drummond, Capt Henry 360, 361, 371
Drummond, Dr 235, 236
Duke, James 352
Dunlop, Alex 381
Dupree, Louis 166, 365
Durand, Lt Henry 15, 197–9, 262, 263, 284, 300, 307, 308, 355
Durba Ghosh 38
Durham, Lord 270

earthquakes 27, 28
East India Company 10–17, 19, 20, 43, 47, 50, 53, 97, 120, 123, 127, 137, 146, 149, 171, 228, 233, 239, 250, 274, 348
  being wound up 381
  deism strong in 147
  revenue from opium 39
  views on Afghanistan 172
Eastwick, Lt 169, 262, 265, 297
Eden, Emily 20, 36, 112, 176, 229, 235, 244, 252, 311, 354
*Edinburgh Review* 233, 327
Edul Khan 176, 193, 347, 371
Ellenborough, Lord 50, 53, 56, 57, 77, 151, 272, 273

ordering survey of Indus 51, 54, 55;
  giving dray horses to Ranjit Singh 78, 79
Ellis, Henry 54, 163
Ellora caves 19, 20
Elphinstone, Mountstuart 11, 12, 14, 18, 19, 21, 27, 39, 57, 59, 74, 98, 99, 101, 128, 132, 151, 152, 194, 225, 273, 284, 342, 344, 377
  and Freemasonry 143
  mission to Sind 60
Elphinstone, Gen William Keith 353, 354, 358, 359, 364, 369, 371, 372, 375
*Elphinstone Castle* (ship) 353
*Emma* (ship) 15
Erzurum 52, 53
Evans, Col George de Lacey 52, 53
Eversmann, Dr 113

Falconer, Hugh 28, 184, 185, 189, 235
Fane, General Sir Henry 173, 242–4, 257, 280
Fane, Lt Henry (son of above) 242, 243, 25658, 263, 265, 267–9, 275, 280, 288
Fane, Lt-Col Henry (nephew of above) 280
Farish, James 267
Fatth Jung Khan, Prince - *see* Saduzai
Fatth Khan (brother of Dost) – *see* Barakzai
Fawkes, Capt 184
Fergusson, Robert 37
Ferozepore 251, 254, 260, 263
Fida Mohammed Khan (formerly Rattray) 191, 204
Finden, Edward Frances 128
Firozuddin, Prince 8
First Afghan War 226, 234, 345, 375
Fitzgerald, Lord 379
Fitzgibbon, John – *see* Clare
Fleming, Admiral 12, 14, 18
*Flying Dutchman* 17
Fontanier, M. 152, 153
Forbes & Co 48, 295, 303
*Fortune* (ship) 47
Fourdonji, Nourozji 166, 177, 377

Fox, Col Charles 314
Franklin, John 28
Freemasonry
  in Afghanistan 142
  in India 23, 27, 35, 139, 146–8
  and the Knights Templar 136–45
  in Montrose 5, 127, 133, 139
  orders of 138–40
  Royal Arch 139

Gandamak 103, 360
Gandava Hills 176, 178, 277, 278
Gangara banking house 132
Ganges canal 185
Ganges river 92
Gardane, General 59
Gardner, Dr 170
Gaurishankar, Pandit 353
Geographical Society of Paris 133
Geological Society of London 28, 129
George I, King 2
George IV, King 83, 126
Gerard, Dr James 97, 99, 102–11, 113, 114, 121, 158, 160, 301
  death of 182, 250
  with malaria 117, 118
  many debts 183
  return to Ludhiana 119
Ghazi Khan, Nawab of Dera 73, 171
Ghazni, fortress of 118, 266, 297–304, 311, 345
  capture by British forces 299–302, 310
Ghilzai tribes 288, 295–8, 316, 323, 344, 345, 356–8, 360, 361, 363
Ghulab Singh, Raja 76
Ghulam (historian) 339
Ghulam Ali 22, 117, 371
Ghulam Haidar Khan (son of Dost) – see Barakzai
Gilchrist, Dr 11, 13
Gillies, Lord 11, 12, 14
Gilmour, David 142
Girishk, fortress of 291, 345
Glasgow University 137
Gleig, Elizabeth 3, 11
Gleig, Rev George 312, 313, 364
Goncalves, Don Jose 166, 200
Gordon (or Carron), Col 173

Gould, Robert Freke 140
Goutt, M. 225, 227
Graham, Emma 130, 131
Grant, Sir Charles 77, 97, 130, 161, 180
Grant, Sir Robert 162, 261
Gray, Capt 358
Gray, Rev James 36
Great Famine (Ireland) 123
Great Game, The 37, 51, 55, 119, 128, 181, 209, 226, 250
Great Panic of 1837 171
Greig, Anne 3
Grey, Earl 124, 125, 130, 180
Griffin, Maj 345
Griffin, Sir Lepel 83
Griffiths, Maj 360
Guelphic Order 308
Gul Mohammed 297
Gulam Hussein 124
Gurkhas 251, 318, 332, 348
Guy's Hospital, London 10, 17

Hadley, George 82
Hafiz Ji 302
Haidarabad 50, 56, 57, 62, 63, 67, 70–73, 80, 96, 161, 168, 169, 174, 254–60
Haidarabad, Amirs of 96, 177, 256, 260
Haj, The 115
Hala mountains 63
Hamilton, Capt Alexander 53
Hamza Khan 356
*Hannah* (ship) 311
Hari Singh, General 77, 99, 100, 155, 173, 248
Harlan, Josiah 102, 204, 212, 218, 219, 225, 312, 315
Hart, Lt 331
Hasan Abdal 185
Hasan Jan – see Lal, Mohan
Hastings, Warren 379
Hathorn, Dr 162
Havelock, Henry 251, 257, 284, 288, 316
Hay, Capt 331
Hazara people 203
Heddle, Dr J.F. 161
Helmund river 291
Hempsall, Robert 17
Herat 100, 103, 109, 150, 163, 176, 182,

*Index* 429

226, 243, 250, 325, 329, 333, 346, 351, 356
  battles over 8, 173, 179, 195, 200, 205, 220
  fall of 222, 230
  rape of princess in 8, 9, 105
  sieges of 206–8, 246, 247, 266, 275
  taxes from 290
  Todd expelled from 347
  treaty of 324
  Wazir of (Yar Mohammed) 117, 118
Hermes Trismegistus 143
Hicks, William 101
Hindu Kush 54, 69, 100, 109, 116, 125, 200, 203, 263, 305, 317, 321, 325, 363
Hindustan, Grand Army of 268
Hobhouse, John Cam 163, 200, 201, 216, 239, 240, 250, 252, 262–5, 270–4, 287, 291, 310, 325, 353, 378, 381
Hogg, James 37, 141, 145
Holland, Lt James 34, 35, 38, 58, 130, 181, 197, 201, 315, 317, 332
  expedition to Sind 39, 44–6, 142
  marriage to Jane Burnes 37, 39
Holland, Lord 314
Holmes, Capt 39
Holmes, Sir John 37
Honigberger, John Martin 80, 112, 118, 156–8, 186
*Hooghly* (ship) 123
Hopkins, Capt 331, 332
Hopkirk, Pter 365
Hough, Maj William 40, 284, 297, 310
Hugel, Charles 40, 80
*Hugh Lindsay* (ship) 151, 152, 246, 267
Humboldt, Alexander von 69
Hume, Allan Octavian 148
Hume, Joseph 3, 10, 11, 13, 16, 17, 25, 29, 123, 124, 148, 352, 378
*Hurkaru, The* 376
Hussan, Muhammad (Wazir of Kelat) 260
Hussan Herati, Mohammad 341
Hyraldghir, Nazir 291

Indian surveyors, secret training of 55
Indus, Army of the 267, 268, 276, 305, 337
  broken up 310
  long supply lines 291
  major losses from 280, 289
  starving 286, 289
Indus river 38, 46, 47, 50–4, 56, 59, 62–7, 70–4, 76, 96, 108, 128, 161, 311
  boat bridges 258, 265, 336
  Burnes' maps of 85, 86, 120
  comparison with Ganges 92
  opening to commerce 170, 172, 195
  second survey of 164–71
  strategic importance of 125
  swollen by monsoons 183
  trade fair at Sukkur 342
Istalif 200

Jabbar Khan, Nawab 103, 104, 109, 118, 119, 142, 181, 182, 195, 197, 204, 213, 216–18, 221, 222, 302, 303, 325, 333, 343
Jacob, George LeGrand 17, 60, 131, 201, 214, 243, 245, 272, 317, 350
Jacobite rebellions 2, 140
Jacquemont, Victor 83, 92, 342
Jafer, Mirza 157, 159, 204, 213
Jagdalak 360
Jalalabad 119, 154, 188, 226, 239, 311, 317, 329, 331, 338, 358–60, 375
Jamrud, Battle of 173, 181, 184, 190, 191
Jan Fishan Khan 360
Jan Mohammed, Sultan – *see* Barakzai, Sultan Mohammed
Jaxartes river 273, 274
Jaysulmir, fortress of 44, 45, 51, 63, 73
  Rawul of 45
Jeddah 152
Jehan, Shah 101
Jenkinson, Anthony 113
Jervis, Major T.B. 25, 85
Jodhpur 45, 51
  Raja of 45
Johnson, Capt 366–71, 373
Johnstone, Sir Alexander 132
Jokrani tribesmen 279
Jugaji (Rana of Nagar) 40
Jugdulluck Pass 310
Julga 334

Kabul 1, 52, 54, 81, 84, 85, 102, 105–8, 118, 121, 130, 154, 156, 164, 168–72, 178, 182, 188, 191, 193–203, 210, 211, 216, 221–7, 245, 306–25, 330, 333, 338, 339, 346, 354, 362–74
    Burnes forced to leave 224–7
    ceremonial entry to 304
    collapse of British morale 274
    command structure dysfunctional 359, 360
    EIC regime in 348–53
    high cost of garrison 312
    lack of money in 318
    occupation of 234
    permanent British Resident in 287
    severe winter 313
    surrendered by Dost 338
    threat of war 219, 220
    under assault 303
Kabul, Qazi of 215
Kabulistan 101
Kacchi 327
Kahun 325, 327
Kakar, Haji Khan 110, 118, 288, 295, 303
Kala Bagh 183, 189
Kalat 327
Kamard 109
Kamran Saduzai, Prince 9, 100, 118, 163, 246, 290, 296, 333, 347
Kandahar 80, 101, 102, 118, 132, 163, 168, 177, 179, 182, 199, 205, 210, 211, 214, 215, 224, 225, 245, 255, 281, 285, 295, 297, 327, 329, 344–7
    British occupation of 288–91, 311, 325
    Sirdars of 224
Kanpur 119, 206, 275
Kara Kum desert 116
Karabagh 334, 335
Karachi 35, 63, 174, 290, 310, 342
    Nawab of 63
Kardera 335
Kars 52
Karshi 112
Karzai, President Hamid 303
Kashmir
    conquered by Ranjit Singh 81
    famed for sexual pleasure 342
    loss of 316, 329
    returned to Afghan rule 365
Kattiawar 25
Kaye, Sir John 38, 229, 237, 377, 378, 381
Keane, Lt E.A.W. (son of Sir John) 280
Keane, Sir John (later Lord Keane of Ghazni) 256, 259, 260, 267–9, 277, 280, 282, 285, 286, 288, 297, 299, 302, 304, 306–10, 314, 340
Keith, Earl Marischal 2, 140
Kelat 37, 80, 155, 175, 234, 244, 260, 275–86, 310, 311, 318, 326, 327, 329, 338, 343
    Khan of, peace treaty with 357
Kelat-i-Ghilzai 345, 347, 348
Kennedy, Dr Richard 267, 277, 289, 306, 315
Kershaw, Capt 301
Khair al-Din, Mullah 169, 170
Khairpur 174, 256–61, 276; capitulation of 269
Khairpur, Amir of (Rustam Khan) 68, 72, 73, 175, 255, 256–60, 276
    treaty with 96, 257, 261
Khaju 116
Khanabad 110
Kharg, island of 237, 246
Khawind 345
Khiva 52, 54, 116, 157, 170, 239, 273, 305, 347
    Khan of 116, 159, 203, 347
    Russian threat to 305, 317–21
Khojuk Pass 287
Khokand 113, 170
Khoord Kabul pass 310, 355, 358, 375
Khorasan 54, 101
Khosa tribesmen 39, 62
Khotkiewicz, Count 69
Khulm 109, 110, 317, 325
Khurruck Singh 188
Khyber Pass 103, 119, 141, 170, 184, 202, 226, 244, 266, 267, 291, 329, 358, 360
    British defeats in 318
    flash flood in 191, 192
Kipling, Rudyard and Freemasonry 141, 142, 145, 147

Kira (or Kheda) 35
Kirki, Battle of 21
Kizyl Kum desert 322
Knights Templar 136–45
Kohan Dil Khan – *see* Barakzai
Kohat 102, 189
Koh-i-Duman 331
Koh-i-Noor diamond 9, 91
Kohistan 8, 105, 201, 303, 304, 324, 329, 333, 335, 336, 340, 348, 365, 373
Kohistani, Ghulam 335
Kotrah 338
Kunduz 108, 110
Kush-Begi, The 114–16, 157, 203, 291

*Lady Holland* (ship) 15
Lahore 53, 62, 70, 76, 77, 84, 85, 93, 99, 119, 239, 256
Lal, Mohan 98–102, 109–12, 132, 167–70, 177, 183, 192, 223, 232, 240, 250, 255–7, 265, 268, 278, 282–4, 288, 295, 299–304, 307, 309, 321–4, 333, 340, 344, 353, 356, 361, 364, 367, 370–3
  in Britain 377, 378
  employed as newswriter 119
  and Freemasonry 147
  as 'Hasan Jan' 99
  in Qochan 117, 118
  a vital asset 374
Lal Suri, Sohan 99
Lansdowne, Marquess of 133, 356
Lawrence, George 306, 337, 356, 362, 369
Lawrence, Henry 229, 237
Leckie, John 59, 70, 77, 78, 81, 85, 92, 146, 265
Leech, Capt Robert 71, 164, 166, 177, 178, 186, 189, 191, 200–2, 214, 224, 226, 235, 260, 277–9, 282, 285, 289, 295, 318, 326, 327, 351, 353
Lehna Singh 76, 188
Leinster, Duke of 144
Lewis, James – *see* Masson
Lewis, Wyndham 126
Lockhart, John Gibson 126
Lodge Canongate Kilwinning, Edinburgh 144, 145

Lodge Perseverance, Bombay 139, 146
Lodge Rising Star, Bombay 146
Logari, Ahmed 70
Logari, Mohammed Khan 70
Lohani caravans 103, 115, 166, 202, 255, 297, 343, 357
Lord, Dr Percival 164–7, 175, 177, 186, 189, 191, 200–3, 213, 226, 227, 235, 240, 244, 256, 257, 266, 290, 291, 306, 310, 314, 317, 318, 323–5, 332, 336, 343
Louis-Philippe, King of France 31, 133, 271
Loveday, Lt 284, 327, 343, 344
Ludhiana 62, 76, 81, 83, 87, 88, 92, 98, 118, 119, 171, 199, 215, 239, 244, 344
Lukput of Mandvi 60
Luni river 39, 42
Lyell, Sir Charles 28, 129
Lynch, Lt 347, 348
Lytton, Edward Bulwer 126

Macaulay, Thomas Babington 97, 229, 233
MacDonald (Ambassador in Persia) 53
McGregor, Capt 235, 309, 331, 360
Mackenzie, Lt Colin 164, 318, 332, 361, 366, 372
Mackeson, Lt 96, 119, 168, 169, 171, 183, 215, 235–9, 318, 360, 372
Mackintosh, Sir James 26
McLeod, Lt 300
Maclise, Daniel 126, 128
Macnaghten, Sir Francis 85
Macnaghten, Sir William 1, 83, 118, 121, 156, 167, 171, 176, 180, 183, 184, 189, 192, 195, 201, 202, 204, 210, 214–37 *passim*, 242–4, 254, 263, 265, 268, 269, 277, 280–97, 303–73
  accusing Broadfoot of cowardice 359
  complaining of overwork 289
  death of 375
  Governor of Bombay 356, 357, 362
  linguistic prowess 85
  negotiating for Peshawar 196–200
  negotiating for withdrawal 374

sending Burnes to Herat 207
signing treaty with Ranjit Singh 238, 239
McNeill, Dr John 25, 118, 119, 128, 130, 150, 151, 167, 171, 173, 179–82, 214, 219, 226, 243, 272, 277, 290, 344, 377
McPherson, Hamish McGregor 177
Maddock, T.H. 262
Mahidpur, Battle of 25
Mahmoud, Shah of Afghanistan 8, 9, 100
Mahomed Amin Khan 321
Mahomed Said, Qazi of Herat 321
Mahratta 21, 25, 52
Major, Capt John 37
Malam Yusuf 152
malaria 36, 99, 112, 117, 139, 182, 383
Malcolm, Admiral Charles 170
Malcolm, Sir John 14, 17, 18, 21, 25, 26, 29–38, 41–46, 50–2, 54, 57–9
  confidence in Burnes 55
  mission to Sind 60
  sending dray horses as gifts 56
Malcolm, Sir Pulteney 150
Malik Qasim, Prince 9
Mandvi (port) 59–61, 66, 162, 167, 178
Mangilaluk 204, 320
Marx, Karl 380, 381
Masjidi Khan, Mir 334
Masonic Order of Heredom de Kilwinning 136
Masson, Charles (James Lewis) 28, 108, 118, 119, 122, 144, 150, 158–60, 168–71, 178–89, 191, 193, 198–200, 204, 208–13, 219–23, 226, 231, 235, 237–40, 244, 256, 262, 263, 283, 284, 327, 344, 365
  granted Royal pardon 130
  suspected of being a Russian agent 343
Maule, Fox 381
Mazanderan 117
Mazar i Sharif 110, 111
Mecca Gate, Jeddah 152
Mehir Dil Khan – see Barakzai
Mehmet Ali Pasha 120, 135, 150, 271
Mehrab Khan (of Kelat) 80, 155, 234, 266, 275–80, 282, 284, 295, 296, 305, 344
  treaty with Burnes 283; to be deposed 286; death of 311
Melbourne, Lord 126, 134, 250, 251, 287
Meshed 116–18
Metcalfe, Sir Charles 38, 56, 77, 82, 121, 161, 167, 173, 347
Mill, James 3, 31
Mill, John Stuart 123, 151, 172, 240, 274, 343, 378
Mir Mohammed Khan 179
Mir Wali 317, 325
Mirza Aga Jan 190
Mirza Ali Khan 105
Mirza Ata 366, 370
Mirza Sami Khan 223
Mirza Sarwar Khan 181
Mitchell, David 7
Mithankot 97, 168, 172, 174–8, 290
Mohammed Khan (nephew of Murad Ali) 71
Mohammed Khan (Sultan of Afghanistan) - see Barakzai
Mohammed Azim Khan 105
Mohammed Mirza, Shah 173
Mohammed Sharif Khan 200
Mohammed Zeman Khan 370, 374
Monteith, Col 358–60
*Monthly Review* 327
Montrose 1–7, 15, 91, 92, 127, 128, 139, 377
Montrose Academy 3, 6, 128, 131
Montrose Burgh Council 4
Montrose Circulating Library 4
Montrose Loyal Volunteers 4
Montrose Museum 60
*Montrose Review* 1, 15, 352
Moon, Sir Penderel 233
Moorcroft, William 77, 101, 102, 108, 110–14, 121, 202, 203, 213, 250
Moore, Thomas 184, 185
Morley, Charles 249
Morpeth, Lord 134
Morris, Lt 65
Mughal Emperors 21
Muhammad Hassan, Wazir 284
Muhin Shah, Sayed 103, 192, 193
Multan banking house 132
Mumbai Asiatic Society 129

## Index

Munshi Mohammed Bakhsh 372
Murad Ali Khan Talpur 24, 29, 67, 68, 70, 93, 132, 325
   assisting Burnes 71, 72
   opposing Indus expedition 62–6
Murad Beg 108–12, 202, 203, 291, 317
Murghab river 116
Murray, Capt 235, 236
Murray, Dr 76, 83
Murray, John (publisher) 125–8, 133, 134, 151, 353
Murri tribe 326

Nadir Shah 200, 248
Nagar, Rana of (Jugaji) 40
Naik Sita Ram 233
Nao Nehal Singh 173
Naqshbandi, Bahaudin 115
Nasrullah Khan 113, 320, 321, 325, 347
Nassir Khan (of Kelat) 176, 327, 344
   peace treaty with 357
Nasu, Mullah 295
National Archives of India 249
National Library of Scotland 132
National Portrait Gallery 128
nautch dancing 82, 175, 187, 353
Navruz, celebration of 223
Nawaz Khan 279, 296, 311, 327, 357
Nehru, Pandit 377, 378
Nesselrode (Russian Foreign Minister) 149, 164, 173, 209, 210, 213, 272, 293, 294, 319, 320, 344
Nicholas I, Tsar of Russia 149, 202, 210, 211, 319
Nicholls, Jasper 318
Nicholson, Lt 325
Nijrow 335, 336
Nizamuddin 159, 160, 212, 213
Nizhni Novgorod 166, 168, 202–4, 210
*Noctes Ambrosianae* 36, 126
Noor Muhal 184
Norris, Charles 44
Nott, Gen 282, 289, 314, 323, 326, 338, 344, 346, 351
Nufusk Pass 327
Nur Mohammed Khan 161, 174, 259

Oates, Capt 131

O'Brien, Smith 379
Ochterlony, General David 25
Omar Khan Lohani 115, 202
Omar, Mullah 288
opium trade 34, 39, 46, 112, 170, 171, 176
Orenburg 23, 69, 149, 166, 211, 239, 322
Osborne, Capt William 82, 83, 235, 236, 280, 342
Oudh, annexation of 233, 234
Outram, James 302, 303, 306, 343
Oxus river 116, 125, 273, 274, 305, 317, 319, 322, 323, 331

Pahawar Mul 321
Pali 39, 42, 46
Palmer, Capt Henry 339
Palmerston, Lord 52, 124, 173. 209, 236, 239, 240, 246, 270–2, 293, 323, 325, 378–82
   alarm at Russian moves 164, 228
   liaisons of 126
   rejecting de Brunow proposals 319
Parkar region 38–41, 43, 44, 50, 57, 96
Parsons, Col 301
Patna 214
Pattison, James 17
Pattison, Lt 282, 286
Pavlovich, Grand Duke 23
Peacock, Thomas Love 262, 274, 322
Peat, Capt 300
Peel, Sir Robert 134, 352, 378, 379
Perovsky, Count 292, 293, 305, 320, 322
Persia
   agreements with Kandahar 205, 217
   alliance with Russia 243
   anti-British alliance in 347
   attacks on Herat 118, 157, 163, 179, 185, 190, 195, 206, 210, 215, 225
   defeated at Herat 8
   possible alliance with Sind 96
   raids by Turkmen 116
   religious shrines in 168
   Russian influence in 32, 82, 84, 106, 130, 150, 167, 175, 223, 224, 230, 267, 268
   Shah of 8, 117, 163, 173, 179, 199, 222
   supporting Dost 182, 196
   threat to Afghanistan 232

Persian Gulf 59, 237, 246
Peshawar 52, 100–5, 168, 180, 185–93,
    208, 215, 220, 226–8, 235, 237,
    245, 248, 317, 328, 329, 351
  as a British Protectorate 349
  conflict over 192–6
  fall of 222, 316
  seized by Hari Singh 155, 156
  Sikh control of 197
  treaty of 120
  revenues from 217
Piggott, Rev 363
Pir Mohammed 208
Pitapur, Thakur of 41
Pitti river 63, 67
Pitumba 63, 65, 266
pneumonia, toll from 314
Pokur (banker) 302
potato, introduction of 314
Potter, Maj 308, 309
Pottinger, Lt Eldred 176, 184, 193, 206,
    222, 226, 237, 264–8, 277, 280,
    290, 348, 355, 356, 371, 372
  the Hero of Herat 246, 247
Pottinger, Major Henry 27, 29, 34, 35,
    41, 43–45, 50, 57, 59–67, 70, 74,
    89, 92, 119, 122, 127, 130, 150,
    158–60, 161–2, 167, 169, 172, 174,
    181, 193, 213, 256–60, 265, 266,
    280, 377
  criticising Burnes' surveys 120
  early expeditions 37–9
  rant against Burnes 261
  Resident in Haidarabad 254
  secret training of Indian surveyors 55
  signing treaties 96
Prinsep, Thoby 81, 235
punctuated equilibrium, theory of 28
Pune 21, 22
Punjab 79, 84–87, 164, 199, 216, 238,
    328, 349, 354
  Burnes' report on 87
  chaos in 317
  cholera in 114
Punjaji (Soda chief) 41

Qizilbash, the 200, 222, 288, 302, 304,
    307, 308, 315, 367, 373, 374

Qochan 117, 118, 206
*Quarterly Review* 128
Quetta 275, 279, 281–6, 289, 311, 326,
    343, 357
Qutab-Alam 266

Raglan, Lord 353
Rahim, Mulla 183, 204
Rahmatulla Khan 109
Rajamundri 228
Rajput tribes 25; female infanticide
    among 26
Raleigh Club 131
Ramsay, Chevalier Andrew 139, 140
Ramsay, Lord James 138, 140
Ramsay, Major-General 5, 6, 89, 90
Ranjit Singh 54–7, 62, 66, 67, 71, 74,
    77, 85, 96, 101, 105, 106, 119,
    141, 158, 161, 163, 168, 172, 178,
    184, 186, 188, 190, 195–97, 208,
    212–27, 230, 234, 236, 248–51,
    269, 273, 288, 307, 319, 328, 342,
    365
  agreement on Peshawar 198, 210
  alliance with Shuja 120, 154
  combining with Dil Khans 192
  conquering Kashmir 81
  death of 349
  delight at dray horses 79, 80
  encouraged by Auckland 231
  jihad from Dost 156
  keen to open Indus 170
  losing ground 173–5, 180
  meeting Burnes 75–8, 99
  meeting Lord Bentinck 89–92
  sexual prowess 82, 83
  signing treaty 238, 239
  status of 84, 87
  suffering a stroke 252
  taking Kashmir 104
  taking Peshawar 222
Rattray (deserter) – *see* Fida
Rawalpindi 99
Rawlinson, Henry 17, 25, 30, 209, 322,
    323, 344, 350, 351, 372
Reform Act, 1832 134
Robert, Capt 92
Robert the Bruce, King 136, 144

Roberts, Brig 308
Robertson, Thomas 317
Roebuck, Thomas 379
Romer, John 59, 60, 63, 64
Rosslyn Chapel 137, 138, 145
Rotas, stronghold of 99
Royal Arch Freemasonry 139, 141
Royal Asiatic Society 26, 29, 129, 132
Royal English Muscovy Co 113
Royal Geographical Society 129, 132, 133
Royal Society of London 123, 129, 137
Rubica (Burnes' servant) 350
Rupar 85, 89–94
Russell, Lord John 134, 377
Russia
   alliance with Kandahar 210
   attacking Herat 185, 199, 205
   attacks on Khiva 239, 319–21, 347
   British view of aims 273
   conflict over Kabul 225
   controlling the Bosphorus 120
   designs towards India 175
   designs on Persia 52–4, 150
   failure of Khiva mission 322
   growth of empire 380
   offering Jabbar Khan money 195
   promising aid to Kabul 227
   withdrawing agents 270
Rustam Khan, Amir of Khairpur 68, 72, 73, 175, 177, 255–60, 276; ceding Baikhar 257, 258

Saduzai royal house 288, 323
Saduzai, Prince Fatth Jung Khan 368–72
Saduzai, Sagdar Jang 345
Saduzai, Shah Shuja 59, 99, 100, 107, 172, 194, 199, 214, 217, 225, 227, 234–6, 243, 251, 254–60, 272, 277–89, 295, 296, 302–5, 310, 315–17, 323–43, 349, 355, 356, 361, 365, 368, 369, 372, 378
   aiming to recapture Afghanistan 119
   alliance with Ranjit Singh 120, 154, 155
   attacked at Ghazni 298
   backed by Auckland 230, 233
   ceremonial entry to Kabul 304
   coming to power 9
   coronation of 291
   description of court 307–09
   exiled 87, 88
   new treaty 287
   receiving tribute from Amirs 237
   restored to power 238, 239, 248, 252
   threat from 149
Saduzai, Taj Mahomed 367
Saduzai, Prince/Shahzada Timur 267, 305, 306, 310, 323, 334, 344
Saigan 318
St Andrews University 229
St Columba's Church, Bombay 363
St John of Jerusalem, Order of 138, 139, 144, 145, 308
St Peter's Lodge, Montrose 5, 127, 133, 138
Sale, Brig Sir Robert 'Fighting Bob' 282, 291, 300, 314, 317, 318, 334, 336, 346, 360, 361, 365
Salter, Col 336
Salu Khan Achakzai 326
Sanders, Major 324
Sarafraz Paydanah Khan 105
Sarwar Khan 115, 276, 297
Scott, Sir Walter 10, 22, 140
Scottish Enlightenment 28, 112
Scottish Freemasonry 146
Scottish Reform Act, 1832 127
*Semiramis* (ship) 246, 267
Semund Khan 105
*Sesostris* (ship) 377
Seton, Capt David 59
sexual morality and practices
   of Avitabile 187
   among British officers 19–21, 82, 83, 364
   of British society 128
   among British soldiers 376
   in Kashmir 342
   among married women 20, 82
   one cause of British failures 375
   of Ranjit Singh 82, 83
Shakespear, Richmond 296, 302
Sharif Khan, Mohammed 103
Shee, Capt 117
Shelton, Col 354, 369, 372, 374

Sher Afzul 298
Sher Mohammed Khan 176
Sherif, Sayyid Mohammed 278
Sherif Khan 367, 373
Sheriffmuir, Battle of 2
Shikarpur 80, 120, 132, 163, 167, 168, 172, 176, 178, 188, 238, 257, 265, 276, 290
Shirin Khan 307, 374
Shuja, Shah – see Saduzai
Shukhr, Mullah 239, 316, 324, 330, 340, 341
Shupaiyan, Battle of 104
Sikunder Khan – see Burnes, Alexander
Simla Declaration 1838 248
Simonicz, Count General 150, 195, 205, 209, 211, 212, 220, 270, 272, 293, 294, 319, 344
Simpson, Brig 267, 328
Simpson, Lt 282–4
Sinclair, Capt 318
Sinclair, Lord (of Rosslyn) 138, 145
Sind 24, 29, 37, 38, 62, 172
   annexation of coast 266
   mission to 161
   possible purchase by Britain 59
   surrendered to Britain 269
   threat of war in 35
Sind, Amirs of 29, 41, 50, 53, 59–62, 70, 71, 80, 89, 92, 161, 167, 174, 197, 254, 268, 273
   links to Persia 168
   opposing Burnes' travel by river 62, 64, 67
   paying tribute to Shuja 237
   plans for attack 188
   treaties with 96
Sind Field Force 58
Sind Irregular Horse 176
Sinyavin, L.G. 292
Sirafrauz Khan 9
Skinner, James 89
smallpox 101
Smith, Adam 341
Smith, Sidney (writer) 134, 352
Smith, Admiral Sir Sydney 137
Sobdar Khan 71, 197, 254
Sobieski, Jan 23

Soda tribes 38, 41
Somnath, temple of 59
Stacey, Col 327
Stevenson, Brig 267
Stewart, Capt Charles Samuel 353
Stirling, Edward 54, 101, 143
Stoddart, Col 113, 114, 157, 209, 222, 246, 247, 277, 291, 305, 320, 321, 326
Sujit Singh 184
Sukhtelen, Count Pavel 69
Sukkur 154, 255, 258, 336, 342
Sultan Mahommed Khan (brother of Dost) – see Barakzai
Surat 22, 35
Sutlej river 89, 90, 96

Taliban 288
Tashkent 113
Tatta 70, 167, 172
Tehran 117, 124
Tezin Pass 310, 360
Thackwell, Gen 267
Thakuri, Pitumba 61
Thar desert 24, 42, 57, 96, 142
Thomson, Capt 267, 278, 299
*Times of India* 148
Timur, Prince/Shahzada – see Saduzai
Timur, Shah 104, 105, 288
Tipu Sultan 233
Tiszkiewicz (Polish revolutionary) 294
Toba, the 105
Todd, Maj D'Arcy 93, 277, 290, 296, 324, 325, 346, 347
Torrens, Henry 228, 229, 240
Treaty of 1809 62
Trebeck, Charles 101, 108, 110–13
Trevelyan, Charles 28, 93, 97, 103, 192, 229, 232, 377
Trevor, Capt R.S. 348, 365, 369
Troup, Capt 366
Tucker, Henry 151
Turkestan 317, 323
Turkmen people 116
Turkmenchai, Treaty of 31, 52
Turnuk river 323
Tutundera 184, 334, 335

# Index

Uch 50, 74, 86, 180
Ullah, Amir 367
Ullah Dad Khan 191
Ullah, Nazir Khan 293, 320, 321
*Undaunted*, HMS 48
Unkiar Skelessi, Treaty of 271
Urquhart, David 164, 380
Usman Khan 348, 355, 356, 367–9
Uzbek, Abdul Salam Khan 367
Uzbek peoples 203, 322, 323, 331, 332
Uzbekistan 274, 322

Valentia, Lord 22
Vellore mutiny 31
Ventura, General 81–83, 152, 178, 213, 214, 236, 353
Victoria, Princess/Queen 123, 124, 130, 196, 250, 251, 371, 377
Victoria and Albert Museum 132

Wade, Capt Claude 62, 76–88, 92, 93, 98, 118, 119, 154–60, 172–8, 181, 183, 192, 195, 196, 208, 213–15, 222, 231, 236, 239, 244, 267, 306, 377
Wade, Maj Hamlet 346, 358
Waghorn (steamship operator) 274
Waiz, Mir 156, 302
Wali, Mir 317, 325, 331–33
Wallich, Dr 218
Walter, Captain 24
Ward, Capt William 37, 122
Warsaw, Grand Duchy of 23
Waterfield, T.M. 310
Waterloo, Battle of 353
*Wellesley* (ship) 266
Wellesley, Arthur – *see* Wellington
Wellesley, Lord 20

Wellington, Duke of (Arthur Wellesley) 21, 31, 52–4, 353
*Westminster Review* 378
Whish, Maj Richard 37, 47
Whitteridge, Gordon 344
William IV, King 124, 134, 137
   death of 196
   granting Masson Royal pardon 130;
   illegitimate children of 126;
Williamson, Capt Thomas 20
Willis, Sgt 27
Wilshire, Gen 267, 289, 310, 318
Wilson, Capt 152
Witkiewicz, Jan Prosper 23, 69, 113, 157, 159, 208–16, 219–22, 228, 246, 247, 262, 263, 270, 272, 277, 319, 320, 343, 380
   death of 292–4
   influence in Kabul 220–5
   nightmare of the Raj 210
Wolff, Joseph 104, 105, 107, 113, 121, 122, 152, 153, 157, 187
Wood, Lt John 164, 166, 167, 170, 174, 177, 178, 184, 189, 191, 200, 202, 203, 226, 227, 235, 238, 256, 258, 318
Woodburn, Capt 345
Wymer, Col 345

Yapp, Malcolm 51, 76, 247
Yar Mohammed (Wazir of Herat) 117, 118, 226, 246, 277, 324, 325, 329, 346, 347, 356

Zabulistan 101
Zeman, Shah 9, 305
Zoroastrianism 143